PREFACE

We are grateful for the favorable reception which the preceding two editions of this work have received. The study of international relations, like the reality which that study seeks to embrace, is changing rapidly, so that a thorough revision of the earlier version seemed appropriate at this time. We have retained much of the basic format of the previous editions. We have made large-scale changes in the contents of the various chapters. Thirty of the 44 selections found in these pages are new.

Like the first and second edition of this work, the present edition is designed primarily to meet the needs of the college or university student who is taking his first course in the field of international relations. We hope that the book will also commend itself to interested citizens outside the academy. To serve the needs of both groups of readers, we have tried to be conceptual rather than factual in our approach. This may persuade some readers that the book is too theoretical and that it provides insufficient coverage of the day-to-day events in international relations that confront us all. Our response is that, in our judgment, it is essential to have a conceptual framework within which these day-to-day events can be organized in such a way as to make sense. We believe neither in the appropriateness nor, indeed, the possibility of a book which will automatically provide a short-cut to understanding and prediction in as complex a field as that which we are studying. But we invite the thoughtful reader to engage with us and with the contributors to this volume in an effort to organize the raw material of international relations—the countless events, occurrences, and happenings that crowd our consciousness, in such a way as to enhance our capability to understand, and eventually perhaps even to predict, actions and reactions in the field of international relations.

We are grateful to many professional colleagues across the country who have provided us with thoughtful comments on strengths and weaknesses of earlier versions of this book. We are likewise grateful to our own students whose reactions to the organization and selections in earlier volumes have provided valuable clues as to what to retain and what to substitute. The line from *The King and I:* "By your pupils you'll be taught" is certainly appropriate in our case. We hope to repay our debt through the changes which we incorporated in the present edition. With it all, the usual disclaimer is in order: errors of omission and judgment are our responsibility alone. We wish we could share that responsibility with others, but we can't.

Finally, we wish to express a lasting debt to our teachers at Yale University who, almost twenty years ago, introduced us to the challenges of trying to understand the world around us as students of the relations among states and other social groups. We single out for special expression of gratitude the late Arnold Wolfers, whose brilliant insights have provided a source of continuing stimulation and challenge to us.

FRED A. SONDERMANN
WILLIAM C. OLSON
DAVID S. McLELLAN

CONTENTS

PART THREE   *Ends and Means in Foreign Relations*   187

The

Theory and Practice

of

International Relations

INTRODUCTION:

THE STUDY OF

INTERNATIONAL RELATIONS

One is naturally reluctant to classify his own special field of study as *the* most important among academic disciplines. This self-restraint is appropriate: given our present state of knowledge, none of us knows enough to claim with confidence that one subject is more significant than another, except in terms of our personal inclinations. Yet most specialists manage to overcome their reluctance. The editors of this volume are no exception and therefore begin by advancing the proposition that if there is any truly crucial set of problems which confronts the student of the contemporary world, it is the set of problems generally spoken of under the heading "international relations." It is not too much to assert that the solution (or lack of solution) of problems in this area of human relationships will shape the design of our future. As matter of fact such solutions (or lack of solutions) may well determine whether there is to be a future at all for the kind of civilization we know. However much many of us might prefer to focus on private or intrasocietal problems, a through understanding of world affairs is a precondition for the preservation of human life and other human values in this last third of the twentieth century.

We live in a world in which over 130 national societies exist. These societies are politically organized as states. The states and the governments which conduct their affairs are the major participating units in international relations. Some of the states are not very powerful if compared with the strongest and most potent states, but they may still be quite strong and effective within limited geographic regions. A few states have sufficient power to participate in international affairs on a global scale. Each unit, however, commands *some* strength, *some* capacity to achieve its goals, either by itself or in concert with others. Each organized human group has such goals, and the crucial point is that the goals of any given human group—such as a state—are not necessarily complementary nor always easily reconcilable with those of another group.

Although in some ways relations *between* states may resemble relations between groups *within* states, there are important differences. There is no easily achievable consensus among the various groups which participate in international relations. Lacking common cultural, social, and historical backgrounds, they lack similar values for the present and common goals for the future. Within a state, order is maintained and violence is prevented through the presence of at least six conditions or institutions: (1) laws—written or unwritten—which reflect the moral judgment of the community, (2) political machinery to change these laws when change is needed, (3) an executive body to administer the laws, (4) courts to settle disputes in accordance with law, (5) superior public force which deters acts of individual or sub-group violence, and (6) "a state of public well-being sufficient that people are reasonable and prudent and are not driven by a sense of desperation to follow ways of violence."[1] One might add an additional factor, which is implicit in this listing: an underlying consensus on acceptable goals and on methods of achieving these goals.

As one considers these preconditions for order and stability within a society, one finds that they are either absent from the international scene or, at best, exist there only in very rudimentary form. International relations thus take place in a special type of environment once described as "one made up of autonomous units without a central authority having a monopoly of power."[2] A good, brief word for this is "anarchy."

It should be added that it is possible to draw the distinctions between domestic and international relations so rigidly as to make them unreal. Not all states contain all of the ingredients mentioned in the preceding list. In particular some of the newer states come to mind as examples where many of them are absent. On the other hand, not all international relationships lack a degree of consensus or institutions to ratify and operate that consensus—American-Canadian relations, relations among the Scandinavian countries, the Benelux countries, and others are cases in point.

Yet the basic distinctions still do apply in most cases, and given the nature of the international environment, the compulsions which operate on participants in international relations are extraordinarily complex and demanding. The problem of effective behavior in international relations is

---

[1] John Foster Dulles, *The Institutionalizing of Peace,* U.S. Department of State Bulletin 34, No. 880 (Washington, D.C.: Government Printing Office, 1956), *passim.*
[2] Frederick Sherwood Dunn, "The Scope of International Relations," *World Politics* (1949), 1, 143.

difficult, very difficult indeed, for the men who make decisions on behalf of states.

In addition a number of significant changes have taken place during the twentieth century (some within the past twenty-five years) that have fundamentally altered the traditional bases of international relations. One such change has been the shift of power from Western Europe to previously peripheral areas—the United States and the Soviet Union. In the immediate post-World War II period, this change was reflected in the nearly complete bipolarization of power, centering upon these two states. In the more recent past, other states and groups of states have assumed or reassumed considerable importance. There are continuing fluctuations in the power distribution among the states of the world, and it would be preposterous to contend that the process of change has come to an end. We also witness continuing changes in the nature of technology (particularly, but by no means exclusively, in the weapons field), and it is by no means clear whether the precise impact of past technological developments is as yet fully understood. The recent past has witnessed the downfall of long-established colonial empires and the emergence, at a bewildering pace, of new states which insist upon independence of action and freedom from entanglement in the conflicts of others. In the areas where the new nationalism has expressed itself in the formation of dozens of new states, we also witness a simultaneous "revolution of rising expectations"—an unwillingness of peoples constituting more than half of the world's rapidly growing population any longer to endure long-accustomed patterns of misery and deprivation. These people and their leaders want improvements, they want them fast, and the means they are willing to employ may not always be those of which others would approve.

Their quest comes at a time when productive capacities and living standards in the more highly developed countries are increasing at a rapid pace, thus widening the gap that separates the countries of the world in terms of access to the benefits which a twentieth-century technical civilization can provide. Their problems are further complicated by the rapid population increase, falling with particular force on many countries which, at this point in their history, can least afford to support additional people.

Finally the last quarter century has witnessed the emergence of the Soviet Union as an immensely powerful nation, with thrust and purpose provided by history, leadership, and ideology. Our era is marked by the efforts of that country (and, increasingly, by the efforts of Communist China) to play an influential and, where possible, dominant part in world affairs. This goal is opposed by several coalitions of states of which the United States is the most powerful member. In recent years the respective coalitions—Communist as well as non-Communist—have demonstrated centrifugal tendencies, making both of them far less cohesive that they were in the period of the late 1940s and the 1950s.

All these events and trends have profoundly changed the international environment. Change is the law of human life; but change with such speed (one is reminded of Stuart Chase's phrase, "'an express-train out of control'") poses most serious problems of understanding and adaptation. It is by no means clear that these problems have yet been met.

With an approximate understanding of some salient features of the environment in which international relationships take place, the problem of defining a particular country's part in that process now also should be clearer. A country's goals may be "reasonable" by its own standards, though not necessarily by those of others. Its capacities may be considerable, although there are always limits on what can be done. It is unrealistic for any country to expect that it can impose solutions which reflect only gain for its own position on all issues, at all times, and in all places. Indeed the task of statesmanship is often to "cut one's losses" and accept the lesser of evils.[3] Within an environment tending toward anarchy, it is necessary for countries to coalesce with other countries in the pursuit of common goals. Such cooperation between legal equals imposes strains and tensions, just as does the opposition between contending states or groups of states. There are only limited alternatives to the solution of international conflict: the ability to arrive at compromise settlements; the willingness to live with unresolved, ambiguous situations; or the employment of some form of bribery or coercion. Two of these alternatives are neither heroic nor glamorous, and the last is complicated by the nature of modern weapons which are too destructive to be used rationally in a total war situation.

Having thus set the stage with a brief description of the nature of international relations and the limitation imposed upon state action by the environment in which those relations take place, it becomes appropriate for us to proceed to a more specific introduction of international relations as a subject of study, to indicate the richness and variety of its material, and to acknowledge some of the many points of view from which the subject can be approached. This is the task to which the following selection by one of the author-editors of this book addresses itself.

[3] A clear exposition of this point can be found in Charles Burton Marshall, *The Limits of Foreign Policy* (New York: Holt, Rinehart & Winston, Inc., 1954).

1. Changes in The Study of International Relations

FRED A. SONDERMANN

Of the many questions which confront the student of this field, one deserves to be singled out for initial consideration. It relates to the definition and the scope of international relations as a subject of inquiry. There seem to be as many definitions as there are writers on the subject. For purposes of this essay we will adopt a definition advanced by Charles McClelland, to the effect that "international relations is...the study of all the exchanges, transactions, contacts, flows of information and meaning, and the attending and resulting behavioral responses between and among separated organized societies, including their components. . . ."[1]

Within the framework of such a definition the study of international relations usually deals with *actors* (states, governments, leaders, diplomats, peoples) striving to attain certain *ends* (objectives, goals, purposes), using *means* (such as diplomacy, coercion, persuasion) which are related to their *power* or *capability*.[2] Two points should be added: first, the relationships take place within an international milieu, which lacks to a substantial degree both the consensual and the institutional ingredients predisposing to peace and order within a domestic environment; and second, in pursuing their goals, actors come into contact—and frequently into conflict—with other actors engaged in similar processes. Not all of the approximately 130 national states of the world are constantly engaged in the same pursuits, to be sure; but more than one state, more than one government, more than one set of leaders or one public is involved in almost any given activity. Whenever a national act deals or attempts to deal with men, groups, governments, and so on beyond the borders of its own state, we are in the presence of an international relationship. This is

Excerpts from "Changes in the Study of International Relations," INTERNATIONAL DIMENSIONS IN THE SOCIAL STUDIES *(Washington: National Education Association, 1968), pp. 101–21. Reprinted by permission.*

[1] *Theory and Problems in Teaching International Relations.* (Unpublished manuscript, San Francisco State College, 1958, no page).

[2] This information is derived from the work of Harold and Margaret Sprout, including *Man-Milieu Relationship Hypotheses in the Context of International Relations* (Princeton, N. J.: Center of International Studies, 1956) and *Foundations of International Politics* (Princeton, N.J.: D. Van Nostrand Co., 1962).

the subject of study of the specialist in the field.

So vast is the subject that even in the present rather early stages of inquiry a considerable degree of specialization has already taken place. Thus alongside the generalist student of international relations, we find specialists dealing with political economic, military, and psychological aspects of such relationships; those dealing with comparative governments and foreign policies of various nations; and those dealing with key relationships in specific geographically limited areas of the world. All of them pursue the same end—that of understanding, and hopefully eventually predicting events in the international realm.

.   .   .

The point of departure for any study of international relations since the end of World War II must be the work of Hans J. Morgenthau of the University of Chicago. The first edition of his *Politics Among Nations* was published in 1948.[3] Discarding many of the assumptions of most previous writers—such as the assumption of automatic harmony between varying interests, the efficacy of law and organization, or the peaceful influence of public opinion—Morgenthau vigorously advanced the proposition that *power* was the central focus for the study of international relations, as it was for its practice. It will help to understand his position to quote from the first chapter of his work:

International politics, like all politics, is a struggle for power. Whatever the ultimate aims of international politics, power is always the immediate aim. Statesmen and peoples may ultimately

seek freedom, security, prosperity, or power itself. They may define their goals in terms of a religious, philosophic, economic, or social ideal. They may hope that this ideal will materialize through its own inner force, through divine intervention, or through the natural development of human affairs. But whenever they strive to realize their goal by means of international politics, they do so by striving for power....[4]

Morgenthau defined power as "man's control over the minds and actions of other men." He proposed further that the objectives of states in international politics could be subsumed under the general category of "national interests," which had to be "other-national," and "supra-national" interests. In what came to be known as the "realist" approach to the study of international relations, Professor Morgenthau and a growing group of scholars adopting the same general stance held that before real advance in our understanding of international politics could be made, it was essential to discard much of the intellectual baggage of the pre-World War II period.

Considering the obvious inadequacy of many of the previous attempts to explain international processes, the clarity of Morgenthau's writings, and the rapidity with which his views were espoused by a number of other writers, it seems fair to say that his views affected the approach of a whole academic generation of international relations scholars. In assessing his work no one can deny that in clearing away some cobwebs which badly needed to be cleared away, he made room for a more lucid approach to the study of the processes which are the subject of our inquiries.

Needless to say all this did not

---

[3] Morgenthau, Hans J., *Politics Among Nations, The Struggle for Power and Peace* (New York: Alfred A. Knopf, Inc., 1948).

[4] *Ibid.*, p. 13.

take place without an intellectual battle which left a number of casualties on both sides—a battle which proceeded under the somewhat oversimplified rubric of "the realists" versus "the idealists." The counterattack of the latter group was that the Morgenthau position glorified power and neglected moral considerations, that it seemed close to the position that "might makes right," and that it therefore left no room for moral judgments. A further charge was that men are driven by many motivations, of which the desire to wield power is merely one, and not always the guiding one. Finally as E. H. Carr had pointed out in his book *The Twenty Years' Crisis, 1919–1939*[5] (which generally follows the realist rather than the idealist tradition), consistent realism has no emotional appeal and in its deterministic approach provides no ground for meaningful action.

This particular intellectual encounter raged for some years at a rather high pitch of involvement and excitement. Whatever one's views on the merits of the debate may be, the discussion took place on Morgenthau's grounds, and he therefore affected the discipline profoundly. Most of today's international relations scholars feel that they have gone beyond his initial formulations—as indeed he himself has done also—and that they have found weaknesses in his emphasis on power and national interest which render these concepts less useful than they had earlier been thought to be. But few would deny that the agenda of international studies was changed greatly by him and others who wrote in the same tradition.

By the mid-1950s, then, the study of international relations had departed considerably from the study of diplomatic history, current events, international law, international organization, and international economics which had been its main foundations in previous periods. Scholars now were primarily concerned with political processes and with the behavior of states and their leaders in pursuing their objectives. . . . A number of new approaches to the study of international relations had emerged since World War II, such as the decision-making process, area studies, various forms and manifestations of behavioralism, game theory, simulation techniques, and content analysis.

A theoretical framework which has commended itself to an increasing number of international relations students (and within which any of the foregoing methods, along with others, can be employed) is that generally referred to as systems theory. It is not easy to outline its basic properties and implications in a limited space. Basically a "system" presupposes that all actions in a given realm are functionally related to one another, that they can be understood only in terms of their relationship to the whole, broader system of which they form a part. Any system has to behave in particular ways and perform particular tasks in order to exist in its specific environment. One of the simpler definitions of a system is that of James N. Rosenau: "A system is considered to exist in an environment and to be composed of parts which, through interaction, are in relation to each other."[6]

A given system has boundaries beyond which exist other systems with which the system is in contact. It also has inputs in the form of demands (for

---

5 Carr, E. H. *The Twenty Years' Crisis, 1919–1939* (London: Macmillan & Co., 1939).

6 Rosenau, James N., ed., *International Politics and Foreign Policy: A Reader in Research and Theory* (New York: The Free Press, 1961), p. 77.

goods, services, the regulation of behavior, participation, and the like) and supports (in the form of taxes, obedience, service, participation, and deference to symbols of authority). These inputs feed into a central mechanism which converts them into policies. The policies emerge as outputs, in the form of allocations and distributions of goods and services, regulations of behavior, and the like. Finally a system has a feedback mechanism by which the results of policies are fed back into the decision-making process.[7]

This is a very simplified version of the intellectual scheme. Whether or not it is possible to think of the international realm as a system is debatable, though the present writer believes that one can do so. It is quite clear, however, that in the analysis of the national units which compose that international sphere, this approach has direct relevance in that it draws attention to certain aspects of the decision-making process, to certain relationships, to the steps which precede and follow decisions, and to the interrelations among many relevant factors which, until the advent of systems theory, were only dimly perceived. Some students of international relations believe, in fact,

that systems theory bids well to become the unifying focus in the study of all human phenomena, including those which fall in the realm of international relationships. Systems theory seems to be developing in a number of the social and natural sciences, and some predict that the coming convergence of these fields will result in a broad conceptual framework from which a new world view of man will emerge.

.   .   .

What emerges from all of this is a field of study which is in flux. A great many persons are pursuing many different lines of inquiry, all of which attempt to add to our understanding of the behavior of men in the massive and complex relations between powerful groups organized into political units and separated by real and by psychological boundary lines. No more exciting challenge has ever confronted the teacher or the student. Our failures are and will continue to be many. Our successes in gaining understanding are intermittent, and each increment of insight only reveals vast new intellectual territories that must yet be conquered. The frontier of all politics, as William T. R. Fox has put it, is endless.[8] It is there, and like other frontiers, it will slowly yield to exploration.

[7] For a particularly valuable essay relating the systems approach to international relations, see Gabriel A. Almond, "A Developmental Approach to Political Systems," *World Politics* (1965), 17, 183–214.

[8] Cited in Warner R. Schilling, "Science, Technology, and Foreign Policy," *Journal of International Affairs* (1959), 13, 7–18.

I

The International System
and
Its Participants

NATION

STATES

Chapter 1

This chapter addresses itself to what we consider to be the basic unit in international relations—the national state.

Defining the national state as the basic unit in international relations is not the only option available to the student of international relations. One could focus on individuals and groups within states such as governments and their personnel, the military, the diplomatic service, important political movements, and interest groups, all of which comprise the political entity to which we attach the shorthand label "national state." One could even focus on the individual citizen. On the other hand one could cite certain international supranational, or "other-than-national" entities, such as international organizations (both public and private) which have varying degrees of influence on the course of events. Movements such as Zionism, institutions such as the Catholic Church, international labor unions, business or professional organizations—and literally hundreds of other entities—all participate in some ways in international relations. The selection by Arnold Wolfers in this chapter takes many of these options into account, and we would not wish to convey by our choice of one of them—the state and its government— that we consider the others irrelevant.

Yet we do choose the state as the basic unit in international relations. And we must begin by making some important distinctions. There is, first of all, the distinction between nation and state.

The term "nation" is an ethnic one, based upon a common heritage, language, culture, and sense of identity. A "state" is a body of people politically organized under one government with sovereign rights. Sovereignty refers to the exclusive jurisdiction that a state possesses within its territory and to its freedom to act in international affairs without subjection to the legal control of another state. From a number of perspectives a state may encompass more or less than one nation; a nation may not possess statehood, but nations and states taken together make up the basic units and bases of power in the international system in which we live. It is the organization of man's activity and loyalty into national communities, that gives international relations its distinctive character.

Second, there is the distinction between states and governments, which can perhaps be dealt with most briefly by saying that governments come and go very frequently, whereas states come and go very infrequently. The student of international relations can usually depend on the continued existence of a given state as a political unit with far more assurance that he can depend on the continued existence of a given government.

Third, we believe it to be important to distinguish between states as they are organized for purposes of domestic government and politics and as they are organized for purposes of international relations. Domestically, there are very nearly as many varieties of organization as there are states. There are federal states and unitary ones, dynastic states and republican ones, democratic states and authoritarian states, states in which the government performs only very limited functions, and states which approach totalitarianism. Yet for purposes of conducting external relations, most states focus their decision-making capabilities in their central government, and it is their capacity to engage in external relations, to formulate goals, to pursue these goals, and to enter into engagements with others that concern us as students of our subject.

Most students of the state as the basic form of political organization agree that there are some generally recognized attributes which make this form of organization recognizable to the observer. A state must, first of all, have a territorial base. The size of that base is fairly irrelevant: Luxembourg is as much a state as is the Soviet Union. (To be sure, there are certain units, such as Monaco, Liechtenstein, Andorra, and so on, which are so small that their status is uncertain; they are sometimes grouped under the label of "dwarf states.") The implication of the territoriality of a state is that the territory is defined, that it is circumscribed, that within it the government has complete jurisdiction.

The second attribute of a state is that it must have a government— one that is capable of governing, capable of entering into international commitments, and capable of abiding by the international obligations that it has incurred. As we pointed out above, the specific form of that government is not of great importance for the student of international relations (except insofar as the form may affect the function of that government's conduct of foreign relations). But what is emphatically important is that the government must have the loyalty and attachment of significant portions of the population in order to govern effectively.

The third criterion of a state is a population. Again, as in the case of territory, there are no clearly defined lower limits nor, of course, upper ones. Populations of states range from a few thousand to China's nearly 800 million.

The final aspect of statehood, sovereignty, is discussed by R.P. Anand in the selection in this chapter, together with its implications and its difficulties.

On the basis of these criteria, how many units are we talking about? The Bureau of Intelligence and Research of the U. S. Department of State issued its latest report on this subject in August 1967, reporting that at that time a total of 131 national states were generally accepted as independent. Within the next year, five new ones were added—Southern Yemen, Nauru, Mauritius, Swaziland, and Equatorial Guinea—which are not included in the figures below. This is a phenomenal growth in numbers since the beginning of this century, with most of the growth occurring in the last twenty-five years. On the eve of World War I, there were sixty-three independent countries in the world. As a result of that war, three states in Europe ceased to exist (Austria-Hungary, Montenegro, and Serbia), but they were replaced by four new states (Austria, Hungary, Czechoslovakia, and Yugoslavia). Poland also reemerged as an independent national state after World War II. Between the wars, several new states emerged, particularly in the Middle East, so that on the eve of World War II, the total number increased to seventy. It is a tremendous, unprecedented jump from such a figure to the 131 with which we are dealing today.

Other interesting facts emerge about today's national states. As of 1967 their distribution by location was as follows:

One hundred and two states lie completely in the Northern Hemisphere; eleven lie athwart the equator, and only eighteen lie completely in the Southern Hemisphere. Fifty-eight countries lie completely in the tropics, forty-seven lie completely in temperate zones, and the remainder straddle both geographic/climatic zones. Twenty-one states are insular, twenty-seven are landlocked, and eighty-three face one or more bodies of water leading to the open ocean. Some of these facts will assume additional relevance after Chapter 5 dealing with geographic considerations has been studied.

The contemporary state system dates roughly from the end of the Thirty Years' War. The temporal rulers of England, France, the German Reformation states, as well as the lesser princes and potentates of Europe, took advantage of the anarchy produced by the religious wars to assume and keep authority within their respective territorial domains. Earlier they had been obliged to bow to the authority of the Pope in religious affairs and to the Emperor of the defunct Holy Roman Empire in secular matters, and they had had to put up with the challenge of powerful feudal lords within their own kingdoms. But henceforth supreme authority or sovereignty came to be identified with the state whose rights, independence, and power derived from what John Herz calls its "territoriality." Once established, sovereignty meant the right of each state to utilize the strength of its people and its resources in whatever way it wished, without regard for any political superior either inside or outside the national territory. This transformation created a world of sovereign, independent states theoretically equal but varying widely in real power, each dependent for its survival upon its own ingenuity and resources and the constellation of forces outside its boundaries.

From that time until the present individual security, diplomacy, international law, war, commerce, and the development of culture and of civilization itself would derive their form and content from the nation-state as the highest sovereign political entity. That system, now extended to the far corners of the earth, prevails in its fundamentals right down to the present day.

Until the United States and Japan entered the international arena as the nineteenth century merged into the twentieth, the nation-state system was virtually limited to Europe. There a common culture and a common respect for the principle of dynastic legitimacy and (following the French Revolution) for the right of national self-determination maintained the system in its principal parts. Fundamentally European security rested on the essential autonomy and defensibility of each national territory. Each of the great states was both large enough to provide its people with living space and strong enough to deter potential invaders. There existed neither the necessity nor the opportunity for unlimited expansion, and the European states could regulate their relations by such methods as limited war and the balance of power. As a basic sense of security took hold in nineteenth-century Europe, it became less imperative for the leaders of its separate units to mobilize their people and their resources for defense. Just as today the expectation of war engenders the very conditions which precipitate war, the expectation of peace in those days fostered peace. But in assessing this period one must not overlook in the European system a safety valve in the form of overseas expansion. Nationalistic and economic pressures could exploit this less dangerous outlet, where even the sharpest conflicts could hardly be regarded as vital.

Thus during the long period in which the international system afforded the major powers an opportunity to develop in comparative peace and prosperity, the nation-state served a most useful and constructive function. Beginning with the nineteenth century, however, certain trends began to undermine the principle of territorial impenetrability which underlay the ability of each state to exist alongside similar powers. These trends had to do in part with difficulties inherent in the application of the principle of self-determination, in part with the perfection of instruments of ideological-political penetration, in part with growing interdependence in the economic field, and in part with the development of weapons of mass destruction. In Chapter 3, "The Structure and Dynamics of the System," we will deal in more detail with some of the consequences of these trends.

1. The Actors in International Politics

ARNOLD WOLFERS

The late Arnold Wolfers was for many years Sterling Professor of International Relations at Yale University. Later he became Director of the Washington Center for Foreign Policy Research, where he served until his retirement in 1965. His death in 1968 marked the passing of one of the founders of the discipline of international relations in America. As an analyst of strategy and foreign policy, he was author of BRITAIN AND FRANCE BETWEEN TWO WARS *(1940)*, DISCORD AND COLLABORATION *(1962), and co-author of* THE ANGLO-AMERICAN TRADITION IN FOREIGN AFFAIRS *(1956)*.

Theorizing about almost any feature of international politics soon becomes entangled in a web of controversy. Even the identity of the "actors"—those who properly can be said to perform on the international stage—is a matter of dispute which raises not unimportant problems for the analyst, for the practitioner of foreign policy, and for the public. If the nation-states are seen as the sole actors, moving or moved like a set of chess figures in a highly abstract game, one may lose sight of the human beings for whom and by

This selection appeared first in Wm. T. R. Fox, ed., THEORETICAL ASPECTS OF INTERNATIONAL RELATIONS *(Notre Dame: University of Notre Dame Press, 1959). It is reprinted by permission of the publisher.*

whom the game is supposed to be played. If, on the other hand, one sees only the mass of individual human beings of whom mankind is composed, the power game of states tends to appear as an inhuman interference with the lives of ordinary people. Or, take the diplomat who sees himself as accredited to an entity called Indonesia or France: he may behave quite differently from the diplomat who considers his mission addressed to specific individuals or to ruling groups or to a people. A statesman accustomed to analyzing international politics in terms alone of state behavior will treat the United Nations differently from one who believes in the rise of international organizations to a place of independent control over world events similar to that control exerted by states.

Until quite recently, the states-as-the-sole-actors approach to international politics was so firmly entrenched that it may be called the traditional approach. After the Napoleonic wars, nation-states, particularly the European "great powers," as they were called, replaced the image of the princes or kings of former centuries as the sovereign, independent, single-minded actors, the movers of world events. To nation-states were ascribed the acts that accounted for changes in the distribution of power, for alignments and counter-alignments, for expansion and colonial conquest, for war and peace —the chief events in international affairs whenever a multitude of sovereigns have been in contact with one another. The concept of a multistate system composed of entities of strikingly similar character and behavior appeared realistic to observers and analysts.

Starting in the period between the two world wars and gaining momentum after World War II, a reaction set in against the traditional states-as-actors approach. This reaction has taken two distinct forms: one new theory has placed individual human beings in the center of the scene that had been reserved previously to the nation-states; the second theory emphasized the existence, side by side with the state, of other corporate actors, especially international organizations. Both reactions have led to valuable new insights and deeper understanding of the dynamics of world politics, but they are in fact supplements to the traditional theory rather than substitutes for it.

I

The individuals-as-actors approach first appeared in the minds-of-men theory of international politics. It was soon to be followed by the decision-making approach which was a reaction against tradition from another angle. Both demanded that attention be focused on individual human beings as actors. Together, the new schools of thought represent a swing of the pendulum from an extreme "state" emphasis to an equally extreme emphasis on the men who act for states. These new approaches must be credited with humanizing international politics by attracting attention to the human element minimized in the traditional approach. It was the aim of the new theories to replace the abstract notion of the state with the living realities of human minds, wills, and hearts. But the result, on the whole, was to substitute one set of abstractions for another because, in politics, it is also an abstraction to examine the individual apart from the corporate bodies by means of which he acts politically.

The minds-of-men approach received its emotional stimulus from two sources: the realization that, in the age of mass communication, propaganda, and ideological movements, there were growing opportunities for the masses to play a significant role in international affairs, and a general desire to see the masses take advantage of these opportunities. To stress men rather than states and thus to focus attention on the common man—traditionally more the victim than the beneficiary of international politics—seemed to offer a way out of conflict, war, and power politics generally. It is not surprising that UNESCO should have become an exponent of the theory, since it was established, as Frederick Dunn points out,[1] with a view to constructing peace in the minds of men. The utopian undertones of many early pronouncements by

---

[1] *War and the Minds of Men* (Harper & Bros., New York, 1950), pp. xi–xiv.

those who espoused the new approach were unmistakable, but should not detract from the contribution which the new approach can make to realistic understanding of world affairs.

The new approach's criticism of the states-as-actors theory turns mainly on the distinction between genuine human needs and what appear to be the a-human interests of the state. There are those who claim that too great an emphasis on the role of states and their interests in power, prestige, territory, and the like, will divert political action from the satisfaction of the common man's real needs and desires to the service of the few who can parade their interests as those of the nation. Is it credible, they ask, that Egyptian fellaheen and Pakistani peasants, desperately in need of food, shelter, and improved conditions of health, should, as their governments contend, yearn for the satisfaction of such "state interests" as the liquidation of Israel or the unification of Kashmir under Pakistani rule, when the pursuit of such interests requires great sacrifices of the masses? Does the state not take on the character of an a-human monster to whom dignity is given gratuitously, if it is regarded as an actor in its own right, at liberty to place its interests above those of the human beings who compose it?

Still, one may question whether the quest for national security and power, for national independence, aggrandizement, or unification is any less "human"—and therefore necessarily less appealing to the masses—than the quest for food, shelter, comfort, and happiness. Actually, the minds-of-men theory and its humanization of international politics must be carried several steps further than its exponents have gone. Any analysis of the dynamics of international politics must take into account the fact that man is more than a private individual concerned only with his personal welfare or with the welfare of his family. Often enough he is ready to compromise his own well-being for the benefit of the groups and organizations with which he identifies himself. Psychologically, nothing is more striking today than the way in which men in almost every part of the globe have come to value those possessions upon which independent national statehood depends, with the result that men, in their public capacity as citizens of a state, are willing to make the most sweeping sacrifices of their own well-being as private individuals in the interest of their nation. Therefore, state interests are indeed human interests—in fact, the chief source of political motivation today.

One can argue that a nationalistic age has distorted men's pattern of values or that the manipulators of public opinion are chiefly responsible for this distortion. Nevertheless, the fact remains that a sufficient number of men identify themselves with their state or nation to justify and render possible governmental action in the name of state interests. . . .

There is, however, nothing absolute or unchanging about the value men attach to state interests. The position of the value of national unification in the hierarchy of values, for instance, especially its position relative to particular private needs and desires, is subject to change and differs from group to group and from individual to individual. Therefore, it is proper to be aware of individuals as the actors behind the scene, so to speak, whenever needs and interests, private or public, come into play in international affairs. Whether a state has a "vital interest"—in access to the sea or in the return of a lost province, for example—depends on the relative values attached by its citizens to these national objectives, on the one hand, and to private interests which would be sacrificed in the pursuit of the national objectives, on the other. In losing sight of the individuals who comprise a state, exponents of the states-as-actors theory may come up with a relatively accurate analysis of national behavior in a period when value patterns remain static, but they are more likely to be mistaken in a period of upheaval when elites and values undergo rapid and radical change.

One wonders today, for instance, whether the bulk of the population in countries facing the risks of nuclear war will long continue to regard as vital, and thus worthy of defense in war, all the state interests they were once ready to place in this category. Signs point to the likelihood that the masses, who have gained greater influence as behind-the-scenes actors, will push for greater restraints upon the pursuit of those state interests—such as national security or prestige—that are seen to conflict with private welfare needs. Such a development will indicate not that individuals are suddenly taking over the function formerly performed by states, but rather that larger bodies of individuals are sharing the role once reserved to the members of small elites who formerly decided what the "national interest" demanded or justified. It always would have been possible to interpret international politics through an examination of the individuals responsible for state action: the "humanizing" approach. But it must be recognized that in the course of the present century the number of these individuals has been greatly enlarged.

The failure to see man in his double capacity, as a private individual and as a political being, accounts for an illusion common among the more idealistic exponents of the minds-of-men approach. They assume that better understanding between peoples opens the safest path to peace, while Dunn has pointed out that peoples who know and understand each other perfectly may nevertheless become involved in war.[2] The explanation for this apparent paradox is not hard to find, provided one thinks in terms of the whole man rather than in terms solely of his private aims and desires. If one were in contact with the people of the Soviet Union today, one probably would find them preoccupied with the tasks of furthering their personal welfare, happiness, and social advancement in much the same way as any similar group of people in the United States. The discovery of such similarities of interest and aspiration tends to arouse a sense of sympathetic understanding; it certainly does not provoke fear or serve to justify policies based on the expectation of international conflict. As a result, people who think exclusively in terms of private individuals and who experience harmonious relationships with citizens of "hostile" countries are inclined to see nothing but unhappy misunderstanding, if not evil, in the way governments act toward one another.

Yet, the fact that Americans and Russians, in much the same fashion, pursue the same goals when acting as private individuals, gives no indication of their aims as citizens who are concerned with the national interests of their respective countries. Here there is far less chance that their aims will be found to be in harmony. Better understanding may in fact reveal the incompatibility of their respective objectives. Thus, it may be revealed that Russians, if good Marxists, want their government to drive capitalism toward its inescapable doom, or, if good nationalists, to secure safe access to warm water ports. At the same time, Russians

2 *Op. cit.,* p. 7.

may find that their American counter-parts demand the containment, if not elimination, of Communist tyranny, and a halt to Russian expansion before it reaches the Mediterranean or Persian Gulf and endangers American security. It appears, then, that to humanize the image of world politics by penetrating to the minds and hearts of actors does not necessarily give us a more peaceful picture of the world. As long as men identify themselves with their nation and cling to such national possessions as sovereign independence, territorial integrity, and national security, the establishment of harmonious private relations across national borders will have little impact on the course of inter-national political events and encounters.

It is therefore clear that an exclu-sive minds-of-men approach with its concentration on the motives and activi-ties of individual actors is inadequate and misleading. It is undeniable that men alone, and not states, are capable of desires and intentions, preferences and feelings of friendship or hatred; men, not states, can be tempted or provoked, can overestimate or under-estimate their own country's power rela-tive to the power of other states, and can establish the goals of national policy and sacrifices consistent with national security. However, although nothing can happen in the world arena unless something happens inside the minds and hearts of scores of men, psychological events are not the whole stuff out of which international politics is formed. If they were, the political scientist would have to leave the field to the psychologist.

The minds-of-men approach, while able to render important and indispen-sable services to a comprehensive theory of international politics, cannot do justice to all the essential events that fill the international arena. There can

be no "state behavior" except as the term is used to describe the combined behavior of individual human beings organized into a state. Not only do men act differently when engaged in pursu-ing what they consider the goals of their "national selves," but they are able to act as they do only because of the power and influence generated by their nations organized as corporate bodies. Therefore, only when attention is focused on states, rather than on individuals, can light be thrown on the goals pursued and means employed in the name of nations and on the rela-tionships of conflict or co-operation, of power competition or alignment that characterize international politics. To abstract from these aspects of reality is as unrealistic as it is to abstract from the events occurring in the minds and hearts of the men who act in the name of the state. But because theory cannot proceed except by means of abstraction, it becomes necessary here to supplement one set of abstractions with another and thus keep in mind the double aspect of events that must be conceived of as emanating simultaneously from indi-viduals and from corporate bodies.

A comprehensive theory does not call for a division of international poli-tics into two compartments, one com-prising the realm of the state as the actor in power politics, the other the realm of the human actors, the masses of common men with their psychological traits and their pursuit of human pur-poses. Instead, all events occurring in the international arena must be con-ceived of and understood from two angles simultaneously: one calling for concentration on the behavior of states as organized bodies of men, the other calling for concentration on human beings upon whose psychological reac-tions the behavior credited to states ultimately rests.

One need only look closely at a feature as significant in high politics and as strongly stressed in the states-as-actors approach as the balancing of power process. Often it has been assumed that a process involving state power and its distribution among nations has a place in the states-as-actors approach alone and can be treated adequately by means of this approach. But if one wishes to answer the question, for instance, whether the United States is in a position today to deter the Soviet Union by balancing the Soviet power, one cannot escape an examination of the psychology of individuals— in this case, of the leaders in the Kremlin. Deterrence can only work in the minds of the men in charge of Soviet policy by convincing them that acts they might otherwise wish to undertake would prove too costly in light of the punishment the United States would, in their opinion, be able and prepared to inflict. It would be foolish, however, to go to the other extreme and try to comprehend the struggle for power between the two countries in purely psychological terms. The Soviet estimate of American resistance to acts of the U.S.S.R. cannot be understood or predicted except as the objective facts concerning the respective power of the two states are taken into account. Moreover, the whole balancing process between the two antagonists, with its tremendous impact on world events, would drop from sight if attention were devoted exclusively to individuals or groups of individuals and to their psychological reactions.

.   .   .

If nation-states are conceived of as the sole actors, it is inevitable that they be treated as if endowed, like human beings, with wills and minds of their own that permit them to reach decisions and to carry them out. More-over, if state behavior is to be intelligible and to any degree predictable, states must be assumed to possess psychological traits of the kind known to the observer through introspection and through acquaintance with other human beings. States must be thought capable, for example, of desires and preferences, of satisfaction and dissatisfaction, of the choice of goals and means.

Actually, the states-as-actors theory postulates a limited number of such traits which, moreover, all states are assumed to have in common. States are presumed to possess a will to survive and a will to power; they live in fear of losing their possessions to others and are tempted by opportunities of acquiring new possessions. Because these basic traits are shared by *all* states, the exponents of the traditional approach can afford to treat these psychological presuppositions in a cavalier fashion. Little attention need be given to traits that, because they are constants or invariants, are incapable of helping to explain any differences in state behavior.

If, as Hobbes assumed, all states were equally and constantly driven by fear that their survival, the most cherished of their state possessions, might be threatened, then the multistate system would of necessity become an all-round struggle for security. If, instead, all states worthy of the name were as eager for expansion as Kjellén maintained, the ensuing struggle would turn on efforts at territorial acquisition and on counterefforts at territorial preservation.

The decision-making approach questions the possibility of reaching realistic conclusions from any such crude and generally applicable psychological presuppositions. Its exponents insist that decisions and actions taken in the name of the state cannot be understood unless one penetrates to the individuals from whom they emanate. In contrast to what is implicit in the views of the opposing school, the basic hypothesis here is that all acts of states, as we are used to calling them, are vitally affected or determined by the particular predispositions of particular decision-makers or of particular groups of participants in the decision-making process. Thus, differences in such individual psychological traits as motivation, value preferences, temperament, and rationality are considered essential variables, and so are differences arising from affiliation of individuals with particular parties, agencies within the state, or with peoples of different culture.

One can illustrate the contrast between the two hypotheses by means of important past decisions in international politics. According to the states-as-actors theory, American employment of the A-bomb over Hiroshima, or American intervention in the war in Korea, could have been foreseen —to the extent that foresight is possible at all—on the basis of the supposed common psychological disposition of states, coupled with an analysis of the existing circumstances which were external to the actors. Those who hold to the decision-making approach, on the contrary, consider it necessary to probe into the personal events that took place within the psyches of men like Stimson, Truman, and Acheson—perhaps also of their advisors, backers, and opponents —and led them to choose one particular course of action rather than some alternative course.[3]

The decision-making approach naturally appeals to the historian who is interested in identifying the unique aspects of past events, which necessitates consideration of all conceivable variables, including the personal traits of particular human actors. But it poses a serious problem for the theorist whose task is not to establish the uniqueness of events but rather to gain a generalized knowledge of behavior in international politics, which means knowledge on a relatively high level of abstraction. Should he not, therefore, abstract from the personal predispositions of those who are instrumental in the making of decisions? If his use of the deductive method, as described earlier, permits him to formulate expectations of probable state behavior that prove relatively accurate, why should he take a long, effort-consuming "detour" of the kind required by the decision-making approach and conduct an extensive empirical investigation into the motivations of a Stimson or a Truman? Could it be that use of the A-bomb against Japan was predictable on the ground that "states tend to use their most powerful weapons," or American intervention in Korea by the proposition that "no great power, if it can help it, will permit its chief opponent to change the distribution of power by the unilateral use of military force"?

At first glance, it would seem as if the actual performance of a particular state could conform only by sheer coincidence with expectations based on extremely crude generalizations about the way states tend to act under given circumstances. Why should the particular individuals responsible for United States policy in 1945 or 1950, men differing from others by a multitude of psychological features—motivations, idiosyncrasies, preferences, temperament— reach decisions of the kind the states-as-actors theory deduces from its

[3] See Richard C. Snyder and Glenn D. Paige, "The United States' Decision to Resist Aggression in Korea: The Application of an Analytical Scheme," *Administrative Science Quarterly,* Vol. 3, No. 3 (December 1958), especially pp. 348, 374.

abstract model? Yet the correlation in many instances between the predictions of theory and actual behavior is not accidental. Such correlation may be expected if two assumptions on which the theory rests are justified by the circumstances prevailing in the real world.

There is, first, the assumption that all men acting for states share the same universal traits of human nature. Specifically, these men are expected to place exceedingly high value on the so-called possessions of the nation—above all, on national survival, national independence, and territorial integrity—and to react in fear against any threats to these possessions. It is also assumed that they share a strong inclination to profit from opportunities for acquisition or reacquisition of cherished national possessions, with national power as the chief means of preserving or acquiring national values. To the extent to which these traits are shared and have a decisive effect on the actions or reactions of statesmen and peoples, they create conformity as if by a kind of inner compulsion.

The second assumption concerns the environment in which governments are required to act. If it is true that the anarchical multistate system creates a condition of constant danger to national core possessions—specifically, to national survival—and, at the same time, provides frequent opportunity for new acquisitions, the actors can be said to act under external compulsion rather than in accordance with their preferences.

It is easy to see that both these sweeping assumptions are not the products of unrealistic fantasies. Attachment to possessions, fear, and ambition —although they vary in degree from man to man and from people to people— can properly be called "general traits of human nature" which are likely to operate with particular strength in men who hold positions of authority and national responsibility. That the condition of multiple sovereignty is one in which states "'live dangerously" is also a matter of common experience and knowledge. The real question is whether internal and external pressures are strong enough everywhere and at all times to transform the actors into something like automatons lacking all freedom of choice. Certainly, to the degree that these compulsions exist in the real world, the psychological peculiarities of the actors are deprived of the opportunity to express themselves and therefore can be discounted as irrelevant to an analysis of international politics.

.   .   .

2. On The Equality of States

R. P. ANAND

Dr. Anand is Head of the Department of International Law at the Indian School of International Studies at New Delhi.

Despite all the inequalities among states—in size of territory or population, economic prosperity or military strength, industrial development or cultural advancement—the Charter of the United Nations, proclaiming its faith "in the equal rights of men and women and of nations large and small", declares in unambiguous terms: "The Organization is based on the principle of sovereign equality of all its Members."

GENESIS OF THE PRINCIPLE OF EQUALITY

This indeed is a reaffirmation of what is supposed to be a most fundamental principle of international law with a long historical lineage. The principle originated during the Middle Ages with the decline of the overwhelming authority of the Holy Roman Empire. Out of the chaos resulting from the disintegration of Christendom, because of the long struggle between Pope and Emperor, emerged nation states without any authority over them. Among different independent states

Excerpts from "Sovereign Equality of States in International Law—I", INTERNATIONAL STUDIES, *Vol. 8 (January 1967), 213–41. Reprinted by permission.*

which dared to call themselves sovereign, there could be no relationship except that of equality....

ENUNCIATION OF THE PRINCIPLE BY CLASSICAL WRITERS

Whether or not Hugo Grotius explicitly declared this principle or made it the underlying theme of his noble system of inter-state relations,[1] it re-

[1] There is a difference of opinion among scholars on this point. Dickinson is firmly of the opinion that Hugo Grotius, the father of modern international law, was not the founder of the doctrine of equality of states. Edwin DeWitt Dickinson, *The Equality of States in International Law* (Cambridge, Mass., 1920), p. 34. This conclusion is affirmed by P. J. Baker in "The Doctrine of Legal Equality of States", *British Year Book of International Law* (London), vol. 4, p. 6. This view is, however, disputed by Frederick Charles Hicks, "The Equality of States and the Hague Conference", *American Journal of International Law* (New York, N.Y.), vol. 2, pp. 531–2. Other writers believe that though Grotius did not deal with the doctrine of equality of states, it was an underlying principle of his system. See Ann Van Wynen Thomas and A. J. Thomas, "Equality of States in International Law—Fact or Fiction?", *Virginia Law Review* (Charlottesville, Va), vol. 37, p. 794.

ceived support in express terms from numerous classical writers, including Samuel von Pufendorf and Emmerich de Vattel. Deeply influenced by the works of Thomas Hobbes and Grotius, and coloured in the prevailing natural law doctrine, Pufendorf's argument was seductively simple: "all persons in a state of nature are equal; the persons of international law are in a state of nature; therefore they are equal."[2]

Thus enunciated by Pufendorf and endorsed by numerous writers during the eighteenth century, the doctrine received a strong support and classical exposition at the hands of Vattel. He declared:

Strength or weakness, in this case, counts for nothing. A dwarf is as much a man as a giant is; a small Republic is no less a sovereign State than the most powerful kingdom.

From this equality it necessarily follows that what is lawful or unlawful for one Nation is equally lawful or unlawful for every other Nation.[3]

. . .

REJECTION OF THE PRINCIPLE BY POSITIVISTS

...the practice of states during the nineteenth century (which was clearly at variance with the theory of equality of states) led many a writer, under the influence of positivism, to deny the efficacy and even the existence of this theory in international law (the sovereign equality of states). Thus, writing in 1885, T. J. Lawrence reached the conclusion that the principle of equality was obsolete:

It seems to me that, in the face of such facts as these, it is impossible to hold any longer the old doctrine of the absolute equality of all independent states before the law. It is dead; and we ought to put in its place the new doctrine that the Great Powers have by modern International Law a primacy among their fellows, which bids fair to develop into a central authority for the settlement of all disputes between the nations of Europe.[4]

A few years later (in 1898), Antoine Pillet concluded that it was futile, as well as a logical mistake, to treat equality as a fundamental right. The assertion that Russia and Geneva have equal rights, said Pillet, "has a primary and very grave defect; it is not just. States are not equal from the point of view of their rights any more than from that of their wealth and their power."[5]

The most serious and uncompromising attack on the principle came from the well-known Scotch jurist, James Lorimer. Pointing out that "the equality of states and their absolute independence have been steadily repudiated by history", he said that "it is a chimera as unrealisable as the union of the head of a woman with the tail

---

[2] See Baker, n. 3, p. 6. Samuel von Pufendorf's *De Jure Nature et Gentium* was first published in 1672.

[3] Emmerich de Vattel, *Le Droit des Gens* (first published in 1758) as translated in Charles B. Fenwick, *Classics of International Law* (Washington, D.C., 1916), vol. 3, p. 7.

[4] T. J. Lawrence, *Essays on Some Disputed Questions in Modern International Law* (Cambridge, 1885), edn 2, p. 232. Quoted in Dickinson, n. 3, p. 141. See also T. J. Lawrence, *The Principles of International Law* (New York, N.Y., 1913), edn 5, pp. 275, 288.

[5] Quoted in Dickinson, n. 3, pp. 133–4.

of a fish".[6] Explaining his point further, he wrote:

Now the equality of all states, the moment they are acknowledged to be states at all, is, if possible, a more transparent fiction than the equality of individuals who are admitted to be jural persons or jural citizens; because in the case of individuals or citizens there are limits to possible size and power, and consequently to equality, which do not exist in the case of states.... To assert that, without any superiority in other respects, a state with ten thousand inhabitants is equal to a state with the ten million inhabitants, or that a state half the size of an English county is equal to a state that covers half a Continent, is just as false as to assert that a thousand is equal to a million, or that the Canton of Geneva is equal to the Continent of Europe.[7]

He, therefore, asserted:

All states are equally entitled to be recognized as states, on the simple ground that they are states, but all states are not entitled to be recognized as equal states, simply because they are not equal states. Russia and Roumania are equally entitled to be recognized as states, but they are not entitled to be recognized as equal states. Any attempt to depart from this principle, whatever be the sphere of jurisprudence with which we are occupied, leads not to the vindication but to the violation of equality before the law.[8]

.   .   .

---

[6] Quoted in Lande, n. 16, p. 260.
[7] James Lorimer, *The Institute of the Law of Nations* (London, 1883), vol. 2, pp. 170–1.
[8] Ibid., p. 260.

PARIS PEACE CONFERENCE OF 1919 AND THE DRAFTING OF THE LEAGUE COVENANT

History bears testimony to the fact that in peace conferences, particularly after great wars, the Great Powers have shown a tendency to take decisions more or less without the consent of small Powers.[9] Although the principle of equality was not openly challenged by anyone and although, on the contrary, it was actually proclaimed expressly by most of the authors of the Covenant, it soon became clear that the Great Powers who had won the war (namely France, Italy, Japan, the United Kingdom, and the United States) were keen on establishing a superior position for themselves in the League. Lord Robert Cecil, the British delegate, who was most critical of the principle of equality, declared "that the Great Powers must run the League, and that it was just as well to recognize it flatly as not".[10] The French delegate was even more clear and blunt:

...the matter is not one to be discussed in the abstract or on the basis of sentiment; but a thing of cold fact; and the fact is that the war was won by Great Britain, France, Japan, Italy and the United States. It is essential that the League be formed around these effective Powers so that at its birth it shall carry with it the influence and prestige of the nations that conquered Germany.[11]

---

[9] Quoted in Rappard, ibid., p. 28.
[10] Quoted in Rappard, n. 73, p. 25.
[11] Quoted in Rappard, ibid., p. 29. See also the Italian draft and the draft by General Smuts in Broms, n. 21, pp. 118–19. Alfred Zimmern, "The Great Powers in the League of Nations", *Problems of Peace* (London, 1935), series 9, pp. 57ff.

Thus, despite verbal affirmation of the principle, it was accepted neither in representation nor in procedure in Paris. Most of the important decisions were made by a "Council of Ten", which at first consisted of two representatives of each of the five Great Powers and which, later, came to have five and, eventually, four members (when the Japanese delegate ceased to participate except in matters of special interest to Japan).[12] The peace treaty with Germany was in fact the work of the Great Powers, and it was left for the small countries only to sign it.

.   .   .

EQUALITY OF STATES AND THE UNITED NATIONS

This reluctance of the Great Powers to include "equality of states" in the League Covenant was noticeably absent during and after the Second World War. Following the Atlantic Charter of 1941,[13] the Four-Power (the Republic of China, the United Kingdom, the United States, and the Soviet Union) Moscow Declaration of 1943 recognized the necessity of establishing a general international organization "based on the principle of sovereign equality of all peace-loving States".[14] Through the Dumbarton Oaks proposals,[15] this later found its way into the United Nations Charter, as we have noted earlier. However, this reiteration of the well-recognized but truncated principle of the law of nations *did not deter the Great Powers from asserting their greatness and special status in*

this new *"Charter of Hope"* established to safeguard future generations from the scourge of war. Advancing the usual argument that they had "special responsibilities" in matters relating to peace and security, they claimed special status for themselves in the United Nations.[16] The small states were told that even if it were true that "all nations are equally interested in the peace of the world", it was certainly not true that they could make equal contributions to its maintenance.[17]

Although equality of representation and voting was generally maintained[18] in the San Francisco Conference[19] called to frame the UN Charter, and, unlike the Paris Peace Conference, small countries were given some bargaining power and a rôle in the framing of the Charter[20], the main purpose of the conference was "no other than to get the smaller nations to agree to a plan of organization based on the proposals worked out by the Big Three or Big Four at Dumbarton Oaks".[21] Following the precedent set in the

12 See Broms, n. 21, p. 118.
13 See Broms, n. 21, p. 155.
14 Louis B. Sohn, *Cases and Materials on World Law* (Cambridge, 1950), p. 1145.
15 Ibid., p. 1146.

16 *Report to the President on the Results of the San Francisco Conference* by the Chairman of the US delegation. Department of State Publication no. 2349 (Washington, D.C., 1945), pp. 66, 67.
17 See Philip C. Jessup, "The Equality of States as Dogma and Reality", *Political Science Quarterly,* vol. 60, p. 531.
18 Cf. Broms, n. 21, pp. 159ff.
19 Fifty Governments were represented in the conference.
20 At San Francisco, said Judge Jessup, the "voice of the middle and small Powers is louder, more insistent, and, again comparatively, more productive of results". Philip C. Jessup, *A Modern Law of Nations: An Introduction* (New York, N.Y., 1948), p. 29.
21 A. Wolfers, "The Role of the Small States, in the Enforcement of International Peace", *Proceedings of the Academy of Political Science* (New York, N.Y.), vol. 21, p. 24.

League Covenant, the Dumbarton Oaks proposals sought not only to give permanent seats[22] on the Security Council of the United Nations to five Great Powers, viz. the United States, the Soviet Union, the United Kingdom, France, and China,[23] but also to reinforce their position by giving them the veto on all the important questions to be decided by the Security Council. Justifying these proposals in a joint statement, the Big Powers declared:

In view of the primary responsibilities of the permanent members, they could not be expected, in the present condition of the world, to assume the obligation to act in so serious a matter as the maintenance of international peace and security in consequence of a decision in which they had not concurred. Therefore, if a majority voting in the Security Council is to be made possible, the only practicable method is to provide, in respect of

non-procedural decisions, for unanimity of the permanent members plus the concurring votes of at least two of the non-permanent members.[24]

This privileged position of the Great Powers and their right of veto were vigorously attacked by small states at San Francisco. They declared this superiority contrary to the "fundamental principles of democracy"[25] and extremely unjust. Such a right (of veto) might lead to a position, they pointed out, similar to that of a murderer who was permitted to vote on his own guilt.[26] Since no nation could be expected to vote for action against itself any case of threat to the peace or breach of the peace caused by itself, the Organization would be powerless.[27] This would establish a world order, said the Mexican delegate, "in which the mice could be stamped out but in which the lions would not be restrained".[28] Although they conceded leadership to the Great Powers, they did not want to be ignored especially when their own interests were involved. As Ezequeil Padilla, the Mexican Secretary of State, said:

The small nations do not pretend to equal participation in a world of unequal responsibilities. What they do desire is that when injustice may strike at the door of small nations, their voices may be heard; and that their complaints and protest against injustice shall not be

---

[22] It is important to note that whereas the states which were given permanent seats in the League Council were actually Great Powers, it was not so in 1945. Thus China, was never considered to be a Great Power, and the United Kingdom and France had lost their Great-Power status as a result of the Second World War. See Weinschel, 'The Doctrine of the Equality of States and Its Recent Modifications", *American Journal of International Law,* vol. 45, p. 423; Harold Sprout, "The Role of the Great States", *Proceedings of the Academy of Political Science,* vol. 21, pp. 284, 286. See also Quincy Wright, "History and Influence of the U.N. Veto", *Virginia Law Weekly* (Charlottesville, Va), 7 December 1961. According to Professor Wright, the Great-Power status in the United Nations does not correspond to any rational criterion for determining Great Powers today. He, therefore, remarks that "the Great Power veto in the United Nations is a product of history, not of reason".

[23] The Charter has recently been amended to include ten non-permanent members in the Security Council.

[24] Report to the President, n. 124, p. 76.

[25] Representative of Cuba, UNCIO Doc., vol. 11 (New York, N.Y., 1945), p. 351.

[26] Mexican delegate, ibid., p. 333.

[27] The Netherlands' delegate, ibid., p. 314.

[28] Ibid., p. 474.

shrouded in the silence and blind solidarity of the Great Powers.[29]

All this had, however, no effect on the Big Powers. On the other hand, the small states were advised to look at the position "realistically".[30] The special position of the Great Powers, they were reminded, corresponded to the "responsibilities and duties that would be imposed upon them".[31] Peace must rest, said the British delegate, "on the unanimity of great powers for without it whatever was built would be built on shifting sands, of no more value than the paper upon which it was written".[32] In any case, the small states were told point-blank that the Charter would be unacceptable to the Great Powers without these special privileges. Thus Senator Connally of the United States dramatically tore up a copy of the proposed Charter and said to the delegates of the small Powers that they would be guilty of the same behaviour if they insisted on opposing the Great-Power veto.[33] He added: "You may, if you wish, go home from this Conference and say that you have defeated the veto. But what will be your answer when you are asked: 'Where is the Charter?' "[34]

Put in this way, the question of voting was no longer a legal one but, as the Norwegian delegate put it, one of "political engineering".[35] The small

Powers were left with no choice except to accept the "evil" of veto and special status of the Great Powers "because the alternative was a thousand times worse".[36] It is important, however, to note that though they "acquiesced" in the proposed voting system for the time being, it did not mean that they "agreed to it". They, therefore, expressed a hope that would be amended in due course.[37]

The privileged position of the Great Powers, of course, gave them numerous powers, not owned by others, and enhanced their status even further than it had been in the League of Nations. Unlike the League Council, the Security Council of the United Nations is endowed with real powers under Chapter VII in connexion with threats to the peace, breaches of the peace, and acts of aggression, and all the Members of United Nations are bound to accept the decisions of the Security Council and to carry them out (Articles 25 and 48) by rendering all necessary assistance, including armed forces.[38] Whereas the Members of the League of Nations possessed the veto in the Council and in the Assembly because of "unanimity rule", all except the Big Five have lost it in the United Nations. Apart from the most important field of peace and security, the special status of the Great Powers in the Security Council gives them further

---

[29] Quoted by Robert Herrara, "Evolution of the Equality of States in Inter-American System", *Political Science Quarterly,* vol. 61, p. 111.

[30] Representative of Great Britain, n. 133, p. 322.

[31] Soviet Representative, ibid., p. 332.

[32] Ibid., p. 475.

[33] Broms, n. 21, p. 160.

[34] Quoted by Broms, ibid. See also UNCIO Doc., n. 133, p. 493; see UK Representative, ibid., p. 475.

[35] Ibid., p. 350; see also Koo, *Voting Procedures in International Political Organization* (New York, N.Y., 1947), pp. 224ff.

[36] Lebanese Representative, ibid., p. 486; see New Zealand's Representative, ibid., pp. 170ff; Peru, ibid., p. 457; Cuba, ibid., p. 460; Honduras, ibid., p. 460.

[37] The Netherlands' delegate, ibid., p. 330. See also representatives of Peru, ibid., p. 166; Cuba, p. 459; Argentina, p. 473; Uruguay, p. 488; Australia, p. 492.

[38] Cf. Eagleton, "Covenant of the League of Nations and Charter of the United Nations: Points of Difference", *Department of State Bulletin* (Washington, D.C.), vol. 13, pp. 263–9.

powers in connexion with the admission (Article 4), suspension (Article 5), and expulsion (Article 6) of Members, the appointment of the Secretary-General (Article 97), and the amendment of the Charter (Article 108).

Nothing more need be said to prove the gross inequality between the Great Powers and the small states in the United Nations. These inequalities did not of course go unnoticed in the San Francisco Conference. The Belgian delegate, Rolin, said that the small states would regard it as ironical, in view of the striking inequalities evident in the Organization, to find at the head of the statement of principles, a bold reference to the "sovereign equality" of all Members. He, therefore, proposed to omit the word "sovereign" found in Article 2, paragraph 1. His proposal was promptly seconded by the delegate from Uruguay, but he suggested that the word "sovereign" should be replaced by the word "juridical". Both of these proposals were defeated,[39] however, and the Charter deceivingly affirmed the "sovereign equality" of all its Members. Considering the fact that the Members of the United Nations have neither equal rights nor equal protection of such rights as they have, Professor P. E. Corbett can hardly be blamed for stating that "the 'sovereign equality' of Article 2, paragraph 1, is a striking manifestation of the persisting appeal of face-saving phrases in international politics", and that, in the circumstances, "it is difficult to attach much practical significance to the salute to the 'principle of equal sovereignty' in Article 2, paragraph 1".[40]

In contrast to the Security Council,[41] the General Assembly, like the League Assembly, has been organized on the basis of the principle of equality and all the Members have the right to equal representation, equal opportunity to participate in discussions, and equal voting power. The Great Powers agreed to this equality between unequal states in the General Assembly because it was supposed to have "no power to take decisions binding on Members with respect to their policies and conduct in their international relations".[42] Although the Charter authorizes the Assembly to take binding decisions in procedural matters, to perform certain elective functions, to admit new Members, and to approve the budget and allocate expenses, its powers are otherwise limited to initiating studies, discussing matters brought before it, and making recommendations to Members and to other organs.[43] The equality in the General Assembly, therefore, would not affect the Great Powers and the special powers they have acquired in other organs.

[40] P. E. Corbett, *Law and Society in the Relations of States* (New York, N.Y. 1951), pp. 264–5. See also Broms, n. 21, p. 166, where he remarks that the term "sovereign equality" "signified merely an act of homage paid to the doctrines of equality and sovereignty of States and that this term was not intended to govern the position between the members of the United Nations in the functional aspect".

[41] There is also no equality of representation in the Trusteeship Council. On the other hand, equality principle is respected in the constitution of the Economic and Social Council. See Weinschel, n. 130, pp. 429–30.

[42] Leland M. Goodrich, *The United Nations* (New York, N.Y., 1959), p. 111.

[43] See Weinschel, n. 130, pp. 432–4.

[39] UNCIO Doc. 784, vol. 6, p. 332.

NATIONALISM

Chapter 2

If we go on the assumption that the state is the major participant in international relations, the next required step is to address ourselves to the question of why it operates as it does.

There are many facets to this problem. Some of them will unfold as the book progresses and will be dealt with in subsequent chapters. But among the answers to the "why" of state behavior, one of the most important is that the state, its government, and the decision makers who run the government are capable of acting in foreign relations because they can count on the loyalty and support of the inhabitants of their state. It is this phenomenon which is generally subsumed under the broad term of "nationalism."

If this assumption—namely, that national loyalty is one of the significant factors which enables decision makers to frame and pursue objectives in their relations with others—is warranted, then it is apparent why a treatment of nationalism is necessary for an understanding of the international system and the behavior of the participants in that system.

There are many definitions of nationalism. Most of them set up a number of criteria, including a common cultural heritage, a common language, a common attachment to a particular piece of real estate, common symbols, common social and economic institutions, a common government (or the desire for one), a sense of attachment, affiliation, even love for one's fellow-nationals, a common interpretation of the group's historical experience, and common hopes and expectations for the future. Other characteristics could be added, but the difficulty is that not all criteria need to be present in any given situation before one can speak of nationalism as being present. There are societies in which several different languages are spoken, where segments of the population have different historical experiences and different cultural patterns, but which still exhibit great attachment to the nation and a high degree of cohesiveness in relations with the outside world.

Some recent attempts to come to grips with the phenomenon of nationalism include K. H. Silvert's suggestion that nationalism has many facets and can be approached, analyzed, and understood from a variety of perspectives. One such perspective is to consider it as a formal, juridical concept, dealing with the relationship between individuals and the state—a relationship of mutual obligations and expectations. Another perspective is to view nationalism as a symbolic concept, approached through identification of differences in the symbols, language, dress, habits, and so on of various groups. Third, nationalism is clearly an ideology, a system of thought about the group's past experience, its present role or mission, and its future expectations and potentialities. Finally nationalism can be understood as a social value defining the loyalty which is thought to be due one's fellow citizens and one's state, and which expresses either tacit or active consent for the activities of the state, both within its own boundaries and in its relations with other states, their governments, and their decision makers. Silvert's own definition of nationalism is that it is "the acceptance of the state as the impersonal and ultimate arbiter of human affairs."[1] This may be a difficult formula to accept for those of us brought up in the tradition that it is the individual rather than the state which is ultimately important, but it describes much of what actually exists in the world, and it is quite in line with the proposition from President Kennedy's inaugural address, widely accepted if insufficiently analyzed and understood, "Ask not what your country can do for you, but what you can do for your country."

The prominent political scientist, Karl W. Deutsch, addressing himself to the confusion surrounding the concept of nationalism, examines the "luxuriant growth of different concepts" but concludes that there is a considerable degree of overlap between various approaches to, and understandings of, the phenomenon with which we are dealing. He describes this overlap in the following terms:

> Most serious writers have agreed that nationality is not biological and has little if anything to do with race. They have suggested that nationality somehow involves some common relationships to parts of men's physical environment—their "country"—and to some events in the past, transmitted to the present as "common" history....(Furthermore) nationality implies some

[1] K. H. Silvert, ed., *Expectant Peoples: Nationalism and Development* (New York: Alfred A. Knopf, Inc. and Random House, Inc., 1967), pp. 18–19.

similar elements inside the minds of every individual participating in it, such as common values, thoughts, or feelings, and...some of these might not be similar but rather complementary: interlocking habits and memories in the minds of individuals inducing them to play interlocking roles of helper and helped, or leader and led.... These interlocking habits and roles (are seen as) linked to actual social institutions.... The further element of a "common attachment to symbols" likewise implie(s) an interlocking relation between those who manipulate these symbols and those who accept them....

On the basis of this common pool of understanding of the phenomenon of nationalism, Deutsch then proceeds to analyze and quantify significant aspects of it in terms of complementary and interlocking processes of social communications, utilizing for his purpose some of the insights, concepts, and methods which the student of international relations finds available in such related fields as communications and information theory.[2]

The student of the history of nationalism points out that affection, devotion, and a sense of belonging to one's group are as old as recorded history and are apparently essential cementing factors for any human group. The experience of the ancient Hebrews and the Greeks is frequently cited in support of the proposition that sentiments and practices resembling those of modern nationalism were not unknown in antiquity. Yet the modern version of nationalism is usually traced back to the development of the modern state in the sixteenth and seventeenth centuries, and the modern version of *mass* nationalism can be said to have come only with the active involvement of large numbers of citizens in the affairs of the states. In that sense it can be said to have been a product of modern means of communication as well as modern means of warfare which required the mass mobilization of large bodies of citizens. Historians of nationalism, such as Carlton C. J. Hayes, Hans Kohn, and others also point to the great variations in the ways in which nationalism has expressed itself, both within and between states. Hayes, for example, traces five *types* of nationalism:[3] (1) the *humanitarian* type, largely a product of the eighteenth century, when national entities were created for the express purpose (if not always with the consequent result) of setting men free, the American and French Revolutions being outstanding cases in point; (2) *Jacobin* nationalism, in which national patriotism became more important than individual freedom, which insisted on a missionary zeal, and which was characterized by fanaticism with respect to national symbols, ceremonies, anthems, flags, shrines, and the like; (3) *traditional* nationalism, arising through the period of imperialism, stressing its moral responsibilities rather than its financial profits; (4) *liberal* nationalism, in which emphasis on individualism was linked with enthusiasm for

[2] Karl W. Deutsch, *Nationalism and Social Communication: An Inquiry into the Foundations of Nationality,* 2nd ed. (Cambridge: The M. I. T. Press, 1966), pp. 27 ff.

[3] Carlton J. Hayes, *The Historical Evolution of Nationalism* (New York: The Macmillan Company, 1950).

reform and belief in utilitarianism; and finally, (5) *integral* nationalism, the exclusive pursuit of national policies in the quest for continuing increases in national power, a system in which the interests of the nation transcended both those of the individual member of that nation and those of the international society, indeed of humanity. None of these types is ever to be found in its *pure* form, of course, but a typology of this kind may be useful in directing our attention to the various forms which nationalism takes amidst the endless varieties and complexities of the modern state system.

Let us conclude by suggesting that nationalism is functional both to the individual, for whom the nation performs many services and to whom membership in a national group bestows considerable values, and also to the group as such, for which nationalism is an important ingredient, a social cement which helps bind it together, particularly in the face of external threats, real or imagined. Whether it is also functional to the international system is quite another question and one about which we would express profound doubts. Examples come readily to mind. Thus in our own country, President Eisenhower's popularity rose after the disastrous U-2 affair of the late 1950s, just as did President Kennedy's after the Bay of Pigs fiasco in 1961, causing the latter to comment wryly that the worse he did, the more popular he seemed to become! These and similar phenomena can be understood not in terms of strict rationality but in terms of the tendency to "rally 'round the flag" in an emergency. It is this tendency that has given governments confidence that actions in international affairs will, in the final analysis, have the approval and support of vast majorities of their own populations. Were this confidence absent, the conduct of external affairs— and therefore the substance of international relations—would be bound to be quite different from the way it is. We may be on the verge of experiencing such a shift, as in the domestic opposition to the Vietnam war, which led to the retirement of an American President; but we are, at most, at the very beginning of an era in which the nearly-automatic support of governments in their foreign relations may become a questionable rather than a certain expectation.

Meanwhile, after all the arguments for and against nationalism have been advanced, after its benefits (mostly domestic) as well as its problems and shortcomings (mostly international) have been weighed against one another, and after one has arrived at a value judgment either in its favor or in opposition, the fact remains that nationalism is alive and thriving— particularly, but by no means exclusively, in the "new" countries of the world—and is an input into the international system which no student of that system, of its structure, its operations, and the behavior of its members, can afford to neglect.

1. What is Nationalism?

LEONARD DOOB

Leonard Doob is Professor of Psychology at Yale University. He is author of BECOMING MORE CIVILIZED: A PSYCHOLOGICAL EXPLORATION, COMMUNICATION IN AFRICA: A SEARCH FOR BOUNDARIES, *and* PATRIOTISM AND NATIONALISM, *from which the present excerpt is taken.*

Nationalism is unquestionably one of the most important problems, if not the most important one, of this century. Surely it would be in better taste not to utter such a flat, modest conviction in the opening sentence of a book. Still whenever a writer voluntarily subjects himself to the joyful misery that writing entails he must feel that his theme merits a very high rating. It seems better, consequently, to make the statement unabashedly than to be coy or cunning. Convincing evidence in support of the claim, moreover, is unfortunately close at hand: nationalism—as well as patriotism—is related to war, is actually and potentially so destructive that it bestows pervasive significance upon any related topic.

Moans about nationalism are as pointless as complaints about disease or mortality. Fine feelings expressed verbally either in a crude or subtle manner do not alter nonverbal facts. Such phenomena must first be understood before they can be affected or controlled. Of course, of course, the

semi-sophisticated must impatiently say, whoever believes otherwise? The banal reminder, alas, is not superfluous in the midst of the stream of spoken and printed attacks upon nationalism which appear almost whenever there is freedom of speech and press. And then, too, not only abuse but sometimes also praise is heaped upon nationalism, which is then viewed as the inevitable culmination of patriotism or God's will. Here, it must be disclosed, no sides are taken, or at least not deliberately. The purpose of this book is the understanding of the psychological foundation of nationalism, especially that of patriotism, through patient analysis. Guidance, control, persuasion come. later, and then only after a dash of value judgment has been added.

And so the writer, miraculously, has required only two introductory paragraphs to purge himself of bias. His conscience is as clear as ever it can be. Let him plunge into the task at hand.

There are various analytic approaches to nationalism, since the topic challenges many learned disciplines. Foremost is the historian, who recounts either minutely or sweepingly the incidents in the development of one or more countries from a particular point in time at which nationalism is claimed to have been either absent or weak to another at which it became very strong or overpowering. In the strict tradition of his craft, this type of scholar emerges with an ordering of detailed events whose very concreteness suggests their singularity. Thus the growth of nationalism in Bolivia has depended upon a rather unique set of circumstances which cannot possibly have been replicated entirely in some other land such as modern Egypt. After he or his colleagues have surveyed nationalism in a number of countries, an historian may summon the intellectual courage to seek general trends in the developmental patterns; details may be singular but, on a higher level of abstraction, they can be grasped as illustrative of a unifying principle. The man producing unification may have been Bolivar in one nation and Nasser in another, and the life histories and the deeds of the two may also have been most diverse; but the two leaders, the induced conclusion states, possessed organizing skill and enough mystique to attract followers, and eventually they both were enthroned as heroes in their lands.

An historical account of nationalism in one or more countries may or may not relate aspects of this phenomenon to a set of specified economic, political, social, or geographical factors. The other social sciences, however, almost always deliberately seek to show that some X associated with nationalism depends upon or varies with some Y or set of Y's. Immediately, it must be noted, much of the literature in those disciplines is admittedly historical too, again with a difference: the growth of one institution is singled out for special emphasis. Consider how policy and behavioral sciences generally deal with nationalism in countries outside the West. Political scientists stress almost exclusively the changes in government and the factors producing and affected by those changes. Economists in their turn concentrate upon the economic changes (preferably, according to the academic fashion of the day, quantitative ones) which allegedly occur before nations can function in the modern world of the United Nations and before they can participate in international trade; for them, nationalism is, more often than not, one of the noneconomic factors affecting economic events. Sociologists and anthropologists move a step or two away from historical analysis and offer the description and analysis of societies which, in the light of some definition, can be considered nationalistic.

The animal of nationalism is so large that a political scientist can focus upon the organization and structure of a nation-state or upon its political parties, an economist upon a country's natural resources or its international trade, a sociologist upon the origins and ideologies of the ruling elite, an anthropologist upon the changes in social organization demanded and produced by nationhood—and all of them may be discussing some section of the same elephant. Although insights from such sources are accepted with grateful acclaim, they are nevertheless not the subject of the present approach. For just as social science disciplines assume but do not systematically focus upon the human beings whose existence obviously is presupposed, so their analyses of nationalism omit or deal only incidentally with the people who live within the nation and who therefore reflect and affect, in varying degrees, their country's development and problems. Without claiming superiority or denying inferiority, this treatise would timidly concentrate upon the psychological foundations of nationalism within all the nationals of a country.

The mere assertion that there are psychological foundations of nationalism may elicit skepticism and disbelief. If the historical development of Bolivia and Egypt are uniquely different, then what reasonable ground exists for believing that Bolivians and Egyptians, who have lived under diverse nationalistic regimes, are psychologically similar? Naturally it is easy to say that the people are different; their languages, for example, are unrelated and so, to the extent that language affects behavior —and to some extent it does—they themselves must differ. Such diversities can easily be discerned and emphasized, but it is much more difficult and likewise important to discover and dissect the underlying similarities.

The foundations of nationalism, then, must be more or less universal for a relatively simple reason: the possession and exercise of similar potentialities and skills require similar attributes. Whether you live in Bolivia or Egypt or, for that matter, in Siberia or Buganda, most though not all relevant aspects of your behavior must be virtually identical if you are successfully to ride a bicycle. The machine's requirements are the critical factors that very definitely restrict the range of variations. Although nationalism is a bit more complicated than a bicycle, it also demands certain kinds of behavior and outlaws others.

The metaphor of the bicycle, however, is applicable to nationalism only by making a basic assumption: the nationalism to which people adapt and which they and their leaders create is everywhere similar, just as all bicycles are very much alike. Is this so? At issue is the tedious question of definition, a question which must therefore be at least tentatively settled forthwith.

DEFINITIONS

Whoever writes about nationalism unveils a private definition in his introductory remarks; hence the literature on the subject is crowded with formal definitions. The following three may or may not be typical, but at least they stem from writers belonging to different disciplines:

An ideological commitment to the pursuit of the unity, independence, and interests of a people who conceive of themselves as forming a community.[1]

A consciousness, on the part of individuals or groups, of membership in a nation, or of a desire to forward the strength, liberty, or prosperity of a nation, whether one's own or another.[2]

A condition of mind in which loyalty to the ideal or to the fact of one's national state is superior to all other loyalties and of which pride in one's nationality and belief in its intrinsic excellence and its "mission" are integral parts.[3]

Three points in the definitions may be effortlessly observed. They contain language, firstly, that is psychologically loaded: "ideological commitment" and "people who conceive of themselves"; "a consciousness"; and "a condition of mind." In fact, some writers, even though they are political scientists, agree with novelists[4] that the distinctive attribute of a nation is the feeling people have toward one another: "The

[1] Lloyd A. Fallers, "Ideology and Culture in Uganda Nationalism," *American Anthrop.*, 63 (1961), pp. 677–86.
[2] Royal Institute of International Affairs, *Nationalism* (London: Oxford University Press, 1939), p. xviii.
[3] Carlton J. H. Hayes, *Essays on Nationalism* (New York: Macmillan, 1937), p. 6.
[4] Israel Zangwill, *The Principle of Nationalities* (London: Watts, 1917), pp. 37–39.

simplest statement that can be made about a nation is that it is a body of people who feel that they are a nation; and it may be that when all the fine-spun analysis is concluded this will be the ultimate statement as well."[5] The acclaimed historian of nationalism quoted above notes that nationalism is used in three other senses: to refer to the process of nation-building, to the theory or ideal behind that process, and to the activities of particular political parties. He stresses, nevertheless, the psychological element, because in his opinion "this is the nationalism which in the twentieth century is most in evidence [and] which colours thought and conditions action in political, social, and cultural spheres, in our domestic politics and in our foreign relations."[6]

Then, in the second place, definitions of nationalism revolve around sociological or political concepts which themselves require explication: "community," "nation," "national state," "nationality." And, thirdly, they are not limited temporally, geographically, or culturally: and group in the past, present, or future may be called nationalistic if it satisfies the requirements that are set forth. This means, therefore, that nationalism has been defined as (1) some kind of psychological state (2) characterizing people in some sort of group (3) anywhere, any time. Established social usage seems sufficiently clear, or can thus be made to appear so.

Before using these three inductions as the bases for formal definitions, however, another trio of distinctions involving types of human reactions must be distinguished. When people respond to a stimulus pattern, they are affected inevitably by their antecedent *predispositions,* which have been called central tendencies, traits, feelings, beliefs, attitudes, response tendencies, etc. Then they may make certain *demands* as a result of what they are perceiving and of these predispositions. Finally, their demands may induce them to take *action,* that is, they exhibit in consequence overt behavior.

In this analysis the predispositions, being subjective and internal, are referred to as *patriotism.* The concept is customarily used in precisely that sense; its most common definition, "love of country," is obviously subjective and psychological. *Nationalism* arises psychologically when patriotism leads to certain demands and possibly also to action. Nationalism is thus not a psychological term as such: the demands and the actions stem from a psychological state, patriotism, but the ensuing demands and actions are politically, socially, economically significant. Now, then, it is finally possible to unfurl two formal definitions reflecting these weighty matters as well as the gems salvaged from the literature:

PATRIOTISM: the more or less conscious conviction of a person that his own welfare and that of the significant groups to which he belongs are dependent upon the preservation or expansion (or both) of the power and culture of his society.

NATIONALISM: the set of more or less uniform demands (1) which people in a society share, (2) which arise from their patriotism, (3) for which justifications exist and can be readily expressed, (4) which incline them to make personal sacrifices in behalf of their government's aims, and (5) which may or may not lead to appropriate action.

These not so innocent definitions immediately raise two questions of fact.

[5] Rupert Emerson, *From Empire to Nation* (Cambridge: Harvard University Press, 1960), p. 102.

[6] Hayes, *op. cit.,* pp. 5–6.

First, is patriotism universal? According to the definition, the answer is likely to be in the affirmative. People are always socialized in groups, one of which is certain to be recognized as a society with its own distinctive culture; they most certainly must come to associate their welfare and that of other groups to which they belong with that society. Patriotism may vary in degree; the traitor may be negatively patriotic; but zero patriotism does not seem probable.

Then, secondly, is nationalism also universal? Here the answer is *probably no*. For the patriotic conviction concerning the relation of welfare and country need not be accompanied by demands and actions. Potentially, however, patriotism can give rise to nationalism; if the beloved society is threatened, then preserving it can quickly become a national policy.

The two definitions are intended to have unlimited scope, so that reference can be made to patriotism or nationalism in the ancient or modern world and in nonliterate and literate societies. To designate a more definite universe of discourse, a modifying adjective can be added, such as classic, Western European, nineteenth-century, African, democratic, communist, or Christian. Or the patriotism and nationalism of a society may be examined piece by piece in terms of geographical regions, strata, or political organizations. *National* either as an adjective (as distinguished from *nationalist* or *nationalistic*) or as a noun will be used without prejudice or psychological overtones simply to refer to any phenomenon associated with a nation, including the inhabitants.

Regrettably the definitions announced above contain words and phrases requiring elaboration. The patriot is said to be "conscious" because, having been made aware of his love of country, he can appreciate the fact that other people share his convictions; but he is only "more or less" conscious since, presumably, unconscious factors always play some role in behavior. The concept of "conviction" also carries psychological overtones: the national has ideals and beliefs concerning his country, himself, and the relation between the two. "Welfare" conveys the importance of patriotism: the person believes that his most valued goals are somehow connected with, or "dependent" upon, his country. In the words of one extremely astute analyst, he gives his "supreme" or "final" loyalty not to "the family, the tribe, the city, [or] the manor" but to his state or nation.[7] Thus the state and not some other group possesses "sovereignty" from the psychological viewpoint.[8]

The groups considered significant within the nation vary from society to society and from person to person, but they undoubtedly include the family and the equivalent of the church. The presence in the definition of a key concept from political science, "power," would emphasize that people are to some degree aware of the state's function in this respect. "Culture" suggests broadly the social heritage and the system of interlocking habits which people acquire during socialization and which both in fact and in fantasy they share with one another. And likewise "society" would indicate that the formal and informal organizations in which people are embedded—the social structure, the groups, the classes—function within the state.

The definition of nationalism, if we may now proceed to that concept, does not indicate the exact nature of

[7] James Clement King, *Some Elements of National Solidarity* (Chicago: University of Chicago Libraries, 1935), pp. 1–2.

[8] Guy E. Swanson, *The Birth of the Gods* (Ann Arbor, Michigan: University of Michigan Press, 1960), p. 20.

the demands people make, for this is a substantive matter which depends on the historical context. Their general content, however, is specified when their origin is attributed to people's patriotism; hence those demands pertain to "the preservation or expansion (or both) of the power and culture" of people's own society. Although patriotism may be an individual matter, nationalism is most definitely social: people must "share" the demands. Noteworthy is the distinction between "preservation" and "expansion." Most nonliterate societies as well as the smaller and more "conservative" nations today are deeply interested in retaining most of the culture and power they already possess. The imperialistic expansion of some nations at the expense of others, on the other hand, is stressed by communist writers: "Imperialism is the period of an increasing oppression of the nations of the world by a handful of 'great' nations"[9]; the bourgeoisie "has made barbarian and semi-barbarian countries dependent on the civilized ones, nations of peasants on nations of bourgeois, the East on the West."[10] The definition implicitly notes that expansionist demands flow from the desire to preserve and strengthen an existing nation by extending its influence; but the wish to preserve need not be accompanied by expansionist demands.

A few additional observations about the definition of nationalism must be briefly made. The assumption is stated that "justifications" accompany nationalist demands. Their nature, however, is not immediately specified but is discussed at length in subsequent chapters. The phrase "appropriate action" calls attention to the fact that

[9] N. Lenin and G. Zinoviev, *Socialism and War* (London: Martin Lawrence, 1931).
[10] Karl Marx and Friedrich Engels, *The Communist Manifesto* (New York: International Publishers, 1930).

action may or may not result from the demands; when there is action, it is "appropriate" in the sense that it represents an attempt to achieve those wishes. The range of ensuing activity that is motivated by patriotism is obviously very great. Thus the appropriate action for patriotic people living under a tyrant is to rebel. But before the rebellion they may simply engage in conspiratorial activity. Or they may seek temporary peace by rationalizing the status quo. In any case, the definition suggests, they stand ready to make personal sacrifices so that their government can be preserved or expanded: secondary drives within them are so strong that under some circumstances or in some situations their goal involves satisfactions to be attained only in collaboration with their contemporaries.

.   .   .

IMPORTANCE

Certainly, then, the role of the outsider—the enemy—in the establishment, the functioning, and the preservation of nationalism is important. It is, nevertheless, difficult to appraise that role because it clearly fluctuates from nation to nation and, within a nation, from situation to situation. A single principle, however, is incontestable: the greater the threat which the outgroup seems to pose, the more significant does that group become in facilitating both patriotism and nationalism.

.   .   .

The threat posed by the outgroup, consequently, may be psychological in nature and hence as dependent upon people's interpretation of a situation as upon reality itself. If they feel generally secure or if they are especially satisfied with their society, they are less likely to feel inclined to take vigorous action either to preserve or expand the power and culture of their nation; they may disregard even hostile outgroups. Under such conditions, their anxiety must first be aroused before they will acknowledge the threat and hence be stirred to nationalistic activity.

The outgroup or the enemy, like every variable affecting nationalism, seldom if ever operates in isolation. When immigrants to the United States cluster together and maintain nationalistic feelings and ties with the country of their birth or origin, for example, the presence of outsiders in their midst promotes cultural unity. But the fact that they are surrounded by strangers with different customs by itself does not determine the strength of their nationalism or the length of time it takes them to become assimilated. Involved is a very complicated interaction between some of the attributes they themselves possess (their skin coloring, native language, religion, education, purpose for emigrating in the first place) and the corresponding attributes of people already living there.[11]

Even during a war the strength of people's convictions concerning the threat offered by an actual enemy fluctuates, of course, from person to person. In addition, if there is more than one enemy, yet another kind of dispersion may appear. Attitude scales, for example, were administered toward the end of World War II to a very restricted group of college students in the Chicago area; their feelings toward Germany were found to vary "much more widely" than those toward Japan.[12] The outgroup, consequently, is not an unambiguous stimulus pattern.

In time of war, however, patriotic convictions are likely to be strongest; does it follow, then, that the influence of the outgroup is greatest at that time? Once more there is a spiraled interaction: stronger patriotism can be considered both a consequence and a cause of international conflict, but patriotism can be powerful without conflict. Certainly, let us once more agree, the nation becomes especially precious when it is attacked; and yet patriots such as the Swiss can love their country without seeking war, and nationalistic demands can be vigorously voiced without threatening to fight. While...wars, especially modern ones, are much too complicated to be traced to single causes, whether they be economic or nationalistic, still the fact remains that the contribution of patriotism and nationalism can be and has been not inconsiderable. Since the French Revolution the number of wars fought between modern nations has been depressingly large; and most if not all of these conflicts have involved goals associated with peoples' patriotic convictions and their nationalistic demands and actions. Warriors everywhere must be loyal to the regime which commands them; and part of basic training is usually a series of communications and experiences designed to promote that loyalty by increasing patriotism. A distinguished student of war once remarked that "to create a spirit ready to participate in the mass massacre characteristic of the most recent wars, cultural, religious, and political motives have been especially enlisted."[13] In his view, then, the contribution of patriotism is noteworthy. After the Soviet Union had been invaded by the German armies, there was a sharp increase in the number of "na-

---

[11] W. Lloyd Warner and Leo Srole, *The Social Systems of American Ethnic Groups* (New Haven, Conn.: Yale University Press, 1945).

[12] A. R. Gilliland and R. A. Blum, "Favorable and unfavorable attitudes toward certain enemy and allied countries," *Journal of Psychology,* 20 (1945), p. 392.

[13] Quincy Wright, *A Study of War* (Chicago: University of Chicago Press, 1942), p. 290.

tional" slogans issued each May Day[14]; since these slogans provide authoritative guides to the regime's information policy, the change can be called symptomatic of the attempt to use patriotism as a psychological device to spur the Russian people to defend not "Communism," "Socialism," "World Revolution," etc., but "Mother Russia." Finally, nationalistic media also sustain the swagger of the victors and the sorrows of the vanquished after each war, with the frequent result that the end of one conflict has been the prelude to the next.

[After]...seeking to determine the factors facilitating patriotism and nationalism, it would be refreshing to be able to present evidence that some of them are generally more important than others.... the presence of an outgroup which appears hostile is extremely important in achieving national solidarity and hence in promoting both patriotism and nationalism; but is it always or usually more important than a common language, a common culture, or infallible leaders? The possibility of a definitive reply has already been eliminated...we do not know, we do not know.

Still let us keep human hopes alive by referring calmly to a rough model of how the problem might conceivably be attacked. Years ago, one investigator first selected a half dozen "elements" of nationalism as the basis for his analysis. He himself then ranked seven modern nations on a scale of "possession or non-possession" of these elements. Thus for one of them, "internal communications," which he determined largely by consulting figures on railroad traffic, he emerged with this ranking: Switzerland, Germany, France, Italy, Spain, and the United States— the seventh country, Great Britain, he did not include in this particular series. Next he obtained ratings from 42 social scientists, editors, and writers in various countries concerning the degree to which the seven countries exhibited what he called "defensive" nationalism; other data simultaneously received from them are not relevant here. Finally, he calculated for the seven countries rank-order correlations between such nationalism on the one hand and the possession or non-possession of the six elements on the other. For two of them, "internal communications" and "historical tradition," the correlations were negligible; but for the remaining four—"geography," "literary tradition," "religion," and "language"—they were satistically significant. In brief, the latter four appeared more closely related to his definition of nationalism than the former two.

The investigator himself, however, is skeptical concerning his own results. He recognizes, for example, that the data from which he derived his index for internal communications are "extremely fragmentary" and that his statistical measures, being based on only seven nations, can be markedly affected by a change in the rank of a single country.[15] In addition, two other defects of the procedure appear in the light of methodological developments since his original analysis. His own rating of the countries with respect to the elements was quite subjective and not submitted to a test of reliability and objectivity. The ratings of the "experts" were not only equally subjective but also most variable. Obviously, therefore, what is needed in order to weight the factors associated with patriotism and nationalism is the application of the

[14] Sergius Yacobson and Harold D. Lasswell, "Trend: May Day Slogans in Soviet Russia, 1918–1943" in Harold D. Lasswell, Nathan Leites, et al., *Language of Politics* (New York: Steward, 1949), pp. 242–43.

[15] King, *op. cit.*, pp. 23–37.

same procedure in a more objective manner to a much, much larger number of representative nations: both the relevant elements and the nationalism of the nations must be more explicitly rated or ranked. In spite of the study's admitted weaknesses and of the time that has elapsed since its inception and publication, nevertheless, the final conclusion of the author seems to be as valid a statement as can be made even now concerning the essential bases for nationalism:

Where all our elements of nationalism are present in a nation to a high degree, the national solidarity of that nation will be high. Where all or a majority of these elements are present to a small degree, the national solidarity is likely to be weak. Nationalism is thus the resultant of various historical, economic, and social forces of which the six here analyzed are by no means the only ones. These forces have worked with varying degrees of intensity in different nations. Where all or most of them have been strong, nationalism is likely to be strong; where all or a majority have been weak, nationalism is likely to be weak.[16]

[16] *Ibid.*, p. 37.

2. The Threat of Nationalism

ARNOLD J. TOYNBEE

Arnold J. Toynbee is an outstanding British historian. He has taught at the University of London and numerous other institutions; has been associated with the British Foreign Office, and has served as Director of Studies for the Royal Institute of International Affairs. His most famous work is A STUDY OF HISTORY. *Among his numerous other books, two may be cited as being particularly relevant to the theme of this article:* NATIONALITY AND WAR *and* WAR AND CIVILIZATION.

Today we are living in a world in which nationalism is effervescing all around us. We do not need to be told of its existence and its power. It thrusts itself on our attention. But we do per-

"Again Nationalism Threatens," THE NEW YORK TIMES MAGAZINE, *November 3, 1963, pp. 23ff.* © *1963 by The New York Times Company. Reprinted by permission.*

haps need to make clear to ourselves just what nationalism is.

It is a state of mind in which we give our paramount political loyalty to one fraction of the human race—to the particular tribe of which we happen to be tribesmen. In so far as we are captured by this ideology, we hold that the highest political good for us is our own nation's sovereign independence; that our nation has a moral right to exercise its sovereignty according to what it believes to be its own national interests, whatever consequences this may entail for the foreign majority of the human race; and that our duty, as citizens of our country, is to support our country, right or wrong.

If this is a correct definition of what nationalism is and of what it implies, it is unquestionably one of the most potent forces in the modern world. At the present moment for instance, French nationalism...is deliberately and effectively obstructing the political unification of the Western peoples.

Political unification offers us Westerners the only hope of being able to hold our own in a world in which we are now losing the technological lead that has given us an ascendancy over the non-Western majority for the last two hundred years. France is one of the Western countries whose future security thus depends on Western political unification. Yet French nationalism today...is giving French national self-assertion priority over Western security (including French security) tomorrow.

The immediate psychological explanation of de Gaulle's passion for French nationalism is not far to seek. What happened in 1940 revealed the nullity of France as a military power. De Gaulle was determined to demonstrate that, in spite of 1940, France can still play a decisive part in world affairs after all.

A similar explanation accounts for China's present mood. From 1840 to 1945, China was trampled on and humiliated by a series of foreign countries—Britain, France, Japan—which were not only far smaller and less populous than China but no more than semi-civilized in Chinese estimation. From the dawn of history until then, China had been the only power, and

Chinese civilization the only civilization, in the Chinese quarter of the earth's surface. So now, in the 20th century, China is determined to reassert herself. She is determined, in fact, to recover the position of pre-eminence in her world which was her normal position in the past.

The present vogue of nationalism in the recently liberated non-Western countries is also not mysterious. Many of these nations did not win their liberation from Western rule without a struggle. They are determined to assert their independence now that they have at last secured it. They are glorying in the new—or renewed—experience of being their own masters.

Moreover, nationalism has prestige in their eyes because nationalism is the ideology of their former Western rulers. They have learned, at first hand, how powerful the Western nations were in the days, now past, of the Western colonial empires. The West's non-Western ex-subjects would like to acquire this Western power for themselves. They guess that the key to it lies in the adoption of Western institutions; and the Western type of national state looks to them as if it were the talisman that confers political power.

As for the Spanish-American peoples, nearly a century and a half has now passed since they liberated themselves from Spanish rule. But they have never felt themselves to be entirely independent. In the 19th century they exchanged Spanish political domination for British, French, Dutch and German economic domination; and in the 20th century they have been overshadowed by the overwhelming power of the United States—a power which is political, as well as economic, throughout the Western hemisphere. Vis-à-vis the United States, Brazil and Haiti are in the same position as the Spanish-speaking Latin-American republics, so that Latin America, as a whole, is today in much the same mood as Asia and Africa.

The psychological explanation of present-day British nationalism is, at bottom, the same as for France. It is true that, in World War II, Britain succeeded in playing the *beau rôle* that France failed to play and, at first sight, it looks as if this ought to have taken the edge off British nationalism in the postwar period. But, in fact, Britain's experience has been the more ironical. Though France was one of the defeated countries and Britain one of the victors, Britain suffered, in the sequel, the same reduction of status as France. Today, the United States and the Soviet Union completely outclass them, and it is probable that China, too, is eventually going to outclass them both again.

Both countries are finding this sudden diminution of their military and political stature painful, and this is the deeper cause of their present nationalistic mood. They are tempted to refuse to face the facts of life. Like the frog in Aesop's fable, they would like to inflate themselves to the size of the Russo-American ox, even at the risk of bursting.

Let us hope that both peoples will get over their present rather childish nationalistic mood. In the course of history, many other peoples have had to reconcile themselves to loss of power, and some have made the necessary adjustment with good grace. Sweden and the Netherlands, for instance, were great powers in the 17th century. Neither of them is a great power today in the material sense, yet both are prosperous and highly respected.

We still have not got to the bottom of the present strength of nationalism, however. The United States and the Soviet Union are *also* in a nationalistic state of mind today, although these are the two countries that are now on top of the world.

Their present nationalism is the antithesis of British and French nationalism. It is not inspired by resentment at the loss of former power; it is inspired by ambition to become the one supreme power in the world by definitively getting the better of the other.

This is, of course, a very old story. It is as old as the national rivalry between Rome and Carthage—and that episode of past history suggests that if the contest between American and Russian nationalism were to be fought out to a finish, the consequences would be as fatal for the victor as for the vanquished. The price paid by Rome for the destruction of Carthage was to wreck herself as well; and, if this was the fate of the victor in a pre-atomic war, it would be his fate *a fortiori* now in atomic warfare.

·   ·   ·

If the human race is to survive, we shall have to make a revolutionary break with the traditional order of priorities in our loyalties. We shall have to transfer our paramount loyalty from our respective national fragments of the human race to the human race itself. This is, of course, going to be difficult —the more so, because we shall have to make the emotional readjustment quickly. We know, however, that such readjustment is possible. It was achieved, for instance, in both the Roman Empire and the Chinese Empire.

When these were first established, the peoples united under them regretted the loss of their previous national sovereignty and resented the fact that they had been compelled to become citizens of a world-state. Eventually, however, loyalty to the world-state came to take first place in their citizens' hearts. Saint

Paul, for instance, was proud of being a citizen of his home town, the city-state of Tarsus, but he was prouder still of being a citizen, as he also was, of the world-state Rome. These past achievements do at least assure us that their repetition is not beyond the power of human nature.

If we, in our time, do succeed in subordinating our national loyalties to a loyalty to the human race, we can turn nationalism from the curse that it now is into the blessing that it might come to be. In a world that has been unified effectively for such essential purposes as the maintenance of peace and the provision of food, national autonomy, subordinated to world government, could play a useful part. If some measure of variety can be combined with an overriding unity, we shall be the gainers by that.

STRUCTURE AND DYNAMICS

OF THE SYSTEM

Chapter 3

We have thus far proceeded on the assumption that the state and its government, characterized by a strong sense of affiliation, loyalty, and support by its citizens, is the major actor in international relations. We have indicated that this is not the only level from which the study of international relations may be approached, but it seems to us to remain the most revealing one.

We must not mislead the reader, however, into believing that all he needs to know is the identity, the values, the capacities, the intentions, and the actual policies of all the states of the world in order .to understand the substance of international relations. In the first place, that task itself would be impossible and, luckily, it is probably unnecessary. One can, indeed one must, establish typologies or categories of actors. Although some of the richness of reality is lost in such an effort, comprehension is increased. Second, states, governments, and decision makers are part of a wider system, and that system itself suggests, perhaps imposes, certain types of calculation and certain forms of behavior upon these actors. The present chapter is devoted primarily to an examination of various structures which such an international system may take. But before we enter upon that task, it may be well to speak about the attempt to think of the various main units, the states, not in individual terms but in terms of categories.

That some ordering and organizing concepts must be used in order to understand and discuss reality is not open to question. Our everyday language in discussing international affairs (and other affairs as well) testifies to this need. We speak of "us" and "them," which is a typology of sorts, and there is usually little question as to who falls into which category. We use labels such as "'friends," "allies," "neutrals," and "enemies." We talk about democracies and dictatorships, capitalist and socialist economic systems. In fact, one of the real problems with our language is that it tends toward polarizing the situation which it seeks to describe and, in its "either-or" orientation, makes insufficient allowance for the vast variety of circumstances and situations which would be far more suitably represented by a continuum than by a polar distribution.

No single attempt to establish categories of states in international relations can be wholly satisfactory for all purposes. Reality is simply too rich and varied for that; and boundaries between categories are always somewhat unreal and fuzzy. Nonetheless the attempt needs to be made in order to speak meaningfully about incredibly complex systems of actions and relations.

A large number of typologies are available to choose from, though not, we must add, without considerable caution. We have already mentioned a few obvious ones. "The free world" versus "the Communist world" is a case where caution seems much needed, because we have to note that the freedom of many units in the former category is open to question, while at the same time the centrifugal tendencies in the latter category have been so pronounced that it seems totally inappropriate to speak of a "Communist world" at all—there are at least two, and probably more. "Haves" versus "have-nots" has been part of the language of popular discourse about international affairs for a long time. We consider these terms to be highly unsatisfactory. Indeed, the distinction between states on the basis of wealth and well-being—a distinction which undeniably exists in reality, of course— creates serious problems of labeling (and not only of labeling, but of understanding the substance which those labels seek to describe). President Truman used to refer to the poorer states (we don't seem to be able to get away from labels ourselves!) as "backward" societies, which did not enchant the leaders or peoples of those societies. Later the term "under-developed" came into usage, but though it was clearly superior to "backward," it still failed to describe reality satisfactorily. In the first place, all countries are underdeveloped in terms of their potentials; and in the second place, many countries which are underdeveloped in the means of achieving certain amenities of life are very rich—very *highly* developed—in terms of their philosophy, their literature, their art. Thus at the very least, the qualifying adjective "economically" should always precede the term "under-developed."

Some students and practitioners of international affairs, such as Presidents Wilson and Franklin D. Roosevelt, used to talk of "peace-loving" versus "aggressive" states—which terms, if they could be made to stick, would be a revealing set of categories for the student of international relations. But unfortunately for those who like their categories simple, it is very hard to make the point that, on any measurable basis, some states are inherently more peace-loving or aggressive than others. The added distinction between peoples and their governments—the former being peace-loving, the latter being aggressive—is equally difficult to sustain.

Arnold Wolfers, who has perhaps done more than anyone else to clarify relevant distinctions among states, has suggested the possibility of categorizing states according to their goals, which he grouped into several broad categories, the most important of which were goals of self-preservation and goals of self-extension (status quo versus revisionist states). This typology appears considerably more useful to us than some of those we have previously cited, as long as one bears in mind that the status quo society of today may well have been the revisionist one of yesterday, and may become so again tomorrow; the same, in reverse, can be said of its counterpart.

Legally, as Anand has indicated in Chapter 1, all states are equal. But actually, of course, they are not; or, in Orwellian terms, if they are equal, then some are more so than others. In Samuel Grafton's words, "Even after you give the squirrel a certificate which says he is quite as big as an elephant, he is still going to be smaller, and all the squirrels will know it and all the elephants will know it."[1] Legal equality has its function in the international system, but it cannot hide the reality of inequality from our eyes. In the book from which the Grafton quotation was taken, W.T.R. Fox himself attempted to establish a typology of Superpowers, Great Powers, Medium Powers, Small Powers (and had to add a fifth miscellaneous category to embrace the variety of other units within the international system). Whether this typology is totally useful is debatable, but that some ordering and organizing concepts must be used is obvious.

As if all of this were not perplexing enough, we must once again call attention to the obvious fact that states, governments, and decision makers are *not* the only actors whose values, capabilities, and behaviors we must take into account. *Within* each society, there are individuals and groups —variously constituted on such bases as race, religion, economic interest, occupation, income, education, section, political preference, and the like— having differential influence on the policies pursued by that society's governmental institutions and those who operate those institutions. In the Soviet Union the Communist Party is a group having the greatest impact on national policies, and within the party, certain sectors have greater impact than others. In the United States there is much talk of a "military-industrial complex" which is said to shape the country's behavior at home and abroad.

Outside, above, and *beyond* national societies, there are all kinds of international groupings, organizations, affiliations which likewise exert in-

---

[1] Quoted in William T. R. Fox, *The Super-Powers* (New York: Harcourt, Brace and Co., 1944), p. 3.

fluence. Intergovernmental international organizations, such as the United Nations, NATO, COMECON, and the European Economic Community play a significant role. The Vatican, representing spiritual authority over more than half a billion Roman Catholics, plays a role which can by no stretch of the imagination be measured merely by answering Stalin's inquiry, "How many divisions does the Pope have?" Zionism as an international movement succeeded in establishing a state where none had existed for over 1000 years. International business, labor, professional organizations—to say nothing of the jet set which is the twentieth-century equivalent of the earlier international aristocracy—all these and many more have their impact on the totality of international relations at any given moment in history, such as this one.

Is it all, then, chaos and utter confusion? Or are there ways in which this total international system can be viewed which, while we bear its complexity in mind, do permit comprehension and perhaps even prediction? We think that the answer is affirmative, and authors in the present chapter think so also. Returning, for the most part, to the level of the state as the level of analysis, Kissinger distinguishes between a *bipolar* international system, one in which overwhelming power and influence are concentrated in two centers, and a *multipolar* one in which power and influence are more widely distributed and shared. He recognizes that the present system must be described differently in different functional areas. Thus he speaks of the system as being *militarily* bipolar but *politically* multipolar. Hoffmann, looking at the same system, comments on the fact that a system which on the surface appears to be so revolutionary and volatile has yet in practice been quite moderate and restrained in the use of force by its participants, particularly by those who command the greatest military strength. Indeed the new fact of nuclear power with unprecedented destructive capabilities has imposed a degree of caution and circumspection upon the two super-powers which in earlier periods was generally associated with a multipolar system of power distribution.

Clearly it makes an enormous difference whether at a given period in time a single state is dominant over its environment (as in the days of the Roman Empire); whether two states predominate (as in the immediate aftermath of World War II); or whether there are several major states, not rigidly aligned with one another, whose relations are marked by both conflict and by cooperation, at least in the sense that they seek to maintain the continued existence of all major participants (as in the Europe of the nineteenth century).[2] The structure of a system has impact not only on the

---

[2] This three-fold scheme is by no means the only one that could be employed. Morton Kaplan examines six states of equilibrium of the international system (though only the first two correspond to historical reality so far): (1) the "balance of power" system, (2) the loose bipolar system, (3) the tight bipolar system, (4) the universal system, (5) the hierarchical system in its directive and non-directive forms, and (6) the unit veto system. *System and Process in International Relations* (New York: John Wiley & Sons, Inc., 1957), p. 21.

major participants themselves but also on all others, whose freedom of action can be enhanced or circumscribed by the number of major actors and their relationships to one another. At the present time, for instance, the enormous military capability of the Soviet Union and the United States and the reciprocal restraint which the capability imposes upon these countries has led to a great strengthening in the position of other states. Alliances which were once cohesive are now disintegrating on both sides. The positions and policies of neutrals are shifting, sometimes in one direction, sometimes in another.[3]

Just as the multipolarity of the nineteenth century gave way to the bipolarity of the post-World War II period, which in turn has given way to another system for which we do not yet have a very good label, so we must expect further and continuous adjustments and changes in the international system. That system, lacking as it does both consensus among as well as directive institutions above its major participants, imposes upon leaders of all states the requirement of basing their respective national policies on what they perceive to be permissible and possible within a given constellation of power and influence.

[3] The concept of the balance of power and the balancing process is dealt with in greater detail in the introduction to Chap. 11.

1. The End of Bipolarity

HENRY A. KISSINGER

Henry A. Kissinger is presently serving as President Nixon's Assistant for National Security Affairs. Prior to assuming that post, he was Professor of Government at Harvard University and Associate in the Harvard Center for International Affairs. His publications include NUCLEAR WEAPONS AND FOREIGN POLICY, THE NECESSITY FOR CHOICE, *and* THE TROUBLED PARTNERSHIP.

...the age of the superpowers is now drawing to an end. Military bipolarity has not only failed to prevent,

From Kermit Gordon, ed., AGENDA FOR THE NATION (Washington, D.C.: The Brookings Institution, 1968), pp. 588–91. Reprinted by permission.

it has actually encouraged, political multipolarity. Weaker allies have good reason to believe that their defense is in the overwhelming interest of their senior partner. Hence, they see no need to purchase its support by acquiescence in its policies. The new nations feel protected by the rivalry of the super-powers, and their nationalism leads to ever bolder assertions of self-will. Traditional uses of power have become less feasible, and new forms of pressure have emerged as a result of transnational loyalties and weak domestic structures.

This political multipolarity does not necessarily guarantee stability. Rigidity is diminished, but so is manageability. Nationalism may succeed in curbing the preeminence of the super-powers; it remains to be seen whether it can supply an integrating concept more successfully in this century than in the last. Few countries have the interest and only the superpowers have the resources to become informed about global issues. As a result, diplomacy is often geared to domestic politics and more concerned with striking a pose than contributing to international order. Equilibrium is difficult to achieve among states widely divergent in values, goals, expectations, and previous experience.

The greatest need of the contemporary international system is an agreed concept of order. In its absence, the awesome available power is unrestrained by any consensus as to legitimacy; ideology and nationalism, in their different ways, deepen international schisms. Many of the elements of stability which characterized the international system in the nineteenth century cannot be re-created in the modern age. The stable technology, the multiplicity of major powers, the limited domestic claims, and the frontiers which permitted adjustments are gone forever. A new concept of international order is essential; without it stability will prove elusive.

This problem is particularly serious for the United States. Whatever our intentions or policies, the fact that the United States disposes of the greatest single aggregate of material power in the world is inescapable. A new international order is inconceivable without a significant American contribution. But the nature of this contribution has altered. For the two decades after 1945, our international activities were based on the assumption that technology plus managerial skills gave us the ability to reshape the international system and to bring about domestic transformations in "emerging countries." This direct "operational" concept of international order has proved too simple. Political multipolarity makes it impossible to impose an American design. Our deepest challenge will be to evoke the creativity of a pluralistic world, to base order on political multipolarity even though overwhelming military strength will remain with the two superpowers.

THE LIMITS OF BIPOLARITY: THE NATURE OF POWER IN THE MODERN PERIOD

Throughout history, military power was considered the final recourse. Statesmen treated the acquisition of additional power as an obvious and paramount objective. As recently as twenty-five years ago, it would have been inconceivable that a country could possess *too much* strength for effective political use; every increment of power was—at least theoretically—politically effective. The minimum aim was to assure the impermeability of the territory. Until the Second World War, a state's strength could be measured by its ability to protect its population from attack.

The nuclear age has destroyed this traditional measure. Increasing strength no longer necessarily confers the ability to protect the population. No foreseeable force level—not even full-scale ballistic missile defenses—can prevent levels of damage eclipsing those of the two world wars. In these conditions, the major problem is to discipline power so that it bears a rational relationship to the objectives likely to be in dispute. The paradox of contemporary military strength is that a gargantuan increase in power has eroded its relationship to policy. The major nuclear powers are capable of devastating each other. But they have great difficulty translating this capability into policy except to prevent direct challenges to their own survival —and this condition is interpreted with increasing strictness. The capacity to destroy is difficult to translate into a plausible threat even against countries with no capacity for retaliation. The margin of superiority of the superpowers over the other states is widening; yet other nations have an unprecedented scope for autonomous action. In relations with many domestically weak countries, a radio transmitter can be a more effective form of pressure than a squadron of B-52s. In other words, power no longer translates automatically into influence. This does not mean that impotence increases influence, only that power does not automatically confer it.

This state of affairs has profound consequences for traditional notions of balance of power. In the past, stability has always presupposed the existence of an equilibrium of power which prevented one state from imposing its will on the others.

The traditional criteria for the balance of power were territorial. A state could gain overwhelming superiority only by conquest; hence, as long as territorial expansion was foreclosed, or severely limited, the equilibrium was likely to be preserved. In the contemporary period, this is no longer true. Some conquests add little to effective military strength; major increases in power are possible entirely through developments within the territory of a sovereign state. China gained more in real military power through the acquisi-

tion of nuclear weapons than if it had conquered all of Southeast Asia. If the Soviet Union had occupied Western Europe but had remained without nuclear weapons, it would be less powerful than it is now with its existing nuclear arsenal within its present borders. In other words, the really fundamental changes in the balance of power have all occurred *within* the territorial limits of sovereign states. Clearly, there is an urgent need to analyze just what is understood by power—as well as by balance of power—in the nuclear age.

This would be difficult enough were technology stable. It becomes enormously complicated when a scientific revolution produces an upheaval in weapons technology at five-year intervals. Slogans like "superiority," "parity," "assured destruction," compete unencumbered by clear definitions of their operational military significance, much less a consensus on their political implications. The gap between experts and decision makers is widening. The decision maker rarely has as many hours to study a problem as the expert has years. The result is that the decision maker runs the risk of unprecedented dependence on his technical staff. He is informed by "briefings," a procedure which stresses theatrical qualities and leaves its target with the uneasy feeling that he has been "taken," even—or perhaps especially—when he does not know exactly how. Decisions may reflect an attempt to ward off conflicting pressures rather than a clear conception of long-range purposes.

In short, as power has grown more awesome, it has also turned abstract, intangible, elusive. Deterrence has become the dominant military policy. But deterrence depends above all on psychological criteria. It seeks to keep an opponent from a given course by posing unacceptable risks. For purposes of deterrence, the opponent's calculations are decisive. A bluff taken seriously is more useful than a serious threat interpreted as a bluff. For political purposes, the meaningful measurement of military strength is the assessment of it by the other side. Psychological criteria vie in importance with strategic doctrine.

The abstract nature of modern power affects domestic disputes profoundly. Deterrence is tested negatively by things which do *not* happen. But it is never possible to demonstrate *why* something has not occurred. Is it because we are pursuing the best possible policy or only a marginally effective one? Bitter debate even among those who believe in the necessity of defense policy is inevitable and bound to be inconclusive. Moreover, the longer peace is maintained—or the more successful deterence is—the more it furnishes arguments for those who are opposed to the very premises of defense policy. Perhaps there was no need for preparedness in the first place because the opponent never meant to attack. In the modern state, national security is likely to be a highly divisive domestic issue.

The enormity of modern power has destroyed its cumulative impact to a considerable extent. Throughout history the use of force set a precedent; it demonstrated a capacity to use power for national ends. In the twentieth century any use of force sets up inhibitions against resorting to it again. Whatever the outcome of the war in Vietnam, it is clear that it has greatly diminished American willingness to become involved in this form of warfare elsewhere. Its utility as a precedent has therefore been importantly undermined.

The difficulty of forming a conception of power is paralleled by the problem of how to use it diplomatically. In the past, measures to increase readiness signaled the mounting seriousness with which an issue was viewed. But such measures have become less obvious and more dangerous when weapons are always at a high state of readiness—solid-fuel missiles require less than ten minutes to be fired—and are hidden either under the ground or under the oceans. With respect to nuclear weapons, signaling increased readiness has to take place in a narrow range between the danger of failure and the risk of a preemptive strike.

.   .   .

2. The International System Today

STANLEY HOFFMAN

Stanley Hoffman is Professor of Government at Harvard University and Research Associate at the Center for International Affairs. His books include THE STATE OF WAR *and* CONTEMPORARY THEORY IN INTERNATIONAL RELATIONS.

I. REVOLUTIONARY OR MODERATE?

At first sight, the international milieu of the 1960s is almost a textbook example of a revolutionary system. If we examine its main *elements,* we find:

(A) Bipolarity, i.e., the existence of the United States and the Soviet Union, whose power far exceeds that of other units and which are sufficiently matched to be placed in the same top league, if one applies to the present system the customary yardstick of power, namely, the capacity to wage war and to inflict damage on an enemy. Whether this yardstick is still decisive in the nuclear age, whether a bipolar structure means an actual dual hegemony in interstate relations, whether indeed the *structure* of the system (i.e., the distribution and hierarchy of power) can be called bipolar, is a matter that will have to be explored later. But we can expect the present international system to be marked, as all previous bipolar systems have been, by a tendency toward instability, due to the dialectic

of reciprocal fear, and inflexibility, due to the dialectic of opposed interests.

(B) An unprecedented heterogeneity in the structure of the system. For the first time, the international system covers the whole planet, but it now includes ingredients of widely different origins and vintage. What Raymond Aron calls the "unity of the diplomatic field" is a fiery unity. Even though the basic unit of modern world politics is the nation-state, this over-all term conceals an extraordinary diversity. For one thing, modern nation-states differ in their degree of integration. Some are states still in search of a nation, marked by serious discontinuities among tribes, ethnic groups, or classes. Others are nations in a formal but not in a substantive sense—i.e., although they have national consciousness, authoritative central power, and social mobility across regional, ethnic, or social lines, there is no consensus on political purposes and institutions. Others are national communities in a substantive sense as well. They also differ in their historical dimensions. Some (well integrated or not) have had an independent existence and an institutional framework for generations or centuries, others are new and ramshackle. Finally, they differ in size, ranging from tiny units that are little more than dots on the map, to traditional territorial states, to what might be called empire-states, huge and often ethnically heterogeneous. Because of this heterogeneity, the distribution of power between and around the United States and the Soviet Union is highly discontinuous and uneven. Consequently the "relation of major tension," the opposition of the two great powers, breeds a permanent danger of conflict through aspiration, expansion or escalation in the various "soft underbellies" that lie between or within the two camps.

(C) Extreme variety in the domestic political systems. Verbal agreement on the two principles of self-determination and self-government conceals fundamental differences over the meaning of democracy, and there are many uncertainties about where the limits of self-determination must be placed and about its relevance in racially or ethnically mixed situations. The variety of regimes is so dazzling that political scientists cannot even begin to agree on classificatory schemes. As for the economic regimes, they range from the most backward societies, where governments have no effective control over economies that are still at subsistence level and/or in foreign hands, to modern societies of mass consumption, heavily regulated by the state. As Henry Kissinger puts it, "When the domestic structures are based on fundamentally different conceptions of what is just, the conduct of international affairs grows more complex. . . . Statesmen can still meet, but their ability to persuade has been reduced for they no longer speak the same language."[1]

(D) Sharp ideological clashes:

[1] "Domestic Structure and Foreign Policy," *Daedalus,* Spring 1966, pp. 503–4.

communism vs. the so-called free world, anticolonial nationalisms of Asia, Africa, and Latin America vs. the West. These are doubly asymmetrical: in each case, one side is heavily ideological and the other rather pragmatic; in each case, the ideological side is on the offensive.

(E) A technological revolution contributes to instability both because it proceeds so fast and because it aggravates the unevenness among nations. There is a technological race among the powerful or would-be powerful, and an increasing gap between the "haves" and the "have nots." And there is a race between what might be called the technological factors of equalization (the revolution in communications which makes of the world an echo chamber, spreads information all over the globe and equalizes concern) and the countless disparities and inequalities—military, economic, political, ethnic, ideological—which distort this revolution and often put it at the service of the most powerful and of the most dissatisfied.

If we turn to the *relations* of the units within the system, we can see why such a milieu is likely to be immoderate in ends and means. All the factors mentioned above contribute to the inflation of objectives, to the rise of universal claims. In a bipolar contest, prestige, power and security are rolled into one; moderate compromises are made difficult (because the contest is acted out in apocalyptic fashion, since any local move may affect the entire field, any hole in the tapestry may lead to its total destruction). When this contest is ideological as well, the distinction between a threat to the physical existence of the foe and a threat to his moral integrity becomes blurred. And the unprecedented heterogeneity of states, political regimes, and economic stages creates total insecurity, in which leaders try to consolidate their power by making enormous demands on the outside world.

The immoderation of means is due to the proliferation of conflict situations. A bipolar contest implies the risk of clashes at any point of contact between the two great powers and elsewhere in the search for supporters. And the heterogeneity of the system makes it likely that border clashes between "empire-states," imperial wars of extension and disintegration, and traditional international wars will all occur. The variety of principles of domestic legitimacy invites clashes between rival conceptions and makes it possible to invoke one of the principles as cover for national ambitions. The unevenness of economic development condemns the poor to do their best to control their resources, and this may be at the expense of the wealthy. Lastly, the ideological substance of the contest leads to generalized intervention in international conflicts and in civil wars. "Total diplomacy" thus requires virtuosity over a range that goes from mere propaganda to the use of force.

This immoderation in ends and means of course results in instability. Both the United States and the Soviet Union, out of reciprocal fear and opposed interests, try to court neutrals, win friends and keep them (hence the proliferation of alliances), and detach the friends of the rival. This need for support from lesser powers (whether for strategic, diplomatic, or symbolic reasons) tends to make the Americans and Russians dependent on their clients; the latter want to safeguard their independence and exploit every possible asset in their position, and this subverts the hierarchy. (The United Nations contributes to this trend.)

One would thus expect each of the "poles" to enjoy a position very close to that which the model of revolutionary systems suggests. One would expect, as a bitter effect of total insecurity, that each would search for at least partial hegemony and full exploitation of its power in order to marshal support, to protect its areas of influence, to stop penetration by the rival, and to penetrate his domain in turn. One would expect that these efforts would lead to a kind of *de facto* partition of the world or to conflagration; at any rate, the likelihood should be a pressuring of all third parties to choose sides—"total diplomacy" in a vertical dimension and ominous deadlock on the horizontal level.

But reality has not gone so far. The present system is also one of relative moderation. Whereas the dynamics have by and large been those of a revolutionary system, the actual results have not differed so much from those of moderate ones. The most important factor here has been moderation in the use of force. The international milieu is saturated with conflicts and violence, and the list of armed conflicts between and within states from 1945 to the Middle Eastern war of 1967 is long and varied. But, on the whole, the use of "brute force" to take and to hold, and the use of force as a means of "coercive violence" to hurt and punish[2] have been kept at low levels and within limits. In the past, multipolarity and homogeneity led to moderation in ends and means; today, relative moderation in means seems to bring back some features of multipolar systems, including some moderation in ends. Demonic or global ends, while maintained intact in proclamations, are pursued only piecemeal. As in the nineteenth century, the great powers have resorted more to

[2] A distinction made, with his usual relentless virtuosity, by Thomas C. Schelling, *Arms and Influence* (New Haven: Yale University Press, 1966), Ch. 1.

threats and confrontations than to war.[3] There is a modicum of flexibility. The system has outlived countless conflicts and confrontations and accommodated drastic changes in the distribution of power; there are some signs of a return to flexibility in alignments and to neutral acceptance of a variety of regimes; there has been a beginning of an erosion of ideology. The two main rivals are beginning to temper their hostility not just with prudence but with cooperation: as in balance-of-power systems, the notion of mixed interests of the great powers spreads.

Do these transformations improve the situation of the great power? Do they decrease its insecurity, giving it greater freedom of choice? Do they at the same time preserve the advantage of hegemony? That is, to they unblock the "horizontal" level while maintaining the effectiveness in the vertical dimension?

II. THE THREE LEVELS OF THE SYSTEM

We can find the answer by analyzing the present international system as a three-level one. The fundamental level —the foundation—is bipolar. But there are two more levels, which we will call *polycentric* and *multipolar,* corresponding to two trends in present world politics, a dominant one that modifies bipolarity, and a secondary, derivative one that challenges it.

A. Muted bipolarity

I refer to muted bipolarity in order to suggest, first, that the bipolar level remains; second, that the bipolar

conflict has been dampened; and, third, that the two poles have not been willing or able to switch from a full bipolar conflict to a full bipolar partnership.

CAUSES. The dominant modification of bipolarity is caused by the convergence of two separate features in the contemporary system: the consecration of the nation-state, and new conditions in the use of force. Those two features emerged only gradually, during the first decade after World War II. Since 1955, the triumphs of decolonization and the nuclear stalemate between Russia and the United States have brought out fully the meaning of these two new developments in international politics.

Virtually the entire globe is now covered with independent states, most of which are or aspire to be nation-states. Sixty years ago, the international landscape was, in cadastral terms, dominated by the big landlords. Today, it resembles those European countrysides so remarkable to the traveler who observes them from the air, with every piece of land cultivated and marked out, with the fields divided into countless strips. This fragmentation has occurred at a time when all the factors of conflict we mentioned before, as well as developments in military technology, have rendered the notion of the "impermeable territorial state"[4] obsolete. Still, the very existence of more than a hundred sovereign units poses formidable obstacles to open, free, and easy penetration of national borders. A border is like a burglar alarm, in that it has value only if there are *other* factors that deter the burglar, such as policemen, or the burglar's sensitivity to noise, or scruples that a ringing alarm would heighten. This is the case today.

[3] Robert E. Osgood and Robert W. Tucker, *Force, Order, and Justice* (Baltimore: The Johns Hopkins University Press, 1967), pp. 89–90.

[4] See John Herz, *International Politics in the Atomic Age* (New York: Columbia University Press, 1959).

First, there is the *nation's* legitimacy in most parts of the world. (It is tempting yet misleading to analyze international politics at a level so abstract that one forgets what stuff the units of international relations are made of, for their nature shapes their goals and the stakes of the contest.) The collapsing colonial empires learned the hard way what resistance to an irresistible claim for national self-determination entails. A world of nations in which most political leaders are engaged in one way or another in the "social mobilization" of their followers is a world in which even the most ruthlessly brutal and expansionist rulers cannot afford to be *too* crude. For, as Hitler's fate showed, any great power that embarks on a policy of destruction of other nations provokes a decisive countervailing response. A would-be conqueror in a world of non-national states did not worry too much about the attitudes of the conquered; but in a world of nation-states, even the cynic will acknowledge that, however much "world public opinion" may be an empty cliché, a statesman's means must be appropriate to his end when the support of other powers is as stake. The burglar himself must pretend that he respects the jewelers' integrity.

Moreover, the nature of the contest between the United States and the Soviet Union makes of the formally independent nation-state a point of saliency, and a beneficiary of the rivalry. Here again, we are dealing not with *any* bipolar competition but with a *specific* struggle. National self-determination is one of the principles of the United States and one of the cornerstones of its conception of world order. We are thus inclined to use it as a weapon against the Soviet Union; but *ipso facto* we also are obliged to take it into account or be embarrassed when we do not, for we cannot afford to blunt a needed tool. And, whereas Communist ideology devotes little attention to the idea of the independent nation and certainly does not rank it as an integral part of its creed, it has used the aspirations to national independence as a club against its enemies. Thus, this fundamentally equalitarian kind of legitimacy, which tends to impart to every nation, whatever its size and resources, a right to existence, obliges both powers to define their competition as one for the "voluntary" support (or non-hostility) of other nations, rather than as one for the enslavement of other territories; the rivalry of Athens and Sparta could afford to be blunter. This does not mean that they are devoid of means of influence, but only that the means are altogether changed. The present contest is well described by the familiar vocabulary: each leading power wants "friends," or clients, or "satellites"—terms that maintain a distinction between actual dependence, which is sought, and formal independence, which is preserved.

Lastly, the effect of the United Nations must not be ignored in this connection. On the one hand, membership in the United Nations has become a concrete symbol of national independence, one of the foundation stones of the Charter. On the other hand, the deadlock between Russia and America and the tendency of each to fan the flames of independence for its own purposes have aided in the well-known increase in the power of smaller nations in the General Assembly.

We may well ask how long and how well the distinction between "friends" or "clients" and "servants" would have lasted, how long and how well the fences between the various plots of land, while frequently crossed or damaged, would have formally persisted if the second great change had not occurred: the appearance of new conditions in the use of force. Here again, we are dealing with an objective and subjective factor. The new attitude toward force reflects both a change of heart and a change in costs.

The change of heart can best be described as a growing sense that resort to force is an illegitimate instrument of national policy. In the West, the horrors of the last world war, the new implications of national legitimacy, the traditional American dislike of the use of force—all explain the thorough discredit of Darwinian theories in whatever form applied to politics. The strength of this feeling is such that even the Communists, in their more pugnacious statements, have adopted it to the point of saying that if or when war comes, it will be due to imperialism's inevitable resort to violence, not to their own preferences.

But even the most sincere repudiation of aggressive war is usually marked by equally sincere qualifications, which pierce the mental barrier to war with holes through which entire armies could pass. Nobody, of course, repudiates defensive war, and in a situation of protracted conflict in which contenders thrust and parry across contested borders and arbitrary partition lines, or around shaky regimes, each belligerent convinces himself that he is on the defensive, or he cleverly tries to put himself there.[5] Nor does the repudiation

of violence extend to so-called liberation wars waged on behalf of the sacred principle of self-determination. Here again, one can easily imagine war provoked by diametrically opposed interpretations of "national liberation" and of aggression or defense; consider Hungary in 1956 if the United States had chosen to act, or Cuba in 1961 if the United States had intervened more openly and the Soviet Union reacted more vigorously. No, I would not stress the deterrent power of this subjective change of heart, were it not reinforced and supplemented by more tangible evidence. The reason these wars did not occur is to be found in the realm of fact, not thought.

The evidence is that the costs of using force have become excessive in two kinds of cases. First, if the aim is to subjugate (or to continue to subjugate) a people that is determined to resist and that has the capacity to organize protracted revolutionary warfare (a capacity which tends to entail outside support), the cost in suppressive military measures will probably be so high as to make statesmen prefer the costs of secession. It may be still too early to celebrate the end of conquest: poor but militarily strong nations may still be tempted by the fruits of conquest; a nation stronger than its neighbors and threatened in its very existence by them may still attempt to buy security, or time, through conquest; and developed nations, which know that economic exploitation and territorial sovereignty can be separated, and that the costs of maintaining sovereignty

---

[5] The Middle East crisis of 1967 is particularly interesting in this respect. As was shown by the failure of the emergency session of the U.N. General Assembly to pass any meaningful resolution, Egypt's acts of May 1967 (whether they were deliberately aimed at provoking a war or merely represented a risky bluff that boomeranged) were judged by a majority of states to have been rash enough to legitimize, or at least to redeem, Israel's resort to preventive war. The Arab argument

that Israel's very existence is an act of aggression that deserves and requires violent suppression (assuredly a major exception to the "change of heart" described here) has obviously failed to convince even many of the Arabs' supporters.

over reluctant foreigners exceed the economic benefits, may still be tempted to conquest for purely strategic reasons, or to subjugate a rebellious partner so as not to lose face. However, the chances of this kind of conquest being attempted are minimal when the prospects of liquidating the rebel in one fell swoop are also minimal or nil.[6]

Second, and more important, there is blinding evidence that nuclear war is, for antagonists capable of inflicting intolerable devastation on one another, a suicidal policy to follow for any purpose whatsoever. Between the United States and the Soviet Union, the two poles of power, fear of nuclear war inhibits the use of force at any level above that of subversion; United States armed forces have never fought Soviet soldiers. Leaving aside American attempts to "communicate" (with some success) to the enemy the message that limited war is the only practicable alternative to the dilemma of humiliation or holocaust in a "hot" test, the residual uncertainty about employing nuclear weapons has itself effectively prevented any confrontation from becoming "hot." Between each of the two main antagonists and the allies or clients of its rival, the fear of provoking a full-fledged (including possibly nuclear) intervention by the rival, in what has been called war by proxy, has also kept the limits of violence low (although much less so than between America and Russia directly). In conflicts between third parties, or in civil wars in which the chief antagonists are not directly involved, the fear of a general war with unpredictable consequences has often led the United Nations, with the tacit consent of the two superpowers, to request and obtain an early end to violence.

Thus, the effect of nuclear weapons so far has certainly not been to compel nations to renounce force (how could they, given the absence of any compelling supranational authority and the proliferation of conflicts among and within states). Rather, it has compelled them to adhere to a considerable amount of both deterrence and self-deterrence in the use of force, and to make the two chief rivals behave at times exactly like partners in a balance-of-power system—i.e., associates with a common interest in not having world peace upset by lesser powers.[7]

In balance-of-power systems, each major power must curtail its ambitions and moderate its means so as not to bring upon itself a damaging response from its rivals. There are important differences in the system today. The margin of deterrence and self-deterrence has increased enormously. Whereas in the balance-of-power system a state that failed to be deterred by the prospect of a coalition against it paid a relatively small and temporary price for its mistake, the cost of miscalculations today could be final. Then too, the hierarchy of big and small states is more complex today. In fact, the United States and the Soviet Union are in a unique situation, both with regard to one another and with regard to the lesser powers. In order to clarify this situation, we must first look at the modern revolution in the nature of power, and at its effects on the structure of the international system.

.   .   .

---

[6] The preceding remarks apply only to wars of conquest or to attempts to safeguard conquest against rebellion. So-called wars of national liberation in which each side sees itself as a champion of freedom are a different problem.

[7] See my *The State of War*, Ch. 8, and "Nuclear Proliferation and World Politics," in Alastair Buchan, ed., *A World of Nuclear Powers?* (Englewood Cliffs, N.J.: Prentice-Hall, for the American Assembly, 1966).

B. Polycentrism

THE DISTRIBUTION OF POWER. The distribution of power among units is, as we know, of great importance in defining the nature of the system. And a system's moderation or immoderation could, in the past, be measured by examining the goals of the major units. Traditionally, a moderate system was a homogeneous, multipolar one, the logic of which led to each unit having restraints on both its ends and means; a revolutionary system was either multipolar (when the great powers had revolutionary ends and means) or bipolar. The very reasons given by Kenneth Waltz for our system's relative stability[8]—the intensity, certainty, and scope of a bipolar contest with, so to speak, no loose ends—are ordinarily reasons for instability and war. Today, for the first time, stability is achieved *despite* revolutionary aims and *despite* apparent bipolarity.

In terms of ultimates, there are today only two poles of power, only two states whose military and economic capabilities permit them to be "present" more or less overtly all over the globe, whose resources as well as policies involve them more or less discreetly in the affairs of all other nations. They exceed all other states in the supply of the power to reward. Only they have full reservoirs of coercive power from which they can draw; only they can destroy one another completely and almost instantly. Only these two states could embroil the world in a general nuclear war; and no important settlements can be reached without their consent.

Now this means that in terms of the capacity to incite a "moment of

[8] See "The Stability of a Bipolar World," *Daedalus,* Summer 1964, pp. 881–909.

truth"—i.e., the aptitude to use fully the coercive power for general war—there is a *latent* bipolar system (latent because of the hesitancy to use this power). Second, this means that while the weight of the two powers is theoretically preponderant and their voice is essential in all matters in which both are involved and power can talk (Germany, disarmament and outer space, Cuba, the Near East, and Southeast Asia), practically, the meaning of this preponderance is reduced by their competition, and their achievements are essentially negative. Each one is able to prevent the other (as well as, *a fortiori,* all others) from achieving goals sought by force or through diplomacy; each one is therefore likely to preserve his preponderance in areas that are, so to speak, on the firing line—such as the two Germanies, each of whose security and political future depends on the effectiveness of its protector's power. *Denials* prevail, *gains* are few. Due to nuclear weapons, the two "poles" enjoy an exceptionally high negative productivity but suffer from a low positive productivity of power. In their mutual relations, they are frustrated not only, as in past bipolar contests, by their very competition, which prevents a moderated duel from becoming a condominium, but also because they cannot freely resort to coercion in order to force one another into either agreement or submission. In relation to lesser powers, each one is able to use its superiority only when those lesser powers have made the mistake of resorting to large-scale force themselves.

We come thus to the notion of an international system where the bipolarity is a *latent* one of *potential* ultimates. The actual manifestations of these ultimates are moments when everyone's heart misses a beat while the superpowers "confront" one another.

No one else much matters then. But these confrontations have been, when direct, nonmilitary. When they are violent, they are so indirect or at such low levels of violence that the final outcome has not been determined by the ratios of the military strength.[9]

As a result, a kind of *de facto polycentrism* occupies the forefront of the stage, in which almost anyone who wants can play. Old-fashioned multipolarity resulted from the distribution of coercive power, but this polycentrism results from the devaluation of coercive power. The "centers" are states many of which lack the traditional ingredients of military might, but which are well supplied in the new factors of power and eager to play the game. Because the fullest use of modern coercive power is for mutual deterrence, these lesser centers can push their pawns between the deadlocked giants. Because the new factors of power are complex and varied, their playing has a flexibility that seems to defy analysis.

This is the most novel element of today's international system. As long as international affairs were dominated by a contest between two rivals, either of which was thought ready to use its military power in order to reach its goal, all other participants were reduced to being anxious dependents or frightened spectators, who hoped that their abstention from the game would help them escape the holocaust. Once it became clear that neither of the two rivals wanted to use (or could easily use) precisely that supply of power that made it one of the "superpower," once it became clear that, being in a bottle, the two scorpions had lost some of their sting, other beasts decided they had their chance.

THE FATE OF THE INTERNATIONAL HIERARCHY. Nuclear bombs have not "equalized" the big and the small. Since there is no "military obsolescence," differences among states in the supply of military power—both in capabilities and in the skill with which they can be used defensively or offensively—continue to matter, even in the intervals between the great confrontations when the bipolar conflict obliterates the polycentric game. So do, of course, differences in economic resources. But if "equalization" is absurd, the coexistence of bipolarity and polycentrism plays havoc with the international hierarchy. For one thing, it moderates the usually exaggerated hierarchy of a purely bipolar system, since the two superpowers restrain themselves from using force to discipline misbehaving partners or ill-behaving neutrals out of fear of how the rival could exploit such a deed in a competition that is necessarily more psychological than military. (The importance of the United Nations in this is not negligible.) For another, the usual possibilities open to small powers in a bipolar system for subversion of the hierarchy are enhanced by the new conditions in the use of force. There are certain new limitations here. Any overt resort to force on their part is likely to recreate a hierarchy at their expense;

[9] The mistake made by Kenneth Waltz in his analysis of the international system (see the preceding footnote)...lies in his failure to distinguish between the supply of power on the one hand, its uses and achievements on the other, and in his analysis of the supply in traditional terms. If the supply of full coercive power were (still) the decisive criterion of the system's structure, Waltz would be right in analyzing the system as bipolar and in charging critics with confusing the structure of the system and relations in the system. But what makes the relations different from those of a typical bipolar system are the diversification of the supply of usable power, and the consecration of the nation-state, i.e., the two features discussed above, which greatly affect even the structure of the system.

and, as in any bipolar system, for reasons of history or geography, many of the smaller powers are strategically, politically, or economically utterly dependent on one of the superpowers' protection and aid, and are thus unable to exploit the basic rivalry or challenge the power to which they cling. However, within those limits, there are many new vistas open to middle and even small powers. Let us examine some of them.

In a pure bipolar system, opportunities for the small states are both created and curtailed by the drive of the two great powers for allies and resources. As Thucydides so clearly showed, a small power too close to one of the rivals and beyond the reach of the other's help was in a tragically determined situation. Opportunities existed only in two cases: when a state submitted to inevitable domination but then subtly blackmailed its leader; and when a state was so luckily located in the field of tension that each "pole" would prefer its neutrality to a conflict for its allegiance. Such opportunities were defensive, precarious, and few. As John Burton correctly puts it,[10] they were "part of the strategy of conflict"; today the opportunities are "part of the strategy of avoiding conflict," and they are better.

One reason is that the transformation of power has strengthened the *defensive* position of smaller states. The inhibitions that now restrict the use of force by the two superpowers protect many more of them from the superpowers' military might. And the deadlock of deterrence assures that a superpower will refrain from overtly threatening their integrity, lest the other intervene and start the machine of

[10] In a book that reveals a fascinating mixture of insights and wishful thinking: *International Relations* (Cambridge University Press, 1966), p. 115.

escalation ticking. Even when the rival superpower is unlikely to help, the smaller nations feel somewhat reassured by their own aura of national legitimacy, which the United Nations reinforces. Moreover, because of the relative security that mutual deterrence gives to the superpowers, these feel less desperately the need for satellites than in past bipolar systems. Also, the compression of the use of force to lower levels and diversion from open coercion serve the smaller nations well, since their capacity to resist at those levels and in those realms is often considerable. Since the basic bipolar contest is not a direct military confrontation, what the smaller powers have to offer (and defend) is likely to be something less than territory and men (diplomatic strength for instance)—i.e., something that it is easier to defend, and whose defense will not inevitably trigger military action on the part of the pressuring superpower. In such a contest, purely diplomatic support may matter more to a superpower than anything more tangible; the weakest of states still has one kind of useful power—the power of its mere existence. These smaller states, whether allies or neutrals, are the real if relatively peaceful battlefields; an uncommitted state that threatens to move toward a superpower's enemy, a minor ally who threatens to obstruct an alliance, are obviously not military threats; their defection would not be a disaster in traditional terms of power. But in the new contest, it is the psychological and diplomatic chessboard that matters. In short, by a remarkable paradox, what conditions the defensive power of the small state is *at the same time* the intensity of the contest between the two larger powers, and its predominantly nonmilitary aspect.

This defensive power is largely provided by internal factors: a small state frequently shows a considerable capacity to resist—indeed to integrate and flourish—under threat, and thus disposes of an increased potential to inflict pain should the threat be carried out. Tito benefited from Stalin's pressure; Albania has survived Khrushchev's displeasure, and France survived America's; and South Africa has not crumbled. Consider in this regard the contrast of the two Cubas. When Cuba became, briefly, a Soviet military base, the potential bipolar system suddenly became actual; in the naked confrontation between the two powers, the United States won, because of its over-all strategic superiority and because it superbly turned the tables. What prevented the confrontation from escalating was, at heart, the fear of nuclear war. Now it is this new, rational recoil before the use of force that explains why, when faced with a hostile Cuba acting *on its own*, the United States has hesitated to apply heavy pressure and why it has failed when it has done so. The Soviet Goliath defied the American Goliath and lost; the Cuban David continues to defy the American Goliath. And the North Vietnamese David has been defying him despite all the bombings.

This example tells us something more. Prevented by the conditions of their rivalry from open coercion the Soviet Union and the United States, each in its own way, try to find ways to reassert their mastery over the smaller states. The Soviet Union does this by encouraging subversion, but this "indirect aggression" is a form of Russian roulette. Whether Communism will ultimately triumph in the subverted state without the help of the Red Army is a gamble. Unwilling to provide such help, the Soviets have therefore switched more and more from covert coercion to seduction. The United States, interestingly enough, has more often resorted to what could be called conspicuous

force (Cuba in 1961, Lebanon in 1956, the Dominican Republic, Vietnam) but it has always done so with inhibitions (both internal and external) that limited its effectiveness. Often, the United States has tried to use the United Nations as an instrument of policy (as in the Congo), but this has obliged the United States to submit to the influence of small states skillfully exploiting the power given them in the voting regulations of the General Assembly.

Second, the transformation of power increases the *offensive* power of smaller states. If they remain nonaligned and act cautiously, they are insured of a modicum of impunity not merely to avoid subservience to the great, but also to realize ambitions of their own. Nations "may now be imperialist on a shoestring."[11] They can exploit their less tangible elements of power, particularly their diplomatic potential in fronts and organizations. They can exploit each rival's interest in keeping them out of the other's orbit in order to get economic aid from both. Moreover, within each camp, the blackmail of weakness is no longer the only form of self-assertion: a restive ally can risk a test of strength (if not of military force).

Thus, the opportunities open to the lesser powers in the present bipolar contest both result from its muffling and contribute to it, for they fill the air with clamors different from the familiar noises of the dominant conflict. These nations enjoy a considerable negative productivity of power—i.e., military safety from the great powers —unless they imprudently overreach the limits of permissible violence, and they can achieve such safety at considerably lower costs than the superpowers, which

[11] Andrew M. Scott, *The Revolution in Statecraft* (New York: Random House, 1965), p. 162.

have to spend astronomical sums on the weaponry, research and development of mutual denials. The lesser powers also have a small but respectable productivity of power, not through overt coercive uses, not in achieving tangible territorial gains, but often, through skillful bargaining, in achieving economic gains and gains in prestige.

We can see, then, why earlier models of international systems have become less than relevant. The bipolar systems of the past led inevitably to war, because the costs of using force were deemed bearable. Today, the rivals tend to move away from the points at which they confront each other directly, to avoid the dilemma of "humiliation or holocaust," and the contest therefore moves toward lower levels and grayer areas—a dilution that gives more of a chance to the smaller states. Multipolar systems of the past, in which rivalries among the strong were similarly muffled and diverted to "frontiers," were marked by a continuing series of moments of truth. In the relations between the weak and the strong, disproportion was more effective; and in the relations among the strong, since there was a greater possibility both of resort to force and accommodation, the positive productivity of their power was much higher. But such moderate systems came to fiery ends—either when (as before 1914) the conditions for a favorable balance of power deteriorated so badly that the major powers divided into groups between which the fatal process of rigidity and escalation would occur, or when (as in 1792 and in the 1930s) one major power tried to disrupt the balance by forcibly imposing its ideas and ambitions on others. In today's system, both bipolar and polycentric, one major power's capacity to destroy without expecting to be destroyed has vanished.

Another change in the interna-tional hierarchy is apparent in the hierarchy of *concerns* of smaller and greater states. The smaller states, feeling stronger in their defenses against threats from the superpowers, are often able and willing to pursue goals beyond mere survival and security. Conversely, the supperpowers, encumbered by their nuclear power, must concentrate as never before on the requirements of security and survival. For, while mutual deterrence provides for survival and security at far lower levels of applied coercion than in the past, the energy and resources spent on *avoiding* the application of massive (nuclear) coercion divert the superpowers from other goals. The might of the strong used to be like the commander's statue appearing at the feast of the puny. Today, it is a brooding presence at the meals of the mighty. (These contrasing trends make terrible mischief, of course, in alliances. The small powers take offense at the preoccupation of the mighty patron with his own security and use it as a pretext to pursue their own ambitions.)

Thus, in the present international system, the superpowers suffer from an acute case of what Aron calls the impotence of power.[12] In a pure bipolar system, small states enjoy a kind of vicarious power to coerce and destroy, thanks to their capacity for embroiling larger states in inexpiable rivalries—the kind of power so well described by Thucydides. But in a moment of truth they stood naked before the armed might of the only states that finally mattered. Athens' warning to Melos rang true: the strong do what they can, the weak what they must. Today, by contrast, the great powers' capacity to destroy is to some extent annulled by

[12] "Macht, power, puissance," in *Archives européennes de Sociologie,* 1964, Vol. V, No. 1, p. 44.

its very nature. So the strong do what they must (and can do only a little more), the weak do a little better than they must.

. . .

C. The emergence of multipolarity

The survival of the nation-state is not just the by-product of what I have called muted bipolarity, the basis for the polycentric level of international relations. The nation-state can also be the elevator to a multipolar nuclear world. The "nuclear revolution" explains why the bipolar system is now more latent than manifest, and why the world appears polycentric at the same time; but the uncertainty of this revolution explains a secondary trend, which leads to nuclear proliferation. This trend is both a reaction against the fragility of the limits on force, and a consequence of the persistence of force.

For the balance of terror is fragile in two ways. For one thing, it could always collapse—hence the desire of other powers to consolidate it by complicating the would-be aggressor's calculations. Yet, to the degree to which it is stable, it both undermines the nuclear protection of third parties and requires a re-evaluation of non-nuclear force—hence the desire of other powers to plug the nuclear hole and to deter the threat of a return to classical war. On the one hand, the persistence of the trappings of force in an armed world, the mileage its possessors can still get out of it, at least in preventing other states from reaching a desired goal, and on the other, the consequences of the "balance of terror" in lessening the protection of the lesser powers, together incite the states that can afford it to seek power themselves in the traditional way and to try to become nuclear

powers. They use the freedom created by the "impotence of power" to build up their own.

At first sight, this appears paradoxical, not only because the costs of acquiring nuclear weapons are high, but because they are compounded by the risks of eventual application. Why invest so much into getting equipment that it is then almost impossible to operate? First, since the two major nuclear powers are capable of annihilating one another, the plausibility of their accepting suicide to protect a lesser power decreases, and the lesser power is tempted to buy an insurance policy of its own. If "peril parity" strengthens mutual nuclear deterrence between the superpowers at the cost of weakening the indirect nuclear deterrence that protects their allies (as well as third parties whose safety is vital to the superpowers), it is the duty of the now less protected state to shore up its position. Second, since in a polycentric world teeming with sources of conflict, there are acute tensions at the "subsystemic" (i.e., regional) level and since force, while muted, is not banned, one side in an international dispute is sorely tempted to acquire nuclear weapons so as either to deny its opponent any gains, or to do at the local level what "peril parity" precludes at the top—exploit a nuclear monopoly or first-strike advantage for offensive purposes. The only development that would thwart such reasoning would be a joint agreement by the superpowers not only to denounce but also to prevent the proliferation of nuclear weapons by joint measures of disarmament, by joint punitive action, or by joint guarantees to the potential nuclear power or its rival—something the competing superpowers have not been able to devise. Third, this trend toward the proliferation of nuclear weapons is a precaution, indeed a reaction, against polycentrism.

The pattern of many new "centers" of power is felt to be fragile, since it results from circumstances that would disappear if the two major powers suddenly moved from deadlock to duel or duopoly; to a middle (or would-be middle) power, it is felt as a nuisance, since it distorts the hierarchy. If polycentrism is unstable and unhealthy, like inflation, then multipolarity, paradoxically enough, is a deflationary remedy.

Thus, the spread of nuclear weapons exploits *and* reacts against the muted bipolar contest and the rise of polycentrism. As long as there is no change in the basic structure of the international milieu, the possession of the *ultima ratio,* nuclear weapons, increases a nation's power of inflicting death and makes it virtually inevitably a party to any settlement of issues in which it has a stake.

The attempt to acquire today weapons that a nation could not easily use and may not want ever to have to use is a way of exploiting the present polycentric system so as to turn latent bipolarity into emergent multipolarity. It expresses the desire to increase the negative productivity of one's power. At present, it is the uncertainty of the balance of terror—the fact that no one knows whether a conventional fuse can be stopped from setting off the nuclear detonator—which keeps the use of force repressed at very low levels. If the balance of terror became much more stable, so that the superpowers' inhibitions against the use of force at higher levels disappeared, then the negative productivity of the power of small states which they owe to the restraints kept on the power of the two poles would decrease, unless they too become nuclear possessors.[13]

The drive toward multipolarity also corresponds to a desire to increase the positive productivity of one's power, by more aggressively exploiting one's new strength or by helping to force the superpowers to make settlements in which their challengers participate.

In the present phase of world politics, the mere threat to become a nuclear power (or a state sharing in the nuclear capabilities of a possessor) or the mere fact that one is known to be capable of becoming one—what might be called the power of holding back—is an asset in the game. While it obviously does not provide a state with all the advantages of being a nuclear power, holding back on the threshold saves the costs and risks of actual nuclear weapons and delivery systems, yet enhances the capacity to extract concessions, guarantees, or support from the superpowers (due to their interest in preventing proliferation) or to prevent issues in which one has a stake from being settled by the superpowers alone. Being on the thin line that separates the polycentric from the multipolar level increases already the productivity of one's power.[14]

What is difficult to know at this stage is whether the emergent multipolar system would be latent, like the present bipolar one, or actual. If it should consolidate the freeze on force—which the stability of the balance of nuclear power on top threatens to crack at the conventional level, and which the uncertainty of this balance threatens to crack at the nuclear level—then the system would still be predominantly polycentric. The new nuclear powers would simply share the bittersweet fruits of that impotence of power which now affects mainly two nations. If, on the other hand, the proliferation of nuclear weapons leads to *more* rather than less

---

[13] See General André Beaufre, *Dissuasion et Stratégie* (Paris: Armand Colin, 1965).

[14] West Germany's case is an exception.

widespread use of force, or to a new hierarchy tied more directly to the military component of power, then the new multipolar system would be the actual one. . . .

III. AN IMPERIAL SYSTEM?

The preceding analysis has tried to explain the relative moderation of the international system. Yet another explanation is conceivable, has indeed gained some popularity, and deserves discussion. Some American officials, as well as political scientists, have developed the notion of the United States as the preponderant world power; according to them, the international system is no longer bipolar, but not for the reasons I have suggested. To be sure, there is a latent bipolarity at the "apocalyptic" level of ultimate military might. But what is apocalyptic —like what is exaggerated, according to Talleyrand—does not matter; at the level of manifest international politics, what matters is not polycentrism and the trend toward multipolarity, but "imperial America." This thesis has been accepted by a number of French commentators. But whereas they tend to fear the effects of American world hegemony, the American writers attribute the relative moderation and stability of the international system to America's combination of firmness (in resisting the forces of disruption) and self-restraint.

Powerful arguments can be made for this thesis. First, in terms of "usable" coercive power, the United States not only has provided capabilities for limited war to match those of the U.S.S.R. but also, as already mentioned, has shown a greater willingness to use them—even by attacking the territory of an ally of the Soviet Union, North

Vietnam, thus far without incurring Soviet retaliation. American naval and air superiority is unquestioned. American soldiers, military bases, and military advisers can be found in more than forty countries. America's huge power to reward has been used through military assistance and economic aid to three-fifths of the world's nations. The Soviet record, in all these respects, is much less impressive.

Second, if we look not at the uses but at the achievements of power, we find that the United States, through the skillful use of the power to reward and more or less subterranean uses of coercive power (for instance, the power to threaten the end of rewards), has succeeded in preserving or establishing friendly or at least nonhostile regimes in all of Latin America except Cuba, most of Africa, and a great part of Asia, not to mention Western Europe. Moreover, in the great non-violent confrontations with the Soviet Union—direct ones as in Berlin from 1948 to 1961, or in Cuba in 1962, "by proxy" as in the Middle East in 1967—the United States has prevailed, either (in 1967) because its opponent happened to back the losing side and chose to accept defeat rather than risk escalation, or else (Berlin and Cuba) because American resolve even more than the balance of military forces (unfavorable in Berlin) gave the United States a decisive edge in "the balance of interests as manifested in the relative capacity of opponents to convince each other that they will support their positions with war, if necessary."[15] Third, if, as George Liska has suggested, an imperial power is characterized by the scope of its interests and involvements and by its sense of task, then the United States does indeed wage "the international

15 Osgood and Tucker, cited, p. 152.

politics of primacy": for whereas its chief rival assuredly has a sense of universal task, the breakup of its camp and the scope of American success have sharply curtailed its effective involvements.

A case can be made to show that what has muffled the bipolar conflict and reintroduced moderation in ends and means into the system is the assertion of American primacy. Both the early American nuclear monopoly, and later the nuclear stalemate, have encouraged the Communist states to use all forms of power except full coercive power in the pursuit of their goals. This could have led to violent instability, had it not been for America's ability to meet and thwart them at every level, and thus to oblige them to recognize, either in their doctrinal statements or in their actual conduct, the failure or limits of offensive violence. It is America's primacy that has led to the disintegration of the enemy's camp As for the troubles in its own, they mark both a futile attempt by lesser powers to challenge American preponderance, and the decline of the strategic and economic importance of other areas for the United States. Thus, stability and primacy can be seen as synonymous: like all empires, America is said to have "a great margin for error," to face only "differences in kinds" and timing of success, but not "alternatives that [spell] the difference between conspicuous success and total failure."[16]

In my opinion, the thesis of "Pax Americana" (seen as the nature of the international system, rather than as merely a tendency in American foreign policy) is an optical illusion. What it suffers from is not, as in the case of the bipolar interpretation, a confusion between the military supply on the one hand and the uses and achievements of power on the other, but a confusion between the kinds of purposes for which power is used and between the kinds of achievements of power—gains vs. denials. It neglects the asymmetries between the two great powers: diplomatic-strategic asymmetry (one side is on the ideological and political offensive, the United States is on the defensive), and geographic-strategic asymmetry (the Soviet Union is a land mass, the United States, so to speak, an island-continent).[17]

Thus, what is interpreted as evidence of primacy is merely the success of the United States in *denying* its adversaries either the establishment of bases close to the United States, or the conquest of areas challenged by them, or the dislodgement of Western economic and political influence in areas once controlled by the West but now politically independent, or the establishment of regimes ideologically allied to the main adversaries of the United States. Now, in order to deny such achievements to its foes, the United States has indeed had, first, to show superior resolve so as to make them back down even when the local balance of force was in their favor; second, to maintain naval and air supremacy in order to protect communications with other continents and to be able to strike at enemy forces coming outside of their land mass, and also to spread its own forces and bases abroad, so as to deter piecemeal aggression by assuring American involvement; third, to strive for a strategic superiority in "nonusable" nuclear power, so as to deter eventual nuclear first strikes against America's

---

16 George Liska, *Imperial America: The International Politics of Primacy* (Baltimore, Md.: The Johns Hopkins Press, 1967), pp. 29–30.

17 For further elaboration, see *The State of War*, p. 165.

allies as well as against itself, and to discourage major Communist non-nuclear military attacks by posing a credible threat of an American first strike. In other words, what appears as "primacy" is largely a superiority in the supply and uses of defensive power. Given the nature of the challenges it has faced—either, as in Korea, a massive military aggression, or, as in the Middle East in 1958 or in the Congo since 1960–62, political anarchy exploitable by Communist forces or powers, or, as in Greece in 1947, economic and social chaos, or, as in the Eastern Mediterranean in the spring of 1967, a risk of active Soviet support to its anti-Western Arab friends—it is not surprising that America has had to use its huge economic power to reward and to develop and use (albeit in limited ways) its military power.

A more widespread use of superior or comparable supplies of power is one thing; world primacy is quite another. For if the negative productivity of American power has been high, three sets of factors make it quite different from primacy. First, the celebrated achievements have often been obtained not merely because of the array of American advantages, but also because of independent factors. Those factors: the proliferation of nation-states and nationalisms and the new conditions in the use of force, hinder the U.S.S.R. (and Red China) as offensive powers more than they hinder the United States, yet they also restrict both the uses and the achievements of American power.[18] Second, in the defensive struggle against Moscow and Peking, American power has not always achieved the denials sought. Military force has not proved a panacea, either in Cuba or, so far, in Vietnam, any more than the combination of economic aid and military supplies had proved effective in China in 1949.

Third, the barrier between denials and gains remains. On the one hand, no Communist nation has been decommunized and while the Soviet bloc has cracked, the United States is now faced with two major challengers instead of one. To be sure, the fear of a major military clash with the United States has led the Soviets to dampen revolutionary violence in many parts of the world; but their preference for dealing with governments rather than revolutionaries is not unrelated to their continuing hope of exploiting those governments' own grievances against Western influence. In the non-Communist parts of the world, the United States has won all the major confrontations except Vietnam, thanks to that "favorable balance of interests"; but then, the United States has never chosen to stage a confrontation within the enemy's domain: there was no East-West crisis over Hungary. On the other hand, while the non-Communist nations assisted by the United States have, on the whole, been kept out of communism, they have not *ipso facto* served the other purposes and interests of American foreign policy. The existence in many countries of "American parties," "economic ties converging at the center,"[19] and military programs directed from Washington does not annihilate the assets which the transformations of the map and of power give to the smaller states: nor does this existence provide the United States with effective means of making others do what we would want them to do, or refrain from doing what we dislike.

18 In one instance—the 1967 Middle Eastern crisis—the Soviet defeat was due clearly not so much to America's actions as to the defeat of the Arab "proxies" by a nation endowed with superior national fervor and the willingness to use force.

19 Liska, cited, p. 24.

The United States has indubitably contributed to moderating the international system by obliging its enemies to delay and fragment the pursuit of their ends and to restrict the scope of the means they could use with some chance of success. The United States' failure in "containment" would have led either to some desperado American escalation that would have brought World War III, or to the primacy of the U.S.S.R., victorious in its search for positive achievements. But America's own "margin for error," while large, may not be so huge as to keep the system safe from potentially immoderate disruptions. These could be caused either by American mistakes, especially in the use of force in situations where the sword opens wounds but does not heal them, or by too unbroken a series of successes in denial, for the Soviet Union can hardly afford to be rebuffed everywhere without trying to snatch some success of its own even at great risks. Room for error stems less from America's imperial primacy than from the transformations of the map and of force, which leave the great powers more serene about local fiascoes, and seem to provide many powers—not only the United States and the Soviet Union but, say, France in the Algeria drama, or China in its present turmoil—with a comfortable margin for mistakes. Indeed, only the superpowers face the peril of crossing the brink.

Finally, the moderating impact of the United States has merely resulted, first, in keeping the international system latently bipolar in terms of general war or essential settlements, and, second, in allowing the spread of polycentrism and multipolarity. If America were serene in her primacy, and the Soviet Union had resigned itself to it, would each of the superpowers show so much of an interest in the *other's* preponderance within its coalition?[20] If order in an imperial system "rests in the last resort on the widely shared presumption of the ultimately controlling power of the imperial state...even if the manifestation of the controlling power is only intermittent,"[21] then we are wide of the mark, for the world seems to have at present two "controlling" powers, each in a different sphere, and wide areas in which neither exercises control, although one may try to score some gains at the other's expense, while the other succeeds in denying control to its rival.

Raymond Aron has argued that, for the West, to achieve survival and peace—deterring one's adversaries from destroying the West, making them accept moderate objectives and means—would be tantamount to achieving victory.[22] Even if one agreed that victory has been won (a statement that would ignore the uncertainties of the nuclear balance, the risks created by polycentrism, and the perils of multipolarity), one would have to distinguish such a victory from imperial primacy. It may be that, in the nuclear age, only a world empire could assure peace, but the limited "victory" won in the past twenty years leaves the world exposed to major hazards, the great powers embroiled in dizzying dilemmas of control, and the international system in a state that bears little resemblance to past configurations.

[20] Osgood and Tucker, cited, p. 171.
[21] Liska, cited, p. 37.
[22] See *Peace and War* (New York: Doubleday, 1966), Part II.

II

The Capability
Inventory

THE MEASUREMENT

OF STATES' CAPACITIES

IN THEIR FOREIGN RELATIONS

Chapter 4

One of the most important and yet one of the most difficult tasks for the student and practitioner of international relations deals with the analysis of the capability of states to formulate and implement their policy objectives.

The task is important because this analysis may help to comprehend facets of relations among states which might otherwise remain incomprehensible. By comprehension we mean either an explanation, usually after the fact, or a prediction. Harold and Margaret Sprout put the matter this way:

> With reference to historical cases, the analysis is designed to answer the question: How was it possible for a given state to exert an influence or to play a role which it did *in fact* exert or play? With reference to the future, capabilities analysis is designed to yield a predictive estimate as to the influence which a state could exert or the international role that it could play, either in a specific postulated contingency or in a postulated overall configuration of political relationships in the Society of Nations.[1]

On one level we can say that since force and the threat of force constitute the ultimate recourse regulating international relations, states can neither afford to neglect the elements which make up their respective force

[1] Harold and Margaret Sprout, *Foundations of International Politics* (Princeton, N.J.: D. Van Nostrand Co., Inc., 1962), p. 163.

inventories, nor can they neglect to consider and compare these with those of other states. This is true, even if items in the inventory are never used. In fact capabilities that are *not* used may be more effective as a deterrent than those that are in use or that have been used.

But a discussion of state capabilities must not be confined, as it has too often been in the past, to elements of and capabilities for physical coercion. Capability has many sides, and such aspects as resources, productive capacity, scientific inventiveness, technological know-how, diplomatic skill, governmental efficiency and stability, cohesiveness, confidence, ideological commitment, and morale are in many instances more relevant to the understanding of an international relationship than the coercive forces at the disposal of the governments involved. The Sprouts define the political potential of states in terms of the *combined* corecive power and non-coercive influence which states can bring to bear on other states.

In analyzing state capability it is useful to caution against the temptation to think in deterministic categories. These appear all too easily in thought and discussion. A country's geographic position, its economic potential, or its military capability, for example, will undoubtedly affect its policies, but the relationship is usually not a direct, automatic, causal one. The Sprouts, in the brief selection from their important work on the subject which is reprinted below, emphasized the point by advocating the use of the term "political potential" instead of the term "power." This is sound advice, not only because of the coercive and military (and therefore restrictive) connotations of the term "power," but also because the term "potential" draws attention to the fact that men in positions of influence and control can *choose* whether or not, and if so in what ways and to what extent, to transform potentialities into actualities.

In fact with the advent of weapons systems of unprecedented destructive capacity we may well have reached a terminal point in traditional capability analysis, because the very power of these systems may render them useless in many situations in which coercive instruments were once quite useful indeed. (This point was made repeatedly in the selections in the preceding chapter.) Hence we are in the presence of a new fact in the study of international relations, in the face of which we may have to make provision in our power calculations for those instruments of force that, because of their magnitude and potency, are in practice unusable. In April 1969, the American Secretary of State, William Rogers, commenting on possible American responses to a North Korean attack on an American plane (following by less that two years a North Korean seizure of an American naval vessel), put the matter succinctly when he spoke of the current international system as one in which "the weak can be rash, but the powerful must be restrained." At first glance this may seem like an upside-down world, but on closer inspection the proposition appears entirely valid.

Some authorities have proposed that environmental factors (capacities, political potential) become important and relevant only as they are perceived and taken into account by policy makers; that the way in which they become important is closely linked to the decision-making formula; that the analysis of state capability consists of calculating the opportunities and limitations which are implicit in the environment of the state under consideration, and that capability calculations are always carried out within the framework of assumptions regarding the objectives and strategies of the state concerned.[2] The latter point is extremely important to bear in mind in the study of this and succeeding chapters. The question whether or not a given country is powerful can never be answered except in conjunction with a statement of the situation, objectives, and relationships within which the power or capability is to be exercised. This draws attention to the fact that capability involves not only the country which attempts to exercise its power and influence, but also the country (or countries) over which such power and influence is to be excercised, and the international system within which the exercise of power and influence takes place.

In attempting to measure capability it is useful to keep certain considerations clearly in mind:

1. The student of international relations should never forget that the ingredients in the comparative analysis are *multiple* and further, that these various ingredients interact with one another. Calculations of the capacity of a give society are almost never soundly based if they are based on only a single factor, be that factor geography, demography, economics, or even military capacity. What is needed is a "grand estimate," involving all the elements which may be relevant for the particular purpose under contemplation. (In this sense, the selection from the work of Karl Deutsch, which cites some examples of single-factor or limited-factors analysis, should be taken as illustrative not of the total process of capability analyses but only of ingredients of such a process.)

2. The ingredients which one must study are *dynamic*; they are always subject to change. Given the present state of research and technological capabilities in many countries, some of these changes may come about with extreme rapidity. This means that evaluations once made must be constantly renewed. Any change in any of the components affects the capability of one society *vis-à-vis* another. Countries rise and decline in their capacity to achieve objectives. The cause for either rise or decline may be internal or external, within or beyond the competence of a country to regulate or control. The student of international relations must be sensitive and alert to all changes in the capability constellation; above all, he must never take the permanency of any situation for granted.

3. The various elements which constitute a country's capability arsenal must be studied on a *comparative* basis with similar elements—or mixes of elements—in specific other countries. It is very tempting and relatively

2 *Ibid.,* Chap 4.

easy to compare a given country with itself at a previous time or stage. This type of auto-comparison is not without value or relevance, because it may provide information about the direction and speed of trends within a society. But the student of international relations is, by definition, concerned with relations *between* societies and hence with comparisons between them. The more specific one is about the comparisons to be made, the more useful the analysis will be. The *margin* of power between two countries is more important than the *absolute* power of either country. Being specific in these matters also permits the student to discriminate more carefully between a variety of possible situations. A country may, for example, be deficient in one aspect of capability as compared with another country, but it may make up for this deficiency in other ways. Country A may be militarily (or economically, or politically) weak compared with country X, but at the same time quite strong when compared with country Y. (As viewed by Liechtenstein, Switzerland is a superpower.

In many cases one must attempt to compare not only single countries but combinations, coalitions, alliances, and groups of countries, a task further complicated by the fact that, in addition to performing the necessary calculations for a number of countries, one must then also estimate the cohesiveness of the groupings involved. The questions that need to be asked in such cases include such difficult ones as: Would the countries stick together? In a specific crisis situation, would they help one another and if so, how and to what degree?

4. Given the complexity of the task, there is considerable temptation to look for short cuts in evaluating a country's capabilities. One cannot say that such short cuts are never useful, but the conscientious student should not be carried away with trying to resolve complex problems by overly simple means. Comparisons of national income or steel production or gross national product are particularly tempting short cuts. They do, in fact, reveal a great deal; and recent studies indicate that there is a high correlation between such factors and numerous other factors, so that knowledge of a limited number of ingredients in the capability inventory can provide a measure of confidence that other ingredients are present or absent as well. Still in the long run there seems to be no substitute for the type of grand estimate spoken of above. One of the reasons for this is that most short cuts tend to overlook what Stephen Jones has called "modifiers" of a power inventory—such factors as quantity, availability, change, sustaining capacity, substitution capacity, and qualitative differences.[3] They also tend to disregard the uses to which the item in question is being put.

5. Let us assume for the moment that all necessary information was readily at one's disposal (an unrealistic assumption, to be sure). At that point another problem would confront us—namely, what value to assign to the various ingredients. Since they are composed of different qualities

[3] Stephen Jones, "The Power Inventory and National Strategy," *World Politics*, (1954), 6, 421–52. Reprinted in second edition of this work.

and types, one cannot simply add them together. It is at this point that assumptions about possible uses of capabilities must enter the analysis. For example, does one assume relatively stable and peaceful relationship? Or does one posit the probability of coercive types of relationships? Does one envisage an active policy on a localized, on a broad regional, or even on a world-wide basis?

6. What all this adds up to is the fact that evaluations of power—grand estimates—cannot in the nature of things be precise. In view of the limitations upon accurate measurement of national power, the evaluative process is best visualized as one in which the ingredients are always in flux both in relation to one another and in relation to those of other countries. All one can hope for is that the questions that are asked be defined as precisely as possible, that the data provided to answer these questions be as complete as possible, and that the assumptions which are made be as explicit as possible. Then if either questions, data, or assumptions are found to be deficient, the necessary corrections can be made.

1. *Political Potential*

HAROLD SPROUT

Harold Sprout is Bryant Professor of Geography and International Relations at Princeton University and a Fellow of the Royal Geographic Society. In collaboration with his wife, Margaret Sprout, he has written such outstanding works as FOUNDATIONS OF NATIONAL POWER *(1945);* MAN-MILIEU RELATIONSHIP HYPOTHESES IN THE CONTEXT OF INTERNATIONAL RELATIONS *(1956); and* FOUNDATIONS OF INTERNATIONAL POLITICS *(1962).*

...I prefer *political potential* to the term *power*. This preference derives from the overriding military connota-

The passage reproduced from an article entitled "Geopolitical Hypotheses in Technological Perspective," WORLD POLITICS, *15 (1963), pp. 188–89 is derived from a fuller statement of the same ideas in* FOUNDATIONS OF INTERNATIONAL POLITICS *(Princeton, N. J.: D. Van Nostrand Co., 1962). Reprinted by permission of the Princeton University Press.*

tion that *power* has acquired in recent years, and that probably cannot be altered significantly now. Political relationships unquestionably include a large element of coercion or threat thereof. But no such concept of power comes anywhere near to expressing the totality of political relationships. Neither hostility (in either a legal or a psychological sense) nor violence (in a military or a quasi-military sense) is a necessary ingredient of relationships universally regarded as political; that is, relationships that exhibit some conflict of purpose or interest, and some exercise of coercion or non-coercive influence. Conflicts of interest divide friends and allies as well as those who regard each other as present or prospective enemies. Governments employ a wide range of tools and techniques to gain their ends, many of which exhibit no property realistically describable as coercion or threat thereof.

It has long seemed to me that a term other than *power* is needed to cover both the military and non-military aspects of political interaction and relationship. For this purpose I have come to favor the term *political potential,* defined in a manner somewhat analogous to the meaning of *potential* in the physical sciences.

In non-scientific discourse, the noun *potential* commonly denotes something that is possible though not yet achieved. This idea of latency is expressed, for example, in the familiar concepts of military potential and industrial potential, terms that refer generally to the magnitude of a community's capacity to mobilize or redirect resources for military or industrial purposes. The idea of latency, or capacity for future achievement, would be more precisely expressed by the noun *potentiality* or the adjective *potential:* for example, the military potentiality of China is so-and-so; or the potential coal reserves of Britain are such-and-such.

In the vocabulary of physical science, the noun *potential* carries a different meaning, a meaning just the opposite of latency. About the closest one can come to expressing it verbally is to define potential as the measure of pressure, or pull, or attraction, or simply effect that one body exerts on another. This concept of potential is also expressed in physical systems by such terms as *voltage* and *gravitation.* This concept is manifestly not strictly transferable to social systems, but it does seem to suggest a fruitful analogy. By this analogy one may think of the combined coercive power and non-coercive influence of a state over other states in the international system as constituting its political potential: that is to say, its pressure, or pull, or attraction, or simply effect on their behaviors. To express this idea I prefer *political potential* to *power,* with its strong connotations of coercion and violence.

The reverse of political influence is political deference. Deferential behavior may be compliance with specific demands. Or it may be reflected in recognition of leadership or superior capabilities in the absence of specific demands. Potential and deference also embrace the idea of political prestige, defined as the attractive, or influential, impact of extraordinary achievements in sports, industry, the arts, science, engineering, etc.

Through time, relationships of influence and deference exhibit patterns that are more or less precisely describable. Many familiar terms of international politics denote such patterns: for example, alliance, coalition, sphere of influence, orbit, satellite, protectorate, command of the sea, bipolarity, Monroe Doctrine, Communist bloc, Atlantic community, European community, neutralism, and many others. . . .

KARL W. DEUTSCH

*Karl W. Deutsch is professor of political science at Harvard University. He is the
author of* NATIONALISM AND SOCIAL COMMUNICATION, POLITICAL COMMUNITY AND
THE NORTH ATLANTIC AREA, THE NERVES OF GOVERNMENT, FOREIGN POLICY IN
WORLD POLITICS, MODERN POLITICAL SYSTEMS, WORLD HANDBOOK OF POLITICAL AND
SOCIAL INDICATORS, *and* THE INTEGRATION OF POLITICAL COMMUNITIES. *He is the
co-author of* GERMANY REJOINS THE POWERS. *He is one of the pioneer contributors
to the disciplines of national and international politics. In 1969–70 he served as
President of the American Political Science Association.*

SOME CONCEPTS ABOUT POLITICS

Among the vast number of human relations, which ones are *political?* What does politics do that other human activities and institutions do not do?

Politics consists of the more or less incomplete control of human behavior through voluntary habits of *compliance* in combination with threats of probable *enforcement*. In its essence, politics is based on the interplay of these two things: habits and threats.

The *habits* of behaving, cooperating, obeying the law, or respecting some decision as binding tend to be voluntary for most people. For habits are part of our nature and of the way we more or less automatically act. Without these habits, there could be no law and no

*Karl W. Deutsch, "On the Concepts of
Politics and Power," in John C. Farrell and
Asa P. Smith, eds.,* THEORY AND REALITY IN
INTERNATIONAL RELATIONS, *pp. 48–57. Reprint-
ed by permission of the* JOURNAL OF INTERNA-
TIONAL AFFAIRS.

government as we know them. Only because most drivers stick to the right-hand side of the road and stop at red lights can the traffic code be enforced at a tolerable cost. Only because most people do not steal cars can the police protect our streets against the few who do. If a law is not obeyed voluntarily and habitually by, say, at least 90 per cent of the people, either it becomes a dead letter, or it becomes very expensive to enforce, or it becomes a noble but unreliable experiment like Prohibition. The voluntary or habitual compliance of the mass of the population is the invisible but very real basis of power for every government.

Although this compliance is largely voluntary, it is not entirely so. If it were, we would be dealing not with politics but with folkways, custom, and morality. In politics, the compliance habits of the many are preserved and reinforced by the *probability of enforcement* against the few who may transgress the law or disobey the government.

Enforcement consists of the threat or the use of rewards or punishments. In practice, punishments are used more often than rewards. Punishments are usually cheaper; some people enjoy applying them under an ideological pretext, such as Communism or anti-Communism; and many people think they are more reliable. Clearly, where most people are in the habit of obeying the law anyhow, it would seem costly and needless to offer them rewards for it; it seems cheaper and more efficient to threaten penalties for the few who disobey. Punishments may deter some transgressors from repeating their offense, but it is more important that they deter others from following their example.

Enforcement usually is not certain; it is only probable. But ordinarily the likelihood of enforcement, together with the compliance habits of most of the population, is enough to keep the proportion of serious transgressions down to a tolerable level. The punishment of nine out of ten murderers might be enough to deter a good share of those who might otherwise commit premeditated murder. And convictions in only one-fourth of the automobile-theft cases might suffice, together with the law-abiding habits of most people, to prevent most automobile thefts.

Even the most certain or most cruel punishments, of course, do not deter those murderers who are too thoughtless, too confident, or too passionately excited to care or think realistically about the chance of getting caught. This fact points up one of the weaknesses of deterrence, whether against murder or war.

The conditions that determine the effectiveness of enforcement are much the same as those that determine the frequency of obedient or law-abiding behavior. Most significant among these are strength of the compliance habits of the bulk of the people, and their willingness to give active support to the government in upholding its commands and laws. Next in importance are all other conditions that influence the relative probabilities of law-abiding vs. law-breaking behavior to which the threat of enforcement is being applied. (E.g., if there is hunger among the poor, more people are likely to steal bread.) The size and efficiency of the enforcement apparatus ranks only third in importance. Least important are the processes of changing rules, passing new laws, or threatening more severe punishments.

However, mass habits of compliance and general social conditions, the most powerful long-run influences on the behavior of the population, are the most difficult to manipulate. Even the size, training, equipment, and morale of the enforcement personnel—the armed forces, police, judiciary, and to some extent the civil service—can be changed only slowly and at great cost. The weakest lever of control thus becomes attractive because it is the easiest to use. Passing another law, threatening a more severe penalty, or relaxing the standards of legal justice are much cheaper and quicker, and hence often more attractive than the longer and harder task of effecting more fundamental changes in the situation.

Politics, then, is the interplay of enforcement threats, which can be changed fairly quickly, with the existing loyalties and compliance habits of the population, which are more powerful but harder to change. Through this interplay of habitual compliance and probable enforcement, societies protect and modify their institutions, the allocation and reallocation of their resources, the distribution of values, incentives, and rewards among their population, and the patterns of teamwork in which people cooperate in the production of goods, services, and offspring.

Rule or Dominion

With this concept of politics clearly in mind, we can readily understand the two related concepts of *rule* or *dominion*. By the rule or dominion of a leader, the German sociologist Max Weber meant the chance or probability of his being obeyed. Of two leaders or governments, according to Weber's reasoning, the one more likely to be obeyed by a given population has more dominion over them.

If we carry this reasoning a little further, we recognize what T. W. Adorno once called "the implicit mathematics in Max Weber's thought."[1] A probability, strictly speaking, is a number denoting the frequency, usually expressed as a percentage, with which events of a certain type (in this case acts of obedience to the commands of the ruler) occur within a larger ensemble of events (in this case the general behavior of the population). Weber's concept of rule can therefore be expressed as a number. At least in principle, it can be measured in quantitative terms.

At the same time, we can see the close relationship between Weber's idea of the chance or frequency of acts of obedience and our own concept of the rate of compliance. The latter concept is somewhat broader, in that it includes passively compliant behavior as well as the more positive acts of obedience emphasized by Weber, whenever such behavior significantly influences the outcome of the political process.

Our concept of *habitual* compliance, however, is somewhat narrower

[1] T. W. Adorno, "Oral Communication," 15th German Congress of Sociology (Max Weber Centenary), Heidelberg, May 1964.

than Weber's "chance of being obeyed," excluding as it does acts of submission to the immediate threat of naked force. People obey a gunman in a holdup or a foreign army of occupation so long as they have guns pointed at them. Weber's concept of "rule" or "dominion" covers such cases of obedience under duress. But it should be noted that the obedience is exacted through processes of force, not of politics. They become political only insofar as the obedient behavior continues after the gunman's or the invader's back is turned. Only then, in the interplay of remembered fear and continuing compliance, are we dealing with politics.

When we say that politics is that realm of human affairs where domination and habitual compliance overlap, we are implying that politics, owing to its double nature, is apt to be an area of recurrent tension between centralization and decentralization. For domination or rule usually can be exercised more easily by centralized organizations; threats of enforcement, too, can be manipulated more effectively from a single center. But the dependable habits of large numbers of people can be created rarely, if ever, through a single center of command; nor can they be created quickly. Habits more often develop from a multitude of different experiences repeated over time in many ways. The centralized use of threats or force rarely creates, therefore, a durable community of politically relevant habits; it is much more often such a community of habits that provides the possibilities for the exercise of centralized power.

THE CONCEPT OF POWER

Recognizing the dual nature of politics also helps us to see the limits of the concept of political power. Some brilliant writers have tried to build a theory of politics, and particularly of international relations, largely or entirely upon the notion of power. This is the approach of classical theorists like Machiavelli and Hobbes, as well as of contemporary theorists like Morgenthau and Schuman. The notion of power as the basis of international politics is also widespread in the popular press and even in the foreign services and defense establishments of many countries. What is the element of truth contained in this notion, and what are its limits?

Power, put simply and crudely, is the ability to prevail in conflict and to overcome obstacles. It was in this sense that Lenin, before the Russian Revolution, posed to his followers a key problem of politics with the question, "Who Whom?" Who was to be the master of actions and events, and who was to be their object and victim?...

Such questions as these, when and of great powers in world politics. The fewer actual encounters that have occurred, of course, the more such rank lists must be built up from hypotheses based upon the past performance and the existing or potential resources of the contestants.

POTENTIAL POWER, AS INFERRED FROM RESOURCES

An example of the relative power potential of two coalitions of nations appears in Table 1.[2] Here the power of the Allied and Axis countries in World War II is measured, or at least suggested, by the millions of tons of munitions that each side produced each year.

The table reveals that the Axis powers produced far more munitions than the Allies in 1938, 1939, 1940, and 1941, but that their lead diminished in 1942 and was decisively lost in 1943,

TABLE 1.

COMBAT-MUNITIONS[a] OUTPUT OF THE MAIN BELLIGERENTS, 1938–1943
(PERCENTAGE OF TOTAL)

Country	1938	1939	1940	1941	1942	1943
United States	6	4	7	14	30	40
Canada	0	0	0	1	2	2
Britain	6	10	18	19	15	13
U.S.S.R.	27	31	23	24	17	15
TOTAL, United Nations	39	45	48	58	64	70
Germany[b]	46	43	40	31	27	22
Italy	6	4	5	4	3	1
Japan	9	8	7	7	6	7
TOTAL, Axis Countries	61	55	52	42	36	30
GRAND TOTAL	100	100	100	100	100	100

a Includes aircraft, army ordnance and signal equipment, naval vessels, and related equipment.
b Includes occupied territories.

asked about actual or possible encounters among a limited number of competitors, lead to rank lists, such as the rankings of baseball clubs in the pennant races, of chickens in the pecking order, the year Winston Churchill aptly dubbed "the hinge of fate." After this turn-

[2] Klaus E. Knorr, *The War Potential of Nations* (Princeton: Princeton University Press, 1956), p. 34.

TABLE 2.

SOME HYPOTHETICAL RANK ORDERINGS OF THE POWER POTENTIAL OF MAJOR COUNTRIES, 1960–63 AND 1980

(Based on Energy Production, Steel Output, and Population) *Index Values: U.S. 1960 = 100* *Computed from:*			
Actual Figures for 1960–63		*Projections for 1980*	
Rank			
1. U.S.	100	1. China	250
2. U.S.S.R.	67	2. U.S.	160
3. China	41	3. U.S.S.R.	120
4. German Federal Republic	15	4. Japan	39
5. Japan	14	5. German Federal Republic	25
6. Britain	12	6. Britain	19
7. France	7	7. France	11
TOTAL	256	TOTAL	624

ing point, the Axis powers fell ever further behind until their collapse in 1945.

Table 2 provides a hypothetical ranking of the power potential of the major nations for the period 1960 to 1963 and projects another one for 1980.[3]

The 1980 estimates are based on projected increases in per-capita steel and energy production and total population in each country. (E.g., for China an annual per-capita steel output of about 400 lbs., or roughly one-half the 1963 level of the U.S.S.R. and of Japan, and a population of about 1,100 million are projected.) No one, of course, can yet be sure whether these projections are realistic. In any case, it seems noteworthy that the power of the strongest single country in both periods is rated at well below one-half of the total power of the first seven countries.

THE WEIGHT OF POWER, AS INFERRED FROM RESULTS

Power potential is a rough estimate of the material and human re-

[3] From data in Wilhelm Fucks, *Formeln zur Macht: Prognosen über Völker, Wirtschaft, potentiale* (Stuttgart: Deutsche Verlagsanstalt, 1965), figs. 37–38, pp. 129–31.

sources available for power. Indirectly, it can be used to infer how successful a country should be in a contest of power, if it uses its resources to advantage. Conversely, the *weight* of an actor's power can be inferred from his success at influencing outcomes in the international system.

The weight of an actor's power or influence over some process is the extent to which he can change the probability of its outcome. This can be measured most easily when we are dealing with a repetitive class of similar outcomes, such as votes in the UN General Assembly. Suppose, for instance, that in the Assembly motions supported by the United States pass on the average of three times out of four, or with a probability of 75 per cent, while those motions not supported by the United States pass only 25 per cent of the time. We then might say that U.S. support can shift a motion's chances of success on the average of from 25 to 75 per cent, that is, by 50 percentage points. These 50 percentage points then would be a rough measure of the average weight of U.S. power in the General Assembly. (The measure is a rough one, and it may understate the real influence of the United States, since anticipated U.S. opposition may be enough to discourage many motions from even being proposed.)

Estimating the weight of power is more difficult when we are dealing with a single event. How much power did the dropping of an atom bomb on Hiroshima, for example, exert in terms of its influence on the Japanese decision to surrender? An outstanding expert on Japan, former Ambassador Edwin O. Reischauer, concludes that the bomb shortened the war by only a few days.[4] To make such a judgment, it is necessary to imagine that the unique event—the attack on Hiroshima at a time when Japan was exhausted and seeking a way to surrender—had occurred many times. One would then try to imagine the average outcome for two sets of hypothetical cases: those in which a bomb was dropped, and those in which it was not.

This might seem farfetched, but it is not. Indeed, it is not very different from the reasoning of an engineer trying to determine why a bridge collapsed, or of a physician trying to determine why a patient died. In order to estimate the effect of what was done, and perhaps to estimate what should have been done, we convert the unique event into a member of a repetitive class of similar hypothetical events. We then try to estimate the extent and probability of alternative outcomes in the presence and in the absence, respectively, of the action or condition whose power we wish to gauge. Finally, we infer the power of the actor in the situation from the power of the act or the condition he controls. Power considered in this way is much the same thing as causality; and the weight of an actor's power is the same as the

weight of those causes of an outcome that are under his control.

Modern governments have greatly increased the weight of their power over their own populations. Taxes are collected, soldiers drafted, laws enforced, and lawbreakers arrested with a much higher probability than in the past. By the same token, the weight of government power in industrially advanced countries usually is much greater than that in the developing nations, although there are wide variations among the latter.

In world politics, on the contrary, the weight of the power of most governments, and particularly of the great powers, has been declining ever since 1945. No government today has as much control over the probable outcome of world affairs as had Great Britain, say, between 1870 and 1935. At present Britain cannot control India, Pakistan, Nigeria, or Rhodesia; the United States cannot control Cuba, and certainly not France; the Soviet Union cannot control Albania, Yugoslavia, or China; and China cannot control Indonesia or Burma.

At a closer look, the weight of power may actually include two different concepts. The first deals with the ability to *reduce* the probability of an outcome *not* desired by an actor. In domestic politics we sometimes speak of "veto groups" that can prevent or make unlikely the passage of some piece of legislation they dislike. In international politics, we find a very considerable veto power of the five permanent members of the UN Security Council formally embodied in the UN Charter. Less formally, we may speak of the power of a government to deny some territory or sphere of influence to some other government or ideological movement. Thus the United States in the 1950's successfully denied South

---

[4] Edwin O. Reischauer, *The United States and Japan,* rev. ed. (Cambridge: Harvard University Press, 1957), p. 240.

Korea to its North Korean attackers, and it is currently denying much of South Vietnam to the Viet Cong.

It should be easy to see why this is so. The specific outcome that we may wish to prevent may not be very probable in the first place. Suppose that Communist guerrillas in an Asian or African country had roughly one chance in three (33 per cent) of establishing a stable Communist regime. In that case, an anti-Communist intervention carried out with limited power—say with a weight of about 28 per cent—could reduce the guerrillas' chances of success from 33 per cent to only 5 per cent. In other words, the probability of their failure would be 19:1. Outcomes that are already moderately improbable thus can be made highly improbable by the application of a relatively limited amount of power. In such situations, the change in the probabilities of a particular outcome will seem quite drastic. The limited use of power will seem to have changed great uncertainty into near certainty and thus to have produced spectacular results.

The same weight of power produces far less impressive results, however, when it is used to promote an outcome that is fairly improbable in the first place. Suppose we wish to produce a stable constitutional, democratic regime in that strife-torn Asian or Africa country of our example. With the knowledge that only about one of every twenty of the developing countries has a stable democratic government, we can estimate that such a venture will have about a 5 per cent chance of success. Thus, applying power with a weight of 28 per cent would still only produce a 33 per cent probability that a democratic regime could be established. We would still be left with a 2:1 chance for its failure.

Even this calculation is far too optimistic. For it has unjustifiably assumed that power to promote one outcome can be transformed without loss into the same amount of power to produce another. We all know very well that this is not true. The power to knock a man down does not give us the power to teach him to play the piano. The power to bomb and burn a village cannot be completely or easily transformed into the power to win the sympathies of its inhabitants, to govern it with their consent, or even less to produce among them the many skills, values, and freely given loyalties that are essential to democratic government.

The more specific a desired positive outcome is, the more alternatives are excluded by it. Hence, it usually is less probable; and, moreover, the application of limited power cannot ordinarily make it highly probable. Limited power is most effective when used negatively to veto or deny some specific outcome. Such a use of power increases the already considerable probability of an entire range of possible alternatives to it, with little or no regard as to which particular alternative happens to materialize.

The power to increase the probability of a specific positive outcome is the power of *goal attainment* and of *control* over one's environment. Like all goal attainment and control, it implies a high degree of self-control on the part of the actor. A charging elephant can smash down a large obstacle, but he cannot thread a needle. Indeed, he cannot make a right-angled turn within a three-foot radius. The greater the brute power, mass, speed, and momentum of the elephant, the harder it is for him to control his own motions, and the less precise his control becomes. Driving offers a similar illustration. The bigger, heavier, faster, and more powerful the car, the harder it is to steer. An attempt to measure its power in terms of its performance would give us, therefore, at least two different ratings: a high one for its power to accelerate and a low one for its power to stop or turn.

Does something similar hold for the power of governments and nations? The larger a country is, the more numerous its population, and the larger the proportion of its population and resources mobilized for the pursuit of some policy (and, we may add, the more intense and unreserved their emotional commitment to that policy), the greater is likely to be its power to overcome any obstacles in its path. But national policies usually require more than surmounting obstacles. Often they aim at specific positive results. They may require, therefore, the pursuit of a constant goal through a sequence of changing tactics, or even the preservation or enhancement of a basic value through a succession of changing goals. The more people and resources have been committed to the earlier tactics, policies, or goals, however, and the more intensely and unreservedly this has been done, the more interests, careers, reputations, and emotions have become committed to the old policy, and the harder it may be for any member of the government, or even for the entire government, to propose a change. Unless substantial and timely precautions are taken, therefore, governments may become prisoners of their past policies and power may become a trap.

This danger tends to grow with the amount of national power and with the breadth and intensity of efforts to increase it. Ordinarily, therefore, the danger of losing self-control is greater for large nations than for small ones, for dictatorships than for democracies, and in wartime—hot or cold—than in peacetime. If this danger is not guarded against, the weight of power in the long run may become self-defeating, self-negating, or self-destructive.

THE IMPACT OF
GEOGRAPHIC CONSIDERATIONS

Chapter 5

Among deterministic theories of national power few have exercised a more seductive and persistent appeal than geography. Until a half century ago the relationship of geographical position to national power appeared to be one of the most stable and predictable factors in international politics. Europe in particular was endowed with such a favorable combination of climate, population, and resources that its economic, technological, and social organization appeared destined to give it unlimited supremacy over the rest of the world. In fact with the exception of North America the rest of the world appeared to be hopelessly limited by geographic and climatic conditions.

The only significant transformation that anyone seems to have perceived was that envisaged by Halford MacKinder, who foresaw in the increasing efficiency of rail transportation a geographically predetermined struggle between the landpower of the Eurasian heartland (designated as the Pivot Area in 1904) and the seapower of the inner or Marginal Crescent.[1] MacKinder believed that the marked improvement in land transport would eventually enable one central authority to control the region from roughly central Europe to the Siberian wastelands, and that such control would affect the greater capacity and flexibility of movement by sea and thereby put the historically dominant Western European powers at the mercy of

[1] Halford J. MacKinder, "The Geographical Pivot of History," (paper read before the Royal Geographic Society in 1904).

whoever controlled Russia and the North European Plain. MacKinder's views, as well as the studies of Friedrich Ratzel, inspired a whole host of geographic determinists, of whom the German geopoliticians were the most notorious with their claim that geographic factors entirely determine the growth and decline of nations.

Most analysts are now highly conscious of the relativity of geography and agree that geography is not the *determining* but merely one of the many *conditioning* factors that shape the patterns of a state's behavior. Nor do contemporary geographers hold to any preconceived notions of what a nation is capable of achieving. The concept generally accepted today is "that the physical character of the earth has different meaning for different people: that the significance to many of the physical environment is a function of the attitudes, objectives, and technical abilities of man himself. With each change in any of the elements of the human culture, the resource base provided by the earth must be re-evaluated."[2]

Harold and Margaret Sprout have elaborated the concept of "environmental possibilism," a term calling attention to the fact that geography, far from being immutable, is capable of being molded to man's purposes. As they point out, it is to be hoped that by achieving a more accurate conception of the man-milieu relationship, the student of international relations will avoid the deterministic pitfalls that have beset geopolitics. Above all it should become clear that the mere analysis of data regarding geographic position, topography, resources, population, climate, industry, and so forth, has no intrinsic political meaning apart from the purposes for which men intend to exploit these geographic and related aspects of their environment. Geography becomes part of the analysis of international relations as a function of the "attitudes, objectives, and technical abilities of man himself." As men are able to view and control their environment in different ways, the relationship of geography to international relations changes.

The Sprouts call our attention to the relationship between capability and intention. The question is: Will countries do whatever they are capable of doing? Or will they, under given circumstances, be content with achieving less?[3] The dominant tendency on the part of practitioners of international relations has been to equate the two, to assume that others (never oneself, always others!) will do the greatest damage they are capable of doing, will inflict the heaviest price they are capable of inflicting, will, in short, both bargain and act to the very limits of their capability. It is this assumption that the worst may happen which is one of the tragic hallmarks of international statecraft—tragic, yet apparently unavoidable, because which statesman, responsible for the lives and fortunes of vast numbers of people, would dare proceed on different assumptions? Thus far it seems to have

---

[2] P. E. James, *American Geography, Inventory and Prospect* (Syracuse, N.Y.: Syracuse University Press, 1954), pp. 12–13.

[3] Harold and Margaret Sprout, *Man-Milieu Relationship Hypotheses in the Context of International Politics,* (Princeton, N.J.: Center of International Studies, 1956).

defied human ingenuity to discover a way of escaping from this dilemma, and while the academic student of international relations may legitimately criticize the tendency to equate capability and intention, and deplore the policies to which this tendency gives rise, he should also attempt to empathize with the policy maker who may feel that he has no alternative but to act on this assumption.

In spite of the relativity with which its role must be viewed, geography *is* related to national power and strategy in many specific ways. The successive technological revolutions of the last half century have changed but they have not eliminated the importance of location, topography, climate, and size. For purposes of clarification Stephen B. Jones[4] has suggested that we look at the influence of geography upon international relations from the two perspectives of inventory and strategy. "Inventory" is Jones' shorthand term designating the power potential which a nation possesses by virtue of its size, population, resource endowment, and industrial base. What is important in inventory is the optimum combination of size, development, and aggregate wealth—the wealth being widely diversified as to type of commodities produced, and distributed in such a manner as to permit a relatively high proportion of expenditure on capital and military goods. Thus Switzerland may have a high standard of living, but it does not possess the massive geographic and economic base upon which great power ultimately rests. "Strategy," as Jones uses the term, refers to the implications that geographic position plus technology hold for international relations. The fact that the United States is separated from the Eurasian continent by several thousand miles of open sea and by the frozen Arctic Ocean still counts for something in the calculations of American and Soviet strategists (though, one assumes, far less than it once did, and Wohlstetter's entire argument, reproduced below, is that it should count for very little indeed.). Similarly, size has positive and negative strategic consequences for a country as large as the Soviet Union, depending on the location of its resources and the efficiency of its transportation system, according to Jones.

In this connection it may be relevant to note the idea, held by many and elaborated by several students of international relations, that there are great technical difficulties involved for a country which attempts to operate far from its home base, regardless of the fact that new means of communications have come to the fore. "There are... limits to the effective radius of political power from any center of the world," writes George F. Kennan, adding that

> There is no magic by which great nations are brought to obey for any length of time the will of people very far away, who understand their problems poorly and with whom they feel no intimacy or origin or understanding. This has to be done by bayonets, or it is not done at all. What I

---

[4] Stephen B. Jones, "Global Strategic Views," *The Geographical Review*, (1955), 45, 499–508. This article was reprinted in the second edition of this work.

am asserting is that universal world dominion is a technical impossibility, and that the effectiveness of the power radiated from any one national center decreases in proportion to the distance involved, and to the degree of cultural disparity.[5]

This view, traditionally held by many students of international relations, is now being challenged. Albert Wohlstetter, in the selection reprinted in this chapter, takes Kennan's formulation as his point of departure and attempts to make the contrary case—namely, that given modern technology, distance no longer imposes the limitations upon the effective expression of power that it once did.

The analytical value of the distinction between inventory and strategy becomes clear if we consider the historical record of the last century. The unification and rapid industrialization of Germany in the last third of the nineteenth century enormously increased its economic, demographic, and industrial inventory. This enabled Germany to resort to war twice within a generation in the confident expectation of achieving a position of hegemony in Europe. From the standpoint of strategy, unification and industrialization enabled Germany to transform the disadvantages of a geographically vulnerable position into the advantages of a centralized power. Belgium and Switzerland afford additional examples of the strategic consequences that location may have upon a country's existence. Because of its location at a point strategically vital to three great powers (Britain, France, Germany), Belgium found itself unable to remain neutral. Switzerland, located just off the main strategic axis of Western Europe, escaped involvement in two successive world wars. The United States and the Soviet Union are accounted the world's major powers in large part because they enjoy the geographic advantages of both a favorable inventory of national assets and a strategic location. It was this combination of advantages that a century ago evoked from de Tocqueville a prophetic observation that both Russia and America would one day hold within their hands "the destinies of half the globe" and that early drew MacKinder's attention to the potential of the Eurasian Heartland which the Soviet Union now controls. And though MacKinder did not foresee the strategic importance that the arctic region would assume with the development of air power, his concepts are so solidly rooted in geographic realities that the Rimland, that great belt or crescent of land that runs from the North Cape through Western Europe, the Middle East, and South East Asia to the Kamchatka Peninsula, is still the main arena of world conflict.

The favorable conditions of climate, topography, resources, and communications by inland seas and overland routes that combined to make Europe and Southern Asia the oldest centers of civilization and power still give them a key position in international politics. Western Europe possesses

[5] George F. Kennan, *Russia and the West Under Lenin and Stalin* (Boston: Little, Brown and Company, 1961), p. 276.

the resources, social organization, industrial capacity, and trained manpower which in the hands of the Soviet Union would represent a dangerous accretion of power. Climate has not dealt as favorably with the Middle East, Africa, and Asia as it has with Europe; this fact, combined with an excess of population has prevented Africans and Asians from effectively developing their rich resources.[6] As a result, those regions remain power vacuums more than power centers. Thus geography establishes the foundations upon which certain aspects of capacity, interdependence, and conflict are based, and its importance should not be underestimated. However, it is the perception, will, and creativity of men that ultimately determine the influence that geography will have upon international politics.

In addition to the selection by Wohlstetter, to which reference has already been made, we reprint in this chapter a brief example of the types of data included in a geographic analysis of a state—the treatment of China by a well known geographer, George B. Cressey; and a selection in which another well known geographer, Richard Hartshorne, addresses himself to the impact of geographic relationships upon both economic and military-strategic relations among states.

We have included the Cressey article in conjunction with Professor Wohlstetter's analysis because together they suggest that China's interest and ability to influence events beyond its ocean approaches (which include Viet Nam, of course) may be less significant than we assume. We may have overrated China's capacity for overturning the existing order in Southeast Asia. The tension thus far developed seems to have come almost entirely from countries indigenous to Southeast Asia: North Viet Nam and Indonesia and not especially from China. It has sometimes been argued that China's acquisition of a nuclear delivery capability is of a more direct threat to the U.S. than the extension of Chinese or Communist influence into Southeast Asia. Yet we are struggling to resist the latter and we can do little about the former (unless the ABM system really counts for a great deal).

---

[6] George H. T. Kimble, "Handicap for New Nations: Climate," *The New York Times Magazine*, September 29, 1963, p. 37ff.

1. A New Concept of Geography and International Politics

ALBERT WOHLSTETTER

Albert Wohlstetter is Professor of Political Science at the University of Chicago. Before that he was on the staff of the RAND Corporation, where he made a number of important contributions to American strategic thought.

For twenty-five years, in a good many remote odd spots in the world, the United States has been locked in battle; or has been seconding some distant and sometimes dubious friend; or trying, by promising help, to deter the start of the trouble altogether. With so many and such far-flung commitments and no sign of letup, it is only natural that there should be a lively debate about their number and extent and how they fit our capabilities. The frustrations of these 25 years of engagements in remote wars, and not only the present long-drawn-out and uncertain struggle in Viet Nam, encourage a new isolationism.

.   .   .

Today, sentiment favoring a withdrawal from international to domestic concerns may be based simply on fatigue; or on the familiar but unanalyzed feeling that very distant troubles are remote not simply in miles but in their likelihood of having any effect on us. But aside from a sense that distant troubles are irrelevant, there are

more substantial beliefs. One belief (very influential, though usually inexplicit) holds that "the effectiveness of the power radiated from any national center decreases in proportion to the distance involved."[1] As a result, areas near the borders of a great power are dominated by that power. In these spheres ("spheres of influence" have figured prominently if rather ambiguously in recent Senate Hearings), a great power can forcibly exclude distant great challengers. The result is, then, a balance which it is futile to try to upset; and unwise: its persistence is a guardian of vital U.S. as well as opposing national interests.

The involvement of the United States in land war in Asia in particular is said to be unthinkable; and today this stricture against land war in Asia is accompanied by references to the limitations suffered by any "air and

---

"Illusions of Distance." Reprinted by special permission from FOREIGN AFFAIRS, *January 1968 issue; copyright: Council on Foreign Relations, Inc., New York.*

[1] These are George Kennan's words. "Russia and the West Under Lenin and Stalin." Boston: Little, Brown, 1962, p. 261. *Cf.* Nicholas John Spykman's statement that "power is effective in inverse ratio from its source," in "America's Strategy in World Politics." New York: Harcourt, Brace, 1942, p. 448. The term "neo-isolationist" is also Kennan's and he applies it to himself. Like him, I do not take it as a term of abuse.

naval power" in opposing a "land power;" and it has been bolstered with much reverent or at any rate unquestioning citation of military authorities like General MacArthur by a good many people not accustomed to such piety. Because the United States, we are told, is a naval power, a kind of whale, or a naval and air power, apparently a sort of flying whale, it would seem it cannot project its strength on the land mass of Asia. In any dispute with a continental power, an "elephant" like China, the only hope for us lies in some negotiated settlement.

Such sweeping injunctions against distant ground wars are voiced not only by doves but by such accredited hawks as Mr. Goldwater. In fact, they fit the views of those whose impatience expresses itself by a desire to get matters over with quickly by bombing rather better than they fit the views of those who are skeptical of exclusive reliance on bombing but hope to reach a quick settlement by negotiations. For the stated limitations of air and sea power would affect both the agreements reached and the application of any sanctions against their possible violation. If it were really true that there were no alternative to negotiation of conflicts in Asia, then the negotiation would not be worth much. It would not represent a bilateral exchange leading to a stable resolution but a unilateral measure at the mercy of the Asian land power. Theories that strength weakens sharply with distance and that air and naval power can do little to affect remote land powers fit the old isolationism a little less awkwardly than the new.

In any case the theory that military strength declines in a straight line with distance has never been correct. Logistics support by water has in general been cheaper and easier than over land. References in earlier geo-political writing to continental land masses, islands and the like, have been in fact a crude means of suggesting some of the differences then current between the logistics of land and water combat. In discussing geography, geopoliticians at best have been talking about the technologies of communications or transport or weapons range. Maxims so derived, however, are not eternal. These technologies have been changing at a rapid clip.

None the less, the agonies of Viet Nam have revived some rather old-fashioned geopolitics. Whatever one's view of Viet Nam (and I have substantial differences with U.S. policy there), the isolationism it has encouraged receives no adequate support from such theories. Distance bears no simple relation either to interests or military strength. In the case of nuclear relations, the defects of the old geopolitical treatment of distance are striking. However, its defects for describing variations in non-nuclear military strength with distance are also crucial.

It was rather common until recently to talk of the comparative disadvantage to the United States in fighting eight or ten thousand miles from home against an adversary whose home base is near the scene of conflict. While these dramatic long-haul distances catch the headlines, neither in current nor in past technology do they determine the matter of comparative disadvantage. This has been documented in detailed studies of the comparative logistics at present levels of technology in several areas of possible non-nuclear conflict—in Thailand, in the Himalayas, in Iran and in Lebanon—and in the actual conflict in Korea.[2]

---

[2] For more detail on these studies, see Albert Wohlstetter and Richard Rainey, "Distant Wars and Far Out Estimates," monograph presented at the American Political

The most striking fact displayed by these studies is that the capacity for long-distance lift of the major powers massively exceeds that for short-distance lift inside the theater, especially in the very short ranges in which the battle would be joined. These bottlenecks inside the theater are largely determined by local factors: climate, terrain, harbors, port unloading facilities, railroads and roads, etc. They are not a function of the long-haul distances. The specific local circumstances and opportunities to change them may favor the combatant that starts from far off or the one that starts from nearby. On the Thai-Laos border the United States can lift, from 8,500 miles away, four times as much as China can from 450 miles away. Various potential combat areas in Iran would show a logistic stand-off between the neighboring Soviet Union and the United States. In the Himalayas, support for Chinese and for opposing forces would be measured in tons per day: the 200,000 tons per day the United States might deliver over the long haul from U.S. ports to Calcutta are not the critical matter.

The figures above describe the rate at which supply can be lifted steadily after the initial build-up. If one looks at rates of deployment and build-up where stocks are accumulated in advance in a potential trouble area, the conclusions are not altered. Moreover, if one looks at the matter in terms of cost, as distinct from capacity,

the minor importance of the long haul appears even more vividly. Adding several thousand miles to the distance at which remote wars are fought increases the total cost of fighting by only a very tiny percentage. It appears, for example, that if the support of U.S. forces in Korea had been 2,000 miles further away, it would have meant adding less than three-tenths of a percent to the total annual cost of the war.

The studies cited deal with recent past technology. The technology of the 1970s will decrease military communication and transport costs further, but especially long-distance costs. Larger payload transport both on the surface and in the air will greatly reduce costs per ton-mile. Fast cargo ships might (Congress and the established shipbuilders being willing) combine with the planned massive increase in air cargo capacity to offer more efficient mixtures of pre-stockage and rapid deployment of men and material for the initial build-up. The C-5A will be operational in large numbers in the 1970s; it will have a ton-mile cost one-tenth that of the DC-3 and will carry $2\frac{1}{2}$ times the payload of the largest jet now flying.

Synchronous communications satellites make the point even more clearly than improved transport.[3] It has long been true in telephony, for example, that a very large part of the costs of long-distance service is traceable to such elements as local switching, operator charges and local lines. Communications satellites make the distance between transmitting and ground stations unimportant so long as both are within line of sight of the satellite, whereas under-

Science Association meeting, New York, September 1966. *Cf.* also Albert Wohlstetter, "Theory and Opposed Systems Design,," to be published in "New Approaches to International Relations," edited by Morton Kaplan. In this connection we are indebted to the work of Mary Anderson, Wallace Higgins, L. P. Holliday, Norman Jones and John Summerfield.

[3] See Leland Johnson's "Some Implications of New Communications Technologies for National Security in the 1970s," presented at the ninth annual conference of the Institute for Strategic Studies, September 29, 1967.

sea cables vary in cost directly with length. Satellites spanning the Atlantic and Pacific will greatly increase the capacity and reduce the costs of sending messages to far-off and isolated locations, and so will make possible a much more detailed and centralized control of classical wars in distant theaters.

If future technology reduces further the difference between fighting a war close by or far off, it can do this not just for the United States, of course, but for other nations as well. This is only one reason that technical developments should not fortify any illusion of omnipotence. We may contest some sorts of war badly almost anywhere, in particular revolutionary wars where recently improved weapons technologies seem to me largely irrelevant (though no more so in Viet Nam than they might be in Colombia or even in Cuba). Military strength is frequently a very poor and self-defeating way of protecting or fulfilling interests. This applies to military strength used nearby as well as military strength used far off. It is plainly better not to have to fight at all. Even more plainly, an ability to fight cannot be directly translated into political authority. Limits in the usefulness of American military strength are clear in relation to countries that are in varying degrees hostile to the United States, such as tiny nearby Cuba—perhaps even more so in relation to America's allies. In spite of the rhetoric about France's slavery to American despotism, General de Gaulle always struck me as a rather masterful slave long before he had even a façade of a *force de frappe*. The point can be made in reference to those allies most menaced and least able to defend themselves. McGeorge Bundy suggests that polemists using words like "'puppet" have never been on the other end of the strings. It is rather more, I should

think, like pushing than pulling strings. The fact that military technology can be projected by the United States and by others at great distances reveals some critical connections between remote parts of the world, but lends no support to the mechanical extension of American political hegemony.

Furthermore, though we can affect matters in some places close to us or far off, we frequently have no discernible interest in doing so. In the last year, the isolationist debate has shifted somewhat from capabilities to interests. A good many places interest none of us very much, and some that interest us can take care of themselves. That's almost always better. No one on either side of the debate is for intervention all over or for total escape. The genuine issues concern the right extent and places of commitment. They cannot be clarified wholesale. And they have not been by the endlessly tedious repetitions and denials of the phrase "policeman to the world."

A great many things—historic, political, ethnic, cultural, sentimental—affect national interests, including a residue of past technologies like the methods of ocean transport that durably linked Great Britain, Spain, France, Portugal and the Netherlands to some of the remotest parts of the world. But future technologies will affect interests too, and on the whole in a direction that makes the new isolationism pure nostalgia. Let me say something on interests of nations in cultural contact, in trade and the movements of capital, and in national safety.

II

Cultural interests have never fallen off directly with distance. Englishmen and North Americans find Australians and New Zealanders quite accessible culturally, and are sometimes greatly puzzled by their immediate neighbors. French contacts with some parts of North America were always considerable and lately seem to be much on the increase. The vast improvements coming in long-distance communications and transport will multiply remote cultural contacts just as they will increase the capacity to project military strength. Civilian supersonic passenger planes, the subsonic high-payload 747 stretch jets, a possible passenger version of the C-5, and the commercial satellites —all neatly parallel in the civilian field the military equipment that makes the problem of getting to a theater of war small compared to getting about in it. Travelers are already used to the sharp contrast between the speed with which they can hurtle between distant airports and the maddeningly slow pace getting to and from the airport, queuing up for tickets, taxis, baggage, porters and traffic lights.

High-payload jets will cover great distances still more quickly and cheaply, but may increase the queues. Supersonic jets will be economic only on long trips. Their principal result will be to bring the remote places closer. It has been pointed out that if sonic booms prevent supersonic aircraft from flying over land, New York will once again, as in the time before the building of the transcontinental railroad, be closer to Europe than to Los Angeles. Passenger traffic in the Pacific should increase still more strikingly. Travel time from Los Angeles to Tokyo may be cut by nearly two-thirds. It will take perhaps forty minutes more than to get from Los Angeles to New York.

For civilian communications as for civil transport, the right map cannot be drawn in kilometers or miles, in what François Perroux calls "banal distance." Buenos Aires is closer now to Europe or the United States than to Caracas or Santiago. Telephone calls from Buenos Aires to Caracas go through New York. Calls between two points in Africa may go through switch points in both London and Paris. The new communications will alter optimal switching points and help local traffic, but in particular will bring together widely separated points.

From the standpoint of economic and strategic interests, one important result of improvements and transport will be to increase the geographical extent of interests and simultaneously to reduce the specific importance of what are now critical bottlenecks at transit points. Suez is an example: reducing the costs of very long hauls cuts the added expense of a detour.

Indeed, most of what I have said about effects on cultural contacts applies quite directly to economic interactions: that is, to the movements of commodities and capital and possibly seasonal labor. Air freight capacity has been increasing rapidly for commodities of high value; the huge cargo aircraft now on the way will make distant air transport economic for new ranges of less valuable commodities. For bulky primary commodities, those that are lowest in value density, like oil, the development of supertankers drastically reduces long-haul costs. The economies of scale are enormous. A tanker with a capacity of 150,000 deadweight tons can move crude oil 5,000 miles at $1.69 per ton compared to $7.29 for a 10,000-ton tanker. Construction costs decrease with increasing tanker size from $220 per ton at 20,000 deadweight tons to less than $70 at 300,000 tons. Operating costs decrease, too, in particular with increased opportunities for automation. In fact, the *Tokyo Maru*, a tanker of about 135,000 deadweight tons, will be operated by a crew of 29, while tankers of 50,000 tons may use

35 men or more. The Japanese in the early 1970s will be constructing 500,000-ton tankers, something like ten times the size of the largest tankers available during the Suez Crisis of 1956. As a result of such changes, not only are detours around gateways like Suez cheaper than they were; they may, because of the limitations of the gateways themselves, be cheaper than the direct route. Suez at present can handle fully loaded tankers only up to 70,000 deadweight tons.

The lowered costs and increased capacity for both long-distance transport and long-distance transmission of messages increase the number of economic alternatives available, and make it feasible to go around choke points. These communications and transport developments reduce interest in specific gateways to remote places, but not the interest in remote places themselves. On the contrary, to the extent that they make links to distant points more reliable, they spread interests more evenly but farther. For example, Japan's growing trade with Europe in manufactures will be less in danger of arbitrary interruption. In reducing the risks of war or peacetime interruption, these technical changes counter one of the chief traditional arguments for economic autarky.

.   .   .

Aside from its theoretical lacks, the belief that technology would reduce the role of trade does not square with available data, even though trade has been hampered by government barriers. World trade in manufactures in the 90 years after 1876, in spite of setbacks in the protectionist and depressed interwar period, increased per capita two or three times. Between 1950 and 1966 it has been increasing even faster than world production of manufactures—7.3 percent compared to 5.3 percent per

annum.[4] For the United States, in spite of claims to the contrary, from the 1870s to the 1960s neither exports nor imports declined relative to G.N.P. in real terms.[5] Similarly within the United States, interregional trade, as Richard Cooper has shown, has grown more rapidly than total output, in spite of an apparent "convergence" in economic structure of the various regions.

What is true of trade seems true also of the movements of capital when not constrained by artificial barriers. Improvements in long-distance travel and telecommunications encourage distant foreign investment by making it easier to manage. Data processing on a large scale may stimulate organizational innovation and in any case makes feasible much more detailed and far-flung control. All of this should continue to encourage the already significant growth of international corporations whose interests extend far beyond any narrow geographical region, and make economic autarky more inappropriate than ever. The distant projection of interest should not be taken, however, as applying only to the capital-rich countries, as an attribute of "imperialism." The underdeveloped world has perhaps even more obvious interests in the distant developed world as a source of aid and as a market for exports. Indeed, as Edwin Reischauer suggests, one of the more disturbing aspects of some of the new isolationism is an implication that "Asians, having their own distinctive cultures and special prob-

[4] See Alfred Maizels, "Industrial Growth and World Trade." Cambridge University Press, 1963, p. 79 ff; for an extension of his data through 1966, see *Monthly Economic Letter,* First National City Bank, New York City, Sept. 1967.
[5] See Robert Lipsey, "Price and Quantity Trends in the Foreign Trade of the United States." Princeton University Press, 1963.

lems, should go their own way, presumably in poverty and turmoil, while we of the advanced nations go our own prosperous and peaceful way."

. . .

Neighborhood in international relations, as Jacob Viner has pointed out, has never guaranteed neighborly feelings, and often has prevented them. Writings on international relations in the eighteenth century and later took proximity as one of the natural conditions of enmity. Indeed, one of the largest defects of regionalism in the postwar period has been a frequent neglect of the hard truths of differences in political interest inside regions and the varying bonds of interests with countries outside. Regionalism, which has seemed a halfway house between nationalism and a utopian universalism has itself sometimes been a kind of utopia for hard-headed Realpolitikers.

. . .

The increasing ease of communication and transport in the future should not be taken as simply irenic, leading to harmony and peace. On the contrary, it means an extension of the "neighborhood" to more remote areas, and such larger neighborhoods need not mean neighborliness any more than the small ones. The possibilities of coercion as well as coöperation increase. Which brings us back to the third interest, that of national safety.

III

National safety is the most critical matter and perhaps the least understood by those who think of it in terms of nineteenth-century and earlier technologies; or by those who conceive of

it exclusively in terms of bilateral nuclear deterrence, the preoccupation of the mid-1950s. One essential here is that improvements in the technology of putting weapons on target and providing logistics affect not merely one's own capabilities and those of one's friends, but those of potential adversaries as well. These changes, then, extend drastically the range at which potential adversaries can do harm. This is most obvious in the case of the technologies for nuclear war. Not only the nuclear capabilities of the two largest powers, but also of others, will extend far beyond any single region, and will permit coercion if unopposed.

But improvements in technology extend the range at which classical, not just nuclear, conflicts may be fought. And as in the case of nuclear technologies, such improvements apply to potential adversaries too. While neither for the nuclear nor the classical case is distance without effect, the effects are complex; and very much more complex than is recognized by linear theories of the weakening of strength with distance. None the less, the upshot of these considerations of technology in the 1970s is that basic interests in safety will extend farther out than they ever have before. . . .

A second essential is that bilateral mutual deterrence is not enough to prevent the international system from deteriorating. Even if a small nuclear force were able to make one country the equal of any other in deterrence, this would leave unsolved the problem of protecting non-nuclear countries from nuclear coercion. A few intrepid proponents of nuclear equalizers might be ready to distribute nuclear bombs to everybody. To most of us, however, the perils are plain in a spread of nuclear weapons rather less than worldwide. A country without nuclear weapons that feels menaced by a nuclear adversary is likely to seek nuclear weapons of its own unless it feels assured of nuclear protection by someone else. Moreover, since any country, nuclear or non-nuclear, is likely to have interests affected by the coercion of some non-nuclear nation—perhaps a neighbor, perhaps a more distant country—the issue of guarantees, of formal or informal commitments for nuclear protection, cannot be avoided.

. . .

In sum, neither military capabilities, nor economic interests, nor interests in cultural contacts, nor in national safety seem likely to be narrowly circumscribed by geography, to be contained for example, by continents. Neither national nor regional autarkies look sensible in either strategic or economic or political terms. Orwell projected for 1984 a world split into a few huge blocs. I find such a prospect neither attractive nor likely to improve the chance of peace. Even inside a single nation sharp regional lines dividing the country into groups with different political, sentimental, ethnic and economic interests make civil war more likely. On a world scale it would be more ominous. Orwell showed his insight by having his huge continental blocs constantly at war. The fact that, so far as technology is concerned, the 1970s do not seem to be marching toward 1984 strikes me, then, as all to the good. There are many forms of coöperation, including, to be sure, some regional ones that are useful for specific and limited purposes. But perhaps it is just as well that the useful sorts of association are "cross-cutting"—that is, likely to vary in membership from one purpose to another.

We all believe in the importance of preserving options, of being able to defer decision in order to make a final resolve on the basis of the utmost in information about alternatives. We feel uneasy about getting involved, about "contracting in." None the less, commitment, foreclosing some options, is essential if we want to keep other options open in the future. The technologies of the 1970s suggest that many of the essential commitments will continue to be long-distance.

The new isolationists sometimes phrase their misgivings about American involvement in distant countries not in terms of traditional geopolitics—the range of weapons and the feasibility of transport—but in terms of our limited knowledge of the problems of these outlying peoples and the limitations of our wisdom, intelligence and perseverance. All of these are, sad to say, limited. But if mileage is today no criterion for increasing either our interests or our capabilities, it is even less plausible to suppose that our degree of knowledge is a simple linear function of distance from home, starting high and falling off very steeply. Sometimes we manage to be rather ignorant of countries close by; and while understanding of other countries is always limited (like self-understanding), we have managed to amass a considerable store of knowledge about some remote spots. It is not evident, for example, that we know more, or are any wiser, about either Haiti or the Dominican Republic than we are about India or Australia. And since we can be greatly affected by distant troubles, we have to deal with them. If we are not adequately informed about them, there is really nothing we can do except to find out more and think harder.

2. A Geographic Analysis I: Three and a Half Million Square Miles

GEORGE B. CRESSEY

George B. Cressey is a well-known geographer who has specialized in the geography of Asia with particular emphasis on China. Among his many publications are LAND OF THE 500 MILLION, ASIA'S LANDS AND PEOPLES *and* HOW STRONG IS RUSSIA?

LAND AND LOCATION

China is the world's third largest country, with an area of 3,657,765 square miles.[1] While China is big, much of it is useless. Mountains, steep hills, and cold plateaus greatly restrict usable land. Plains and rolling basins cover less than 50 per cent of the country, and two-thirds of this percentage is arid. Barely 15 per cent is potentially usable for agriculture. China's 500 million live in a country which is impressive on the map but which is not so good in reality.

China shares the summit of Mt. Everest, 29,028 feet,[2] with Nepal, and

From LAND OF THE 500 MILLION *by George B. Cressey, (copyright 1955: Mc-Graw-Hill Book Company), pp. 30–32. Used with permission of McGraw-Hill Book Company.*

[1] The USSR leads, with 8,597,000 square miles; then comes Canada with 3,843,-144 square miles. China is followed by Brazil, with 3,286,170 square miles, and the United States, with 3,002,387. Prior to the loss of the Mongolian People's Republic, China covered 4,380,535 square miles. [When Alaska and Hawaii were admitted to statehood, the area of the United States increased to 3,614,-210 square miles.]

[2] The conventional elevation for Mt. Everest has been 29,002 feet. The above figure was officially announced by the Surveyor-General of India in 1955.

also includes the world's second lowest elevation, the Turfan Depression at −928 feet. Within this six-mile range in altitude there are many types of land surface: desert sand dunes, alpine glaciers, broad alluvial plains, and precipitous canyons. Loess hills and limestone karst are uniquely developed. The chief types of topography not represented are the souvenirs of continental glaciation and active volcanoes.

From the interior highlands flow three of the world's longest rivers, the Yangtze, Hwang, and Amur. Other large areas have no drainage to the sea, since evaporation exceeds precipitation and the few streams wither as they flow toward the center of their basins.

Where is China? To the Chinese, the answer is simple; it is here, and the proper name for the country is the Central, or Middle Kingdom. To outsiders, China is "somewhere else"; perhaps it is no more than a large yellow spot on the map. Europe looked eastward and spoke of the Far East. With equal appropriateness Americans might term China the Near West. By ship Shanghai lies 18 days west of San Francisco, but by plane it is only as many hours away. When one looks at a globe, however, it becomes clear that the shortest route to China from Europe or North America does not lie east or west, but northward.

China has traditionally dominated eastern Asia; she may come to lead in the western Pacific. Perhaps this sentence summarizes her space potential. Within a radius of 2,000 miles from Shanghai, China holds possibilities of continuing leadership. In the area surrounded by India, the Soviet Union, Australia, and the United States, China's leadership is threatened only by Japan.

It appears to a geographer that for many decades to come, the world will be dominated by the North Atlantic area. The leadership once held by the Mediterranean and then by Europe has shifted to the countries around this ocean. The Pacific Basin will surely grow in importance, but it does not appear probable that it can catch up with the Atlantic. If this suggests that China is not likely to lead the world, it need not mean that China cannot have a great future in her own area.

China is like a huge oasis. On all sides she is surrounded by the most perfect of physical barriers. To the east and south lies the widest of the oceans. To the west is the highest of all plateaus. To the north lie nearly a thousand miles of desert. China has had trouble with some of her immediate neighbors, all of whom she regarded as barbarians, but no invasion from outside eastern Asia has occurred until modern times. Foreign commerce before the twentieth century was negligible.

In so far as classical China had a front door, it was the westernmost gateway of the Great Wall, poetically named the Jade Gate, since through it passed caravans bringing jade to China. Here entered Marco Polo and the first Europeans; out from this gateway passed Chinese pilgrims in quest of Buddhism. Shanghai was merely a fishing village;

it and the other coastal cities were China's backdoors.

With the arrival of the Europeans who came by sea, China has had to make an about-face. Shanghai, Tientsin, Dairen, and Canton are the new front doors. In the space of a century China has been obliged to reorient her life, to adjust the thinking of millions of people, the economy of millions of square miles, and the tradition of thousands of years. The ocean, rather than the interior frontiers, has dominated her foreign relations during the past century. China's current interest in the Soviet Union thus represents something of another reversal, one which is not in keeping with the modern emphasis on maritime contacts.

Mainland China borders the sea for 3,300 miles. On her landward side, the frontier extends for 9,300 miles, of which 3,050 faces the Union of Soviet Socialist Republics and 2,400 borders the Mongolian People's Republic.

Transit facilities across the land and sea boundaries differ notably. China has some twenty-five seaports, not all fully modern, which are capable in all of caring for hundreds of steamships in a day. Across the land frontiers there are only a few areas with railways, each of them off-center. Two lines lead to Indochina. Three lines cross into Korea. The Soviet Union is reached over either end of the old Chinese Eastern Railway, built as a short cut across Manchuria for the Trans-Siberia Railway, and there will be another link with the completion of the line through Sinkiang. A new railway across Mongolia provides a short cut to Siberia. Not a single paved highway crosses the border, and the total of usable automobile roads scarcely exceeds a dozen. The capacity for overseas commerce is a thousand times greater than that for overland trade.

During normal years between the First and Second World Wars, China exchanged a few goods with Korea, and there was a small transit across Indochina. Some soy beans were exported through Vladivostok, but business with the Soviet Union was negligible. The total foreign commerce through all overland gateways for a year probably did not exceed that through Shanghai during a day or two. This is a matter of geography, not of politics. Mountains, deserts, and distance permanently isolate interior China, and the expense of shipment by rail or truck, and certainly by air, will always exceed the cost by sea. China's orientation toward the Pacific seems assured.

3. A Geographic Analysis II: The Functional Approach in Political Geography

RICHARD HARTSHORNE

Richard Hartshorne is Professor of Geography at the University of Wisconsin. He is a Past President of the Association of American Geographers and author of THE NATURE OF GEOGRAPHY *as well as many scholarly articles.*

In the analysis of a state-area the need to consider its economic relations with outside areas arises from the fact that in many respects a state operates, must operate, as a unit economy in relation with other unit economies in the world. The difficulties arise because, while it must operate completely as a political unit, a state-area operates only partially as an economic unit.

The first problem is to determine to what extent the economy of one

From Richard Hartshorne, "The Functional Approach in Political Geography," ANNALS *of the Association of American Geographers, 40 (June 1950), pp. 122ff. Reproduced by permission from the* ANNALS *of the Association of American Geographers.*

state-area is dependent on that of others, though the mere analysis of self-sufficiency is only a beginning. If one says that the United States produces a surplus of coal and iron, but is dependent on foreign countries for much of its supply of tin, nickel, and manganese, of sugar and rubber—such a statement, even in precise percentage figures, tells us directly little of importance. If a country has plenty of coal and iron it can normally secure the other metals mentioned from wherever in the world they are produced. Under abnormal conditions of war, or threat of war, it is essential to know that the manganese normally comes from the Transcaucasus in the Soviet

Union, the tin from British Malaya (but can be obtained in Bolivia), whereas the nickel comes from adjacent Canada. Natural rubber supplies are available in adequate amounts only in one remote region—Malaya-East Indies —but nearby Cuba can supply most of our sugar needs.

In general, the geographer will analyze the economic dependence of one state-area on others in terms of the specific countries concerned and their location and political association in relation to the state he is studying.

Since all sound trading is of mutual advantage to both parties, to say that one state is economically dependent on any other necessarily implies also the converse. But the degree to which any particular commodity trade, shipping service, or investment is critically important varies in terms of the total economy of each of the two states concerned. It is only in this sense that the common question "Is a particular state economically viable?" has any validity, since every state above the most primitive level is in some respects critically dependent on others.

The problem is far from simple, but perhaps we can suggest two generalizations. As between two countries that differ greatly in the size of their total national economy, the economic relationships between them are more critically important for the lesser country (though this might not be true under war conditions). This is true because these economic relationships, which may be taken as equalized through international balance of payments, will form a larger proportion of the total national economy of the lesser state. An obvious example is found in the relation of Eire to Great Britain, of Cuba to the United States.

The second generalization rests on the fact that the critical significance of the trade depends on the possibility of alternatives, of finding other sources for needed supplies or other markets for products which must be sold to maintain the national economy. Most popular discussions tend to think only of the former, whereas under the capitalist profit-system under which most international trade operates, it is the latter that is more significant. The reason is that for most commodities of world production there are alternative sources of supply at moderate increase in cost; there may not be alternative markets even at greatly reduced selling prices.

Finally we may note that relatively few areas of the world now produce a surplus of manufactured goods requiring a high degree of technological development and these constitute therefore a relatively limited market for the surplus of primary products of farm, forest, and mine which can be produced widely over the world. Consequently the countries producing primary products, even the very necessities of life, may find it more difficult to find alternative markets for their products than the industrial countries producing articles less essential to life. With wider spread of industrialization over the world, this situation would of course be altered, conceivable reversed.

It should not be assumed however that these rough generalizations will provide the answer in any given case. Consider the problem posed by the independence of Austria after the dissolution of the Habsburg empire—a problem which Austria still faces. To survive as a viable economic unit, Austria needed to maintain with the adjacent regions, re-organized as independent states, a high degree of economic relationship. Its position in competition with otherwise more favored regions of industrial Europe, made it peculiarly dependent on markets immediately to the east. For these eastern neighbors such relationships were also necessary for the maximum economic progress, but were not vitally necessary to economic life. If, for political reasons, and to develop their own industries at greater cost, they preferred not to trade freely with Austria, they had the choice of the less profitable plan, whereas for Austria the alternative was economic collapse.

In the nineteenth century, international economic relations, though both supported and retarded by state action, were generally operated as the private business of individuals and corporations. With the depression of the 1930's, the rise of totalitarian states, and the last war, there has been an increasing tendency for the state itself to direct the operations of international trade and investment. In these respects states function increasingly as economic units so that the economic relations among them become increasingly important in the politico-geographic analysis of the state.

. . .

STRATEGIC RELATIONS

In no phase of political geography does the geographer experience such difficulty in maintaining his geographic point of view or in keeping his eye focussed on problems he is competent to study as in the field of strategic relations. Strategy obviously depends on national power and this is a subject on which the geographer feels ready to contribute his share, in "geographic foundations of national power." But in so doing he is migrating into a field whose core and purpose is not geography, but military and political strategy. Further, to answer the questions raised in that field—e.g., "How strong is a state?"—one must analyze not only the geographic conditions, but a wide host of other factors including the effect of party systems on the conduct of foreign policy, morale of fighting troops, effectiveness of personal leadership, size of standing armies, and number of fighting planes.

It is therefore not merely an intellectual exercise to attempt to distinguish between political geography and the study of the power of states (to which geography has much to contribute); it is a problem of practical importance for the individual geographer concerned to outline a unitary field of political geography in which he may competently work.

The literature of political geography provides no clear answer, so far as I can find, to this problem. Certainly the development of Geopolitik greatly confused the problem for the German geographers, and those of our own colleagues who have hoped to establish a purified field of geopolitics have inherited that confusion. Some writers evidently solve the problem by simply omitting any consideration of strategic relations. But surely this produces an incomplete study. In the analysis of the external relations with other state-areas, we must certainly recognize that the state-area, as a unit, has vitally important strategic relations with the other areas of the world.

I therefore approach this problem with no assurance that we have a satisfactory answer.[1] But in this progress

[1] As examples of attempts to handle this problem in specific cases, reference may be made to two studies, by the writer, one written early during the last war (though published somewhat later), the other just after the end of that war: "The United States and the 'Shatter Zone' of Europe," in Hans W. Weigert and V. Stefansson, *Compass of the World*, New York, 1944, pp. 203–14; and "The Geopolitical Position of the United States and the Soviet Union," *Education*, (October 1946): 95–100.

report, it may be appropriate to present as current thinking even very tentative conclusions.

Every state-area in the world lives in a strategic situation with other states, a situation that may be in part created by its own actions and policies, but in major part is determined for it by those other states.

Thus Switzerland in modern times has been a unit area of relatively small offensive power, though not inconsiderable defensive power, situated in the midst of a group of larger neighbors, each fearful of expansion of power by the others. In this situation Switzerland has found its best hope for security in a policy of armed neutrality because such a neutralized area was in the mutual interest, defensively, of the neighboring powers. In a much earlier period, in the sixteenth and seventeenth centuries, when Austria was the only major power bordering Switzerland, and many of its neighbors were small states, the Swiss Confederation followed a very different policy of strategic relations, frequently allying itself with any of various neighbors in conflict with the others.

The strategic relations of a state, in other words, must be adjusted to the particular strategic situation in which it finds itself at any time. With the unification of Germany in 1871, the strategic map of Europe was changed no less than the political map. Because that new unit increased in economic production, population, and power faster than any of its neighbors, and was able to establish close strategic relations with Austria-Hungary, forming a solid block of power across Central Europe, all the other states of Europe including Great Britain, were forced to change their strategic relations with each other.

Within the last five years the United States has found itself forced to abandon one of its most time-honored principles of international relations— that of having no strategic relations in peacetime with any states outside of the Americas. The new relationships entered into under the North Atlantic Pact followed an appraisal of the new pattern of space-relationships of power as created by the changed system of states in Europe. It might be significant, though now too late, to ask whether an equally realistic appraisal of that situation in 1938 or 1939 would not have shown the need for a similar strategic association at that time.

Whatever reaction the reader may have to that idea, our concern in this theoretical discussion is merely to illustrate the type of problem that seems appropriate for inclusion in the analysis of the political geography of a state-area. In studying the relations which such an area, operating as a unit, enters into with other areas, we are concerned with engagements which it has, or has not, made with other units, whether for defensive or offensive purposes. Interpretation of these associations necessarily involves an appraisal of the space relationships of all the strategic areas involved, whether as power units or as territories of passage. The problem is logically inherent in the political geography of states and its geographic quality seems clear.

.   .   .

POPULATION AND
ECONOMIC CHANGE

Chapter 6

What is the relationship between population and a nation's capabilities to formulate and effectively pursue objectives *vis-à-vis* other nations?

> Population is...a nation's greatest resource.... What greater asset can a nation have than a multitude of able-bodied citizens, ready to stoke its furnaces, work its mines, run its machinery, harvest its crops, build its cities, raise its children, produce its art, and provide the vast array of goods and services that make a nation prosperous and content? On the other hand, what greater liability can a nation have than a mass of surplus people, living in hunger and poverty, scratching at tiny plots of land whose produce will not feed them all, swarming into cities where there are no more jobs, living in huts or dying in the street, sitting in apathy or smouldering with discontent, and ever begetting more children to share their misery? The relationship between numbers and wealth and power is not simple, but surely it is significant.[1]

Although the quotation seems to us to overstate the case, it does serve the purpose of effectively calling attention to many aspects of the population-policy continuum. We are not only concerned with numbers, but also with age distributions, sex distributions, education, training, skills, health stan-

---

[1] Katherine and A. F. K. Organski, *Population and World Power* (New York: Alfred A. Knopf, Inc., 1961), pp. 3–4.

dards, and productive capabilities (and tax-paying capabilities should by no means be omitted as an important datum, given the incredible\expense of many means of contemporary statecraft).

There was a time not too long ago when some students of international relations studied population trends almost exclusively as an index of national power. The population profile, meaning the proportion of men and women in various age brackets, is still important because it tells us what proportion of the population is available for military service and for the labor force (although different countries vary in their policies of utilizing women for such purposes). Forecasts and projections inform us what these proportions are likely to be twenty or thirty years hence.

Yet it has become increasingly apparent that population does not automatically determine a nation's power position: the huge and growing populations of India and China, for example, have been and may continue to be sources of weakness rather than strength to those states. Almost all students of international relations agree that population is but one of the many variables that account for a nation's power and prosperity. In this sense, therefore, the population element is no different from geography or from any of the other ingredients of national capability which are examined by the student of international relations, and we return to the proposition advanced earlier: the ingredients of a country's capability arsenal are always multiple.

Population is one of these ingredients. And if there is any one factor which distinguishes our age from previous eras, it lies in the unprecedented population growth throughout the world, falling with particular impact upon the economically less-developed areas that for the most part can least afford to support their rapidly growing numbers. If the size of a country's population exceeds the capacity of the existing productive resources to support it, or if it hinders the efficient exploitation of those resources, or limits the opportunities for growth in the country's productive capacities, then it is a source of weakness rather than of strength. There must be some balance or equilibrium between population and resources which permits a society to generate an economic surplus over and above the subsistence level before a state can start on the long road to economic development. Before we can properly assess the relationship of a state's population to that state's capacity to formulate and achieve foreign policy goals, we must know many things, including the proportion of the national wealth available for capital investment, education, and scientific research; the proportion of the population that is actually educated, in what fields and at what levels; and the capacity of a population to adapt to social change.

The serious and growing imbalance between population and resources is one of the most intractable problems in the field of international relations. There was a time when the swollen populations of India and China could be treated as strategically unimportant. The United States and the European powers with the climate and resources conducive to industrial development were also those which had most successfully mastered the processes of population control. Beginning in the eighteenth and continuing through the nineteenth century, the European and North American resource base expanded more rapidly than the population, thereby providing a surplus for investment, education, and science. As a result, the United States, Great Britain, and Germany emerged as leading industrial powers. By the end of the 1930s the Soviet Union was ready to join the select circle. The case of Japan's early development is instructive, because that development was achieved in the face of great population pressures. This indicates once more that population is not the only relevant factor to be taken into account in predicting development trends. More recently Japan has been in the forefront of countries taking active measures to control their population growth.

A few countries, then, succeeded in developing the social organization, capital, skills, science, and technology necessary to exploit their own resources and those of much of the rest of the world. As a result of their superior technology, much of the mineral wealth and raw materials of the rest of the world flows unceasingly toward these several centers. Meanwhile underdeveloped countries are experiencing great difficulties both in controlling their population growth and in reaching the take-off stage for self-sustaining economic development.[2]

However, unlike in the past, the plight of the less developed countries can be ignored no longer. As we know from scenes of mob violence in Latin America, the Middle East, Africa, and Asia, the urban masses have become conscious of both their deprivation and their power. Political independence had brought a rising demand for economic development and better standards of living. Some of the implications of population growth for political viability are traced in the article by Sondermann below. As populations continue to grow and as the inequalities of wealth, income, and education persist, we can expect dissatisfactions to lead to grave political unrest. Thus population pressures in underdeveloped countries become a threat to stability, and even if the West were prepared to deal with those problems with intelligence and moderation, we must expect a long period of revolutionary unrest and political instability.

In this connection many Western students of international relations have failed to take sufficient account of what one Soviet theorist has called "the role of the popular masses in international relations."[3] We are so accustomed to thinking of states and governments as the only legitimate international actors that the role of the street mobs in Cairo, Bagdad, Caracas, and Havana tends to take us by surprise. The Soviet Union fre-

2 W. W. Rostow, *The Stages of Economic Growth: A Non-Communist Manifesto* (Cambridge: Cambridge University Press, 1960).

3 Y. Arbatov, "The Role of the Popular Masses in International Relations," *International Affairs* (Moscow, September, 1955), 54–67.

quently manages to identify itself with the explosive aspirations of vast numbers in the less developed lands. The Soviets and the Chinese believe that dissatisfaction, unrest, and rebellion in Africa, Asia and Latin America will benefit the long-term aspirations of the Communist movement. They may be right.

The population problem, then, is not a figment of the imagination or of the Cassandra complex of scholars. It exists; it is grave; it is bound to become worse because even the most effective current program of control would not make itself felt for twenty to thirty years. Ideally, therefore, any program should have started at least two decades ago! The problem is an extraordinarily touchy one to deal with. The sanitary-medical revolution which, by prolonging life expectancy, has brought about the population increases cannot be undone. In fact it is likely to continue to extend lives and thereby increase populations. When penicillin, other antibiotics, DDT, and other medicines are available to cure, at a minimal cost, such age-old enemies of life as tuberculosis, malaria, and a host of other diseases, no one can responsibly advocate or realistically expect that these means will not be used. Efforts at population control must therefore be directed toward the other end of the life-cycle, the control of births or, more properly, of conception. This is surely the most private matter imaginable, and governments have been understandably reluctant to intrude into this sphere. Yet there are more and more governments which do recognize the seriousness of this problem and are taking steps to cope with it. But most of these programs are woefully inadequate.

States have traditionally equated a large population with national power; the thought patterns of centuries are hard to break. The Western powers are confronted with the particular problem that the less developed, newer societies are the ones most affected. These societies and their governments tend to suspect that Western interest in population limitation in their countries is engendered by the calculation of continued dominance, and these suspicions are carefully fanned by Communist parties. Under these circumstances it is very difficult for a country such as the United States, or her Western allies, to pursue policies *vis-à-vis* less developed countries other than to let them know that we would be willing to render assistance in handling the problem if requested to do so.

In the unlikely event that anyone should still imagine that the problem is far removed from us, let it be added that even for the industrially developed countries, all is no longer clear sailing. As early as 1952 the report of the President's Materials Policy Commission, *Resources for Freedom*,[4] pointed out that civilian and military consumption was so great that even a country as rich as the United States faced severe shortages of important resources.

---

[4] *Resources for Freedom,* Summary of Vol. I of a Report to the President's Materials Policy Commission (Washington, D.C.: U.S. Government Printing Office, 1952).

According to this report we had completed our transition from a raw materials *surplus* nation to a raw materials *deficit* nation, and our dependence upon overseas sources of supply was bound to increase. The countries of Western Europe were and are in an even more difficult position. The Soviet Union, a relative newcomer to industrial maturity, has only begun to exploit its potential resources and is unlikely to face major resource problems for some time. Therefore, though the United States enjoys a large industrial lead over the Soviet Union, it faces the need to establish economic and trade relations with resource-rich underdeveloped countries in order to guarantee a continued supply of basic materials.

Since World War II American companies have acquired large holdings in Latin America, Africa, the Middle East, and Southeast Asia, now threatened by the rising tides of nationalism, spurred on by the deprivations occasioned by the population increases. The United States government has pursued enormous stockpiling programs. These activities can prosper only if the underdeveloped peoples believe that they are getting a fair deal. Thus, far from being unrelated problems, the quest for economic development among the underdeveloped countries and the Western resource position upon which our security and prosperity depend are but two sides of the same coin.

1. Implications of Population Growth

FRED A. SONDERMANN

(This paper deals with the political and economic implications of rapid population growth.)

. . .

The populations of almost all countries are growing, and although the growth rate in some developed countries is higher than in some underdeveloped countries, this paper will concentrate on the political implications of population growth in the underdeveloped states of the world,[1] because growth rates by themselves do not clarify the nature of the problem. The most densely populated states are

From *"Political Implications of Population Growth in Underdeveloped Countries,"* THE COLORADO COLLEGE STUDIES, *1961, pp. 12–24. Reprinted by permission.*

[1] No attempt will be made to define the term "underdeveloped states" in detail. Broadly, the category includes all of Africa except the Union of South Africa, the bulk of Central and South America, mainland Asia except Siberia, and the islands of the Pacific except Japan, Australia, and New Zealand.

among the most highly developed and the most stable politically. The crucial element is the relation between resources (broadly defined) on the one hand and population on the other; and in the underdeveloped areas of the world this relationship is at its most critical stage. In part the problem can be described in the words of Professor Kingsley Davis, University of California demographer, who recently wrote.

Population growth will tend to be greatest where people are poorest. In this desperate situation, the less developed nations will hardly be squeamish about the means they adopt to further their national goals. Caught in the predicament of having an ever larger share of the world's people and an ever smaller share of the world's resources, they will be driven to adopt revolutionary policies.[2]

For purposes of analysis, the subject will be divided into the domestic and the international political implications of population growth. One must be aware, however, that these two facets cannot be neatly separated, because each impinges upon the other. Domestic pressures may lead to foreign adventurism of various kinds, and foreign influences may affect the domestic situation and the way in which it is perceived and handled.

II

Any political system must perform certain minimum functions to justify itself. Traditionally these functions have been defined in terms of providing external security and internal order. The Preamble to the American Constitution is a good traditional definition of a government's purpose. Recently the task of assuring the well-being of the members of society has been added to the functions of government and interpreted in broader terms than the vague reference to the general welfare which we find in our own Constitution. The Welfare State is not just an American phenomenon; in various forms and based upon various definitions it is found around the world. Peoples everywhere, and most especially those in the less developed countries, are anxious to achieve higher living standards, with all that such standards imply—and demand. This quest for higher standards is given particular urgency by the fact that many of these countries have recently attained political independence. A "revolution of rising expectations," to use Adlai Stevenson's phrase, has thus been superimposed upon a nationalistic revolution in vast areas of the world.

Until recently it has always been possible to blame the manifestly unsatisfactory living standards in these countries on the colonial powers, and to charge them (often unjustifiably) with deliberately maintaining a situation of need and deprivation in the colonies for the greater glory and profit of the home countries. Now, however, this argument has reached the point of diminishing returns, and the new, frequently inexperienced governments must deliver on their own.... [I]t is extraordinarily difficult for an underdeveloped society to reach a point at which there is a sufficient increase in savings and productivity to make a raised standard of living possible.[3] In fact, these new governments—many

[2] Kingsley Davis, "The Other Scare: Too Many People," *The New York Times Magazine*, March 15, 1969, p. 13.

[3] Industrialization might help reduce the problem, but it is itself complicated by the existence of the problem. Ashish Bose, "The Population Puzzle in India," *Economic Development and Cultural Change*, VII (April 1959), 230–48.

without a trained administrative corps, without capital, without experience— are expected to perform feats which even long-established systems would find difficult. . . .

The very fact of vast population increases accounts for many specific demands upon governments, demands extraordinarily difficult to satisfy. They include:

demands for development of industry and modernization of agriculture, with the trained manpower for both occupations;

demands for greatly expanded educational facilities;[4]

demands for increased opportunities for productive employment;

demands for adequate housing;

demands for social welfare policies in such fields as food, health, and sanitation;

demands for support of the very young and the very old sectors of the population, which increase disproportionately (because of advances in medical care) in an expanding population.

Since it is difficult for highly developed societies such as our own to meet some of these demands, we can imagine the magnitude of the problems confronting governments of underdeveloped states. But simple comparisons are misleading, because none of the underlying strengths in education, values, history and tradition, capital accumulation, and governmental experience which characterize American society and form the underpinning for our efforts to cope with domestic problems are found in the countries under discussion.

For this very reason, observers must consider what kinds of political organizations are likely to result from the pressures upon governments to perform their increased functions. The crux of the problem is that the demands can be met only after a long series of extremely hard steps that are necessary to bring about the rapid economic development of a society. The decisions which will have to be made are extraordinarily difficult, because they deal with such things as delayed satisfactions and enforced savings for capital accumulation and investment. The question is whether the peoples of the underdeveloped countries will make such decisions voluntarily, or whether the decisions will have to be made (and enforced) by an elite which understands the nature of the problem and is willing and able to take the actions which it requires.

We are, in effect, dealing with the question of whether a democratic society is capable of making the necessary decisions. All we can say is that we do not know the answer to it. In extreme situations of short duration people who understand the crisis are often capable of making tough, self-sacrificing decisions. But the crisis with which we deal here, while extreme, is long-range rather than immediate; each day—indeed, each hour—makes it a little greater, but the increments are neither dramatic nor easily perceived. In such a situation, will the inexperienced governments of the new countries be able to (and, equally important, will they want to) impress their uneducated publics with the seriousness of the national, rather than the individual, problem?[5] They probably will not; and

---

[4] For detailed discussion of just this one phase of development, see Harold L. Geisert, *World Population Pressures* (Washington, 1958), p. 39.

[5] A pessimistic view is presented by Professor Davis, in these terms: "A leader who rests his political career on the whims of ...swollen cadres of youth is usually incapable

if this proves to be the case, then the outlook for democratic government in the underdeveloped countries is dim.

The assumptions made so far are 1. that increased populations press increased demands on their governments; 2. that, paradoxically, governments are able to put themselves in a position eventually to meet such demands only by immediately demanding serious deprivations of their publics; and 3. that governments are unlikely to take this unpopular position, and publics are unlikely to accede voluntarily to the demands which such a position would entail.

If these assumptions are even approximately valid, then it would seem to follow logically that the governmental system most appropriate to such a situation is an authoritarian rather than a democratic one; one that is based upon the enforced decisions of relatively few rather than upon the policies agreed upon by the relatively many. The international implications of this conclusion will be considered in the following section. For the United States it means that our society might consider providing a somewhat clearer example of making voluntary sacrifices for the national welfare, and that we must learn to deal with regimes which differ from our own political and ideological preferences. Hamilton Fish Armstrong recently com-

mented on this problem in the following terms,

Democracy is a relative term everywhere, but as Mr. Dooley might have said, it is more relative in Asia. Let us not be too disturbed by this. In countries where perhaps nine-tenths of the people cannot read; where any experience they have had with self-government has usually been within the family, the village, or the tribe; where villages live in isolation, separated by jungles, deserts, mountains or seas; where the average income of a family is something like $100 a year and that mostly in kind, not money; where the population grows by over 2% per year; where most countries have no trained civil service; where the social services of the state, itself new and inefficient, are rudimentary or non-existent— in these conditions what we call democracy can develop only by slow stages. Even when the governing clique in the capital and the little knot of articulate intellectuals there are sincere in their admiration for representative government (and often they are) they must begin by creating rudimentary organs and build upwards cautiously, layer by layer.[6]

III

Two aspects of the international consequences of rapidly rising populations in underdeveloped countries will be discussed here: 1. what countries experiencing population pressures do to other countries, and 2. what other countries do to countries which experience rapid population growth.

In doing so, we may start with the observation that countries have tradi-

---

of making solid economic improvements. He is driven to embrace the safest and most inflammatory of all issues—nationalism. He can persecute and expropriate the foreigners, the Jews, or the Christians. He can threaten war on neighboring states. He can play the Communists against the free world to get emergency funds for staving off calamity or for buying weapons. He is the unstable political offspring produced by the monstrous marriage between rapid population growth and national destitution." "Analysis of the Population Explosion," *New York Times Magazine,* September 22, 1957, p. 78.

[6] "Thoughts Along the China Border— Will Neutrality Be Enough?" *Foreign Affairs,* XXXVI (January, 1960), 257–58.

tionally felt that a large population enhances a country's position among the other states of the world, because a larger population means a greater reservoir of productive manpower, larger markets which facilitate more efficient and economical production and distribution of goods, greater chances of producing inventors, scientists, and other men of great ability,[7] and a greater population base with which to fight a conventional war. For all these reasons, countries have almost invariably interpreted a population increase as a strengthening of their position vis-à-vis other powers.

In a situation in which population presses upon resources, and in which there is no short-range prospect of dramatically increasing the available resources, only two alternatives seem possible: migration or expansion. If the first of these does not take place the second is apt to. Professor Quincy Wright's statement points in this direction: "Differentials of population pressure in neighboring areas, if generally known to the inhabitants of the overpopulated area and if maintained by artificial barriers to trade and migration, tend to international violence. . . ."[8]

---

[7] Except that some of the world's outstanding statesmen have come from smaller countries, which might lead one to assume that supply follows demand in the vital commodity of statesmanship. The smaller and weaker countries need capable statesmen more than those countries which have had margins of safety for their leaders' mistakes.

[8] Quincy Wright, *The Study of International Relations* (New York, 1955), p. 364. Professor Davis expresses the same view: ". . .excessive population growth seems to intensify the struggle for scarce raw materials, to build up explosive migration pressures, and to encourage *lebensraum* wars, and. . . communism is making its greatest conquests precisely in the impoverished and crowded countries." "The Other Scare: Too Many People," *New York Times Magazine*, March 15, 1959, p. 114.

If this violence is to be avoided, what chance is there for migration to relieve the population pressures which will increasingly characterize the underdeveloped countries? There are four major obstacles to migration as a solution to the overpopulation problem:

1. As long as most countries consider population as a power factor, they will be reluctant to permit the emigration of large numbers of their younger and more productive citizens (who presumably would be the ones most interested in migrating).

2. Potential receiving countries, for reasons of their own (such as cultural homogeneity, fear of being overwhelmed by alien populations, fear of competition for jobs, fear of infiltration by alien doctrines, perverted racial ideas, etc.) usually do not want large numbers of immigrants, particularly from the countries suffering most from overpopulation. There are, after all, only a limited number of developed, underpopulated areas which—given present technology—lend themselves to additional settlement. These include North and parts of South America, Siberia, Australia, and possibly some parts of Africa and the Near East, although here care would be necessary to avoid merely transferring the problem of underdevelopment from one area to another by resettling vast numbers of people. In this context, the United States has little justification for pointing a finger of scorn at the immigration policies of other countries. . . .

3. Large population movements over a short time always involve great human suffering and tragedy. And in order to come close to solving the present problem, the movements would have to be enormous. According to one estimate, merely to keep the proportions of underdeveloped to developed countries at the 1950 level would require migration of over 700 million people

by the year 2000 A.D.[9] There has never been a population movement of this magnitude in the history of mankind, and human migration on such a scale seems inconceivable.

4. Finally, international migrations create alien minorities within states, thus further complicating an international situation which is sufficiently tense even without this additional ingredient of conflict.

Thus, migration scarcely seems to provide an answer to the problem. Yet it is safe to predict that migratory pressures are bound to increase. The demand in underdeveloped countries for admission to industrial, highly developed areas will become very great indeed, and the more developed societies must either adjust to that demand or propose acceptable alternatives. Since migration does not seem to be an answer,[10] it seems reasonable to expect various kinds of international disequilibrium, as indicated in the other alternative, namely, expansion brought about by aggression set off by population pressure. In this context, one automatically thinks of Japan in the 1930s, but might it not be equally realistic to think of China in the 1970s? And is it any great comfort to reflect that perhaps the Russians are thinking of this possibility too, which might explain their haste to settle Siberia?

[9] By comparison, between 1846 and 1932, 60 million people left Europe—little more than one years addition to world population. Political and Economic Planning, *World Population and Resources* (London, 1955), p. xxxiii. For a straightfaced but nonetheless morbidly hilarious discussion of sending surplus populations into outer space, see Garrett Hardin, "Interstellar Migration and the Population Problem," *Journal of Heredity,* I. (March–April, 1959), 68–70.

[10] A very comprehensive—and discouraging—analysis of migration as a possible solution to the population problem is presented in J. O. Hertzler, *The Crisis in World Population* (Lincoln, Nebr.: 1956) Chapter 8.

The disastrous consequences of continued population pressures in the underdeveloped countries stagger the imagination. It can be argued that these consequences can be avoided, given more rapid economic development of these countries, which would provide more adequately for the now-existing populations and could be expected, in time, to bring about a levelling-off in birth rates. But the immediate consequence of economic development has thus far always been a greatly increased rate of population growth. Thus the crucial factor in the equation is the time element. Is there time enough, and can it be used effectively enough, to bring population increases and industrialization into some kind of balance which would assure political stability? The answer to this question lies, in part, in how well the more highly developed countries understand the nature of the population problem of the less developed countries and what they are willing (not able!) to do to help solve it.[11]

This introduces the second aspect of this discussion: what other countries do to those states suffering from overpopulation. Here one must be particularly concerned about the impact and appeal of Communism. Specifically, what is the nature of the Communist appeal to these areas?

In the first place, the Communists argue that such problems as overpopulation and underdevelopment are the fault of the former colonial powers and their present Western allies, that they are reflections of the inability of the capitalist economic system to satisfy basic human needs. Secondly, the Communists describe birth control as a capitalist device to keep Asian and African

[11] The assumption here is obviously that much more could be done to stimulate the development of underdeveloped countries; that in large part the problem is one of policy, not of capacity.

countries weak—a strong argument, since small populations are traditionally associated with national weakness, and an attractive argument since birth control is artificial and sexual relations without it easier and more natural. They argue pointedly that developed countries such as the United States are unwilling to practice comprehensive birth control schemes on their own. Hence, advocacy of such a scheme for underdeveloped countries can rather easily be pictured as a typical capitalistic trick.[12]

Such arguments are bound to evoke a strong response. Substantively more important, however, are Communist arguments based on descriptions of the rapid improvement in living standards in the socialist societies as compared to the slower progress in capitalist economies. The comparison between India and China is frequently cited, with one country attempting to raise its standards through relatively free political institutions, while the other uses totalitarian methods. The contest is still in the balance, although the signs point to a substantially greater improvement in the Chinese condition than in that of India. (There is no way, however, to check on Chinese statistics). If present Soviet and Chinese plans come even close to succeeding, they are bound to provide formidable arguments to the peoples of underdeveloped areas to adopt at least some of the economics, if not the politics, of Communist States.[13]

.   .   .

[12] Morton Clurman, "Will Births Outstrip Mankind's Resources?" *Commentary*, 13 (March 1952), p. 287. . . .

[13] Karl Sax, Harvard botanist, calls attention to the old Chinese proverb, "It is difficult to tell the difference between right and wrong when the stomach is empty," and to the literal translation of the Chinese word for "peace"—"food for all." *Op. cit.*, p. xi.

2. Trends in World Inequality

BRUCE M. RUSSETT

Bruce M. Russett is Associate Professor of Political Science at Yale University and Director of the Yale Political Data Program. He is the author of the WORLD HANDBOOK OF POLITICAL AND SOCIAL INDICATORS, TRENDS IN WORLD POLITICS, INTERNATIONAL REGIONS AND THE INTERNATIONAL SYSTEM, *as well as numerous other studies and articles.*

REVOLUTIONS AND INEQUALITY

Most people believe that revolutions arise as a reaction to great inequalities of wealth or income. Perhaps so, but all situations of great inequality are by no means equally likely to end in revolution. Many instances of the grossest repression continue for decades or even centuries without serious revolt; other cases of much milder inequity may result in violent upheaval and bloody revenge upon the former dominant group. The peculiar mixture of circumstances that produce revolution is still only imperfectly understood; undoubtedly it varies under different historical conditions and different incentives to revolt. Nevertheless certain common elements do seem always to be present:

1. Inequality in the distribution of something that is widely valued, like money, farm land, political power, or even respect.

2. The possibility of comparison.

From TRENDS IN WORLD POLITICS, *(New York: The Macmillan Company, 1965), pp. 106–23. Reprinted with permission.*

Those who are poor must have some means of knowing that others live very much better; they must see that others are better off and have some basis, however distorted, of recognizing their own poverty.

3. Some means of communicating with others who feel themselves deprived, so as to make joint action possible.

4. Some possibility of success, at least in the minds of the potential revolutionaries. No matter how downtrodden, men will seldom revolt in large numbers unless they see a reasonably good chance to succeed. Now the meaning of "reasonably good" may vary with the circumstances, and desperate, badly oppressed men will certainly take greater chances than men who are fairly well off. Also, potential revolutionaries seldom can evaluate their chances with perfect accuracy. They are human, fallible, and may take chances that objectively would not be justified.

As citizens of the richest country on earth, where even ordinary people have a standard of living which surpasses that of all but a fraction of the world's population, Americans cannot ignore the problem of inequality and its implications for world politics. People in underdeveloped countries are becoming increasingly aware of their poverty; they know that by comparison with the nations of Europe and North America they are poor, and they think that somehow they can find the means to raise their living standards. The questions of crucial importance to world peace are: to what extent will the improvement in these countries' economic conditions keep pace with increasing demands, "the revolution of rising expectations," and, in cases of shortfall, what kinds of solutions are the world's poor likely to seek?

Because much of the world is poor while parts of it are rich does not mean that the rich necessarily planned it that way in any kind of greedy or diabolical plot. Few of us, who are the world's privileged, can honestly say that we have any major control over the system, that we deliberately oppress anyone, or that if we individually tried to change the world's distribution of income in the direction of greater equality we could actually succeed. As far as we are concerned there simply *are* rich and poor; "the poor are with you always." We (or our fathers) have worked hard for what we have, and we did not steal it (usually); poor people, in our own country as elsewhere, are poor because they lack the skills, the education, the capital, or the opportunities to better themselves. Sometimes we say too that poor people in our country are poor because they lack the intelligence or the ambition to improve their status. To whatever degree that is true in America, however, there is no reason to believe that Americans are as a nation more intelligent than Chinese, or even more ambitious—providing that you present the average Chinese with an opportunity where ambition will do him some good.

Marxists have tried to explain world inequalities in terms of their theory of how capitalism operates. According to the Communists, capitalists in industrial countries are faced with an ever declining rate of profit. Many firms fail, and the remainder become larger and more monopolistic. Capitalists become fewer, the proletariat becomes larger, and the downfall of the capitalist system is ever more imminent. The capitalists, says Lenin, try to postpone their doom by exporting capital. They find both markets and labor in the backward countries of the world, and persuade their own governments to take over political control of them as colonies. The people in these countries are brought under the capitalist system and impoverished; the capitalists of the advanced countries gain a respite, and for a time, the workers in the imperialist states may find their condition improving. Capitalists—or, more precisely the capitalist system, for individual capitalists are merely driven by economic forces and are not personally evil—are thus to blame for the impoverishment of the underdeveloped states, and only by the overthrow of capitalism will they escape poverty.

Now this argument is sometimes persuasive to inhabitants of poor countries, but it ignores some important if inconvenient facts. The acquisition of colonies by America and Britain in the late nineteenth century was not primarily the result of capitalists' demands for markets; on the contrary, many industrialists opposed imperialism for fear that it might result in war that would be bad for business. Since the end of World War II almost all of the former colonies have achieved political independence, but few of them are developing more rapidly as independent states than they did as colonial territories. In fact, many, like the Congo

(Leopoldville), Burma, Indonesia, and Algeria, have stagnated under independence. Marxists might maintain that though politically sovereign in theory they are still in economic bondage to the foreign capitalists who control their import and export trade. But actually there is little evidence that a colonial past makes much difference in the rate or level of development in African and Asian countries. Thailand, though long independent, is not notably more wealthy than her neighbors. Afghanistan and Ethiopia were never colonies (except for about five years for Ethiopia), nor were they ever seriously penetrated by Western capitalism. They also are notably neither poorer nor richer than neighboring states that were colonies. It is true that in many instances the colonial powers failed to develop their colonies other than to the degree that was necessary to build raw material exporting industries and to tighten political control. But neglect of development is not the same as active impoverishment, for which there is little evidence.

Western states therefore cannot fairly be blamed, as villains, for the low living standards of most of the world. The wealth of the West is absolutely unique in world history. Medieval Europe was probably not much better off than modern Southeast Asia or the Middle East. In the Renaissance and, much more substantially in the Industrial Revolution, Western Europe embarked on a period of rapid development without precedent, a process whose causes we still do not thoroughly understand. But the result of Europe's development has been to create an enormous gap between the Western industrial nations and Asia, Africa, and Latin America. Unless this gap begins fairly rapidly to narrow, part of the necessary foundation for a revolutionary situation will have been laid.

THE DISTRIBUTION OF WORLD WELFARE

In fact, the gap has been narrowing very slightly, despite popular opinion to the contrary. It has been a common expression that "the rich get richer and the poor get poorer" (or, in one variant, "the poor get children"). This certainly was true during the nineteenth and early twentieth centuries, when rapid economic development continued at a much faster pace in the West than in Africa and Asia—in many parts of the East per capita income hardly grew at all.[1] But by the middle of this century the situation had begun to change. Table 7.1 presents estimates of G.N.P. per capita for 30 important countries in 1950; it also presents projections for G.N.P. per capita in 1975.

How do we go about making projections? One method would involve true *prediction*; making estimates based upon a detailed knowledge of the situation in each country and of the conditions that will affect economic growth in coming years. Now obviously this kind of demand is totally unreasonable. The prospects for economic growth depend upon the unemployment situation, on political policies, on international developments, and on a host of other factors that cannot be predicted with any degree of accuracy. We cannot reasonably say even who will win the next Presidential election, let alone what his policies will be and what effects they will have. (Considering the importance economic growth has played as an issue in recent campaigns we surely do think political acts really affect it.)

[1] See Simon Kuznets, "Regional Economic Trends and Levels of Living," in Phillip Hauser (ed.), *Population and World Politics* (New York: The Free Press, 1958), pp. 79–118.

TABLE 1 G.N.P. PER CAPITA*

1950		1975	
United States	$2300	United States	$3550
Canada	1750	West Germany	2900
Britain	1200	Canada	2600
Belgium	1000	Czechoslovakia	1950
France	750	Belgium	1875
Netherlands	675	Britain	1800
West Germany	600	France	1750
Argentina	500	U.S.S.R.	1625
Venezuela	480	Netherlands	1475
Czechoslovakia	450	Venezuela	1400
U.S.S.R.	400	Italy	1330
Italy	350	Poland	1300
Chile	340	Japan	1140
Poland	320	Yugoslavia	925
Spain	290	Spain	700
Brazil	235	Brazil	500
Mexico	225	Chile	480
Colombia	220	Argentina	455
Turkey	200	Mexico	395
Japan	190	Colombia	390
Philippines	185	Philippines	335
Yugoslavia	165	Turkey	305
Egypt	135	Egypt	285
Indonesia	120	China	190
Thailand	85	Indonesia	170
Nigeria	70	Thailand	130
Pakistan	70	Burma	115
India	70	Nigeria	95
China	50	India	85
Burma	45	Pakistan	75

* In this table and those following the source of the data and the rates of change is Bruce M. Russett *et al., World Handbook of Political and Social Indicators* (New Haven, Conn.: Yale University Press, 1964). In a few cases change rates are estimated. All G.N.P. figures are in 1957 dollars.

Another method, which does not involve one in making impossible judgments about the consequences of a million and one factors, is to compute the rates of change in something like G.N.P. over a given past time and project these same rates into the future. Assume, in other words, that the situation in the future will change at the same rate as in the past. Such a procedure is only one of *projection,* not *prediction.* It says what would happen *if* the rates remained unchanged, but does not predict that they *will* be unchanged. It is therefore a method of "persistence forecasting." By its very nature this method of course cannot identify any change in trends, and it is therefore less useful the longer the projection one attempts. Here, however, we shall attempt projections only for a moderate time span, to 1975. We shall project from around 1960, using the rates that applied in the decade 1950 to 1960. In the tables you will find only the figures for 1950 and 1975, but they are based on actual developments up to about 1960. By this procedure we see what the world would look like in 1975 *if* past trends continued. Because some past trends cannot or will not continue, some of our projections will look peculiar, but they can nevertheless assist us in identifying problem areas and trends of particular consequence.

We find some rather startling changes between the situation of 1950 and that projected for 1975. The United States will, if these projections are correct, remain the richest country in the world, but it will be followed fairly closely by West Germany. If they are even approximately accurate, by 1975 the Soviet Union and Eastern Europe will have a per capita product not far short of the projected average for much of Western Europe, and very far above the 1950 Western European average. Communist China will also have made very significant gains, and Japan's per capita G.N.P. will be well above that of Europe in 1950. Most of Latin America (except for stagnating Argentina) will show real but modest gains (Venezuela, however, shows the effects of a rather high growth rate). But major segments of the non-Communist underdeveloped world—India, Pakistan, and Indonesia, for example—are likely to grow only very slowly in per capita G.N.P.

Actually, of course, there is no reason to believe that these projections will be borne out just as they appear here. It seems reasonable, for example, to expect the growth rate for several European countries to be slower in the 1960's than it was in the previous decade, as postwar recovery is com-

pleted and the early stimulation of the Common Market wears off. Probably also the Communist countries will not do quite so well as would appear. Much of the success of Soviet-type economics in achieving rapid industrialization is due to their ability, through totalitarian political controls, to maintain a higher level of investment and a lower level of consumption than their people would freely choose if given the opportunity. But to some degree they are assisted by the ability to adopt or adapt technological advances that are developed in other more advanced countries.[2] The more economically developed the Communist countries themselves become, the harder it is to continue development without a massive and expensive scientific base. Though the Russians have built just such a base their efforts seem unlikely to compensate them entirely for their losses in ability to borrow technology. Declines in East and West European growth rates were actually in evidence in the early 1960's, and they are not fully reflected in our projections, nor is the very serious floundering of Communist China's "great leap forward" in the late 1950's and early 1960's. . . .

TRENDS IN INEQUALITY

So far we have been able to look at projected changes in the rankings of various countries, and to see changes in the absolute levels of possession of goods like radios. . .but have lacked a good way of talking about our central interest —inequalities. What we need is a mea-

[2] Much of the Soviet Union's technology is fully as advanced as that in the West, but important segments, especially agriculture and consumer goods production, could still benefit enormously from the use of European or American methods.

sure, a summary index, to say whether one pattern of distribution is more or less unequal than another. One possibility would be simply to say what proportion of the world's G.N.P. was held by, for instance, the richest 10 per cent of the world's population in 1950 and compare it with the projected distribution for 1975. That would be helpful, but it would tell us only about that single point in the distribution, the richest 10 per cent.

Another and more widely useful possibility is to make use of the *Lorenz curve* and the *Gini index*. A Lorenz curve is drawn by plotting on graph paper the points in a cumulative distribution of percentages. The poorest countries in 1950 were Burma and China. Together they held 28 per cent of the population of the world (we will here speak of our list of 30 countries as the "world," although actually they have only a little more than 80 per cent of the world's population) but less than 4 per cent of its G.N.P. We can continue this way up to all countries *except* the United States, which together account for over 92 per cent of the world's population but less than 54 per cent of its G.N.P. The cumulated percentage of population is given along the horizontal axis and the cumulated percentage of the value along the vertical axis. The 45-degree line represents the condition of perfect theoretical equality, where each percentile of the population would have an equal share in the cumulated total of the value. Thus under perfect equality each 10 per cent of the population would have exactly 10 per cent of the G.N.P., and so on. How far, in fact, the curve for a particular distribution departs from the "line of equality" gives us a visual measure of the inequality involved.

Now the Lorenz curve provides an extremely useful way of showing the complete pattern of a distribution, but it is difficult to compare whole curves for any substantial number of distributions, and it is especially difficult to interpret curves that cross each other, as the ones for G.N.P. and radios do in Figure 1. We can, however, measure the *area* between the cumulated distribution and line of equality. This gives us the Gini index, a simple measure of the total inequality of a distribution. The Gini index calculates over the whole population the difference between an "ideal" cumulative distribution (where all shares are equal) and the actual distribution. The Gini index may vary from 0 to 1.0; the higher the index the greater the inequality.[3] It should be clear, of course, that use of the line of equality in our calculation does not imply that we consider perfect equality to be a desirable goal. That is quite a different question; we merely use it because we must have some base line against which to measure real-world distributions. At the bottom of each of the graphs you will find the Gini indices for the distributions in each year. Notice how literacy is distributed quite equally around the world, but G.N.P. and radios much less so.[4]

We find a small over-all decrease in the inequality of the world's distribution of G.N.P., but only from a Gini index of .66 to .62—hardly enough to be very meaningful given the margin of error involved in any projection of this sort. The improvement, remember, is

[3] The Gini number for a Lorenz curve is actually twice the area mentioned divided by the area (10,000 for 100 by 100 axes) of the whole square. The formula is

$$G = \frac{2\int_0^{100} (x - f(x))\, dx}{10,000}$$

where x is the cumulated population percentage and $f(x)$ is the height of the Lorenz curve.

[4] The curves for radios and especially hospital beds are not strictly comparable with the others, because data was missing for several poor countries and the degree of inequality is understated.

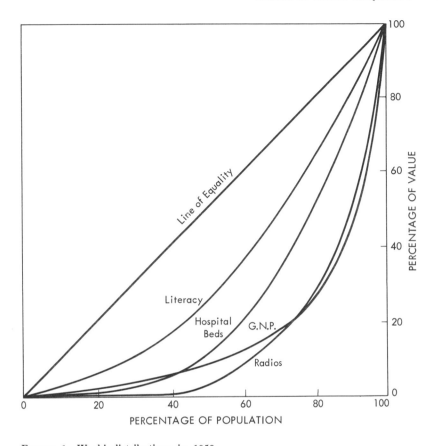

FIGURE 1   World distributions in 1950.

	Gini Indices		
G.N.P.	.66	Literacy	.30
Hospital beds	.49	Radios	.68

concentrated in two areas—Western Europe and the Communist bloc. France and Germany appear to make important strides toward the American level, and Eastern Europe reaches levels typical of rather mature industrial powers. But Communist China, and perhaps Egypt and Burma, are the only poor countries to show substantially raised living standards in these projections. In other words, though the middle countries tend to catch up with the richer ones, and though Communist China is, according to this projection, more than keeping pace, the gulf between the poor coun-

tries and those of Europe is widening, and seriously so. Such large under-developed countries as India, Indonesia, Nigeria, and Pakistan show only very moderate improvement, at a rate far below that of European nations and less even than the United States. With health conditions, however, the situation is rather different. The Gini index for the distribution of hospital beds remains at .49, and some of the underdeveloped states, such as Nigeria and India, appear to make the most progress. This implies that many citizens of poor countries will live longer, and perhaps

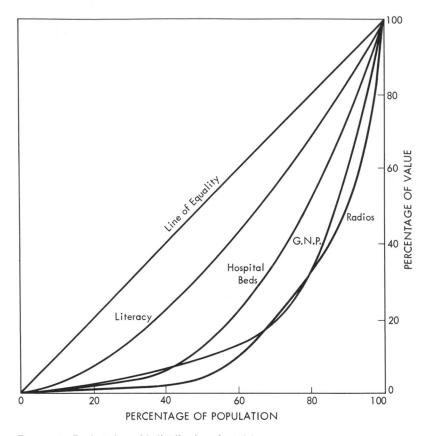

FIGURE 2   Projected world distributions in 1975.

	Gini Indices		
G.N.P.	.62	Literacy	.24
Hospital beds	.49	Radios	.68

be healthier, but still remain very poor. But we do not have information on several important countries, particularly Pakistan and China.

All our data on access to mass communications certainly show a world that is much more closely linked together than in the past. The Gini index for radios remains the same (.68), but every country shows major increases on the absolute index of radios per thousand inhabitants. If we assume a potential audience of perhaps four persons per radio (probably not an overestimate, at least in an underdeveloped area) even such relatively backward countries as Egypt will have over half their population regularly exposed to this modern medium. And for literacy we found not only a sharp improvement in conditions in most underdeveloped areas but even a notable decline in the already low Gini index, from .30 to .24. High levels of literacy (50 per cent or more) will very shortly come to characterize all but the poorest countries, and even they will have sizable educated elites.

In other words, some of the conditions for a revolutionary potential will be stronger than they were. Communications will be such as to make it very easy, for many poor people in backward areas, to become aware of just how impoverished they are. They will also have the means of communicating with others, both in their own countries and elsewhere, who feel themselves deprived. In this sense joint action will become possible. Furthermore, serious inequalities will persist. There will not have been enough time to modify them significantly, and in any case the trends are not in the direction of important modification in the case of the underdeveloped non-Communist states. (One important goal—better health conditions—will be much nearer achievement, however.) We cannot know whether these developments—wider communications, continued inequalities of income —will go far enough to make the danger of world conflict between haves and have-nots become really serious, but at least the risk will be higher than it was in the not-so-distant past.

POWER AND REVOLUTION

The other factor that we listed as a common element in revolutionary situations was some possibility of success. Would a group of underdeveloped countries, acting together, conceivably have the power to create a situation that would be potentially dangerous for the peace and stability of the world? Here we can look again at our basic index of national power—total G.N.P. Table 2 shows the percentage distribution of world G.N.P. in 1950 and in 1975.

Some of the changes here are quite startling. China very clearly rises to fourth place behind only the United States, the U.S.S.R., and West Germany. Japan and Italy also rise substantially; Britain drops from third to a poor sixth, and India falls from eighth to eleventh place. And although the United States remains first, the gap between it and the Soviet Union changes from a relationship of almost five to one to one of less than two to one. As a group, the countries of the European Common Market fall not far short of the Soviet Union. To repeat: the rankings are more reliable than the actual percentages, which exaggerate the difference between developed and underdeveloped countries. Also, there is no reason to believe that these projections will really be borne out quite as they appear here. Those for Western Europe and the Communist nations may be too high; it is possible the one for the United States will prove slightly low. But based as they are on actual trends through 1960 they cannot be wildly out of line.

On the whole we find that the relative power position of the Communist countries, especially if they can act together, will be greatly improved. Even if China must operate alone without active Soviet support for expansionist moves, she will be very much stronger than any other Asian power or combination of Asian states. India, which many Westerners have seen as a potential counterweight to the Communist Chinese, will be dangerously inferior in basic productive resources. A slower-than-anticipated rate of economic growth for China would modify this conclusion, but not enough to provide much comfort. As early as 1962 the Chinese took great pains to demonstrate their superiority by deliberately attacking India and inflicting a serious if limited defeat on Indian troops along the border.

The threat of a major violent

TABLE 2 PERCENTAGE DISTRIBUTION OF TOTAL WORLD G.N.P.

1950		1975	
United States	46.4	United States	33.0
U.S.S.R.	9.5	U.S.S.R.	18.2
Britain	8.1	West Germany	7.1
France	4.2	China	7.0
West Germany	3.8	Japan	4.9
China	3.6	Britain	4.2
Canada	3.3	France	3.7
India	3.3	Italy	2.8
Italy	2.1	Canada	2.6
Japan	2.1	Brazil	2.4
Brazil	1.6	India	2.1
Belgium	1.2	Poland	1.9
Indonesia	1.2	Czechoslovakia	1.2
Argentina	1.1	Spain	1.0
Poland	1.1	Indonesia	.9
Spain	1.1	Mexico	.9
Mexico	.9	Netherlands	.8
Netherlands	.9	Yugoslavia	.8
Czechoslovakia	.7	Belgium	.7
Pakistan	.7	Venezuela	.7
Philippines	.5	Philippines	.6
Turkey	.5	Argentina	.5
Egypt	.4	Turkey	.5
Yugoslavia	.4	Egypt	.4
Chile	.3	Pakistan	.4
Colombia	.3	Colombia	.3
Nigeria	.3	Chile	.2
Thailand	.3	Nigeria	.2
Venezuela	.3	Thailand	.2
Burma	.1	Burma	.1

conflict along rich-poor lines seems much exaggerated, at least for the next few years. The non-Communist under-developed nations simply will not have the power to challenge the wealthier states, even if they should have the ambition. Only an extraordinarily rash leader could try, even in combination with a large bloc of such countries. (This is even more true if we remember that the non-Communist poor nations lack nuclear weapons, which adds immensely to the power disparity.) This does not mean that discontent may not seethe, for it is very likely to do so given the trends in income and communications access that we have noted. This discontent may lead to major efforts, especially within the United Nations, to make the developed states contribute greater sums in foreign aid. It may lead to public bitterness, to propaganda attacks on the rich powers, and possibly to a kind of racism.... the most dangerous political cleavages are those where class or status divisions coincide with splits based on some other factor like race.

These trends may also lead to the kind of domestic instability in underdeveloped countries on which Communists thrive. Dissatisfaction with the progress achieved by non-Communist governments may very well inspire Communist revolutions or the takeover of power from democratic leaders by the military. Ofter this may be justified in terms of anti-Communism, as has sometimes been the pattern in Latin America. . . .

SCIENTIFIC AND TECHNOLOGICAL DIFFERENTIALS

Chapter 7

There is a close linkage between scientific and technological capability and all the other aspects of a country's capability inventory. In the selection reprinted in this chapter, William T.R. Fox spells out many aspects of that linkage. In an introductory way we wish to call attention to the relationship between science and technology and the other items in the capability inventory which are dealt with in this section of the book.

The relationship between scientific-technological capability and geography lies in the fact that the former can make profound changes in the constellation and significance of the latter. The building of canals, the improvement of communications systems, and the conquest of climate are but examples of the many ways in which geography can be altered through the application of modern science and technology. As for resources, scientific discoveries and technological applications affect not only their availability (for example, through devising economical means of extraction and use), but profoundly affect the needs for certain types of resources. Thus, for example, uranium was always present in the earth's crust, but it did not become an important raw material until less than thirty years ago when it was required in the production of atomic materials.

We have already referred to the impact of scientific developments on population, primarily through medical discoveries. The development of new ways to combat disease has led to a vast increase in the world's population.

Similarly scientific findings may provide avenues for solving the problem of conception control, although it must be added that social, religious, and cultural patterns and values are bound to complicate the task and may perhaps even negate the possibilities that science has made or will make available.

With reference to the reciprocal relationship between scientific findings and the economic and military capacities of states, suffice it to state, categorically, that the development of the modern economic-industrial machine has been dependent on its scientific and technological underpinnings, and that military capabilities are increasingly affected by developments in science and their applications in military technology. Conversely, of course, the needs of industry and the military have spurred scientists to new efforts and have channeled those efforts into appropriate directions.

These, very briefly, are some of the reasons why such great significance has come to be attached to a state's scientific and technological capabilities. The implications are important not only for the highly developed countries, but perhaps even more so for the less developed areas of the world which in many cases build their expectations on the assumption that it may be possible for them, by applying the findings of modern science and technology, to make a quantum jump from backwardness to a high level of development.

Science and technology have affected not only the capabilities of states and the availability of certain means of pursuing and attaining goals, but they have also affected other aspects of international relations, including the very structure of the international system and the definition of purposes and objectives of states. Scientific and technological capability also has become an important element in the prestige position of countries within the international system. Prestige is an intermediate goal of policy because it can be used as a means for the achievement of other goals. Hence no government can afford to take questions of prestige lightly. In recent decades prestige increasingly has become associated with scientific discoveries and their applications. The Soviet launching of the first Sputnik in 1957 is an excellent example of how a country's international prestige position suddenly improved as a consequence of a scientific-technological achievement of the first magnitude. The race to the moon (whatever else may be said for or against it) must in part be judged not only on the basis of scientific curiosity or of military advantage but also on the basis of the prestige which will accrue to the country that wins the contest.

At the same time we must caution against the tendency to make science and technology the single determining factor in capability analysis. For one thing it is not really an independent variable but is closely attached to other elements. Standards of health, education, social structure, systems of rewards or risks all affect the status of scientific research and the technological applications of the findings of that research. Many major changes in the character of international relations have been the result of non-technical factors. Some recent analysts of the role of science and technology in international relations have come too close to establishing a theory of scientific determinism which would be as inappropriate as theories of economic (or any other) determinism have been in the past.

There nevertheless remains a large element of significance that attaches to the scientific and technological capabilities of states. It is not only a matter of the fund of human talent a given state possesses but the proportion of this fund that can be induced to pursue a career in science and technology, the capacity to train these people, the most efficient ways of allocating them to various phases of the process (such as basic research, applied research, education, and administration); and finally, the capacity of a society to support research at given levels. One of the interesting problems that arises here relates to the impact of governmental activities on the scientific-technological function. In a number of ways governments can encourage or discourage bright persons to enter the field of scientific discovery and technological application; they can make such careers attractive or unattractive. Governments have increasingly addressed themselves to such problems, not always with total success.

A continuing question relates to the diversion of talent into channels which are of greatest immediate usefulness, as against the allocation of resources to pure research, where results are uncertain and may be long-range in character. To what extent does the availability of funds determine the nature and direction of research? To what extent does it add to the strength of a country to divert scientists from academic careers or careers in private industry to pursue careers in and for the government. Are there costs involved which may be invisible but are not therefore unimportant?

Another very serious problem relates to the diminishing role that the layman, including the political leader, can play in making important decisions. Many aspects of a country's economy and many more aspects of a country's military status have become so complex and technical that such traditions as civilian supremacy in policy making appear to be undergoing great change.

Military policies are formulated in an environment that is increasingly affected by developments in military technology and by the civilian and military elites associated with that technology. Rapid advances in science and technology cause strains on the policy process in two major respects: 1. with regard to American foreign and military policies the problem of development of military instruments that are relevant to our national policy objectives is exacerbated by rampant extensions in the range, complexity, and destructive power of modern weapons systems; 2. with respect to our domestic political system the secrecy and technical complexities inherent in the new weapons technology impose limitations on the responsiveness of military policy to traditional democratic control arrangements.[1]

[1] David W. Tarr, "Military Technology and the Policy Process," *Western Political Quarterly* (1965), XVIII, No. 1, 135ff.

In his final presidential address General Eisenhower warned against the growing strength of the "military-industrial" complex. The dilemma is that a scientific and technological society cannot help but develop appropriate elites for its operation. The concept of the garrison state is part of the intellectual arsenal of the student of modern government. The question now arises whether there is not an equal, or perhaps even greater, probability of the coming of the laboratory state, in which important decisions are really made long before they reach the point of official concern and before they reach public consciousness.

The chance that this may happen—that, in fact, it may already be happening—firmly draws attention to the need for contemporary societies to stress scientific and technological virtuosity, but also to do more—to devote equal attention to the understanding of social processes within and between societies, and to the understanding and appreciation of the qualitative aspects of life that draw their sustenance from the humanitarian disciplines.

Another aspect of the problem, too, commands attention because of its relevance to an understanding of certain contemporary international concerns. Governments are, as we have noted, concerned about the state of scientific research and technological applications of such research in their societies. They therefore maintain a close watch on the movement of scientists, technicians, and other categories of persons who are deemed important to the operation of the national economy and defense. For some years now the problem of the brain drain has been on the agenda of a number of nations, whose governmental and other elites are concerned about an outward movement (usually in the direction of the United States) of trained scientists, technicians, managers, and other skilled personnel. This phenomenon has been in evidence in the less developed countries which can least afford to lose any portion of their small reservoir of such manpower; it has likewise assumed increasing importance in the case of Western Europe, which has traditionally been in the forefront of scientific and technological progress.

1. Science, Technology, and International Politics

WILLIAM T. R. FOX

William T. R. Fox is Professor of International Relations and Director of the War and Peace Institute at Columbia University. Dr. Fox is the author of THE SUPER POWERS *and more recently co-author with his wife, Annette Baker Fox, of* NATO AND THE RANGE OF AMERICAN CHOICE, *as well as many other studies and articles.*

As the superpowers of the 1960's have been discovering that they can neither make war on nor make peace with each other, the arms race between them has been giving way to a space race, itself part of a larger science and technology race. The space industry is today one of the world's greatest, even though there are only two major customers for its product, the governments of the Soviet Union and of the United States. Leadership in that industry is a hallmark of superpower status, but the entrance fee and the annual dues are both so high that the space club will remain small.

The Soviet-American science race is only the most dramatic reason for a student of world politics to pay close attention to changes, and especially to

differential changes, in the world's science and technology. There is probably no other resource that can be made to serve so many alternative national purposes as a nation's scientific and technical manpower. There is no better indicator of tomorrow's wealth and power than today's science capability. Indeed, this resource is so fungible and so precious that if one wanted to plot the position of states of the world in the 1980's along a curve of economic advancement (and of per capita influence in world politics), a very good measure would be the proportion of each country's whole population enrolled as university-level scientific and technical students in the 1960's.

"Science and world affairs" is by no means an unworked area. Christopher Wright's survey made in 1962 listed some 350 items.[1] What he modestly called "a tentative guide" was followed in 1964 by a less selective State Department Foreign Service Institute bibliography.[2] It listed more than

This essay was prepared for delivery as the Keynote Address at the Eighth Annual Convention of the International Studies Association, New York City, April 14, 1967. It is very largely a by-product of the author's participation in the organizing phase of the program of Columbia University's new Institute for the Study of Science in Human Affairs. The support of that Institute is gratefully acknowledged. The essay is reprinted from Vol. 12, #1 of the INTERNATIONAL STUDIES QUARTERLY, *by permission of the Wayne State University Press.*

[1] "A Tentative Guide to Writings on Science and World Affairs," Council for Atomic Age Studies (New York: Columbia University, 1962).

[2] *Bibliography on Science and World Affairs* (Washington, D.C.: U.S. Government

two thousand items. Where there is so much smoke there must be at least a little fire.

Nothing very useful can be said about science in general and how it is related to international politics in general. There are, however, two ways of identifying particular relationships between science and world politics about which useful things *can* be said. One may list conventional topics in the academic study of international relations and then ask about the scientific and technological aspects of each of these conventional topics. Alternatively, one may list the main headings appropriate to the study of science affairs and ask about the international political aspects of each of those topics.

A conventional course in international politics might include several lectures on basic power factors. One of the most important would deal with the degree of industrialization of the more than one hundred sovereign states. The Industrial Revolution did not occur everywhere at the same time or at the same rate. One of the most important ways in which the influence of any particular scientific or technological development upon industrial society has affected world politics derives from the transient effects of that development while one or only a few states are able to utilize it. Consider, for example, the probable effects on world politics if Nazi Germany had had as much success in nuclear technology as it had in rocket technology. Or consider how different Western Europe might look today if both the United States and the Soviet

Union had had atomic weapons in the period 1945 to 1950, so that the United States could not have held an atomic umbrella over the then almost completely unarmed Europe without risking two-way atomic war. Being first in science has a political significance which it did not have in earlier times.

Another whole set of effects derives from the unequal benefits which a given technological advance permanently confers once it is fully assimilated into the world political system. Compare the effects of the Industrial Revolution on coal-and-iron rich England and on coal-and-iron poor Ireland. A recurring theme in the geopolitical writings of the 1940's was the disparate effects of a transportation revolution on the great powers in their competition with each other, the improvement in the relative efficiency of overland transport as against overseas transport which was felt to have had a major influence in reshaping the whole international order.[3] Great continent-size states, such as the United States and Russia, could be integrated politically and economically. Centrally located Germany could gain power in the age of the railroad, at the expense of less centrally located European power competitors. But it does not take science leadership to enjoy the natural advantages in location or resource which a new technology may ultimately confer. Otherwise, the citizens of oil-rich Kuwait would hardly enjoy in 1968 an average income about equal to that of citizens of the United States.

Printing Office, November, 1964). One reason why this bibliography is so large is that modern science operates on world politics largely indirectly via technology, so that "science and world affairs" turns out to be "science, technology, and world politics."

[3] See, for example, Harold and Margaret Sprout, eds., *Foundations of National Power* (Princeton, N. J.: Princeton University Press, 1945), Chapters IV, V and VI for pertinent selections not only from their own writings but from those of William T. R. Fox, Nicholas J. Spykman and Robert Strausz-Hupé.

There may be another set of lectures dealing with the actors in world politics. Here it might be appropriate to consider how scientific and technological changes affect the relative importance of local, national, and transnational groups in world politics. It seems clear that for most of the past two centuries the advancing technology of communication and transportation—the technology of the railroad, the telegraph, the mass newspaper, the motor car, the airplane, radio and television—has increased mobility and contact within individual countries relatively more than it did between countries. This may no longer be true in Western Europe, and the increasing efficiency of world-wide networks of communication and transportation may be creating politically important transnational communities and interest groups of various kinds.

One student of the impact of atomic age inventions on our state system, John Herz, has concluded that these inventions are causing the demise of the territorial state.[4] This ought to mean that the nation-state will decline in importance as one of the categories of actors in world politics and that only the superpowers or the bloc actors will be important in the future. Unfortunately, or perhaps fortunately, some of the territorial states do not seem to have gotten the word. Herz wrote before the balance of terror had begun to appear quite stable and before lack of discipline and polycentrism had become apparent on both sides of the Iron Curtain. The technological gap between the United States and its Western European NATO partners which has attracted so much attention in the press

[4] *International Politics in the Atomic Age* (New York: Columbia University Press, 1959).

recently also helps to explain some of the Western polycentrism. The United States government does not appear to be greatly concerned about closing this gap, even though the gap is a threat to alliance solidarity and thus limits the efficiency of performance of the bloc actor in today's bipolar competition.

The proliferation of new states in the non-European world raises questions as to how small a state can be and still enjoy access to the benefits of advanced science and technology, and to what extent the problems created by the new pattern of micro-sovereignties can be overcome by the desire for such access. In theory, either common services arrangements of the Kenya-Uganda-Tanzania type, or functional international organizations such as the World Health Organization, open the way for a solution to these problems.

As one turns to discuss the Western state system itself, and particularly the transformation of our multiple sovereignty system from a balance of power system to a loose bipolar system, one may speculate on the role which scientific and technological changes have played in this transformation. To do this one must engage in an activity which might be called "hindcasting" or, perhaps more elegantly, "retrospective forecasting." Let us imagine that there had been no such thing as two world wars. How different would the world of 1967 look? Would the secrets of atomic energy have been discovered sooner or later, and on which side of the Atlantic Ocean? Would not the pace of scientific and technological advance have quickened in the twentieth century without the spur of war and defense mobilization? Is there any reason why the advantages of scale in research and development which the United States and perhaps also the Soviet Union enjoy today would not also be enjoyed by a

United States and a Russia which had avoided participation in two protracted world wars? One cannot separate out the strand of scientific and technological change from all the other dynamic forces, but it is instructive to make the effort.

Governing ideas in world politics may also be derived from the science of the time, sometimes spuriously. For example, social Darwinism, the doctrine of the survival of the fittest, provided a rationale for foreign policies with untold human costs. For Darwin himself the survival of the fittest referred to a competition between species and not between members of the same species who happened to differ only slightly in the color of their skin, eyes, and hair, and sometimes did not even differ that much. Query: Are there similar vulgarizations of twentieth-century science which today corrupt thinking about foreign affairs?

Scientific and technological changes affect the institutions for the settlement of interstate disputes. The slow-acting sanctions of Article 16 of the League Covenant would have been wholly ineffective in any conflict in which irretrievably decisive events occurred in the first hours of military action. If technology has rendered League of Nations style collective security obsolete, it has had an even more devastating effect on the utility and cost of general war as a device for resolving disputes among first-ranking powers. Query: Are newly available scientific and technological resources being effectively harnessed to the task of strengthening other kinds of institutions for resolving international disputes?

Part of the answer may be found by examining the ways in which the new science and the new technology have altered the objectives of foreign and military policy. If even for the first-ranking powers it is something called deterrence rather than something called victory by which a government hopes to avoid military defeat, then reciprocal deterrence may be performing some of the tasks formerly handled by war or by a functioning machinery of collective security.

There are North-South problems as well as East-West problems. The promise of science is shaping both the sense of what advanced industrial countries can do about less developed countries and the demands which the less developed countries are making on the advanced ones. The stigmata of new sovereignties may be a national university, a national airline, a national steel mill, and a national delegation at the United Nations larger than the staff of the Foreign Office in the national capital; but ecological, demographic, and nutritional studies may be more important in the management of the rising and as yet unfulfilled expectations of the burgeoning populations outside North America and Europe.

All this is rather conventional speculation, but it does suggest how much work can be done by students of international politics, using conventional categories of analysis and conventional methods of social science research. Students of international relations are hampered by lack of science literacy and by the limited demands which they can make upon natural scientists for help in overcoming this scientific illiteracy. The natural scientists can make them better students of international politics. Students of international politics, however, cannot make natural scientists better scientists, though they may occasionally make them more effective citizens.

Let us now approach science and international politics from the other direction. Let us list some of the main categories for the study of science affairs and ask something about the world political aspect of each of those topics. Thus, one might identify for discussion such topics as the following: (1) science and the scientific method in the study of international politics; (2) national and transnational scientific communities and their impact on the world political process; (3) members of the scientific establishment as advisers to governments (and to international organizations) in decisions affecting the world political process; (4) scientific considerations affecting decisions in the world political process; (5) decisions about science as an institution in the modern world made by national governments and international organizations; (6) the dream of science as the way out of "politics"—science and a depoliticized world; (7) science and technology as semi-independent variables in world politics; and, above all, (8) the problem of cutting down innovative-adaptive time in adjusting to scientific and technological change.

The political scientist has always been under some pressure, a good deal of it self-administered, to live up to the pretensions of the name of his discipline. Others may be skeptical of how scientific political science is and perhaps not even understand how little pretension was involved in the development of the discipline's name. If it is presumptuous to talk about a science of politics, it is even more so to talk about a science of international politics. One can, however, talk about the role of science in international politics. The scientific method, and particularly the need for conducting and reporting on research in such a fashion that another scholar can replicate as much of it as he wishes and make his own judgment about the accuracy and objectivity of the prior research, have long operated to keep the student of international politics honest. But when one talks about science and the study of international politics, one is taking about something more specific. The new paradigms of science have stimulated the construction of new paradigms for the study of world politics. A most obvious example is the effect of Norbert Wiener's cybernetic studies on Karl Deutsch's conception of politics. Deutsch conceives of politics more as a steering device than as a power competition.[5] Many statesmen will be glad to learn that they are not mere politicians but helmsmen on the spaceship Earth.

Scientific advances have affected the study of international politics in another way, for they have altered research technology as well as research paradigms. Data collection, data classification, data storage, data retrieval, and data manipulation all take forms hardly imaginable only a few years ago. The study of international relations is inevitably affected by the culture of science in which it now has to be carried on.

One cannot, perhaps, speak of the American science community or the international science community as new actors in the world political process. Scientists are no more likely to agree about United States policy in Vietnam or United States policy toward the test ban than are international lawyers or professors of international politics. The national and international science communities have, however, begun to develop interests in questions of public policy, so that even where scientists disagree, the disagreement tends to take the form of arguing about the significance of various scientific considerations.

[5] *The Nerves of Government* (New York: Free Press of Glencoe, 1963).

The student of world politics needs to know who are the policy-sensitive and policy-influential members of these national and international scientific communities.[6] He needs to understand the consequences of international contacts between scientists from various countries. Pugwash conferences, first sponsored by the Canadian-born, Russian-sympathizing American capitalist, Cyrus Eaton, are only the most dramatic example. The student of functionalism may find interesting data in the Pugwash experience. It is ironic that social scientists, for whom meetings with their opposite numbers on the other side of the Iron and Bamboo Curtains might be a professionally useful experience, have no Pugwash conferences to report. One need not, however, accept the explanation which J. Robert Oppenheimer once gave that perhaps social scientists do not have anything to say to each other.

Morton Grodzins invented the colorful term, "traitriot," to describe the patriot-traitor that each of us is.[7] He described a group of psychiatrists who were asked how they would handle information relevant to national security which they stumbled on in their doctor-client relationship. They reconciled the requirements of the Hippocratic oath and of loyal citizenship in a variety of ways. Grodzins might equally well have been talking about the guilt-ridden scientists of Los Alamos who made atomic weapons to be used against Adolf Hitler in a European war and saw them

used against an almost defeated Japan in an Asiatic war. How much one or another of us ought to be willing to risk national security in order to slow down the nuclear arms race is only partly a matter of technical judgment, as public disagreements among world renowned American physicists constantly remind us. Even in weighing a potential sacrifice of national interest in relation to a potential gain in some transnational interest, we are, as moral men with plural values and plural loyalties, behaving as "traitriots." The policy perspectives of influential scientists are as worthy of study as those of high-level military men, diplomats, and professional politicians. The unexplicated value preferences of a statesman's scientific advisers pose the same kind of problem for the responsible statesman-politician as the unexplicated value preferences of other expert advisers.[8] The professional civil servant, the professional diplomat, and the professional soldier who have for more than a century been learning how to give value-neutral advice may have lessons to teach the newcomers to the policy process.

Query: Do social scientists, and particularly students of international relations, perhaps feel that they are at

[6] On the composition and characteristics of the American science community and on government use of scientific advice, see Robert Gilpin and Christopher Wright, eds., *Scientists and National Policy Making* (New York: Columbia University Press, 1964).

[7] See "The Traitriot," Chapter 12 in his *The Loyal and the Disloyal* (Chicago: The University of Chicago Press, 1956), pp. 208–16.

[8] See especially Warner R. Schilling, "Scientists, Foreign Policy and Politics," in Gilpin and Wright, *op. cit.,* pp. 144–74, and the references there cited to the conflicting advice which Henry Tizard and F. A. Lindemann gave the British government in 1942. See also Warner R. Schilling, "The H-Bomb Decision: How to Decide Without Actually Choosing," *Political Science Quarterly* 76 (March 1961), pp. 24–46; Robert Gilpin, *American Scientists and Nuclear Weapons Policy* (Princeton, N.J.: Princeton University Press, 1962); and Harold K. Jacobson and Eric Stein, *Diplomats, Scientists and Politicians: The United States and the Nuclear Test Ban Negotiations* (Ann Arbor, Mich.: University of Michigan Press, 1966).

least as much entitled to whisper directly into the ear of the statesman-politician as the natural scientist? Do the social scientists fear about the natural scientists what they have sometimes feared about soldiers, that if the physicists are too close to the seat of power, their advice may exhibit what Alfred Vagts has called the "vice of immediacy," so that the statesman-politician gets fractional advice to deal with whole policy? Is it the secret desire of students of world politics that they should stand between the statesman-politician and all other experts, including natural scientists and soldiers, because they believe that their distinctive talent is to be able to advise on *whole* policy? So far, they have not succeeded in getting the President to appoint a social science adviser to serve alongside his natural science adviser.

The American student of world politics may sometimes wonder how the Americans wandered into a race with their British and French friends to see on which side of the Atlantic the first supersonic transport would fly. The science and technology race, ever since the trauma of Sputnik, was supposed to be between the two sides of the Iron Curtain and not between the two sides of the North Atlantic. Whether a social scientist would have had any better luck than a natural scientist in making that point if he had been in a position to advise the highest level of policy makers, there is no way of knowing. In any case, the characteristics of those scientists who are part of the national policymaking establishment need to be described at least as carefully as the national and international science communities do.

There is need to study not only the scientists in the policy process, or the scientific community as a group actor, but there is also need to examine considerations relative to science which

enter into policymaking. Here one can make a rough two-fold division between the role of scientific considerations in making national policy, and particularly national security policy, and the way in which government decisions are made which constitute the science policy of the country. Only then can we come to understand the role of mobilized science in an era of total diplomacy and limited war.

Scientific and technological change is a semi-independent variable in the equations of world politics because decisions of national governments and occasionally those of international organizations affect the rate, the direction, and the mass of the effort which goes into producing the change. In the past, it was left largely to the economic historian to describe the impact of major technological changes on the social system in which they took place; but an economic historian magisterially writing about the early industrial revolution and the relative rise in English power, which in the course of a century or two gradually became visible, does not quite meet the needs of the 1960's and 1970's.[9] In a time perspective of centuries the impact of wars, even world wars, on changes in the international order may seem slight as compared with the great scientific and technological changes of recent centuries. It was earlier suggested that nuclear energy, the computer, and micro-electronics generally might well be producing many of the same effects we now see whether or not the mass carnage of 1914–18 and 1939–45 had taken place. One cannot, however, go far with this line of argument. Otherwise, it might be difficult to explain why nations provide such massive support to

[9] See John U. Nef, *War and Human Progress* (Cambridge, Mass.: Harvard University Press, 1952).

their scientists in an effort to be the first to discover a new scientific principle or to complete the development of a scientific device.

Some social scientists were more nearly correct than some natural scientists in projecting the political consequences of the great events at Hiroshima and Nagasaki. They appear to have understood better than the scientists who advocated "one world or none" that even nuclear weapons cannot persuade a representative of a great power to yield his country's veto in an international organization.[10] They saw more readily than at least some natural scientists why co-existence was likely to be the order of the day for some time to come, why the real choice in the post-World War II world was not "One Rome or Two Carthages" but "Two Romes or None."

In a headlong race to be first in scientific advances, secrecy can only have a short-term utility. If, however, a short period is enough to implement irreversible decisions of the first importance, then recommendations for the long run which fail to take account of the short-run problem are inappropriate. Not only the atomic bomb but the proximity fuse, radar, LST's and the artificial harbor for the Normandy landings were the product of what Churchill called "the wizard war." The computer and micro-electronics are in the 1960's playing an analogous role, in helping to keep the balance of terror stable. In all these cases, by answering short-run technological problems, time was bought in which to discover answers to long-run political problems.

One should at least examine the possibility that Soviet-American competition in the science race is having a benign effect on world politics, whatever the intentions of the men who have ordered that the science race be run. It diverts at least some energies away from simply piling up armaments for the arms race itself. Samuel P. Huntington has suggested that only quantitative arms races are dangerous.[11] Certainly the science race tends to keep the arms race qualitative, thus keeping each side from feeling that it is sufficiently prepared to resort to trial by battle. There is always the "weapons system after next" to be made operational before one can ever begin to think of being so fully prepared as deliberately to choose war. The science race may, however, yield clues as the contenders' respective capabilities with such great clarity that a trial by battle becomes unnecessary. Furthermore, there may be some incidental peacetime payoffs. Perhaps the intensive development of the fuel cell, ostensibly for interplanetary travel, will so transform interborough travel between the various parts of New York City as to transform today's gray smog and aerial sewer into tomorrow's bright blue skies. The thrill of new worlds to conquer which the science race brings into view, not just the world of outer space but the world of Antarctica, the world of inner space (here one may pause to shed a tear on the grave of the Mohole project, which might have told much about the Earth's interior) and the race to make the world's deserts bloom—all these competitions may take some of the heat out of bipolar military competition.

[10] See, for example, Bernard Brodie, ed., *The Absolute Weapon* (New York: Harcourt, Brace and Co., 1946).

[11] "Arms Races: Prerequisites and Results," in Carl J. Friedrich and Seymour Harris, eds., *Public Policy: Yearbook of the Graduate School of Public Administration, Harvard University* (Cambridge, Mass.: Graduate School of Public Administration, 1958), pp. 41–86.

One must not overstate the case. The science race can be destabilizing and it can make the state system resistant to change. Even though secrecy can have only a short-term utility in the science race itself, a short period may be enough to implement irreversible decisions of the first importance. Recommendations for the long run which fail to take account of the short-run problem are inappropriate.

It was a science race which has today made the one big war totally unacceptable, but the science race has neither eliminated nor solved problems that in an earlier day seemed to make that big war worth fighting. Thus, the science race may have promoted the "deceleration of history." All over the world there are problems too important to ignore, but not important enough to cause Washington and Moscow to choose to destroy each other. So history slows down, the problems remain, and some of them grow daily more menacing.

If the science race has decelerated one kind of history, it may have accelerated another. The dizzy pace of technological advance has certainly contributed to the erosion of the physical, biological, and cultural resources of a planet on which over three billion human beings live but on which only a few hundred million enjoy a standard of living made possible by consumption of non-recurrable mineral resources. The science race may be a problem generator and a problem preserver, especially if it has brought about what Walter Millis has called "the hypertrophy of general war."[12]

The science race, on the other hand, has sometimes solved problems for governments and social scientists.

[12] This is the title of the concluding chapter of his *Arms and Men* (New York: Putnam, 1956).

Thus, the twin developments of "the spy in the sky" and ballistic sea power have transformed the problem of international inspection into the struggle to achieve some kind of international regulation of atomic energy. The first has made Soviet secrecy seem somewhat less important to the Americans. Ballistic sea power, on the other hand, has made American openness somewhat less of an advantage to the Soviet Union. Thus the two superpowers have a more nearly equal interest in arrangements to exchange information. Also, the fact that counter-city strikes are technically easier than counter-force strikes means that retaliation capability rather than efficiency in inspecting down to the last few concealed atomic weapons provides the true protection against the nuclear aggressor. Some technological advances may, of course, exhibit both aspects. They may solve one problem while creating another. Reclaiming the world's wastelands, perhaps in largest part through de-salinization and cheap energy for transporting the de-salted water, may possibly give the world a much needed extra decade or two in which to cope with the population explosion. It also may be destabilizing. Quest for territory seems to have become a much less potent source of conflict with the world's most fertile areas all divided up; but if there are to be new fertile areas, what reason is there to believe that neighboring states will find it easy to agree on how these new areas are to be divided?

Whether one looks down one road to disaster at the end of which is a thermonuclear Doomsday or down that other road which ends in a population explosion, it is clear that we need institutions and policies to shorten the innovative-adaptive time with respect to scientific and technological changes, some of which are going to come anyway and others of which can be made to come if we choose to have them. Herman Kahn has already led the way in manufacturing hypothesized history of post-explosion events and more generally in writing scenarios for alternative futures.[13] Daniel Bell has painted in broad brush strokes the picture of the post-industrial society.[14] We need not believe that only domestic politics will be affected by the emergence of this post-industrial society. We need not believe in the utopian dream of a depoliticized world made possible because science has provided the way out. Science does have its uses in the contemporary race with the twin disasters of the atom bomb and the fertility bomb. Malthus has been proved wrong now for almost 200 years, but without the most creative use of our scientific and technological resources, it will fall to this generation to have proved that both he and Hobbes were right after all.

Science does beckon us to a new view of world politics. Thirty years ago it was possible for a distinguished political scientist to write that "politics is the study of who gets what, when, and how."[15] The implication that politics (including world politics) is a "zero-sum game" struggle for power or that there is an iron fund of values to be contested does not in fact describe accurately the views of Harold Lasswell, the coiner of the who-gets-what phrase. No living political scientist has a broader view of the potentials of political science for improving main's lot, but the zero-sum game view of politics was widely prevalent then and has been since. A political scientist writing in the 1960's, one who has since been appointed to one of the highest posts occupied by a political scientist in the Executive Branch of the American federal government, that of Under Secretary of Housing and Urban Development, has written, "Today no national political system can afford to concentrate on distributive and allocative problems."[16] I understand this to mean that a modern political system including a world political system must, in the same writer's words, "have the capacity to translate basic scientific knowledge into workable, effectively engineered design and structure." For national political systems of at least the first-ranking powers this means that "decision-makers must have the assurance that the society they direct maintains technological innovation at least on a par with its major competitors." For the world as a whole the minimum requirement is set by the competition of national systems not with each other but with nature itself. A world of plenty may or may not be a world of peace; but unless certain minimum aspirations of less advantaged peoples are met, the prospects for peace and order will be dim indeed. It will take a technology tailor-made for developing areas to satisfy these minimum aspirations.

---

13 *On Thermonuclear War* (Princeton, N.J.: Princeton University Press, 1960); and *Thinking About the Unthinkable* (New York: Horizon Press, 1962).

14 "The Post-Industrial Society," in Eli Ginsberg, ed., *Technology and Social Change* (New York: Columbia University Press, 1964), pp. 44–59. See also, "Notes on the Post-Industrial Society (I)" in *The Public Interest*, No. 6 (Winter 1967) and (II) in No. 7 (Spring 1967).

15 Harold D. Lasswell, *Politics: Who Gets What, When, How* (New York: McGraw-Hill Book Co., Inc., 1936).

16 Robert C. Wood, "Scientists and Politics: The Rise of an Apolitical Elite," in Robert Gilpin and Christopher Wright, *op. cit.,* p. 54.

2. The Future of the Strategic Arms Race: Options for the 1970's

Dr. Rathjens has served as Staff Special Assistant to the President for science and technology. He is presently director of the Weapons System Evaluation Division of the Institute for Defense Analyses.

SUMMARY

Although American strategic forces were built up rapidly during the early 1960's, their level has been almost constant during the last two years. In contrast, Soviet strategic forces have recently been growing at a fast rate, although according to most measures of strategic strength, the United States continues to have "superiority." In the present context, the concept of "superiority" may have outlived its usefulness. The present strategic balance might be more meaningfully characterized as one of "sufficiency" in strategic forces in the sense that each side can inflict unacceptable damage on the other, regardless of the conditions under which nuclear war might develop. Thus, further increases in strategic force levels are not likely to offer either country new political options. Yet on both sides there have been vigorous research and development programs that now make probable the deployment of new strategic systems.

There was hope a few years ago that during the early 1970's the strategic balance might become stabilized, with both the Soviet Union and the United States willing to base the planning of their strategic forces on the view that they could serve little purpose other than to deter a Soviet-American thermonuclear war. It now seems possible that this hope of stability based on mutual deterrence may not be realized: there is no evidence that the expansion in Soviet strategic forces is tapering off; technological advances have made possible new strategic weapons that are likely to be deployed; and the emergence of China as a nuclear power may be a stimulus to the expansion of strategic forces.

At the heart of the difficulty in moderating the arms race is the fact that the United States is likely to react to any deployment of new strategic forces by the adversary by making compensating or over-compensating improvements in its own capabilities; the same is probably true of the Soviet Union. Indeed, because of the time required to translate decisions into operational capability, both sides often react in anticipation of *possible* adversary deployments. The problem is exacerbated by the great uncertainty of each side about its adversary's capabilities and intentions. These factors

Prepared for the Carnegie Endowment for International Peace (December 1968). Reprinted with permission from the author and Massachusetts Institute of Technology.

must be taken into account in any attempt to control the arms race by agreement—and in unilateral decisions regarding new weapons choices.

Some of the weapons systems that now appear on the horizon, particularly anti-ballistic missile (ABM) defenses and multiple individually targetable reentry vehicles (MIRV's), are likely to introduce large uncertainties into the calculus of the strategic balance, and thus are especially likely to stimulate adversary reaction or over-reaction.

Despite the lateness of the hour, it may still be possible to head off a new escalation of the arms race. However, this may require a reversal of some decisions already made. The most promising approach would be through negotiations between the superpowers, although the importance of reciprocal unilateral restraint regarding new weapons choices should not be discounted. It should be added that strategic arms talks, even if they do not result in a formal treaty, may still serve a useful purpose if they help dispel some of the uncertainties that fuel the arms race.

In any case, fundamental clarification of U.S. objectives is required as a basis for making specific decisions regarding weapons choices and negotiating positions. In this connection we are confronted with two difficult dilemmas: that of reconciling our desire to minimize damage to ourselves in the event of war with our desire to escape the adverse consequences that may flow from developing damage-limiting capabilities; and that of minimizing the likelihood of escalation while relying on it as a deterrent.

There is a desire on the part of both Americans and Russians to try to limit to very low levels damage to their own countries in the event of war, and a desire on each side to ensure that it will emerge from a nuclear war less damaged than its opponents. Yet attempts to develop and deploy forces that might contribute to the attainment of these specific objectives are likely to have two adverse effects: an increase in the probability of thermonuclear war; and a build-up in strategic forces leading not only to greater expense for both sides, but probably even to an increase in the total damage that each might expect in the event of war.

As for the second dilemma, the consequences of thermonuclear war are rightly judged so horrible that major efforts to avoid it are justified. Yet there is a tendency in the United States and elsewhere to rely on the danger of escalation as a deterrent to limited aggression, particularly in Europe—a tendency that is incompatible with minimizing the possibility of a thermonuclear war occurring.

It is suggested that it is in the interest of the United States to resolve this second dilemma by moving away from reliance on the likelihood of escalation as a deterrent to limited aggression.

As regards the first dilemma, we should give greater weight than we have in the past to curtailing the action-reaction cycle that drives the arms race, even at the expense of our deep-seated desires for "superiority" and for development of effective "damage-limiting" capabilities. If the Soviet Union can accept similar limitations on its objectives, there would appear to be a basis for negotiations to limit strategic armaments.

This neither requires nor implies a resolution of the fundamental political differences that pervade Soviet-American relations. But moderating the pace of the strategic arms race may make possible cooperation in other areas and help to accelerate a resolution of some of these political conflicts.

ECONOMIC

CAPABILITY

Chapter 8

It would be difficult to list in detail all the aspects of a country's economic situation which contribute to, or detract from, its capacity in international relations. Entire courses in economics are focused on such a task. It would also be difficult to separate many of the economic ingredients of state capacity from the other aspects of a society treated earlier, such as geography, resources, population, and scientific-technological development. These are all intertwined and interdependent. Nevertheless in attempting to identify specific economic factors one would have to take into account a country's industrial capacity, the amount of its capital available for investment purposes, and the investment opportunities presented at home and abroad, as well as its gross national product (the monetary value of the total of goods and services produced) and the mix of that product. For example certain production is entirely oriented toward national security purposes and thus directly contributes to a state's ability to achieve its objectives in relations with others. Other aspects of production may have an indirect relationship, and still others either have no relationship at all or perhaps only a most tangential one. In fact the diversion of resources to some kinds of production may even detract from the possibility of attaining maximum strength in a society's international relationships.

In comparing the form of economic organization of a given state, in its relevant functional and dysfunctional aspects, with forms practiced elsewhere, such considerations as the type of planning characteristic of the country and the way in which production and income are distributed throughout the population need to be taken into account. Countries differ in their attitudes toward innovation in the economic sphere. Tax structures differ, as do labor-management relations. There may be religious, cultural, or ideological impediments to the full utilization of a country's economic potential, as in the case of India. Until recently France has been cited as an·example of an economy based heavily on the small family firm, emphasizing small-scale, high profit-per-unit production, and de-emphasizing risk-taking with large production for uncertain markets.[1] Cultural patterns may significantly affect the degree to which a given economy may enable a state to become and remain a regional or world power.

The state's ability to utilize human and material resources depends largely on the economic structure and organization of a society. The catalog of alternatives ranges from complete state control (seldom fully achieved, except at a certain phase of textbook Marxism) all the way to completely private decision making (also seldom reached, except in the speeches of American campaign orators). The Marxist theory, simply stated, is that capitalism breeds imperialism which, in turn, breeds war; that in the quest for economic advantage, markets, resources, and investment opportunities, the governments of capitalist countries, spurred on by the needs and desires of their business communities, have no alternative but to become externally aggressive. There are variations on this theme, including certain low-level scandal theories which propose that wars are the result of capitalists' influences over statesmen (war profiteers, merchants of death, and the like). The trouble with this theory is that it very frequently does not stand up to historical investigation; numerous international conflicts, such as those in Korea and Vietnam, make almost no sense at all if one were to attempt to explain them on the basis of economic motivation.

One distinguished student of international affairs, Quincy Wright, has argued that capitalist societies have been relatively peaceful, in large part because the central idea of capitalism is to separate government and business. In the modern period, Wright holds, war has more frequently been initiated by states dominated by agrarianism or by a form of socialism than by those dominated by capitalism.[2]

Doubts about simplistic Marxist explanations of international tension and conflict may equally apply to opposing over-simplified theories, such as the one that free enterprise is, by definition, peaceful and that it is so efficient as to eventually overcome any other form of economic organization. As to the first point, it is important to remember that war is essentially a political phenomenon, not an economic one, arising out of the contacts and

---

[1] David S. Landes, "Observations on France: Economy, Society, and Polity," *World Politics* (1957), Vol. 9, 329–50.

[2] Quincy Wright, *A Study of War* (Chicago: The University of Chicago Press, 1942), Chap. 32.

frictions of states regardless of their form of economic organization. As to the second point the question must be raised whether an economy such as that of the United States is always efficient in ways germane to international relations, or whether its efficiency lies in the satisfaction of wants and desires that have only indirect relevance to the country's external power position. This raises the related question as to whether the capitalist model is necessarily the most appropriate for countries that are just beginning the economic development process.

To most Western observers a system of state planning such as that of the Soviet Union is in many ways less efficient than that of the United States. Whatever shortcomings one can identify in the Soviet economic system, it has not broken down and it has, at least in major respects, succeeded in what it attempted to do, namely, to transform the country into a first-rank industrial power. The example of the Soviet Union, and increasingly that of Communist China as well, carries a potent appeal to peoples in the underdeveloped areas who want development, want it fast, and are sometimes not as particular about means of achieving it as statesmen in the more highly developed Western societies might prefer them to be. The drive for economic development in the emerging countries is enormously complex and expensive. Much depends, therefore, on the ability and willingness of the more highly developed countries to offer support to the less advantaged. Such support may, on occasion, be given as a purely humanitarian gesture, but the usual pattern is to provide it for reasons of concrete political advantage.[3] A state's capability to render such assistance is largely dependent on its own economic strength. Obviously highly productive and wealthy countries are in a better position to carry out large-scale and long-term assistance programs than countries that have grave economic problems of their own. It may be safely suggested that the economic competition among highly developed states for influence over and support by less developed ones will assume increased importance in the years to come.

In a world which is increasingly oriented toward economic growth and development, a reputation for economic stability, high productivity, a high rate of growth, and an equitable distribution of product and wealth is to be prized very highly. One should take note here of the controversy concerning the relevance of actual versus potential economic capacity. In the past it has usually been possible for a country to bring its *potential* capacity to bear in the event of an international conflict situation. This has been the experience of the United States in two world wars. Whether or not, and if so to what extent, this is still the case today is the subject of serious controversy. The selections by Klaus Knorr and James R. Schlesinger both concern this very point, Knorr assuming the position that the concept of economic potential is still viable, while Schlesinger poses serious questions

[3] See Herbert Feis, *Foreign Aid and Foreign Policy* (New York: St. Martin's Press, 1964), especially Part Three, "What to Ask of Recipients of Aid," pp. 115–73.

about this, stressing the concept of the pre-attack capacity of states instead. The resources, population, skills, and industrial base of a country together constitute what is traditionally known as economic potential for war, which Knorr defines as "the capacity to produce military forces and supplies in time of war and thus to add substantially to, and often to multiply, the amount of combat power maintained in peacetime." As the line between war and peace has become increasingly blurred, economic potential encompasses the wherewithal to support a whole spectrum of security programs ranging from the narrowly military through defense support and economic assistance to education and scientific research. Differences in economic potential then would refer to the relative capacities of two or more powers to provide the necessary productive resources to support foreign economic aid and development programs and a high level of investment in appropriate industries as well as a military establishment.

Ultimately the test of a state's economic capability in international relations is a military one. As Edward Hallett Carr observed in relating wealth to war:

> Economic strength has always been an instrument of political power, if only through its association with the military instrument. Only the most primitive kinds of warfare are altogether independent of the economic factor. The wealthiest city-state could hire the largest and most efficient army of mercenaries; and every government was therefore compelled to pursue a policy designed to further the acquisition of wealth. The whole progress of civilization has been so closely bound up with economic development that we are not surprised to trace, throughout modern history, an increasingly intimate association between military and economic power.[4]

No matter how rich a country may be, its effective power depends upon the effectiveness with which it utilizes its natural resources, and this in turn depends on its level of economic development and social organization. In 1914 the German armies, though heavily outnumbered by the Russians, were able to defeat them in part at least because of the superior productivity of German industry. A generation later German armies of equally superb equipment and morale were incapable of subduing a Russia that had by then acquired modern weapons and supporting industry. Forced industrialization of backward Russia had brought it abreast of its most dangerous Western foes. To achieve this goal Stalin had concentrated upon the development of Soviet heavy industry at the expense of light industry and consumer goods. From a level of steel production less than one quarter that of Germany's in 1914, the Soviet leaders raised Russian production until it exceeded Germany's in 1940. That, plus American lend-lease was enough to give the U.S.S.R. the industrial means necessary to prevail.

[4] Edward Hallett Carr, *The Twenty Years' Crisis, 1919–1939* (London: The Macmillan Company, 1951), p. 113.

Although the economic capability of states is germane to international relations in diverse ways, one that is of increasing significance is clearly the quest for economic well-being that increasingly characterizes every society in the world. Virtually all societies have become welfare states, in actuality or as a goal for the near future. This has two implications. Peoples in all countries demand and expect services and advancing standards of well-being, and if these demands are satisfied, the nation is strengthened. But if those services and standards are not forthcoming, dissatisfactions will arise which will undermine the morale and the stability of a society, thus rendering it less effective in attaining its objectives in international relations.

1. The Concept of Economic Potential for War

KLAUS KNORR

Klaus Knorr is Professor in the Woodrow Wilson School of Public and International Affairs, Princeton University, and a frequent government consultant. He is an outstanding authority on the economics of international resources, and indeed on the economic aspects of international relations in general. He is the author of WAR POTENTIAL OF NATIONS *(1956), and* NATO AND AMERICAN SECURITY *(1959).*

...Military potential...is the ability of a nation to divert resources to defense in both formal peace and war. Economic (including technological) capacity is, of course, one constituent of military potential in this sense. But before concentrating on this particular factor, its relation to other major constituents must be clarified. The production of military power demands an input of manpower and other productive resources which would otherwise be directed to non-military output or, marginally, remain idle. But at no time, not even when engaged in total war,

WORLD POLITICS, *X (1957), 49–62. Reprinted by permission.*

can a nation allocate all resources to the production of combat power. The proportion which can and will be diverted to this purpose depends a. on the structure and productivity of these resources and b. on the nation's will to provide for military power, i.e., to pay the price for military strength. This price is to be paid not only financially but in terms of foregoing the satisfaction of a wide range of interests—consumption, leisure, comfort, safety, etc. —that conflict with the commitment of resources to the production of military power. The will to provide for military power is therefore another constituent of a nation's defense potential.

Furthermore, given any degree of

willingness to pay this price (including the discipline with which the population supports government measures), the output of military power depends upon the efficiency with which the diverted resources are employed. Hence, organizational ability and especially administrative competence represent a third major constituent of military potential. To illustrate, the amount of military power maintained by the United States at any one time is not only a function of the country's productive capacity. It also depends on the size of the defense budget (which permits a proportion of this capacity to be allotted to the output of combat power, and which is contingent upon a political decision reflecting the price the American people are willing to pay for defense), and on the efficiency with which every defense dollar—and, indeed, every non-defense dollar—is spent. As will appear in the following, any realistic analysis of economic and technological potential for defense must pay heed to these interrelationships.

II

While it is useful to theorize on the general meaning of military potential and on the general ways in which this concept can be put to predictive and manipulative use, practical application calls for an immediate descent from the general to the particular. In real life, a nation has no such thing as a military potential or an economic defense potential which is the same for all possible situations calling for the use of military power in formal peace or war. At present, for example, there are countries which have a relatively high potential for fighting with non-atomic weapons on their own territory or in nearby theaters of war; but they have a very low potential for conducting war with non-atomic arms in distant theaters of operations and a still lower, or zero, potential for waging thermonuclear war. It cannot be stressed too strongly that the analysis of the war potential of any particular country or alliance must begin with specific assumptions about the kind of situation demanding the use of military power. If we are interested in military potential, we must relate our analysis to the likely situations that require, or will require, a military effort. At the present time, and using the United States as an example in the following analysis, it is reasonable to concentrate on three such situations: 1. the long-run maintenance of an adequate defense establishment (which, in fact, it is hoped will deter aggression without jeopardy to vital American interests abroad); 2. involvement in limited wars; and 3. the outbreak of unlimited war. For illustrative purposes, we may furthermore assume that the first two situations demand a diversion of resources from the civilian to the military sector of the economy amounting to from 8 to 12 per cent and from 14 to 18 per cent of the Gross National Product (GNP), respectively.

Obviously, the basic factors governing economic defense potential are the same for the two first situations, in the sense that a nation endowed with a high economic defense potential for fighting limited war usually also enjoys a high potential for maintaining a strong military posture in the absence of formal war. The main conditions that make up economic defense potential for limited war are:

(1) The volume of the GNP

The absolute volume is patently significant, since the economic effort for defense will be measured as a proportion of total capacity for producing goods and services. The volume of GNP per capita, or per head of the labor force, is a rough index of the productivity of labor and helps in estimating how much civilian consumption can be compressed in an emergency in order to release productive factors for the defense section. Clearly, it makes a difference whether the GNP per capita is the equivalent of $2,000, $800, or $100 per year.

(2) The rate of growth of the GNP

This datum will help in estimating changes in economic defense potential over time. Growth will result chiefly from increases in the labor force, from the rate of savings and investment, and from technological innovation. These three factors each have their own bearing on economic defense potential—e.g., a country with a high rate of savings and investment may be able to sustain the conduct of limited war by temporarily switching resources to the military sector entirely or largely from investment, rather than from consumption.

(3) The structure of output

The most relevant condition is the degree to which the normal product mix approaches the output mix required for waging limited war. This includes the value of industrial as against agricultural, mining, and service production; of heavy as against light industrial production; within these categories, of production of the many goods of special importance to defense such as arms, aircraft, electronics, and fuels; and the growth rate for all of these key products.

(4) The flexibility of output

It is important to know the relative ease and speed with which output patterns can be modified and, especially,

the output of key military supplies be expanded. To the extent that this depends on the flexibility of an economy rather than on government policy, the main factors are the organizational ability of management, the mobility of labor, and the state of such industries as construction, transportation, and machine tools which facilitate the conversion of plant from one output mix to another or the shift of labor from one plant or locality to another.

(5) Science and technology

The current pace of technological innovation in weapons production is unprecedented in history and is indeed so swift that a nation's endowment in scientists and technicians, the rates and quality of their training, the distribution of this precious personnel over various research fields, and its division between pure and applied research have become major constituents of economic defense potential.

(6) Size and structure of the defense budget

This factor will in large measure determine a country's ready capacity for producing military supplies and skills required in limited war.

(7) The size and structure of the tax burden

Both the magnitude of tax revenues in relation to the national income and the tax pattern affect the ease with which the financial instrument can be used in an emergency for allocating additional resources to defense production.

It should be noted that the degree of national self-sufficiency, as against dependence on foreign supplies, is considered as part of the "structure of output." For industrial nations, this problem is chiefly one of foodstuffs and primary commodities. Normally, there should be no problem so far as the long-range maintenance of defense forces in time of formal peace is concerned. But as the Suez Canal crisis and the sharp rises of raw materials prices during the Korean War showed, dependence on foreign supplies may be a very serious handicap in time of limited war. Yet, since most primary materials are storable, and since participation in international trade tends to raise labor productivity and the GNP—another determinant of economic defense potential—self-sufficiency achieved by a deliberate cut-back of foreign trade is distinctly less of an asset than when it is the natural outcome of comparative production advantages.

In view of the number of main conditions affecting the economic war potentials of nations, it is immediately apparent that there is no magic key to the estimation of war potential. An estimate of any one condition cannot be expected to yield more than partial results. For instance, a mere comparison of the GNP of two countries—although it offers valuable information—is not only difficult technically but also of narrowly limited value by itself.

When the conditions of economic defense potential are discussed, reference is often made to conditions that are not actually economic, but constituents of administrative capacity or of the nation's will to provide for military power. Thus, how large an input of productive resources is needed to generate a given amount of military strength depends in large measure on the administrative efficiency with which defense dollars are spent. The flexibility of the output mix depends on administrative competence, which is a considerable element in lead-times, whenever new admixtures of military end-items are urgently required.

The maintenance of a large-scale defense effort in time of formal peace must, in the long run, rest on a commensurate degree of taxation, so that there are no consumption and investment dollars in excess of what can be spent on consumption and investment goods at current prices. If the defense effort is not put on a pay-as-you-go basis whenever full employment prevails, inflationary pressures will result and, if strong and prolonged, they will have various debilitating consequences. Whether the defense effort will or will not be mounted on a pay-as-you-go basis is not, of course, an economic but a political and psychological problem (and, since public attitudes are subject to government leadership, it is an administrative problem as well). This crucial factor of the will to provide for defense is frequently slighted in American discussions of how large a defense budget the "economy" can stand. What the "economy" can stand is something quite different from, though not unrelated to, what the electorate will stand. Provided the electorate agrees to be taxed for a defense effort requiring year after year, say, 12 per cent of the GNP, the question is whether or not this tax load (in addition to taxes for the civilian purposes of government) will undermine the "soundness" of the economy. The economy might suffer if high taxes engendered a fall in the rate of savings and investment (public as well as private) and, in a private enterprise economy, weakened the incentive to work, innovate, and employ productive resources efficiently. Such ill consequences would slow down the rate of economic growth in, and reduce the flexibility of, the economy and thereby diminish economic defense potential over time.

Contrary to the assurance with which such deleterious effects are frequently predicted, we know unfortunately little about the circumstances under which they would represent a serious risk. We do know that the high tax rates levied in the United States since the outbreak of the Korean War have not prevented a very high rate of economic growth; that the effects on the incentives and the savings of high-income groups as a whole have been minor; that harmful effects of severe taxation depend on the structure of taxation as well as on its level; and that, in democratic communities, the slackening of the electorate's will to provide for defense in peacetime is likely to keep taxes from reaching the level at which these subversive risks to the economy would become serious. . . .

2. Economic Growth and National Security

JAMES R. SCHLESINGER

James R. Schlesinger, Senior Staff member at RAND, has served as a research associate of the Foreign Policy Research Institute and as a consultant to the Naval War College. A leading authority in the field of monetary and fiscal policy as it relates to national security, he has written widely for professional and scholarly journals.

In the past year, the discussion of economic growth as an answer to the security and other problems facing the United States has suffered some eclipse as a consequence of the recession and the need to take action to prevent economic retrogression. Despite the distrac-

ORBIS *V (1962), 453–69. Reprinted by permission. This paper may be regarded as an early by-product of a broader research project on "Professionalism and Natural Security," which is being assisted by a grant from the Social Science Research Council, to which the writer would like to express his indebtedness. Remarks akin to those in some sections of the paper were made in a lecture at the Industrial College of the Armed Forces on March 17, 1961.*

tions of the recession, an underlying belief persists that overall economic capacity is likely to prove determinative in the power struggle between the West and the communist world. In the United States this conviction seemingly goes unchallenged from either end of the political spectrum, largely because it draws upon a common element in the American credo—the optimistic assumption about human nature that the exertions and energy of the typical citizen will never be undermined in a society which continues either to protect individualism and incentives (right) or to provide social justice (left). On this question, the American creed appears to have taken little account of either historical experience or humanistic knowledge.

Many economists have tended to accept the proposition that security is dependent upon growth—partly, no doubt, because they are products of the American society and value-system, but more importantly, perhaps, because through professional training they have been indoctrinated with the presupposition that given a system of ends, the more resources available, the better will those ends be accomplished. Other things being equal, such would be the case with respect to the defense problem, but other things are never equal. By concentrating on aggregate resources, economists tend to overlook certain qualitative changes which growth may induce—changes which lessen a society's capacity to deal with its security problems. When such matters are taken into account—at least in the case of a society with such vast resources as the United States—the easing of the strain on resources made possible by growth may, on balance, contribute relatively little.

The first objective of this paper is to challenge the widespread supposition that military potential advances monotonically with increases in economic capacity. Changes within certain ranges of aggregate income are vastly more important than larger changes in other ranges. Just as in geophysical terms the freezing point of water is critical and the distinction between 31° and 33° is vastly more significant than the much larger temperature change, say from 0° to 31°, so in politico-economic terms a critical point is reached when capacity levels are attained which can provide a nation with a full-fledged nuclear striking force. Just as phenomena such as glaciation can be explained only in terms of the critical point, so the power struggle can be analyzed only in terms of the economic critical point, which clearly demarcates those nations which are world powers from those that are not. Only the United States and the Soviet Union have passed that point today, and for the present it is somewhat futile to compare other powers to them in terms of worldwide influence. In the short run the relationship between economic capacity and power is a discontinuous one. It differs from the relationship implicit in the older concept of economic potential for war, for which many Americans have an emotional penchant, in that the latter would measure all nations by the same yardstick—thereby providing a gradual transition from Andorra to the United States.

A second objective is to inquire what connection exists between American security and economic capacity and growth under present conditions and in the foreseeable future. In the abstract, additional resources should permit the expansion of military power, but historically speaking, the correspondence between the two has rarely been close. The *will* to employ resources effectively is indispensable—as is evidenced by present American strategic weaknesses despite the country's immense economic superiority. Nuclear weapons have, if anything, reduced the dependence of power on annual productive capacity, because in a nuclear war forces-in-being will be the most important determinant of the outcome. Since advance preparations are essential, impressive forces-in-being may over time be provided by a power with an industrial base relatively modest by American standards. After the initial blow had been struck, its rival would have no opportunity to convert its superior capacity to war purposes. Substantial economic capacity may still provide the flexibility which permits a speeding up of preparations when an emergency has been detected—an advantage which may have some relevance for the United States today—but it is offset by the disadvantage that a power whose reaction time is reduced in this way is likely to be more careless about early preparations and to rely on its presumed capacity for rapid adjustment.

For the United States, which already possesses so impressive a reserve capacity, growth is not the critical variable, and the continued emphasis upon it has tended to distract our attention from other, more pressing problems. The effects of growth, moreover, are complicated; in some ways growth may tend to lessen security. There is something, for example, in the public's instinctive notion that Red China would possess an awesome advantage, if (as the public assumes) it should shortly possess a nuclear striking force, for its poverty implies that it would offer fewer enticing targets in terms of urban-industrial concentrations than would a developed industrial power. Nikita Khrushchev himself has opined that the Soviet Union, more recently arrived at urban-industrial status, could more easily survive a thermonuclear war than its American rival because of the greater Soviet ability to revert temporarily to an economy not greatly removed from subsistence agriculture. There is some truth in this supposition of the increased vulnerability of an urban-industrial society (though it is surprising to have it put forward by a proponent of Marxist-Leninist philosophy). What it suggests, however, is the need for an urban-industrial civilization to make more careful advance preparations to reduce its vulnerability. Happily, such a society will have the resources to undertake these steps.

In addition to the possibility of increased vulnerability, growth has social side-effects which may reduce the capacity for defense. Those who argue that more rapid growth is essential to American security reach their conclusion by ignoring such side-effects and by extrapolating the presumed positive effect on power of additional economic capacity. It is perhaps not inappropriate to raise the question whether in America's present position the negative effects of growth do not outweigh the positive. Many people conceive of growth as a Cold War weapon. At best it is a low-confidence weapon which has little relevance under present American conditions unless it is associated with the provision of strategic capabilities.

I

The presumed connection between economic and military capabilities reflects the fact that "in modern times many different causes contribute to render the defence of the society more expensive." This statement is drawn not from one of our contemporaries but from Adam Smith. Though the latter recognized that economic power had not always been determinative and that previous history was replete with instances of the conquest of civilized by barbarous nations, he did argue that "in modern war the great expense of firearms gives an evident advantage to the nation which can best afford that expense and consequently to an opulent and civilized over a poor and barbarous nation."[1] It is but a step from this statement to the notion of the economic potential for war (EPW), the doctrine that wars are won through the conversion of economic capacity to the production of war material. With the coming of the Industrial Revolution, the dominance of economic power came increas-

---

[1] Adam Smith, *The Wealth of Nations* (New York: Modern Library, 1937), p. 669.

ingly to be stressed—a tendency which reached its apogee in World War II, which was in so many respects a war of production and of material attrition. Just as it is said that "the battle of Waterloo was won on the playing fields of Eton," so it can be said with substantially less exaggeration that the battles of the Rhine and the Philippines were won in the factories of Detroit (two statements which, incidentally, in their own way reflect characteristic differences in the British and American cultures).

The triumphant role of economic capacity in World War II fostered careful study of EPW and the allied concept of the mobilization base, as well as a sublime confidence in the degree of security provided for the United States by its productive power. But the world had already changed. Future wars were not likely to be wars of material attrition, but either nuclear wars, which would be fought primarily by forces-in-being and in which there would be no time for mobilization, or limited wars, wherein a nation's full power would not be committed. Deterrence, moreover, was believed to be a relatively simple matter. A society had only to build up a stock of A-bombs and a retaliatory striking force; this could be done with a given outlay irrespective of over-all capacity. As long as it could be assumed that power could be immobilized through a balance of terror, aggregate economic strength would count for little.

The hypothetical world of frozen power relationships which were to characterize the anticipated nuclear stalemate never came into existence. Hopes or fears of its coming were jarred by a revolution in military technology which so reduced the size of the H-bomb that it could be placed in a missile and delivered to any point on the earth's surface. An attack of enormous power and speed could thus be launched virtually without warning, thereby placing a tremendous premium on the first strike. Achieving stability in deterrence is no longer a simple matter; it is necessary to protect the nation's retaliatory capacity against an initial attack—i.e., to provide a second-strike force. A small number of exposed bases, particularly bases close to the enemy lines and susceptible to an attack of enormous weight, will no longer do. It would permit, or even entice, an enemy to destroy our nuclear power by a first strike.

This possibility has led to recognition of the need for a larger and better protected strategic striking force. Quite naturally it has increased interest in a greater number of bases, hardened and dispersed, and in increased mobility of weapons. It has also led to interest in another form of deterrence: the preparation for disaster which involves emphasis on civilian defense and recuperative capacity. For, if an enemy knows we have prepared to cope with disaster, this increases the credibility of our nuclear threat, since presumably it reduces our unwillingness to become involved in a nuclear encounter.

Changes of this sort have led to renewed interest in economic capacity as a possible determinant of the "victor" in a nuclear-age struggle. Economic capacity, it is argued, is needed to provide maximum dispersal and hardening of bases, more weapons, and civil defense preparations including protection of the economy, which may require so vast a project as the building of underground cities. Deterrence may now involve so great an expense, to use Adam Smith's phrase, that once again an evident advantage is provided to the nation which can best afford that expense.

II

How important is economic capacity? Belief in its cruciality has recently revived, and its earlier interment as a determinative force now seems premature. To be sure, the newer interpretation, unlike the older concept of EPW, places emphasis on the *pre-attack* utilization of capacity. Reserve capacity is now regarded as relevant primarily in that one power may be reluctant to make a provocative move for fear of stirring a more vigorous defense effort on the part of its rival. To be specific, America's capacity for a substantial expansion of its military establishment provides something of a restraint on aggressive Soviet actions. Due to fear of Soviet economic development, the revised version also lays greater stress on long-range economic growth. Even with such qualifications, however, the question arises whether the revival has not gone too far.

Contemporary discussion of the bearing of growth on security fails to distinguish between three different ways in which such influence may occur:

1. growth may take place in consumption-patterns or the development of industries specifically related to the defense posture of the United States

2. growth may add to taxable capacity, thus providing revenues to finance defense-related government expenditures, and

3. growth may be of the common or garden variety, associated with the creation of industrial capacity and the supplying of consumer goods and services not directly related to the nation's defense posture.

Of the three possible influences currently only (1) is of great importance. Its predominance should occasion no surprise, for it has always been true that devoting additional energies to defense-related activities will improve the defense posture of the nation taking such steps. Such use of national energies is not necessarily related to over-all capacity, which is merely permissive, but depends instead upon the will to employ resources for strategic purposes. For reasons that will become clear shortly, in the nuclear age many types of outlays serve strategic purposes—not only expenditures which enhance military capabilities, but also outlays for family shelter and food storage, public and private buildings with deep basements, plant and equipment located away from main target areas, improved transportation facilities, and the like. Unless growth spills over into such activities, it will add little to security.

Most of the commentators who emphasize the importance of growth for security are, however, thinking in terms of (3). Ordinary economic growth did have great significance when material attrition was a principal aspect of warfare and sufficient time might exist for conversion of industrial facilities. It still, for obvious reasons, possesses substantial domestic political appeal, but under present conditions it has little relevance for security. In fact, it may be argued that the increased specialization in the economy associated with higher incomes, when new facilities are concentrated in prime target areas, detracts from security by increasing vulnerability to attack.

The more sophisticated political observers recognize the irrelevance of (3) and lay the greatest stress on (2). Conditions can be hypothesized under which limited taxable capacity could undermine our defense efforts. Though this is the primary concern of many observers, the emphasis would seem to be misplaced. This is not a critical factor at the present time, and even with modest rates of growth all the revenue requirements for an effective defense program in the foreseeable future can readily be handled. Putting aside the desirability of expansion of certain security-related capacity, it would seem wise to conclude that the concern over America's (allegedly) lagging growth rate is overdone.

There may be legitimate reasons to doubt whether America's productive facilities will actually be turned in the direction of defense-related types of output. Yet, there is no reason to doubt that these facilities are more than adequate to achieve in short order the desired levels of production in these lines. In addition, potential revenue sources seem ample to satisfy anticipated demands. Even with present capacity, the American economy could readily support defense expenditures running well over $100 billion a year. In fact, under emergency conditions, by facilitating the transition through controls, the economy could probably support expenditures of more than $250 billion a year on a temporary basis without destroying the fabric of our kind of economic system. By the end of the decade, normal economic expansion would permit defense expenditures running to $175 billion annually without undue strain.

Military spending appears likely to be a fraction of such a sum. The "high" projection of defense spending for 1970 by Eisenhower's Budget Director, Maurice Stans, just before leaving office was but $47 billion.[2] This may appear to be a "low" Republican estimate. It *is*—being based on the assumptions that deterrence is a static position,

[2] *Ten-Year Projection of Federal Budget Expenditures,* Bureau of the Budget, Executive Office of the President (January, 1961), p. 26.

that defense costs will fall as our missile strength is built up toward present targets, that there is no need for costly counterforce strategies, and that our missile force-requirements will be unaffected by Soviet defensive measures. Such assumptions appear debatable, to say the least, though it is to be noted that the Kennedy Administration, despite the vehemence of its criticism of the nation's defense posture in the campaign, during its first months in office accepted roughly the force-levels contemplated by its predecessor and left largely unaltered the budget estimates for fiscal 1962. It was only the crisis in the summer of 1961 that induced a change in attitude and brought an increase of some $6 billion in planned expenditures. It is to be noted, also, that the build-up, especially in missile forces, is by no means spectacular, and that defense spending still remains well below 10 per cent of Gross National Product. Even if the present efforts are substantially expanded, however, it seems clear that no contemplated increase in spending on the military functions of the Department of Defense would strain our capacity.

In certain respects, present-day advances in military technology are expense-saving, thereby permitting a more economical military establishment. The main barrier to be overcome is development of the nuclear weapons-systems. Once the initial developmental costs are surmounted, missiles provide a relatively cheaper form of deterrence than do bombers, not merely because of reduced manpower and maintenance outlays, but because, at least at present, one avoids the heavy costs of saturating the enemy's defenses entailed by bomber attacks. The procurement cost of missiles is low. A Titan costs $5.1 million, a Minuteman $3 million, and a Polaris $1.1 (though the pro-rated shares of the cost of the Polaris submarine, costing $105 million, make the last system a *relatively* expensive one). Staggering destructive power thus becomes available at moderate cost. One need only imagine the kind of defense posture that could be maintained in the mid-sixties with budgets running to $100 billion per year. Titan missiles by the hundreds and Minutemen even more numerous would bristle in countless hardened sites. Mobile Minutemen would be moved at random over the nation's railroad network. Fleets of Polaris submarines would cruise beneath every sea. Presumably the yield of such weapons will be increased in time. The effect would be "awesome"—to use General Eisenhower's term. Such a force could not be destroyed by a Soviet first strike. It seems most unlikely that the Soviets would launch such an attack, if the counterblow (consisting of, say, a 4,000 megaton attack) would push Russia back to 1929, if not to the days of the Mongols. Until a defense against missiles is uncovered, a force so constituted could almost certainly deter direct attack.

For various reasons the adequacy of fiscal capacity in meeting the requirements of military spending alone may no longer be a complete test of the sufficiency of expenditures on security or of economic growth. A princial reason for asserting that more rapid economic growth may be necessary for defense purposes is the recognition that the increased power of nuclear weapons gradually adds to the complexity and expense of providing a credible deterrent and, what for some purposes is intertwined, the possibility of a sizable part of the population surviving an attack and making good the damage in a decade or two. Such considerations have been stimulated by Herman Kahn's monumental book, *On Thermonuclear*

War.[3] The general position taken therein is: (1) providing a sizable second-strike force is essential though expensive, (2) there is a possibility that war will break out and society can reduce damage and improve its post-attack position by taking defensive steps, and (3) such defensive steps will be necessary to enable the country to resist provocations and blackmail. If the Soviet were able to protect its population and we were not, this nation would face a series of Munichs. Such protective measures are expensive: Underground shelters will have to be built to permit the bulk of the population to survive. Food will have to be stocked—perhaps a two or three year supply. Careful planning and organization will be necessary to maintain morale (and order) in the post-attack period. Enough industrial capacity will have to be placed underground to permit the society to recuperate with fair rapidity.

Kahn's analysis has been objected to, sometimes hysterically, on grounds that it is immoral in rationally contemplating the possibility of a thermonuclear exchange. Nothing could be further from the truth. No doubt, in the Clausewitzian tradition his view represents the extreme extension of military logic, but it is the function of the analyst to examine all of the possibilities. Such a logical exercise is desirable, but one should be aware of possible divergences between the logic and the probabilities. One comment in particular seems appropriate. Kahn may well be overstating the possibility either of a calculated first strike on the United States or of Soviet nuclear sabre-rattling designed to wrest concessions from a frightened West. Political leaders in the past have been bolder at times than their military ana-

[3] Herman Kahn, *On Thermonuclear War* (Princeton: Princeton University Press, 1960).

lysts, but they have also been less bold. These are times which are likely to inspire caution. The risks are very great. The existence of early warning, for example, means that an attacker must fear that the defender's missiles will be on their way and his bombs will fall on empty launchers. Moreover, there would appear to be a fair possibility that society would fail to survive a massive attack as an organized entity, and this possibility would seem greater for a totalitarian society in which control would be loosened in the post-attack period. For any society the problems of morale and of organization would be staggering. Historically Russian leaders, though inclined to stern threats, have been cautious in their actions. It would appear odd if such caution were to be reduced after the advent of The Bomb. Why should the Soviet leaders today rashly jeopardize communist and Soviet gains on what might be a fatal plunge?

Nevertheless, it seems wise to conclude that a sizable program for civil defense and post-attack recuperation should be launched. First, the exchange of blows *might* occur—and it is desirable to minimize the long-run effects of such a cataclysm. Second, Kahn is correct in stating that for some types of deterrence to work, a nation must indicate that it would be willing to accept a blow, which means it must prepare for an attack. Otherwise it would be forced through a series of diplomatic retreats without its ever actually being attacked. The kinds of outlays necessary to reduce the vulnerability of the society in thermonuclear war should be made.

This brings us back to the expenditures specifically related to the defense posture of the United States discussed under (1) above, which include private or government expenditures for shelter space, the storage of food and other vital supplies, or capital

equipment which would survive an attack and facilitate recuperation. Locating plants away from main target areas simultaneously increases the capacity available in a post-attack period and by reducing vulnerability weakens the inducement for attack. At present far too high a proportion of new plants is located in the standard metropolitan areas. The government might well encourage firms to locate new plants in the smaller towns well away from target areas. In addition, the possibility of distributing surplus foods for storage near consuming, rather than producing, areas is too obvious to require more than a mention. A third important step is made possible by the high rate of technical obsolescence of capital equipment in American industry. Since the productive life of such equipment need not be finished, the more valuable items —machine tools, for example—might be stored rather than scrapped and placed in industrial depositories away from the main industrial areas. A requirement to this effect might even be imposed upon firms as part of the projected investment credit program of the administration. It would provide the United States with an important advantage over the Soviet Union, where relatively little equipment is declared obsolete until its productive life is exhausted.

These are examples of quick, inexpensive steps that may be taken to improve the defense posture of the United States. Some may be essential to national survival, but clearly they are not dependent upon economic growth. These steps, including an ambitious and costly civilian defense program, should be taken. But such programs will not exhaust our fiscal capacity. Relative to overall resources, one should be aware of how small the demands of even an expensive program would be. Kahn, who is not inclined to be niggardly, presents a hypothetical budget for 1975, inclusive of nonmilitary defense, of $100 billion[4] which is within our present capabilities. This figure may represent something of a limit, though it must be remembered that Kahn is thinking in terms of the cumulative effects of budgets over a fifteen-year period on our posture, and the longer the delay in inaugurating preparations, the greater will annual expenses be. Nevertheless one finds it difficult to envisage expenditures running much in excess of $100 billion at the end of the decade. Such a figure would represent about 15 per cent of GNP—and it would not constitute an undue strain on our economic capacity.

One additional reason exists for arguing that more rapid economic growth is essential for military security. We are in the infancy of the development of modern weaponry. The power that falls behind in the technological race will probably lose. For example, the development of a reasonably effective defense against missiles by either side would bring a sizable and perhaps a decisive shift in the power balance. Consequently, it may be argued, research and development in the long run is the crucial variable, and the larger the Gross National Product, the larger can be R&D expenditures. In dollar terms, the argument approaches a truism. How significant is it in real terms? The essential ingredient in R&D is scientific personnel. Employment costs of such personnel, without any increase in their number, will automatically reflect growth of the GNP because of the increase in the per capita incomes. With larger percentages of GNP spent for R&D, more personnel can be hired. But the critical limit in terms of specific resources is brainpower; only a very limited portion of the population appears to possess that talent for *useful* scientific research. With brainpower so limited, it is a question whether a nation which spent more than, say, 5 per cent of GNP would be doing any more at the margin than misallocating resources. The limits on the economy's absorptive capacity for R&D expenditures are inherent in the society's curve of intelligence distribution.

Nevertheless, it seems unlikely that the nation will be called on to test these limits during the next decade. R&D expenditures now run about 2.5 per cent of GNP, about half of this representing spending for the defense establishment.[5] The balance, most of which is spending by industry, is undoubtedly inflated because of the loose definition of R&D, which includes expenditures for "product improvement," styling, etc. It is anticipated that during the next decade the proportion of R&D effort devoted to defense activities will fall. Even if it were to rise, however, it could perhaps triple without crossing the brainpower limit. In any event, R&D activities will not be a factor necessitating an expansion of overall economic capacity.

Thus one may conclude that economic capacity is not the critical variable determining the military security of the United States, since it already possesses sufficient capacity to take care of foreseeable strategic requirements. Without undue concern for economic growth, the United States can provide the means for protecting itself against its foe. It has been the absolute growth of the Soviet economy which permits the USSR to mount a nuclear threat that imperils us. Our own growth rate,

---

[4] *Ibid.*, pp. 512–21.

[5] For present and projected expenditures for research and development, see Dexter M. Keezer, "The Outlook of Expenditures on Research and Development During the Next Decade," *American Economic Review* (May, 1960), esp. pp. 357–62.

under present conditions, is relatively unimportant. Soviet missile might would constitute a threat irrespective of the size of our GNP. To be sure, as Soviet defense expenditures grow, the United States will be required to put up "more," but this would be true irrespective of our growth rate. The United States has the capacity to increase expenditures on defense. The real problem is overcoming the traditional reluctance of democracies to divert resources to strategic purposes. That is fundamentally a political rather than an economic problem—and although growth eases the problem somewhat by lessening the need for increasing tax rates, it does not solve it. The courage and the persuasiveness of leadership are essential.

It is clear that a more rapid growth rate would provide Americans with the psychological balm of feeling more secure. Aside from the emollient provided by the avoidance of higher tax rates (which we could surely stand), it is difficult to state precisely why. The reason for feeling safer and less uncertain is different from the old one of providing for massive wartime production. It represents a type of insurance against unknown risks associated with a Malthusian-like projection of defense needs. In the final analysis, even the amount of reassurance it provides may be exaggerated because of failure to take account of the negative side-effects of growth.

III

It is frequently contended that even if growth is not presently critical for defense purposes narrowly construed, it is essential for financing certain specialized activities which may be related to security. Education is the most frequently cited example, though others may be found. On close examination it appears that this contention erects a sizable superstructure of hope and alarm on a limited basis of fact. A principal reason for the misconceptions that exist is that statistics on economic growth, which are market-oriented measures, become increasingly loosely related to the growth of real output in specialized services, as economic growth takes place.

To be sure, the ability to finance education is vital. Other influences, to which it is not always good form to draw attention in a democracy, such as educational standards or the intelligence and energy of those to be educated, are perhaps of greater importance. Still financing is essential, and up to a point increases in expenditures, made possible by growth, will encourage intellectual progress. The chief influence, however, lies not in terms of absolute expenditures, but in permitting a larger *proportion* of the nation's energy to be devoted to intellectual effort. When incomes are rising, increased expenditures are necessary merely to maintain the total energy devoted to education. Consequently, economic growth which permits larger expenditures on education need not result in an improvement in the result.

Much of the expansion of GNP these days reflects changes in the evaluation of service-type returns. The assumption of the statistician must be that changes in quality are reflected in the price, but under the impact of growth it is not unlikely that quality and price (or real and nominal production) move in opposite directions. In some areas—the services of physicians, for example, where quality depends upon expanding knowledge—enormous increases in output are possible. Increase in doctors' incomes, moreover, reflects higher capacity operations, increased efficiency, improved division of labor, as well as increased knowledgeability. But what about those sectors *where quality of service depends upon devotion to pro-*

fessional goals, integrity, the willingness to sacrifice? Here the economic progress of a society, in terms of the available comforts and the ease of making one's living, is quite likely to cause retrogression. The effect may be observed in groups as diverse as research workers, students or military personnel.

In science, it is a common complaint among older researchers that the younger generation, tempted by suburban homes, family life and social activities, is less dedicated to professional goals than was its predecessor. No doubt, there is a good deal of false nostalgia in such observations, but they are also suggestive of the competing claims on the scientist's energy associated with economic growth.

In education, the most important determinants of the quality of the ultimate product are the energy, the co-operation and the intelligence of the recipient. All too frequently, economic growth and the comforts it provides as alternatives, in fact the very ease of attending an educational institution, have meant a corresponding decline in the student's willingness to work hard. The problem of investment in human capital is a difficult one.[6] The chief cost is that of personal dedication and energy; money costs are a smaller part of the whole. The American assumption that money provides the key to increased capacity is probably most wide of the mark on such matters.

Similar observations may be made about military personnel. In the military establishment, one must be prepared to lay down one's life, if necessary, and to accept frequent transfers and other

[6] Cf. Theodore W. Schultz, "Investment in Human Capital," *American Economic Review* (March, 1961). In the writer's judgment, Professor Schultz simplifies the problem by overlooking the importance of the contribution of participants, as well as expenditures, in human capital formation.

disruptions of family life, including lengthy separations. Economic growth and rising incomes permit men to enjoy the luxury of avoiding such discomforts. The resignation rate of officers in recent years no doubt reflects the civilization of the military establishment and the easier transferability of talents to civilian life, but it also reflects the greater ease of making a living in the civilian life, the availability of certain comforts and prestige without sacrifice, and growing pressures for the "normalization" of family life. Rising consumption standards for the populace have increased the cost that the officer must pay in terms of alternatives foregone. Since one thing needful in the officer is the willingness to make sacrifices, many of the present difficulties of the military establishment may be attributed to economic growth.

Economists, because they desire to limit themselves to measurable aggregates, have tended to take too material a view of resources, and consequently ignore the issue posed by the efficiency of the population. Implicitly, though invalidly, they assume that other things remain equal as income expands. Yet the cost and the ultimate worth of services such as education may be wholly unconnected. Whenever dedication enters, nothing is measurable in regard to services. The only thing that can be stated is that the GNP figure ought not to be taken too seriously; it is not an adequate measure of what the nation can or cannot accomplish.

Those who assume that economic growth is conducive to security fail to take account of concurrent trends. The leisure and luxuries provided by economic growth sap the energies of a population. A public grown accustomed to high living standards may be too "spoiled" to accept sacrifice. Yet if a nuclear war is unlikely, if limited war, guerrilla wars and subversion (in short, dirty warfare) constitute the likely shape of future conflict, then capacity for endurance becomes the essential element in defense. Consequently one may argue that the side-effects of growth militate against security.

Many contemporary phenomena—including educational problems, the difficulties of the armed forces, and even economic growth itself—are symptoms of a more fundamental malady: the lessened energy and drive of the American public. Recognition of this underlying reality may explain the appeal of references to sacrifice in public statements. But, speeches aside, whenever the difficulties facing the nation are considered, the solution automatically proposed is—economic growth. It can solve all our problems—education, security, depressed areas, etc. Just as in the forties it was argued that "the only cure for defects of democracy is more democracy," so at present many believe that the only cure for side-effects of economic growth is more growth.

Even the popular pastime of searching for the "national purpose" reflects the deeper malady. A nation which has a national purpose does not have to establish study commissions to devote energy to uncovering the national purpose and how it can be achieved; it goes about its job. The national purpose is built into the value systems of individuals; it does not have to be propagandized or even analyzed (save by scholars). Discussion of what is the national purpose is another luxury item made possible by substantial resources and, one may observe, generally consumed in comfortable homes or over comfortable restaurant tables.

Failing energies, the refusal to face actual problems, and the assumption that solutions are to be obtained by economic means are not characteristic of the United States alone. These are ailments of Western society generally.

A more dramatic illustration may be found in France, where the officer corps, unlike its American counterpart, has been isolated from the general community and has not shared in rising living standards or changes in values. Consequently a widening gap exists between the army and contemporary French society, tenuously bridged by President De Gaulle. A group bearing military values has become estranged from a society which in its view is incapable of sacrifice, service and obedience. The officers are embittered by that ease and comfort made possible by recent economic growth; they spurn the compromises that a satisfied, comfortable society is eager to make. It is a commonplace to observe that recent French history can only be understood in light of an army which has been overseas for twenty years, engaged continually in warfare, and yet in its own view has not been given the support necessary to win a war during that period because of the defects of the society from which it sprang.

Brooks Adams, who argued in his *Law of Civilization and Decay* that societies are undermined by peace permitting economic virtues to destroy military virtues, possesses contemporary relevance. Growth is a two-edged sword. The luxuries made possible by growth foster a lackadaisicalness and a heedlessness of the future reminiscent of Tennyson's *Lotos-eaters*.[7] Nothing fails like success. The high living standards which sap energy breed complacency.

[7] Round and round the spicy downs the
   yellow Lotos-dust is blown.
 We have had enough of action, and
   of motion...
 Let us swear an oath, and keep it
   with an open mind,
 In the hollow Lotos-land to live and
   lie reclined
 On the hills like Gods together, careless of mankind.
                              Tennyson

The general assumption among economists and laymen that the nation would be more secure if resources were greater is but a wry half-truth. To be sure, *ceteris paribus,* additional resources would permit more effective preparation for possible hostilities, but it is also true that, *ceteris paribus,* a populace with lower consumption standards and less demanding expectations will be in a better position to cope with external pressures. One is reminded of Sir Charles Snow's observation, "We are becoming existential societies...living in the same world with future-directed societies."[8] The lack of resources can be compensated for, the growth of "existential views" unfortunately cannot be. In the long run a nation's chief resource is the national character. Increased material resources are but a poor substitute where the sense of duty or sacrifice has failed and where the soothing rationalizations of politics are welcomed by the public as balm in Gilead.

[8] Sir Charles Snow, *Science and Government* (Cambridge: Harvard University Press, 1961), p. 80.

THE MILITARY DIMENSION

Chapter 9

The contemporary student of politics and strategy wonders whether Clausewitz's famous aphorism that "war is nothing but the continuation of political relations by other means" retains its original meaning. Clausewitz wrote in an age when the concept of limited war was rooted in the temper and technology of the times. But in the memory of living men the political interests of victor and vanquished alike have twice been swept away by the force and passion of total war. And now man has added nuclear weapons and intercontinental ballistic missiles to his arsenal, whose destructiveness raises serious doubts as to whether all-out war can still be contemplated as a viable alternative in the pursuit of political objectives.

In fact the difficulty of using massive nuclear weapons in the pursuit of specific political objectives may well lead to a revision of relevant capability analysis. No one has yet developed an approach which would permit countries to dispense with such weapons; they appear to be essential as deterrents and as symbols. Yet it is by no means clear what, if any, positive functions are served by having them—how, in other words, their possession can be translated into concrete political advantage. Indeed weapons of such massive destructive capacity appear to carry with them the greatest inhibitions on their employment. The argument that force is not the most effective way of exercising power because it calls forth violent resistance is particularly appropriate to the kind of force that is available to some countries today and that seems bound to become available to more countries in the future, despite strong efforts to prevent nuclear proliferation by treaty.

But in spite of this one is still compelled to examine international relations in the light of war-making capability, because of what the sociologist would call a cultural lag—man's inability to adjust on short notice to drastically changed circumstances. "No single weapon—however revolutionary—suffices to change human nature; political trends depend on men and societies as much as on weapons. . . ."[1] Because nuclear weapons happened to be developed at a moment in history when two states were overwhelmingly more powerful than all the others, the anarchy of the system was for a time reduced to a precarious bipolar balance of nuclear terror. Since then other powers have entered the nuclear club or may do so, so that one of the mockeries of the modern age is that peace itself seems to rest upon the mutual fear inspired by the magnitude of nuclear destructiveness. States have arrived at such a deadlock in their search for security that peace seems to depend upon the degree to which rival states can maintain the so-called balance of terror. On the other hand nuclear weapons in the hands of many can only add to the insecurity and instability of the entire international system.

Although in a sense apprehension of what others can do has always been a basis for restraint in international behavior, this is a dubious foundation upon which to rest one's hopes for continued peace and stability. The system is highly volatile; there are no guarantees against the kinds of miscalculations, destructive impulses, or even accidents which could blow it up.

So long as war lurks in the background of international politics, the question is not whether states require military power but how much and what kinds of military power are most appropriate for achieving a given state's objectives. The answers to this question involve more than calculations of relative technological or productive capacity. The psychology engendered by an arms race profoundly affect the entire international climate; an arms race, like war itself, seems to possess its own inner dynamic. Military superiority seems to transform itself from a means to an end. Diplomats must negotiate from what Secretary of State Acheson called "positions of strength," yet often policies of building positions of strength are pursued with such energy and dedication that the ultimate purpose—negotiation and settlement—tends to be overlooked. As one leading analyst of power politics has put it, "The most serious wars are fought in order to make one's own country militarily stronger, or more often, to prevent another country from becoming militarily stronger, so that there is much justification for the epigram that 'the principal cause of war is war itself'."[2]

[1] Raymond Aron, *On War* (Garden City, N.Y.: Doubleday Anchor Books, 1959), p. 2.

[2] Edward Hallett Carr, *The Twenty-Years' Crisis, 1919–1939* (London: Macmillan & Co., Ltd., 1951), p. 111.

How can statesmen and strategists avoid this dilemma? One set of criteria by which a nation might sanely and safely measure its military power has been suggested by Louis Halle: (1) to have adequate force available, and *known* to be available, for deterring or successfully meeting any threats to its vital interests; (2) to leave no doubt in the minds of others that it has the will and competence to use this force effectively; and (3) to leave no doubt in the minds of others that its force is under responsible control.[3] The policy maker, confronted by an enormous range of weapons in the hands of a potential enemy and restricted by the scarcity of resources available to him, must choose among a baffling host of weapons systems whose adequacy is difficult to determine because of the availability of countervailing systems to others. Uncertainty as to what constitutes the most effective distribution of the components of military power obliges the major powers to prepare for more than one type of war. Nuclear powers must still arm for conventional wars in the hope that nuclear conflicts can be avoided.

In announcing the "massive retaliation" policy, Secretary of State Dulles complained that it was too bothersome and too expensive to prepare for conventional *and* nuclear wars, for limited and unlimited wars, for wars in the tropics, in the Arctic, and places in between. While one can sympathize with those who must confront such problems, the powers have found that there is no substitute for a balanced weapons system permitting a wide range of alternative uses, if they can afford it. Few states, unless their national survival is clearly at stake, are anxious to build up their weapons systems to such a magnitude as to require them indefinitely to forego many other values. Nor can any nation afford to neglect the broad range of ancillary conditions upon which modern military power must rest: education, health, basic scientific research, capital investment, strategic intelligence, foreign aid as a means of supporting alliances and overseas bases, and so on down a long list. However compelling any concept of "adequate" levels of military power may be, it must ultimately be weighed against corresponding values in other directions. Sacrifices which have to be made to achieve greater security are directly experienced; the benefits are only very indirectly experienced, mostly in terms of the absence of greater insecurity. In this contest between directly felt satisfactions and benefits, it takes an act of will to decide in favor of the expenditure of manpower, wealth and resources to attain nothing but, at best, a lower level of insecurity.

A related factor in the measurement of military capabilities is that of mobilized versus potential military strength. Historically no nation has ever been fully mobilized in peacetime. Normally peace-time levels of military strength are set according to prevaling assumptions about the amount of military power necessary to achieve national goals. The higher a nation

[3] Louis Halle, "The Role of Force in Foreign Policy," *Social Science* (1959), 30, 203–8.

rates goals which are attainable only through military power or the greater its sense of insecurity, "the larger will be the amounts of military strength that are preferred."[4] Some societies, such as the Spartan or more recently the German, have placed a high value on military virtues and as a direct consequence of this value pattern, were able to sustain the costs of mobilization. Soviet society was in a quasi-mobilized state for decades after the October 1917 revolution, calling for great sacrifices in peacetime as well as in war for the attainment of national goals. Only in recent years have Soviet leaders been forced to acknowledge that the burden of all-out military preparedness cannot be sustained indefinitely in the face of a population striving for more of the values of a consumer-oriented society.

Today the distinction between mobilized and potential military strength is less significant because the great powers must maintain a large ready capability even in time of peace for any and all military eventualities. If protection and deterrence are to be achieved, the advent of nuclear striking power now requires that a large share of the industrial might of a state be devoted to military ends long before war becomes imminent. Even so, military priorities are still far more ambiguous and contingent in time of peace than in time of war.

Military power is meaningful only in relation to strategy, and strategy is meaningful only in relation to national objectives. It is a course of ruination for a country to develop costly strategies which have little or no relation to the permissible or attainable goals. A nation uncertain about its objectives will squander its economic substance and engage in untenable and irresponsible strategies that alienate public opinion at home as well as abroad.[5]

As the magnitude of the security problem grows and the military claims upon the lives, resources, and direction of society increase, there is the latent danger of the transformation of national life in the direction of the garrison state. But there is an even more subtle aspect to the problem, and that is the risk that military considerations will take precedence over political considerations in the conduct of foreign policy itself. "When we recall," writes Bernard Brodie, "that both sides prior to the first World War failed utterly, with incalculable resulting costs, to adjust adequately their thinking to something as evolutionary as the machine gun, and that such failures have been characteristic rather than exceptional in the history of war, we can hardly be sanguine about the adjustments to be made to such a change as represented by developments in nuclear weapons."[6]

Time and again societies have turned the most crucial decisions

---

[4] Klaus Knorr, *The War Potential of Nations* (Princeton, N.J.: Princeton University Press, 1956), p. 21.

[5] See Charles M. Fergusson, Jr., "Military Forces and National Objectives," *Military Review* (1955), 30, pp. 194–204. Reprinted in part in the second edition of this book.

[6] Bernard Brodie, "Nuclear Weapons: Strategic or Tactical?" *Foreign Affairs*, (1954) 32, No. 2, p. 219.

affecting their destiny over to incredibly busy men limited by training, experience, or responsibility, with little or no motivation to examine the non-military concomitants of international politics. In 1914, European diplomats handcuffed themselves to the mobilization schedules of the general staffs; in 1939, it was the folly of the Maginot line; in 1949, it was American surprise at the rapidity with which the Soviet Union achieved a nuclear explosion; in 1960, it was the hotly debated credibility gap.

Generals and admirals, often extremely capable, are frequently the first to recognize the inherent limitations of their profession and request the political leadership to specify guidelines for policy, yet unless such guidelines are provided, defense planners may gradually lose sight of the limits of their viewpoints. Those viewpoints must always be subject to criticism from outside structures of a military hierarchy governed by habit, tradition, interest, and formal authority.

In summary the assessment of military power must be conducted within the context of political purposes and human values, not outside it. The honest realist who accepts the proposition that military power is a concomitant of the state system assumes the obligation to appraise that power by the strictest canons of *both* political necessity *and* human values.

1. Military Power

E. H. CARR

Edward Hallett Carr, a distinguished British statesman, historian and scholar, is currently a Fellow of Trinity College, Cambridge. Among more than a dozen major works in the field of diplomatic history and international relations, his book THE TWENTY YEARS' CRISIS, 1919–1939 *is a landmark. He recently completed an extensive study entitled* WHAT IS HISTORY? *(1963).*

...The supreme importance of the military instrument lies in the fact that the *ultima ratio* of power in international relations is war. Every act of the state, in its power aspect, is directed to war, not as a desirable weapon, but as a weapon which it may require in the last resort to use. Clausewitz' famous aphorism that "war is nothing but the continuation of political relations by other means" has been repeated with approval both by Lenin and by the Communist International; and Hitler

THE TWENTY YEARS' CRISIS, *1919–1939 (London: Macmillan & Co., Ltd., 1951), pp. 109–11. Reprinted by permission.*

meant much the same thing when he said that "an alliance whose object does not include the intention to fight is meaningless and useless." In the same sense, Mr. Hawtrey defines diplomacy as "potential war." These are half-truths. But the important thing is to recognize that they are half true. War lurks in the background of international politics just as revolution lurks in the background of domestic politics. There are few European countries where, at some time during the past thirty years, potential revolution has not been an important factor in politics; and the international community has in this respect the closest analogy to those states where the possibility of revolution is most frequently and most conspicuously present to the mind.

Potential war being thus a dominant factor in international politics, military strength becomes a recognized standard of political values. Every great civilization of the past has enjoyed in its day a superiority of military power. The Greek city-state rose to greatness when its hoplite armies proved more than a match for the Persian hordes. In the modern world, Powers (the word itself is significant enough) are graded according to the quality and the supposed efficiency of the military equipment, including manpower, at their disposal. Recognition as a Great Power is normally the reward of fighting a successful large-scale war. Germany after the Franco-Prussian War, the United States after the war with Spain, and Japan after the Russo-Japanese War are familiar recent instances. The faint doubt attaching to Italy's status as a Great Power is partly due to the fact that she has never proved her prowess in a first-class war. Any symptom of military inefficiency or unpreparedness in a Great Power is promptly reflected in its political status. . . .

These facts point the moral that foreign policy never can, or never should be divorced from strategy. The foreign policy of a country is limited not only by its aims, but also by its military strength, or, more accurately, by the ratio of its military strength to that of other countries. The most serious problem involved in the democratic control of foreign policy is that no government can afford to divulge full and frank information about its own military strength, or all the knowledge it possesses about the military strength of other countries. Public discussions of foreign policy are therefore conducted in partial or total ignorance of one of the factors which must be decisive in determining it. . . . Many contemporary books and speeches about international politics are reminiscent of those ingenious mathematical problems which the student is invited to solve by ignoring the weight of the elephant. The solutions proposed are neat and accurate on the abstract plane, but are obtained by leaving out of account the vital strategic factor. . . . If every prospective writer on international affairs in the last twenty years had taken a compulsory course in elementary strategy, reams of nonsense would have remained unwritten.

Military power, being an essential element in the life of the state, becomes not only an instrument, but an end in itself. Few of the important wars of the last one hundred years seem to have been waged for the deliberate and conscious purpose of increasing either trade or territory. The most serious wars are fought in order to make one's own country militarily stronger or, more often, to prevent another country from becoming militarily stronger, so that there is much justification for the epigram that "the principal cause of war is war itself." . . .

2. Changing Attitudes Towards War

BERNARD BRODIE

Bernard Brodie is Professor of Political Science at the University of California at Los Angeles. Previous to that he taught at Yale University and was on the staff of the RAND Corporation. He is the author of a number of distinguished contributions to international relations, including SEA POWER IN THE MACHINE AGE *and* STRATEGY IN THE MISSILE AGE. *Professor Brodie has held numerous visiting professorships and consultantships.*

. . .

World War II was not followed by a literature of disillusionment or rejection. But neither was there any special glorification of the war; it had been too costly and bitter for that. The prevailing mood following World War II was that the use of military power was legitimate if, but only if, the ends it served were essentially anti-war ends —as for example preventing or resisting aggression, which is to say deterrence. This idea was enshrined in the enforcement provisions (Chapter VII) of the U.N. Charter.

One of the important changes that World War I began and World War II completed was the liquidation from positions of power, if not from existence altogether, of that aristocratic and monarchical caste that had previously ruled affairs in most of Europe and in Japan. This caste had derived many of its moral and political values, including attitudes towards war, from the Middle Ages. The virtual wiping out of this formerly powerful caste in those nations which it previously controlled is a change of enormous consequences for the behavior of governments which I think we too frequently overlook.

Another cataclysmic event in World War II was the advent of nuclear weapons, which were at once recognized by almost all people for the terribly revolutionary things that they are. They were greeted with the most apprehension by the very people who at that time had a monopoly of them.

For some years the government and people of the United States felt that they had reason to worry whether the Russians would be as sensitive to the horrible dangers of nuclear warfare as we felt ourselves to be from the outset, but by now the answer has clearly been accepted to be in the affirmative. Actually the Chinese too have been sending similar signals—like their vehement denial in late 1963 of Khrushchev's charge (following their denunciation of him for retreating from the Cuban missile crisis) that they did not understand the horrors of nuclear war.[1]

From Henry A. Kissinger and Bernard Brodie, BUREAUCRACY, POLITICS, AND STRATEGY, *Security Studies Project, University of California, Los Angeles, 1968. Reprinted by permission.*

[1] The relevant Chinese note of September 1963 is translated and reproduced in *Survival*, Vol. 5 (Nov.–Dec. 1963), pp. 263–68.

We are now some years further away from World War II than the beginning of that war was from the end of World War I, which was just under twenty-one years. The ending of World War II is already more than twenty-three years in the past. The world has since known a number of wars, and some of them have been difficult and prolonged enough for those engaged directly in them, but in comparison with the two world wars, they have all been small.

The United States has been mainly involved in the Korean War of 1950–53, and in the Vietnam war that still goes on today. In the case of Korea, we backed into a kind of war that ran counter to one of our axioms of the time that "all modern wars must be total wars," and we did so out of a kind of helpless feeling that our position of world leadership left us little choice to do anything else. The aggression which we intervened to counter, on the whole successfully, was indeed brusque and arrogant. Our Secretary of State had early in 1950 described our "defense perimeter" in terms which left Korea outside, and even though we had no direct treaty commitments to defend it, our initial responses were guided by the conviction that someone did have to resist aggression and that there was no other nation which could do so effectively. That we managed, after these decisions were made, to get the United Nations involved more as a cover than as a meaningful source of assistance occurred through a mere diplomatic fluke —which took the form of the Soviet delegate to the United Nation's Security Council boycotting that body while the critical votes were being taken.

The Korean War was the first example of modern limited war, about which there has since been a good deal of theorizing. By modern limited war— as distinct from earlier types—we mean a kind of war in which at least one of the powers involved is a major power and is deliberately refraining from using the most powerful and terrible military capabilities under its control, especially nuclear weapons. Of the Korean War, we must remember also that our military leaders in Washington considered it throughout the period of the most active hostilities to be, in the words of General Omar Bradley, then chairman of the Joint Chiefs of Staff: "the wrong war, at the wrong place, at the wrong time, and with the wrong enemy." By this statement he was giving voice to the conviction then strongly felt in Washington that the real enemy was the Soviet Union, and that the aggression in Korea has been simply a *ruse de guerre* to absorb our attention and forces in that far-off area while the Russians prepared a massive attack against Western Europe, which for a while was considered imminent. This was a huge and potentially dangerous misreading of Soviet intentions, but we do seem to have adopted a more mature official outlook in the years since.

The Vietnamese War has had similar yet distinctive characteristics. We got involved the way we did mostly out of the feeling that after the French defeat and departure, there was again no one else to do what we thought needed doing, which was to carry out what we called "containment."[2] There were various other related attitudes and perhaps fixations, such as notions bound up in the so-called "Domino Theory." Neither in Vietnam nor in Korea were the dimensions of our ultimate com-

---

[2] The word "we" refers in the first instance to Administration attitudes, including the presidencies of Eisenhower and Kennedy as well as Johnson, but it is worth remembering that dissent from Administration actions concerning Vietnam was hardly voiced prior to 1966 and remained a minority opinion in the United States at least until the Tet Offensive of early 1968.

mitment at all foreseen in the beginning; even so the commitment in both wars was kept very far short of full mobilization.

In both wars we have shown ourselves willing to settle for a negotiated compromise peace while exercising massive restraint against the militarily inferior enemy. In the Korean War we never bombed beyond the Yalu River, although the major enemy was China. In the case of Vietnam, we refrained not only from the use of nuclear weapons, which we now had in enormous numbers, but from any attempt at invasion of North Vietnam. The bombing in the North, at this writing largely suspended, has always been of a controlled and relatively constricted kind, and we have also exercised great restraint on the shipping lanes leading to Haiphong.

I mention these points not to attempt in the least degree to justify our political and military intervention either in Korea or Vietnam, but rather to point out that the United States, which is a very great power, is practicing a kind of behavior marked by conspicuous military and political restraint such as would have been totally unthinkable prior to 1914. Some of course hold that we have been too restrained, and have thus made ourselves militarily ineffective; but the tide of opinion is all in the opposite direction. Any future president of the United States, at least in the next decade or so, is likely to view the personal disaster of President Johnson in Vietnam as a compelling reason for not intervening in like manner somewhere else, rather than as a good reason for throwing off restraint. And surely if there has been any degree of enthusiasm for the war in Vietnam or elsewhere, it has not been particularly noticeable. The same was true of Korea.

I do not wish to concentrate attention mainly on American experience since World War II, except insofar as that experience is vivid to us. With respect to the changes of attitude I have emphasized, I do not see that the experience of France either in Vietnam or later Algeria was much different. In both cases the public attitude in the metropolitan country became one of being thoroughly fed up with a military operation abroad which was simply not prospering. In the case of Algeria it is all the more remarkable in that this territory had been considered legally a department of metropolitan France for very many years. If we consider the Middle Eastern war of June, 1967, the attitude of the Israelis before the event seems to be well summed up by one of them who was quoted as saying: "If there is a war, we will win; but who needs it?" And if the Arabs had a markedly greater degree of enthusiasm, it was not reflected in the verve of their fighting.

Thus, certain attitudes towards war which national governments used to be able to count upon, or feel obliged to take into account, have gone out of fashion or even out of existence since 1945, and even more markedly since 1914. The kind of mindless fervor which brought people out on the streets when their national government declared war seems quite definitely a thing of the past, except possibly in Cairo. Personal heroism is of course always respected, but rather little is made of it nowadays, and war heroism seems not to enjoy a much higher status than peace-time heroism.

National glory is clearly no longer a commodity of much importance in the minds of statesmen trying to decide for or against resort to arms in particular instances. Conquest of foreign territories, the passion for which has been one of the greatest war markers since ancient times, seems no longer to move people as a suitable reason for giving up the relative comfort and safety of peace. Even the regaining of lost territories, or what we used to call *irredentas,* the thirst for which so inspired French foreign policy from 1871 to 1914, tends to be put in perspective when the means of regaining them involve the chance of nuclear war. In Germany today there is universal persuasion that reunification, though desirable, must be accomplished *ohne Krieg*—without war. For this reason among others, the danger of war today within the European community, the former cradle of modern wars, seems lower than at almost any other time in history—a factor which has much to do with the decay of both NATO and of the Warsaw Pact.

How then must we relate the changes I have described, as well as many others that I do not have space to mention or develop, to the probabilities of war in the future, or rather to the probabilities of specific kinds of war among specific nations? In order to do so, we should want to start with an exploration of the basic causes of war, about which much has indeed been written. But if we do so we will immediately find that by far the greater portion of it is scientifically rubbish. What should be abundantly apparent by now is that the approach to the study of the causes of war is inevitably a highly eclectic approach, necessarily combining with a deep and accurate understanding of history such modern insights as psychology, cultural anthropology, and political science may offer.

3. The World Today: Twenty Years Later

COLONEL CHARLES M. FERGUSSON, JR.

Colonel Charles M. Fergusson is on the staff of the United States Army War College. He is the author of numerous articles, including "The Study of Military Strategy" (MILITARY REVIEW, April 1965) and "Military Forces and National Objectives" (MILITARY REVIEW, 1955), which appeared in the second edition of this book.

With the light of a thousand suns the nuclear age dawned at 0530, 16 July 1945 on the New Mexican desert at Alamogordo. Man had set off his

MILITARY REVIEW, *45 (July 1965), pp. 3-10. Reprinted by permission.*

first atomic device. The European phase of the greatest war in history had already ended with the surrender of Nazi Germany on 7 May. The blast in New Mexico was to signal the end of the war in the Pacific.

[More than] twenty years have

now elapsed, years of neither peace nor war, a period which has come to be called the cold war. At periodic intervals, it seems highly desirable to take stock of one's situation. As Abraham Lincoln once observed, "If we could first know where we are and whither we are tending, we could better judge what to do and how to do it."

It seems...appropriate, therefore, ...to assess some of the major factors existing in the world situation today and to consider some of the military implications growing out of this situation.

It is appropriate to begin this assessment of the world situation by noting the significance of war itself. World Wars I and II have come to be called the civil wars of the West. It is tragic to recall that these wars were initiated by Western, Christian, industrial nations. Although many changes have occurred since World War II, the legacy from the war is everywhere evident—witness the two Germanys, two Vietnams, two Koreas, and two Chinas.

POWER SHIFT

Europe emerged from World War II in a severely weakened state. Power shifted out of Europe—westward to the United States and eastward to the Soviet Union. A large part of Eastern Europe was physically occupied by the Soviet Union and today remains, to a greater or lesser extent, under the domination of Soviet tanks.

The Western European nations, victors and vanquished alike, were seriously weakened. Their colonial empires melted away rapidly as a result of this weakness and the antiwhite, anticolonial attitudes which had been strengthened by the war. Today, the most populous European nation, West Germany, ranks only ninth in population among the nations of the world. Or, stating it another way, none of the eight most populous nations today is European.

The two World Wars apparently have proved congenial to the fortunes of communism. World War I provided the opportunity for seizing control of Russia, which thus became the first Communist state. And although suffering severely during World War II, the Soviet Union emerged from that war with enhanced prestige and power, a power to be reckoned with throughout the world. The Soviet Union and her Communist allies moved quickly into the vacuums created in Europe and Asia by the rapid removal of German and Japanese power.

As for the United States, the war ended the Great Depression and stimulated a period of unprecedented economic prosperity. It gave great impetus to scientific and technological development, producing, among other things, the nuclear weapon. It greatly increased our power, both absolute and relative, and also increased our willingness to utilize that power. It literally forced us into the active leadership of the non-Communist world—it seems on a permanent basis.

SCIENCE AND TECHNOLOGY

Of even greater importance than war—but not unrelated to war—is the impact science and technology have had on the world situation. Directly or indirectly, most of the world's realities—for good or for ill—stem from the pervading impact of science and technology, and they have permitted man in certain limited areas of the world to conquer his nonhuman environment. Ironically, just when science and technology had made it feasible to overcome man's traditional enemies of fire, famine, flood, and disease, science compensated for this success by producing the nuclear weapon, giving man something new to worry about.

. . .

The world has become a much smaller place since the end of World War II. At that time, the range of transportation was measured in hundreds of kilometers: today, that range is measured in thousands of kilometers. In 1945 man's fastest speed was measured in hundreds of kilometers per hour; today, manned orbiting satellites exceed 28,163 kilometers per hour.

With regard to communications times, the world has shrunk even smaller. Until the recent past, message time was identical to travel time; today, news can be transmitted almost instantly around the globe. Moreover, with television and *Early Bird,* we can sit in our living rooms and watch events as they actually happen all over the world. It is becoming increasingly difficult for us to understand how the Battle of New Orleans could be fought two weeks after the Treaty of Ghent had ended the War of 1812.

POWER OF EXPLOSIVES

The power of explosives has also increased tremendously. The nuclear weapon represented a growth in the power of explosives which was different in kind, as well as in degree. And it is sobering to realize that a single weapon carried by a single vehicle can release greater energy than that of all the explosives used in all of the wars that have taken place during the entire history of the world.

No one can, without considerable difficulty, exaggerate the importance of the big bomb. It has changed the mean-ing of geography. For the first time in many years it has made the United States vulnerable to sudden, direct attack. It has required vast additional outlays for new weapons without their really being able to replace the older, more conventional types of military force. Most of the major differences between nations today involve the nuclear weapon in one way or another. The Sino-Soviet split and the current French-American differences can be cited as examples.

. . .

One can hardly describe the current world situation without recognizing the reality of communism and the Communist nations.

The gains of the Soviet Union in the early postwar period are particularly remarkable considering her inferior power position relative to the West, the absolute American monopoly of the nuclear weapon during this period, and the destruction suffered by the Soviet Union during the war. Also remarkable and unexpected was the Soviet's rapid development of the atomic weapon, the thermonuclear weapon, and the *Sputnik* satellite.

"POLYCENTRISM"

It seems clear that the Communists have enjoyed successes and have also suffered failures. Today, we see the Communist world rended by what has come to be called "polycentrism." But the fact remains that communism continues to present a great threat to the non-Communist world. Had it not been for the United States' efforts, it seems all but certain that much more of the world would have fallen to the Communists since World War II. And even today, in spite of Communist troubles and the Free World effort, the issue remains in doubt on many frontiers. It is sobering to speculate on what would happen if United States power did not exist on the frontiers of freedom—in Vietnam, Korea, Germany, Turkey, and Greece.

Although communism poses much more than a military threat, its military implications are many and varied. The Soviet nuclear capability poses the only direct military threat to the United States in the foreseeable future. The Communist nations have shown the ability and willingness to allocate great resources to military purposes in peace as in war, and they have demonstrated many alternative ways of employing force, particularly guerrilla and anti-guerrilla warfare.

They have shown a respect for force but also a willingness to use it whenever and wherever it suited their purposes. The Soviet Union has shown considerable talent for getting other Communist nations and Communist leaders in non-Communist nations to do her bidding.

FOREIGN POLICY

Soon after World War II, the weakness of the Western European nations and the seriousness of the Communist threat became evident. American power had to be applied actively to keep our allies and erstwhile enemies away from Communist domination.

As a result, the United States abruptly changed her foreign policy and proceeded to provide massive support —including U.S. troops—to many threatened areas. In this process the United States entered into alliances with many other nations throughout the world.

In general, our postwar policy has been remarkably successful in Europe but less so elsewhere. But even in Europe, as our allies became more prosperous, and as the Soviet threat was thought by them to have diminished, some of them, notably the French, have become increasingly independent, leading to some disarry in the alliance. General Charles de Gaulle, for example, vetoed the admission of Britain into the European Common Market in January 1963, recognized Communist China a year later, and...articulated and pursued policies that deviated substantially from those held by the United States and most of the other NATO allies.

One of the great questions of the day is how to deal with allies. What kind of arrangement, organization, and integration is needed? What kind is feasible? How much leadership is the United States able and willing to exercise?

. . .

Military force is quite clearly very much a part of the current world situation. Military operations have recently occurred or are now occurring in many widespread areas—Vietnam, Laos, Yemen, Malaysia, Cyprus, and the Congo. We are constantly being reminded of the reality of the nuclear weapon. Military leaders have assumed a large role in many nations, and not only in the developing nations.

The continuing importance of military force seems all but certain. Because there are many more players on the world stage—more people, more nations, more leaders, and progressively more in prospect—the stage grows ever smaller. A number of the nations are experiencing revolutions of several varieties; for others, their expectations greatly exceed their capabilities.

Since there are more military

forces available, and so many disputed boundaries, almost any kind of conflict is possible—from thermonuclear war to cold war penetrations. It does seem likely that the situation of nuclear plenty will tend to make more limited types of conflicts likely. But even these limited conflicts will be conducted under the umbrella of the big bombs. This nuclear situation tends to provide less powerful nations with considerable room for maneuver against the more powerful nations, as witness the remarkable ability of Cuba to defy the United States and the Soviet Union, as well as the United Nations in 1962.

Military affairs now assume a greater importance than ever before. At the same time, because of the devastation that nuclear war would bring to all participants, the primary military mission has become one of deterrence, or what has been called the non-use of military force. This is, indeed, a significant change in military strategy.

Although peace has been a national objective for most nations for most of the time, it comes closer now to being the national objective. Peace is still by no means an absolute objective, but it is much closer to an absolute objective than in pre-bomb days.

For the first time in many years, the United States is vulnerable to a direct attack of unprecedented suddenness and severity. Moreover, the United States is committed to the defense of many other nations. These nations are vulnerable not only to direct attack, but to many other types of threats as well.

For the first time in our peacetime history, the United States is devoting massive amounts of resources to military force. Forces must be ready at all times. No longer can the United States rely on allies or geography to provide time for mobilization.

Because of the increased importance of military force and the vast resources devoted to it, more people are interested in military decisions. The military profession no longer belongs to the uniformed officer. Intelligent citizens in all walks of life are interested—and quite properly interested—in military decisions. The military officer is having to learn to share his profession with statesmen, politicians, scientists, academic strategists, diplomats, economists, and bureaucrats.

There is an important international aspect of this sharing. To the extent that U.S. forces serve to defend or to implicate other nations, it follows that these nations and their citizens have an interest—and again a proper interest—in such forces.

We should note, too, that science and technology continue to exercise a profound impact on military force. The contribution that physical science can make to military force has long been recognized, and if any lingering doubt existed on that contribution, World War II demolished it completely. But today, science and technology are also being applied increasingly to military strategy and to management. Techniques of economic analysis, war gaming, mathematical models, systems analysis, and automatic data processing are realities and are clearly here to stay.

The age in which we live has been called many things. It has been called the Age of Crisis, the Age of Revolution, the Age of Insecurity, the Age of Nationalism; it has been called the Age of the Masses—masses of people, mass education, mass communications, mass production, and mass destruction; it has been called the Age of Explosions—explosions of nations, explosions of people, explosions of weapons, explosions of knowledge.

Our age seems to be all of these

things. It also seems clearly to be an age in which the challenge to the military officer is greater than at any other time in history.

4. What is the Threat?

COLONEL IRVING HEYMONT

Colonel Irving Heymont, U.S. Army, Retired, is a veteran of World War II and the Korean War. He has also served with the North Atlantic Treaty Organization and on the faculty of the U.S. Army Command and General Staff College. He is presently with the Research Analysis Corporation of McLean, Virginia.

A major problem in long-range military studies and cost effectiveness analyses is a proper delineation of the threat. The problem stems from the uncertainties of the future, the diversity in areas where U.S. forces must be prepared to operate, and the diversity in potential enemies. Disregard of these problems could lead to forces prepared to fight the wrong kind of war at the wrong time and place, and with serious vulnerabilities. General Edward Braddock's defeat by the Indians in Pennsylvania in 1755 was, in part, a result of the failure of British force planners to anticipate properly the requirements of colonial frontier warfare.

Planning the composition of military forces is based on the existing or potential military threat to the execution of national policy. In the period following the Civil War, U.S. Army forces were designed primarily to secure the Western frontier and to maintain

MILITARY REVIEW, 47 (April 1967), pp. 47–55. Reprinted by permission.

seacoast defenses. Following the Spanish-American War, the strength and composition of the U.S. military forces changed in keeping with the new national policy based on a secured Western frontier and maintenance of overseas possessions.

The major source of information on the threat is usually a threat study. This is a formulation and analysis of the expected or real situation from which to derive the combination of enemy capabilities that can be used to counter a proposed U.S. military capability. Other source materials include target arrays, foreign technology, and long-range forecasts. A target array is a representation of any enemy force in a specific situation that usually includes a scenario, a portrayal of dispositions, and a target analysis. A foreign technology forecast describes anticipated foreign scientific advances of military interest.

Any intelligence estimate—threat studies are types of such estimates—of future enemy activities is a set of conclusions projected into the future. The projection is based on the enemy's previous behavior in comparable situations, his expected behavior based on indications, and estimates of what he is physically capable of doing. These conclusions are founded on information that is either incomplete or uncertain or both.

Even if the intelligence information available at a given time were complete and accurate, there is still no certainty that the enemy will not change his mind. We have pursued the development of major weapons and organization systems with much fanfare only to cancel them for valid reasons. . . .

TENTATIVE CONCLUSIONS

In preparing an intelligence estimate, the estimator creates one or more hypotheses to explain the available information. The hypotheses are tentative conclusions on the significance of the information. By weighing the known information for pertinency and validity, and by testing with new information, the estimator finally selects one hypothesis, perhaps modified, as the best explanation of all the available information. This hypothesis rests on assumptions that cover many aspects including accuracy of information and validity of previous judgments on enemy behavior. Such assumptions are necessary, but they are not always the only logical ones that can be made. A change in the basic assumptions would probably lead to different hypotheses and different conclusions.

Threat source materials are often misused because of failure to recognize that they do not consider the impact on the enemy of the specific friendly capability that is under study. This misuse often results in disregard of enemy countermeasures or countermoves. For example, standard target

arrays for a potential mechanized enemy for the 1965–70 timeframe cannot consider all possible friendly developments or enemy responses during that period. This does not imply that standard target arrays are useless, but, rather, that their limitations must be understood.

One method sometimes mistakenly used in formulating a threat study is known as "mirror image." This method is based on the implied assumption that "if we can do it—so can our opponent." With this technique a technology forecast of friendly developments is modified slightly, coupled with some assumptions on the political context, and presented as the enemy threat. Such a procedure incorrectly assumes that the United States and the enemy have the same objectives, resources, and economic and political restraints. For example, current U.S. objectives call for greater mobility for ground forces, and extensive use is being made of helicopters. It does not necessarily follow that a potential enemy can or will do the same. His objectives might be satisfied by his current capabilities or greater use of existing or improved armored personnel carriers.

The major variables in the threat are time, the enemy forces, the locale of potential conflicts, the type of warfare, the political context, and developments in technology. Each variable influences the nature of the total enemy threat and the other variables within the total threat. A variation in the political context may change the composition and strength of the potential enemy or only change the weapon systems available to the enemy. There is further variability within the enemy factor because of the possible enemy countermeasures or countermoves.

Time influences the validity of all threat source materials. Estimates for the near timeframe are usually more valid than those for later periods because, within certain limits, the enemy's capability to depart from present patterns is restricted by time. It takes time to develop systems to the point of operational readiness, to develop new doctrine and tactics, and to retrain and reorganize forces. For the later periods, time is less restricting and additional options become available because of new technological developments. It is difficult enough to predict what our antitank weapons will be 15 years hence, much less predict with certainty what a secretive enemy will then have. It is usually impossible to prepare—with confidence —threat studies, target arrays, or enemy technological forecasts beyond about 10 years except to indicate broad trends.

The threat study used must cover the same timeframe as the expected useful lifespan of the system under study. Judging the effectiveness of a new kind of division by use of a threat model based on a Korean situation enemy and tactics of 1950–53 may lead to false conclusions.

CHANGES IN THREAT

Another pitfall is to assume that the enemy threat will remain constant during the time period under study. The threat may change because of the introduction of new enemy capabilities or changes in the over-all strategic concept. The useful lifespan of the 120-millimeter antiaircraft gun was cut short by the introduction of jet aircraft. It is difficult to foresee all changes in the enemy threat and their timing, but the possibility of such changes, as they affect the system under study, must be considered.

Enemy forces may vary significantly depending on the political context of the time period under study. In a given time period, one potential enemy may be equipped with highly developed air defense missiles and extensive ground and air mobility means. In the same time period, there may also be other potential enemies who are equipped only with simple weapon systems. All significant enemy forces must be considered in judging the effectiveness of alternatives unless there are obvious reasons to the contrary. Nothing is gained by measuring the effectiveness of a proposed system for defense against low-flying supersonic aircraft in an environment where the enemy forces do not have modern weapons available.

COMMON ERROR

Consideration should not be restricted to only one enemy unless the system is intended to be employed against only that type of enemy. A common error, when employing only one kind of enemy in an effectiveness model, is to generalize to other enemies....

Examination of effectiveness is also degraded by use of a target array that does not depict all logical tactics of the enemy.... All the pertinent elements of the entire enemy force must be included in considering enemy operations. An examination of enemy attack capabilities should not be limited to one class of weapons such as surface-to-surface fires. Close air support, if available to the enemy, must also be considered. Treating only some enemy capabilities, but not all, usually leads to false measurement of effectiveness.

The enemy must be credited with some degree of ability to react to new friendly capabilities. Guerrilla forces faced with a new airmobile capability should not be expected to continue to employ the same tactics used against a roadbound enemy. The introduction of a tank main weapon with greatly increased accuracy or lethality can be expected to result in some changes in the enemy's tactics.

The significant feasible enemy countermeasures and countermoves must be developed for each specific study because each new capability opens new possibilities for countermeasures and countermoves. These must be developed to supplement target arrays and threat studies that are prepared without consideration of the system under study. The countermeasures and countermoves should be formulated by specialists in intelligence of the potential enemy and in friendly and foreign technology, economics, and the type of military operations involved. The formulation of countermeasures and countermoves is a form of cost effectiveness analysis from the enemy point of view. . . .

QUALITATIVE UNCERTAINTY

Nations do not have perfect information of their potential enemy, and they do not always either react or react appropriately to the information they possess. History is full of examples of nations that failed to take advantage of available information because of institutional processes, incredulity, and human failures. Although this qualitative uncertainty cannot be reduced to a probability figure, it should not be disregarded.

It is equally as dangerous to overestimate the enemy's capabilities as it is to underestimate them because overestimates do not necessarily lead to insurance and safety. . . .

INDIRECT INFLUENCES

Changes in the political context can also have important indirect influence. An internal defense operation can be transformed into a different conflict by a change in the political context. Such a change could alter the enemy capabilities, the locale of the operation, and even the kind of warfare. The insurgents are usually initially weak in air defense weapons. In studying equipment for use in counterinsurgency operations that exploit this weakness in air defense, examining only the current air defense capabilities of the insurgents is inadequate. The political context must also be examined to determine if any reasonable changes could result in the insurgents receiving increased air defense capabilities. The purpose is not to predict whether the insurgents will or will not receive air defense weapons, but, rather, to determine the possible results if they did receive them. Similarly, the study of any new capability must consider what significant changes in the political context, if any, will alter the effectiveness of the capability under study.

TECHNOLOGICAL DEVELOPMENTS

Variability in both friendly and enemy technological developments poses great uncertainties in planning for the future.

The forecasting of trends in science and technology and their influence on military affairs cannot be reduced to a scientific method. Progress in science is not like the growth of population or the development of backward economies where trends are well recognized and reliable predictions are possible. Progress in scientific knowledge cannot be foretold since a breakthrough may or may not occur at any moment. When a breakthrough does occur, it usually opens new fields both in further scientific ideas and in technological applications. Nevertheless, it is possible to analyze scientific developments and to evaluate their possible military implications if one is aware of the limitations imposed on such considerations.

The uncertainties regarding enemy technological developments can be readily appreciated by comparing them with the uncertainties of our own future technological developments where full information is available. For example, the *Skybolt* missile had been under development for many years before it was abandoned because of technical difficulties and changed operational needs. Furthermore, estimates on the operational availability of new systems have been more in the nature of guesses. The *Mauler* air defense system, even before being cancelled, was well behind the estimated development schedule.

Enemy technological developments, despite the uncertainties involved, are an integral part of the threat. The uncertainties about which development he is pursuing, operational availability, and the probability of his making unanticipated technological breakthroughs cannot be dismissed because there is a lack of firm information. Treating these uncertainties is difficult, but failure to do so can lead to poor decisions. During World War I, the Allied failure to anticipate the development of the tank led to near disaster.

...It is often feasible to reduce the volume of [these] combined uncertainties to a manageable number and range by carrying three threat estimates through the study: "optimistic" and "pessimistic" estimates that bracket the range of uncertainty, and a "best estimate" that has the highest confidence of likelihood of occurring. These terms are not rigorous, and subjective judgment is required. Using these three estimates assists in determining the sensitivity of the effectiveness of any individual alternative to the assumptions about the threat variables.

In dealing with the "pessimistic" estimate, it should not be assumed that the enemy will always react to cause us the most harm. What is worst for us is not necessarily the best for the enemy. For example, the enemy's massing of his air defenses in one area may be the worst action from our viewpoint. However, it is not necessarily the best for the enemy, because of the vulnerability that ensues in other vital areas. The enemy use of low airburst nuclear weapons in certain terrain may bring both his and our forces to a standstill.

Failure to consider properly the threat factor leads to faulty preparations. Victories of tomorrow can only come from today's proper vision.

III

Ends and Means
in
Foreign Relations

FOREIGN POLICY

OBJECTIVES

Chapter 10

One of the most difficult problems in the study of international relations is to explain why nations behave as they do.

Thus far in this book we have dealt with the problems that arise when autonomous units confront each other in an environment where there is neither consensus on ends and means nor institutions that can regulate or prescribe the course of relations that ensues as a result of this confrontation. We have dealt with some aspects of the capacity of states to formulate, pursue, and achieve objectives in their relations with other states. All this has been difficult enough, but now we must confront the even more difficult task of grappling with the definition of goals and, having done that, with the methods that can be used to attain those goals.

In doing so we approach the problem specifically from the point of view of the participating units—the states and their governments. It is not the only level of analysis from which the problem could be broached. We could also speak of the goals of the international system in general, or more specifically of the goals of those who are responsible for operating certain international institutions such as the Secretariats of organizations like the United Nations or the European Economic Community. Their goals often differ from those of the national states which comprise their membership. But although the international system does exercise an influence on the behavior of its participants, the weight of influence is in the opposite direction, and the specific definition of states' goals is, in the final analysis, performed by the separate states themselves, which is to say that it is performed by their leaders.

Let us begin with two propositions: one from the "real" world, and one which deals with the way in which this real world has been perceived by those who have studied it. The first proposition is that states are multi-purpose organizations. This is obviously true in their domestic concerns. The Preamble to the American Constitution—characteristic of its *genre*—lists no less than six fairly broad types of goals (a more perfect union, justice, domestic tranquility, common defense, general welfare, and liberty), and not only the basic documents but the actual behaviors of other governments run along very similar lines. In their external as in their internal operations, states and their governments have multiple goals. These may include the protection and safety of citizens, the advancement of economic interests, the enhancement of prestige, the conclusion of various types of political, military, economic agreements with certain other states, and so on down a long "shopping list" of objectives.

The second proposition is that in talking about state objectives, we operate on the basis of many assumptions but little tested knowledge. This is an area in which it is very tempting to base an entire theoretical construct of international relations on assumptions about the motivations of individuals, groups, governments, and states, but it is very difficult to prove that those assumptions correspond to objective reality in an invariable and therefore predictable fashion. The selections reprinted in this chapter constitute, in our judgment, some of the most fruitful and suggestive work that has been done in this area of our concern—but there is not a great deal of work from which to choose. More often than not, motivations are implied or assumed rather than studied and explicated.

To begin with, we make the following assumptions: (1) that the activity of individuals is, consciously or not, goal-oriented; (2) that varying factors, internal and external to the actor, influence the definition of his goals as well as his chance for attaining those goals; and (3) that all groups involved in international relations have, as we indicated earlier, multiple objectives, the ingredients of which may at times be contradictory or mutually exclusive. In order to make sense of a statement of goals, therefore, one must know: (1) how terms are defined, (2) what priorities are given to various objectives, and (3) what specific resources can and will be devoted to their attainment. Some students, in fact, go so far as to suggest that because of built-in problems and ambiguities (and also because of the hard-to-resist temptation to speak in terms of glittering generalities which have no operational meaning), the definition of general policy aims is less important than the day-to-day pursuit of concrete, immediate objectives.[1] After one reads some of the flowery but essentially meaningless

---

[1] Charles Burton Marshall, *The Limits of Foreign Policy* (New York: Holt, Rinehart and Winston, Inc., 1954).

statements of objectives made by leaders of many societies, one can readily understand this preference; yet the editors of this volume proceed on the different assumption that the clarification of aims is an important precondition for evaluating the appropriateness of concrete policies.

But the problems remain, and the fact of the matter is that most terms in common usage to describe long-range objectives contain—and conceal—seriously disqualifying ambiguities. "Survival" and "self-preservation" of a given state are often cited as the *sine qua non* of its policy. But, one might well ask, what is the "self" that is to be preserved? For that matter what do terms such as "preservation" or "survival" mean? Do they refer to the maintenance of a momentary status quo, or do they also take into account changes in the internal composition or external position of states? Another term that is frequently used to describe state objectives is "independence." It has, to be sure, reference in real life. Especially for the newer countries, the stress on independence is strong and understandably so. Yet to be wholly realistic one must conclude that no country, not even the most powerful one, is ever fully independent of decisions made in other countries, over which only very imperfect control can be exercised. Just how "independent" was the United States on December 8, 1941? Just how wide was its range of options in responding to the Japanese attack of the preceding day? The decision to engage in a war with Japan was then made in Washington, to be sure, but the real decision had been made weeks before—in Tokyo (which, in turn, was basing *its* "independent" decision on prior moves that had been made elsewhere, including Washington—and so on).

"Territorial integrity," another term often used to define state objectives, is no less free of ambiguity and difficulty. It fails to specify precisely which territory is to be protected and against what. Taking the case of the United States again as an instructive example—and one with which students are apt to be most familiar—does the term "territorial integrity" imply that this country would defend only its own territorial boundaries, perhaps three miles out to sea? If so, what about the territories of states to which it is bound by alliance obligations? What about foreign bases which were established for the specific reason of protecting the national realm? What about the proposition that "our" frontier lies on the Elbe; or the preceding British proposition that her frontier lay on the Rhine?

Some students of international politics maintain that all human behavior, including therefore behavior in the international realm, is characterized by a "power drive." Bertrand Russell, for example, wrote that "of the infinite desires of man, the chief are the desires for power and glory," and added that some human desires, unlike those of animals, "are essentially boundless and incapable of complete satisfaction."[2] Other competent observers agree, and although some of them might not classify the power drive as either

[2] Bertrand Russell, *Power: A New Social Analysis* (New York: W. W. Norton & Co., Inc., 1938), pp. 9–11.

unlimited or omnipresent, they feel that the concept of power provides the best organizing focus for the study of relations among individuals and groups, including the massive and complex groups whose interaction is the subject matter of the study of international relations.[3]

Yet in our judgment there is reason for caution before accepting this or any other single-motive explanation of behavior and applying it to the infinite variety of patterns found in international relations. Certainly considerations of power are important. Probably they are seldom, if ever, completely absent from the minds of statesmen. But this is not the same as claiming for them a first priority in each and every type of situation. Much will depend upon how power is defined—and·anyone who has ever attempted such a definition will know that he is dealing with a slippery concept. If it is equated with physical force alone, one finds that many contemporary international relationships simply cannot be explained at all by sole reference to relative possession of physical strength. Maybe it was so in an earlier day, when Thucydides could write that "the strong do what they can, and the weak suffer what they must"; but we live in a different world in which an American Secretary of State can say (and quite correctly, we believe) that now the weak can afford to be rash, but the powerful have to be restrained!

If power includes, as it must, not only physical but also psychological, economic, and even moral ingredients, then one may wonder whether the concept has not become too broad to be useful for purposes of analysis, which would argue not for abandoning it but for breaking it down into smaller and therefore more manageable constituent parts.

Among other objectives which may underlie the policies of states are those of aggrandizement and expansion—either physical, economic, cultural, or ideological. Again, no doubt, these are frequently important goals of states in international relations, and it might be a worthwhile exercise to try to establish categories of states according to the frequency with which they engage in actions designed to achieve one or more of these aims. Yet one should hesitate before drawing conclusions from such categorizations. It is not easy to divide the states of the world into neat categories such as "peace-loving" versus "aggressive," "satiated versus unsatiated," "haves versus have-nots," and so forth. The difficulty is that states change over time not only in their actions but in their motivations as well—or at least so we assume. Such cases as Germany, Japan, probably the Soviet Union, and for that matter probably the United States come to mind to buttress this statement. Also states which behave in certain ways in one area, at one period, or with respect to one problem may behave quite differently in other areas, at other times, and on other issues. A presently non-expansionary state, for example, may simply be one that is content with the fruits of past expansionary policies.

---

[3] Hans J. Morgenthau, *Politics Among Nations* (New York: Alfred A. Knopf, Inc.), succeeding editions.

The problems inherent in the task of defining goals of state behavior are clear. The solutions to these problems are less obvious. Given the complexity of the subject, Hans J. Morgenthau has suggested a solution by employing the concept of national interest as a guide to the analysis of a country's behavior in international relations.[4] In alerting us to distinctions from subnational or supranational interests, the concept is undoubtedly useful. The difficulty with it is that one can scarcely think of any instances, in practice or in theory, where a country would do anything *but* pursue its national interests; but the specific definition of what is in the national interest, how it is to be defined, and what implementing actions it suggests or requires must still be performed. Thus even after one has said "national interest," one has really only pushed back the question of defining the motivation which underlies state behavior. The next task must inevitably be the precise definition of that national interest. Thomas W. Robinson, in the selection reprinted in this Chapter, page 199, on that subject, addresses himself to that task, with what seems to us to be a fair degree of success. Similarly the article elaborating George F. Kennan's views on the American vital interests introduces an ingredient of specificity into the discussion which lends itself to a deeper understanding (if not necessarily agreement) of what broad terms such as "national (or vital) interest" mean.

The more adequate conceptualization and categorization of objectives thus seems to be an outstanding need for the student of international relations. This is particularly true as it is difficult to distinguish between "objectives" and "policies," or between "ends" and "means." Much semantic confusion ensues as a result of this difficulty. The various categories have a way of shading off into one another. Some objectives may be so immediate that they are easily confused with specific policies. Some policies may be so long-range in nature as to be tantamount to objectives of states.

One possible partial way out of this problem may be to distinguish between objectives and policies in terms of *time*. This would involve the distinction between immediate objectives, corresponding to short-term policies; intermediate objectives, corresponding to longer, but still limited-term policies; and long-range objectives, corresponding to permanent policies. Another tool of analysis that may be useful in the interpretation of state objectives would be to distinguish a given country's aspirations from the point of view of their *object*. Thus a country's objectives for itself would certainly differ from those held for potential allies, neutrals, and potential or actual adversaries. (Notice, however, the ambiguity of such terms as "potential," "allies," and "adversaries." One's allies at one time may become one's adversaries at other times, and vice versa; one's potential adversaries are, conversely, also one's potential allies.)

Relatively few professional students of world politics have grappled

4 Hans J. Morgenthau, "Another 'Great Debate': The National Interest of the United States," *American Political Science Review* (1952), 46, pp. 971–78.

with this complex topic. The selections reprinted in this chapter constitute some of the most useful work on the subject to date. But much more work clearly remains to be done before either the theorist or the practitioner of international relations can begin to be satisfied with his knowledge concerning the important question of the objectives of states in their international relations.

1. The Goals of Foreign Policy

ARNOLD WOLFERS

It might seem that the mere existence of a multitude of nation-states, each capable of independent decision and action, would suffice to explain the peaceless state of the world and the power struggles that fill the international arena. Undoubtedly, the anarchical condition inherent in any system of multiple sovereignty constitutes one of the prerequisites of international conflict; without it, there could be no international relations, peaceful or nonpeaceful. Yet, in the last analysis, it is the goals pursued by the actors and the way they go about pursuing them that determine whether and to what extent the potentialities for power struggle and war are realized. This can be seen by imagining two extreme sets of conditions, both theoretically compatible with a multistate system, in which, as a consequence of the wide differences in the objectives pursued by the states in question as well as in the means they are

From DISCORD AND COLLABORATION (Baltimore: The Johns Hopkins University Press, 1962), pp. 67–73. Reprinted by permission.

willing to employ, the chances of peace would stand at opposite poles.

Starting at one pole, one can postulate a situation in which all actors are entirely satisfied with the established state of international affairs, and are content, therefore, to concern themselves exclusively with domestic matters. In this case, they would have no incentive to make or press demands on others. As a consequence, there would be no rational cause for conflict or for disturbances of the peace. Needless to say, this is a utopia. In some historical instances, however, conditions so nearly approached this extreme that to some observers the utopia appeared within reach, while in other times various schools of thought held it up as at least a goal toward which policy should be directed.

Thus, since the days of Cobden, free-traders have argued that if governments ceased to interfere with commercial activities across borders the chief source of international conflict would be removed. Others have pleaded instead for economic autarchy which, by eliminating the need for international economic intercourse altogether, would make economic demands on others unnecessary. Then again, the satisfaction of demands for national self-determination, one of the cornerstones of Woodrow Wilson's peace strategy, was expected to eliminate a potent cause of international conflict. If every nation had the government of its choice and if every ethnic group were united within the boundaries of a single state, demands for more territory or for independence, objectives most conducive to war, would lose their *raison d'être*. It might be added that some have advocated policies of isolation and neutrality on the same grounds: a condition of dissociation among nations would reduce their interdependence and thus minimize the occasions for conflict. My purpose here is not to determine whether such policies are practical or desirable, but to draw attention to the close relationship between foreign policy objectives and the incidence of tension that might lead to a resort to violence.

This close relationship appears confirmed if one moves to the other pole and postulates that nations are engaged in making exacting demands on one another and are prepared to fight rather than give in. Actually, to be able to predict very serious threats to the peace, one need only assume that a single powerful actor within a multistate system is bent on attaining goals of territorial expansion or dominion over others, because resistance to any drive toward acquisitive goals of this nature is almost certain to materialize. The stage is thus set for clashes that justify a high expectation of violence.

Before looking into the kinds of goals or objectives that nations tend to pursue in their external activities, one semantic hurdle must be taken. It is customary to distinguish between goals and means, a custom I intend to follow to a certain extent; yet it is impossible to draw a sharp line of demarcation between the two ideas. All means can be said to constitute intermediary or proximate goals, and few goals if any can be considered ultimate, in the sense of being sought as ends in themselves. Even when a nation aims for a goal as highly valued as national independence, it can be argued that the nation is seeking such independence as a means of providing its citizens with benefits other than national independence itself.[1]

To make things more complicated, what constitutes a means or intermediate goal in one context may be a remote if not ultimate goal in another, with specific objectives changing places from one instance to another. Thus, enhanced power may be sought as a means of obtaining more territory, while the acquisition of more territory in turn may be desired as a means of enhancing national power. In the case of Europe prior to the establishment of NATO, the question was whether what was needed most was higher productivity as a means of increasing defensive strength or conversely whether more defensive strength providing a greater sense of security was not a prerequisite of greater efforts toward higher productivity.

Because the objectives a nation seeks to reach can range from the most

[1] Percy Corbett, for instance, points out that "for democratic purposes it seems worthwhile to insist that the prime object of foreign policy...is the welfare of the individuals and groups organized as a national society" and goes on to conclude that "insofar as territorial integrity and political independence are judged to minister to that welfare, they may well be described as the mediate and instrumental objective to which foreign policy is especially directed." "National Interest, International Organization, and American Foreign Policy," *World Politics*, Vol. V, No. 1 (October, 1952), p. 51.

immediate means to the most remote or ultimate ends, all goals will be taken to fall within the scope of this chapter with the single exception of power and influence. The justification for this exception should become clear when the unique position of these two values as the means *par excellence* for the attainment of all other foreign policy goals is discussed. The fact that power may be turned into an end in itself will be taken into consideration in that connection.

Despite the difficulties and complications arising out of the way ends can serve one another as means, it often becomes necessary to inquire whether a nation is seeking certain results from its policy primarily for the results' own sake or merely as means of reaching more remote goals. If a nation is helping others through economic aid to raise their standard of living, it may make a great deal of difference for the chances that such aid will be continued or extended whether the nation extending the aid considers economic improvement abroad as being desirable in itself, or promotes it merely for the sake of cementing its alliance with the assisted country or of drawing that country over to its own side. To take another example, there has been uncertainty in Europe whether American support for European integration implies that the United States believes such integration to be a good thing in itself—worthy therefore of continued support, cold war or no cold war—or whether greater European unity is valued solely as a means of strengthening Western defenses. Then again, the importance of aim or purpose may be illustrated by a question that has led to much controversy. Some see the Soviet Union supporting revolutionary movements abroad because world revolution *per se* is the goal of Soviet policy; others maintain that the aim is to bolster the security of the Soviet Union as a nation-state, and the revolutions can count on Soviet support only when and where they are expected to enhance the power of the Soviet Union and its alliances. Frequently, of course, a single means can serve to promote two or more concurrent ends. The Soviet leaders being both the rulers of Russia and the leaders of world communism may be unable themselves to distinguish between their national and world revolutionary goals and interests.

As soon as one seeks to discover the place of goals in the means-end chain of relationships, almost inevitably one is led to probe into the dark labyrinth of human motives, those internal springs of conscious and unconscious actions which Morgenthau calls "the most illusive of psychological data."[2] Yet if one fails to inquire why actors choose their goals, one is forced to operate in an atmosphere of such abstraction that nothing is revealed but the barest skeleton of the real world of international politics.

It is understandable that historians have devoted so much time to probing the motives of actors. Although the success of an act such as an effort to pacify an area does not depend on the nature of the motivation, overt behavior remains unintelligible except in relation to motivation. An act of intervention may be the same in its outward appearance whether it is motivated by imperialist design or by the desire to help a people throw off the yoke of a tyrannical government. However, when other governments are making up their minds how to react to such intervention or deciding what to expect from the intervening nation in future contingencies, they cannot avoid seeking to dis-

[2] Hans J. Morgenthau, *Politics Among Nations: The Struggle for Power and Peace* (3rd ed., Alfred A. Knopf, New York, 1960), p. 6.

cover what it was that prompted the particular action.

If nations are seen to desire a wide variety of accomplishments and gains ranging all the way from such ambitious ends as empire or predominance to mere trade advantages, opportunities for cultural exchanges, or voting rights in international organizations, one might expect that whatever a nation values and can attain only from other nations will automatically be transformed into a foreign policy objective. This is not the case. Leading statesmen may give expression to hopes or ideals of their people, but these hopes do not, thereby, become what properly can be called policy goals. They will become goals only if the decision is reached that some national effort involving sacrifices, or the risk of sacrifices, is to be made for their realization. All goals are costly. Therefore an aspiration will not be turned into a policy goal unless it is sufficiently cherished by those who make and influence policy to justify the costs that its attainment is expected to require in terms of sacrifices. The American people, or influential Americans, may place high value on the liberation of satellite peoples; the question is whether such liberation is valued highly enough to turn it into an American foreign policy goal for which a high price possibly would be paid.

Picturing aspirations and goals at opposite poles is not accurate. One might better regard them as the two ends of a continuum that runs from mere hopes to goals of vital interest. "Liberation," declared a goal of American policy at the beginning of the Eisenhower Administration, is more than a mere hope as long as it is promoted by propaganda that risks enhancing East-West tension; when one speaks of peaceful liberation one implies that the goal is not considered vital enough to justify a resort to force. World revolution is not merely a hope, but a goal of Soviet foreign policy. Yet, while it may be close to the pole of vital goals usually assumed to justify the resort to violence, it may be sufficiently removed from this pole to keep Soviet policy-makers from initiating a war for the sake of its promotion. Statesmen are well advised to keep in mind that threats to the peace may arise if other nations are left uncertain whether or not national spokesmen who proclaim national aspirations have actually decided to turn a particular aspiration into a policy goal, possibly a goal deemed vital enough to warrant risking or sacrificing the peace.

In analyzing international politics, there would be no need to concern oneself with the problem of goals if nation-states were single-purpose organizations. If they were, states would never consent to make sacrifices for purposes—such as the promotion of peace—that obviously do not constitute their sole objective. It should be added, however, that even if foreign policy were directed predominantly toward a single goal, such a goal would not monopolize the entire activity of states, except in the extreme emergency of a war. Always there would remain the many domestic goals which no government can ignore and which compete for resources with whatever external purposes the nation may be pursuing. Often these domestic objectives place the severest restraints on external aspirations, as one can gather from any parliamentary debate in which the demand for financial appropriations to meet the needs of external pursuits runs up against demands to increase social benefits or to reduce taxes.

Appearances to the contrary, there is no division of opinion among analysts of international politics about the fact that the policy of nations aims at a multitude of goals. Some exponents of realist thought have been misunderstood to hold that power or even maximum power represents the only significant goal. Authors like Nicholas Spykman and Hans Morgenthau have contributed to this misapprehension, the first by stating on one occasion that "the improvement of the relative power position becomes the primary objective of the internal and the external policy of states,"[3] the latter by his statement that "the aspiration for power is the distinguishing element of international politics."[4] However, Morgenthau also stresses that power is only an immediate aim or chief means of foreign policy,[5] while Spykman, relating the quest for power to the task of survival, mentions the existence of other objectives that are "geographic, demographic, racial, ethnic, economic, social and ideological in nature."[6]

The goals of national independence, territorial integrity, and national survival which figure so large in the foreign policy of all nation-states are not uniform in scope or character and must, therefore, be treated as significant variables. Governments conceive of these cherished values in more or less moderate and in more or less ambitious and exacting terms. A good illustration is offered by colonial powers. Only those among them who insist that their "colonies"—or some of them—are not colonies at all but an integral part of their national territory are led to treat the preservation of these areas as a requirement of national survival and thus as a vital goal that justifies almost any sacrifice. The new postcolonial states present another illustration of differences in outlook among different actors. Some insist that any continuing ties with the mother country are unacceptable because such ties would defeat the goal of sovereign independence; others favor "union" or commonwealth types of association in the interest of economic welfare, provided the goal of sovereign equality is attained.

The goal of national survival itself is given a wide variety of interpretations by different countries or countries facing different conditions. Nations intent upon keeping their involvement in international conflicts at a minimum are inclined to consider their survival at stake only when their own territory comes under the threat of attack or actually is attacked. The idea of "indivisible peace" which would require them to participate in collective action against any aggressor anywhere has little appeal to them. In contrast, a nation engaged in a global struggle, as the United States is today, will tend to regard any shift in the balance of power that favors its adversary as at least an indirect threat to its own survival. As a consequence, it may consider its survival at stake in a conflict over remote and intrinsically unimportant islands such as Quemoy and Matsu or over legal rights in West Berlin on the ground that, by an assumed domino effect or chain reaction, defeat at any one point will lead to defeat at every other point, until in the end all chances of survival are nullified.

• • •

[3] Nicholas John Spykman, *America's Strategy in World Politics: The United States and the Balance of Power* (Harcourt, Brace & Co., New York, 1942), p. 18.

[4] Morgenthau, *op. cit.*, p. 31.

[5] *Ibid.*, p. 27.

[6] Spykman, *op. cit.*, p. 17.

2. The National Interest

Thomas W. Robinson is a member of the Social Science Department of the RAND Corporation, specializing in Soviet and Chinese domestic politics and foreign policy, and in the theory of international relations.

. . .

In this paper, we shall attempt to contribute to the solution of two... problems: application of [Morgenthau's] theory to the real world, and use of international relations theory to study the communist orbit. We shall examine, in the context of Sino-Soviet relations, Hans Morgenthau's national interest formulation as representative of the best which the "traditional" approach has to offer. Sino-Soviet relations were chosen because: (1) the states in question are communist; (2) they are at different "stages" of political development; (3) they are powers of consequence in world politics; (4) the data situation is much improved over a few years ago, thanks to the Sino-Soviet dispute.

II. HANS MORGENTHAU'S CONCEPTION OF THE NATIONAL INTEREST

In discussing Morgenthau's view of the national interest, let us divide the subject as follows: (1) Definition and

From INTERNATIONAL STUDIES QUARTER-LY, *11 (June 1967), pp. 137–51. Reprinted by permission from the Wayne State University Press.*

analysis of the national interest; (2) basic statement of the relation between interest and power; (3) national interest and morality; (4) propositions about the national interest; (5) national interest and nuclear weapons; (6) national interest and international organization.

A.1. Definition and analysis of the national interest

At first it seems that Morgenthau uses the term "national interest" in many different ways to cover a bewildering variety of meanings. This seems to be evidenced by the following array of terms: common interest and conflicting interest, primary and secondary interest, inchoate interest, community of interests, identical and complementary interests, vital interests, legitimate interests, specific or limited interests, material interests, hard-core interests, necessary and variable interests.[1] Upon further

[1] (Note: All footnote references are to Hans J. Morgenthau; the author's name will therefore not be repeated).

a) Common and conflicting interests: *The Restoration of American Politics* (Chicago: The University of Chicago Press, 1964), p. 203; "Alliances in Theory and Practice," in Arnold Wolfers, ed., *Alliance Policy in The Cold War* (Baltimore: The Johns Hopkins Press, 1959), p. 188.

investigation, however, these terms can be collapsed into two general categories —the national interests of a single nation and the degree of commonality of interests among two or more nations. Under the heading of the national interest of a single state we can group together several interests, according to: (1) the degree of primacy of the interest; (2) the degree of permanence of the interest; (3) the degree of generality of the interest. These may be represented according to the following diagram:

	primary(a) secondary(c)
permanent	specific(b) general
variable	specific(b) general

(a) includes as synonyms: vital, legitimate, hard-core, and necessary national interests;

(b) includes as synonyms: material and limited interests;

(c) includes as a synonym: non-vital interests.

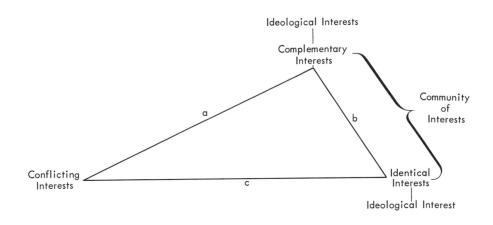

b) Primary and secondary interests: *The Impasse of American Foreign Policy* (Chicago: The University of Chicago Press, 1962), p. 191; "The Crisis in the Western Alliance," *Commentary*, Vol. 35 (1963), pp. 185–98.

c) Inchoate (rudimentary, incipient) interests: *The Restoration of American Politics, op. cit.*, p. 198.

d) Community of interests: *Ibid.*, p. 204; "Alliances in Theory and Practice," *op. cit.*, p. 189.

e) Identical and complementary interests: *The Impasse of American Foreign Policy, op. cit.*, p. 173; "The Impotence of American Power," *Commentary*, Vol. 36 (1963), p. 385; "Alliances in Theory and Practice," *op. cit.*, p. 189; *In Defense of the National Interest* (Chicago: The University of Chicago Press, 1950), p. 146.

f) Vital interests: *Dilemmas of Politics* (Chicago: The University of Chicago Press, 1958), p. 274.

g) Legitimate interests: *The Impasse of American Foreign Policy, op. cit.*, p. 214.

h) Specific (limited) interests: "Alliances in Theory and Practice," *op. cit.*, p. 201.

i) Material interests: *Ibid.*, p. 188.

j) Hard core interests: *Dilemmas of Politics, op. cit.*, p. 66.

k) Necessary (permanent) and variable interests: "Another 'Great Debate:' The National Interest of the United States," *The American Political Science Review*, Vol. XLVI (1952), p. 973.

Thus, for example, primary interests can be either permanent or variable in time as well as specific or general. This gives us eight different types of interests which a given nation may hold. Note, however, that only three adjectives are needed to describe a national interest. For instance, an interest can be designated as primary, permanent, and specific, or secondary, variable, and general (but not, note, as primary, permanent, and variable or secondary, specific, and general). All of the interests of a given nation expressed at any given moment are called the total interests of that nation.[2]

The degree or lack of commonality of interests between two or more states, may be represented geometrically as in the previous page's diagram.

Thus, there exist three continua of interests between two or more nations, represented by the sides a, b, and c of the triangle. Inchoate interests cannot be represented since, by definition, they have yet to be expressed. Once they are defined they will appear as an interest representable as a point on one of the lines of the diagram. Ideological interests are always built on the foundation of some commonly-felt interests. This is shown in the diagram.

It remains to define more closely each of the interests mentioned. We have the following six "national" interests.

a. *Primary interests* include protection of the nation's physical, political, and cultural identity and survival against encroachment from the outside.[3] Primary interests can never be compromised or traded. All nations hold these same interests and must defend them at any price.[4]

b. *Secondary interests* are those falling outside of *a* but contributing to it. For example, protecting citizens abroad and maintaining proper immunities for a nation's diplomats are secondary interests.

c. *Permanent interests* are those which are relatively constant over long periods of time; they vary with time, but only slowly.[5] For instance, Great Britain for many centuries has had an interest in the freedom to navigate the seas and in a narrow definition of coastal waters.

d. *Variable interests* are those which are a function of "all the cross currents of personalities, public opinion, sectional interests, partisan politics, and political and moral folkways" of a given nation.[6] In other words, they are what a given nation at any particular time chooses to regard as its national interests. In this respect the variable interest may diverge from both primary and permanent interests. For example, Great Britain in 1938 chose to regard certain events bearing on the security of Czechoslovakia as not within its interest.

e. *General interests* are those which the nation can apply in a positive manner to a large geographic area, to a large number of nations, or in several specific fields (such as economics, trade, diplomatic intercourse, international law, etc.). An example would be the British interest in the maintenance of a balance of power on the European continent.

f. *Specific interests* are those positive interests not included in *e*. Specific interests are usually closely defined in time and/or space and often are the

---

[2] "Alliances in Theory and Practice," *op. cit.,* p. 188.

[3] *Dilemmas of Politics, op. cit.,* pp. 50, 51, 66, 178; "Another Great Debate," *op. cit.,* p. 973.

[4] *The Impasse of American Foreign Policy, op. cit.,* p. 291.

[5] *Dilemmas of Politics, op. cit.,* p. 66.

[6] *Ibid.,* p. 66; "Another Great Debate," *op. cit.,* p. 973.

logical outgrowth of general interests.[7] For instance, Britain historically has regarded the continued independence of the Low Countries as an absolute prerequisite for the maintenance of the balance of power in Europe.

We also have the following three "international" interests:

g. *Identical interests* between nations obviously are those national interests (that is, one or more of *a* through *f* above) which those nations hold in common.[8] For example, Great Britain and the U.S. have had an interest in assuring that the European continent is not dominated by a single power.

h. *Complementary interests* between nations are those which, although not identical, at least are capable of forming the basis of agreement on specific issues.[9] England has an interest in maintaining the independence of Portugal from Spain as a means of controlling the regions of the Atlantic Ocean off the Iberian peninsula, while Portugal has an interest in British maritime hegemony as a means of defense against Spain.

i. *Conflicting interests* are those not included in *g* and *h*. It should be noted, however, that today's conflicting interests can be transformed tomorrow, through diplomacy, occurrence of events, or the passage of time into common or complementary interests.[10] The same thing might be said about the possibility of transforming identical or complementary interests into conflicting interests.

A.2. *The relation between interest and power*

In Morgenthau's political theory, the starting place for a discussion of most subjects is a consideration of human nature. This is the case also with his derivation of the basic proposition of his theory that politicians and statesmen, if they wish to be successful, must in the first instance equate their own and their states' interests with the pursuit and use of power. The derivation of this proposition is as follows. Since human nature is imperfect, society also is imperfect, as it is human nature writ large. Hence, abstract moral principles can never be realized fully but can only be approximated through the balancing of interests and by temporary settlements. Two good methods exist to this end. On the one hand, one can attempt to set up a system of checks and balances among the various contending parties. On the other hand, one may strive for the lesser attainable evil in preference to the absolute good which is always beyond reach.[11] In international relations, too, this method must be followed. Foreign policy goals must not range beyond the power available, for although national desires for good and for evil are infinite, the resources for obtaining them are strictly limited. It is therefore necessary to distinguish desirable goals from essential goals. The list of essential national goals is called the total national interest. Once this is done, it remains only to establish a hierarchical order among them according to the purposes of the nation and

---

[7] "Alliances in Theory and Practice," *op. cit.,* p. 191.

[8] *Ibid.,* pp. 188, 189, 191; *In Defense of the National Interest, op. cit.,* p. 146; "The Impotence of American Power," *op. cit.,* p. 385; *The Impasse of American Foreign Policy, op. cit.,* p. 173.

[9] *In Defense of the National Interest, op. cit.,* p. 146; *The Impasse of American Foreign Policy, op. cit.,* p. 173.

[10] *The Restoration of American Politics, op. cit.,* pp. 198, 203.

[11] *Dilemmas of Politics, op. cit.,* p. 261; "Goldwater—The Romantic Regression," *Commentary,* Vol. 38 (1964), pp. 65–68.

then to allocate the power resources of the nation accordingly.[12]

Bringing the desires of a nation into line with the power available for their pursuit, and the designation of those interests which are to be pursued at all costs, is the focus of Morgenthau's theory of international politics and of his statement of political realism.[13] This is all that is meant by "the concept of interest defined in terms of power."[14] It is, therefore, not a vague concept with no real meaning, as alleged by some. It is merely prudence operating in international relations, resulting in "a rational, discriminating understanding of the hierarchy of national interests and the power available for their support."[15] It is true that these interests tend to be relatively constant over long periods of time. This is due to: (1) the nature of the interests themselves, especially the primary interests defined above; (2) the relative constancy of the political environment within which policies made in pursuit of those interests operate; (3) the limited number of policy alternatives available to pursue them.[16] Since these are by no means constant, even the most "permanent" interests change in time. The fact is that national interests are constant only as long as the latter two factors themselves do not vary. In other words, although the national interest is a prime variable, it is dependent on the state of the political environment and on the variation in the number of policy alternatives available. It is the relative constancy in these just as much

as the root desire to protect one's national security and identity that allows Morgenthau to conclude that by thinking in terms of interest defined as power "we think as [the statesman] does, and as disinterested observers we understand his thoughts and actions perhaps better than he does. . . ."[17] It is not necessary, for instance, to know all the secrets of the Chinese foreign office, in order to know China's national interests in regard to Korea or Formosa.[18] But Morgenthau also concludes, as we shall see below, that many components of the national interest may change very quickly, when, as at present, the political environment and the available policy alternatives themselves fluctuate rapidly. The implication is clear that in periods of rapid change, we shall have much more difficulty in putting ourselves in the shoes of statesmen and figuring out, on the basis of a national interest analysis what their policy was, is, or will be. Finally, the national interest is by no means the only factor to be considered when making or ascertaining policy. The relative power of the parties concerned is the other primary element and we must also consider such factors as personalities of the members of the decision-making groups, national traditions, and situationally-based "opportunities" that may suddenly appear.[19]

. . .

A.4. Propositions about the national interests

Morgenthau makes use of national interest analysis in many different contexts, and we can only illustrate the

---

[12] *In Defense of the National Interest, op. cit.,* pp. 117–18.

[13] *Dilemmas of Politics, op. cit.,* pp. 47, 50, 51, 54; *Politics Among Nations* (New York: Alfred A. Knopf, 1963, 3rd edition), p. 5.

[14] *Ibid.,* p. 14.

[15] "War With China?" *The New Republic,* Vol. 152, April 3, 1965, p. 14.

[16] *Dilemmas of Politics, op. cit.,* p. 66.

[17] *Ibid.,* p. 67; *Politics Among Nations, op. cit.,* p. 5.

[18] *Dilemmas of Politics, op. cit.,* p. 308.

[19] "Another Great Debate," *op. cit.,* p. 969.

mode of analysis here by selected examples. These will be divided into three parts:

A. War and the use of force;
B. Alliances;
C. Diplomatic negotiations.

A. USE OF FORCE. War and peace form a continuum of means by which nations pursue their interests.[20] Whether a nation protects those interests by peaceful or violent means, however, is not only its own choice but is also a function of certain objective conditions over which it has no control.[21] Every great power—even in the nuclear age—must at times defend its national interests with the threat or use of force.[22] Still, although it often occurs that the interests of nations are irreconcilable (and diplomacy has had a chance to show that they are), war can sometimes be avoided merely by the passage of time.[23]

B. ALLIANCES. The purpose of an alliance is to explicate and make precise an existing community of interests among two or more nations,[24] and to transform that community of interests into legal obligations. It follows immediately that if there is no such community of interests—either common or complementary—either the alliance will fail or naked power must be substituted; and the latter does not provide a firm foundation for any alliance.[25] An alliance, of course, is a function of the large variety of interests—primary, permanent, variable and so on—that

every nation possesses. The generality and duration of a given alliance will therefore depend on the relative strengths of those interests which favor the alliance and those that oppose it. Such an estimation must be made by every statesman when he considers whether or not to engage in alliance ties.[26] The advantage of pursuing the national interests through alliances, of course, lies in the translation of inchoate, common, or complementary interests into common policy[27] and in bringing the nation's power directly to bear on questions of national interest.

Alliances can be classified, in regard to their relationship to the interests of the nation involved, according to the following table:[28]

National Interest	Alliances
1. Type of shared interest: identical (common), complementary, ideological	Identical or complementary and/or ideological
2. Increment of power and benefit added: mutual increase one-sided increase	mutual alliance one-sided alliance
3. Degree of totality of national interests covered: primary or general secondary or specific	general alliance limited alliance
4. Coverage of national interests in terms of time: variable national interests permanent national interests	temporary alliance permanent alliance
5. Degree of effectiveness in operation in terms of common policies and actions.	operative or inoperative alliance

---

20 *Dilemmas of Politics, op. cit.,* p. 256.
21 *The Impasse of American Foreign Policy, op. cit.,* p. 186.
22 *Ibid.,* p. 44.
23 *The Restoration of American Politics, op. cit.,* p. 202.
24 *Politics Among Nations, op. cit.,* p. 182; "Alliances in Theory and Practice," *op. cit.,* p. 186.
25 *Ibid.,* p. 206.

26 *Ibid.,* p. 191.
27 *The Impasse of American Foreign Policy, op. cit.,* p. 123.
28 "Alliances in Theory and Practice," *op. cit.,* p. 189; *Politics Among Nations, op. cit.,* p. 182 .

Presumably the types of alliances noted here are polar types so that, for instance, one could also speak of alliance which is *more* complementary than ideological, *rather* one-sided, *somewhat* limited, of *medium* duration, and *partially* operative. Presumably, also one can write the history of a given alliance in terms of the variability of these factors. Morgenthau adduces the following propositions concerning the relation of alliances to national interests.

1. The degree of generality of common interests expressed in alliance form is inversely related to the duration of the alliance: general alliances (founded on general interests) will be of short duration while limited alliances will be long-lasting.[29]

2. The relative degree of primacy of national interests expressed in an alliance is inversely proportional to the power of the nation: a weak nation and a strong one will enter into an alliance to defend primary and secondary interests, respectively.[30]

3. In this case, however, the weaker is dependent on the stronger; this will be tolerable only if there is complete identity of interests between the two, a condition which is rare.[31]

4. Even though an alliance may be based on equality (that is, not one-sided in the distribution of power and benefits), it will not succeed unless (a) there is an identity of interests, reflected in the goals of the alliance and (b) an awareness of this identity exemplified through "common measures" and "spontaneous cooperation."[32]

5. A one-sided alliance, where one party receives most of the benefits and the other party carries most of the burden, often results from complementary national interests. Treaties of guarantee are often of this variety.[33]

6. The degree of cohesion of alliances is a function only of the relative community of interests felt by the participants and not of the degree of integration achieved or of the quality of legal ties expressed in the alliance.[34]

7. Not every community of interests need be codified into an alliance.[35] Conversely, the existence of certain legal ties binding one nation to another can never overbalance the national interests of the nation; at some time these may lead the nation to pursue policies fundamentally opposed to those by which the nation is legally bound.[36]

8. Ideology is related to interest in alliance in the following manner. An ideological commitment is often added to an alliance already firmly grounded on specific common or complementary interests. In this case it will probably strengthen the alliance. It may, however, weaken it by "obscuring the nature and limits of common interests that the alliance was supposed to make precise and by raising expectations bound to be disappointed for the extent of concerted policies and actions." If, however, a community of interests is absent, an alliance based on ideology alone will be stillborn.[37]

9. The interests that unite two nations

[29] "Alliances in Theory and Practice," *op. cit.*, p. 191.

[30] *Ibid.*, p. 190.

[31] "The Crisis in the Western Alliance," *op. cit.*, p. 186.

[32] "The Impotence of American Power," *op. cit.*, p. 385.

[33] "Alliances in Theory and Practice," *op. cit.*, p. 189.

[34] *The Impasse of American Foreign Policy, op. cit.*, p. 219.

[35] "Alliances in Theory and Practice," *op. cit.*, p. 186; *Politics Among Nations, op. cit.*, p. 182.

[36] *In Defense of the National Interest, op. cit.*, p. 144.

[37] "Alliances in Theory and Practice," *op. cit.*, pp. 188–89.

against a third and therefore the alliance built on their base are usually precise concerning the designation of the enemy but relatively vague concerning the concrete objectives and policies to be pursued against that enemy.[38]

C. DIPLOMATIC NEGOTIATIONS AND PEACEFUL SETTLEMENT. Conflict of interest, to Morgenthau, is the basic factor of international society. Morgenthau defines diplomacy as the technique for accommodating such conflicts of interests.[39] Diplomacy attempts to make the best of a bad situation by attempting to reconcile one's own national interests with those of the other side; that is, it first attempts to define the differences of those interests and then tries to delimit, codify, and emphasize common and complementary interests. At the same time it separates commonly held interests from conflicting interests and manipulates conditions so as to minimize the danger stemming from those conflicts.[40] Negotiations are an attempt to reconcile divergent interests through a process of give-and-take in which either or both sides concede minor points while leaving the substance of their interests, or else one side receives through compensations from the other at least the equivalent of what it concedes.[41] National interest is directly related to diplomacy not only through definition but in the probabilities as to whether the outcome will be peaceful or not. For only those agreements will last which express the common or complementary interests of the parties concerned and they will last only so long as

"their terms coincide with those interests."[42] Although relative power is also a central factor in the outcome of negotiations[43] (from which the conclusion is immediately apparent that settlements must be negotiated only by those whose interests and power are involved, and by no others), it is less important to a successful (i.e. peaceful) outcome than the ability to reconcile apparently irreconcilable interests. The supreme task of diplomacy, therefore, is to "assess correctly the chances for peaceful settlement by ascertaining the vital interests of the opposing nations and their relations to each other."[44]

There exist three possible outcomes of diplomatic negotiations between two nations according to the type and degree of compatibility of interests involved. These are either: primary and incompatible (i.e. conflicting) interests, in which case negotiations are impossible; primary and compatible (i.e. either common or complementary) interests, in which case negotiations redefine seemingly incompatible interests; secondary (compatible or incompatible) interests, in which case a compromise is arrived at through trading of interest for interest.[45] Such a compromise may or may not be fruitful. A misleading settlement occurs when one of the parties, pursuing a policy end through appeasement, misjudges its interests or those of its opponent as well as misjudging the power situation. The result is that the nation may surrender a vital interest without

---

[38] *Ibid.*, p. 187.
[39] *Dilemmas of Politics, op. cit.*, p. 274; *The Restoration of Amercian Politics, op. cit.*. p. 202.
[40] *Ibid.*, pp. 203–4; *The Impasse of American Foreign Policy, op. cit.*, p. 214.
[41] *Ibid.*, p. 190.

[42] *Ibid.*, p. 173; *In Defense of the National Interest, op. cit.*, p. 146.
[43] *The Impasse of American Foreign Policy, op. cit.*, p. 171.
[44] *In Defense of the National Interest, op. cit.*, pp. 136, 149.
[45] *The Impasse of American Foreign Policy, op. cit.*, p. 191; *Dilemmas of Politics, op. cit.*, pp. 274–75; *The Restoration of American Politics, op. cit.*, pp. 202–3.

obtaining anything worthwhile from the other side.[46]

A.5. National interest and nuclear weapons

It was stated above that the primary interest of all nations consists in the security of national territory and in the safeguarding of the lives and values of the citizens. This is true in the nuclear age as it was true previously. But in contrast to the era which ended in 1945 it is no longer physically possible to guarantee this result.[47] This is due, of course, to the technological revolution in transportation, communication, and war, and in particular to the advent of nuclear weapons.[48] In consequence, all nations—large, small, communist, non-communist—for the first time have an overriding common interest in the avoidance of war.[49] Nuclear weapons have not modified the range of traditional interests pursued by powers, nor have they changed the problems associated therewith. They have, however, modified the means for pursuing those interests: for the most part these must now be peaceful (and therefore) diplomatic in character.[50] All nations whether they like it or not, now must redefine their national interests in terms of the interests of all the others; for contemporary war not only means possible defeat in the traditional sense but also certain destruction of domestic society and of the political regimes and civilizations built on them.[51] This means, in particular, that nations will no longer go to war (and thus will not risk their existence) in pursuit of secondary interests. Now these must all be subjected to the process of diplomatic settlement.[52]

This process of redefinition and accomodation is imperative not only because of the nuclear-technological revolution but also because of the post-World War II political revolution. The latter has wrought five basic destabilizing transformations in the international political system, which together and separately serve to make precarious the connection between violence and foreign policy. These are: (1) expansion of the formerly Europe-centered balance of power system to include the entire world; (2) transfer of the center of gravity of that system to the extra-European peripheries; (3) collapse of the previous multipolar system into a bipolar one; (4) disappearance of the crucial role of the balancer, formerly held by Great Britain, without prospects for a successor; (5) the rise of Asia and Asian nationalism as a major factor in world politics.[53] These radical changes indeed have made the present era revolutionary and force every nation to modify its conduct accordingly. Instead of ignoring these factors of revolution or working in opposition to them (policies which were possible before 1945), it now becomes the interest of each nation to work with these powerful forces and, if possible, direct them

---

[46] *In Defense of the National Interest, op. cit.,* p. 137.

[47] *Dilemmas of Politics, op. cit.,* p. 178.

[48] *In Defense of the National Interest, op. cit.,* pp. 152–60.

[49] *The Restoration of American Politics, op. cit.,* p. 283; *Dilemmas of Politics, op. cit.,* p. 277.

[50] *The Restoration of American Politics, op. cit.,* p. 138; *Dilemmas of Politics, op. cit.,* p. 277.

[51] *The Restoration of American Politics, op. cit.,* p. 275; *In Defense of the National Interest, op. cit.,* p. 162.

[52] "Cuba—The Wake of Isolation," *Commentary,* Vol. 33 (1962), pp. 427–30.

[53] *In Defense of the National Interest, op. cit.,* pp. 40–52.

toward the attainment of national goals.[54]

The nature of alliances also changes in the nuclear age. Previously, nations became allied with one another because they shared some common or complementary interests. Today, on the other hand, alliances—especially those made between one of the bipolar core powers and a peripheral member of its system—carry unacceptable risks to the smaller, less powerful nation. Therefore, in contrast to the past, nations with similar interests today may *not* ally.[55] For instance, European nations today have an interest in *separating* themselves from the United States, or at least not allying themselves too closely.[56] There is thus a tug of war between, on the one hand, the common interest felt among the alliance partners against Soviet pressures and, on the other, the interest in not coming under bombardment in a nuclear war between the giants. So far the interests felt in common have overbalanced the divergent ones but the trend is in the other direction.[57] (Presumably, many of these same pressures are also being felt in the Eastern bloc.) Thus, in the nuclear age, alliances tend to lose their efficacy as instruments for the pursuit of the national interest and as a result nations tend to become more and more isolated from each other.

A.6. National interest and international organization

However, there is an instrument for pursuing the national interest that may take up the slack. This is the United Nations, to which Morgenthau turns next.[58] As we have noted, national interests in the nuclear age do not change, except for the addition of the overriding interest to avoid thermonuclear war. The two core powers in a bipolar world must pursue their national interests by retaining their allies (or at least not allow them to join the opposite camp) and preparing for conflict with the enemy. On the other hand, they must justify their interests and policies to their allies—who now have interests different from the core power—by means of appealing to the general interests of all. These general interests may or may not in reality agree with those of the core power but they must be appealed to nevertheless. This usually means that the core power must ideologically justify and rationalize its interests in terms of supranational interests.[59] The United Nations, a supranational institution, is a good place to pursue this task. The United Nations thus becomes an arena both for the traditional pursuit of national interests, and the rationalization thereof. Nations, to be sure, must be careful to submit for United Nations debate and consideration only those problems for which they *a priori* are sure of obtaining Security Council approval. This means, of course, that issues of dispute between the two camps will not be submitted for solution to the United Nations.[60] But because all matters are debatable by the organs of the United Nations, the national interests of the core powers and the policies made in accordance with them must be defined in terms transcending these interests. That is,

---

[54] "We are Deluding Ourselves in Vietnam," *New York Times Magazine,* April 18, 1965, p. 85.

[55] "The Four Paradoxes of Nuclear Strategy," *The American Political Science Review,* Vol. LVII (1964), p. 33.

[56] "The Crisis in the Western Alliance," *op. cit.,* p. 185.

[57] "Alliances in Theory and Practice," *op. cit.,* p. 193.

[58] *The Impasse of American Foreign Policy, op. cit.,* p. 122.

[59] *In Defense of the National Interest, op. cit.,* p. 104.

[60] *The Impasse of American Foreign Policy, op. cit.,* p. 121.

these two powers must appeal to those whose support the core power seeks on the basis of national interests of the latter and not on the basis of interests in common with the core power,[61] for the United Nations is an instrument for the pursuit of those national interests which nations have in common.[62] Treating the United Nations instrumentally, however, has the somewhat unintended effect of "blunting," "reformulating,"

[61] *Ibid.*, pp. 124, 126.
[62] *Ibid.*, p. 125.

and "adaptation" of policies made in consonance with the national interest. While this does not of course preclude continued pursuit of the national interest outside of the United Nations, that organization does have a real, if subtle, effect on the interests of nations.[63] This is a liability to the core powers since it limits their freedom to define those interests.[64]

[63] *In Defense of the National Interest, op. cit.*, p. 104.
[64] *The Impasse of American Foreign Policy, op. cit.*, p. 127.

3. Vital Interests

MARVIN KALB

Marvin Kalb is the C.B.S. News Diplomatic Correspondent in Washington.

It is perhaps a measure of Congressional respect for Kennan's credentials that he was among the first to be invited to testify before Senator Fulbright's belatedly inquiring committee, despite his persistent criticism of Congress's "interference" in foreign affairs. It might have seemed contradictory for Kennan to seize an opportunity to use the platform of the Senate to carry his

From "The Vital Interests of Mr. Kennan," THE NEW YORK TIMES MAGAZINE, *March 27, 1966, pp. 31ff.* © *1966 by The New York Times Company. Reprinted by permission.*

views on Vietnam to the American people over the head of the Johnson Administration. Not to Kennan. He felt so strongly that the State Department's policy on Vietnam was wrong that he chose to ignore the contradiction. He obviously wanted to encourage debate. He fully succeeded.

His performance was Kennanesque: orderly, sober, intelligent, sincere, provocative. He opposes a military escalation of the war almost as much as he does a "precipitous and disorderly withdrawal." He feels American policy should be aimed at "liquidating" our involvement in Vietnam. He is dismayed by the thought of Vietnam, "a remote and secondary theater of activity," harming our relations with the Soviet Union, a "prime concern," and threatening to "damage" our relations with Japan, which is "of vital importance to us and indeed to the prospects generally of peace and stability in East Asia." In his view, Vietnam "unhinges" our world policy.

Kennan sees the world in terms of "prime" (sometimes he uses the word "vital") and "secondary" areas of concern. There are to him a finite number of "vital" concerns for every nation (for the U.S. the number is five) and an infinite number of "secondary" concerns. Any self-respecting state must learn to distinguish between the two, never allowing itself the luxury of human beings: to be swept along by emotional or legalistic considerations toward major commitments that hold the promise of only minor rewards.

"The Administration speaks of its 'commitment' to Vietnam," Kennan said recently during a lengthy conversation in a musty Washington club for retiring and returning diplomats. "Well, as a teacher, I have a 'commitment,' too— to my students—to raise the questions and to offer my views on current problems."

With this justification, Kennan proceeded to attack the Administration's policy and to construct a vision of the world which conflicts with Dean Rusk's at virtually every point. Kennan profoundly disagrees with the Secretary of State's oft-repeated contention that Vietnam is the Ethiopia of the nineteen-sixties, that its collapse to Communism would be a body blow to American national interest almost equal to the submission of West Berlin to Russia. "Dean is a nice man, sincere and intelligent," Kennan said, choosing his words carefully, "but his historical parallels are completely misconceived. The notion that we must stand up and fight in Vietnam or risk losing the allegiance of our allies around the world is flagrantly unsound.

We have geopolitical interests in Europe of a wholly different order from our interests in Vietnam. That is why I hate to see the Ethiopian parallel fall from the lips of a Secretary of State. Such a moralistic viewpoint has little or nothing to do with history or policy."

He said he believes that Europe's confidence in the United States would remain unimpaired as long as "we did not retire in disgraceful disorder." The Vietcong must not be awarded a "spectacular victory," but neither must we "be locked into unpromising positions."

Kennan also criticized Pentagon strategy in the war, once mentioning Defense Secretary McNamara by name. The idea of bombing North Vietnam to gain a "diplomatic advantage" is merely a form of "military escapism," he said. In South Vietnam "control by night is the only real control"; therefore it is "sophistry" to claim "partial control" over 50 or 60 per cent of the land. He agrees with New York's Senator Robert F. Kennedy that the Vietcong should be granted a role in Saigon's Government. This would be "regrettable," but the outcome would hardly be "tragic."

.   .   .

Throughout his long career Kennan has developed a very special view of America and the world which helps in understanding his thinking about modern diplomacy—more particularly, these days, his thinking about Vietnam, the outlines of which emerged in his Senate testimony. Kennan divides the world into five regions, as noted earlier —all of "vital importance" to the United States because each is capable of producing a modern war-making machine (Kennan poetically uses the term "the sinews of war"). They are the United States itself, and Great Britain, Germany, Russia and Japan, which because of their "sinews" have the means of imposing "grievous" harm upon the American people.

Of course, he recognizes that the list of vital areas may grow. Industrialization, the necessary prerequisite for any war-making machine, may engulf other regions, and they in turn may threaten American interests in different parts of the world. But, at the moment, there are to him only five such areas of "vital" concern, and of these, only Russia has fallen into the hands of an "adversary." It is "absolutely vital" to the over-all interests of the United States that none of the others do. Russia can be "contained." Therefore America should be "vitally" concerned only with these regions; all others are peripheral, South-east Asia included. (Kennan favored American intervention in Korea, because Korea is the gateway to Japan, a "vital" area.)

Kennan sees all of the upheavals which convulse the seventh floor of the State Department and darken headlines throughout the world through the convenient—if occasionally distorted—prism of this theory. He acknowledges that China may one day evolve into a war-making country, but he feels that day is still a long way off. Within the context of his theory, it would have been "infinitely more harmful" to the "interests" of the United States for Italy to have gone Communist in 1948 than for China to have turned Maoist in 1949. Such an event on the Tiber could have jeopardized friendly control of the Rhine and, ultimately, of Britain, two "vital" areas; that outcome would have been "tragic."

Kennan readily admits that his five-region theory may be fallible and that, like a whole generation of American diplomats and commentators, he is Europe-oriented. In his mind, Asia (with the exception of Japan), Africa and Latin America have decades to go before they reach the level of industrial development at which they can begin to produce the "sinews of war" capable of hurting the American people.

But is it not possible that the Communists could aim to gain control of the underdeveloped world, thus outflanking the United States? Possible, but unlikely, Kennan replies, because there is no such thing any longer as a unified Communist movement. No single fountainhead of Communist inspiration exists. Every Communist party is "obliged" to follow a "reasonably independent course." Thus, every party is potentially Titoist and therefore "unlikely" to unite with other Titoist nations in a common drive against the United States. Besides, Kennan feels that all of the Communist nations are now more absorbed in national self-development than in national expansion.

"I can think of nothing we need more at this stage," he wrote in March, 1965, "than a readiness to relax; not to worry so much about those remote countries scattered across the southern crescent, to let them go their own way, not to regard their fate as our exclusive responsibility." When it was suggested to Kennan that he might be following the classic pattern of the nineteen-thirties' liberal turning into the nineteen-sixties' conservative—or even isolationist—all he could do was smile. "Call me a quasi-isolationist, if you wish," he said.

. . .

With a detectable note of sadness, Kennan seems to realize that one of the cruelest ironies of his life is that he conceived of the policy of containment only to see it nurture the spirit of anti-Communism he finds so antithetical to what he considers the best interests of the United States. Anti-Communism helped to produce not only McCarthyism but also the rationale for America's involvement in all of the Vietnams of the world, and Kennan is deeply embarrassed about his role in the evolution of these events.

Moreover, Kennan has always felt that containment has been misunderstood. It was interpreted—"improperly," he feels—as the theoretical justification for establishing military alliances, for rearming West Germany, for creating "unreal blocs," such as the Central Treaty Organization, the Southeast Asia Treaty Organization or even the North Atlantic Treaty Organization, the sacred cow of State Department planners. Those were not what Kennan had envisaged at all. He claims he always meant "political containment," not a military kind of containment.

Kennan is a bit mystical about "political containment." He seems to recognize that military power was necessary to contain the Soviet Union but he is clearly uncomfortable about Washington's dependence upon military power alone to hold a foreign adversary in check. He likes to think in terms of "economic forces" and "national interest" and "historical trends." Military might alone bothers him. He points to the Marshall Plan, Point IV, and the economic aspects of the Truman Doctrine as the kind of policy which holds out exciting prospects for American diplomacy. The deportment of American power in different parts of the world seems too Prussian for Kennan, too brutish for his vision of America.

When he wrote the "X" article, Kennan was thinking in political terms: of the upcoming Italian elections, the civil war in Greece, the growing power of the French Communist party and, most important, the division of Berlin and Germany and, through them, Europe. "There is only one Europe." Kennan believes that "for as long a time as Germany remains divided, war could erupt in Europe and burst into a nuclear catastrophe." The seeds of major war, he feels, are still planted in the division of Germany, not in the division of Vietnam.

Throughout the conversation, Kennan seemed like a father trying desperately to disown a child. He believes that containment had merit when applied to the Soviet Union. It did, in fact, lead to a gentle mellowing of communist excesses, despite too heavy a reliance, as he sees it, upon military containment. But he is still uncertain about whether containment can be applied to other nations with similar results.

He realizes that the United States is trying to "contain" China. Even China says that the United States is trying to contain her, but adds that India, Japan and the Soviet Union are helping, too. But Kennan has the feeling that the policy, as applied to China, is probably fallacious.

.   .   .

POWER

AND

INFLUENCE

Chapter 11

As we have seen, the international political scene is characterized by the presence of an increasing number of autonomous
units, each of which pursues certain self-defined (and sometimes ill-defined)
goals, restrained as little as possible by others and apparently not at all
by abstract moral principles. While the power and position of one's own
state must be placed in the context of the power and position of various
other states within the evolving international environment, there is no
assurance that the goals, and particularly the means and options, selected
by the leaders of the respective governments in pursuit of those goals will
always harmonize. Indeed it is precisely because disharmony frequently
occurs that so much potential or actual international conflict exists.

Given the possibility of interstate conflict—a possibility that is seldom
very remote—each government must constantly be concerned not only
with its own economic, military, and political strength and influence, but
that of others as well. The power of states in international relations is
relative; hence their leaders must at all times be concerned with their own
state's comparative position *vis-à-vis* that of other states.[1] The studied
attempt on the part of statesmen, in light of these realities and of their
perception or understanding of them, so to adjust their country's power

[1] Some preliminary observations about the structure of the international system,
and the way in which that structure affects the behavior of participants were raised in
Chap. 3.

position as to serve its greatest advantage is often referred to as "power politics," and the comparative relationships of the strength of the actors on the stage of world politics as the "balance of power." The ongoing adjustment of the various factors of power, both as conscious acts of decision makers and as an automatic sequence of events, has been characterized by W.T.R. Fox and others as the balancing process. This kaleidoscopic process, which is taking place all the time in our dynamic world of shifting power relationships, is a basic feature of the international system.

Several variations of meaning and usage of the term "balance of power" exist, but fundamentally there seem to be two: balance may connote an equal (or essentially equal) distribution of power between sides, as a scale is "in balance," i.e., *equilibrium;* or it may mean *preponderance,* in a manner analogous to having a balance in the bank, in the sense of possessing a surplus of assets over liabilities.[2] Yet neither of these conceptions covers one of the historically most effective applications of balance of power principles, that by Britain over a period of many decades when she endeavored to hold the balance by placing the weight of her strength and influence on the scales of European politics. By standing against the stronger powers in the scale, Britain thus sought to bring about the equilibrium between her potential enemies that would leave her safe and secure.

For many states an uneasy equilibrium may be all they can aspire to with any hope of achievement. Even this is beyond the capacities of some who can only hope that a more powerful opposing neighbor may be engaged elsewhere or be otherwise unprepared to bring his whole power to bear upon their weak defenses. This common situation often explains why certain smaller and weaker states can get away with so much in their relationships with larger and stronger powers. Just as the United States benefited from this kind of situation (Europe's preoccupation with her internal balance of power throughout the nineteenth century), weak states benefit today from balance of power policies and uncertainties between the Soviet Union, the United States, and other major powers. They may have little quantifiable power, but they exercise considerable influence upon events:

Occasionally the leaders of a state either can, or think they can, acquire the capability successfully to threaten and dominate its neighbors, so that they can altogether ignore the balancing process. Conversely, such statesmen as Woodrow Wilson have condemned the whole idea of power politics and have sought to create a new kind of world system, based upon law rather than upon power. Statesmen after World War II endeavored

---

[2] For instructive treatments of the balance of power in theory and practice, based upon examples drawn from historical situations, see especially Hans J. Morgenthau's discussion in any of the editions of *Politics Among Nations* (New York: Alfred A. Knopf, Inc.).

once again to establish a new kind of world system, and for a time it appeared that the United Nations, including at least in its early years all of the Great Powers (as the League of Nations had not), might succeed. Soon international politics came to be dominated by the Cold War—a bipolarization of world political forces into one of two camps, the American or the Russian. While certain observers profess to discern the beginnings of the emergence of new weights on the scales, others regard the enhancement of Chinese and European strength merely as refinements and complications of an international system still bipolar in its fundamental character. In contrasting the present configuration with that of the interwar period, Hugh Seton-Watson has observed:

> Between the world wars there were seven Great Powers—five in Europe (Britain, France, Germany, Italy, Russia), one in Asia (Japan), and the United States of America. Since 1945 there have been two giant Powers, the United States and the Soviet Union. Admittedly the old Great Powers of Western Europe are still factors to be reckoned with, and in Asia there are two countries of vast population, China and India, which are capable of reaching giant power status within a few decades. But the two giants of today overshadow the world in a manner that is new in human history.[3]

Historically the more frequent manifestation of the balance of power has taken the form of a multiple balance in which a larger number of states, fairly evenly matched, have shifted their alignments to correspond with their changing perceptions of the intentions of others. The operation of this balancing process over considerable time has resulted in the prevention of conflicts which might well have destroyed one or more of the participating states. Each state involved is interested not only in maintaining or improving its own power position in absolute and relative terms but also in preventing other states from becoming so strong that they might at some future time become dangerous. Participants in such a multiple balance of power system thus tend to coalesce against stronger members and come to the aid of weaker states which are threatened. Since coalitions are flexible, all participants proceed with caution and circumspection lest the impression of unreasonable ambition on their part antagonize other members of the system and bring about a coalition between them. At least this is the theory of the multipolar balance. Critics of the theory and especially of the practice in the form of balance-of-power policies argue that, far from preserving peace and protecting the participants, it has always sooner or later brought on war, defeat, and mutual destruction. It may be that the key to the argument lies in whether, without the application of the balancing principle, wars

[3] Hugh Seton-Watson, *Neither War nor Peace* (London: Methuen & Co., Ltd., 1960), p. 9.

would have come *sooner* or *later*; no one has professed lately to see in it the formula for permanent peace.[4] But one must ask whether a given State has to be involved in the balancing process whether it endeavors to carry out a balance of power policy or not.

A bipolar balance is usually regarded as being inherently even more brittle, unstable, and dangerous than a more complex system. The apparently simplified bipolarity of the immediate postwar era may be giving way to a new configuration in which a growing number of states refuse to commit themselves to either side. Close attention to foreign office pronouncements and to propaganda claims and threats reveal that both systems, if not actually breaking up, are at least facing basic internal challenges. The Americans have been frustrated by French intransigence; the Russians have seen the initiative if not the control of world Communism pass from Moscow to Peking; and both blocs are rejected, resisted, or used by new states determined to join neither one.

States have employed a variety of methods to establish or maintain either a fairly equal distribution of power with other states or a situation or preponderance. One of these has been termed "compensation," which consists in giving a state the equivalent of something of which it has been deprived. Another method involves a division of weaker states among much stronger states, so that the underlying power ratio among the dividing powers is essentially maintained, e.g., the various divisions of Poland in the eighteenth and twentieth centuries. Also instructive in this regard was the division of Africa among contending European colonial powers during the past century. As a method for keeping power relations constant (for everyone, that is, except the unfortunate victim), this has proved effective only if the dividers are in fact interested in preserving a balance; in the case of the Munich agreement of 1938, four European states truncated a fifth without its consent, but instead of preserving peace, this only served temporarily to postpone war. A third method takes the form of agreements to establish buffer zones or states between actual or potential antagonists, areas over which both parties exercise agreed-upon degrees of influence. In the past Persia (Iran) has been an example of this, and recent proposals for "disengagement" contemplate this type of solution to the conflict between the U.S.S.R. and the anti-Soviet coalition. More frequently, states conclude alliances and even construct interlocking systems of alliances (if, as in the case of the United States today, a sufficient number of other states possess similar interests, intentions, and especially, security requirements). Such

---

[4] One of the most distinguished of the post-war generation of scholars, Kenneth Thompson, has observed that "it is a sobering fact that the nineteenth century was perhaps the most peaceful of modern centuries; the twentieth, by contrast, has been an epoch of unparalleled bloodshed," and that what characterized the earlier, more peaceful century was a "system of old-fashioned balance of power." "Collective Security Reexamined," *American Political Science Review* (1953), Vol. 47, 413.

alliances may be purely defensive—to protect and preserve a given power position; or they may be offensive—designed to exert pressures to alter a given power situation and construct a new one.

Assuming greater and greater significance is still another approach, represented by attempts within a state to strengthen its own power base relative to others by increasing or improving social cohesion, industrial and economic productivity, economic self-sufficiency, and armaments. This internalized approach is normally easier and hence more common than attempts to weaken the other side through the use of economic, psychological, political, or military means, especially when the contending powers possess the ability to annihilate one another should nuclear war break out between them.

In the balancing process states seek "equilibrium plus" in making power calculations *vis-à-vis* others. Any power position is difficult, even impossible, to measure with any degree of precision. Hence, since there is always a chance for error, each state tends to try to ensure that *its* error is on the side of safety and accordingly tries to acquire more than enough of the factors of power needed to guarantee its security. A surplus of power if attainable is (like a surplus of funds) considered desirable, even if there are no immediate plans for its use. It provides psychological satisfaction, and, more significantly, it constitutes a reserve which can be drawn upon should there be necessity or opportunity to do so.

In assessing the viability of the balance of power, one must not forget the basic purposes which underlie the pursuit of power policies. First of all the objective is to prevent another state or group of states from becoming so powerful as to threaten one's own security (however defined), or even one's own system of basic values, or possibly one's continued existence as a viable society. Second, any statesman wishes to see his own state powerful enough to withstand demands that others may make upon it. Third, he may hope to make certain demands upon others and have those demands honored.

The entire concept of balance of power as a stabilizing force in international politics has been criticized for its unreality, its imprecision, and its inherent danger. Despite such criticism, power politics continues and will continue to be pursued. In terms of the processes which actually do exist in interstate relations, the balance of power is among the facts of international life. Regardless of one's value preferences, it seems evident that sophisticated policy makers of all countries really have no choice but to pursue some type of balance of power policies in order to protect and advance the interests of their state in a context in which these interests are constantly subject to challenge.

1. The Capacity to Influence

J. DAVID SINGER

J. David Singer is Professor of Political Science and Research Political Scientist for the Mental Health Research Institute at the University of Michigan. He is the editor of HUMAN BEHAVIOR AND INTERNATIONAL POLITICS *and of* QUANTITATIVE INTERNATIONAL POLITICS *and the author of* DETERRENCE, ARMS CONTROL AND DISARMAMENT *as well as numerous articles in professional journals.*

Students of international politics often state that power is to us what money is to the economist: the medium via which transactions are observed and measured. Further, there seems to be a solid consensus that power is a useful concept only in its relative sense; such objective measures as military manpower, technological level, and gross national product are viewed as helpful, but incomplete, indices. The concept does not come to life except as it is observed in action, and that action can be found only when national power is brought into play by nations engaged in the process of influencing one another. Until that occurs, we have no operational indices of power, defined here as the *capacity to influence*. In this paper,[1] then, my purpose is to seek a clarification of a formal, analytic model of bilateral inter-nation influence.

. . .

I. SOME GENERAL PROPERTIES OF INFLUENCE

In trying to clarify what we mean by influence, and to articulate its dominant properties, the first point to be noted is that all influence attempts are *future-oriented*. The past and present behavior of the potential influenc*ee* (whom we will label B) may be of interest to A (the influenc*er*) and will certainly affect A's predictions of B's future behavior, but there is nothing A can do about controlling such actions.

From "Inter-Nation Influence: A Formal Model," AMERICAN POLITICAL SCIENCE REVIEW, *57 (June 1963), pp. 420–30. Reprinted by permission of The American Political Science Association and the author.*

[1] This paper was originally prepared for the International Studies Division of the Institute of Defense Analyses. The views expressed are not necessarily those of the Institute, the Arms Control and Disarmament Agency, or the Department of Defense. The author wishes to thank Caxton C. Foster for his assistance both at the conceptual and the graphic level, and Lloyd Jensen for help in surveying the literature on social power.

He[2] may *interpret* the past and present behavior of B in a variety of ways, but obviously he can no longer *influence* it.

The second general observation is that influence may or may not imply a modification of B's behavior. While the tendency (there are exceptions) in both political science and social psychology is to define an influence attempt as one in which A seeks to *modify* the behavior of B, or to identify A's influence over B in terms of "the extent to which he can get B to do something that B would not otherwise do," there are several objections to this restricted meaning.[3] One is that it excludes that

very common form of influence which we might call perpetuation or "reinforcement."[4] That is, it overlooks the many cases of inter-personal and inter-group influence in which B is behaving, or is predicted to behave, in essentially the manner desired by A, but in which A nevertheless attempts to insure the continuation of such behavior, or the fulfillment of the prediction, by various influence techniques.

The second (and more elusive) objection is that it implies no difficulty in A's prediction of what B will do in the absence of the influence attempt. If A could, with a very high degree of confidence, predict how B will act if *no* attempt to modify or reinforce is made, then reinforcement measures would be unnecessary and influence would only be attempted when changes (from predicted to preferred) are sought. For a multitude of reasons, ranging from the complexity of the international system to the theoretical poverty of the disciplines which study that system, such predictability is a long way off. Consequently, A will tend to seek insurance against the possibility of an error in his prediction as long as he is modest in evaluating his predictive abilities.

This leads in turn to a third difficulty, if not objection, which is the probabilistic nature of all predictions. Even if the "state of the art" in international relations were well advanced, there would still be no *certainty* (*probability* = 1.0) on the part of A that B will behave in the predicted fashion.

---

[2] Throughout this paper, we will often use the singular personal pronoun to denote a nation, but it will always be understood that the nation is not a person and is not capable of perceiving, predicting, and preferring in the literal psychological sense. Thus all designations will, unless otherwise specified, refer to those who act for and on behalf of, the nation: the foreign policy decision makers. We are not, however, accepting the proposition of the "methodological individualists," who deny the empirical existence or conceptual legitimacy of the group or nation. Their point of view is articulated in Floyd H. Allport, *Social Psychology* (Boston, 1924), while two persuasive refutations are Ernest Nagel, *The Structure of Science* (New York, 1961) and Charles K. Warriner, "Groups are Real: A Reaffirmation," *American Sociological Review,* Vol. 21 (October 1956), pp. 549–54.

On the choice of the nation-as-actor, see Arnold Wolfers, "The Actors in International Politics," in W. T. R. Fox (ed.) *Theoretical Aspects of International Relations* (Notre Dame, University of Notre Dame Press, 1959) and J. David Singer, "The Level of Analysis Problem in International Relations," *World Politics* Vol. 14 (October 1961), pp. 77–92.

[3] This definition is tentatively employed in Robert A. Dahl, "The Concept of Power," *Behavioral Science,* Vol. II (July 1957) pp. 201–15; Dahl tends to use "power" and "influence" interchangeably. The emphasis on change or modification is also retained by John R. P. French and Bertram Raven, "The

Bases of Social Power," in Dorwin Cartwright (ed.) *Studies in Social Power* (Ann Arbor: Institute for Social Research, 1959) pp. 150–67.

[4] We will use this word in its generic sense, rather than in the various specialized ways found in such psychological theories as conditioning, learning, and S-R.

Consequently, there will always be some incentive to attempt to influence.

Having made the case for both the modification and the reinforcement types as legitimately belonging in the influence attempt category, however, it would be misleading to suggest that they are of equal significance in inter-nation relations. The fact is that if A's decision makers are *reasonably confident* that nation B either *will* behave in a fashion *desirable* to A or *not* behave in an *un*desirable fashion, the incentive to attempt to influence B will diminish, and A may conserve its limited skills and resources for application elsewhere. As the forces at work in A's foreign policy processes move A's decision makers in a pessimistic direction, there will be an increasing application of A's available resources to the influencing of B, until the point is reached where A predicts that *no* influence attempt would be successful.

A third preliminary observation is that inter-nation influence is far from a one-way affair. In the first place, while A is planning or attempting to influence B, B is itself exercising some impact on A's behavior. The very classification of B by A as a potential influencee imme-diately leads to some degree of influence by B upon A, even when B makes no conscious influence attempt. And in the second place, the international system is neither a dyad (duopoly) nor a multi-tude of dyads. For analytical purposes, it is often convenient to scrutinize only two nations at a time, but we cannot forget that all are influencing all, directly or indirectly, merely by sharing the same spatial, temporal, and socio-political environment. Thus, the system is characterized not only by reciprocity but by multiple reciprocity. For the sake of simplicity, however, we will restrict the analysis which follows to direct bilateral relationships between nations of more or less equal power, in which influence or influence attempts are a conscious effort of the national decision makers.[5]

Finally, we might distinguish be-tween an influence *attempt* and the *outcome* of such an attempt. Not only are they not the same phenomena, but they are described and measured in terms of different variables. An influ-ence attempt is described primarily in terms of: (a) A's *prediction* as to how B will behave in a given situation in the absence of the influence attempt; (b) A's *preference* regarding B's behavior; and (c) the techniques and resources A utilizes to make (a) and (b) coincide as nearly as possible. The outcome of such an attempt will be a function not only of (c) above, but also (d) the accuracy of A's prior prediction; (e) B's own value, utility, or preference system; (f) B's estimate of the proba-bilities of various contemplated out-comes; (g) B's resistance (or counter-influence) techniques and resources; and (h) the effects of the international environment.

II. THE INTERNATIONAL SYSTEM AS AN INFLUENCE ENVIRONMENT

Before turning to more refined characteristics of influence, let us place its general properties, as noted above, in their larger setting within the inter-national system.

[5] "Power" may be measured in a mul-titude of ways: relative or absolute, perceived or objective, potential or present; and many criteria may be used in making such measure-ments. Furthermore, the distinction between "fate control" and "behavior control" made by John W. Thibaut and Harold H. Kelley in *The Social Psychology of Groups* (New York, 1959) is quite relevant here. Thus, the U.S. certainly has the power to decide the ultimate *fate* of Cuba, for example, but lacks the power to exercise effective and continuing control over Cuba's day-to-day *behavior*.

THE CAPACITY TO INFLUENCE

The fact that nations invest a great deal of their energies in attempts to influence one another is perfectly obvious, but *why* this should be so is somewhat less apparent. One of the most frequently recurring themes among the peace-makers is that all would be well if nations would only "live and let live." The naïveté of this prescription becomes evident, however, when we recall that such a doctrine can only be effective if one of the following conditions is present: (a) each nation is so completely isolated from all the others that the activities of one have almost no impact on the others; or (b) each is so completely self-sufficient that it has no dependence upon the goals or behavior of the others in order to meet its own "real" and perceived needs. Neither of these conditions characterizes the international system, and it is doubtful whether they ever did. Not only do nations rely heavily upon one another for the commodities (tangible and otherwise) which are sought after, but it is extremely difficult for any nation to trade with or steal from another without this inter-action having some impact on some third party.

But this is only part of the story, and it is the part which is equally applicable to relations among many other forms of social organization. The international system has another characteristic which distinguishes it from other social systems: each actor has the legal, traditional, and physical capacity to severely damage or destroy many of the others with a considerable degree of impunity. In inter-personal, inter-family or other inter-group relations, regardless of the culture, normative restraints and superior third-party governors are sufficient to make murder, plunder and mayhem the exception rather than the rule. But in inter-nation relations the gross inadequacy of both the ethical and the political restraints make violence not

only accepted but anticipated. As a consequence, the scarcest commodity in the international system is security—the freedom to pursue those activities which are deemed essential to national welfare and to survival itself.

To be more specific then, we might assert that under the survival rubric the highest priority is given to autonomy—nations are constantly behaving in a fashion intended to maximize their present and future freedom of action and to minimize any present or future restraints upon that freedom. In such a system, no single nation can afford to "live and let live" as long as the well established and widely recognized anarchic norms are adhered to, acted upon, and anticipated by, most of the others. Any social system must contain some inevitable competition and conflict, but in the international system they are handled in a more primitive fashion. Moreover, there seems to be only the barest correlation between the way a nation pursues its interests and the nature of its leadership or its sociopolitical institutions. To suggest otherwise would be, to quote an excellent analysis of the problem, to commit the "second-image fallacy."[6] Rather, we might more accurately conclude that the international system itself is the key element in explaining why and how nations attempt to influence the behavior of one another.

III. PERCEIVED BEHAVIOR AS A DETERMINANT IN INFLUENCE ATTEMPTS

Though the international system is definitely one in which influence and

[6] See Kenneth N. Waltz, *Man, the State, and War* (New York, Columbia University Press, 1959) and the review article based on it: J. David Singer, "International Conflict: Three Levels of Analysis," *World Politics*, Vol. 12 (April 1960), pp. 453–61.

counter-influence attempts are a dominant characteristic, our interest is in analyzing the factors which tend to produce any given such attempt. The first prerequisite for an influence attempt is the perception on the part of A's decision-makers that A and B are, or will be, in a relationship of significant interdependence, and that B's future behavior consequently could well be such as to exercise either a harmful or beneficial impact on A.

Not too long ago, most nations were in such a relationship with only a handful of other nations. Even in today's highly interdependent world, one still finds, for example, little interaction between Paraguay and Burma or Egypt and Iceland. Moreover, no nation has the resources to engage in serious efforts to influence a great many of the others at any given time; we select our influence targets because of the perceived importance of our relationship to, and dependence upon, them. In addition, there is a particular tendency to concentrate such efforts upon those nations with which we are already in a highly competitive and conflictful relationship, devoting far fewer resources to those with whom our relations are either friendly or negligible.

Not only do our perceptions of interdependence and conflict-cooperation strongly determine whom we will attempt to influence, but, as subsequent sections will suggest, they affect the types of influence attempt we will make and the likelihood of success or failure in that attempt.

IV. PREDICTED BEHAVIOR AS A DETERMINANT IN INFLUENCE ATTEMPTS

The second determinant is that of the *predictions* which A's decision-makers reach regarding the nature of B's future behavior: what is B likely to do, in the absence of any conscious influence attempt by A? This expectation may be of two rather distinct types. One deals with the affirmative *commission* of an act, and the other deals with the more passive *non-commission* or *omission* of an act. In the first case, illustrations range from the American expectation that, in the absence of any conscious influence attempt by ourselves, India might endorse a troika arrangement for arms control supervision, to the fear that the Soviet Union might employ military force in an effort to drive us out of Berlin. In the second case, we think of such examples of non-commission or failure to act as Germany *not* meeting its ground force commitment to NATO, or mainland China *not* participating in a disarmament conference to which it had been invited. Though one can often describe expected acts of omission as ones of commission (*i.e.*, Germany *refusing* to draft more soldiers or China *rejecting* the conference bid), and with somewhat greater conceptual straining even describe acts of commission in the semantics of omission (India *not rejecting* the troika, or the Soviets *not refraining from* force) one or the other of these two emphases is almost always more obvious and salient to the influencer, as discussed in the next section.

V. PREFERRED BEHAVIOR AS A DETERMINANT IN INFLUENCE ATTEMPTS

Finally, and perhaps most important, there is A's *preference* regarding B's future behavior. Without preferences, the perception of B's present behavior and predictions regarding his future behavior have only limited importance to A and would exercise only a minor impact on A's tendency to invest in an influence attempt. Here we might illustrate by reference to the contingent predictions suggested above. The United States prefers that India *not* accept the troika plan, and that the Soviets *not* use force in Berlin; we care much less what administrative arrangements New Delhi *does* accept, or what other techniques the Kremlin *does* apply in Berlin. Our main concern is that they *not* do the specified, but partially likely, act from among a number of possible acts. For us, removing or reducing the likelihood of what they *might* do is much more salient than which one of a host of alternative acts they select in its place. Conversely, the concern of our decision-makers (as the potential influencers) over what the Germans do *not* do with their limited manpower, or what the Chinese do *not* do regarding a disarmament conference is much less than our concern that they *do* engage in the act which we prefer. The salience of what they *do* do is higher for us than the salience of what they do *not* do, because of the nature of our preferences.

To illustrate this crucial distinction further, let us suppose that A predicts that B is about to supply weapons to an insurgent group opposing the government of an ally of A's; A's concern is not so much what else B does with these weapons as with seeing that B does *not* supply them as predicted. B might, at this juncture, scrap them, sell them to a neutral nation outside the immediate conflict area, or give them to an ally, and A would have a much less intense concern over which of these alternatives B selected. In another— and very real—case, A might want desperately to prevent its major adversary B from supplying nuclear weapons to an ally of B with whom A has had a number of disastrous military encounters in the past. Whether B gives these nuclear weapons to another ally, converts them for peaceful uses, or retains them in its own arsenal is of much less

moment than that they *not* be supplied to the feared recipient. In both these cases, avoiding or preventing a specific outcome is of considerably greater salience to the influencer than is the remaining range of alternatives open to B.

VI. PERCEPTION, PREDICTION, AND PREFERENCE: THEIR COMPOSITE EFFECT

So far, we have discussed individually the way in which A's perceptions, predictions, and preferences will tend to move him toward an influence attempt *vis-à-vis* B. What are the implications of combining these three sets of variables? More particularly, what are the possible combinations, and what is the effect of each upon: (a) the motivation of A to undertake an influence attempt, (b) the relative amount of effort required for success, and (c) the techniques and instruments A will employ?

As the following chart will indicate, there are eight possible combinations of influence situations, four dealing with cases in which A prefers that B *do* a certain act (*X*) and four in which A prefers that B *not* do a particular act, but do almost anything else (non-*X* or *O*) instead. The first four might be called *persuasion* cases, and the latter four *dissuasion*. Since each of these eight cases would seem to pose a different type of influence problem for A and call for varying combinations of techniques, let us list and label them as in Figure 1.

In cases 1 through 4, A prefers that B do act *X*, and in cases 5 through 8, A prefers that B *not* do act *X*, but do *O* (anything else but act *X*). Cases 1 and 5 are relatively simple and normally would call for no impressive influence attempt: B not only is already acting or not acting as A prefers, but the predic-

	Persuasion Situations: A Prefers X				Dissuasion Situations: A Prefers O			
	1	2	3	4	5	6	7	8
Preferred Future Behavior	X	X	X	X	O	O	O	O
Predicted Future Behavior	X	X	O	O	O	O	X	X
Perceived Present Behavior	X	O	X	O	O	X	O	X

FIGURE 1. Types of Influence Situations.

tion is that such behavior will continue into the relevant future. Cases 2 and 6 are, however, slightly more interesting: again B's predicted behavior is seen as congruent to that which A prefers in the future, but A observes that for the moment B's behavior is different from the preferred or predicted. And in cases 3 and 7, B's present behavior *is* what A prefers, but the prediction is that it will *not* remain so without any effort on A's part. Finally, in cases 4 and 8 we have the most difficult situation for A: he perceives B not only as not behaving as preferred, but as unlikely to do so in the future, without some effort on the part of A. These, then, are the eight typical situations confronting a potential influencer, ranged more or less in order of increasing difficulty.

VII. THE INFLUENCEE'S DECISIONAL CALCULUS

Having examined the varieties of influence situations, we should notice one other consideration prior to evaluating the range of techniques available to the influencer in these situations. This is the influencee's decisional calculus: the abstract dimensions upon which he (*i.e.*, those individuals who, alone or together, act on behalf of the target nation) weighs a range of conceivable outcomes in any influence situation. For every outcome which any decision-maker can conceive of as possible, there are at least two such dimensions. The

degree to which he likes or dislikes the prospect is called the *utility* or *disutility*, and the likelihood which he assigns to its ever occurring is called the *probability*. Both of these are, of course, subjective variables: preferences and predictions of the influencee (B).

In the abstract, the combined judgments which the influencee makes along both of these dimensions will determine his contingent expectations and thus his response to the influence attempt. Before combining them, let us examine each in somewhat more detail. As to the subjective utility dimension, we proceed from the assumption that an individual or a group does—implicitly or explicitly—have a set of benchmarks by which it is able to arrange conceivable outcomes (be they threatening, rewarding, or more typically, both) in some order of preference. These benchmarks usually derive from value systems and goal structures and, though they are by no means uniform from nation to nation, those relevant to foreign policy behavior tend to have a great deal in common. For example, outcomes that appear to restrict short-range freedom of action will almost invariably be placed very low in any such utility scale; they will be assigned a high *dis*utility score. Conversely, those which seem likely to minimize the power of some other competing nation (A, C, or D), and hence reduce that competitor's capacity to restrict one's own (B's) freedom, are normally rated high on utility. If we go much beyond these basic drives of nations, however, we get into the peculiar webs of their secondary goals and their varying formal and informal ideologies.

We may pause, though, to point out that national preferences are by no means fixed and permanent. Not only do successive parties and factions in a particular nation bring differing preference structures into office, but even the same sub-group or individuals undergo value changes while in power. Consequently, we must not overlook the usefulness to A of seeking to induce attitudinal (especially value and preference) changes in B's elites as an alternative means of influencing B's existing preferences, or of seeking to change them now in order to make it easier to appeal to them later.

Nations do not, however, commit themselves to actions merely because one possible outcome of such actions seems to be extremely attractive or because it may avoid an extremely *un*attractive outcome. No nation has the unlimited resources and skills which such behavior would require. They must compare these possible outcomes not only in terms of a *preference* ordering, but also in terms of their estimated *likelihood*. And just as there are important differences between nations in the matter of assigning utilities and disutilities, there are equally important (but more subtle) differences when it comes to assigning probabilities to future events. Some are more willing than others to play the "long shot," and pursue an objective whose probability of attainment may be quite low. On the other hand, there do seem to be strong similarities here, as in preference ordering. A perusal of recent diplomatic history strongly suggests that most nations are remarkably conservative in foreign policy; *i.e.*, they seldom commit resources and prestige to the pursuit of

an outcome which seems improbable—no matter how attractive that outcome may be. Individuals, on the other hand, reveal far greater ranges of risk-taking propensities, with many getting a large measure of psychological satisfaction from the low-probability-of-success decision.[7]

The point which concerns us here, however, is that—despite idiosyncrasies on one or the other dimension—nations *combine* both sets of considerations in responding to an influence attempt or in any other choice situation. In graphic terms, we might depict this combining process as in Figure 2.

Suppose that A is attempting to influence B by the use of threatened punishment in order to deter B from pursuing a certain goal (*i.e.*, A is trying to induce *O*). If B attaches a high utility to the outcome which he is pursuing while the threat which A makes would—if carried out—constitute a loss whose disutility is of apprximately the same magnitude, these two considerations will tend to cancel out and the important dimension becomes the probability of each outcome actually eventuating. If B estimates that the probability of A carrying out the threatened punishment is quite low (let us say .25) and that he therefore has a .75 probability of pursuing his goal *without* A executing the threat (perhaps its cost to A is seen as quite high) the resultant product would tend to make B adhere to his original intention. Though he realizes that there is *some* chance that A will act to punish him, the combined probability and disutility is so much less than the combined probability and utility of A's *not* acting, that B decides to take the gamble.

[7] See Ward Edwards, "Utility and Subjective Probability: Their Interaction and Variance Preferences," *Journal of Conflict Resolution*, Vol. 6 (March 1962), pp. 42–51.

PROBABILITIES

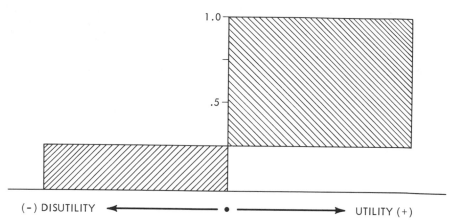

FIGURE 2. Influencee's Decisional Calculus.

This is, of course, a rather abstract model, and it not only deviates from the kinds of articulate, as well as implicit, calculations which policy makers employ, but it oversimplifies the choice situation with which nations are ordinarily confronted. For example, B must normally weigh his utility-times-probability product against not only the disutility-times-probability of A's *threatened* punishment but against a range of greater or lesser punishments which A is capable of inflicting and against the probability of each of these occurring.[8] Furthermore this model assumes that choice situations and influence attempts, as well as their possible outcomes, occur at discrete and identifiable moments in time. The assumption is extremely useful for analytical purposes, but it pays insufficient attention to the overlapping and highly unpredictable time scale along which such situations and alternate outcomes may occur. Finally, it ignores three important quantitative considerations. One of these

is the relative weight which a given set of decision-makers might assign to each of the two dimensions; in their implicit fashion, nations do differ in the degree to which they emphasize either the probability or the preference element in their appraisal of an outcome. Moreover, these two dimensions are by no means psychologically independent; the more highly valued an outcome is, the greater the tendency to exaggerate the probability that it can be achieved (the wish is father to the thought), and conversely, when a probability looks very low, the tendency will be to downgrade the attractiveness of the associated outcome. Thirdly, there is the tendency toward polarity: as subjective probabilities move up or down from .5 they will be exaggerated in the direction of either the certainty (1.0) or the impossibility (0.0) end of the scale. Recognizing these limitations does not, however, invalidate this influencee's decisional model. It merely reminds us that it cannot be employed for either descriptive or predictive purposes in a purely mechanical way. But used in a careful, self-conscious fashion it can be helpful to both the study and the execution of

[8] Among the outcomes to be considered are those which might impinge on the domestic setting or upon one's allies or any Nth powers.

the decision process. For the scholar, much of the confusion and mystery of that process could be clarified, and for the policy maker, regardless of the weights and values he attaches, it could identify the range of alternatives and indicate the implications of each. It might even lead to consideration of a larger number of alternatives and hence mitigate one of the greatest causes of diplomatic disaster—the prematurely restricted repertoire.

VIII. INFLUENCE TECHNIQUES

Up to this juncture, we have delineated some of the general characteristics of inter-nation influence, identified its three major dimensions alone and together, and articulated a submodel of the influencee's decisional considerations. Now let us turn to the two broad classes of technique available to the influencer: threat and promise. Each may be used either to modify or to reinforce, although, as we shall see later, not with equal efficacy. Each has an appropriate role, but careful choice must be made in determining which is best suited to the various classes of influence situation.

By *threat* we mean the communication to the influencee (B) by the influencer (A) that if a certain preferred act (X) is not taken, or non-act (O) is not avoided by B, there is a given probability that A will act to punish B in a particular fashion. That punishment may take the form either of withholding a reward, denying a preference, or positively damaging that which B values.[9]

[9] One quite successful attempt has been made to draw an analytic distinction between punishment and denial, but it seems less relevant here. In *Deterrence by Denial and*

By *promise* we mean the communication to B that if he complies with A's preference, A will, with some given probability, act to reward B. Again, that reward may range from withholding a contemplated punishment to the enhancement of one or more of B's values and preferences.

Threat and punishment and promise and reward go together, but the distinction must be constantly kept in mind. Threat and promise refer to nothing but contingent, probable future events, while punishment and reward are concrete acts that already have taken, or are in the process of taking, place. Thus punishments and rewards may be threatened or promised respectively, and they may be contemplated by both A and B, but they have none of the empirical concreteness in a future situation that they have in past or present situations.

In inter-nation influence, reward and punishment for past or ongoing behavior may be said to serve primarily as a link between B's experiential present and his anticipated future. The outcomes which accompany particular actions in B's past and present serve as predictors of such associations in the future. Therefore, the use of rewards and punishments by A should be devoted, among other aims, to increasing the *credibility* of the promises and threats which he transmits to B. This is not to suggest that credibility-building is the only relevant use for reward and punishment in attempting to influence an opponent of approximately equal power. Present-oriented techniques

Punishment (Princeton, Center of International Studies, 1959) and in *Deterrence and Defense* (Princeton University Press, 1961) Glenn Snyder refers to retaliation as punishment, while denial refers to the costs inflicted upon B (the deterree who was not deterred) while trying to gain his military objective.

	Persuasion Situations: A Prefers X				Dissuasion Situations: A Prefers O			
	1	2	3	4	5	6	7	8
Preferred Future Behavior	X	X	X	X	O	O	O	O
Predicted Future Behavior	X	X	O	O	O	O	X	X
Perceived Present Behavior	X	O	X	O	O	X	O	X
Reinforce or Modify	R	M	R	M	R	M	R	M
Punish?	No	P	No	Yes	No	P	No	Yes
Reward?	Yes	No	Yes	No	Yes	No	Yes	No
Threaten?	P	Yes	Yes	Yes	P	Yes	Yes	Yes
Promise?	Yes	Yes	Yes	Yes	Yes	Yes	Yes	Yes

FIGURE 3. Hypothesized Relevance of Influence Techniques.

might also serve the supplementary purposes of (a) hastening an influencee's *shift* from non-preferred to preferred behavior, or (b) reinforcing current preferred behavior if there is some indication that it might not continue.

. . .

The most obvious undesirable side effect of threat is that it may often do no more than "modify the form of antisocial behavior which is chosen."[10] In other words, by making one path of behavior which is undesirable to A seem unattractive to B, A may merely drive B into other behavior which, while more attractive to B than the action which has been associated with impending punishment, is equally undesirable to A. And for A to threaten B for so wide a range of anticipated acts could either exceed A's capabilities or create such a dilemma for B that he has no choice but to carry out the action and accept (or retaliate for) the consequences.

As to the effect of threat on B's capacity to respond rationally, a number of disturbing findings appear. First of all, threat often exercises a negative influence on B's capacity to recognize

signals and communications accurately. Not only might B become less able to identify and respond to neutral messages, but he may also lose some of his ability to recognize subsequent threats. Thus, threats might well make it difficult or impossible for A to convey the very messages upon which his capacity to influence B must rest.[11] An equally dysfunctional result is that of "cognitive rigidity:" the inability of B to respond efficiently and adequately to changing stimuli, and a consequent breakdown in B's problem-solving capacity.[12] This experiment also suggests that the ultimatum is a particularly dangerous form of threat, inasmuch as the subjects dropped markedly in their capacity to respond appropriately when the experimenter reduced the time allowed for making that response.

Similar results were found when subjects were threatened with a physical shock. The threat of this highly undesirable possibility produced a high level of stress and markedly hampered their

[10] Alex Comfort, *Authority and Delinquency in the Modern State* (London, Routledge and Kegan Paul, 1950), p. 74.

[11] Charles D. Smock, "The Relationship Between Test Anxiety, Threat-Expectancy, and Recognition Thresholds for Words," *Journal of Personality*, Vol. 25 (1956), pp. 191–201.

[12] Sidney Pally, "Cognitive Rigidity as a Function of Threat," *Journal of Personality*, Vol. 23 (1955), pp. 346–55.

problem-solving capacity.[13] The stress induced by threat has also been reported as not only degrading an actor's predictability but his own confidence in that predictability as well.[14]

On the other hand, there is a tendency among some observers of international relations to exaggerate the dysfunctional effects of threat and to ignore the very real role it does and must play in the contemporary international system. These critics forget that most of the influence and social control situations from which they analogize take place in an ordered, hierarchical environment in which influence is normally based on legitimate authority, recognized roles, and accepted norms. To illustrate, one of the more thorough analyses of social power lists five major bases of such power: reward power, coercive power, legitimate power, referent power, and expert power.[15] Of these five, reward often requires more resources than are found in a highly competitive influence relationship between equals, legitimate power can only be exercised through the frail channels of international law or organization, referent power is generally absent between rivals, and expert power is seldom recognized by national decision-makers. Coercion via threat is, by process of elimination, one influence technique upon which we must continue to rely

until we have markedly modified the international system.

A point worth noting in this connection has been demonstrated in a number of experiments on group performance under varying degrees of stress. The results "indicated that the performance of the group was best under mild stress."[16] If threat produces stress (as we assume), the absence of threat may often be as detrimental to successful influence attempts as too heavy a dose of it. The lesson seems to be to use enough threat to generate stress, but not so much as to produce high anxiety. If the upper threshold is crossed (and it varies from nation to nation and situation) we are likely to generate the sort of undesirable effects which reduce B's rationality. The less rational B is, the less likely he is to consider the entire range of alternative actions open to him, and the less likely he is to analyze adequately the implications of each such alternative. Anxiety induced by excessive threat may be said to contract B's repertoire of possible responses as well as his ability to predict the payoffs associated with each.

In the same vein, we have some experimental results which indicate the impact of threat upon group cohesiveness. While it is generally true that external threat exercises a unifying effect, there are some important exceptions, and when cohesiveness in B is reduced, some serious problems arise.[17] Admittedly, internal divisions may lead to a diminution in B's power *vis-à-vis*

[13] Robert E. Murphy, "Effects of Threat of Shock, Distraction and Task Design on Performance," *Journal of Experimental Psychology*, Vol. 58 (1959), pp. 134–41.

[14] Alvin Landfield, "Self-predictive Orientation and the Movement Interpretation of Threat," *Journal of Abnormal and Social Psychology*, Vol. 51 (1955), pp. 434–38.

[15] John R. P. French and Bertram Raven, "The Bases of Social Power," in Dorwin Cartwright (ed.), *Studies in Social Power* (Ann Arbor, Institute for Social Research, 1959).

[16] John T. Lanzetta, "Group Behavior Under Stress," *Human Relations*, Vol. 8 (1955), pp. 29–52.

[17] For example, Albert Pepitone and Robert Kleiner, "The Effects of Threat and Frustration on Group Cohesiveness," *Journal of Abnormal and Social Psychology*, Vol. 54 (1957), pp. 192–99.

A, thus enhancing the credibility of threat even further. But on the other hand, a drop in B's relative power is not necessarily a precursor to compliance. Moreover—and this is a frequently overlooked consideration—the creation of divisions within B may make an intelligent response to A's influence attempt almost impossible. When B's top elites are in firm control of their nations, they are more capable of (a) making rational choices and (b) making the concessions necessary to A's successful influence attempt. Conversely, when they are preoccupied with critics, conspirators, and powerful "inevitable war" factions at home, they must resist influence attempts in order to stabilize their shaky power base.

Another point that seems to emerge in regard to the role of threat, (and to a lesser extent, promise) is that B must be provided with two categories of information. One is the precise nature of the action which A prefers to see B take (X) or avoid (O); without this information B is unable to respond in a mutually advantageous fashion. The other is the availability of alternatives, and this is particularly relevant in the dissuasion situation.[18] For A to try to dissuade B from a given action (to induce O) when B must clearly do X or something similar to X, without helping B to ascertain which O acts are available to B and acceptable to A, is to call

for a probable showdown. If B is completely thwarted, he has little choice but to resist.

Also worth considering, in terms of the limitations of threat, is the fact that A may well be able to modify B's decisional calculus in the appropriate fashion and still fail in his influence attempt. Even though, in the time period implied by the effort to modify or reinforce, B might find A's preferences the most attractive alternative behavior for himself, he may nevertheless refuse to comply. The explanation lies primarily in the context of longer-range considerations on B's part: precedent. B (or A, when in the B role) may be concerned that his compliance under threat will set a precedent. Each time that B does the rational thing and complies with the preferences of A, he increases A's propensity to believe in the efficacy of threat, and to utilize it again and again. As a result, B has an additional reason to do the thing which is, in the specific and discrete influence situation, irrational. Moreover, B must combine his refusal to comply with a more-or-less immediate counter-influence effort, in order to compel A to re-allocate those resources which might otherwise be used to carry out his threat. In a simplified way, this is what an armaments race boils down to: threat and counter-threat, coupled with the drive toward ever-increasing military capabilities with which to resist these threats.

IX. CONCLUSION

Without laboring the need for an empirically based theory of inter-nation influence, it should not be amiss to note that its lack is both a cause of intellectual embarrassment to political science and a menace to the human race. For the policy-maker to select

---

[18] Daniel Katz, "The Functional Approach to the Study of Attitudes," *Public Opinion Quarterly* Vol. 24 (1960), pp. 163–204. Note that this does not preclude the use of influence by ambiguity; it calls for clarity regarding A's preferences but permits ambiguity regarding A's behavior if B does not comply. Highly suggestive in this regard is Thomas C. Schelling, "The Threat That Leaves Something to Chance," in *The Strategy of Conflict* (Cambridge, Harvard University Press, 1960).

intelligently from among a wide range of alternative decisions, he must be able to predict their outcomes with *some* degree of reliability. Such prediction requires far more than the "hunches" by which we operate today; having no sound criteria for behavior choices, the policy-maker will tend, as he has in the past, to adopt those policies which have the most powerful or persuasive advocates, regardless of the accuracy (or even the existence) of the "theory" upon which those policies are allegedly based.

And as long as the nations continue to base their policies on so flimsy a foundation, our understanding will be incomplete, our predictions unreliable, and our policies deficient. I would not want to exaggerate the reliability of any theory we might build, nor minimize the difficulties of injecting it into the policy process, but neither we nor our adversaries of the moment can afford these present deficiencies. The probabilities of error are already much too high, and the disutilities could be disastrous.

2. Reciprocal Influence

AMITAI ETZIONI

Amitai Etzioni is Professor of Sociology at Columbia University, where he is also associated with the Institute of War and Peace Studies. His books include MODERN ORGANIZATIONS, POLITICAL UNIFICATION, *and* THE ACTIVE SOCIETY.

The pattern of events between June 10 and November 22, 1963, provided a partial test of a theory of international relations. The essence of the theory is that psychological gestures initiated by one nation will be reciprocated by others with the effect of reducing international tensions. This tension reduction, in turn, will lessen the probability of international conflicts and wars.

"The Kennedy Experiment," THE WESTERN POLITICAL QUARTERLY, *20 (June 1967), pp. 361–80. Reprinted by permission.*

Examining this theory in light of the 1963 experiment, I ask: (a) What are the main propositions of the theory? (b) What initiatives were actually taken by the United States in the experiment period, and how did the Union of Soviet Socialist Republics react? (c) What were the effects of these initiatives and responses on inter-bloc relations, and to what degree did these effects conform to the expectations of the theory? (d) What other factors, not accounted for by the theory, could have produced all or part of these effects? (e) What factors limited both the scope and the extent of the experiment, and under what conditions could it be replicated or extended?[1]

A PSYCHOLOGICAL THEORY OF INTERNATIONAL RELATIONS

The theory views the behavior of nations basically as that of persons who have strong drives that motivate their pursuit of goals, influence their choice of means, and distort the communications they send and receive. It suggests that nations, when in conflict, tend to be caught in a spiral. The hostility of one as perceived by the other evokes his hostility, which in turn is perceived by the first side, further increasing *his* hostility. Arms races, in which the participant countries increase the level of their armaments because the other countries are doing so, are viewed as an expression of such upward spiraling of hostile reactions.

Psychological analysis of international behavior has been so discredited[2] that most political scientists and members of sister-disciplines might find their patience tried when asked to examine such a theory. It should therefore be stressed from the outset that the evidence provided below, although partial, provides some new support for some elements of the psychological approach. While the more extreme version of the theory remains unsupported, a moderate version is strengthened enough to stand among the major hypotheses on international behavior that are to be explored further. After a brief recapitulation of the theory and its two versions, the evidence speaks for itself.

According to both versions of the theory, a high level of hostility generates psychological blocks that prevent the sides from facing international reality. Various defense mechanisms are activated: for one, a high level of tension tends to produce a *rigid* adherence to a policy chosen under earlier conditions, e.g., the sides increase armaments and hold to a hostile posture ("cold war"), though armaments have been procured beyond military needs, and hostile feelings are no longer justified in view of changes in the character and intentions of the opponent.[3] These changes are *denied,* another mode of defensive behavior, to make the continuation of the earlier policy psychologically possible.

Further, fears of nuclear war, *repressed* since they are too threatening to be faced, express themselves in stereotyping and paranoia, indications of which advocates of the theory find in the conduct of nations locked in a state of international tensions. *Stereotyping* is represented by the divisions of the world into black and white, good and bad,

---

[1] This article grew out of my work at the Institute of War and Peace Studies at Columbia University. I am grateful for the research assistance of Sarajane Heidt and Robert McGheean. Since this article was written two books have appeared which provide additional documentation for the points made but seem not to affect the conclusions reached: See Theodore C. Sorensen, *Kennedy* (New York, Harper and Row, 1965), esp. chap. XXV, and Arthur M. Schlesinger, Jr., *A Thousand Days* (Boston, Houghton Mifflin, 1965), esp. pp. 888–923. Additional treatment of this subject will be included in my *The Active Society: A Theory of Societal and Political Process* (New York: Free Press of Glencoe, forthcoming).

[2] See, for example, Kenneth Waltz, *Man, the State, and War* (New York: Columbia U. Press, 1959), chap. III.

[3] Gabriel A. Almond, *The American People and Foreign Policy* (New York: Praeger, 1960), p. xvi.

nations,[4] and the manipulation of information by selecting among and distorting the content of communications, so that positive information about one's adversary is ignored and negative information about one's own side disregarded. Blocked or distorted communication between the sides thus prevents "reality-testing" and correction of false images.

Stereotyping is often accompanied by *paranoia*. Whatever the adversary offers is interpreted as seeking to advance his own goals and as a trap for us. If the Soviets favor complete and general disarmament, this in itself brings Americans to point to disarmament as a Communist ruse.[5] A possibility of a genuine give-and-take is ignored. The same repressed fear, the psychological analysis continues, causes even reasonable concessions to the other side, made as part of a give-and-take, to be seen as submission or, to use the political term, appeasement. The labeling of bargaining behavior as disloyal or treacherous impedes negotiations that require open-mindedness, flexibility, and willingness to make concessions even though not sacrificing basic positions and values.

What could a therapy be? How, the psychologists ask, can the vicious circle of hostile moves and countermoves be broken? The answer is similar to psychoanalytic technique—increased and improved communication. Communication can be increased by visits of Americans to Russia and Russians to America, exchange of newspapers, publication of American columns in Soviet newspapers and vice versa, by summit conferences, and the like.[6] Communication will become less distorted and tensions will be reduced if one of the sides begins to indicate a friendly state of mind. While such indications will be initially mistrusted, if continued they will be reciprocated, reducing hostility which in turn will reduce the counter-hostility, thus reversing the cold war spiral. Once the level of tension is reduced, and more communication is received from the other side, there will be an increased ability to perceive the international reality as it is, which will further reduce tensions. Joint undertakings are also favored because psychological experiments with children have shown that the introduction of shared tasks helps to reduce hostility.[7] International cooperative research, joint exploration of the stars, oceans, and poles, joint rather than competitive development aid, are hence favored.[8]

There are significant differences in the extent to which this theory claims to explain international behavior. Strongly put, it suggests that "war starts in the minds of man" and "the situation is what we define it to be." In this interpretation, the causes of war are psychological and can be fully explained

---

[4] Urie Bronfenbrenner, a psychologist, found that when American school children were asked why the Russians planted trees alongside a road, they responded that the trees blocked vision and "made work for the prisoners," whereas *American* trees were planted "for shade." *Saturday Review,* January 5, 1963, p. 96.

[5] On disarmament as political gamesmanship, see John W. Spanier and Joseph L. Nogee, *The Politics of Disarmament* (New York: Praeger, 1962), chap. 2.

[6] These ideas are also held by non-psychologically oriented writers. For example, see C. Wright Mills, *The Causes of World War III* (New York: Simon & Schuster, 1958), pp. 103ff.

[7] A study often cited in this context is Muzafer and Carolyn Sheriff, *Groups in Harmony and Tension: An Integration of Studies on Intergroup Relations* (New York: Harper, 1953).

[8] See discussions of the International Cooperation Year—for instance, the *Washington Post,* March 7, 1965.

in psychological terms. Arms are merely an expression of these attitudes of mind.[9] If attitudes are modified, arms will either not be produced or have no threatening impact. The people of New Jersey, it is pointed out, do not fear nuclear arms held by New Yorkers.

More moderate versions of the theory view psychological factors as one aspect of a situation that contains economic, political, and military dimensions as well. Just as triggers without hostilities do not make a war, so hostilities without arms cannot trigger battles. Moreover, even if armaments were initially ordered to serve a psychological motive, once available they generate motives of their own to propel hostile postures and wars. Thus one can hold the psychological theory with varying degrees of strength.[10] Osgood, in most of his writings on this subject, has advanced the stronger version,[11] while

this author subscribes to the more moderate one.[12]

A second line of variation centers on where the blame for triggering the spiral is placed. Some writers tend to view the sides as equally at fault with no "real" reason for a cold war other than misunderstanding. For example, Stalin only wished to establish weak friendly governments on his Western borders, a desire which the West misperceived as expansionistic. Others tend to put more of the blame on the West or on the East. All of these interpretations can be coupled with the psychological analysis on the grounds that regardless of the initiator and whether the initial cause was real or imagined, the same process of psychological escalation is at work. The therapy, hence, remains the same. To insist that the side that triggered the process be the one to take the initiative to reverse it, is viewed as immature behavior.

Next, there are important differences in the steps suggested to break the cycle. It is generally agreed that measures which require multilateral negotiations are not appropriate for the initiation of tension reduction. The high level of hostility and mutual suspicions invariably disrupts the negotiations, and the mutual recriminations that follow increase rather than reduce the level of international tensions. Unilateral steps are therefore needed. The im-

---

[9] In a statement typical of this line of argument, Erich Fromm points out: "This time the choice between violent-irrational, or anticipatory-rational behavior is a choice which will affect the human race and its cultural, if not its physical survival.

"Yet so far the chances that such rational-anticipatory action will occur are bleak. Not because there is no possibility for such an outcome in the realistic circumstances, but because on both sides there is a thought barrier built of clichés, ritualistic ideologies, and even a good deal of common craziness that prevents people—leaders and led—from seeing sanely and realistically what the facts are, from recognizing alternative solutions to violence. Such rational-anticipatory policy requires...a serious examination of our own biases, and of certain semipathological forms of thinking which govern our behavior." Erich Fromm, *May Man Prevail?* (Garden City: Anchor Books, 1961), p. 8.

[10] For a discussion of various versions of this approach, see Arthur I. Waskow, *The Worried Man's Guide to World Peace* (New York: Anchor Books, 1963), pp. 74–82.

[11] Charles E. Osgood, *An Alternative to War or Surrender* (Urbana: U. of Illinois Press, 1962), esp. chap. III. See also John H.

Kautsky, "Myth, Self-fulfilling Prophecy, and Symbolic Reassurance in the East-West Conflict," *Journal of Conflict Resolution,* 9 (March 1965), 1–17; Raymond A. Bauer, "Problems of Perception and the Relations Between the United States and the Soviet Union," *Journal of Conflict Resolution,* 5 (September 1961), 223–30.

[12] Amitai Etzioni, *The Hard Way to Peace* (New York: Collier Books, 1962), esp. chap. 4, and *Winning Without War* (Garden City: Anchor Books, 1964), esp. pp. 21–26, 62–68, 209–12.

portant differences between the two versions of the theory concern the nature of these steps. Jerome Frank, for instance, stresses that the initiatives must be clear, simple, and dramatic to overcome the psychological barriers,[13] for any minor concessions will be seen as a trap to encourage the opponent to lower his guard. Actually, in Frank's judgment, unilateral renunciation of nuclear weapons might well be the only sufficiently large step to break the vicious cycle.[14] More moderate interpretations call for significant reductions of arms as initiatives; still more moderate interpretations seek to restrict the unilateral steps to purely symbolic gestures not involving any weakening of the military strength of the initiator even though some arms reduction, such as the cutting of arms surpluses, might be recommended.[15]

Finally, there are those who believe that the transition from a "cold war" to a "stable peace" would be achieved by a chain of unilateral initiatives followed by reciprocations by the other side, while others believe that such exchanges would open the way of effective multilateral negotiations. The unilateral-reciprocal approach, it is suggested, is needed to create the atmosphere in which important international accommodations such as broad-based arms reduction schemes can be introduced, but those in themselves cannot be introduced in this way because the unilateral-reciprocation approach can carry only comparatively simple communications, and the sides are unlikely to make major arms reductions unless those of the other side are made simultaneously.[16]

. . .

[Professor Etzioni then lists American initiatives and Soviet responses, beginning with President Kennedy's speech at the American University on June 10, 1963, in which be outlined "A Strategy of Peace" and announced that the United States was stopping all nuclear tests in the atmosphere and would not resume them unless another country did. This speech was published in full in *Izvestia* and *Pravda*, and Premier Krushchev made a speech on June 15, welcoming the Kennedy initiative and announcing that the Soviet Union had ordered a halt in the production of strategic bombers. The Soviets also removed their objection to a Western proposal to send United Nations observers to Yemen, and Russia reciprocated by not testing in the atmosphere. The test-ban treaty itself was signed on August 5, 1963; it was followed by a number of tension-reducing proposals on both sides as well as a reduction in trade barriers between East and West. In October, a resolution was passed in the General Assembly prohibiting the orbiting of nuclear bombs, with the support of both major nuclear powers. In short, there was evidence that the theory of graduated reciprocation in the reduction of tensions was working.]

[13] Jerome Frank, "Breaking the Thought Barrier: Psychological Challenges of the Nuclear Age," *Psychiatry,* 23 (1960), pp. 245–66.

[14] *Ibid.,* pp. 263–65.

[15] *The Hard Way to Peace, op. cit.,* esp. chap. 7.

[16] *Ibid.,* pp. 95–98. Others view unilateral reciprocation as a much more encompassing measure. Schelling points out another difference in the policy's use—as a communication method (which can convey hostility as well as good will) and as a treatment of international conflicts. His approach is that of a communication method. Thomas Schelling, "Signals and Feedback in the Arms Dialogue," *Bulletin of the Atomic Scientists,* January 1965, pp. 5–10. . . .

THE PSYCHOLOGICAL IMPACT

The first steps in June 1963 did not produce what later became known as the Soviet-American *détente*, or the 1963–64 thaw in the cold war. In accord with the preceding psychological analysis, they were rather received with much ambivalence and suspicion. The *New York Times* seems to have reflected accurately the mood the author observed in Washington at the time, when it stated on June 16, 1963, that

...there was a new threat of international peace in the air this week, the kind of threat that leaves sophisticates smirking and the rest of us just dumbfounded. The "accommodators," as outraged Republicans call them, were simply delighted. The "cold warriors," as the accommodators call them, regarded conciliation as a shrewd new tactic.[17]

Thus, even the initiating side was not convinced that there really was a new line, and, if we may assume that Russian authorities read the *New York Times,* they too could hardly have been immediately persuaded.

In line with the theory, Kennedy's initiation speech included recognition of Russia's achievements ("We can still hail the Russian people for their many achievements—in science and space, in economic and industrial growth, in culture and in acts of courage") and suffering ("And no nation in the history of battle ever suffered more than the Soviet Union suffered in the course of the Second World War"). These statements seemed to have weakened the rigid image that was typical of the cold war period.

[17] *New York Times,* June 16, 1963.

The impact of the speech was felt outside the seats of government. In the United States, "from around the country came a generous flow of messages echoing all these responses, but more approving than not. And from around the globe came new bursts of hope kept alive by quick signs of interest in Moscow."[18] A *New York Times* correspondent in Moscow reported that "the ready approval of its contents by ordinary Russians was evident in the reactions of Muscovites who lined up at kiosks to buy newspapers."[19] But the main turning point came when the test treaty—considered an important "breakthrough" —was successfully negotiated. That at first hopes for a treaty ran low, and that it took great effort to obtain it only increased the significance of its ratification.

The treaty to partially ban thermonuclear tests was the central gesture of the Kennedy experiment. Until it was reached, gestures and counter-gestures were met with caution, if not skepticism. When in early July Khrushchev offered a ban on tests in sea, air, and space (as was ultimately agreed), but coupled this offer with a suggestion of a non-aggression pact between the North Atlantic Treaty Organization and the Warsaw Treaty Organization, the *New York Times* referred to the offer as "Another Booby Trap?"[20] A week later, discussing the test treaty negotiations, the same source reflected the mood in the capital: "If these talks are successful, it is generally believed that a new chapter in East-West relations will open. But there are grave doubts on all sides that such a new chapter is indeed at hand."[21] Thus, a test ban was viewed as having major tension-reduction potential, but

[18] *Ibid.*
[19] *Ibid.*
[20] *Ibid.,* July 7, 1963, p. 1E.
[21] *Ibid.,* July 14, 1963, p. 1E.

there was much doubt whether it would be achieved. A Washington reporter still refers to the *détente* at this point with a question mark and explores at length the possibility "that the Soviet Union did not really want an agreement"[22] (i.e., was negotiating in bad faith). An American report from Moscow indicated that "Mr. Khrushchev would also hope that conclusion of a partial test-ban treaty would create an atmosphere in which he could negotiate other advantageous agreements, especially on Germany."[23]

The treaty was negotiated in July, signed in August, and ratified in September. Thus, for more than two months, it served as the focus for discussions about Soviet intentions, the possibility of peaceful co-existence, and the dangers of nuclear war; and the Senate hearing helped to keep the debate alive. Its ratification was therefore not merely one more gesture in an international sequence of pseudo-events,[24] but a major educational act. The American public that entered the period with ambivalent attitudes toward a test-ban treaty, remembering the arbitrary resumption of testing by the Soviet Union in 1961, after three years of voluntary moratorium, as well as the 1962 Cuban crisis, was now strongly in favor of the agreement. Louis Harris reports that a national poll taken in July, before the negotiations on the treaty had begun, found that 52 per cent of the population strongly supported a treaty. This percentage had risen to 81 by

September when the treaty was ratified.[25] The tone of the press also changed; there was now an "official amity" between the United States and the Soviet Union.[26] While some newspapermen, accustomed to sudden shifts in international winds, continued to be cautious, a report from Moscow stated:

As Secretary of State Rusk left the Soviet Union today, after six days of discussions with Soviet leaders, it appeared almost certain to Western observers here that a surface of calm would descend on East-West relations.... The prospect, it is believed, is for a long period of manifold negotiations at all levels and in many cities and countries on all sorts of issues.... The feeling is that the Russians are generally interested in maintaining the current state of improved relations with the West. They are believed to be hoping for a minimum of friction.[27]

The correspondent who had reported smirking and dumbfoundedness over any possible thaw in June now stated that "we have cleared the air and cleared the atmospheres and warmed the climate and calmed the winds."[28] The test-ban treaty had allayed many of the doubts about Russian intentions.

Following the signing of the treaty came a number of new proposals to improve East-West relations and further extend the *détente*. While none of these materialized in this period, the repeated and frequent offering of various tension-reduction measures had some effect in itself. Actually, hopes rose so quickly that late in August, Secretary of Defense

---

[22] *Ibid.*, p. 5E.

[23] *Ibid.*

[24] This concept was introduced by Daniel J. Boorstein in *The Image* (New York: Atheneum, 1962), esp. pp. 9–12. A pseudo-event has the following characteristics: it is not spontaneously initiated; it is manufactured largely for publicity purposes; and it is intended to be a self-fulfilling prophecy, to create its own consequences.

[25] *Washington Post*, September 16, 1963.

[26] *New York Times*, August 4, 1963, p. 1E.

[27] *Ibid.*, August 11, 1963, p. 3E.

[28] *Ibid.*, September 22, 1963, p. 8E.

McNamara warned that it was perilous to relax in a "euphoria," and Kennedy cautioned in September that the test ban was "not the millennium."

By late October, almost no new American initiatives were taken, and those of the Soviet Union were not reciprocated. The press referred to a "pause in the thaw"; there was a marked slow-down in tension reduction though efforts continued, as we shall see, to preserve the measure of *détente* that had been achieved. The assassination of President Kennedy and the beginning of the election year ushered in a year of more or less stable semi-*détente*.

What are the conclusions from this brief and incomplete test of the theory? Certain of the central hypotheses were supported: (a) unilateral gestures were reciprocated; (b) reciprocations were proportional; (c) unilaterally reciprocated gestures reduced tensions; (d) unilateral reciprocated gestures were followed by multilateral-simultaneous measures, which further reduced tensions; (c) initiatives were "suspected," but, when continued, they "got across"; (f) the gestures and responses created a psychological momentum that pressured for more measures, a reversal of the cold war or hostility spiral; (g) when measures were stopped, tension reduction ceased (we shall see the significance of this point below); (h) the relatively more consequential acts were initiated multilaterally or were transformed from an initially informal, unilaterally reciprocated basis to a formal, multilateral one.[29]

Not all the assumptions and derivations of the theory were as clearly supported. Most important, it is impossible to tell, without re-running history

for "control" purposes, whether multilateral negotiations could have been successfully undertaken without the "atmosphere" first having been improved by unilateral steps. The fact, however, that both the test treaty and the space ban were first introduced on a unilateral-reciprocal basis and that even in the reduced tension condition these measures were hard to defend before Congress, suggests that, if not preceded by tension reduction, they either might have failed, or the risks of failure would have been sufficiently high for the Administration to refrain from introducing them. (Attempts to advance a test ban in earlier periods failed.)[30]

Also, the Kennedy experiment was only a partial application of the theory: the gestures were not the clear signals a full test of theory would require. Thus, for instance, to gain the Senate's consent for a test-ban treaty, its value for American security was stressed.[31] It would allow, it was said, stopping of testing while we were ahead both in number of tests and weapons technology. Further, President Kennedy made it clear that the United States would "vigorously and diligently" pursue its underground nuclear test program.[32] The wheat deal was interpreted in a similar fashion,[33] e.g., as a show of Russia's weakness. Further, during the whole period, American observers provided various interpretations of the gestures as other than efforts to com-

---

[29] *The Hard Way to Peace, op. cit.,* pp. 99 ff. That this was necessary was a point of some debate. See Waskow, *op. cit.,* pp. 75ff.

[30] Spanier and Nogee, *op. cit.,* chap. VI.

[31] United States Senate, Committee on Foreign Relations, *Nuclear Test Ban Treaty: Hearings on Executive M, 88th Congress, 1st Session, August 12–17* (Washington, D.C.: G.P.O., 1963). pp. 97–109.

[32] *Documents . . . , op. cit.,* 1963, no. 27.

[33] *New York Times,* October 14, 1963, p. 1E.

municate a desire for peaceful co-existence (e.g., the *détente* exacerbates the Soviet-Sino rift). While a policy is often supported by a large variety of arguments, and the self-serving ones are usually emphasized when facing Congress, their preponderance could not but have had negative side-effects on Soviet-American relations. Also, the same gestures would have been more effective had they been introduced with less hesitation, and if Soviet initiatives had been met with less ambivalence.

Above all, since the process was halted, one cannot tell whether psychological measures open the door to "real" give-and-take or are essentially meaningless in the absence of basic and lasting settlements of differences and conflicts. The fact remains, however, that gestures that were almost purely psychological in nature led to an American-Soviet semi-*détente* lasting from June 1963 until now. Whether more of the same could have brought about more fundamental changes cannot be learned from this case.

.   .   .

DIPLOMACY

Chapter 12

Some years ago Hans J. Morgenthau, writing on "The Art of
Diplomatic Negotiation,"[1] advanced the proposition that a
nation which exists among other nations can deal with the outside world in
one of three ways: it can deny the importance of the links between itself and
other countries—which will lead to a policy of isolation and non-participation;
it can deny the equality of other nations and try to impose its will on
others by coercion—which will lead to a policy of hegemony and imperialism;
or it can attempt to pursue interests in contact with other countries, on the
assumption that there are possibilities of defining, redefining, adjusting, and
accommodating varying interests of countries to one another. This is the
function which, in Morgenthau's judgment, diplomacy serves.

There are almost as many definitions of diplomacy as there have been
writers on the subject. The most basic approach to defining and describing
the process is to think of it as a form of continuous contact between states
based on a system of permanent representation. The Oxford Dictionary
describes diplomacy as "the management of international relations by negotiation." Other writers focus more on the ingredients of diplomacy, taking of
"the application of intelligence and tact," and other desirable attributes of
successful diplomacy and skilled diplomats. Perhaps the definition which

---

[1] In L. D. White, ed., *The State of the Social Sciences* (Chicago: The University
of Chicago Press, 1956), pp. 404–14.

most closely relates method to substance is that diplomacy "represents the accumulative political, economic, and military pressures upon each side, formalized in the exchange of demands and concessions between negotiators."[2]

No matter how the process is defined or described, what we are dealing with is a method by which states conduct their relations with other states; it is not the *substance* of policy that concerns us here but one of the ways in which policy is being implemented.

Space limitations prohibit us from dealing in detail with the history of diplomacy. Some students consider the angels to have been the first diplomats, mediating between God and man. We have no ready response to this observation, other than to concede that if it is valid, then the quality of the service has declined somewhat. Inter-state and inter-governmental relationships are referred to in the Bible, in the histories of the Greek city-state, and throughout subsequent periods. But these relationships were, for the most part, episodic, centered on particular problems, and did not have the character of permanence which is a characteristic of modern diplomacy. Historians usually suggest that a recognizably modern pattern of interstate relationships originated among the Italian city-states of the Renaissance, that it was then taken over by other European states (France, Spain, England), and that from there it spread to the far corners of the world. While the substance and content of what is being discussed, transacted, and negotiated by diplomats differs widely, of course, the forms and methods in use today are remarkably uniform across the globe.

The past has undoubtedly left its mark. The Byzantine influence, which was perceptible in the conduct of diplomacy on the part of the Italian states, infused a certain amount of mysticism and secrecy into the process (though it should be added immediately that secrecy is certainly functional, quite aside from diplomacy's historical roots). Harold Nicolson points to the impact of what he calls the "French method" of conducting diplomatic relations, a method which he believes was particularly adapted to the conduct of relations between civilized states and which he describes by such adjectives as courteous, dignified, continuous, confidential, gradual, and experienced.[3]

Kenneth W. Thompson describes the background of diplomacy in the following terms:

> For the better part of four centuries the statecraft of Europe displayed certain salient features. In theory at least, it sought to mitigate and reduce conflicts by means of persuasion, compromise, and adjustment. It was a diplomacy rooted in the community of interests of a small group of leaders

[2] Ernst B. Haas and Allen S. Whiting. *Dynamics of International Relations* (New York: McGraw-Hill Book Company, 1956), p. 135.

[3] Harold Nicolson, *The Evolution of Diplomatic Method* (London: Constable & Co. Ltd., 1954), pp. 48–71.

who spoke the same language, catered as often to one another as their own people, and played to one another's strengths and weaknesses. When warfare broke out, they drew a ring around the combatants and sought to localize and neutralize the struggle. The old diplomacy...carried on its tasks in a world made up of states that were small, separated, limited in power, and blessed, ironically enough, by half-hearted political loyalties. Patience was a watchword; negotiations were as protracted during war as in peace. Everyone took for granted that negotiations and talks would be initiated, broken off, resumed, discontinued temporarily, and reopened again by professionals in whose lexicon there was no substitute for 'diplomacy'."[4]

Needless to say much—though not everything—has changed since that kind of description was applicable. Nonetheless certain basic functions of diplomacy and diplomats have been remarkably persistent. These include transmissions of information and viewpoints between governments; the representation of policy-positions vis-à-vis others; the protection of interests of citizens; and, importantly, the negotiation of existing differences of opinion and policy through the process of finding fomulae which can accommodate those differences. All this sounds a great deal easier than it actually is. Actually, all practitioners argue and observers agree that diplomacy is a tough and demanding business which requires the utmost in skill, craftsmanship, patience, and many other qualities. It is not, as Nicolson has rightly observed, "the art of polite conversation." (Although courtesy is generally considered an important ingredient of diplomatic discourse, it is not the substance of it; and at times, in fact, calculated harshness may be extremely effective.)

Given the conditions of modern international life, the role of the diplomat has changed. No longer is he the independent agent far removed from the seat of his own government that he once was. Now the home office is no farther away than the nearest scrambler telephone or teletype. The improved communications systems not only reduce the independent decision-making capabilities of the professional diplomat but also make top-level negotiations more easily possible than was the case in the past. Foreign ministers and heads of state meet more frequently now than in past periods for direct discussions, consultations (Davis' description of a summit conference, reprinted below, is a case in point), and even negotiations. In addition the existence of international organizations has provided diplomacy with a new locale in which to operate.

Many observers of contemporary international relations are concerned about some trends generally subsumed under the overall rubric of "The New Diplomacy." Open negotiations, based on Woodrow Wilson's misconceived and misunderstood formula of "open covenants openly arrived at,"

---

[4] Kenneth W. Thompson, *Christian Ethics and the Dilemmas of Foreign Policy* (Durham, N.C.: Duke University Press, 1959), pp. 81–82.

top-level summit negotiations, the increasing interest which large numbers of citizens in many countries take in the details of diplomatic negotiations, and what has been called the "democratization" of foreign policy—all these are developments whose impact is debatable. The influx of new styles of diplomatic procedure such as those described by Gordon A. Craig in the selection below, the relative decline of traditional customs and courtesies which were quite functional even if (or perhaps just because) they were often misunderstood by the public, and above all, the new conditions of world politics with the presence of immense threats to stability, indeed to survival—all these have transformed the practice of diplomacy, making it at one and the same time more important and less effective in dealing with the explosive problems of our age.

Some observers see in a revival of the art and practice of diplomacy something like a "last and best hope" for mankind. This may overstate the case, and it may be as much the result of disenchantment with all other methods that have been tried as it is the consequence of a full and fair evaluation of the potentialities of diplomacy itself. Others have consigned diplomacy as a means of managing international relations to the graveyard of history; the obituary may be premature. We consider diplomacy as an important continuing, ongoing process in international life. We consider it to have considerable potential for the management of international relations and for the channeling of conflicts and disputes. And although we would refrain from overestimating its potentialities, we would likewise caution against an unwise and premature abandonment of a process which, for all its shortcomings, has served the world well and continues to do so.

1. Totalitarian Approaches to Diplomatic Negotiation

GORDON A. CRAIG

Gordon A. Craig, Professor of European and Diplomatic History at Stanford University, is a frequent contributor to scholarly journals. His works include FROM BISMARCK TO ADENAUER: ASPECTS OF GERMAN STATECRAFT *(1958) and* EUROPE SINCE 1915 *(1961).*

In a treatise that is justly admired by students of diplomacy, François de Callières wrote in 1716: "The art of negotiation...is so important that the fate of the greatest states often depends upon the good and bad conduct of negotiations and upon the degree of capacity in the negotiators employed.... It is not necessary to turn far back into the past to understand what can be achieved by negotiation. We see daily around us its definite effects in sudden revolutions favorable to this great design of state or that, in the use of sedition in fermenting the hatreds between nations, in causing jealous rivals to arm against each other so that the *tertius gaudens* may profit, in the formation of leagues and other treaties of various kinds between monarchs whose interests might otherwise clash, in the dissolution by crafty means of the closest unions between states: in a word, one may say that the art of negotiation, according as its conduct is good or evil, gives form to great affairs and may turn a host of lesser events into a useful influence upon the course of the greater."[1]

Since these words were written, changes in the methods of communication, in the nature of international society, and in the distribution of political power within the states that comprise it have profoundly affected the forms and the techniques of diplomatic negotiation; but its importance as an instrument of national power has in no way been diminished. There is no easier way to demonstrate this than to consider the role of negotiation in the history of the totalitarian states of the first half of the twentieth century. The failure of the Fascist and National Socialist governments to understand or take advantage of the uses of negotiation was not the least important cause of the difficulties that in the end overwhelmed Italy and Germany; whereas the Soviet regime's ability to devise new techniques of negotiation and to adapt traditional ones to its own purposes carried it through the hazards of

In A. O. Sarkissian, ed., STUDIES IN DIPLOMATIC HISTORY AND HISTORIOGRAPHY *(London: Longmans, Green & Co. Ltd., 1961), pp. 107–25. Reprinted by permission of the editor and of the author.*

[1] *The Practice of Diplomacy,* being an English rendering of François de Callières' "De la manière de négocier avec les souverains," presented with an introduction by A. F. Whyte (London, 1919), pp. 7, 16.

the inter-war period and, after the Second World War, consolidated and expanded the position won by Soviet arms.

I

The deficiencies of Fascist diplomacy and the amateurishness of its leaders' ventures into negotiation may be explained, in part at least, by the fact that the first years of Mussolini's political life were spent as a journalist. The talents that are required to make a man a good newspaperman are different from those that one expects to find in a competent diplomat. Cavour is one of the rare individuals who have possessed both kinds, and Mussolini, in this and other respects, was no Cavour. The Duce's newspaper experience left him with a tendency to be preoccupied with style rather than with substance, with a hankering after sensational strokes and dramatic coups that would look good in headlines, and—although this hardly accords with that cynicism that newspapermen are traditionally supposed to possess—with an excessive regard for newspaper opinion and a dangerous sensitiveness to newspaper criticism.

Mussolini's fundamental attitude toward diplomacy, and the attention he paid to its purely verbal aspects, were bound up, in a curious way, with his editorial policy for *Il Popolo d'Italia*. He once explained how he had impressed upon that journal, "in thousands of articles, headlines, drawings and sketches inspired by me, a polemical and aggressive character, one of continual battle";[2] and, after he became chief of state, he seemed to feel that it was only fitting

that this should become the characteristic mark of every aspect of Fascist policy, including foreign policy. He was forever talking about "the Fascist style" which he equated with courage, resolution, action, forcefulness, dynamism. "Note that I do not love the hesitant and conventional form," he said in December 1925. "I affirm."[3]

This dislike of the hesitant and the conventional extended to those forms of diplomacy which sought, with a minimum of public display and a maximum of deliberation and reflection, to solve European problems in the first postwar decade, as well as to the frequent attempts made, at Geneva and elsewhere, to reach collective agreements by means of multilateral negotiation. All of these were, in a phrase frequently used by the Duce's son-in-law, "contrary to our diplomatic style."[4] Mussolini's prejudice against multilateral negotiation can probably be traced back to the chastening experience of his first diplomatic venture, when, at the Lausanne Conference of November 1922, his *gaucheries* were received by the other delegates with an amusement that bordered on scorn.[5] But there can be little doubt that it was rooted also in his belief that the satisfactions to be gained from collaborative diplomacy in the interest of general appeasement were not worthy of Fascist Italy, which must dazzle the world with spectacular triumphs of its own.

During the first decade of his regime, however, Mussolini could not afford, and did not attempt, to base his policy upon these prejudices. The de-

---

[2] Herman Ellwanger, *Sulla lingua di Mussolini* (Verona, 1941), p. 22.

[3] Benito Mussolini, *Scritti e discorsi* (Milano, 1934–39), V, 321 ff.

[4] Galeazzo Ciano, *L'Europa verso la catastrofe* (Verona, 1948), p. 338.

[5] See Harold Nicolson, *Curzon: The Last Phase* (London, 1934), pp. 288 ff.

fiant, and only partly successful, stroke at Corfu in August 1923[6] was not imitate in the years that followed; and, if Mussolini was prone to ringing declarations of imminent action, he generally allowed the word to stand for the deed. Thus, in February 1926, when he electrified Europe by a clear threat of military action north of the Brenner unless an end was made to criticism of his policy in the South Tyrol by the Austrian and German parliaments, he backed down quickly when the Austrians proposed to bring the matter before the League of Nations, delivering a second speech in which, behind "a characteristic parade of truculence," he converted his earlier menaces into "an inoffensive intimation that he would defend himself if attacked by others."[7]

Throughout these early years, the exigencies of domestic policy reduced Mussolini's dynamism to what has been called a "random and uncoordinated striking-out in all directions in the hope of scoring points on the cheap."[8] The best that can be said of it is that it did no real harm to Italy's basic interests, since Mussolini was content to leave the bulk of the diplomatic business of the state, which was, as elsewhere, carried on by the continuous negotiations that go on in embassies and foreign offices, in the hands of the professional foreign service and the permanent officials in the Palazzo Chigi. By making concessions to their leader's vanity, these officials were able to moderate his outbursts and control his ambitions, while cementing relations with those Powers, like Great Britain, who

were willing to respect Italy's traditional interests and even to assent to modest increases in her influence in Africa and eastern Europe.[9]

All of this changed when the deterioration of economic conditions in the early 1930s, and the consequent disruption of European power relationships, opened new vistas to Mussolini's eyes and made him impatient with old restraints. The dismissal of Grandi as Foreign Minister in July 1932 marked the inauguration of a new policy of all-out revisionism and, simultaneously, the beginning of that decline of the influence of the professionals in Italian diplomacy that was to reach its nadir in the Foreign Ministry of Galeazzo Ciano.[10] As their role diminished, negotiation became almost a forgotten art in the Italian service, a tendency encouraged by the belief that the goals Italy now sought must be attained not by diplomacy but by heroism.

Even the atmosphere of conventional courtesy that customarily reigns in the diplomatic corps and is conducive to the useful exchange of views was dispelled by Ciano. Once he had become Foreign Minister, he seems to have determined to realize his father-in-law's stylistic ideals and insisted that Italian diplomats must henceforth make their behaviour reflect the approved *tono fascista*.[11] The meaning of this phrase is elusive; it seems to have meant a proud and militant bearing that would impress the foreigner with the dignity and strength of the new Italy. Its practical effect was to make ambassadors dispense with traditional forms and usages of polite intercourse (Ciano

[6] See Gaetano Salvemini, *Prelude to World War II* (New York, 1954), pp. 44 ff.

[7] A. J. Toynbee, *Survey of International Affairs*, 1927 (Oxford, 1929), p. 199.

[8] H. Stuart Hughes, "The Early Diplomacy of Italian Fascism," in *The Diplomats, 1919–1939*, edited by Gordon A. Craig and Felix Gilbert (Princeton, 1953), pp. 224 ff.

[9] *Ibid.*, pp. 216 ff.

[10] See especially Felix Gilbert, "Ciano and His Ambassadors," in *The Diplomats*, pp. 512 ff.

[11] Raffaele Guariglia, *Ricordi, 1922–1946* (Napoli, 1950), p. 193.

insisted on the deletion of even the most conventional expressions of good will from ambassadorial declarations),[12] to be constantly on the alert for slights to Italy's honour, to adopt a hectoring tone in delivering communications and complaints to the governments to which they were accredited, and, in general, to conduct themselves, especially in countries that were not bound by ideological or more formal ties to Italy, as if they were in an enemy camp.

This made it virtually impossible for envoys abroad to perform effectively their duties of representation, reporting and negotiation. Representing Italian interests seemed now to consist for the most part of continual protestation against criticisms of Fascism, even when they were made by private citizens; and this, as one Italian diplomat noted, was ludicrous, when one remembered that Fascist Italy was "all too prone to criticize, injure, jeer at, and menace all the peoples of the world, and not in private conversations, but in manifestations of an official character and in articles in a press which the whole world knew was rigidly controlled by the government."[13] Ambassadorial reporting degenerated into demonstrations of conformity to Fascist style; and the reports from posts like Belgrade, Sofia, and Bucharest in the last years of the peace contained little of interest except descriptions of the ambassadors' success in bullying their hosts.[14] Finally, the possibilities of ambassadorial negotiation of any kind were handicapped, not only by this new cult of bad manners, but also by the apparent belief in the

Palazzo Chigi that, in certain capitals —Paris, for example—an attitude of disdainful reserve was all that should be expected of a Fascist diplomat. "What ought I try to accomplish in Paris?" asked Guariglia as he left for his post in November 1938. "Nothing," answered Ciano. "It will be difficult," the ambassador replied, "but I will do my best."[15]

The subordination of diplomacy to the *tono fascista* was even more patent in the negotiations that Ciano carried on personally at Mussolini's orders. In these he appears to have been more interested in the speed with which an agreement could be reached and the publicity that could be garnered from it than in anything else. In general, his negotiations were amateurish in technique and dangerous in result.

. . .

II

In retrospect it would seem that the weakness of Italian diplomacy arose from the essential frivolity of the officials charged with the task of conducting it; and, behind Ciano's shocked protest, upon learning in August 1939 of Hitler's intention of going to war, that "no indication had been given by Germany, either in the conversations at Milan, or in the talks during his visit to Berlin, that the situation in respect of Poland was so grave,"[16] lies a pathetic admission that he had not mastered the art of negotiating even with his own allies.

Adolf Hitler can hardly be accused of Ciano's kind of *leggerezza*. He both understood what could be gained by negotiation and, at various times in

12 *Ibid.*, pp. 255 ff.
13 Emanuele Grazzi, *Il principio della fine* (Roma, 1945), p. 13.
14 Ministro degli Affari Esteri, *I documenti diplomatici italiani* (Roma, 1952 et seq.), 8th series, Vol. XII, Nos. 100, 177, 672, 819.

15 Guariglia, *op. cit.*, p. 357.
16 *German Documents*, series D, VI, No. 43.

his career, demonstrated his ability to use it, in ways of which Callières would have approved, "in the dissolution...of the closest unions between states" and "in the formation of leagues...between monarchs whose interests might otherwise clash." His faults as a statesman are, therefore, of a different order from Mussolini's. He is to be criticized, not for lack of diplomatic proficiency, but rather for the fact that he refused to be content with the great gains that negotiation could bring to his country, but sought greater ones in war.

Despite the suspicion with which he was viewed by professional diplomats when he came to power, Hitler showed considerable facility in the use of diplomatic means during his first years. In the unfolding of his policy, there was, for one thing, little of the incoherence that had characterized Italian policy in the 1920s. Hitler was aware that the revisionism and expansion upon which his heart was set could be pursued only after the home front had been stabilized and Germany's armed forces built up. While the *Gleichschaltung* was being carried out, therefore, and the Versailles Treaty undermined, the Führer encouraged foreign states to believe that his government would effect no radical break with the policy of the past. This he did, in the first place, by retaining the existing Foreign Ministry staff and by relying on diplomats who were known abroad and whose continued employment would have a reassuring effect.[17]

In the second place, unlike Mussolini, Hitler was not given to complicating the work of his diplomats in the field (whose task, essentially, was to explain away the brutalities of his domestic programme and to portray him as a force for European order) by inveighing against the international *status quo*. His public pronouncements at this stage were pacific, disarming, even ingratiating, designed to divert foreign attention from his real intentions and to blunt criticism of, or split possible opposition to, his policies, by promising concessions or hinting at willingness to make agreements desired abroad.[18] Hitler realized that the public statements of heads of government were not the least important of modern channels of negotiation, and he showed great skill in using this means of advancing his purposes and supporting the efforts of his envoys at Geneva and foreign posts. It was by this means that he was able, after his withdrawal from the Disarmament Conference and the League of Nations in October 1933, to mislead the other Powers by his professed willingness to consider any schemes of arms limitation that they might propose; and this channel was also used with effect in persuading states which criticized his withdrawal from the collective security system to enter bilateral negotiations with him.

In the last-mentioned area of negotiation, Hitler's first years were marked by two successes that were admirably designed to protect him from collective counteraction as his policy evolved. These were the pact with Poland, which drove a wedge into France's eastern alliance system,[19] and the Anglo-German naval agreement of June 1935, which split the Stresa Front

---

17 Karl Dietrich Bracher, "Das Anfangsstadium der Hitlerischen Aussenpolitik." *Vierteljahrshefte für Zeitgeschichte*, 1957, pp. 69–70.

18 A good example is Hitler's speech of 17 May 1933 concerning Germany's stand on disarmament. See *The Speeches of Adolf Hitler*, edited by Norman H. Baynes (Oxford, 1942), II, 1041–58.

19 Richard Breyer, *Das Deutsche Reich und Polen, 1932–1937* (Würzburg, 1955), pp. 106 ff., and 113.

and destroyed the last possibility of reprisals for Hitler's violations of the arms clauses of the Versailles Treaty.[20] The notable feature of these examples of "dynamic" diplomacy is that there was nothing impulsive about them. The possibility of a treaty with Poland seems to have been in Hitler's mind as early as April 1933;[21] in September he instructed his Foreign Minister to talk with his Polish opposite number about "the best means of creating a better atmosphere in the relations between the two states"; and in November he authorized the formal negotiations that eventuated in the treaty of 26 January 1934.[22] The idea of a pact with Britain had interested Hitler for an even longer period, stretching back before his coming to power; and, after he became Chancellor, he took it up and played an important role in pushing the naval negotiations to a successful issue. His private talks with Lord Allen of Hurtwood in January 1935, with the British Ambassador in February, and with Sir John Simon in March, and his public address of 21 May 1935 certainly made a more important contribution to the pact's conclusion than the tactics used by Ribbentrop when he led the German delegation to London in June.[23]

After the middle of 1935, when Germany's growing military might supplied an authoritative backing for her diplomacy, Hitler was never again as dependent upon negotiation as he was in his first years; and, after 1936, when he was given his first proofs of the weakness and indecision of the western democracies, his tendency was to rely more upon military pressure than upon negotiating skill and persuasiveness. The tone of German diplomacy now began to change; Hitler's public statements on foreign policy became menacing; and, especially after Ribbentrop became Foreign Minister in February 1938, the style of Foreign Ministry communications became peremptory and sometimes arrogant.[24] Ribbentrop himself had such an exalted conception of his role that he was led to indulge in astonishing displays of bad manners when he felt that his dignity had been hurt.[25] Aside from this, he had no real sympathy for genuine negotiation. As Attolico once said, he could see nothing but his own version of the facts;[26] he had no patience with lengthy deliberations, being desirous of headlong decisions;[27] and he was interested, not in agreements of mutual advantage, but only in settlements that were imposed upon his *vis-*

---

[20] See, for instance, the speech of 21 May 1935 in *The Speeches of Adolf Hitler,* II, pp. 1218–46.

[21] Herbert von Dirksen, *Moskau, Tokio, London: Erinnerungen und Betrachtungen zu 20 Jahren deutscher Aussenpolitik, 1919–39* (Stuttgart, 1950), p. 123.

[22] Republic of Poland: Ministry for Foreign Affairs, *Official Documents concerning Polish-German and Polish-Soviet Relations, 1933–39* (London, 1940), pp. 11–24; *German Documents,* series C, II, Nos. 84, 87, 88, 217, 218, 219.

[23] See W. Malanowski, "Das deutsch-englische Flottenabkommen vom 18. Juni 1935 als Ausgangspunkt für Hitlers doktrinäre Bündnispolitik," *Wehrwissenschaftliche Rundschau,* 1955, p. 416; D. C. Watt, "The Anglo-

German Naval Agreement of 1935; an Interim Report." *Journal of Modern History,* 1956, pp. 157, 159 ff.

[24] This change was apparent even in the language of professionals like Ernst von Weizsäcker, the Under Secretary. See the language in which he "categorically refused" to accept a French protest after the Prague coup of March 1939. *German Documents,* series D, VI, No. 20.

[25] See Paul Schmidt, *Statist auf diplomatischer Bühne, 1923–1945* (Bonn, 1949), pp. 457 ff.

[26] *Documenti diplomatici italiani,* 8th series, XII, No. 503.

[27] Ernst L. Presseisen, *Germany and Japan: A Study in Totalitarian Diplomacy 1933–1941* (The Hague, 1958), pp. 198, 208.

à-vis, or treaties of alliance that were directed against third powers.

. . .

III

In sharp contrast to Hitler's approach to negotiation is that of the Soviet Union. Far from preferring the arbitrament of war to decisions made at the council table, the Soviets have generally valued diplomacy for its ability to win great triumphs at small risk and have shown virtuosity, not only in mastering its procedures and forms, but also in devising formidable negotiating techniques of their own.

In the first stages of the Soviet experiment, there was, it is true, some tendency to regard diplomacy as an outworn bourgeois institution, and Leon Trotsky actually spoke of shutting up the Foreign Office completely.[28] This mood soon passed, and, from the days when G. V. Chicherin led a top-hatted and striped-trousered delegation to the Genoa conference of 1922, the Soviet Union has made full use of all the possible channels of diplomatic negotiation and shown complete command of the time-tested methods of the profession.[29] The official Soviet history of diplomacy says proudly: "Soviet diplomacy is master of its technique. In its relations with Foreign Powers, it defends the interests of its country in the most worthy manner; and, with an incontestable authority and with impeccable special skills, it conducts negoti-

ations and concludes agreements advantageous to its country."[30]

One need only think of some of the diplomatic successes won at moments when the Soviet Union was vulnerable to outside pressure, or threatened by outside attack, to admit the justice of this. In the first ten years after the Bolshevist revolution, the Soviet Union often faced the possibility of complete diplomatic isolation. It escaped this by its success in persuading England and other countries to enter negotiations for trade agreements, by the subsequent treaties of recognition concluded with the major Powers, by continuous negotiation in areas like Afghanistan, the Middle East and Poland for protective or diversionary purposes, and by the masterful cultivation of the association with Germany that was inaugurated so sensationally at Rapallo in 1922 and confirmed by the Treaty of Berlin in 1926.[31] These successes were won for the most part by patient negotiation and the skilful use of the techniques of classical diplomacy, especially the art of playing upon the differences of other powers or appealing to their greed or their apprehensions. In the use of the traditional arts of bargaining, Soviet negotiators, in these early days and later, showed themselves the equals of their adversaries, sometimes to the surprise of the latter;[32] and in preparing their case

---

[28] Theodore H. von Laue, "Soviet Diplomacy: G. V. Chicherin, Peoples Commissar for Foreign Affairs," in *The Diplomats,* p. 235.

[29] A number of western studies of diplomacy, including Sir Ernest Satow's *Guide to Diplomatic Practice,* and Jules Cambon's *Le Diplomate,* were translated into Russian in the interwar years and used in training courses.

[30] V. P. Potemkin *et al., Histoire de la diplomatie* (Paris, 1946–47), III, 787.

[31] The latter treaty in particular played a part in the initiation of the negotiations that led to the Nazi-Soviet pact in August 1939. See *German Documents,* series D, VI, Nos. 406, 490, 579, 607.

[32] Thus, during the negotiations for American recognition of the Soviet Union in November 1933, the British Ambassador in Washington could write: "M. Litvinov has proved somewhat of a surprise to the State Department. I learn on good authortiy that

before the opening of negotiations, in mastering the agenda and the technical aspects of items included on it, and in tactical adroitness in exploiting the legal aspects of existing agreements which bore on current negotiations, they sometimes showed an embarrassing superiority of performance, as the first post-Second World War meetings of the Foreign Ministers showed all too clearly.[33]

Despite the excellence of their training in the external forms of diplomacy, and their skill in using it, Soviet negotiators have always had a fundamentally different approach toward diplomacy from that of their western colleagues. To them diplomacy is more than an instrument for protecting and advancing national interest; it is a weapon in the unremitting war against capitalist society. Diplomatic negotiations, therefore, cannot aim at real understanding and agreement; and this has profound effects upon their nature and techniques.[34]

For one thing, it means that not all of the negotiations entered into by the Soviet government are intended to eventuate in settlements, a fact that irritates or baffles some western diplomats and seems to represent a complete denial of the purpose of diplomacy.[35] Negotiations may be begun, or agreed to, by the Soviets, not as a means of promoting agreement on an issue, but of delaying it, pending the clarification of problems in other areas or the successful completion of other talks. They may be started out of mere speculation, as a means of eliciting the views, defining the interests, or testing the tenacity of the parties on the other side. They may be designed for purely propaganda purposes, as "elaborate stage plays" to edify and win the sympathy of the uncommitted part of the world.[36] Because of this, as Philip Mosely has written, the first task of the diplomats who engage in talks with Soviet negotiators is to try to discover whether the latter have instructions to negotiate seriously or, indeed, have any instructions at all, beyond a general directive to make propaganda for the Communist cause.[37] If they do not, the result is apt to be what a British Foreign Secretary has

---

he has been showing himself the toughest of negotiators. He has evinced no trace of any ambition to achieve a personal success. He has had the blandest, but firmest, of retorts ready for any question, and has appeared quite ready to depart empty-handed at any moment." *British Documents,* 2nd series, VII, no. 542. Speaking of Molotov's conversations in Berlin in November 1940, Paul Schmidt wrote: "Molotov had a certain mathematical precision and unerring logic in his way of speaking and presenting arguments. In his precise diplomacy he dispensed with flowery phrases and, as though he were teaching a class, gently rebuked the sweeping vague generalities of Ribbentrop and, later, even of Hitler." *Statist auf diplomatischer Bühne,* p. 516.

[33] Newspaper reports of the meeting of Foreign Ministers in London in 1945 would seem to bear this out. See, more recently, "Topics of the Times," *New York Times,* July 26, 1959; and John Foster Dulles, *War and Peace* (New York, 1950), pp. 27 ff.

[34] See Stephen D. Kertesz, "Diplomacy in the Atomic Age," *Review of Politics,* 1959,

pp. 132 and 193; and "American and Soviet Negotiating Behavior" in *Diplomacy in a Changing World,* edited by Stephen D. Kertesz and M. A. Fitzsimons (Notre Dame, 1959), pp. 144 ff.

[35] "I have 'done' many conferences in my life but never went into one without some hope of a fairly quick result. No one could say the same today. Results are often not expected, and often not even desirable...." Lord Vansittart. "The Decline of Diplomacy," *Foreign Affairs,* 1950, p. 184.

[36] Henry A. Kissinger, "Reflections on American Diplomacy," *Foreign Affairs,* 1956, p. 46.

[37] Philip E. Mosely, "Some Soviet Techniques of Negotiation," in *Negotiating with the Russians,* edited by Raymond Dennett and Joseph E. Johnson (New York, 1951), p. 274.

described, in a moment of exasperation, as "negotiation by equivocation."[38]

Even when Soviet diplomats have been instructed to seek a settlement, the subsequent negotiations are apt to diverge in marked respects from the rules that have traditionally guided diplomatic intercourse in the western world. Soviet diplomats do not subscribe to Callières's belief that there exists between negotiators a *commerce d'avis réciproque*.[39] Bound themselves by rigid directives that allow little flexibility they cannot understand the freedom of manoeuvre permitted to western diplomats. Moreover, since they regard their opposite numbers as ideological enemies, they are bound to view all their moves, however trivial, with suspicion[40] and to regard any means that promise to win advantage over them as legitimate.

These things being so, negotiations with the Soviets have generally been marked by an almost automatic Soviet opposition at the outset to all proposals from the other side of the table, followed by persistent and uncompromising advocacy of the Soviet point of view. The tactic of initial rejection extends to the most innocuous suggestions made by the partner in negotiation, since the Soviets apparently believe that "the trivial is the first line of defence on which to meet the enemy assaults that always aim at the cru-

cial."[41] In September 1929, when Arthur Henderson presented M. Dovgalevsky with a list of questions that he felt should be discussed and settled before the resumption of diplomatic relations between their two countries, the Soviet representative came to the second meeting with a list of his own, with the questions in quite a different order, and proceeded to fight, with a zeal out of all proportion to its object, for his arrangement.[42] This sort of thing has been normal practice and has come to be expected by western negotiators.

The stoutness with which the Soviets hold to their own proposals has become proverbial. "Anyone accustomed to dealing with M. Litvinov," Sir Esmond Ovey wrote from Moscow in December 1929, "will remember how he frequently appears to be on the point of agreeing to suggestions made to him, but in practice, when pressed for any definite statement, he invariably reverts to his original point of view."[43] Similar statements have been made in more recent times about the persistence of Molotov and Gromyko.[44] Nor has this inflexibility in negotiation been easily shaken by non-diplomatic means. It is true that, in the years 1940 and 1941, during the almost continual Soviet-German negotiations about the disposition of eastern Europe, the Soviet Union was forced repeatedly to yield to German gains, in face of *faits accomplis* backed by the threat of force.[45] But in the inter-war years and in the period

[38] Selwyn Lloyd, describing Gromyko's tactics during the London talks of July 1959. *New York Times,* July 22, 1959.

[39] *The Practice of Diplomacy,* pp. 20–21.

[40] Writing of Molotov's behavior at the London meeting of the Foreign Ministers in 1947, Herbert L. Matthews said: "He is innately suspicious. He seeks for hidden meanings and tricks where there are none. He takes it for granted that his opponents are trying to trick him and put over something nefarious." *New York Times,* December 7, 1947.

[41] Nathan Leites, *A Study of Bolshevism* (Glencoe, Ill., 1953), pp. 55 ff.

[42] *British Documents,* 2nd series, VII, No. 20.

[43] *British Documents,* 2nd series, VII, No. 43.

[44] See Sidney Gruson's remarks on Gromyko's negotiating style, in *New York Times,* July 26, 1959.

[45] See *The Initial Triumph of the Axis,* pp. 319 ff., 364 ff.

since 1945, other cases of this are hard to find; and attempts to bring non-diplomatic pressure to bear on the Soviets, far from succeeding, have sometimes merely given them an opportunity to claim loudly and publicly that they were being threatened by imperialist Powers. When the British government sought in 1933 to intimate in private negotiations that they would break off economic relations unless the Soviets released British engineers who were accused of wrecking and espionage, the Soviet government replied with press releases claiming "gross external pressure" and persisted in their course.[46]

The granting of concessions in the hope of eliciting concessions in return has had no more effect in persuading Soviet negotiators to modify their positions. In the fruitless Anglo-French negotiations with the Soviet Union in the summer of 1939, the western governments repeatedly conceded points described by the Soviet negotiators as being of fundamental importance, hoping that this would facilitate agreement, only to discover, once they had done so, that new points were now of fundamental importance to the Russians, whose intransigence was in no wise diminished. This led Lord Halifax to question the genuineness of the Russian desire for a treaty and to complain to the Soviet Ambassador that "the Soviet Government had not budged a single inch, and we had made all the advances and concessions. Saying 'No' to everything was not my idea of negotiation."[47] In the years since 1939 other diplomats have learned, as the British did then, that yielding points, or even changing one's original position for reasons other

than the presentation of new evidence, merely encourages the Soviets to hold fast.[48]

Soviet inflexibility is generally combined with the skilful use of tactics designed to wear out the patience or weaken the judgment of their adversaries. Among these tactics is the use of bad manners, not out of personal or ideological vanity, which was responsible for the discourtesies of Ribbentrop and Ciano, but with the calculated intention of disconcerting their partners in negotiation, throwing them off balance, and thus betraying them into ill-advised decisions. It was a convention of the old diplomacy that one pretended not to notice the artifices employed by one's adversary and accepted the verbal formulas with which he covered them.[49] The Soviets have no patience with this kind of tolerance. "I may be mistaken," said Sir Anthony Eden at the Moscow conference of Foreign Ministers in 1943, "but..." "You *are* mistaken," Molotov interrupted harshly, breaking the thread of Eden's argument and destroying its effect.[50] By this kind of crude attack upon the rules of elementary courtesy and by false accusations, name-calling and the imputation of the worst possible motives to their adversaries, Soviet negotiators have been able on occasion to obscure the real issues at stake, to divert the course of discussion to subsidiary points, and even to bully a conference into accepting their point of view. Deliberate assault upon the values and forms of the old diplomacy is a means by which the Soviets seek to impose their views and their standards

[46] *British Documents,* 2nd series, VII, No. 306.

[47] *Ibid.,* 3rd series, VI, No. 135: *The Eve of the War 1939,* p. 454.

[48] John N. Hazard in *Negotiating with the Russians,* p. 46.

[49] See François Walder, *Saint-Germain ou la négociation* (Paris, 1958), p. 110.

[50] Philip E. Mosely in *Negotiating with the Russians,* pp. 283 ff.

on the rest of the world, and they have not been entirely unsuccessful.[51]

The most successful Soviet tactic is their use of time. Kurt Schumacher once said to an American diplomat, "The day you Americans are as patient as the Russians, you will stop losing the cold war."[52] American negotiators, and western diplomats in general, have found it difficult to learn this lesson and have sometimes, in their anxiety for a happy conclusion to talks, seized upon illusory concessions or grasped at dangerous "agreements in principle" in order to be able to claim a success.[53] This weakness is something the Soviets are constantly watching for; and, because they are free from parliamentary or public pressure, they are usually able to hold their ground calmly, while insinuating into the foreign press charges that their adversaries are needlessly protracting negotiations. Since they have often been dealing with democratic countries in which there are parties or pressure groups sympathetic to the Soviet Union, these tactics have frequently been effective.

The practice of prolonging negotiations for months and even years, coupled as it sometimes is with a shifting of the centre of negotiation from the ambassadorial to the ministerial level and from there to the levels of heads of state, often has the effect of blurring the outlines of the issues at stake and making less precise the original points of difference. The Soviets make the most of this by issuing press communiqués which are designed to confuse the general public and which often impute to their opponents views that weaken their position while strengthening the Soviet case. This kind of tactics was used with effect in the repeated and protracted negotiations in the 1920s over the question of the Russian debts and enabled the Soviet Union to avoid payment without penalty. A more recent example of their use was afforded when, at the end of his visit to the United States in 1959 and his talks with the President about the Berlin problem, Premier Khrushchev informed the press that he was satisfied that the President recognized that the existing situation in Berlin was "abnormal."[54] The President may indeed have used this term, for the Western Powers have never denied the abnormality of the Berlin situation, while attributing it to the failure to unite Germany. He did not, however, mean to suggest that this abnormality could be corrected by withdrawing Western troops from the city or altering its status to the advantage of the East German regime, although this was what Khrushchev implied. But so many talks had been held on the subject since the original Berlin note, and in so many different places and with so much publicity, that it was not easy for newspapermen to detect the distortion immediately; and, once it had been printed, it could be cited, and has since been cited, as a significant American admission of the fundamental weakness of the western position in Berlin. One

[51] See Lord Strang, *Home and Abroad* (London, 1956), p. 206.

[52] Charles W. Thayer, *Diplomat* (New York, 1959), p. 96.

[53] A good example is afforded by the attitude of the Labour Party during the Anglo-Soviet trade negotiations in 1924, when they were so eager for agreement that they forced the Foreign Office to accept an unworkable formula. See Philip Viscount Snowden, *An Autobiography* (London, 1934), II. 680–86. See also remarks of John Foster Dulles before the National Press Club in January 1958. *Department of State Bulletin*, February 3, 1958.

[54] Max Frankel in *New York Times*, September 30, 1959.

of the main tasks of those engaged in negotiations with the Soviet Union consists in keeping the record straight, so that it can be revealed to the public at any time without tactical disadvantage to them,[55] and so that their position will not be eroded by unwitting concessions imposed on them by imputation.

These techniques of negotiation helped protect the Soviet Union in its most vulnerable years, defended its interests in the period before the outbreak of the Second World War, and won from its Allies more than adequate compensation for the losses it suffered in that war. But these have not been the only effective weapons in the Soviet diplomatic armoury; and, in a more thorough analysis of Soviet negotiating behaviour, attention would have to be paid to other methods that have helped consolidate the war-time gains and now threaten to expand them. These would include the new methods of economic diplomacy, which have been used with undeniable success by Soviet negotiators of agreements for technical assistance and aid to underdeveloped countries,[56] and the various techniques of public negotiation, with particular reference to their use in the United Nations.[57] Even in a brief account it can be noted that the Soviet Union has effectively emulated Hitler's use of the public statement as a means of negotiation and has employed the exchange of letters between heads of state for the same purpose. Indeed, it might almost be said that by these means the Soviet Union has been able to be a party to negotiations to which she has not been

invited, for, by timely use of threats against NATO members,[58] of proposals for disengagement of Soviet and Allied troops from central Europe,[59] or of invitations to summit conferences,[60] she has forced the periodic meetings of the NATO Council to discuss *her* views, *her* policies, *her* proposals rather than their own, and to spend time and energy combating the divisiveness promoted within the alliance by her tactics.

IV

Some years ago, when Sir Harold Nicolson delivered his Chichele Lectures on the evolution of diplomatic method, he said: "I have not observed that... the Soviet diplomatists and commissars have evolved any system of negotiation that might be called a diplomatic system. Their activity in foreign countries or at international conferences is formidable, disturbing, compulsive. I do not for one moment underestimate its potency or its danger. But it is not diplomacy: it is something else."[61]

There are doubtless many who would agree with Nicolson in lamenting the decline of the older diplomacy and in refusing to consider the Soviet Union's way of conducting international relations as diplomacy at all;[62] but the

[55] On this, see Thayer, op. cit., p. 98.

[56] Klaus Knorr, "Ruble Diplomacy," *Memoranda of the Center of International Studies* (Princeton, 1956).

[57] See Kertesz in *Review of Politics*, 1959, p. 376.

[58] Editorial, "Soviet Atomic Diplomacy," *New York Times*, March 28, 1957; editorial, "Soviet Campaign," *ibid.*, December 13, 1958.

[59] See Gordon A. Craig, "Germany and NATO," in *NATO and American Security*, edited by Klaus Knorr (Princeton, 1959), pp. 254 ff.

[60] *Department of State Bulletin*, June 2, 1958, pp. 906 ff.

[61] Harold Nicolson, *The Evolution of Diplomatic Method* (London, 1954), p. 90.

[62] "Diplomacy could flourish only so long as there was a loose, tacit and general agreement to behave *more or less* like gentlemen." Vansittart in *Foreign Affairs*, 1950, p. 185. It is interesting to note that Adolf Hit-

question of nomenclature need not be debated here. What is clear is that the

---

ler, at least before he came to power, felt a fundamental incompatibility between Soviet and Western diplomacy. In 1932 he wrote: "I look upon...Soviet diplomacy not only as being unreliable but, above all, as being incapable of being considered of the same nature as the foreign political activity of other nations, and, in consequence, as being something with which one cannot negotiate or conclude treaties." Thilo Vogelsang, ed., "Hitlers Brief an Reichenau vom 4. Dezember 1932," *Vierteljahrshefte für Zeitgeschichte*, 1959, p. 434.

Soviet approach to negotiation has been less impulsive, more systematic and more effective in its results than that of either Italian Fascism or German National Socialism. In an age when war is no longer acceptable as a continuation of policy by other means, and when the importance of reaching settlements short of war is undeniable, the Soviet methods of negotiation would appear to deserve as much study by western diplomats as their own diplomatic tradition has received from their professional colleagues within the Soviet Union.

2. Democratic Approaches to Diplomacy

WILLIAM C. OLSON

As the range of alternatives open to a democracy narrows with its awareness of great peril, the competence of the ordinary citizen in the making of great decisions tends to come more and more into question. At the same time, as the Cold War settles down to a war of ideology in which the concept of the sovereignty of the people finds itself pitted against the concept of an elite vanguard of the proletariat, the necessity for nurturing viable democratic institutions of survival becomes ever

Excerpts from "The Public Ingredient in Statecraft," WORLD POLITICS *10 (1958),* 318–26. *Reprinted by permission.*

more apparent. Noted contributors to the subject of open discussion of foreign affairs have recently advanced some of their most telling arguments on this question of the role of the people in foreign affairs.

The very familiarity of Lippmann's [views] renders unnecessary any but a brief recapitulation of his thesis with reference to foreign policy. The malady of the democracies is the devitalization of the governing power caused by the unwarranted intrusion of the public into the policy-making processes of the great powers of the West. Because its opinion about events moves more slowly than the events themselves, the public is invariably concerned (when it is concerned at all) about situations which no longer exist. Emotional involvement further complicates matters, negatively through the propensity of leaders to portray wicked national enemies as deserving of passionate hatred, positively by the penchant for utopian dreams of a new Golden Age after the current war to end wars makes the world safe for democracy. Drugged by propaganda, the public never learns from experience, so that the deadly cycle of unreadiness frantic preparation—demobilization goes on and on. Intimidated and insecure, politicians advance "only as they placate, appease, bribe, seduce, bamboozle, or otherwise manage to manipulate the demanding and threatening elements in their constituencies." Their decisions rest upon what is popular, not what is good or right. Combined pressures of unknowing mass opinions and of "boss-ridden oligarchies" (Lippmannese for representative assemblies) enfeeble the executive leadership of most democratic states, which have fallen victim to an internal revolution reversing the proper relationship of the rulers and the ruled. Democratic foreign policy fails *because* it is democratic.

[Sir Harold] Nicolson also regrets the passing of the *ancien régime,* particularly the "old diplomacy" in which he himself was schooled, and the emergence of what he terms the "Wilsonian" or the "American" method of diplomacy. This unfortunate transformation came about through the internalization of foreign policy, "the belief that it was possible to apply to the conduct of *external* affairs, the ideas and practices which, in the conduct of *internal* affairs, had for generations been regarded as the essentials of liberal democracy." By the end of World War I, the now-domi-

nant Americans added their distrust of diplomacy (especially of the secret variety) and their missionary zeal for egalitarianism to the prevailing sentiment against war. The idealistic and "dangerous" Wilson preached that covenants should not only be open, but be openly arrived at, and that diplomacy should be conducted in full view of the public. This, perhaps the "most confusing of all the fallacies that we owe to President Wilson," continues to corrode the international effectiveness of the Western powers. At Paris he may quickly have perceived that negotiation and policy were two different things, but the public never has grasped the distinction. Furthermore, the stability characteristic of the old diplomacy has given way to "utmost instability." In televised negotiation, rational discussion is suspended in favor of endless propaganda harangues addressed not to the other delegates but to the public back home. Assailing the view that the people are always right and that their misfortunes are due to professionals, the British writer revises Lincoln's phrase to read, "although it may be difficult to fool all the people all the time, it is easy to fool them for a sufficient period of time to compass their destruction." Here Nicolson comes very close to Lippmann's conviction that the public instrusion into foreign affairs has brought on "something which can be called an historic catastrophe."

George Kennan, . . . former Director of the Policy Planning Staff of the State Department, asserted in 1951 that much of our "trouble" stems from the degree to which executive leadership in Washington feels itself beholden to short-term tides of popular judgment. Public opinion (or what passes for it in official circles) "can be easily led astray into areas of emotionalism and subjectivity which make it a poor and inadequate guide for national action."[1] Later, he candidly argued in favor of a freer hand for "the ruling group,"[2] stating that America "must take a tighter control of its own life and evolve a greater sense of purpose with regard to the shaping of its own development."[3]

Turning more directly to foreign affairs, Kennan notes how many dislike the fact that governments, not peoples, engage in foreign affairs, and yearn for more direct people-to-people relations, unmarred by meddling interference from government. Because of the inevitable association of power with responsibility, Kennan argues that only governments can speak responsibly in foreign affairs. Yet, because a government represents the dominant political faction as well as the nation as a whole, its pronouncements and programs abroad reflect not only the nation but competing political forces within it. To follow a constructive course in international relations often runs counter to the dictates of the internal political struggle. The more democratic a country is, the more this tends to be so. A regime which is "strong and authoritative" (Kennan does not say "authoritarian") may more easily undertake an intelligent course than one caught in the throes of domestic politics.[4]

Despite certain differences in emphasis (e.g., Nicolson devotes a great deal of attention to historical aspects of diplomacy), there is no mistaking the essential oneness in the viewpoint of these critics of public interference in statecraft. The criticism has aroused Henry Wriston to a vigorous defense of what he proudly calls "democratic diplomacy." Where Lippmann "brooded upon the events" which have precipitated the decline of the West, Wriston praises the "adaptability, resourcefulness, imagination, and skill that made it possible for a people civilian in thought and habit to mobilize their energies to win victories in two successive wars over nations steeped in militarism." Public opinion, far from being the source of a disastrous collapse of Western civilization, lies at the very foundation of a successful American system. Scholars, professionals, and "tired commentators" who propose schemes for the elimination of politics in diplomacy in favor of their own particular brand of *expertise* overlook the facts of life; "it is absurd to find men arguing for such a utopian program while pretending to deal realistically with world problems." The professional diplomat, like the professional soldier, must subordinate his will to that of the people. As Wriston sees its function, public opinion "is not expected to deal in nuances, in procedures, in techniques. Actually it needs only to respond to situations in clear and simple terms. For example, public opinion must decide that the United States is to go it alone or have a 'career in the world'; it must determine to let the devil take the hindmost or temper competition with cooperation; it must agree or refuse to pay the bill for deterrent armaments; it must weary of the stridency of the chauvinist, the exploiter of issues—and show its disapproval; ... it must bring the moral simplicity of the golden rule to bear upon international issues."

---

[1] *American Diplomacy, 1900–1950,* Chicago, 1951, p. 93; reviewed by Grayson Kirk in *World Politics,* V, No. 1 (October, 1952), 110–15.

[2] *Realities of American Foreign Policy,* Princeton, 1954, p. 44; reviewed by William G. Carleton in *World Politics,* VII, No. 4 (July, 1955), 627–39.

[3] *Realities of American Foreign Policy,* p. 110.

[4] *Ibid.,* p. 44.

II

Morality, in one form or another, plays an important role in each of these interpretations. In a phrase that has often been quoted, Kennan characterized the most serious fault in past policy formulation as being the legalistic-moralistic approach to international problems, involving "the carrying-over into the affairs of states of the concepts of right and wrong, the assumption that state behavior is a fit subject for moral judgment."[5] Explicitly rejecting this criticism, Wriston cites as both genuine and significant the "profound moral commitment" of the Marshall Plan, the winning of the Battle of Britain "by heart, by courage, by faith," the "soul force" of Gandhi which defeated every other kind of power, and the "faith in the reality and vitality of spiritual forces" exemplified by Eisenhower at Geneva. Kennan denies that he ever meant to suggest that the United States neglect certain fundamental moral concepts characterizing the very spirit of our way of life in promulgating its foreign policy, but does oppose the assumption that our particular set of moral values, growing out of our own traditions and religious groupings, are necessarily valid for people everywhere.[6] Nor would such an assumption be made by Wriston, who asks that policy be based upon moral considerations as well as the more tangible factors of power, arguing that the "human spirit cannot be entered upon a balance sheet, nor weighed, nor measured, nor counted." He is highly critical of analysts of foreign affairs who, in listing factors of national power, appear to neglect the

moral element. Unlike the other authors, Wriston identifies morality with public opinion: "Democracy itself finds its roots in the equality of men, which is explicable upon no basis except religious grounds. Public opinion provides the strongest foundation for diplomacy when spiritual strength is given its rightful position of priority among all the factors that shape policy." Contrast this with Sir Harold, who is weary of the "egalitarian illusions" of Americans. To the venerable British diplomatist there is a moral element involved, but it lies more subtly in a belief that "Americans possess more virtue than any giant Power has yet possessed." In an earlier book on diplomacy, Nicolson argued that it "is not a system of moral philosophy. ... The worst kind of diplomatists are missionaries, fanatics and lawyers. ... Thus it is not religion which has been the main formative influence in diplomatic theory; it is common sense."[7] Lippmann, in using the moral argument *against* democracy in the conduct of foreign affairs and associating virtue only with an elite imbued with the "public philosophy," finds in contemporary public influence on foreign policy the very antithesis of morality in politics.

This is the heart of the matter. One's moral philosophy applies to issues involving the governing of men by men. Diplomacy may not itself be a system of moral philosophy, but the goals and objectives of diplomacy necessarily reflect the moral predispositions and judgments of the nation and its political leaders. Democracy is a normative concept. Either people have a right to govern themselves, taking the consequences of their decisions, or they do not, in which case a paternalistic elite

---

5 *American Diplomacy, 1900–1950*, p. 100.

6 *Realities of American Foreign Policy*, p. 47.

7 *Diplomacy* (London, 1939), p. 50.

could better perceive and pursue the national interest. Few national problems fail to derive, in some way, from international relations; to eliminate foreign policy from the area of legitimate concern of the people is to eliminate the democratic principle itself. If the guiding ideal is to be government *by* the people, then foreign policy must be their concern; if it is to be merely government *for* the people, then the executive should be supreme, in diplomacy as in other aspects of statecraft. But in the latter case, the elitists would have to make a case for efficiency as well as for morality, for the elite systems of this century have hardly distinguished themselves by their finesse and permanence in foreign affairs, to say nothing of their moral rectitude. As Churchill is said to have observed, democracy is the worst form of government ever devised, except for every other form.

Despite philosophical differences, the authors reach essentially the same conclusion on one point: the necessity for the enhancement of professional diplomacy if the United States is to maintain (in Wriston's view) or to regain (in Lippmann's) its leadership of the West and the world. Nicolson venerates the old French method of diplomacy which, as it was developed by Richelieu and Callières, combined a centralized authority for policy formulation with a professional service for its implementation. Dignified, gradual, sensitive to the realities of power, it attached importance to experience and knowledge, but did not assign any role or responsibility to the people. Kennan, though apparently resigned to some degree of amateurism in American foreign affairs, nevertheless pleads for the "principle of professionalism" in order to produce a corps of officers of unparalleled quality. By deploring the eclipse of executive power which has undermined the au-

thority of leaders to speak and act for the nation, Lippmann clearly indicates the necessity for a return to executive leadership and responsibility, which obviously implies more professionalism and responsibility in the handling of foreign affairs. By devoting one half of his book to the professional diplomat, Wriston confirms the trend, exemplified in his own special assignment in 1954 as chairman of the Public Committee on Personnel for the State Department, toward establishing professional diplomacy as a permanent feature of the American process.

III

None of the authors deals with one crucial aspect of this concept of professionalism in a democracy. Does not this concept encompass sensitivity to, and systematic analysis of, public opinion in both the country to which the diplomat is accredited and, perhaps even more importantly, the country which he represents? One of the alleged abuses of American diplomatic practice which led to the "Wristonization" of the Foreign Service was a tendency of officers long away from home to represent the outside world to America more than the other way around. Now, to the discomfiture of some of them, FSO's are required to serve terms at Washington desks, the better, presumably, to sense the changing moods and patterns of American life and the better, presumably, to represent their homeland when they once again take assignments in the field. Yet, if the process is nothing more than one of political and sociological osmosis, whereby the specialist is supposed somehow to "sense" the political milieu of his own country, it is scarcely likely to produce the kind of result envisioned by those who brought him home. Public opinion analysis, though hardly yet a science, has advanced far enough to provide something better than that.

If part of the diplomat's initial training and continuing responsibility were to include careful attention to the stresses and the harmonies among the many different strands that make up the fabric of public opinion, he would be better able to interpret his country to foreigners and to analyze the directions into which public pressures may be forcing the policies of the government he represents. Very little is accomplished simply by deploring the fact of democratic control, for it is a fact. Rather, a useful and essential task, along with raising the level of public understanding of foreign affairs, is heightening the degree of comprehension of the public mind on the part of the professional. This should be part of the meaning of professionalism in democratic diplomacy. Even if the professional is to be given more leeway, as Kennan and Nicolson advocate, he must know the range and limitations of his support, so that "leeway" or "freedom of action" are not taken to be a kind of exclusive authority appropriate only to an aristocracy. And, as C. J. Friedrich has pointed out with reference to Sir Eyre Crowe's disparagement of its role in diplomacy, public opinion has long had an influence on policy, whether the professional diplomatist has been willing to admit it or not.[8]

Analysis of national opinion abroad, or at least relevant segments of it, has for some time been an accepted responsibility of legations and embassies, and was a well-used technique in HICOG. Much less attention seems to have been paid to the analysis of opinion at home.[9] Does the evidence, unfortunately all too abundant, that the American people are emotional, shortsighted, and subject to manipulation by irresponsible politicians merely serve to confirm existing elitist predispositions among some diplomats, who soberly believe that only men like themselves are capable of comprehending and serving the national interest? Yet Kennan himself, while rejecting as unreliable the short-term judgments of the public, seems to concede that in the long run the public judgment is sound.[10] It is difficult to see just how an analytically valid distinction can be made in these terms, since the polls have largely been confined to essentially short-run situations. To be sure, the public may be characterized as possessing certain rather basic predispositions toward the outside world and, at the same time, as developing new attitudes with reference to immediate issues, such as the Girard case. The combination of these, as they impinge upon one another, make up the national will. Only by developing sensitivity to the several kinds of manifestation of public opinion can the diplomat (or anyone else, for that matter) know the range of public acceptance within which foreign policy must operate. And

---

[8] C. J. Friedrich, *Constitutional Government and Democracy* (Boston, 1946), pp. 589–90.

[9] During the foreign aid hearings in the spring of 1957, it was revealed that the Secretary of States confidential emergency funds had been used ot take a sample of public opinion purporting to reveal overwhelming support for continued foreign aid. The House Government Operations Committee later issued a statement reporting that, since 1943, the Department of State had "illegally" spent more than one-half million dollars on polls on various foreign-policy issues, and severely criticized the Bureau of the Budget for failing to prevent this practice. *House Report 1166*, August 14, 1957; *Congressional Quarterly*, XV, No. 33 (week ending August 16, 1957), 976.

[10] *American Diplomacy, 1900–1950*, p. 93.

if he either misunderstands or rejects the very nature of democratic society, a nation which cherishes democratic values and procedures can ill afford to entrust its representation to him.

From this it follows that to the degree to which the diplomat is called upon to heed public opinion, the national interest dictates that the level of public sophistication be continually elevated. No doubt this carries with it the danger of a kind of "hidden persuasion" by the social engineer skilled at manipulating the mass mind for his own purposes. Yet it can also be the kind of adult education represented by world affairs study and discussion groups like those encouraged by the Foreign Policy Association, for example, which are increasingly active from one end of the country to the other. In resting his case Wriston cites, as the key to the improvement of American foreign policy, public enlightenment through voluntary associations, pressure groups, the now world-conscious daily press, and through what de Tocqueville long ago observed as the American tendency to treat every conversation as a town meeting.[11]

There is still another dimension which must be developed if democratic diplomacy is to be cultivated. This involves public acceptance of the legitimate role, the intelligence, the loyalty, and the integrity of the professional. In this respect we may be better off now than we were several years ago, at a time when Lippmann, writing his book, could observe the clever nurturing of public distrust of the diplomat for purposes of political advantage. To respect the professional's sphere of competence is quite a different matter from turning the affairs

of state over to him completely, giving him an unfettered hand to control the national destiny. If the diplomat continues to be the whipping boy of American politics he can neither respect nor represent the American people. They have an obligation to him, just as he has his obligation to them.

IV

Taken together, these divergent commentators on the crisis in Western diplomacy provide a welcome antidote for those zealots who, caught up in the ebullience of the Cold War, would either endanger America to save democracy or sacrifice democracy to save America. The value of the public philosophy as expressed by Walter Lippmann lies in its reminder that the privilege of democracy can be ruinous unless tempered by responsibility. The value of democratic diplomacy as elaborated by Henry Wriston lies in its promise that, in the ideological struggle in which the West is locked, the noble concept that government by the people shall not perish from the earth may yet prevail. Thus, in a deeper sense, both schools of thought are "right" as analyses of a critical problem in foreign policy. The solution of the problem lies not in the creation of a superdiplomat, or even a super-Secretary of State who carries the foreign policy of the country under his homburg, where it is unresponsive to the political process. It lies rather in the continual development of a more enlightened and more sensitive public, and an educational system capable of producing both responsible laymen with a basic understanding of international relations and also highly trained and highly motivated specialists capable of practicing the difficult art of democratic diplomacy.

[11] Wriston's more recent article, "Education and the National Interest," *Foreign Affairs*, XXXV, No. 4 (July 1957), 564–80.

3. The New Diplomacy

PAUL C. DAVIS

Mr. Davis is a senior staff member of the Institute of Naval Studies. He is a contributor to UNITED STATES REPRESENTATION ABROAD *(published in 1965 by the American Assembly).*

. . .

It may seem puzzling to have selected a summit conference as a case for the examination of modern diplomacy. A summit conference is, after all, but one mainfestation of diplomacy, and in the long sweep of history perhaps a unique one at that. For purposes of analysis, however, it is peculiarly opportune because a summit conference is a microcosm of the diplomacy, the foreign policies and the strategies of the major states, telescoped in time, focused in intensity, bringing the power and methods of each to bear upon common problems.

Nor are its processes so entirely distinct from normal diplomacy as the common criticisms of "summitry" would suggest. Issues, techniques, public and private representation, ceremonial actions, and the personal impact of leaders are manifestations which summit conferences share with foreign ministers' conferences, state visits, missions of special emissaries, and the day-by-day conduct of diplomacy by resident pleni-

From "The New Diplomacy: The 1955 Geneva Summit Meeting," in Roger Hilsman and Robert C. Good, eds., FOREIGN POLICY IN THE SIXTIES *(Baltimore, Md.: The Johns Hopkins Press, 1965). Reprinted by permission.*

potentiaries. If the summit conference is unique, its uniqueness lies in its apparent brevity[1] (with all that implies about accomplishment), the public expectations and attention it invites, and the aura of publicity in which it proceeds. Even in these respects it differs from most forms of diplomacy only in degree. Of these apparently unique features of the summit conference I shall have a good deal to say.

It is not my purpose, then, to scrutinize the summit conference as a special phenomenon. I want rather to see what one particular summit conference can teach us of the general nature of modern diplomacy, in order to see how diplomacy can more effectively be used as one of the foreign policy instruments.

I say "modern diplomacy" for the significant reason that there is a widespread sentiment among those with experience in diplomacy—and they tend to be the only ones who write about its nature—that diplomacy has changed for the worse. Their criticism usually rests on three propositions. The first is that diplomacy properly has as its sole

[1] Apparent" because as I develop in the concluding section of this paper, the actual conference is but one phase of a negotiative process.

aim accommodation, or the reaching of agreement in accordance with mutual interests, and that an unhealthy tendency to conduct diplomacy for "victory," for prestige, or for other allegedly irrelevant purposes has become the norm. Thus Sir William Hayter (who, incidentally, participated in the summit conference of 1955) says: "The Russians always negotiate for victory. It never occurs to them that the proper object of negotiation is not to defeat your opposite number but to arrive at an agreement with him which will be mutually beneficial."[2]

The second proposition grows naturally out of the first: negotiations, to be successful, must be, as they once were, conducted quietly, "far from the madding crowd." Publicity tends to compel rigidity in negotiation, for a negotiator's departure from previously announced positions is popularly construed as appeasement. Today there is altogether too much publicity, they assert. Often they imply that we must somehow exorcise the modern press or that the diplomats could by sheer exercise of will induce silence. Some, recognizing that public silence is impossible, try to distinguish between "good" and "bad" publicity, between the airing of issues to educate the public or to learn its will, and publicity intended to create hostility or embarrass opposite numbers.

In the third place these critics bemoan the use of conferences "for propaganda." This they see as something different from and more insidious than the mere "vice of publicity." In their minds the cold war has brought with it a misconception that the function of conference diplomacy is to provide an

occasion for fighting a war of words. It is not always clear whether the implication is that propaganda is conducted without purpose. At the least the proposition seems to suggest that diplomacy and propaganda, like oil and water, do not mix.

These are serious criticisms uttered by very responsible people. It is one of the purposes of this study to discover what light the 1955 Geneva Meeting of the Heads of Government[3] sheds on the validity of this indictment.

Beyond this, the Geneva Conference was quite generally thought to have had profound significance, yet involved no substantive agreement. The mystery of its pay-offs and its influence in the absence of agreement challenges our curiosity, and suggests that here if anywhere insights could be had about the nature of modern diplomacy. As we shall see, the anomaly of its impact is explainable in terms of a complex interplay of psychological and substantive factors which distinguish the new diplomacy from the old.

. . .

[In subsequent portions of the manuscript, here omitted, the author addresses himself to the subject of preparations for the conference and the actual conduct of the conference between the heads of the four governments. His conclusions follow.]

CONCLUSIONS

At the outset we cited three propositions widely maintained by diplomats of experience as to the proper char-

2 Sir William Hayter, *The Diplomacy of the Great Powers* (New York, 1961), p. 28. Also Lester Pearson, *Diplomacy in the Nuclear Age* (Cambridge, Mass., 1959), p. 42.

3 Hereafter referred to for brevity as the Geneva Conference or simply the conference. The Geneva Meeting of Foreign Ministers, which grew out of it and took place the same year (Oct. 27—Nov. 16), is referred to hereafter as the Foreign Ministers' Conference.

acteristics of diplomacy and the conditions which have recently degraded it.

The first was that diplomacy should properly limit itself to the quest for accommodation. Applying this proposition to summit meetings, Sir William Hayter has said: "The truth is that if there is a desire to settle, a Summit meeting is unnecessary, while it is useless if there is no such desire."[4] This point merits brief review in the context of a second question. Since the Geneva Conference did have wider purposes than accommodation, were the pay-offs of those purposes significant or was the conference, as Sir William Hayter would prognosticate, indeed useless? What did each participant want? What did he get?

President Eisenhower valued the first conference as the occasion to create conditions of mutual confidence as a prelude to accommodation in the second. He succeeded notably in achieving a new "spirit" at Geneva, but how much this influenced the Soviet leaders is problematical. If there were vacillations in the rigidity of Bulganin and Khrushchev under the magnetism of the President, these reaped no obvious fruits. All we can record with confidence is that the new spirit did not advance the substantive negotiations. It did not even stimulate the Russians to take a new initiative in their own interest at the Foreign Ministers' Conference; their defensive strategy precluded that. It may even have forced them to be more rigid at the conference than they had intended. The President viewed the "spirit" as an accommodative move, meant only to influence the Russian leaders. In this it proved nugatory, whereas its symbolic effects were great.

Secretary Dulles sought in vain

4 Sir William Hayter, *The Diplomacy of the Great Powers*, p. 67.

through his negotiative propaganda not to reach accommodation, but rather to weaken the Soviet hold on the European satellites. He failed both because of Soviet negotiating tactics and because his objective conflicted with the President's. Geneva was a manifestation of the thaw in Eastern Europe, but the thaw owed far more to the Soviet decision to liberalize its controls than to the maneuvers of Dulles. His purpose was not accommodative. On the other hand his nonaccommodative aims proved unproductive.

French hopes of deferring German unity benefitted from Soviet rigidity on this issue. But neither the French aim nor its result can be characterized as accommodative. Accommodation assumes change. The French success lay in changing nothing. Indeed a far more significant pay-off in the eyes of the French was the relaxation of tensions. Not only were the French leaders more driven to the conference by their public than were other governments; the public response to the "spirit of Geneva" was probably greatest in France.

Eden's purpose was to gain a settlement of modest nature—limited demilitarization. He hoped from it both a substantive accommodation and a contribution to mutual confidence which might lead to further settlements. It was viewed in this light by all parties and was seriously negotiated. Eden's aim was, then, accommodative, and we have no reason to discredit it as a meaningful effort. It fits Sir William Hayter's prescription well. We must, however, recognize that the other participants did not place it high among the reasons for the conference.

The Russians went to Geneva to perform a blocking action in Europe and through diversion to gain time for their Asian offensive. In this they were mildly successful. They would have been more so had they conducted the second conference as adroitly as the first. Certainly they needed no conference in order to postpone German reunification: simple inertia could have accomplished that. But the relaxation of tensions in Europe was well worth the effort, and it is difficult to visualize another way which could have been as dramatic and as persuasive of their sincerity as the Geneva Conference.

The Russian leaders no doubt viewed the symbolic pay-offs of Geneva as closely related to their more concrete global strategy. For Western leaders many of the symbolic pay-offs were ancillary. This difference notwithstanding, the symbolic pay-offs are in many respects the most interesting for what they suggest as to the limits of *accommodation* as the prime occupation of diplomats.

Clearly, the almost total acceptance of the idea that there had been a tacit agreement against nuclear war, and its variant that the likelihood of war had receded, have had consequences for the post-1955 style of East-West negotiations which are incalculable. They reach beyond the modest aims of accommodation. Geneva marked the beginning of a flexibility in the strategy of both major powers, which has opened up great opportunities, great uncertainties, and great risks. It led to an alteration in strategies and negotiating styles. While this change has embraced elements that are accommodative, it has also included elements which are far more ambivalent and complex.

This ambivalence is exemplified in the contrast between the promise and the fate of the "spirit of Geneva." For the slogan, "spirit of Geneva," which was received at its inception so euphorically in so many places, afterward acquired an opprobrium probably in the main deserved. Over-dramatization, partly by the President but more particularly by journalists, gave rise to self-deception in the West. The "spirit" which President Eisenhower wanted only for the negotiations became in fact a public trauma. This could have had unpleasant consequences but the new mood proved insufficiently structured for that, and new events quickly brought a more sober view of the dimensions of the cold war. Had the "spirit" been used after the Foreign Ministers' Conference to reinforce Dulles' aim of subverting the satellites, it might have had greater effect, though Hungary showed how little we could have capitalized upon it. In any event, the "spirit" was not immediately very productive, perhaps was even counter-productive, but revealed the possible dimensions of policy leverage which diplomatic conferences will afford once the planned use of such atmospheres becomes better understood.

The second ancillary pay-off— Open Skies—was an intended one. But it was a spill-over nonetheless, because it was not consistent with the President's object of creating a climate of confidence for further negotiation. Open Skies nonetheless illuminated the possibilities of symbolic negotiation. It revealed for just a moment the tremendous vulnerability of the Soviet Union to the well-conceived psychological operation: one which appeals superficially to dramatic and simple truth while it exporses beneath the surface basic flaws in Soviet society. Though the President gave Open Skies the appearance of an accommodative move, it was in fact an offensive cold war maneuver, and for a time was a successful one.

In sum, to view the Geneva Conference as an effort at accommodation would be greatly to distort its character. Probably no one save Eden can be thought to have played the traditional diplomat in a quest for what can fairly be called accommodation. Both purposes and results ranged beyond the traditional pattern. Yet neither can be thought either irrelevant or insignificant. The Geneva Heads of Government Meeting was a significant milestone in post-war world politics, not only because the participants pursued an unprecedented variety of objectives, but also because the pay-offs, intended and accidental, successful or not, were strategically significant.

The symbolic pay-offs were among the most interesting. Perhaps no other event in the cold war so mesmerized the public, or so suddenly transformed expectations, popular and elite, about the possibilities of future policy. This, it might be alleged, is the very danger to which such conferences are subject. But that can only be judged by the ways leaders profit from this newly discovered capacity to restructure opinion. It reveals that leaders are not necessarily prisoners of an inflexible public opinion. There is an interplay that the conventional statesman has too often failed to exploit by giving the public appropriate opinion-molding cues. There are occasions, it seems, when leaders can escape the power-dissipating pressures of conflicting interest groups and acquire through dramatic symbolism the chance to act strategically and decisively in the name of a universal consensus—a consensus such as Rousseau once favored as the prime mover of states. The summit conference may occasionally serve this purpose, particularly when the issues are elemental and universal.

The second proposition held essential to conventional diplomacy was that diplomatic negotiation should be conducted quietly, to avoid rigidity. It is difficult to conceive how the first such meeting since Potsdam could possibly have been held in quiet. Not alone was it bound to excite public expectations. The impetus to bring the conferees together included and probably required the pressures of publicity and propaganda. When nations have endured a long period of hostility one cannot simply leap into amiable negotiations without overcoming the resistances posed by the suspicions of leaders, the opposition of political factions, or public distrust.

Extensive publicity during the negotiations might have been avoided. The leaders used the press positively if somewhat uncertainly, revealing most of the formal discussion daily. Did it prove inhibiting? The first conference, far from being forced into rigidity by its openness, was conducted in a friendly and flexible manner. Not only did this flexibility favorably influence the public, but public reactions (as in the case of Open Skies) compelled a flexibility of response on the part of some participants which they did not privately feel. The second conference [of Foreign Ministers in October] was characterized by rigidity, but this arose from the private negotiating purposes of the participants, not from public pressures. Public acclaim for the "spirit of Geneva" was not transformed into pressures on the Western foreign ministers to yield; public opinion proved both unstructured and highly adaptive to the new pessimistic turn of events. It appears that whether rigidity is induced by public opinion depends on a variety of environmental factors, and often as much on leadership aims and estimates as on the excesses of public fervor.

The press, which was made privy to much of the negotiation, far from constituting a distractive element, reflected the views of the diplomats quite accurately (though admittedly with simpler optimism).

The third proposition of the conventional diplomat is that conferences are often mistakenly conducted "for propaganda," as a forum for the invective of the cold war. To deal with this charge effectively requires examination of larger aspects of the interplay of diplomacy and propaganda, which we discuss below. Suffice it to say at this point that both propaganda and diplomacy are usable for a number of purposes. Perhaps the diplomatist means really to question the wisdom of those purposes. Insofar as propaganda supports diplomacy, its range of purposes is as wide as those of the particular diplomacy it supports. And at Geneva these purposes were wider than those the conventional diplomat finds suitable.

The possible purposes of diplomacy go even beyond those embraced by the West in the Geneva Conferences. A conference may be used, for example, to seek to avert war (by clarification of intentions and capabilities or by ambiguous or frank preventive ultimata); to enhance prestige or diminish an opponent's; to illuminate public opinion or allay public fears; to assess the adversary's strategy or take the measure of his strength of will and mind; to achieve delay, diversion, subversion, or deception; to register or confirm an objective situation; or even to reach accommodation on substantive issues. There are as many symbolic as substantive purposes possible, and there is no a priori reason why one kind of purpose need be less useful than another.

The Western uses of diplomacy at Geneva were, then, many. But they did not have the strategic sweep of the Russian and their accomplishments suffered by the fact their objectives were evident to the Russians. Negotiative propaganda is *meant* to be evident, but the larger purposes to be served by the particular diplomacy need not be.

There will always be propaganda going on at the time of negotiations (and for that matter negotiations in

one form or another go on continually too). Some of the propaganda will not be directly related to the negotiations. If it does violence to the negotiative aims this is quite likely an accidental spill-over, such as often develops between our various policies; otherwise the propaganda must be truly purposeless, which is an absurdity. There will also be propaganda directly related to the negotiative aims. If we are clear which diplomatic aims we have, the choice of an appropriate propaganda becomes a rational exercise in policy execution. Propaganda must serve to facilitate the object of the diplomacy. If we are seeking simply "to gain propaganda advantage," this is probably not a deficiency in the propaganda itself but in the precision of the diplomatic objective. Many diplomats probably entertain this vague notion of the functionlessness of propaganda, a notion which propaganda planners by their laxity all too frequently reinforce.

If diplomatists need not limit themselves to diplomacy conventionally defined, it is equally true that propaganda need not be conducted only by the "conventional" propagandists. This is one of the points which the Geneva Conference best illustrates. The American negotiative propaganda was not conducted by a propaganda agency. Indeed it could not have evoked the necessary responses if it had been. Top leaders are inevitably propagandists, and the Geneva case suggest that they are often consciously so. In this modern age of symbolic communication, in which most life is experienced vicariously, propaganda cannot be restricted to a narrow range of officially identified propaganda media. Nor if it could be, would it be effective in its purpose.

If we look at the Geneva Conference as a total process this supportive interplay of diplomacy and propaganda becomes evident. Neither conference was a discrete event in itself. It was a continuum[5] consisting of three phases: preparation, conduct, and exploitation. In all three phases both diplomacy and propaganda played a part. In the preparatory phase diplomatic correspondence and diplomatic conferences took place, including a preliminary meeting between East and West. But propaganda received priority. Propaganda was used first to make the conference possible, then to negotiate and delimit the agenda, and finally to establish and communicate the basic aspects of the respective agenda positions.

In the conduct phase, though conventional person-to-person diplomatic intercourse was the normal mode of communication, many of the pay-offs were sought through symbolic action. This is to say they were aimed at influencing leaders indirectly through public pressures, and not solely concerning the agenda. In the exploitation phase, propaganda media were the main but not exclusive vehicles. In all three phases, real targets were mixed (sometimes mass, sometimes leadership), and the medium of communication used is not necessarily a clue to the target. It is an arbitrary convenience to think of public communication as propaganda, hence intended for the masses, and to think of personal communication as diplomacy, hence meant for the leadership. In reality, there was negotiative communication and non-negotiative communication, and both were communicated person-to-person as well as by the mass media.

At this point conclusions as to the

[5] Actually part of the larger continuum of the policy process, evident in the difficulty I have had in finding a starting point, end, or geographic limits of the process. Nonetheless, it was relatively isolable as a unique aspect of the larger process.

precise nature of negotiative propaganda and its function are in order. Negotiative propaganda is designed to focus leaders' thoughts upon the scope of the agenda and the considerations affecting one's negotiating position, and to influence their perceptions and expectations concerning both so that one's diplomatic aim may be served.

Negotiative propaganda is conducted publicly when one (a) has an obligation or occasion to speak publicly for an ancillary purpose; (b) wants to commit oneself publicly as a bargaining device; (c) has an obligation or occasion to speak publicly for an ancillary purpose; or (d) when silence might be disadvantageously construed, typically when one is the cue receiver in a negotiative communication process.

In the present case, non-negotiative propaganda was of two kinds. First was the cumulative, non-strategic propaganda which the information agencies conducted normally, some of which no doubt had relevance to the conference though handled in accordance with the routine policy planning procedures. This we did not examine. Second was the single instance of the Open Skies proposal. Because of the attention-getting forum in which it was announced and the audience officially addressed, it was strategic in character. It could, however, be thought negotiative only had its primary intent been to influence the disarmament negotiations of the two conferences. The Russians pretended to treat it so and in fact we did as well. But its aim was actually to influence public attitudes about the nature of a closed society, and by reshaping popular images of the Soviet Union to gain a general initiative in the conduct of our global strategy. It was indeed inconsistent with the immediate American aim and cannot therefore properly be thought negotiative. For these reasons

Open Skies should be classified as strategic non-negotiative propaganda.

The combination of audiences which the "modern diplomatists" addressed is instructive. Mr. Dulles often talked publicly for the ears of Khrushchev, and Khrushchev in turn replied publicly for the ears of Eisenhower or Dulles. At the first conference, Eisenhower offered the "spirit" to his opposite number and Open Skies to the public. But the Russians and the press converted the "spirit" into symbolic propaganda, and indeed Eisenhower was unable to keep its negotiative separated from its symbolic consequences. All seemed at least partly conscious of these distinctions. No Western leader used negotiative communications so consciously as Dulles. But when he failed in his diplomatic aims (German reunification and weakening the Communist Bloc), he did not carry out fully his final shift to symbolic propaganda. For this the close support of the United States Information Agency would have been required, and it is unlikely that Dulles saw symbolic communication as other than a one-man task.

I have said earlier that at Geneva the old diplomacy mingled with the new. I do not suggest that the Geneva Conferences were in any sense a consciously rationalized model of modern diplomacy. At the same time, Soviet diplomacy is in this context not, as some have suggested, a gauche and amateur old diplomacy but a modern Marxist diplomacy. It has the limitations *and* the advantages of the Marxist

perspective, of which the great advantages are clarity and unconventionality of objectives and the skill to conceal the objectives. Western diplomacy is at a transitional stage. American diplomacy has abandoned the old but not yet perfected the new. It supports a new range of purposes. It does not yet derive these purposes from a broad strategy, for that strategic perspective does not yet exist. Nor has it yet fully elaborated the role of propaganda in modern diplomacy. Our leaders are experimenting with the interplay of propaganda and diplomacy as the modern American statesman becomes his own natural propagandist.

This interplay, so evident in the international conference, is naturally less evident in day-to-day personal diplomacy, but hardly ever absent. The international conference, however, enjoys advantages over representative diplomacy akin to those enjoyed by the television political debate over whistle-stop speeches. The widened range of negotiative purposes that we have enumerated can find their full play best when public attention is focused as only a foreign minister's or summit conference permits. There will no doubt always be scope for quiet negotiation, notably when the prospects of accommodation are evident. But for the wider range of diplomatic aims, especially (but not exclusively) when they deal with adversary states, the international conference is probably here to stay and governments will probably continue the process of rationalizing this kind of modern diplomacy as a communicative process.

COMMUNICATIONS

Chapter 13

With the diminishing usefulness of methods of outright physical coercion, states have turned to other means of trying to achieve their goals in international relations. One of these alternatives involves the attempt to persuade or influence the minds of leaders as well as of the general population of other countries. Propaganda may be too narrow a term for this, since it is usually thought of as being directed at enemy or hostile people. The term "psychological methods," which refers to a broad range of activities, is more useful although, as W. Phillips Davison suggests below, the term "political communication" would perhaps be more appropriate to describe this facet of contemporary foreign policy implementation. In a more or less technical fashion, propaganda may be defined as the manipulation of facts and symbols to attain desired effects in the minds of an audience. The dividing line between propaganda and psychological warfare is shadowy although the degree of hostility implied may be more marked in the latter than the former.[1] A clearly related method is that of subversion. Although subversion may take overt physical forms, its relevance to the present discussion is that it represents an attempt to enlist individuals and groups within some countries to work for the advantage and interests of other countries in terms of communicating information, ideas, images, and expectations.

[1] See M. A. Linebarger, *Psychological Warfare* (Washington: Combat Forces Press, 1948), *passim*.

Communicational targets, however, may be both foreign and domestic. Domestically, a government makes use of all kinds of communications media to rally the people of its country in support of its policies, because those policies will be effective internationally only to the degree that it is known by others that they have the support of important publics at home. For example, Woodrow Wilson's position at the Paris Peace Conference was weakened by the results of the Congressional elections of 1918 and the clear indications from opposing senators that they would not support the results of the negotiations in which he was engaged. Even dictatorships must demonstrate support by their people in order to put up an impressive facade during crises with other countries.

When communications are directed at foreign publics, two types of results or consequences are sought: in cases where another government is hostile to the purposes of the government employing the psychological methods, such methods are designed to create internal opposition and dissension, thus weakening the support which those policies enjoy domestically. Similarly, psychological methods may be used to encourage and promote policies which are advantageous to the state that utilizes and applies these methods. For example it is not at all unusual for one government to help cement the prestige and reputation of a friendly government in another country through such means as appropriately timed state visits, declarations, and policy moves known to be popular in that country.

As is obvious from this discussion, the use of psychological methods or communicational approaches can be both defensive and affirmative. A given government will use them not only to create positive support for its policies, but also to ward off the negative effects that the use of similar policies by other states might have in the absence of countervailing efforts.

Political communication and the systematic use of psychological methods is not an entirely new development in international relations. Bismarck, for example, made use of the press in order to bring about a certain state of affairs between Prussia and France. During World War I, stories of atrocities, reports of starvation due to blockade, and even President Wilson's Fourteen Points were designed, in whole or in part, to produce changes in the opinion of important public sectors across national boundaries and through them in the official attitudes of important countries. World War II saw an extension and refinement of such methods, and in the contemporary period of chronic tension their use has not only proliferated but has become highly sophisticated in its orchestration of subtle and powerful techniques.

Certain new and arresting developments are taking place in the communications field as it impinges upon international relations. One student of the subject has suggested that the real innovation may be "the frank recognition of propaganda as a regular branch of government alongside economic and military departments,"[2] and despite the continuation of a marked degree of suspicion and doubt on the part of legislators, this idea is accepted even in democratic countries. Among the new elements is the availability of new and vastly improved technological means of communication, permitting a far greater scope for the application of psychological methods. In addition, pioneering research activity by psychologists has yielded more—and more reliable—information about how men's minds can be influenced (though it is not clear that governments and other agencies involved in the application of psychological methods always act on the basis of the new findings). But perhaps the most fundamental development lies in the fact that the conduct of foreign relations in many countries has become democratized, in the sense that various publics are involved in one way or another. The public at large may not participate actively in the decision-making process, but it has certainly become increasingly influential in setting the general directions and tolerable limits within which policy makers must operate. This being the case, it has not only become more profitable for governments to attempt to influence the beliefs and actions of masses of people across national boundaries but more foolhardy for them to ignore or de-emphasize the wishes or moods of their own people.

The key question to be asked of any operation, of course, concerns its effectiveness. Whether a given method is effective or not depends on a number of considerations. It depends on the validity of the assumptions that underlie its use. In this connection the analysis by W. Phillips Davison of the Graduate School of Journalism at Columbia is most valuable and instructive, because the author not only outlines the false assumptions on which much of political communication has been based but also presents some important findings from recent social science research that indicate more appropriate policies in terms of content and audience. These are necessary and useful cautions against the indiscriminate use of propaganda or too great reliance on it.[3] Nor is it correct to argue that the most effective propaganda tells the biggest lies, effective though the "Big Lie" may be, especially in the short run. Daniel Lerner has pointed out that truth in propaganda is a "function of effectiveness," the basis for decisions about the use of falsehoods or factual statements being the "estimate of what will work" most effectively.[4]

It is often argued that democratic societies find themselves at a disadvantage in psychological contests with non-democratic adversaries. For one thing they lack the clearly defined ideological base which totalitarian

---

[2] John B. Whitton, "Propaganda in Cold Wars," *Public Opinion Quarterly* (1951), 15, 142–44.

[3] See Ralph K. White, "The New Resistance to International Propaganda," *Public Opinion Quarterly* (1952), 16, 539–51.

[4] Daniel Lerner, *Sykewar* (New York: George H. Stewart, 1949), p. 26.

states possess. One of the main ingredients of liberal democracy is the willingness to tolerate, in fact to encourage, diversity of belief. The report of a special committee appointed by President Eisenhower is instructive here in that it argued that the pursuit of effective psychological warfare was based on certain preconditions, including fanaticism, utmost flexibility and maneuverability, and a great deal of money; included also was the willingness to proceed "with no holds barred and no questions asked." Inspection of this list will reveal that autocratic regimes are more likely to satisfy all these requirements, with the possible exception of money, than are democracies. Furthermore there are no democratic equivalents to the disciplined Communist parties found in most countries of the world.[5]

As we have seen, the decision to make use of modern psychological methods in international relations is essentially to engage in an exercise in communications. The crucial ingredients in this process can be summarized in the following questions:

1. *Who* does the communicating? Is it best for cross-national communications to be performed by governments or by private agencies? In the same context the question arises: Who controls the in-flow of communication into a given country and the circulation of information within the country? Who, to use a phrase employed by students of the communications process, are the "gate-keepers," and how do they behave?

2. *What* is to be communicated? Here, of course, the clear rule is that the content of communication must depend on a large number of factors in the total process. Most notably, it must depend on the audience to which the communication is to be directed.

3. *To whom* is the communication addressed? Is it geared to mass audiences or to specific audiences, at home or in other countries? If the object is to influence specific publics, how are they to be singled out? What are the relevant characteristics of the audiences, and how can the message be most appropriately geared to appeal to them? Should the major efforts be directed to audiences in countries which are hostile to one's purposes, countries which are friendly, or countries which do not fall into either of these categories?

4. *What media* are to be employed in communicating the message? The answer to this question depends in part on the content and the audience of a message.

5. What are the *results* which a given act of communication achieves? One must assess these results both in terms of the intended and the unintended consequences. On the basis of this kind of assessment, future strategies must be evolved.

However advanced methods of communications may become, they are, by themselves, probably not likely to replace other methods of projecting

[5] Arthur Krock, "Why We Are Losing the Psychological War," *The New York Times Magazine,* August 8, 1957, pp. 12ff.

policy effectively in the world arena. The political-diplomatic instrument, the use of economic means, and even the employment—actual or potential—of force will always play significant roles in international relations. Psychological approaches can facilitate or hinder the achievement of results, but they cannot substitute for the other ways in which a state attempts to gain its ends. It is perhaps best to speak of communications as supplementary and facilitating to other policies rather than as substitutes for them. They can help attain given ends if their employment is skillfully combined with the use of other methods of achieving policy goals to which statesmen turn in the modern conduct of foreign relations. As Karl Deutsch of Harvard has observed, "The credibility of a government, a national elite, or a national system of mass media, in the international arena as well as in domestic politics, may well depend in no small part on the extent to which its messages correspond to the actual impact of reality on the populations, groups, and other governments concerned."[6]

6 Karl W. Deutsch, *The Analysis of International Relations* (Englewood Cliffs, N.J.: Prentice-Hall, Inc., 1968), p. 110.

1. *Political Communication as an Instrument of Foreign Policy*

W. Phillips Davison

Heavily affecting the conduct of United States propaganda activities from the time of Tom Paine to the present have been certain conceptions about what information can do, how it affects behavior, and how it should be used. First, it is clear that Paine's view of the press (now including radio, television, and motion pictures) as a power

PUBLIC OPINION QUARTERLY, 27 (1963), pp. 28ff. Reprinted by special permission of PUBLIC OPINION QUARTERLY, Princeton, New Jersey.

that governs the sentiments of mankind has been and continues to be widespread. According to this mode of thought, propaganda is an effective instrument for influencing opinion. True information will correct misconceptions regarding the United States and United States policy. Communist propaganda will be counteracted if its falsity can be demonstrated. If hostile propaganda is not countered, according to this view, it can exert a dangerous influence on impressionable minds.

A second common conception about propaganda activities is that they should be aimed at a mass audience. If enough people can be persuaded to adopt a given opinion, then the policy of their government will be affected, at least in a democracy. Mass attitudes are thus seen as the primary target of propaganda.

A third popular idea is that propaganda should be directed primarily to audiences who hold opinions different from those of the propagandist. These are the people who need to be won over. Tom Paine proposed to convert the British to the American point of view. The Committee on Public Information in World War I sought to undermine enemy morale. The expression "psychological warfare," widely used in World War II, carried with it the implication that the audience was composed largely of hostile elements. Propaganda leaflets were sometimes referred to as "paper bullets." More recently, the arsenal of American propagandists has been said to contain "truth bombs."

It should be emphasized that these views about propaganda, while widely held in the United States and in some other countries, are not entertained by all professional practitioners of the art. Many personnel in the U.S. Information Agency would not subscribe to them, or would endorse them only in part. The Soviets have shown that they look at propaganda very differently. Nevertheless, as far as democratic countries are concerned, these conceptions are so generally accepted among the public that they heavily influence the conduct of foreign information programs. . . .

During the past few decades social science research has increasingly led to questions about the validity of these popular conceptions. Some appear to be misleading, others to require considerable refinement. More and more evidence has piled up to indicate that the mass media are effective instruments of persuasion only under rather special circumstances, and that the primary capabilities of propaganda lie in a very different direction.

First, it is now widely accepted by social scientists that information by itself is not usually able to reverse established attitudes.[1] If an attitude is useful to a person, if it helps him maintain his personal integrity or a satisfactory social adjustment, even very skillful and sustained propaganda will ordinarily be unable to shake it. People defend themselves resourcefully against information with which they disagree. They do this in part by refusing to expose themselves to unwelcome communications, by forgetting them, by distorting them, or by finding counterarguments. The editorial preference of a large majority of American newspapers for Republican candidates ever since 1932 has not succeeded in preventing the election of Democratic presidents in all but two national contests since then. Almost a generation of sustained Communist propaganda does not seem to have been successful in making convinced Communist out of most people in Eastern Europe.

On the other hand, it has become clear that information can have a very significant effect in strengthening and nourishing attitudes that already exist. People look for communications that reinforce their predispositions, and wel-

[1] Much of the experimental research on mass communications has been summarized by Joseph T. Klapper in *The Effects of Mass Communication* (New York: Free Press of Glencoe, Inc., 1960). Because of the volume and diffuse character of research in this field, individual studies will not be cited here, except by way of example.

come information that proves them right and helps them to take actions they are inclined to take anyway. Voting studies have been particularly important in showing that individuals expose themselves to propaganda with which they agree, and that this propaganda strengthens them in their convictions and helps to get them to the polls.[2]

Information can also play an important part in establishing new attitudes on new subjects, and can sometimes change lightly held attitudes. People who know nothing or very little about an issue can often be swayed *if*, and it is a big if, a communicator is able to gain their attention. This is one reason why American films have been so important in shaping attitudes toward the United States. Many of the people in foreign countries who see these films do not give their attention to very much other information about this country. The importance of information in establishing new attitudes is also one reason why the emerging countries will be such an important arena for propagandists in the coming years. In these countries, opinions on world issues are just beginning to be formed.

At the same time that research has shown that well-grounded attitudes rarely change as a result of propaganda alone, it has also indicated ways that attitudes can and do change. Attitudinal shifts usually occur when the situation in which a person finds himself changes, when his old attitudes are no longer useful to him, and when new attitudes are likely to bring him into better adjustment with his environment. Thus,

combat replacements who were assigned to established units in World War II gradually altered their attitudes in the direction of those held by the men in the established units to which they were assigned.[3] People whose economic situation changes often adopt new political attitudes that serve their new interests better. Research on the opinions that people in different nations have of each other suggests that positive or negative attitudes frequently reflect good or bad relations between the governments involved. Friction between governments can lead to a hostility between peoples, and good intergovernmental relations often lead peoples in the states involved to have more favorable images of each other.[4] Basic attitude changes are thus usually brought about by changes in the social, political, or economic environment—*not* by propaganda.

These observations, which will have a very familiar ring to those acquainted with the social scientific literature, suggest the need for radical revision in some of the popular conceptions about propaganda that were described above. The most rewarding target for propaganda is ordinarily not the individual with differing opinions, but rather the person who shares at least partly the views of the propagandist or whose attitudes have not yet become firmly established.

Does this mean that communications are of little value as an instrument in foreign policy. One might conclude that little is to be gained by preaching to the converted and to the indifferent. On the other hand, it can also be

---

[2] The familiar pioneering study that inspired much of the research in this area was conducted in Erie County, Ohio, in the 1940 election. Cf. Paul F. Lazarsfeld, Bernard Berelson, and Hazel Gaudet, *The People's Choice* (New York: Columbia University Press, 1948).

[3] M. Brewster Smith, "The Combat Replacement," in Samuel A. Stouffer *et al.*, *The American Soldier* (Princeton, N.J.: Princeton University Press, 1949), II, 243–72.

[4] William Buchanan and Hadley Cantril, *How Nations See Each Other* (Urbana, Ill.: The University of Illinois Press, 1953).

argued that one gains a great deal. By reinforcing the convictions of those who are already favorably disposed, by providing them with evidence that their beliefs are correct, and by giving them information about what they might do to achieve their goals, the propagandist can often stimulate action on the part of people who are in basic agreement with him. This action tends to change the social environment and thus may affect hostile elements within that environment also, since some of those who were previously opposed to the propagandist are likely to change their attitudes to conform to the new situation. To take an example from election campaigns, a Democrat who is surrounded by enthusiastic, well-organized, and vocal Republicans is more likely to change his voting intention than if his associates do not feel strongly about their political opinions or keep these opinions to themselves. The propagandist can play an important part in stimulating both enthusiasm and organization.

ORGANIZATIONS AS USERS OF INFORMATION

The fact that propaganda can help to promote organization is perhaps more significant in the foreign policy context than the fact that it can affect individuals. This is because unorganized individuals rarely have political significance; only if they work together, talk together, or vote together are they likely to have an effect on the political scene. Organizations are much more important, and they are large users of communications. As the literature of industrial sociology and public administration emphasizes, upward, downward, and lateral communication within an organization is vital to its successful functioning. Furthermore, organizations require an enormous amount of information originating outside themselves if their members are to do their jobs properly. Many organizations make use of communications from abroad. Industrial and scientific groups try to obtain the information that will be most useful to their work, regardless of where it originates. Governments are particularly large consumers of political information from abroad, as is testified by the volume of diplomatic reporting and the voracious appetite of all foreign offices for media that contain news about foreign areas. Private organizations concerned with foreign policy likewise require large quantities of international news.[5]

If propagandists can provide information that is useful to existing organizations, or if they can help new organizations to form, they are much more likely to have a significant political impact than if they focus their attention on influencing individuals. The worldwide Communist propaganda apparatus is an outstanding example of this. It works in close conjunction with existing Communist organizations by providing them with information about the party line, by helping to train and indoctrinate those already recruited, and by assisting in the attraction of new members.

The United States information services also devote substantial attention to serving foreign organizations. They furnish political groups in new countries with material about the workings of democracy. They help to supply the leaders of friendly nations with information they require to make daily decisions. They assist in training new personnel for a wide variety of organi-

[5] Much of the research on the interest of American organizations in information from abroad is cotnained in the five volumes edited by Alfred O. Hero, *Americans in World Affairs Communications* (Boston: World Peace Foundation, 1959 and 1960).

zations.[6] Their work in providing information that helps emerging countries to develop new institutions of industry and commerce, and to expand old ones, has great long-term political significance.

A dramatic instance of the organizational importance of communications is afforded by the work of the British Broadcasting Corporation and certain other Allied agencies during World War II. One of the chief tasks of these agencies was to encourage resistance movements in German-occupied Europe. The BBC initially promoted the formation of resistance movements by letting individuals on the continent know that they were not alone—that there were others who shared their opinions. It urged all those who were resistance-minded to get together and form groups. It then attempted to provide political and technical information that would be useful to these groups. It gave them news that was relevant to their activities and that was likely to support their morale. It also let them know about techniques that had been used successfully to interfere with Nazi military operations. In this case, a foreign source provided not only *external* communications to a group of organizations but in some cases provided *internal* communications as well. That is, it enabled members of groups that had no reliable internal channels to keep in touch with each other.

A SUMMING UP

Social science research thus suggests that the principal target of

6 The most recent general treatment of the U.S. Information Agency is that of Wilson P. Dizard, *The Strategy of Truth* (Washington, D.C.: Public Affairs Press, 1961). Important parts of the United States foreign information program are also conducted by the Department of State, the Department of Defense, and the Agency for International Development.

propaganda should not be a mass of individuals whose attitudes are to be changed, but much more a set of groups and organizations that are to be assisted. This is not to say that the propagandist should be unconcerned with individual psychology. The opposite is the case. But he should think of inidivduals primarily as members or potential members of politically significant bodies. His task is to identify organizations that require certain types of information and then supply this to them. The information in question may not be political at all—it may be about disease prevention or farming techniques—but its effects are likely to be political. He may be considered a persuader, in that he may ultimately affect attitudes, but it is more useful operationally to think of him as a purveyor of information that can be used to achieve both his goals and those of his audience.

It is not enough that this approach, if indeed it is correct, should be understood by those who are engaged in using political communication as an instrument of foreign policy. Many officials in the U.S. Information Agency and other organizations carrying on foreign information programs already appear to look at their tasks substantially in the way suggested here. If these people are to do their jobs efficiently, however, a working philosophy such as this will have to be more generally accepted by Congress and by the public. As long as American propagandists are expected to convince Communists that they should turn into democrats, to persuade street mobs in foreign nations that they should stop anti-American demonstrations, or to explain away racial discrimination in the United States, they will have a more difficult time getting on with their less spectacular but ultimately more important functions.

Finally, it should be apparent

from the way the words "propaganda" and "propagandist" have been used in the foregoing that they are not intended to carry a pejorative connotation. The expression "propagandist" has been employed in this paper to refer to anyone who uses an information program to help achieve his goals. Thus, the most objective news file can be considered propaganda under certain conditions, for instance, if it is provided to assist a friendly foreign government in making wiser decisions.

The low esteem in which propaganda is held by the public in this country is itself a block to the more efficient utilization of political communication as an instrument of foreign policy. But that is another story. At this point it is sufficient to observe that propaganda has not always occupied a low estate in the United States. The Committee of Foreign Affairs, of which Tom Paine was Secretary, grew out of the Committee of Secret Correspondence of the Continental Congress. Thus, in this country, propaganda might be considered the senior foreign service.

2. The Importance of the Audience

RAYMOND A. BAUER

Raymond A. Bauer is Professor of Social Psychology at the Harvard Graduate School of Business. His publications include THE NEW MAN IN SOVIET PSYCHOLOGY *and* HOW THE SOVIET SYSTEM WORKS *(with Alex Inkeles).*

I should like to present a few ideas which have grown out of the work of the Program of International Communications at Massachusetts Institute of Technology. Since these thoughts are group products, this paper could as

From "The Communicator and the Audience," JOURNAL OF CONFLICT RESOLUTION, *2, (March 1958), pp. 67–77. Reprinted by permission of the* JOURNAL OF CONFLICT RESOLUTION *and the author. An earlier version of this paper was delivered at the tenth anniversary of the founding of the Department and Laboratory of Social Relations, Harvard University, February 9, 1957.*

appropriately have been presented by any one of several colleagues whose names will be mentioned in the course of this paper.

If we may judge by the glee with which physicists greeted the recent demolition of one of the theoretical underpinnings of their trade, it would seem that limited chaos is a sign of health in a science. When old models prove too simple, we expand them and add new variables. In the short run we are delighted when our work substantiates our theories. In the long run, however, it is the discarding of theories and assumptions that marks the milestones of advance. On these grounds, research in the field of social communications may be viewed with a great deal of satisfaction. A high proportion of individual pieces of research are so inconclusive that they have forced on us these ever more elaborated models of the communications process. May I cite just one major example: It is now generally conceded that the Erie County study of the 1940 elections compelled us to discard certain simple assumptions about the direct impact of the mass media upon the mass audience. The idea of the "two-step flow of communications" was introduced, and this initiated a search for opinion leaders. But opinion leaders proved not to be a single class of persons all of whom exercised their influence in the same way. We are now thrown back on looking for networks of interpersonal communication. Not only has the communications model been expanded, but the study of informal communications has now blended into basic psychological research on interpersonal influence and sociological studies of the primary group (1).

The same sort of revision is gradually taking place with respect to the classic formula of communications research: "Who says what to whom and with what effect?" Originally, communications research implicitly gave the major initiative to the communicator. The main question asked was: What sort of communications and media are most effective and under what circumstances? It would be incorrect to say that the audience was *ignored,* but it was certainly accorded very little initiative. Audiences (if I may use this term to embrace also "readers"), however, have proved intractable. They make their own decisions as to whether to listen or not to listen. Even when they

listen, the communication may have no effect, or it may boomerang. More and more, researchers have had to shift their attention to the audience itself to find out what sorts of people they are dealing with under what circumstances.

I would like to go further and suggest that in the future we may come to regard the audience more and more as a system of response potentials and the communication as a signal which triggers off the response highest in the hierarchy. Or, to shift language a bit, what was once regarded as a "stimulus-bound" situation looks more and more like a "response-bound" situation. I am not proposing that this is all of what happens in *all* communications, but I *am* proposing that we are likely to find that it is profitable to look at a high proportion of communications not as *changing* behavior but as triggering the organism to do what it was very likely to do in any event. If this view of the audience is correct, it is of course not the result of, nor can it be tested by, any single crucial experiment; it is rather the reflection of the impact of a long series of research findings.

Our own attempts to understand a series of problems in the field of international communications have suggested to us the desirability of entertaining seriously the following propositions concerning the role of the audience in communications: (1) The audience influences the way in which the communicator organizes new information and thereby what he himself may remember and/or believe at a later point in time. (2) A communication once completed has an existence external to the originator. It is a sample of his behavior which he must often reconcile —as a result of social or of internal pressure—with other behavior. On this latter point we need only remember the story of Franklin Roosevelt asking

Samuel Rosenman to reconcile one of his early speeches with later policy. After some deliberation, Rosenman told him that the only solution to his dilemma was flatly to deny having made the first speech. (3) Communications are seldom directed to a single manifest audience. Secondary audiences or reference groups, usually internalized and often imaginary, are important targets of communication and may at times play a decisive role in the flow of communications.

These propositions are not new discoveries. They may be found in the sociology of C. H. Cooley and of G. H. Mead, the psychiatry of Harry Stack Sullivan and others, and the essays of writers on communication. The rationale for presenting them in this context is twofold. First, practical problems of communications research have suggested to us their utility; second, it appears that it is presently possible to bring to bear on these propositions more systematic data than have been employed in the past. Much of what I have to say will consist of reporting of work we have done and are planning to do and of pointing to established areas of research and to individual studies which contribute with varying degrees of directness to the testing of these propositions, their implications, and their practical significance.

I. EFFECT OF THE AUDIENCE ON ORGANIZATION AND RETENTION OF MATERIAL

Our first proposition is that audiences influence the way in which a person organizes new information and thereby what he himself may remember and/or believe at a later point in time. The functional approach to per-ception and remembering which has been so attractive to social psychologists in the past decades has led them to investigate the relationship of man's needs and interests to the way he perceives and remembers the "blooming, buzzing confusion" around him. Is it not equally plausible that one will organize new information in terms of its intended use in interpersonal relations, that a person who intends to communicate on a topic will organize and remember material on that subject as a function of his image of the audience he has in mind?

This question was posed by Harry Grace in a paper published in 1951 (8). He asked subjects to remember an array of objects which they were later to report to an experimenter. Some of the subjects were told that the person to whom they were to report was a woman; the control subjects were told nothing about the characteristics of the person to whom they were to report. It was anticipated, since some of the items might be "embarrassing" to report to a woman, that those subjects who were briefed on the sex of the experimenter would remember fewer of these items than would control subjects. Grace's data were not so conclusive as one might hope for, but he had nevertheless posed a meaningful question.

As often happens, the same question occurred to us without our having been aware of Grace's earlier work. While we were trying to organize our thoughts concerning the impact of foreign travel on American businessmen, Ithiel Pool suggested the possibility that a person might never formulate his impressions of a foreign country systematically until he was in the position of having to communicate them to someone else. In this event, the first audience to whom he addressed himself would influence the way in which he would organize his information and the terms in which he would couch his conclusions. In this way the audience would influence what he would later remember and believe. Let us consider the position of a man confronted with a new batch of information or with old unorganized knowledge, i.e., items of information which he has not previously related to each other. He is now in a position in which he views this information, whether "old" or "new," as something he may have to communicate to another person. He has a set to communicate to an audience of which he has a specified image. It is a basic assumption of both content analysis and effective public speaking, as well as the object of common-sense observation, that the communicator adapts his statements to his audience, taking into consideration its interests and expectations for purposes of more effective communication. That this set to communicate may affect what he later remembers is given plausibility by the voluminous experimental literature on the effect of set on perception and retention.

One of the major problems of design in studies of the influence of set on remembering has been to prevent rehearsal of the material between periods of recall. From the standpoint of communications research, we would assume that such rehearsal is precisely what happens in the real life-situations in which we are interested. Therefore, it presents no design problem. Cooley long ago spelled out the process that we would guess to be at work. The anticipated audience would serve as—in Cooley's words—an imaginary interlocutor with whom the subject would hold internal conversations in anticipation of the eventual communication (4, esp. pp. 61–62). In the course of these internal conversations the material ought to be "reworked" to bring it

closer to the form in which it was intended to be communicated. Cooley contended that the human personality is formed via such internal conversations with audiences real and imagined. Our goals are more modest. We should like to know what happens to the particular batch of new or newly organized information about which we have been talking. Is retention of this information indeed affected by the person's image of the audience to which he expects to communicate? The audience, in a fashion, coerces the individual into playing a role. Does this also mean, as the work of Janis and King on the influence of role-playing on attitudes (9, 13) suggests, that the subject's attitudes are changed in this process?

We have so far undertaken only one piece of research directed at the question of the influence of the audience on what is remembered of new, incoming information. This was an experiment reported by Claire Zimmerman and myself (19). The design evolved out of a joint Harvard-M.I.T. seminar consisting of Miss Zimmerman, Ithiel Pool, Jerome Bruner, George Coelho, and myself.

The experimenter presented herself in the classrooms of a number of colleges and universities, as a representative of one of two fictitious organizations: the National Council of Teachers, identified as interested in improving the teachers' lot, or the American Taxpayers Economy League, identified as interested in saving taxpayers' money. Her organization, she said, was seeking speakers to address its members on the topic of teachers' pay, and she had arranged with the instructor to have them write sample speeches during class time one week from that day. In the meantime, she said, her organization was also interested in how well people remembered material on this topic. She then read a short passage to them—in half the instances favoring, and in the other half opposing, teachers' pay raises. There were thus four groups of 18 persons, each involving all possible combinations of materials and "audiences" both favoring and opposing raises in teachers' pay. She then asked the subjects to write from memory the passage she had just read to them, as close to verbatim as possible. On returning the next week she asked them again, before writing the sample speech, to write down the passage as literally as they could. This was an experiment in remembering, but under conditions where the subjects anticipated communicating the material to an audience of specified characteristics.

Our prediction was that, at the end of a week, subjects would remember more information in those instances in which the passage and the intended audience were on the same side of the issue (we called this a situation of "congruence") than they would if the passages to be remembered and the audience for whom they were to write a speech were in conflict (a situation we labeled "incongruent"). Thus a subject would remember more arguments in favor of raising teachers' pay if he were anticipating a favorable audience than if the intended audience were interested in saving the taxpayers' money. There were no differences among the groups in their initial recall immediately after

the presentation of the material. However, there were differences in the expected direction at the end of the ensuing week. Our hypothesis was supported comfortably beyond the 0.01 level of statistical significance. Schramm and Danielson have since replicated the basic experiment at Stanford University, using as subject matter a quite different issue, that of lowering the voting age to eighteen. The results once more hold up beyond the 0.01 level (17).

A subsidiary hypothesis was that this "audience effect" of selective remembering would be maximal for persons primarily concerned with the audience and minimal for persons primarily involved in the subject matter. The complete design mentioned above was carried out on both graduate students of journalism (supposedly oriented by selection and/or training to be sensitive to the characteristics of the audience) and on students in teachers' colleges (presumably highly involved in the issue of teachers' pay). The basic hypothesis held up for both groups. But the effect, as predicted, was greater among the graduate students of journalism. The difference in effect was, again, statistically significant beyond the 0.01 level. The journalism students' rate of forgetting in a situation of "incongruence" was *double* that in a situation of "congruence." These results appear to be not only statistically but practically significant (see Table 1).

TABLE 1

MEAN ANGLES CORRESPONDING TO PERCENTAGE LOSSES FOR ALL GROUPS BETWEEN FIRST AND SECOND RECALL TRIALS*

	TAX AUDIENCE		TEACHER AUDIENCE	
STUDENTS OF	Incongruent Raise Salary Arguments	Congruent Do Not Raise Salary Arguments	Incongruent Do Not Raise Salary Arguments	Congruent Raise Salary Arguments
Journalism	55.44	26.85	54.79	27.30
Teaching	40.05	26.81	41.09	25.88

* From Zimmerman and Bauer (19, p. 244).

Since the completion of this experiment, several other pieces of work starting out on entirely different tacks have been done which testify to the effectiveness of a set to communicate on the organization and retention of information. Zajonc, in a study directed at an understanding of cognitive processes (18), has found that persons who anticipate communicating a body of material organize it differently from persons who anticipate being communicated *to* on the same subject. Furthermore, by specifying that the other persons (i.e., those to whom the subjects are supposedly going to communicate or who are going to communicate to the subjects) are opposed to the subjects' own position on the issue, he was able to effect still further changes in the organization of the material. Thus in Zajonc's work, not only is the communicative set per se found relevant, but the qualitative image of the intended audience is also of importance to the way in which new information is handled.

Jones and Aneshansel (10) became interested independently in the question of the relative influence on retention of experimental subjects' own values and their intention to use controversial material for communication. They told some of their subjects that they were going to have to use the material presented to them in rebuttal to arguments with which they were to be confronted later. Their subjects remembered significantly more material counter to their own values when they were told they would have to use this material in an argument. Under control conditions the usual results were found. Subjects remembered more material in line with their own beliefs.

These several findings all seem to say that it is possible to affect what a person will recall of new information by telling him he will have to communicate on the subject and that his image of the audience will affect what is remembered. This indicates that the audience can, in fact, have an enduring effect on the communicator that extends beyond its influence on the form and content of individual messages.

Is it "perception" or "remembering" that is affected? All these studies suffer from the usual difficulty of distinguishing between perception, retention, and recall. In the instance of the Jones and Zajonc studies a very early effect was observed which might possibly reflect the initial organization of incoming material, i.e., perception. In the Zimmerman experiment, however, there was no observed effect on initial recall of the material. But there was a pronounced "audience effect" at the end of a week. This suggests that conscious or unconscious rehearsals of the anticipated speech resulted in accommodation of the newly acquired information to the values and expectations of the intended audience. It makes sense in light of this to look at the intended audience as an induced reference group of high salience. Presumably one's habitual reference groups regularly evoke similar internal conversations, although this process is somewhat more difficult to study.

However, we must again complicate matters. Image of the audience, information, and communicator's values appear to be in a state of active interrelationship in which any one of the elements may affect any one or combination of the others. Communicators committed strongly to the subject matter may "distort" their image of the prospective audience to bring it more in line with either their own values or the content of the incoming information and thereby reduce the "audience effect." Thus the teachers' college students were more likely than the journalists to report "objectively incongruent" audiences as "neutral" with respect to the material they were given to memorize. Furthermore, those subjects who "neutralized" an incongruent audience remembered more of the material. Because of the limited number of cases that fell in these categories, the differences in Zimmerman's data are not statistically reliable, and, in fact, some of the findings are presently ambiguous. They do, however, suggest this line of speculation.

Whereas it was previously proposed that reference groups, by acting as internal audiences, affect what one remembers (and possibly one's attitudes), it seems likely also that the individual's image of a reference group is formed and changes in the process of these internal conversations. On controversial issues, this may eventually produce a schematization of reference groups in which positive reference groups are seen as "all white" and negative reference groups are seen as "all black." This proposition, also, seems amenable to systematic study.

There are indications also that the set to communicate may have a dampening effect on the impact of the individual's own values. Most of the experiments on the influence of personal values on remembering and perception accept implicitly the position that pleasurable material will be remembered better than disagreeable material. That which is consonant with the individual's personal values is taken tacitly by most of the investigators to be pleasurable to the individual. Direct test of the proposition that agreeable material will be better remembered has produced conflicting results in quite a number of experiments. The possibility that positive results of the influence of personal values on remembering and perception

may be due, at least in part, to greater familiarity with consonant material may be bypassed for the moment in deference to a point more crucial to the present argument. Reinforcement of one's self-image or ego-defense is only one of the possible motives that may influence one's set toward incoming information. This is already implied in the notion of "perceptual vigilance" with the suggestion that under some circumstances the threshold for so-called "contravaluant" material will be lowered. Jones and Aneshansel make the same argument I am making now, and say: "The functionalist might suggest that we examine the total context in which perception (or learning) takes place, in an effort to determine those conditions which promote lowered thresholds for threatening material (perceptual vigilance) and those which promote higher thresholds (perceptual defense)." It will be remembered that in their experiment positively valued material was better remembered in the control situation, but negatively valued material was better remembered by the experimental subjects who were told they were going to have to use the material in a later argument. Zimmerman's data also indicated that when subjects were given instructions that they would have to communicate on the topic of the material they were to memorize, this set to communicate dampened the effect of the subjects' personal values. Teachers' college students, for example, remembered material opposed to raising teachers' pay as well as they remembered material favoring raising teachers' pay. Pending more direct evidence, it is reasonable to assume that a majority of them favored high salaries for the profession they were about to enter.

To summarize the discussion of this point, I have presented evidence, argument, and speculation to the effect that one's image of the audience to which material is to be communicated affects how this material is organized and/or retained. The influence of the communicative set seems on occasion to offset the role of the individual's personal values and beliefs. However, the audience does not operate independently either of the content of the information in question or of the communicator's values. In some instances the communicator apparently accommodates his image of the audience so as to reduce the perceived incongruence between it and his values and information. Other investigations, of course, have indicated that under some circumstances his values influence what he remembers.

Present evidence is at best not definitive. We have in plan further experimentation to test on larger samples some of the findings which are statistically unreliable; to ascertain to what extent Zimmerman's results reflect forgetting in any meaningful sense as opposed to a response set induced by the fact that the subjects were actually prepared to write a speech; to determine how lasting is the "audience effect" on what is remembered and whether or not attitudes are influenced. Our comparison of teacher's college students with journalism students was a lucky shot in the sociological dark but tells us less of the psychological factors which may be involved. It will be necessary to look into the psychological characteristics which differentiate persons of varying degree of "audience susceptibility" and audience resistence.

II. COMMUNICATION AS PERSONAL COMMITMENT

It is a commonplace that people on occasion say things other than precisely what they feel in their hearts. In psychological literature this circumstance has been memorialized in the distinction between "private" and "public" attitudes. Even the most honest and thoughtful person, confronted by different situations, will, quite sincerely, say different things on the same topic. What is relevant to one person in one situation is not what is relevant to another person in another situation. A disingenuous politician may well argue that he does not preach civil rights in the South because his audience is not interested in the topic. Regardless of the motives involved or the amount of disparity between private belief and public statement, the fact remains that a statement once made constitutes some degree of personal commitment.

It is easy to see how a public figure may be haunted by some utterance of his and be forced to extremes of ingenuity to reconcile it with other of his statements. We need but recall the incident mentioned previously when President Roosevelt asked Rosenman to explain away an earlier speech of Roosevelt on balancing the budget. More pertinent for us, however, is the possible effect of such commitments on the communicator's own attitudes.

Probably the most relevant body of research is that on compliance to group norms. Students of group dynamics have devoted a considerable amount of attention to the conditions under which an individual will shift his belief—at least on the overt level—to conform to the majority opinion in his group. It was Festinger who, a few years ago, called attention to the fact that overt compliance to group norms is not synonymous with covert compliance, i.e., change in private opinion (5). It is therefore interesting to note that in a recent book Festinger devotes two chapters to the discussion of the conditions under which forced compliance leads to change of private opinion (6, chaps. iv and v). He cites experimental work of McBride and Burdick and Kelman's work on the effect of response restriction on opinion change (12).

My own work on political loyalty in the Soviet Union (discussed in 1), and Bettelheim's earlier study of Nazi concentration camps (2) offer clinical evidence of opinion change when individuals are forced by external circumstances into a given line of behavior. In the light of this work on the effect of forced compliance on opinion change, it is reasonable to hypothesize that the audience, by evoking a commitment from the communicator, may have the second-order effect of causing him to accommodate his own beliefs to that commitment. This process, it would seem, is continuous with the one referred to above in which the audience affects the way in which the communicator organizes and retains information. The difference, however, is that one effect occurs in anticipation of the communication and the other follows after it. While it is easy to draw this distinction analytically, it may be difficult to draw empirically in practical situations, if an individual is involved in several successive communications.

From our contact with elite communications in this and other countries it seems to us that occurrences like the following sometimes take place. A prominent man is invited to deliver a ceremonial speech. In some instances a subordinate may draft the speech, and the speaker is rather indifferent to the content. He only wants it to be a good speech, appropriate to the occasion, that is, not blatantly divergent from his own values. On occasion the speech makes quite a hit, and the speaker is invited to make more speeches on the topic. Soon he is committed even in his own mind to this position and becomes an active advocate of it.

This sort of occurrence is probably rare among the general populace. However, among elite communicators of the sort we have been studying, this may be a problem of genuine practical significance. We have been struck with the frequency with which a public figure, bent on holding or gaining a position of influence, will deliberately seek out issues which may interest his constituency. When he hits on a successful issue and is rewarded, he becomes a vigorous proponent of that issue and in many cases converts himself even more firmly to that belief. This is exemplified in the instance of one ardent congressional spokesman for protectionism who told us that he had tried several issues on his constituency but found them uninterested until he evoked an enthusiastic response to a speech in favor of high tariffs. He has since made this his business.

We have no immediate research plans in this area. But, because of its seeming significance among elite communicators, it appears that we ought to take a closer look at the potential coercive force of the audience in evoking commitments and producing attitude change.

III. REFERENCE GROUPS AS SECONDARY AUDIENCES

Our third and final point is that messages are seldom directed to a single manifest audience but that reference groups, acting as secondary audiences, have an influential and occasionally a crucial role in the flow of communications. The importance of secondary audiences is a matter of common experience and has often been commented on anecdotally. Anyone who wishes to refresh himself on their role in everyday life need only leaf through a few casually selected doctoral theses. It has been my experience in reading them that I could identify certain pages written for Professor A, for Professor B, and certain others for Professor C, even though none of these gentlemen obviously was going to read the thesis.

As I have said, the importance of secondary audiences has been commented on frequently in anecdotal fashion but seldom studied systematically. Systematic work on reference groups—to which I am referring in this context as potential secondary audiences —has been confined largely to their influence on the attitudes of the subjects under investigation. But, unless we consider the interview situation in which the attitudes were evoked as an instance of communication, there has been little direct research on the role of reference groups or secondary audiences in the flow of specific messages. Daniel Lerner has pointed out (14) that the reviews of *The American Soldier* were influenced by the reference groups of the reviewers. More recently, Herbert Gans has presented a case study of the role of the reference groups of various moviemakers in the production of the movie *The Red Badge of Courage* (7). But such examples are few.

In an attempt to get at the actual role played by secondary audiences in the flow of communications, Irwin Shulman, a research assistant at M.I.T. and himself a journalist, interviewed newspapermen immediately after they had finished writing a story for their newspapers. At first he asked, "Who reads stories like this?" In response to this question he got stock answers derived from the newspaper's readership surveys. Then he shifted to asking, "While you were writing this story did you think of any person or group?" The answers to this question were quite different from those to the former question. The persons or groups of whom

they actually thought while writing the story were seldom the "average middle-class man who buys this newspaper." The number of interviews was not sufficient for statistical analysis. Yet the qualitative evidence suggested that there was a patterning to these secondary audiences with respect to the type of communicator and story involved. Let me put the case more conservatively: There was in these interviews at least enough evidence that these secondary audiences are more than "noise" in the communications system to encourage us to continue the investigation.

The fact that many, possibly not all, journalists in Shulman's sample thought of secondary audiences while writing did not by any means demonstrate that these secondary audiences influence the content of what is written. An experiment was conducted with journalism students who were asked to write news stories out of a set of disjointed facts (16). The conditions of the experiment and the findings are too complicated for brief summarization. However, Pool and Shulman demonstrated that the reference groups and persons evoked were systematically and predictably a function of the material presented to the subjects of the experiment; and, much more interesting, the distortions which occurred in the handling of the material were a systematic function of idiosyncratic images which individual subjects imagined.

Both the results of Zimmerman's experiment, suggesting internal conversation in rehearsal of a speech, and Shulman's and Pool's work indicate the utility of thinking of reference groups as internalized audiences which are targets of imaginary conversations. While the existence of negative reference groups has been mentioned in the literature, almost all attention has been paid to positive reference groups. Reference groups have usually been treated as groups whose acceptance is sought or who are used as positive yardsticks for self-assessment. Our own orientation and data suggest that negative reference groups should be given more serious attention and that reference groups should be regarded as groups which one wants to influence in *any* fashion, whether it be to gain their approval or to persuade them to one's own position.

IV. CONCLUSION

The general import of these remarks is that there is something to be said for expanding our model of the communications process. I have proposed the utility of three propositions and presented evidence for both their plausibility and their practical import. These three propositions are, in summary, (1) images of audiences, both real and imaginary, external and internal, affect the way in which we organize and retain information and what we believe; (2) the audience often commits the speaker to a public position to which he may subsequently accommodate his private belief; and (3) finally, one seldom has in mind a single audience, and secondary, reference-group audiences may often exert the determining influence in the organization and retention of information, as well as in the flow of communication. In the simplest words, the communicator may actually be addressing himself to someone other than the manifest audience.

It will be remembered that our interest in this expanded model of communications was generated by concern with the practical problem of the impact of foreign travel on American businessmen. It is our belief that this view of the communications process will continue to have practical implications in the field of international relations. In the recent conduct of our own foreign policy, observers have commented, the utterances of American officials, while ostensibly directed abroad, were actually directed at domestic American secondary audiences. Also, in international relations audience *images* play a crucial role. Negotiators between nations, in all probability, carry in their heads highly stereotyped images of their opposite numbers. Their absorption and retention of information will be much affected by the intervention of these images. Coelho has, partially out of the stimulus of these ideas, done a doctoral dissertation on the role of audience images as reference groups in the accommodation of Indian students to the United States (3).

While we may talk about such practical implications abstractly, it will take a considerable amount of empirical work to establish what part audience images actually play in international affairs.

References

1. BAUER, R. A. "Brainwashing: Psychology or Demonology," *Journal of Social Issues* (in press).

2. BETTELHEIM, B. "Individual and Mass Behavior in Extreme Situations," *Journal of Abnormal and Social Psychology,* XXXVIII (1943), 417–52.

3. COELHO, G. *Acculturative Learning: A Study of Reference Groups.* Ph.D. thesis, Harvard University, 1956.

4. COOLEY, C. H. *Human Nature and the Social Order.* New York: Charles Scribner's Sons, 1902.

5. FESTINGER, L. "An Analysis of Compliant Behavior." In M. SHERIF and M. O. WILSON (eds.), *Group Relations at the Crossroads.* New York: Harper & Bros., 1953.

6. ———. *A Theory of Cognitive Dissonance.* Evanston: Row, Peterson, 1957.

7. GANS, H. J. "The Creator-Audience Relationship in the Mass Media: An Analysis of Movie-Making." In M. ROSENBERG and D. M. WHITE (eds.), *Mass Culture.* Glencoe, Ill.: Free Press and Falcon's Wing Press, 1957.

8. GRACE, H. A. "Effects of Different Degrees of Knowledge about an Audience on the Content of Communication," *Journal of Social Psychology,* XXXIV (1951), 111–24.

9. JANIS, I. L., and KING, B. T. "The Influence of Role Playing on Opinion Change," *Journal of Abnormal and Social Psychology,* XLIX (1954), 211–18.

10. JONES, E. E., and ANESHANSEL, JANE. "The Learning and Utilization of Contravaluant Material," *Journal of Abnormal and Social Psychology,* LIII (1956), 27–33.

11. KATZ, E., and LAZARSFELD, P. *Personal Influence.* Glencoe, Ill.: Free Press, 1955.

12. KELMAN, H. C. "Attitude Change as a Function of Response Restriction," *Human Relations,* VI (1953), 185–214.

13. KING, B. T., and JANIS, I. L. "Comparison of the Effectiveness of Improvised versus Non-improvised Role-Playing in Producing Opinion Changes," *Human Relations,* IX (1956), 177–86.

14. MERTON, R. K., and LAZARSFELD, P. (eds.). *Continuities in Social Research: Studies in the Scope and Method of "The American Soldier."* Glencoe, Ill.: Free Press, 1950.

15. OSGOOD, C. E. *Method and Theory in Experimental Psychology.* New York: Oxford University Press, 1953.

16. POOL, I. DE S., and SHULMAN, I. "Imaginary Audiences and the Creative Process." Cambridge, 1957 (mimeo.).

17. SCHRAMM, W., and DANIELSON, W. "Anticipated Audiences as Determinants of Recall," *Journal of Abnormal and Social Psychology,* LVI (1958), 282–83.

18. ZAJONC, R. *Cognitive Structure and Cognitive Tuning.* Ph.D. thesis, University of Michigan, 1954.

19. ZIMMERMAN, CLAIRE, and BAUER, R. A. "The Influence of an Audience on What Is Remembered," *Public Opinion Quarterly,* XX (1956), 238–48.

ECONOMIC METHODS

Chapter 14

Many past discussions tended to explain international relations primarily or exclusively in terms of economics. Imperialism particularly was considered to be an economic phenomenon. The Marxist interpretation was that an overly-productive capitalist system searched for safe places to invest surplus capital, to obtain needed raw materials for its industrial needs, and to find markets for its finished products. Governments, it was argued, engaged in aggressive imperialism to acquire and dominate areas which could provide these opportunities. Marxist theory suffered a blow when historians were able to show that it was often the other way around: that governments, in pursuit of political and strategic advantages, had urged financial interests to penetrate into other areas, so that the governments would then have a pretext for becoming politically involved there.[1]

Between the two world wars, great emphasis was placed on economic methods to preserve the peace, such as the League of Nations system of economic sanctions designed to discourage potential aggressors. But the sanctions imposed against Italy during the Ethiopian War were imperfectly applied, and failed to stop or even greatly hinder Mussolini's conquest in East Africa. The widely accepted interpretation that America had entered

[1] Eugene Staley, *War and The Private Investor* (Chicago: University of Chicago Press, 1935).

World War I for economic reasons led to an attempt to prevent future involvement through the ill-fated neutrality legislation of the 1930s; these laws not only failed to work but must bear part of the blame for the deterioration of European political relations in the 1930s.

These and other experiences persuaded some analysts and statesmen to conclude that economic aspects of international relations could largely be disregarded, and that the political-strategic sphere was all that mattered. But this extreme swing of the pendulum could not be sustained in light of the obvious fact that economic considerations *do* play a significant part in the relations between states. The observer of international affairs who disregards them holds and presents a warped picture of the processes involved in these relations, and the policy maker who fails to heed their lessons may lead his country to disaster.

Inasmuch as states employ economic policies in various ways and for diverse purposes, one needs to distinguish between economic policies pursued for purely economic reasons, for political or strategic reasons, or for some combination of reasons. It would be just as misleading to regard economics merely as a handmaiden to politics as to assume political motivations for all economic actions; but it would be even more erroneous to disregard the intimate relationship between economic policies and political considerations in foreign policy. One must avoid the temptation to consider single lines of policy—be they diplomatic, economic, or psychological—as being most common or most fruitful.

Policy is projected into the international sphere multidimensionally, and economic methods in international relations are most effective when they are combined with other methods of policy. Yet there may be times when they are in tension or contradiction, or are incompatible with political requirements. Although one cannot make sweeping assertions that either politics or economics always prevails, it does seem clear that in recent years political (including the military and strategic) considerations have most often been given priority.

This being so, it is sometimes difficult for the policy maker to make effective use of the economic means at his disposal. There will always be some internal opposition in his own country from groups which fear that they may be adversely affected by the employment of one or another method of economic pressure. Although a given policy may be to the benefit of the economy as a whole, sections of the economy may suffer. Needless to say opposition will be more effective within a democratic rather than an authoritarian society, though it is not completely precluded in the latter. There may be some advantage in the fact that economic methods are difficult to employ, for otherwise policy planners might be tempted to overutilize them. The risk in this would be that real problems would be concealed. If a country uses economic pressures in the expectation that these pressures *alone* will yield the desired results, it will frequently find that this is not so and that economic methods have to be combined with other measures of policy to be effective.

Many types of economic pressures may be employed including, *inter alia:* (1) financial manipulations to diminish the value of an opponent's currency and enhance that of one's own country; (2) economic penetration of weaker countries on the part of more powerful ones with the eventual objective of exerting pressure on the government of the penetrated society; (3) exploitation of a strategic economic position through such policies as price-fixing, dumping, the imposition of quotas, exchange controls, and so forth; (4) the boycott—a refusal to buy from another country; (6) the use of economic subsidies, about which more will be said below; (7) preëmptive buying of goods produced in other countries in order to withhold them from other purchasers; and (8) stockpiling of important goods.[2]

But by far the most common method of economic pressure has been the imposition of tariffs on the importation of specified goods from other countries. Most economists are agreed that from the viewpoint of the health of the international economy free trade would be of the greatest advantage to the greatest number of countries. Flying in the face of this expert judgment, however, tariffs have traditionally been used to serve a number of domestic or foreign policy ends of the government that imposes them. Tariffs may be imposed as revenue-raising procedures; they may be enacted to protect national industries for economic, political, or strategic reasons; and they may be designed to injure (or threaten to injure) trading patterns of certain other countries in order to achieve some economic or political concessions.

Just as alliances have been formed in the military sphere, groups of states have combined in the economic sphere in order to take advantage of larger trading areas and to overcome the crippling effects of tariff and other economic barriers. The most impressive achievement is seen in the European Economic Community ("Common Market"), though groupings in other areas also exist. The question is whether once large free-trade regions have been established it will be possible to reduce impediments to free-trade between those regions, or whether regional arrangements will in fact be used to create such impediments against trade with countries outside the group. Efforts at over-all reductions of tariffs, such as the Organization for Economic Cooperation and Development, attempt to link the economies of several trade areas.

Operations under the General Agreement on Tariffs and Trade, designed to promote world-wide improvements, attempt to counteract the tendency to divide the world into competing free-trade areas. While programs of economic assistance to other countries have historical antecedents, the scope

    2 Charles C. Abbot, "Economic Penetration and Power Politics," *Harvard Business Review* (1948), 26, pp. 410–24.

of such programs and the vigor with which they are being enacted and conducted constitute a new element in the relations between countries. This has become one of the most significant of economic methods used in international politics. A growing number of new states, having within their borders more than sixty per cent of the world's population, have found themselves to be economically underdeveloped, their traditional societies having concentrated upon the production of agricultural goods and the extraction of raw materials for export. Their value systems have held little expectation for progress. Consumption has approached production levels, thus leaving insufficient surplus capital for investment that could promote economic growth. The rising nationalism which produced many of these units as separate states has demanded economic and social betterment. Improved communications have awakened the peoples of these countries to the possibility that the way in which they have traditionally lived is not the only way to live. They see that other societies enjoy many more of the material benefits that contemporary civilization can bestow, and they are insisting upon improvement on a large scale in a short time. Yet for a very great number of reasons, the process by which a society can raise its standards of productivity and of living is a long and complex one. It requires strenuous exertions on the part of the country itself. It also requires large-scale assistance from other countries.

Efforts have been afoot since the end of the World War II to improve conditions in the underdeveloped areas of the world, to permit them, in Rostow's phrase, to reach the "take-off" phase of economic development and growth.[3] The United States and other economically advanced countries, including some in Western Europe as well as Israel and Japan, have developed programs of assistance to new states, albeit on too small a scale to bring about rapid transformations of their economies and societies. The Soviet Union has developed a highly concentrated and selective foreign aid program. Red China has entered the scene. Numerous programs under the auspices of the United Nations, its specialized agencies (such as the World Health Organization, the Food and Agriculture Organization, and UNESCO) are likewise designed to contribute toward an alleviation and eventual solution of the problem.

None of these programs, either by themselves or combined, can suffice to bring about needed improvements as rapidly as the peoples living in these areas desire. The world is confronted with what has been termed a "revolution of rising expectations"—a set of demands by the peoples of the underdeveloped areas, composing a majority of the world's population and growing at a rapid pace, who want and expect change. They want it quickly, and they are not always too concerned about just how the develop-

---

[3] W. W. Rostow, *The Stages of Economic Growth* (Cambridge: Cambridge University Press, 1960), *passim*.

ment occurs, especially in terms of political consequences. Yet long-term rapid improvement in living standards is extraordinarily hard to bring about, for as Rostow and others have pointed out, this requires not only external assistance, but a shifting of internal values and patterns. Furthermore, the medical revolution of our age has brought about dramatic decreases in death rates, reflected in sharply rising population figures particularly among the young and the old. This in turn means that education, health care, provisions for old age, and other social welfare programs place growing demands upon new states.

The rate of increase in economic productivity must outpace the rate of population increase. To bring about greatly increased productivity requires vast capital investments many of which, such as roads, harbors, and more efficient administrative systems, may not yield immediate returns.

Since surplus capital in amounts sufficient for such investment is not generally available within the new countries and since foreign private investors are reluctant to invest money where there is political and social unrest (particularly when investment opportunities in more highly developed countries are good), the only feasible alternative is aid from other governments or international development agencies. Neither has as yet provided assistance on a sufficiently large scale, and both are imposing increasingly exacting conditions of one kind or another.

Relations between the emergent and the economically more mature areas of the world are becoming a most serious contemporary and future problem. Astute observers suggest that just as the East-West conflict was characteristic of the first two post-war decades, so North-South tension (between the more and the less developed countries) will mark much of the remainder of the century. Strain between the more and the less developed countries would exist irrespective of the East-West confrontation, but the fact that the more highly developed states of the world *are* antagonistic toward each other contributes to the tension. The underdeveloped world is in a sense an arena for their competition, because the United States, the Soviet Union, Communist China, and the allies of these countries compete for influence in and over the less advanced states. All sides assiduously attempt to win their approval and support. The outcome of the cold war between the contending blocs may well be decided in the underdeveloped but aroused emergent countries throughout the African, Latin American, and Middle Eastern sectors of world politics.

1. Economic Development:
Rival Systems and Comparative Advantage

JOHN KENNETH GALBRAITH

J. Kenneth Galbraith, Professor of Economics at Harvard, has had a distinguished record of public service since 1940. He was economic advisor to the National Defense Advisory Commission, director of the Office of Economic Security Policy of the State Department, and served as United States Ambassador to India under President John F. Kennedy. His books include THE AFFLUENT SOCIETY, THE LIBERAL HOUR, *and* THE NEW INDUSTRIAL STATE.

One of the well-observed features of economic development in the 20th century is the need to choose between two broad political and economic designs. This choice, one from which developing nations of the 18th and 19th centuries were conveniently exempt, is between Western constitutional organization on the one hand and Marxian and neo-Marxian polity and economic organization on the other.

These are not, as everyone knows, homogeneous alternatives. Wide differences separate a state such as Poland, where the agriculture, and hence close to half the economy, remains in private hands and subject to market influences, from the far more completely socialized economy of the Chinese mainland. There are similar distinctions between the non-Marxian economies, which, in this case, are enlarged by terminological preference and political semantics. In Scandinavia, the United Kingdom and modern India the word "socialism" is politically evocative. As a result politicians try to

Department of State Bulletin, XLVII (1962), 13–17.

find as much of it as possible. In the United States, steps that would elsewhere be identified with socialist enlightenment—social security, agricultural price guarantees, even the public development of public power sites—are firmly for the purpose of making private enterprise function better.

Also one must be cautious in speaking of a "choice" between the two designs. Geography and the proximity of military power have had much to do with the decision. Had Poland, to select a country not unaccustomed to movement, been radically relocated after World War II to approximately the position of Paraguay, her subsequent economic and political history would have been rather different. Individuals do commit themselves as a matter of free choice to a Marxian political and economic design. But nations have rarely done so in the normal course of unmanaged elections—a reluctance, incidentally, which was foreseen by both Marx and Lenin.

Nevertheless these broad alternatives exist. My purpose is to weigh their advantages and disadvantages from the standpoint of the developing country. I am aware that an American ambassador will not be considered by everyone a wholly impartial judge. And even in this liberal and sophisticated gathering there would doubtless be eyebrow-lifting if my evidence were to lead me to the wrong conclusion.

But the choice merits serious assessment. Much of the present literature consists of declarations of superiority by one side or the other. We share with the Communists a strong faith in the value of robust assertion. Were the advantage all on our side, we would have little reason to worry. But we do worry, and it might be well, accordingly, for us to have a moderately unemotional appraisal of what we have to offer the developing nations as compared with the Communists.

THE GOAL OF DEVELOPING COUNTRIES

The goal of the developing country can be quickly stated: It is to bring itself as rapidly as possible into the 20th century and with the apparatus of individual and group well-being— food, clothing, education, health services, housing, entertainment, and automobiles —which is associated in every mind, urban and rural, bourgeois and Bolshevist, with 20th-century existence. Here and there are some that demur. But in my observation the most monastic Christian, the most contemplative Buddhist, and the most devout Gandhian cannot be considered completely secure against the charms of the bicycle, motor scooter, or transistor radio.

The things associated with modern civilization are now denied by backwardness and poverty. The task of the two systems is to overcome this poverty.

The causes of poverty, in turn, are not simple—although the problem has suffered prodigiously from over-simplification. One cause, clearly, is an oppressive social structure which channels return from the many to the few and which denies the individual the natural reward of his efforts at self-improvement. Another is a feeble, nonexistent, or corrupt apparatus of public administration which denies to the country the things —law and order, education, investment in roads, power, manufacturing—which are possible only where there is effective public authority. Or poverty may be itself a cause of poverty; it denies the country capital for investment, revenues for education, or purchasing power for consumer products which, in turn, are an incentive to effort. Thus poverty perpetuates itself. Such are the fundamentals that both systems must attack. It is unlikely that the same causes operate in the same form and with the same intensity in any two cases. An effective attack, therefore, requires not only efficient remedies but effective diagnosis of the condition to be cured.

Both systems agree on a number of important points. It is common ground that a shortage of capital is a likely cause of stagnation. Both agree on the need for a massive volume of investment to initiate and stimulate not only economic but social advance. There is agreement also that this investment should be in accordance with a carefully conceived plan. (Here we have paid the Soviets the compliment of appropriating an important idea.) There is increasing agreement that a principal object of this investment must be in the education and cultural improvement of people themselves. The visitor to the more remote parts of Soviet Asia is immediately impressed by the volume of resources going into schools, colleges, adult education programs, and other forms of cultural extension as part of the attack on the traditional backwardness of these areas. If, in the years following World War II, we thought too much of investment in terms of physical capital and too little of the importance of a literate and educated populace, this is an error we are now correcting.

There are, however—and this will doubtless come as a relief—important differences between the two approaches, and these are vital. The first lies in the diagnosis of the causes of poverty and the related remedy. The second difference is in the way development is organized. The third is in the political and constitutional environment of development. Let me take up each of these differences in turn.

DIAGNOSING THE CAUSES OF POVERTY

In the Marxian view poverty is principally caused by institutions which chain the country to its past—which hold it in colonial subjection, which exploit and subjugate the masses and deny them the reward of their labor, which make government not the efficient servant of the many but the corrupt handmaiden of the few.

In the predominant Western view the poor are the victims of their poverty. All societies have capacity for growth; the poor society lacks the resources to invest in growth. Having less than enough for its current needs for food, clothing, and shelter, it has nothing for investment in education, improved agriculture, transportation, public utilities, or industrial enterprise.

Each of these views leads naturally to a prescription. If institutions hold a country to its past, the answer is the elimination of these institutions. If the problem is the self-perpetuating

character of privation, the answer is to provide the catalyzing resources—specifically, economic aid and assistance in its use—which the country cannot supply to itself.

This is the first difference. The Marxian emphasis is on the institutions that inhibit progress and the need to eliminate them. Our emphasis is on the self-perpetuating character of poverty and the catalyzing role of aid. It will be noted that each system has a cause and remedy that is not without convenience to itself. The Soviets, at least until recently, were short of capital. They had a revolution which could be exported at moderate expense. Accordingly it was convenient to associate backwardness with colonialism, feudalism, and repressive capitalism, all of which could be eliminated by revolution. By contrast, we had capital. This we could export with greater ease than comprehensive social change.

The second difference is in the way development is organized. Although there is room for some national preference, and heresy cannot be entirely eliminated, the Marxian commitment is still to state ownership of the means of production—of land, capital plant, and natural resources. Private ownership of productive resources and their use for private gain is one of the retarding institutions. Its elimination leaves the state in possession and this continues. Incentives to individual and group effort are strongly supported. But incentives which use the device of property ownership to combine reward for individual effort with reward for management of property are excluded in principle and in large measure in practice.

The non-Marxian design for organizing development is not so easily characterized. In the past many countries—Japan, Germany, Canada, and to a remarkable degree also the United

States—have made state ownership of canals, turnpikes, railroads, electric power and other utilities, and even steel mills the fulcrum of development policy. India, Egypt, and some South American countries are taking the same course today. However, the main and indeed overwhelming reliance in non-Marxian development, both in agriculture and industry, is on private ownership of productive plant. This is true of countries such as India which choose to describe themselves as socialist.

WESTERN ADVANTAGE IN PROVIDING CAPITAL

The foregoing differences are sufficiently sharp so that we can relate them to results. And in Eastern Europe and China, not to mention the much older case of the Soviet Union, there is now an ample experience of Marxian development on which to draw.

Two major advantages lie with the Western or non-Marxian alternatives. There is, we have anciently been advised, a certain physical difficulty in extracting blood from a stone. This, however, is comparatively easy as compared with getting savings out of a poor society. When people do not have enough to eat, they are loathe to forego any part of their meal in order to eat better in the future. Pleas on behalf of children and grandchildren leave the man of simple, uncomplicated intelligence unmoved; he reflects that starvation will prevent his having children and, *pro tanto*, grandchildren as well. But Marxian no less than non-Marxian societies must have savings; without them there can be no growth. Accordingly, the Western pattern of development, with its prospect of assistance from outside the country, eases one of the most painful problems of development. This is why economic

aid has become such an important feature of Western foreign policy. It is the process by which savings are transferred from countries where saving is comparatively unpainful to those where it is very painful. It exploits one of the major advantages of our system.

The Communist countries are not without resources in this respect. The Soviet Union, though its capacity has been far less than ours, has spared some savings for other countries. Communist economic and political organization deals more effectively—or ruthlessly—with unproductive and excessively luxurious consumption, of which there is always some and may be much in the poor country. And Communist organization can, within limits, squeeze blood from its turnip. The penalty is the pain, and this cannot be avoided. The rioting in Poland in 1956 which brought Mr. Gomulka to power was occasioned in large measure by the enforcement of a rate of saving that was too grim for the people to bear. These last years on the Chinese mainland have evidently been ones of serious trouble and tension. Part of the problem is inherent in socialist organization of agriculture to which I will advert in a moment. But some has certainly been the consequence of squeezing a large volume of savings out of a very poor population.

The larger consequence is that Marxian development risks the alienation of the people as non-Marxian development does not. It seems doubtful if a majority of the Chinese people are very pleased with their government and would vote for it in an uninhibited poll. By contrast, in India, after a decade of development, there has been an overwhelming vote for the government that led the task. If the Indian Government had to subtract the $7.3 billions it has received from the West in overseas loans and grants since independence from the meager incomes—an average of about $70 per year—of its own people, its popularity might well have suffered. We see in India, in remarkably clear relief, the advantages of the Western design in providing capital.

WESTERN ADVANTAGE IN AGRICULTURE

The second and equally substantial advantage of Western development is in the matter of agriculture. Industry, on the record at least, is fairly tolerant as to forms of organization. American industry works well under private ownership. Even the most reluctant among us must agree that the Soviets have made considerable progress with socialism. So no decisive contrast can be registered here. But the undeveloped country is, by definition, a pastoral or agrarian community. The agricultural policy is, accordingly, vital. And it is far from clear, as a practical matter, whether it is possible to socialize a small-scale, densely populated, peasant agriculture. Even in the Soviet Union the agricultural problem has not been wholly solved. And here, at least, there is no serious talk of catching up. Each year we insouciantly extend our advantage in manhour productivity without effort and somewhat to our regret. Outside the Soviet Union, agriculture has been even more of a problem. Poland and Yugoslavia have had to revert to private ownership. In China, by all external evidence, the effort to socialize agriculture has brought a serious crisis. Certainly it has forced her to turn to the West for the largest food imports in history.

There are good reasons for this failure. Farmers, when they are small and numerous, cannot be brought unwillingly into a state-run system of agriculture for they can defeat any system that is available for their control. The employees of a factory, like the men of an army, are subject to external discipline. Failure in performance can be detected, judged, and penalized. (The same rule holds for certain types of plantation agriculture.) A scattered peasantry, carrying on the diverse tasks of crop and especially of livestock husbandry cannot be so regimented. As a consequence, productivity falls off. Working for others the farmer works at the minimum rather than the maximum and the difference between the two is enormous. He can be made to work at the maximum by giving him land to work and rewarding him with the fruits of his labor or some substantial share to consume or exchange as he wishes. But this is to restore individual proprietorship—private capitalism—which its doctrine excludes.

One day the Marxian economies may succeed in socializing agriculture —no effort is being spared. And the ability of the small man in agriculture to sabotage a system he dislikes or which treats him badly is not confined to communism. It is the reason for the low productivity and backwardness of the latifundia of Latin America and the feudal domains of the Middle East. But the fact that it accepts independent agricultural proprietorship is the second clear advantage of Western development.

ELIMINATING RETARDING INSTITUTIONS

I come now to a disadvantage of Western development. The Marxian alternative, I have noted, emphasizes the destruction of the bonds that tie the economy to the past. Our emphasis is on capital, education, technical assistance, and the other instruments that allow of change. Until recently, at least, we have been tempted to suppose that any society is a platform on which, given these missing elements, development can be built.

In fact, institutions do chain economies to the past, and the breaking of these chains is essential for progress. The promise that this will be done is a valid and an appealing part of the Marxian case. There is no chance of agricultural development in the underdeveloped and hence agricultural country under systems of absentee landlordism, with the workers or sharecroppers confined by law and tradition to a minor share of a meager product. And feudal systems of farming extend their corrupting influence to government, to the provision of public sinecures to those who lack a claim on the land, to the milking of middle-class and industrial enterprise, and to the destruction of incentives, and the morale of the society itself. "In our country," a South American guide once told me, "those who do the least get the most. I hear that in the United States it is the other way around. It's a better system." Progress does require the radical elimination of retarding institutions. If elimination can be had from no other source, the Marxian alternative will sooner or later be tried. The revolution they offer here, we should remind ourselves, is less the Russian Revolution than the French Revolution.

POLITICAL ENVIRONMENT

I come now to the final point of comparison—one, unfortunately, which has been much damaged by bad rhetoric. From the earliest days of their development, personal liberty, equal justice under law, and constitutional government have been important to Englishmen and to Americans. They haven't been the concern of everyone, but we have never supposed they were the fad of the esoteric and privileged minority.

And so it is in the underdeveloped country today. The Andean Indian and the landless worker in the Indian village do have a preoccupying concern with keeping themselves fed. But the general yearning for the dignity of democratic and constitutional government is very great. No people who live under a dictatorship ever feel themselves to be first-class citizens.

There can be little question that most people believe that liberty and constitutional process are safer with the Western than with the Marxian alternative. We haven't, in my view, made as much of this advantage as we might. But the Communists are under the considerable handicap that their alternative involves a step into the dark. And while the details are obscure, most people know that it does not involve free selection of rulers by the governed, *habeas corpus,* equal justice under law, and a voluntary return to other economic arrangements should the experiment prove unpalatable.

MAKING USE OF THE ADVANTAGES

On first assessment, then, the advantage of the non-Marxian alternative for the developing country is considerable. It promises at least a partial avoidance of the pain that for the poor country is inherent in finding savings for investment and growth. It promises an acceptable and viable system of agriculture rather than a certain unpalatable and possibly unworkable one. And it offers personal liberty and constitutional process. Against this the Marxian alternative promises a more rigorous attack on the institutions—the unproductive claims on revenue and especially the feudal control of land—which exclude change.

But this is not a game where one can count the cards and decide the winner. Some cards count for more than others, and there is the unfortunate possibility that some good cards will not get played.

The Marxian promise can be decisive. That is because the things we offer are only effective and attractive after the retarding institutions are eliminated. In a country where land and other resources are held by and operated for the benefit of a slight minority and where the apparatus of government serves principally to reinforce such privilege, aid is not of much use. It will also benefit not the many but the few. Our promise of independent proprietorship is obviously nullified so long as land remains in the hands of the few. And personal liberty and constitutional government have little meaning in countries where government is of the privileged for the rich.

We must, in short, meet the Marxian promise of reform of retarding institutions. We cannot organize revolution. We can place our influence solidly on the side of reform. Having done this, our cards give us a clear advantage. To be sure, we must play them. We must make good with aid on our promise of a less painful savings and investment process. We must give firm support to the small farmer. We must be clear in our commitment to constitutional process and personal liberty. We cannot suppose that these are wanted only by people of Anglo-Saxon origin of good income. And we must not excuse dictatorship on grounds of anticommunism or convenience in the absence of visible alternatives. The price of doing so, as we have so painfully learned, is disaster magnified by postponement.

These are highly practical matters. If there are no advantages in our alternative, it won't be chosen. The first resort to the Marxian alternative in this hemisphere was in a country where the concentration of wealth and land ownership was extreme, where these had extended a corrupting influence to other economic life and to government, and where dictatorship had been endemic. This being the experience with the Western alternative, it was not remarkable that so many were so little perturbed by the alternative. India, in face of formidable difficulties, is firmly committed to development on the Western model. That is because already in British India and over the whole country at the time of independence there was a strong attack on retarding institutions—especially on the feudal claims of princes, zamindars and great landlords, and government which was an extension of this landed power; because a substantial measure of peasant ownership had replaced the old system; because aid from outside eased the problem of supply capital; and because people felt secure in the protection of constitutional guarantees and representative government.

The lesson is clear. The advantages are with us. We must, however, have confidence in them and exploit them to the full.

HANS MORGENTHAU

Hans J. Morgenthau is Albert A. Michelson Distinguished Service Professor and Director of the Center for the Study of American Foreign Policy at the University of Chicago. A frequent consultant to the U.S. Department of State and the Defense Department, he is the author of many books, among them POLITICS AMONG NATIONS, DILEMMAS OF POLITICS, *and* THE PURPOSE OF AMERICAN POLITICS. *His realist critique of international relations greatly affected the study of that subject in the United States.*

Of the seeming and real innovations which the modern age has introduced into the practice of foreign policy, none has proven more baffling to both understanding and action than foreign aid. The very assumption that foreign aid is an instrument of foreign policy is a subject of controversy. For, on the one hand, the opinion is widely held that foreign aid is an end in itself, carrying its own justification, both transcending, and independent of, foreign policy. In this view, foreign aid is the fulfillment of an obligation of the few rich nations toward the many poor ones. On the other hand, many see no justification for a policy of foreign aid at all. They look at it as a gigantic boon-doggle, a wasteful and indefensible operation which serves neither the inter-ests of the United States nor those of the recipient nations.

The public debate on foreign aid has contributed little to understanding. In the spring of every year the nation engages in such a debate, carried on almost exclusively in terms of the amount of money to be spent for purposes of foreign aid rather than of the substantive purposes which a policy of foreign aid is supposed to serve. The Administration tries, as it were, to sell a certain amount of foreign aid to Congress, and Congress refuses to buy that amount. Congress generally appropriates about ten per cent less than what the Administration has requested, and the Administration spends what is appropriated as it sees fit within the general categories authorized. Only when glaring abuses and inefficiencies are uncovered, as for instance in our foreign aid to Laos, is the question of the substance of our foreign aid policy raised in public, and even then it is put in the negative terms of remedying the abuses and inefficiencies rather than in the positive

AMERICAN POLITICAL SCIENCE REVIEW, *56 (June 1962), pp. 301–9. Reprinted by permission of the American Political Science Association and Professor Morgenthau. The paper was originally prepared for the Public Affairs Conference Center, University of Chicago.*

terms of the purposes our foreign aid policy may be supposed to advance and the kinds of measures best calculated to serve these aims.

It is in fact pointless even to raise the question whether the United States ought to have a policy of foreign aid— as much so as to ask whether the United States ought to have a foreign political or military policy. For the United States has interests abroad which cannot be secured by military means and for the support of which the traditional methods of diplomacy are only in part appropriate. If foreign aid is not available they will not be supported at all.

The question, what kind of policy of foreign aid we ought to have, can then not be evaded. As it has developed in recent years, the kind we have is fundamentally weak. It has been conceived as a self-sufficient technical enterprise, covering a multitude of disparate objectives and activities, responding haphazardly to all sorts of demands, sound and unsound, unrelated or only by accident related to the political purposes of our foreign policy. The United States, in short, has been in the business of foreign aid for more than two decades, but it has yet to develop an intelligible theory of foreign aid that could provide standards of judgment for both the supporters and opponents of a particular measure.

I. SIX TYPES OF FOREIGN AID

The first prerequisite for the development of a viable foreign aid policy is the recognition of the diversity of policies that go by that name. Six such can be distinguished which have only one thing in common: the transfer of money, goods and services from one nation to another. They are humani-tarian foreign aid, subsistence foreign aid, military foreign aid, bribery, prestige foreign aid, and foreign aid for economic development.

Of these distinct types, only humanitarian foreign aid is *per se* nonpolitical. The aid which governments have traditionally extended to nations which are victims of natural disasters, such as floods, famines and epidemics falls in that category. So do the services, especially in the fields of medicine and agriculture, which private organizations, such as churches and foundations, have traditionally provided in Asia, Africa, and Latin America.

While humanitarian aid is *per se* nonpolitical, it can indeed perform a political function when it operates within a political context. The foreign aid that private organizations provide will be attributed for better or worse to their respective governments insofar as humanitarian aid emanating from a foreign country is recognized by the recipient country or its inhabitants to perform a political function. Thus the agricultural aid which the Rockefeller Foundation has provided for many years to certain Latin American countries is likely to take on under contemporary conditions a political function which it did not perform previously. The same has from the beginning been true of the work the Ford Foundation has been doing in India. By the same token, humanitarian aid extended by a government may have political effects.

Subsistence foreign aid is extended to governments, such as those of Jordan and Niger, which do not command the resources to maintain minimal public services. The giving nation makes up the deficit in the budget of the recipient nation. Subsistence foreign aid is akin to the humanitarian type in that it seeks to prevent the breakdown of order and the disintegration of organized society. But it also performs the political function of maintaining the *status quo,* without, however, as a rule, increasing its viability. Where a political alternative to a nonviable regime may exist, subsistence foreign aid diminishes the chances of its materializing.

Bribes proffered by one government to another for political advantage were until the beginning of the nineteenth century an integral part of the armory of diplomacy. No statesman hesitated to acknowledge the general practice of giving and accepting bribes, however anxious he might be to hide a particular transaction. Thus it was proper and common for a government to pay the foreign minister or ambassador of another country a pension, that is, a bribe. Lord Robert Cecil, the Minister of Elizabeth, received one from Spain. Sir Henry Wotton, British Ambassador to Venice in the seventeenth century, accepted one from Savoy while applying for one from Spain. The documents which the French revolutionary government published in 1793 show that France subsidized Austrian statesmen between 1757 and 1769 to the tune of 82,652,479 livres, the Austrian Chancellor Kaunitz receiving 100,000.

The Prussian Ambassador in Paris summed up well the main rule of this game when he reported to his government in 1802: "Experience has taught everybody who is here on diplomatic business that one ought never to give anything before the deal is definitely closed, but it has only proved that the allurement of gain will often work wonders." It is worthy of note that the first appropriation act adopted by the first Congress of the United States in 1789 included a modest contingent fund for such purposes.

Much of what goes by the name of foreign aid today is in the nature of bribes. The transfer of money and services from one government to another performs here the function of a price paid for political services rendered or to be rendered. These bribes differ from the traditional ones exemplified above in two respects: they are justified primarily in terms of foreign aid for economic development, and money and services are transferred through elaborate machinery fashioned for genuine economic aid. In consequence, these bribes are a less effective means for the purpose of purchasing political favors than were the traditional ones.

The compulsion of substituting for the traditional businesslike transmission of bribes the pretense and elaborate machinery of foreign aid for economic development results from a climate of opinion which accepts as universally valid the proposition that the highly developed industrial nations have an obligation to transfer money and services to underdeveloped nations for the purpose of economic development. Thus, aside from humanitarian and military foreign aid, the only kind of transfer of money and services which seems to be legitimate is one ostensibly made for the purpose of economic development. Economic development has become an ideology by which the transfer of money and services from one government to another in peace time is rationalized and justified.

The present climate of opinion embraces another assumption as universally valid: that economic development can actually be promoted through such transfers of money and services. Thus economic development as an ideology requires machinery that makes plausible the postulated efficacy of the transfer for the stated purpose of economic development. In contrast to most political ideologies, which operate only on the verbal level and whose effects remain within the realm of ideas, this political ideology, in order to be plausible, requires an elaborate administrative apparatus serving as an instrument for a policy of make-believe. The government of nation A, trying to buy political advantage from the government of nation B for, say, the price of 20 million dollars, must not only pretend, but also act out in elaborate fashion the pretense, that what it is actually doing is giving aid for economic development to the government of nation B.

This practice of giving bribes as though they were contributions to economic development inevitably creates, in the giver and the recipient, expectations which are bound to be disappointed. Old-fashioned bribery was a relatively straightforward transaction; services were to be rendered at a price, and both sides knew what to expect. Bribery disguised as foreign aid for economic development makes of giver and recipient actors in a play which in the end they may no longer be able to distinguish from reality. In consequence, both may come to expect results in terms of economic development which in the nature of things may not be forthcoming. Thus both are likely to be disappointed, the giver blaming the recipient for his inefficiency and the recipient accusing the giver of stinginess and asking for more. The ideology, if taken for reality, gets in the way of the original purpose of the transaction, and neither side believes that it has received what it is entitled to.

For the past decade, military aid took the lion's share of the foreign aid programs of the United States. A shift in favor of nonmilitary aid occurred during the 1961 session when Congress appropriated somewhat over 2 billion dollars for military aid, while the total voted for all the other foreign aid programs ran in excess of 3 billion dollars. To the latter amount must be added the equivalent of approximately 1 billion dollars in foreign currencies, the proceeds of the sale of agricultural commodities abroad, to be used for economic grants and loans to purchasing governments.

Foreign aid for military purposes is a traditional way by which nations buttress their alliances. Rome used to receive tribute from its allies for the military protections it provided. The seventeenth and eighteenth centuries are the classic period of military subsidies, by which nations, and especially Great Britain, endeavored to increase the military strength of their allies. Glancing through the treaties of alliance of that period, one is struck by the meticulous precision with which obligations to furnish troops, equipment, logistic support, food, money, and the like were defined. The loans which France extended to Russia after the conclusion of the alliance between the two nations in 1894 fall in the same category. This traditional military aid can be understood as a division of labor between two allies who pool their resources, one supplying money, matériel, and training, the other providing primarily manpower.

In contrast to traditional practice, military aid today is extended not only to allies but also to certain uncommitted nations. The military aid the United States has been giving to Yugoslavia is a case in point. The purpose is here not so much military as political. It seeks political advantage in exchange for military aid. It obligates by implication, the recipient toward the giver. The latter expects the former to abstain from a political course which might put in jeopardy the continuation of military aid. Military aid is here really in the nature of a bribe.

What appears as military aid may also be actually in the nature of prestige aid, to be discussed below. The provision of jet fighters and other modern weapons for certain underdeveloped nations can obviously perform no genuine military function. It increases the prestige of the recipient nation both at home and abroad. Being in the possession of some of the more spectacular instruments of modern warfare, a nation can at least enjoy the illusion of having become a modern military power.

As bribery appears today in the guise of aid for economic development, so does aid for economic development appear in the guise of military assistance. In the session of 1961, for instance, Congress appropriated 425 million dollars for economic aid to stategic areas, and it is likely that in the total appropriations of over 2 billion dollars for military aid other items of economic aid are hidden. This mode of operation results from the reluctance of Congress to vote large amounts for economic aid in contrast to its readiness to vote virtually any amount requested for military purposes. Yet the purposes of aid for economic development are likely to suffer when they are disguised as military assistance, as we saw the purposes of bribery suffer when disguised as aid for economic development. The military context within which such aid is bound to operate, even though its direct administration be in the hands of the civilian authorities, is likely to deflect such aid from its genuine purposes. More particularly, it strengthens the ever-present tendency to subordinate the requirements of aid for economic development to military considerations.

Prestige aid has in common with modern bribes the fact that its true purpose, too, is concealed by the ostensible purpose of economic development or military aid. The unprofitable or idle steel mill, the highway without traffic and leading nowhere, the airline operating with foreign personnel and at a loss but under the flag of the recipient country—all ostensibly serve the purposes of economic development and under different circumstances might do so. Actually, however, they perform no positive economic function. They owe their existence to the penchant, prevalent in many underdeveloped nations, for what might be called "conspicuous industrialization," spectacular symbols of, and monuments to, industrial advancement rather than investments satisfying any objective economic needs of the country.

This tendency sheds an illuminating light upon the nature of what is generally referred to as the "revolution of rising expectations." We are inclined to assume that the urgent desire to improve one's lot by means of modern technology and industry is a well-nigh universal trend in Asia, Africa, and Latin America. Actually, however, this trend is universal only in the sense that virtually all underdeveloped nations want to appear as having achieved industrialization, while only a fraction of the population, and frequently only small elite groups within it, seek the social and economic benefits of industrialization and are willing to take the measures necessary to achieve them. For many of the underdeveloped nations the steel mill, the highway, the airline, the modern weapons, perform a function that is not primarily economic or military, but psychological and political. They are sought as the outward show of modernity and power. They perform a function similar to that which the cathedral performed for the medieval city and the feudal castle or the monarch's palace for the absolute state. Nehru is reported to have said, when he showed Chuo-En-Lai a new dam: "It is in these temples that I worship." And the more underdeveloped and less viable a nation is, the greater is likely to be its urge to prove to itself and to the world through the results of prestige aid that it, too, has arrived in the mid-twentieth century.

The advantage for the giver of prestige aid is threefold. He may receive a specific political advantage in return for the aid, very much like the advantage received for a bribe. Also, the spectacular character of prestige aid establishes a patent relationship between the generosity of the giver and the increased prestige of the recipient. The giver's prestige is enhanced, as it were, by the increase of the recipient's prestige. Finally, prestige aid comes relatively cheap. A limited commitment of resources in the form of a spectacular but economically useless symbol of modernity may bring disproportionate political dividends.

The giver of foreign aid is therefore well advised to distinguish between prestige aid and aid for economic development, though both are justified by the prospective recipient in terms of genuine economic development. The prospective giver, if unaware of the distinction, is likely to fall into one of two errors. By mistaking prestige aid for aid for economic development, he may waste human and material resources in support of the latter when the purpose of prestige aid could have been achieved much more simply and cheaply. Or else he may reject out of hand a request for prestige aid because he cannot justify it in terms of economic development, and may thereby forego available political advantages. The classic example of this error is the American rejection of the Afghan request for the paving of the streets of Kabul as economically unsound. The Soviet Union, pursuing a politically oriented policy of foreign aid, did pave the streets of Kabul.

II. FOREIGN AID FOR ECONOMIC DEVELOPMENT IN PARTICULAR

None of the types of foreign aid discussed thus far poses theoretical questions of great magnitude; rather they raise issues for practical manipulation which can be successfully met by common sense tested by experience. Foreign aid for economic development has been the primary area for theoretical analysis and speculation, and these have been primarily of an economic nature. Economic thought, true to its prevailing academic tradition, tends to look at foreign aid as though it were a self-sufficient technical enterprise to be achieved with the instruments, and judged by the standards, of pure economics. And since Western economic development, from the first industrial revolution onwards, has been due to the formation of capital and the accumulation of technical knowledge, we have tended to assume that these two factors would by themselves provide the impetus for the economic development of the underdeveloped nations of Asia, Africa, and Latin America. This tendency has been powerfully supported by the spectacular success of the Marshall Plan, the political origins and motivations of which were easily forgotten in its justification as a strictly economic measure for the provision of capital and technological know-how. Yet it is not always recognized that this success was made possible only by the fact that, in contrast to the underdeveloped nations of Asia, Africa, and Latin America, the recipients of Marshall aid were among the leading industrial nations of the world, whose economic systems were but temporarily in disarray.

The popular mind, on the other hand, and, through it, much of the practice of foreign aid have proceeded from certain unexamined assumptions, no less doubtful for being deeply embedded in the American folklore of politics. Thus the popular mind has established correlations between the infusion of capital and technology into a primitive society and its economic development, between economic development and social stability, between social stability and democratic institutions, between democratic institutions and a peaceful foreign policy. However attractive and reassuring these correlations may sound to American ears, they are borne out neither by the experiences we have had with our policies of foreign aid nor by general historic experience.

The first of these assumptions implies that underdevelopment is at least primarily the result of lack of capital and technological know-how. Underdevelopment is regarded as a kind of accident or at worst as a kind of deficiency disease, which can be taken care of through subcutaneous injections of the missing ingredients. Yet a nation may suffer from deficiencies, some natural and insuperable, others social and remediable, which no amount of capital and technological know-how supplied from the outside can cure. The poverty of natural resources may be such as to make economic development impossible. Nations such as Jordan and Somalia are in all likelihood permanently incapable of economic development for that reason. Many of the nations which are the perennial recipients of subsistence aid are likely to fall in the same category.

A nation may also suffer from human deficiencies which preclude economic development. As there are individuals whose qualities of character and level of intelligence make it impossible for them to take advantage of economic opportunities, so are there nations similarly handicapped. To put it bluntly: as there are bums and beggars, so are there bum and beggar nations. They may be the recipients of charity, but short of a miraculous transformation of their collective intelligence and character, what they receive from the outside is not likely to be used for economic development.

Other nations are presently defi-cient in the specific qualities of character and intelligence that go into the making of a modern economic system, even though their general or inherent capabilities qualify them potentially for the necessary transformation sometime in the future. They are, to use a rough analogy, in a medieval stage of cultural development, still awaiting the equivalent of the moral and intellectual revolutions which in the sixteenth and seventeenth centuries created the cultural preconditions for the economic development of the West. Yet we tend to take the existence of these preconditions for granted, forgetting that without the secularization and rationalization of Western thought and society the industrialization of the West would not have been possible.

A civilization, such as the Burmese, which deprecates success in this world because it stands in the way of success in the other world, puts a cultural obstacle in the path of industrial development, which foreign aid by itself cannot overcome. Saving, that is, the preservation of capital or goods for investment or future use, has become so integral a part of our economic thought and action that it is hard for us to realize that there are hundreds of millions of people in the underdeveloped areas of the world who are oblivious of this mode of operation, indispensable to economic development. We have come to consider the productive enterprise as a continuum in the betterment of which the individual owner or manager has a personal stake. Yet in many underdeveloped areas the productive enterprise is regarded primarily as an object for financial exploitation, to be discarded when it has performed its function of bringing the temporary owner the largest financial return in the shortest possible time. Foreign aid poured into such a precapitalistic and even prerational mould is less likely to transform the mould than to be forced by it, in ways hardly predictable in advance, into channels serving the interests of a precapitalistic or prerational society.

The economic interests which tend to prevent foreign aid from being used for economic development are typically identified with the ruling groups in underdeveloped societies, which derive their political power in good measure from the economic *status quo*. The ownership and control of arable land, in particular, is in many of the underdeveloped societies the foundation of political power. Land reform and industrialization are in consequence an attack upon the political *status quo*. In the measure that they succeed, they are bound to affect drastically the distribution of economic and political power alike. Yet the beneficiaries of both the economic and political *status quo* are the typical recipients of foreign aid given for the purpose of changing the *status quo*. To ask them to use foreign aid for this purpose is to require a readiness for self-sacrifice and a sense of social responsibility which few ruling groups have shown throughout history. Foreign aid proffered under such circumstances is likely to fail in its ostensible purpose and, performing the function of a bribe to the ruling group, to strengthen the economic and political *status quo*. It is more likely to accentuate unsolved social and political problems than to bring them closer to solution. A team of efficiency experts and public accountants might well have improved the operations of the Al Capone gang; yet by doing so, it would have aggravated the social and political evils which the operations of that gang brought forth.

Given this likely resistance of the ruling group to economic development, foreign aid requires drastic political change as a necessary condition for its success. Foreign aid must go hand in hand with political change, either voluntarily induced from within or brought about through pressure from without. The latter alternative faces the giving nation with a dilemma. On the one hand, to give foreign aid for economic development without stipulating conditions that maximize the chances for success will surely maximize the chances for failure. On the other hand, to give aid "with strings" arouses xenophobic suspicions and nationalistic resentments, to be exploited both by the defenders of the *status quo* and the promoters of Communist revolution.

Furthermore, once one has decided to bring about political change in opposition to the ruling group, one must identify some alternative group as the instrument of political change. Sometimes, the only choice is among alternative groups which are equally unattractive. Sometimes, and not infrequently, the absence of any available alternative group leaves only the choice between creating one or doing nothing.

Finally, the promotion of drastic social change on the part of the giving nation may create the indispensable condition for economic development, but it also conjures up the spectre of uncontrollable revolution. In many of the underdeveloped nations peace and order are maintained only through the ruthless use of the monopoly of force by the ruling group. Determined and skillful foreign intervention may find little difficulty in weakening or even removing altogether the power of the ruling group. It is not so easy to finish what has thereby been started. While the interventionist nation may be able to control events up to the point of instigating drastic reform and revolution, it may well prove unable to control the course of the revolution itself. More particularly, a democratic nation, such as the United States, is greatly handicapped in competing with Communists in the control of a revolution. The revolution may start, as it did in Cuba, under the democratic auspices of unorganized masses dedicated to social reform and supported by the United States, and may in the course of its development be taken over by the highly organized and disciplined Communist minority, the only organized and disciplined revolutionary group on the scene.

Successful foreign aid for economic development may have similarly unsettling political results. Economic development, especially by way of industrialization, is bound to disrupt the social fabric of the underdeveloped nation. By creating an urban industrial proletariat, it loosens and destroys the social nexus of family, village and tribe, in which the individual had found himself secure. And it will not be able, at least not soon, to provide a substitute for this lost social world. The vacuum so created will be filled by social unrest and political agitation. Furthermore, it is not the downtrodden peoples living in a static world of unrelieved misery who are the likely protagonists of revolution, but rather those groups that have begun to rise in the social and economic scale have not enough to satisfy their aroused expectations. Thus, economic development is bound to disturb not only the economic *status quo* but, through it, the political *status quo* as well. If the change is drastic enough, the social and political effects of economic development may well bring about a prerevolutionary or revolutionary situation. And while the United States may have started the revolutionary process, it will again be uncertain under whose auspices it will be ended.

The United States faces a number of formidable handicaps in trying to control social and political change in the underdeveloped nations either as a prerequisite for, or a result of, foreign aid for economic development. First of all, as a Western capitalistic nation, the United States is a conservative power both domestically and internationally, and must appear particularly so to the underdeveloped nations. Both in its civilization and its social and economic structure, it belongs to that complex of nations which until recently were able to hold Africa, Latin America, and the outlying areas of Asia in a condition of colonial or semicolonial dependency. It has military alliances with these nations, and while it has generally shunned and even opposed outright colonial policies, it has actively and successfully participated in the semicolonial exploitation of backward nations. Thus the resentment against the former colonial powers attaches also to it and its policies of foreign aid are frequently suspect as serving in disguise the traditional ends of colonialism.

Furthermore, the United States, by dint of its pluralistic political philosophy and social system, cannot bring to the backward nations of the world a simple message of salvation, supported first by dedicated and disciplined revolutionary minorities and then by totalitarian control. In the nature of things, the advantage lies here with the Communist powers. They are, as it were, specialists in exploiting a revolutionary situation, which is bound to cause us embarrassment. For while the Communists are able to direct a revolution into the desired channels through their use of a disciplined minority, we, even if we are convinced that revolution is inevitable and therefore do not oppose it, tend to look on it with misgivings since we cannot control the direction it will take.

The Communist powers have still another advantage over the United

States in that, at least on the surface, their problems and achievements are more meaningful to the underdeveloped nations than ours. The Soviet Union has achieved, and Communist China attempts to achieve, what the more enlightened underdeveloped nations seek: a drastic increase in national output through rapid industrialization. The Communist powers use totalitarian control as their instrument and Communist doctrine as rationalization. Seeking the same results, the underdeveloped nations cannot help being attracted by the methods which brought about these results elsewhere. In contrast, the slow process, stetching over centuries, through which the nations of the West achieved a high standard of living through industrialization must appeal much less to them. That appeal is further lessened by the economic processes of the free market and the political processes of liberal democracy through which in large measure Western industrialization was achieved. For these processes require a degree of moral restraint and economic and political sophistication which are largely absent in the underdeveloped nations. The simple and crude methods of totalitarianism must appear to them much more congenial.

Thus we arrive at the disconcerting conclusion that successful foreign aid for economic development can be counterproductive if the social and political goal of the giving nation is the recipient's social and political stability. In some cases at least, the failure of American aid for economic development may have been a blessing in disguise in that it did not disturb a stable *status quo* whose continuance was in our interest. Such aid, intended for economic development, actually performs the function either of a bribe or of prestige aid. Here again, however, these functions are likely to be impaired by disappointed expectations of economic development on the part of the giving and the recipient nation.

It is equally a moot question whether successful foreign aid for economic development is conducive to the development of democratic institutions and practices. Without stopping here to examine the complexities of the relationship between democracy and economic development, it is enough to observe, as recent history has made clear, that no necessary causal relationship exists between the two. The most impressive example is the Soviet Union. Its rapid economic development has gone hand in hand with totalitarian government, and a case could well be made for the proposition that the former would have been impossible without the latter. It is more likely than not that where the intellectual and moral preconditions for economic development are lacking in the population at large and are present only in a small elite, as is true in many of the underdeveloped nations, the imposition of the will of that small minority upon the majority of the population is a prerequisite not only for the start of economic development but also for sustained economic growth.

As concerns the promotion of a peaceful foreign policy, economic development is likely to be counterproductive if a political incentive for a belligerent foreign policy is present. The contrary conclusion derives from the popular, yet totally unfounded assumption that "poor" nations make war on "rich" nations for economic advantage and that "rich" nations are by definition peaceful because they have what they want. In truth, of course, most wars have been fought not for economic but political advantage, and, particularly under modern technological conditions, only economically advanced nations are capable of waging modern war. We did not consider the Soviet Union a military threat as long as it was economically underdeveloped; it became one when its economic development had transformed it into a modern industrial power. Similarly, Communist China today, except to its immediate neighbors, is only a potential military threat by virtue of its economic potential, both likely to be activated by economic development.

Foreign aid for economic development, then, has a very much smaller range of potentially successful operation than is generally believed. Its success depends in good measure not so much upon its soundness in strictly economic terms as upon intellectual, moral, and political preconditions, which are not susceptible to economic manipulation, if they are susceptible to manipulation from the outside at all. Furthermore, the political results of successful foreign aid for economic development may be either unpredictable or counterproductive in terms of the political goals of the giving nation. In any event, they are in large measure uncontrollable. Foreign aid proffered and accepted for purposes of economic development may turn out to be something different from what it was intended to be, unless it is oriented toward the political conditions within which it must operate. Most likely, it will turn out to be a bribe or prestige aid, or else a total waste. To do too much may here be as great a risk as to do too little, and "masterly inactivity" may sometimes be the better part of wisdom.

III. CONCLUSIONS FOR POLICY

The major conclusions for policy to be drawn from this analysis are three: the requirement of identifying each concrete situation in the light of the six different types of foreign aid and of choosing the quantity and quality of foreign aid appropriate to the situation; the requirement of attuning, within the same concrete situation, different types of foreign aid to each other in view of the over-all goals of foreign policy; and the requirement of dealing with foreign aid as an integral part of political policy.

The task of identifying concrete situations with the type of foreign aid appropriate to them is a task for country and area experts to perform. Can country A not survive without foreign aid? Is its government likely to exchange political advantages for economic favors? Would our military interests be served by the strengthening of this nation's military forces? Does this country provide the non-economic preconditions for economic development to be supported by foreign aid? Are our political interests likely to be served by giving this nation foreign aid for purposes of prestige? Can a case be made for foreign aid in order to alleviate human suffering? What kind and quantity of foreign aid is necessary and sufficient to achieve the desired result?

To answer these questions correctly demands first of all a thorough and intimate knowledge and understanding of the total situation in a particular country. But it also requires political and economic judgment of a very high order, applied to two distinct issues. It is necessary to anticipate the receptivity of the country to different kinds of foreign aid and their effects upon it. When this analysis has been made, it is then necessary to select from a great number of possible measures of foreign aid those which are most appropriate to the situation and hence most likely to succeed.

In most cases, however, the task is not that simple. Typically, an underdeveloped country will present a number of situations indicating the need for different types of foreign aid simultaneously. One type given without regard for its potential effects upon another type risks getting in the way of the latter. One of the most conspicuous weaknesses of our past foreign aid policies has been the disregard of the effect different types of foreign aid have upon each other. Bribes given to the ruling group, for instance, are bound to strengthen the political and economic *status quo*. Military aid is bound to have an impact upon the distribution of political power within the receiving country; it can also have a deleterious effect upon the economic system, for instance, by increasing inflationary pressures. Similarly, the effect of subsistence foreign aid is bound to be the support of the *status quo* in all its aspects. Insofar as the giving nation desires these effects or can afford to be indifferent to them they obviously do not matter in terms of its over-all objectives. But insofar as the giving nation has embarked upon a policy of foreign aid for economic development which requires changes in the political and economic *status quo,* the other types of foreign aid policies are counterproductive in terms of economic development; for they strengthen the very factors which stand in its way.

This problem is particularly acute in the relations between prestige aid and aid for economic development. The giving nation may seek quick political results and use prestige aid for that purpose; yet it may also have an interest in the economic development of the recipient country, the benefits of which are likely to appear only in the more distant future. Prestige aid is at best only by accident favorable to economic development; it may be irrelevant to it, or it may actually impede it. What kind of foreign aid is the giving country to choose? If it chooses a combination of both it should take care to choose an innocuous kind of prestige aid and to promote economic development the benefits of which are not too long in coming. Afghanistan is the classic example of this dilemma. The Soviet Union, by paving the streets of Kabul, chose a kind of prestige aid that is irrelevant to economic development. The United States, by building a hydroelectric dam in a remote part of the country, chose economic development, the very existence of which is unknown to most Afghans and the benefits of which will not appear for years to come.

It follows, then, from the very political orientation of foreign aid that its effect upon the prestige of the giving nation must always be in the minds of the formulators and executors of foreign aid policies. Foreign aid for economic development, in particular, which benefits the recipient country immediately and patently is a more potent political weapon than aid promising benefits that are obscure and lie far in the future. Furthermore, the political effects of foreign aid are lost if its foreign source is not obvious to the recipients. For it is not aid as such or its beneficial results that creates political loyalties on the part of the recipient, but the positive relationship that the mind of the recipient establishes between the aid and its beneficial results, on the one hand, and the political philosophy, the political system, and the political objectives of the giver, on the other. That is to say, if the recipient continues to disapprove of the political philosophy, system, and objectives of the giver, despite the aid he has received, the political effects of the aid are lost. The same is true if he remains unconvinced that the aid received is but a natural, if not inevitable, manifestation of the political philosophy, system, and objectives of the giver. Foreign aid remains politically ineffectual—at least for the short term—as long as the recipient says either: "Aid is good, but the politics of the giver are bad"; or "Aid is good, but the politics of the giver—good, bad, or indifferent—have nothing to do with it." In order to be able to establish a psychological relationship between giver and recipient, the procedures through which aid is given, and the subject matter to which it is applied, must lend themselves to the creation of a connection between the aid and the politics of the giver which reflects credit upon the latter.

The problem of foreign aid is insoluble if it is considered as a self-sufficient technical enterprise of a primarily economic nature. It is soluble only if it is considered an integral part of the political policies of the giving country—which must be devised in view of the political conditions, and for its effects upon the political situation, in the receiving country. In this respect, a policy of foreign aid is no different from diplomatic or military policy or propaganda. They are all weapons in the political armory of the nation.

As military policy is too important a matter to be left ultimately to the generals, so is foreign aid too important a matter to be left in the end to the economists. The expertise of the economist must analyze certain facts, devise certain means, and perform certain functions of manipulation for foreign aid. Yet the formulation and over-all execution of foreign aid policy is a political function. It is the province of the political expert.

It follows from the political nature of foreign aid that it is not a science but an art. That art requires by way of mental predisposition a political sensitivity to the interrelationship among the facts, present and future, and ends and means. The requirements by way of mental activity are two-fold. The first is a discriminating judgment of facts, ends and means and their effects upon each other. However, an analysis of the situation in the recipient country and, more particularly, its projection into the future and the conclusions from the analysis in terms of policy can only in part be arrived at through rational deduction from ascertainable facts. When all the available facts have been ascertained, duly analyzed, and conclusions drawn from them, the final judgments and decisions can be derived only from subtle and sophisticated hunches. The best the formulator and executor of a policy of foreign aid can do is to maximize the chances that his hunches turn out to be right. Here as elsewhere in the formulation and conduct of foreign policy, the intuition of the statesman, more than the knowledge of the expert, will carry the day.

REVOLUTION
AND
INTERVENTION

Chapter 15

Despite two generations of on-again, off-again anxiety about the intentions of "certain foreign powers" to overthrow the United States by violent revolution, there is still a tendency here (as elsewhere) to look at international relations exclusively in terms of the *external* relations of states, as if they were billiard balls bouncing about on the pool table of world politics. To be sure one is aware, often by personal experience, of tourism abroad, of the exchange of students, and of a wide range of transnational cultural and financial influences, but when it comes to foreign policy, most people think of diplomats of one country dealing with diplomats of many other countries as representing completely separate political entities. Indeed one of the first expressions the new student of world politics encounters when he studies the Charter of the United Nations is "the sovereign equality of all its Members," and as he heads further on in Article 2 he discovers in paragraph seven that "Nothing contained in the present Charter shall authorize the United Nations to intervene in matters which are essentially within the domestic jurisdiction of any state." But if he concludes from this that intervention in the affairs of one state by another is outmoded, or that revolution has only domestic encouragement, he has much to learn.

Max Beloff of Oxford University reminds us that little is new in the practice of international affairs, and that intervention, which he defines as the attempt by one state to affect the internal structure and external behavior of other states through various degrees of coercion, has been prevalent in the history of world politics, right down to the present day.[1] As Beloff has observed, intervention is one of the devices which is expected to be used in any system of international relations which is competitive in nature. Intervention may not be pervasive throughout the system, but that it will exist in one form or another at some place at some time is almost a foregone conclusion. State A may feel threatened by the possibility that certain aggressive elements within State B may assume leadership, and intervene to insure the continuation of a friendly regime. Given the openness of world communication and the general distaste in other parts of the world for interference with the internal affairs of another country, State A is usually careful to arrange an "'invitation" from its neighbor to help it maintain its freedom. Yet if the government of State B has already been overturned, intervention by State A has to take the form of "liberation" of the people of State B from the usurpers of legitimate authority, which in this case means an authority which can be expected to respect the wishes of the intervening power. But is it intervention when State A merely involves itself in the affairs of State B without in any way appearing to coerce its leadership?

In endeavoring to find a definition of intervention which distinguishes between a number of closely related patterns of behavior, Howard Wriggins, Director of the Southern Asian Institute at Columbia, suggests a spectrum with "influence" at one end, running through "involvement" and thence to "intervention" at the other, with influence being the more "benign" of the extremes, and intervention connoting "action in another's territory."[2] An extreme case of intervention is what Wriggins calls the "clandestine" variety, whereby State A endeavors to direct the course of State B's policy without the latter's knowledge that this is what is happening. So understandably outraged are leaders in State B when this form of intervention is laid bare that may well charge that aggression has taken place, even if military forces are not actually brought into play. Here, as in the case of the definition offered above by Beloff, a distinction needs to be made between the objective and the means used to achieve it, for not only does intervention imply an attempt to influence or to manipulate the internal affairs of another state, but it also requires hostile action or at least the threat of it. The importance of this distinction is readily seen in the contrast between the attitude of a government, especially a weaker one in dealing with a stronger one, regarding what is proper in those relations, and the attitude of its internal opposition, which either honestly or for purposes of domestic political advantage tends to regard any degree of unusual involvement by a foreign power as outright intervention. This is particularly true in the field of

[1] Max Beloff, "Reflections on Intervention," *Journal of International Affairs* (1968), 22, No. 2, 198. This entire issue of the *Journal,* a periodical put out by the students of the School of International Affairs at Columbia University, is devoted to "Intervention and World Politics."

[2] Howard Wriggins, "Political Outcomes of Foreign Assistance," *Journal of International Affairs* (1968), 22, No. 2, 217–18.

economic assistance—foreign aid—when and to the extent that it becomes military in nature.

It is the Marxist-Leninist assumption that intervention in the affairs of the less developed countries by the capitalist powers is inevitable and implicit in what Lenin called the "highest stage of capitalism"—imperialism. While the term "imperialism," like "colonialism," has been exorcised from the self-descriptive rhetoric of the Western powers, the Communists and their sympathizers throughout the world see foreign aid as but one more manifestation of what they regard as an historical process which will only end with a series of terrible wars between the capitalist states and the eventual triumph of world communism in their stead. What was imperialism yesterday is intervention through economic assistance today and then military control tomorrow. No doubt most, if indeed not all, Western statesmen are sincere in protesting this interpretation of their behavior, but the contention that their policies do often constitute intervention is difficult to contradict, as the brilliant analysis by Morgenthau in the previous chapter illustrates.

For their part the Communist powers (or, more accurately, that giant among them, the U.S.S.R.) are demonstrably more interventionist than any of the Western powers, at least when neighbors on their most sensitive borders are concerned, as the Czechoslovakian people have so recently and so painfully learned. The presence of Soviet troops in Prague provides an illustrative contrast to the absence of Communist Chinese troops in Vietnam, even though obviously the two situations are in many ways not at all analogous. From the point of view of the nature of intervention, the interesting point of difference is the illustration that the latter case may provide of State A (China) intervening in the affairs of State C (South Vietnam) by utilizing the forces of State B (North Vietnam). This complex set of relationships is rendered even more complicated by the activity of State D (the U.S.S.R.) on behalf of North Vietnam, through Communist Chinese territory, at a time when China and the Soviet Union are at ideological, political, and even military loggerheads. The presence of State E (the United States), responding, according to its leaders, to the plea of State C (South Vietnam) to prevent intervention by B, C, and D (the Communist states), shows how complex this subject can be, especially when it is the United States which is considered by much of world opinion to be the interventionist power.

Revolution may or may not represent a form of intervention, although even when it is not intervention, it is usually so regarded by the government against which the revolution is aimed. That is to say, a revolution may very well occur simply as a result of widespread and acute dissatisfaction within the borders of a given country.

Depending upon the location and power of the country within which a revolution takes place, Communist or otherwise, there is a certain degree of international interest in the outcome. But when the revolution occurs as a direct result of the activity of an outside power, then the international system is instantly alerted and vitally affected, regardless of the size and geographical placement of the country involved. Preventing the outbreak of such revolutions has occupied almost as much attention on the part of the government of the United States as the prevention of (or victory in) a third world war. Authorities differ on whether a very poor country is more or less likely to succumb to the blandishments of local Communist parties than one which is merely poor, or perhaps just not as rich as it would like to be, but this has not prevented the expenditure of vast sums of money and the diversion of a great deal of talent to make viable existing governments all over the world. Not too much attention has been paid to what kinds of governments they were, just so they were not Communist and could be persuaded not to become so.

Although only one revolution has to date produced a Communist regime in the Western hemisphere, there have been numerous coups, revolts and other illegitimate governmental turnovers. As a rule these have been on behalf of or opposed to military juntas; the characteristic revolution has been neither totalitarian nor democratic, but military. Yet, as one student of Latin American politics has observed,

> Outside the North Atlantic area, the armed forces are more likely than not to be among the most important power contenders in any political system, and military regimes are at least as widespread as either totalitarian or democratic ones. It is surprising, therefore, that until recently this phenomenon has attracted little attention from students of politics. Though there has been some speculation about the causes of military intervention, our actual knowledge of the subject is meager indeed.[3]

Once again the student of international phenomena must rely on fundamentals and seek the underlying causes and the long-term consequences of revolution, whatever form it may take, and of intervention, be it military, economic, or a combination of both of them. What conditions make a revolution within a country more likely? Under what circumstances is a government susceptible to outside efforts to control or influence the course of its policies? Is it inevitable, as the Marxists contend, that class antagonism will produce violent revolution and dictatorship of the proletariat? Is it in the nature of international competitive systems, as some political analysts insist, that intervention is part of the scheme of things? Some insight into these questions, as well as others related to them, will be found in the selections which follow.

[3] Robert D. Putnam, "Toward Explaining Military Intervention in Latin American Politics," *World Politics* (1967), 20, No. 1, 83.

1. A General View on Intervention

Louis J. Halle

Louis Halle served as a member of the Policy Planning Staff of the U.S. Department of State from 1952 to 1954. He is presently on the faculty of the Graduate Institute of International Studies in Geneva, Switzerland. He is author of numerous books and articles of which the latest, THE COLD WAR AS HISTORY, *is a distinguished contribution to the understanding of the post-World War II era.*

...In the world as it is today, the government of a country is the responsibility of the people in that country.... If a dictatorship is to be ousted from power, and another kind of government put in its place, the prime agent in accomplishing the change must be the population that lives under it. It follows that the propriety of placing the responsibility on foreign governments is doubtful except in extraordinary cases.

The foreign government lacks not only legal jurisdiction but competence as well. It cannot have the knowledge and sensitivity to judge what kind of government is best for people of a culture different from what it represents. To be truly native, a government must be native-bred.

I am equally doubtful of the competence of any government, our own included, to apply the moral test and grade other governments accordingly. The notion that there are only two kinds of government in the world, the good and the wicked, is illusory. All govern-ments are bad by the accepted standards of individual behavior.... They are necessary evils, and the degree of their evil varies from easily tolerable to intolerable. It would not be easy to know where the line should be drawn between acceptable and unacceptable, and I doubt that any government is capable of justly discriminating.

Under the circumstances, the rule in international affairs has been to accept the existence of a foreign government, whether one approves of it or not, where it appears to be accepted by the people under it, who have the primary responsibility.... Washington cannot conduct tests in the jurisdiction of other governments to determine whether their decisions have the "support" of the people. The best it can do is to judge general acceptance, and this only by the absence of popular rebellion on any significant scale. The overwhelming majority of the Spanish people may abhor their present government (I cannot tell whether they do) but they accept it in submitting to its authority. Washington can hardly refuse to accept what they themselves accept.

Finally, there is the tacit assumption that by overthrowing bad govern-

"On Dealing with Franco," New Republic, September 24, 1962. Reprinted by Permission of THE NEW REPUBLIC, © *1962, Harrison-Blaine of New Jersey, Inc.*

ment one gets good government. Unfortunately experience does not bear
this out.

In our dealings with Spain, as
normally in our dealings with every
other country in the world, we are not
offered a choice of governments with
which to deal. If such a choice were to
be offered, it would have to be by the
active initiative of the Spanish people.
...it is not the business of the U.S. to
select the government of the Spanish
people; and it is not its business to
reject the government that they themselves accept, however unhappily. In its
relations with Spain it has to deal with
the one constituted Government of Spain
because there is no other government
to deal with. This may have evil consequences, as any alternative course of
action might have consequences equally
evil or more so. With a view to these
considerations, and to our own disaste
for the Spanish form of government, it
would be well for us to make a point
of avoiding gratuitous cordiality in such
relations. We would find, however, that
we could not effectively deal with the
matters involved in our myriad necessary relations with Spain while following a policy of publicly insulting her
officials.... Being courteous to fools and
scoundrels is a universal necessity of
politics. Being courteous to one's ideological opponents is often a necessity
of international politics. Otherwise this
inflammable world might quickly burn
up.

2. Patterns of American Intervention

LINCOLN P. BLOOMFIELD

*Lincoln P. Bloomfield is Professor of Political Science at the Massachusetts
Institute of Technology. He is author of* THE UNITED NATIONS AND U.S. FOREIGN
POLICY, *co-author of* INTERNATIONAL MILITARY FORCES, *and of* KRUSCHEV AND THE
ARMS RACE, *as well as author of numerous monographs and articles dealing with
peacekeeping and the arms race.*

A decade ago we had one picture
of what the general lines of U.S. policy
in our epoch were and would likely
continue to be. Instability in the developing world had a kind of fixed significance for both Moscow and Washington.

*"Future Small Wars: Must the United
States Intervene?"* ORBIS, *12 (Fall 1968), pp.
669–84. Reprinted by permission. An earlier
version of this material was prepared in connection with a conference sponsored by the
Browne & Shaw International Studies Division of Bolt, Beranek and Newman, Inc.,
under contract to the Office of the Assistant
Secretary of Defense for International Affairs.
The judgments expressed herein are the
author's own.*

Each seemed destined to play a fore-ordained role, one fomenting conflict, the other counterattacking. U.S. interests appeared to be relatively unchanging, with European concerns in the accustomed catbird seat, and counter-insurgency the new magic by which nuisance wars would be disposed of. Inspiring the whole scene was a sense that the United States of America was fulfilling its God-given mandate to show the way, if necessary with a billy-club —a mandate celebrated by Americans from Jonathan Edwards ("Providence intended America to be the renovator of the world") to John F. Kennedy ("We in this country, in this generation are—by destiny rather than choice— the watchmen on the walls of freedom"). American omnipotence, in other words, was satisfactorily accompanied by omniscience, and there was no reason to believe that the 1960's would be all that different from the 1940's and 1950's.

The picture has changed with dazzling rapidity. Much of the following discussion reflects newer beliefs about what the past in fact meant and what the future might bring. But the final sobering thought is that our new perspectives, too, are transitory and subject to profound alternation as the 1960's give way to the 1970's.

II

Fifty-four local conflicts have taken place since World War II—small wars or near-wars, involving no direct U.S.-Soviet military confrontation. Some are still going on, such as the Arab-Israeli conflict, and those in Kashmir and Cyprus. The rate is not necessarily high: the only new ones during the last two years were the renewed Arab-Israeli fighting in 1967 and the civil war in Nigeria. Over 90 per cent of them occurred in the developing areas. Less than half were characterized by a prime communist element, even in insurgency situations. Yet U.S. military power was involved, directly and indirectly, in almost one-fourth of these small wars.

Already changes are discernible in the patterns of local conflict. It used to be that the easiest cases to predict were the inevitable decolonizations, some peaceful, some violent. But now only the Portuguese African territories remain a pressure point, and even here history could make liars out of some of us by arranging for Angola and Mozambique not to explode, i.e., to become happily biracial, or perhaps to be protected for twenty-five years by white South African power.

Neither is the old category of automatic Soviet mischief-making, countered by automatic U.S. opposition, necessarily valid for the 1970's. Note the word automatic—not adventitious or serendipitous, which accounts for the Soviet position in such places as Cuba, the UAR, Algeria, Nigeria and Somalia. In all of these cases other people made their own revolutions and then looked around for outside support. (The United States did the same after *its* revolution, and found it in Jacobin France, to the disgust of the conservative European powers. This analogy is pregnant with possible meaning for Americans.) An increasingly valid distinction can be made between local conflicts in which the Soviets meddle for quick profit and cheap influence, such as those now disturbing various parts of the Moslem world, and conflicts in which communist regimes, established of, for and by communists, are at stake, such as Hungary in 1956, Korea in 1950–1953, and currently North Viet Nam and Czechoslovakia.

The sources of deliberate insurgency-fomenting will more likely be Peking, Hanoi and Cuba. Of these only China has or is likely in the 1970's to have nuclear weapons. Conflicts fomented by Hanoi or Cuba have so far been unable to trigger direct Soviet or Chinese involvement, and thus do not raise the same danger of escalation one fears in those threatening a U.S.-Soviet collision. But whether or not touched off by communist arsonists, "wars of liberation" will be in the forefront in the 1970's, as colonial problems were previously. This leads to the second change in the local conflict picture.

This second change is an outgrowth of the virtual end of decolonialization. The Congo collapse in 1960 was its harbinger. A second generation of leaders and ideas is already making its appearance in the less developed countries. The "morning after" phenomenon is becoming institutionalized, with less and less hope that promised growth rates and modernization effects will soon, if ever, be achieved. This revolution of risen expectations will be continuously fueled by growing literacy, radio, television, UNCTAD conferences, and technical assistance operations. It is ironic that a form of stability has manifested itself in inherently unstable situations such as that in the southern half of Africa or the eastern half of Germany. Paradoxically, the reverse may also be true. Inherently hopeful situations characterized by national independence, aid programs, growing school populations, and concerned citizens, may well be the ones most likely to generate violence in the period ahead. In this sense West Africa, Southeast Asia and the Persian Gulf are not much different from Detroit, the Chicago South Side, Bedford-Stuyvesant, or Roxbury: they all illustrate Kropotkin's aphorism that the hopeless do not revolt (but once hope is born, watch out!).

Anyone requiring persuasion that change and turmoil will be the order of the day should study the ages of men who rule important parts of the world, often where there is no tradition of peaceful transmission of power. The science of gerontology will not save them from a certain fate (and might give us important clues to their behavior in the meantime): Chiang Kai-shek is 81, Salazar (recently incapacitated and removed from power) is 77, Charles de Gaulle 76, Franco 75, Ho Chi Minh 75, Tito 75, Jomo Kenyatta 74, Mao Tsetung 74, and Ulbricht 74.

It seems inevitable that a decade of turmoil, revolution, small wars and attempted takeovers lies ahead. The failure of overnight modernization will create more fertile soil for "wars of liberation," and the latter, while often arising out of genuine revolutions, will also be fomented or egged on by Peking, Hanoi or Havana, and rather nervously supported by an increasingly stability-favoring USSR.

The United States, for its part, is not going to be able to drop out, and is not going to wish to expend its treasure and reputation in an endless succession of unilateral interventions. How can a policy be found that mediates between the imperatives? The past supplies a number of clues—but some of them are misleading.

On the evidence of the postwar local conflicts, the United States has acted according to a clear and even predictable pattern. Before the Viet Nam war became massive and eventually intolerable, several linked propositions could be asserted with confidence, notably that U.S. interests as a general rule favor stability and are opposed to violent conflict.

U.S. interests toward local *interstate* wars outside Europe have usually converged with international norms in favoring conflict control. But this has not been the case where vital interests appeared to be endangered by direct Soviet or Chinese advantages.

With respect to most *internal* wars, U.S. interests have derived from strategic concerns, e.g., regional security, U.S.-Soviet-Chinese relations, and modernization. Rather than invariably being subordinate to conflict-control policy, they have tended to depend on pragmatic assessments of probability of success, accessibility of the area, and the actual need for U.S. intervention. Wherever communist takeover was not a prime issue, the United States did not have a primary interest as to which faction won.

Both where the United States was relatively indifferent to the outcome, and where it was committed to victory for a given side, the crucial independent variable inhibiting this country's willingness to manipulate rather than suppress internal and interstate conflicts has often been a perceived danger of great-power escalation.[1]

Will this pattern continue? What, if anything, is changing? And where will such changes leave U.S. interests with respect to the local conflict process?

Most students of the problem would probably agree that, as of the late 1960's, at least one thing has changed: there is no longer a virtually unanimous consensus among American leaders that the United States has an automatic role as policeman to a refractory and unruly world in default of collective security and collective peacekeeping.

We can dismiss as *démodé*, at least for this planning period, the recent intoxication of some Americans by the heady wine of *imperium* (with or without the actual empire). There was an archaic, if not lunatic, ring to the revelation in February 1968 of the Army-sponsored study by Douglas Aircraft entitled *Pax Americana,* supposed to deal with "world power configurations to be used as a basis for the United States to maintain world hegemony in the future. . . .[2]

But even after dismissing the mysticism and the neurotic Herrenvolkism of the latter-day Beveridges and Mahans, there remains a vital question of the extent to which the United States has a responsibility to intervene in local conflicts for unneurotic reasons: to prevent a larger war, or to oppose injustice, or to preserve friends from defeat or extinction. There is also the issue of what it *must* do in order to get the international community to meet its responsibilities, or to see that the various world power balances are not dangerously overturning, to the point they were by 1529 when the Turks were at the gates of Vienna, or 1806 when Napoleon had conquered most of Europe, or 1939 when Hitler seemed invincible. According to policy planner Zbigniew Brzezinski, U.S. involvement is a historic given on grounds of both fate and responsibility: "Our global involvement and our preponderance of power is such that our disinvolvement would create international chaos of enormous proportions. Our involvement is a historic fact—there is no way of ending it."[3]

   .   .   .

. . .But cogent warnings come from the State Department's Director of Intelligence and Research: Thomas Hughes argues that our overseas policy must not "suppress the pent-up revolu-

---

[1] See Lincoln P. Bloomfield and Amelia C. Leiss, *The Control of Local Conflict* (Washington: GPO, 1967), II, Chapter II, which appears in revised form in *Controlling Small Wars: A Strategy for the 1970's* (New York: Knopf, 1969).

[2] *New York Times,* February 17, 1968.
[3] Zbigniew Brzezinski, "The Implications of Change for United States Foreign Policy," *Department of State Bulletin,* July 3, 1967, p. 4.

tions which the century's politics require"; that "over time our national interest has been compatible with insurgencies more often than with counter-insurgencies"; and that "depriving people for the first time in history of the option to use force for social change is a serious and in many ways presumptuous effort."[4]

Perhaps the United States does find itself on the wrong side of the revolutions of the twentieth century, forced by some ghastly accident of history to play the role of Holy Alliance, while the most notable enemies of political freedom—the communists—somehow get away with parading as liberals. If this is an exaggeration, it is an exaggeration of a home truth that worries a multitude of Americans. The election campaign of 1968 signaled that many interpretations of the American role were up for re-examination. To define the interests of the United States in the local conflicts of the decade ahead, some pointed questions have to be asked anew. Some are astonishingly fundamental, such as: What keeps the peace of the world? All but the most egregious doves know that maintenance of the balance of power is one of the eternal verities of international life, and that failure to live by that verity brings on calamitous wars. But what balance of power? or balances? Do we mean only the balance between worldwide communists and worldwide noncommunists? What about balances between North Viet Nam and Communist China? Mainland Asia and offshore Asia? Arab Moslems versus non-Arab Moslems plus Israelis? Western Europe versus Eastern Europe? Or Europe versus the USSR? *Or*—Europe versus North America?

The point of these questions is self-evident, and unless one can answer them lucidly, there can be no policy for this country that represents rational judgments about intervention or nonintervention, caring or not caring, Asia or Europe, unilateral or multilateral undertakings.

It seems obvious that there are multiple balances, as well as an overall superpower balance that, once tipped, slides everything and everyone downhill toward World War III or, if we manage to avoid that, toward World War IV in the developing regions. Having accepted this situation, there then exists a clear responsibility to prevent the overturn of those balances and that balance. But whose responsibility? And if we assume the responsibility as in part ours—as American liberals earlier embraced it—can we live with it shorn of the once valid inflammatory and misleading rhetoric of a worldwide ideological battle?

Finally, if we do accept continuing responsibility commensurate with our size and wealth (though not necessarily our wisdom and understanding), how do we tell when a local conflict is truly a perturbation of the balance of power structure, requiring to be met and rectified? What, in 1968–1978 reference, is "aggression," and how can we always distinguish it from bush-league neighborhood feuds we hear about only because of Huntley-Brinkley's news stethoscope, not because they are important. Given that (as Thomas Hughes pointed out in the same remarkable speech) "internal violence is normal for most countries," how do we distinguish "aggression" from other unpleasant and even frightening events: peasant revolts, slum riots, student glandularity, and other manifestations of not-necessarily-communist oppression, misery, discontent, racial resentment and nationalist

---

[4] Thomas L. Hughes, remarks entitled "The Odyssey of Counter-Insurgency" to Foreign Service Institute, July 3, 1967, p. 25.

spirit? How do we arrange to keep remembering John F. Kennedy's axiom that "Those who make peaceful revolution impossible will make violent revolution inevitable."?

In operational terms, even if we become wiser and more sophisticated about relaxing while watching tribal blood flow or any other shaking of the comfortable status quo, where should the line be drawn? How "quietist" can the United States be in a turbulent world without encouraging incipient turmoil and destabilizing thrusts by the enemies of freedom into the soft mass of discontent? To accept as policy guides the predictions of those who say "No more Viet Nams" could be immoral and, even worse, stupid. We would do well to remember what John Stuart Mill said more than a hundred years ago on the subject of nonintervention:

> The doctrine of non-intervention, to be a legitimate principle of morality, must be accepted by all governments. The despots must consent to be bound by it as well as the free states.
>
> Unless they do, the profession of it by free countries comes but to this miserable issue, that the wrong side may help the wrong, but the right must not help the right.
>
> Intervention to enforce non-intervention is always rightful, almost moral, if not always prudent.
>
> Though it be a mistake to give freedom to a people who do not value the boon, it cannot but be right to insist that if they do value it, they shall not be hindered from the pursuit of it by foreign coercion.

Isolationism is not necessarily bound to follow Viet Nam. For one thing, we have an alliance system we cannot undo quickly even if we wanted to. For another, as a nation we have a generally better understanding of the need to maintain balances of power than we have had since the early nineteenth century. And even when the United States has looked away from Europe, it has invariably found Asia and the Pacific in its field of vision.

A modulated American approach to local conflict would still leave a wide range of policy options for the United States. Washington can regard some local conflicts as not likely to upset a balance significant to the peace, and ignore them. It can view others in the light of increasing awareness that, on the record so far, neocolonialism is hard to impose. Why not let the Russians (or Chinese or French or Egyptians) fall on their faces instead of us? Perhaps we can "win" sometimes without even competing, just as the Soviet Union (France, Cuba, et al.) have scored points with people around the world despite our bigger gifts, our nobler attitude, and our genuine commitment to the good life.

Against this must be balanced the cases where the United States *must* act. Unilateral military intervention may still be the only way to cope with local conflict situations where the vital security interests of the United States are genuinely in jeopardy. But what still must be answered is whether, if intervention is required at times, it must be by the United States alone or virtually alone; whether adequate nonmilitary intervention early in the conflict would obviate the need for later military intervention; and whether multilateral peacekeeping and peacemaking should not have a more significant role in the decade ahead in confronting this range of issues.

III

The national interest in respect to local conflicts may be seen as a function of several tangible considerations: whether a direct treaty commitment binds us to another; whether sworn enemies of the United States are bound to benefit directly from a given outcome; whether ready reaction forces are available. Another potential "involver" is the solemn pledge entered into under Article I, Chapter I of the United Nations Charter, "to take effective collective measures for the prevention and removal of threats to the peace, and for the suppression of acts of aggression or other breaches of the peace. . . ." But it is uncommonly hard in this century to organize a genuinely collective effort along these lines, even in the face of blatant aggression, probably because most aggression nowadays is not blatant, and may not even be aggression in any traditional sense of people in different uniforms, or from distinctly separate territorial entities, or even, in moral terms, wearing black and white hats.

Experts are currently debating whether new technology that drastically cuts the ton-mile cost of distant interventions does not cancel out the old rule that interests vary in inverse ratio to the distance from one's shores. But somehow an explosion in Central America or Canada seems more likely on the face of it to alert U.S. planners than one in Botswana.

In addition there is the matter of vital economic interests abroad. But it is difficult to think of items on which this country is so directly dependent as to allow the need for them to overcome vital political-security considerations.

If we construct a scale that weights potential conflicts in terms of these criteria for U.S. interests—explicit treaty obligations, communist profit with its presumed bandwagon effect, available U.S. forces, and distance—we could predict that, for example, the United States would have approximately three times more "interest" in what happened in Korea than Ethiopia. On *prima facie* grounds Washington would have a greater reason for intervening if Haiti or Guatemala "went communist" than if the Federation of South Yemen did so. One could assume that the United States would be likelier to act unilaterally to keep Panama from collapsing than the Sudan or Somalia. It would become enmeshed sooner in ethnic-religious warfare in Palestine than in racial-tribal warfare in Southern Africa.

Conversely, U.S. interest in tranquilizing measures, pacification, UN diplomacy, even arbitration and adjudication would be greatest at the low end of the scale, remote from places where a box-score with Moscow or Peking is kept and where the bandwagon and the dominoes are found—say, the Horn of Africa, the Congo, Nigeria, Zambia, Burma, or Algeria vs. Morocco.

But are these calculations eternally true? Can we predict today what U.S. interests will be a decade hence? And if we do, does not that lead us to a self-fulfilling prophecy? Note that the weighting of cases can be changed significantly by changes in two of the variables, and eventually three. Geography cannot be changed. But U.S. forces can be readily redeployed. The likelihood of distinct, direct Soviet or Chinese gains that are "zero-sum" for this country can change. Even more importantly, American *perceptions* of the degree of likely gain by Moscow or Peking from a given outcome of a conflict in Africa, Asia or the Middle East—or by Hanoi in Southeast Asia or Castro in Latin America—can alter. Finally, over time U.S. treaty commitments can be modified.

Moreover, U.S. interests can, in effect, be created by the initial decision to become involved. It has become increasingly clear that definition of vital interests and subsequent intervention have sometimes taken place as a *result* of arms or expertise transfers to the developing countries, rather than vice versa. Who in 1948 would have predicted an American interest in Viet Nam vital enough to warrant sending half a million U.S. soldiers to defend that country? And who that same year would have predicted that U.S. interests in the defense of Israel would become so shaky in the face of changing times that Washington's first instinct in the third round of fighting in 1967 would be to announce its neutrality?

. . .

A final corrective to the sliding scale version of Washington's critical list of local conflicts is that such a list is not by any means a mirror-image of the probable target list maintained in Moscow, Peking, Hanoi or Havana. . . .

IV

In this epoch U.S. interests in local hostilities arise first of all out of a concern that the most powerful of America's self-identified adversaries is in conflict with us in the developing regions.

In the late 1960's one is entitled to wonder how the Soviet Union is playing its role. It looks increasingly as though Moscow does not run risks threatening the collision of strategic nuclear forces. It seems true also that the USSR, in contrast with China, supports bourgeois nationalist leadership and movements in the less developed countries, in many places scorning the local communists who are often outlawed and/or in jail. The Soviets are known to disapprove of Castro's militant and violence-provoking tactics in fomenting Latin American revolution.

Perhaps Moscow actually *is* operating a conflict control strategy, as it claims. Premier Kosygin spoke of this to the UN General Assembly in 1967:

A seemingly small event, or so-called "local wars," may grow into big military conflicts. This means that every state and government should not only refrain from bringing about new complications by its actions—it must undertake every effort to prevent any aggravation of the situation and, moreover, the emergence of hotbeds of war, that should be quenched whenever they appear.[5]

But something else is happening too. The same week Kosygin spoke, *The Economist*, in an editorial trenchantly entitled "Bears Can't Fly," predicted that Soviet abstention from trouble in the developing areas would be signaled by failure to prepare for it logistically:

The combination of an offensive ideology with a defensive strategy is apt to produce...diplomatic defeats. To avoid more Cubas and Sinais the Russians will have either to resist the temptation to take on commitments in the Third World (which includes encouraging 'wars of liberation'), or else to acquire the military capacity this sort of policy calls for. This means building aircraft-carriers and acquiring staging posts for airborne troops. It will be a bad omen for East-West relations if there are signs that they have chosen the second way out of their dilemma.[6]

Today there are such signs. Soviet amphibious and airlift capabilities have improved. Landing forces are being trained. Soviet naval activity in the

[5] *New York Times,* June 19, 1967.
[6] June 24, 1967.

Mediterranean has increased substantially since the Middle East war of 1967.

As with most Soviet phenomena, at least two explanations can be found for this one. Perhaps Moscow is mounting a new drive for dominance around the world, this time under the umbrella of mutual nuclear deterrence. We seem, as a Yugoslav commentator recently wrote, to be witnessing "the increasingly obvious effort of the USSR to break out of the bounds of the continental Eurasian geostrategic shell without relying directly on nuclear missiles of intercontinental calibre." But as others have warned us in recent years—notably Marshall Shulman—the Soviet shift may well be a result of Moscow's calculations that the *United States* has adopted a basic strategy of intervention in any and all "small wars" in the developing regions to enhance American influence and control. . . .

V

Even if one of the communist states is actively engaged in a local conflict, must the United States necessarily intervene? The United States tends to react sharply in this type of situation, and is not likely to prefer conflict control measures such as peacekeeping. There will continue to be instances where unilateral U.S. intervention may be imperative to keep the balance of power from being dangerously overturned. This is what responsibility has to mean, and this is why, regardless of the congeries of failures with respect to policy execution, it was right for the United States not to turn away when the Hanoi-directed operations in South Viet Nam became a serious threat of forceful takeover by terror.

But having said that, we should add that the most important single component of policymaking in Washington in the years ahead may be the degree of sophistication and objectivity molding the *perceptions* of those who decide what shall be done in regard to local conflicts. Perhaps no one continues to believe in monolithic communism (except possibly Senator Thomas Dodd, who spoke of it in the Rusk hearings of early 1968). Many have come to agree with Thomas Hughes, who warned: "Let us also beware of the tendency to exaggerate the genuine communist influence on internal violence when that influence itself is no longer cohesive, is often divisive, and is frequently only one element among many others."[7]

It will no longer serve American interests to react in blind opposition to revolutions wherever significant communist involvement or potential gain is perceived. In Viet Nam, for instance, a shrewd American strategy for "victory" would equally require that we do everything possible to set Hanoi against Peking, to the point of making this one of our prime objectives. If it worked, the postwar situation would favor broad American interests, above all in preventing a coalescing of hostile power on the Asian mainland which could encourage dangerous alterations in the regional power balance.

The battles are by no means over. Communism as a doctrine continues to rely on anti-Americanism; in practice it quenches political freedom, and it still has remnants of international cohesion. It might be a decade too soon to act on Senator Fulbright's belief that

. . .American interests are better served by supporting nationalism than by opposing communism, and when the two are encountered in close association it is in our interest to accept a communist gov-

[7] Hughes, *op. cit.*, p. 29.

ernment rather than to undertake the cruel and all but impossible task of suppressing a genuinely national movement.[8]

But the counterstrategy is not to let the communists pose as the supporters of nationalism and the United States as the enemy, nor to let them posture as the advocates of genuine political reform. The United States must help to advance revolutionary processes in ways that steal the thunder from the extremists; this should *always* be the aim of reformers. Both in American ghettos and in local conflicts, we did not realize until recently that our winning strategy was reform rather than simply containment. The meaning of reform has become better understood; only its implementation continues to evade us.

U.S. interests are going to require a whole series of new policies in the economic and social, psychological and political spheres. U.S. political interests require us to find and support acceptable local leadership. Lee Kuan Yew, Eduardo Frei, Kenneth Kaunda—these are the types with which to "win"; note that they were at one time or another

[8] William J. Fulbright, *The Arrogance of Power* (New York: Random House, 1967), p. 78.

jailed by the white "reformer," or opposed by white Westerners as "too radical." Batista was disliked by most Americans, but the world believed he was our man. Diem was efficient, but when he embarrassed us we dumped him. We support the Portuguese regime in Angola because it is there, and because "we have to work with the people in power" who eventually become our "friends." The CIA long ago learned that this was not necessarily true. Activist politicians up to and including de Gaulle have balanced temporary embarrassment against national interest and swallowed transient unpopularity when necessary.

In dealing with local conflicts, U.S. interests require that we adopt as moral Canning's aphorism that a nation has no permanent friends or permanent enemies, only permanent interests. Agonizing choices will continue to confront us in internal conflict situations. As a nation that sensibly avoids a tragic view of history, the United States tends to believe that in revolutionary situations there must be a third force, between the extremes, that is congenial to our values. Perhaps there are in fact no Kerenskys to be found in modern-day revolutions. But that does not force us to support either the Tsar or the Bolsheviks.

3. An Interpretation of the Chinese View on Intervention

DAVID MOZINGO AND THOMAS W. ROBINSON

The authors are on the staff of the RAND Corporation.

I. INTRODUCTION

On September 3, 1965, *People's Daily,* the official organ of the Chinese regime, published a major article expounding the strategic principles of the Chinese revolution. Entitled "Long Live the Victory of People's War," this 17,000-word article by Marshal Lin Piao, China's Minister of Defense, was issued to commemorate the twentieth anniversary of the defeat of Japan in World War II. It followed the publication earlier this year of important articles by top Chinese Communist military leaders, including Lo Jui-ching, Ho Lung, and Liu Ya-lou. In these earlier articles, China's military leaders attempted to draw parallels between the present world situation and that prevailing in former years when China and the Soviet Union won historic victories over the imperialist enemy. These articles reiterated a major theme in Peking's pronouncements of the past several years: that the military-political strategy formulated nearly thirty years ago by Mao Tse-tung is still applicable to many revolutionary situations today.

The Lin Piao editorial is the most recent and important instance of this habitual application of past Chinese Communist revolutionary experience to the contemporary world scene.[1]

It has long been recognized that, in the politics of Communist states, where insistence on secrecy and rigid controls over public pronouncements is an elemental facet of political life, esoteric communications serve a special function. When rigorously analyzed, the timing, content, style, and ideological character of statements by Communist leaders often suggest insights into their problems and attitudes— insights more significant than the superficial content of a particular speech or article. On the surface the Lin Piao article is an exposition of the Chinese leaders' strategic revolutionary doctrine directed primarily to the contemporary Communist-led revolutionary movements in Asia, Africa, and Latin America. This interpretation is self-evident, for "Long Live the Victory of People's War" is a definitive summation of the accumulated strategic and tactical doctrines the Chinese Communists for-

"Lin Piao on People's War: China Takes a Second Look at Viet Nam," RAND Memo RM-4814-PR, November 1965. Reprinted by permission.

[1] A table of parallels drawn in the Lin Piao article between the Chinese civil war, the Vietnamese conflict, and the world revolutionary scene is provided in Appendix A.

mulated in the "Second Revolutionary Civil War" (1927–1936), "The War of Resistance Against Japan" (1937–1945), and the "Third Revolutionary Civil War" (1946–1949), that Peking now related to that of the underdeveloped world as a whole against "United States imperialism." Lin Piao asserts that the basic political-military doctrines successfully applied by the Chinese Communists against "Japanese imperialism" can in the present international situation be the basic guide lines for the people of Asia, Africa, and Latin America in their struggle against "U.S. imperialism." Thus, just as the Chinese Communists encircled and defeated the Japanese invaders from their revolutionary bases in the Chinese countryside, so the contemporary world revolution in Asia, Africa, and Latin America occupies the "rural base areas" from which it will ultimately encircle and defeat "the cities of the world," the imperialist strongholds of North America and Western Europe. This surface content of the Lin Piao article merely explicates what has been implicit in Chinese pronouncements for some time.

.   .   .

The Lin Piao article, it seems to us, it a major statement of Peking's views on the war in Vietnam. Not only the content of the article but also its timing leads us to the conclusion that this should be the main interpretation. By September 1965, the Communist world had had an opportunity to estimate the effects of the U.S. bombardment of North Vietnam and the U.S. commitment of approximately one hundred and fifty thousand troops to South Vietnam. "Long Live the Victory of People's War" constitutes Peking's judgment on what should now be done by Hanoi and the Viet Cong in the light of these U.S. actions. The following basic conclusions about Peking's

view of the war in Vietnam emerge from close analysis of the Lin Piao article:

1. The war has now developed a fundamentally new character. Since the massive U.S. intervention it is no longer essentially a civil war between non-Communists and insurgents but must now be treated as a full-fledged national war of resistance against U.S. imperialist invasion. The Communists' main enemy is now the United States, not the Saigon government.

2. The Viet Cong's present tactics are wrong from both the military and political standpoint. Now that the United States is the major enemy, Peking argues, the Viet Cong for political reasons should abandon such practices as terrorism, forced conscription, assassination, and confiscation in favor of the same multi-class appeals and united front tactics that the Chinese Communists themselves adopted in the war against Japan. On the military side, the Viet Cong should abandon mobile warfare and go over to the strategic defense, retreat to revolutionary bases in the countryside, and carry on smaller-scale but protracted guerrilla warfare.

3. The Viet Cong can win this struggle only if they rely primarily on their own resources and their own revolutionary spirit. Help from the socialist countries is important (and Peking pledges more assistance to revolutionaries in the future as China becomes stronger) but the decisive factor must be the strength and determination of the Vietnamese Communists themselves.

.   .   .

III. THE BROADER CONTEXT : CHANGES IN CHINA'S POLICY

The authors believe that the extent to which the Lin Piao article openly expounds the Chinese Communist strategic doctrine in the war with Japan strongly suggests that Peking for a long time has had serious disagreements with Hanoi about the proper way the Vietnam revolution should have been conducted. In the past, Western observers have frequently asserted that Communist tactics in Vietnam have been modeled after those of the Chinese Communists. But that is not true, particularly with respect to political tactics, which were always the fundamental and distinctive part of the Maoist revolutionary weapon. The VC's policies of terrorism, forced conscription, assassination, confiscation, and no alliances with non-Communist elements contradict the entire political line of Chinese revolutionary doctrine.

While the revolution in South Vietnam was developing favorably, Hanoi was evidently reluctant to yield to Chinese claims that their revolutionary techniques were more appropriate than those devised by Ho Chi Minh. Now that the situation in South Vietnam has changed radically for the worse, the Chinese, through Lin Piao's article, seem to be saying to Hanoi: "Your tactics are wrong and you had better come around to our way of thinking if you expect to win." If the VC's military and political tactics both change in the months ahead to conform more closely with the classic Chinese model, this would suggest Peking has won the argument on revolutionary strategy. If the VC does not change, this would indicate the existence of a major difference between Hanoi and Peking that could have very significant effects on their relations. If the Chinese feel the issue to be critical they may attempt to exert pressure on and inside the North Vietnamese Party, and if that has no effect they may feel compelled to reappraise their entire commitment to Hanoi's war in the South.

While the authors have stressed the importance of the Lin Piao article as a key to the Chinese view of the nature of the war in Vietnam and how it should be treated, they believe this significant document also reveals a great deal about Peking's perception of how this war is related to some of its basic international problems. Although in the Lin Piao article the Chinese do not conceal either their pessimism about the present stage of the war or their insistence that the VC adopt new tactics, they are confident about the long-range prospects of revolution both in Vietnam and elsewhere. The article tells the Vietnamese Communists that they must expect setbacks, ups and downs, and yet heavier blows from the U.S. "imperialists." But the Communists will win if they adopt the correct strategy, remain determined, and rally the entire population behind a war of national resistance. Drawing lessons from their war against Japan, the Chinese assert that the United States cannot successfully stamp out the Communist revolutionary bases because its limited ground forces, with worldwide commitments, will not be able to augment the thinly spread forces already in Vietnam and hence will not be able to accomplish their mission. Like the anti-Japanese war in China, the war in Vietnam is linked to a broader world struggle that will weaken the United States and therefore aid the Vietnamese. By tying down U.S. forces over a long period, says China, the Vietnamese are making a major contribution (and it is their duty to make it) to the defeat of the United States everywhere. Similarly the revolutionary struggle in other countries aids the Vietnamese.

It is no doubt very discouraging to Hanoi to learn that Peking now sees the successful outcome of the struggle in Vietnam ultimately turning on the more distant global defeat of the United States. In the meantime the Chinese contend it is the Vietnamese Communists' duty to keep up their end of the struggle indefinitely.

"Long Live the Victory of People's War" also provides insights into Peking's estimate of the U.S. purpose in Vietnam. Many in the United States have reasoned that their government's actions in Vietnam have been designed to strengthen a negotiating position so that it would be possible to reach a solution enabling the United States to withdraw without suffering an unacceptable political defeat. The estimate of U.S. intentions contained in the Lin Piao article is altogether different. Lin shows clearly that Peking regards the United States as having entered Vietnam to stay, to turn it into an American colony, and to prove by a decisive victory over the Viet Cong that the United States, if necessary acting alone, can invalidate China's doctrine of revolutionary war anywhere in the world.

Peking's estimate does not indicate that the Vietnamese will be able to win a quick victory over the United States; on the contrary, victory will be a long time coming. In effect, the Lin Piao article expresses China's acceptance of a contest with the United States on these terms. More important, it recognizes that China, since she is not able to defeat the United States frontally, should wage war with the United States by proxy. The contest must be between other revolutionary peoples and the United States, not between America and China directly. The Chinese leaders realize that American strategic superiority and China's relative industrial weakness preclude an early frontal challenge. Therefore they prefer the lower risk policy of indirect conflict, at least in those areas where China's vital national interests are not directly and seriously threatened. Revolutionary war-by-proxy on the tactical level and military caution on the strategic level

are thus mutually reinforcing features of China's political-military philosophy.

Before the large build-up of U.S. ground forces in South Vietnam began, Peking's public statements, it is true, did threaten the possibility of direct Chinese intervention in support of the revolutionaries, and offered "volunteers" if the VC requested them. But the key message that also came with these statements was that China would willingly fight the United States directly only if the latter attacked China. In the authors' view such threats are primarily intended to deter the United States from further escalation of the war in Vietnam. They are not simply bluff or propaganda, but serious efforts to restrain the United States from further enlarging the scope of the war. They can be interpreted as efforts to limit the war rather than as signals of China's intention to intervene. Had the Chinese wanted to emphasize the threat of their intervention, the Lin Piao editorial was the place to do it. But a striking feature of this major policy statement is precisely the absence of those threats of possible intervention that Peking had alluded to on several occasions in the preceding months. The reason for this significant omission—which can only have been deliberate—must be that by choosing to concentrate its main efforts in the South, the United States itself has helped to confine the war just where China wants it to be fought—in South Vietnam. After telling the VC how to win their war, Peking's main aim is to make sure the war remains limited as far as possible to South Vietnam. The best way to accomplish both these objectives is to tie down American ground forces in South Vietnam and then beat them with "people's revolutionary war" tactics.

"Long Live the Victory of People's War" should not be interpreted as meaning China would not intervene in Vietnam under any circumstances. We have already mentioned the existence of areas in which China has a vital interest. Her strongest threats to intervene have come in response to the U.S. bombing of North Vietnam. If bombing should ever reach a level at which the North Vietnamese regime was in danger of collapse or unable to assist the revolutionaries in the South, China might feel forced to intervene. Her interest in North Vietnam's security is probably stronger than her desire to see an early and successful conclusion to the revolutionary issue in South Vietnam. Although China prefers war-by-proxy with the United States in the South, this does not mean she would remain passive in the event of a serious threat to an allied state on her own borders, whatever the superiority of American power that could be brought to bear there.

Finally, the positions expressed in the Lin Piao article provide some insights into the political relationship between Peking and Hanoi. The implied Chinese criticism of the way the war in South Vietnam has been run so far tends to support those who have argued that Peking is not really the off-stage director of a Hanoi-VC cast of puppets. If anything, Lin Piao's article reveals the lack rather than the extent of China's control over the Vietnamese. In arguing that Hanoi and the VC must continue the war no matter what the costs, and primarily on a self-reliant basis, Peking betrays a doubt as to its own ability to prevent the Vietnamese Communists from considering the possibility of terminating the war at some point. There are no hints of Chinese commitments or guarantees sufficient to induce the Vietnamese to continue the struggle if at some future time they should view the revolutionary effort as no longer in their own interests.

North Vietnam would seem to be in a position where she will soon be forced to choose between two lines of action, neither of which can be completely to her liking. It seems clear that the Chinese have offered the following advice: The war must be continued but it must also be confined if possible principally to yourselves and the Americans. The war will be painful and it will go on indefinitely but as revolutionary war breaks out in other countries you will move closer to victory. China, in addition to supplying aid directly, is making her major contribution to the Vietnamese struggle by energizing revolutionary war in other countries where prospects for an anti-"U.S. imperialist" struggle look promising. The less candid Russians have said nothing to contradict the Chinese views, but we may suppose they would offer a different analysis. It seems logical to infer that Moscow's advice to Hanoi would be essentially the following: The Americans will continue to invade the South and pound you to pieces by air. Moreover, neither we nor the Chinese are likely to go to war with them over your revolutionary ambitions in the South. Why don't you call off the revolution for the time being? You can no longer win at an acceptable price anyway. If you call off the insurgency—and you don't have to negotiate this—the Americans in the absence of a war will be very hard pressed by their own and other people to withdraw their army of occupation from Vietnam. The South Vietnamese, furthermore, are so divided that after the Americans leave they will again fight among themselves and you will then be able to exploit the turmoil by violence or political means. North Vietnam will be stronger, the socialist camp will be stronger, and the Americans, once out, are not likely to come back again.

To the Vietnamese, Russian advice of this kind comes too close to the position both Russia and China took at Geneva in 1954. These two powers forced Ho Chi Minh to settle for half of Vietnam when all of the country could well have been in his grasp had the struggle continued. The expected internal collapse of South Vietnam, predicted by Moscow and Peking, did not materialize and therefore, in 1959, Hanoi reactivated the revolution. If the Soviet Union offers basically the same advice today as it did a decade ago, the Vietnamese would be profoundly suspicious. On the other hand, in addition to having a revolution to win, Ho Chi Minh now has the North Vietnamese state to preserve. The Soviet advice would make better sense in terms of protecting a decade of socialist progress. The Chinese advice no doubt appeals to Hanoi's aspirations to reunify North and South. In the Soviet-Chinese contest for influence in Vietnam, the decisive factor may be the extent of Hanoi's nationalistic dedication to unifying the country by revolution. That is clearly the question Peking has put to Hanoi in the Lin Piao article: How much are you willing to give to win your revolution?

FORCE:
ITS THREAT, USE, AND
RESTRAINT

Chapter 16

The uses of force—actual or potential—are many and varied, old-fashioned sabre rattling being but one. Force constitutes an omnipresence behind negotiations between states. It can enable states to make threats and gain concessions. It can be used to deter other states from doing these things. Its ultimate application is to wage war, and the ultimate task of world statesmanship is to restrain its use and prevent war.

Of all the types of relationship which may exist between states, war is the least attractive. Quite possibly it is also the most significant, because it entails the possibility of rapid changes in the structure of the international system. In recent times the nature of war has changed drastically, primarily because of the changing technology of war but also because of changing concepts about the purposes of war. In former times (the sixteenth through the nineteenth centuries), wars were fought with limited means—mostly because no other means were available—and for limited objectives. The participants in an armed conflict took it for granted that, with minor rectifications and changes, the postwar environment would resemble the prewar scene. War, in other words, was important but not crucial; its outcome made a difference but not usually the difference between survival and extinction. With the coming of total war by and against whole populations for total stakes, previous concepts of war have had to be revised, and the need for reevaluating war as an instrument of policy has become urgent.

In considering the use of force and violence and the institution of war in international relations, one is compelled to raise serious questions concerning not only war's morality but also its practicality as a method of conducting relations among states. Yet one must also admit that the threat of force and its use in war have been instrumental in achieving the present distribution of power and values and that not all of the consequences have been detrimental to order and progress. H. L. Nieburg has advanced some extraordinarily discomforting thoughts on the periodic necessity for the use of violence in relations among states. The uncomfortable, almost tragic, fact is that without the threat—and, according to Nieburg, the periodic use—of violence, given status quo would tend to remain frozen; anxiety about the breakdown of law and order tends to moderate the demands of political leaders, enabling the informal political processes of negotiation, concession, compromise, and agreement to take place. This is a useful caution signal not to let our personal inclinations get in the way of our scholarly analysis.

Of the many theories of the causes and occasions of war, most leave much to be desired. For example, one can identify a "who-done-it" theory of war, which assumes that there is a villain or group of villains who can be identified and legitimately punished. The "devils" may be governmental leaders, the press and an inflamed public, the big businessmen, warlords, or munitions makers.

Another widely held misconception is the notion that at any given moment countries are either at war or at peace with one another, the existence of a state of war being certified by a formal declaration of hostilities. But the United States alone has been engaged in more than a score of undeclared wars, of which the Korean and Vietnamese conflicts are only the most recent examples. Clear distinctions between war and peace are further blurred by the practice of warfare by means other than armed force—such as psychological, political, economic, or subversive warfare. The very term "cold war" indicates that the simple war-peace dichotomy is insufficient. Relations among states can be thought of as occupying various points on a continuum, with a friendly absence of violence on one end and total violence without restraint on the other, often with neither extreme being reached.

Those who subscribe to the Marxist-Leninist view hold that wars are caused by the capitalist powers at a certain phase in their respective development. Others believe that wars are caused by racial, religious, or cultural differentiations that give rise to frictions. The Marxist-Leninist thesis has been discredited by evidence that in many instances capitalists have opposed war as an undesirable disturbance of normal economic processes. Nor is there conclusive evidence to substantiate the view that interracial, interreligious, or intercultural wars are more frequent than intraracial, intra-religious, or intracultural ones. The almost infinite variety of recent conflicts is admirably summarized in the treatment by Kenneth Thompson below.

More plausible is the hypothesis that wars may be caused by individuals and groups who actually desire it. The Fascists sought to glorify war and to ennoble those who died for the fatherland on the field of battle. The resort to force frequently appears to a nation's leaders to be the only suitable remedy for some situations. In other instances the threat of force may offer a tempting device to utilize in order to achieve stipulated goals. Individuals may even accept war as a means of escape from unsatisfactory conditions of everday existence. It has not thus far been possible to make peace as meaningful a symbol as war, in the sense that people in general are willing to work and sacrifice as much for one as for the other.

The most obvious cause of war is probably war itself, or rather the expectation of war. In an environment approaching anarchy, with wars having frequently occurred in the past, each state must consider the possibility that war may occur in the future. To protect a state against such an eventuality, its leaders take such steps as the acquisition of bases, strengthening of armaments, or concluding alliances. Noting this, other states find their insecurity increased and follow suit. Tension may soon reach a point of open hostility. Ironically, as Kenneth N. Waltz's article demonstrates, force is less visible where power is most present.

Although it is difficult to formulate generalizations about the cause or causes of war, war is and always has been a fact of international life. Few (if indeed any) among the older states in the world have not engaged in war at one time or another. Nor is resort to violence specific to international relations. It occurs within states as well, albeit on a smaller scale and with different kinds of weapons. The amity-violence continuum exists within any political entity except that within well ordered communities the situation more often tends toward amity within a context of law. In international relations, as we shall see in the next chapter, the restraining influence of law is less, if indeed it exists in any meaningful way at all.

Within the relatively brief history of the so-called Western state system (the system of independent sovereign states), there have been profound changes in the conduct of warfare. In the seventeenth century wars were fought by hired mercenaries or small professional armies. By the eighteenth and nineteenth centuries wars began to involve large portions of the population and mass armies. To motivate conscripts wars needed a cause other than selfish or dynastic gain, so the ideological component came to be stressed more and more, a trend which has intensified down to the present day. As has been pointed out by Morgenthau, war has become total in at least four respects: (1) it involves total populations emotionally; (2) it involves total populations actively and physically; (3) it is conducted against total populations (for example, saturation bombings during World

War II, which killed more civilians than actual warfare killed military personnel); and (4) it is fought for total stakes, reflected in the insistence on unconditional surrender in World War II.[1] All this has meant total resistance and recourse to any and all means of prevailing over real or imagined enemies.

The advent of weapons of total destructive capacity inevitably has led to reevaluation of war as a means of policy. War is a means to an end, not an end in itself. The objective is not to obtain victory alone (even though victory may be a necessary precondition), but to produce conditions after the war that are either more congenial than those which had existed or, minimally, the establishment of conditions that are more congenial than those which would have existed had the war not been fought. Thus to say that "in war there is no substitute for victory" is to posit, at best, an intermediate goal. The real question is what comes after victory is achieved: Will it be possible to establish (or reestablish) an environment in which victorious states can function and prosper? The new destructive capability of weapons systems raises grave doubts about whether victory in a nuclear exchange is likely to provide a better world. Indeed it is a commonplace to contemplate the possibility of the end of civilization or even of the human race as a result of nuclear war. No wonder more thought is being devoted to alternatives to total warfare—non-military contests (competitive coexistence) whose conflicts are conducted by diplomatic, political, economic, or psychological means, and limited or localized wars.[2]

Since total war may be irrational, has it therefore become impossible? Unfortunately not, for the idea that what is unreasonable is impossible is the counterpart of the equally false notion that whatever is necessary is also possible. It assumes that men always act rationally and that pathological behavior patterns, such as those of Hitler, will never recur in international relations. But there are other reasons why wars, including major wars fought with nuclear weapons, may still be possible. One side or the other may miscalculate the effects of an aggressive action, convincing itself that it can get away with achieving its goals through the use of force. Or one side may believe that the other side is about to launch a military action and that it must strike first; this is the doctrine of preemption and was effectively applied in the six-day war by Israel in 1967. A war may break out, not because of a miscalculation arrived at by deliberation (however faulty), but simply by accident, remote though this may seem. Or one side or the other may achieve a genuine technological breakthrough in weapons, delivery systems, or defense capabilities which might drastically shift the

---

[1] Hans J. Morgenthau, *Politics Among Nations* (New York: Alfred A. Knopf, Inc., 1948), Chap. 20.

[2] See Raymond Aron, *On War* (New York: Doubleday Anchor Books, 1959), pp. 70–71.

present uneasy balance[3] and make war once again appear to be a rational policy choice. Also just as the monopoly of nuclear weapons soon gave way to duopoly and as America and Russia have since then been joined by Great Britain, France, and China as nuclear powers, other states may well be on the threshold of joining the nuclear club, despite the efforts of statesmen to prevent it. Local, limited conflicts may grow in area and scope (such as in the Middle East) until they embrace powers with nuclear capabilities. One can easily imagine that nuclear weapons may not be used at the outset of a war, but it stretches the imagination to assume that a country would prefer losing a war or its very existence to using its full arsenal.

There is, then, no assurance that the use of war as a method of achieving goals in international relations will soon end. But one is left with the inescapable judgement that wars, whatever utility they may have possessed in the past, normally do not function well in the present era. The task of statesmanship[4] and of informed citizenship therefore seems to be that of creating alternatives to an age-old method of international relations which has now become counter-productive.

[3] Albert Wohlstetter, "The Delicate Balance of Terror," *Foreign Affairs* (1959), 37, pp. 211–34.
[4] See especially Arnold Wolfers, "Statesmanship and Moral Choice," *World Politics* (1949), 1, pp. 175–95, reprinted in the first and second editions of this book.

1. Uses of Violence

HAROLD L. NIEBURG

Harold L. Nieburg is Professor of Political Science at the University of Wisconsin-Milwaukee. He was formerly associated with Illinois State University, the University of Chicago, and Case Western Reserve University. His publications include NUCLEAR SECRECY AND FOREIGN POLICY, IN THE NAME OF SCIENCE, *and* VIOLENCE, LAW AND THE SOCIAL PROCESS.

· · ·

The argument of this essay it that the risk of violence is necessary and useful in preserving national societies.[1] This specifically includes sporadic, uncontrolled, "irrational" violence in all of its forms. It is true that domestic violence, no less than international violence, may become a self-generating vortex which destroys all values, inducing anarchy and chaos. However, efforts to prevent this by extreme measures only succeed in making totalitarian societies more liable to such collapses. Democracies assume the risk of such catastrophes, thereby making them less likely.

Violence has two inextricable aspects: its actual use (political demonstrations, self-immolation, suicide, crimes of passion, property, politics, etc.), or its potential use. The actual demonstration of violence must occur from time to time in order to give credibility to its threatened outbreak, thereby gaining efficacy for the threat as an instrument of social and political change. The two aspects, demonstration and threat, cannot be separated. The two merge imperceptibly into each other. If the capability of actual demonstration is not present, the threat will have little effect in inducing a willingness to bargain politically. In fact, such a threat may provoke "preemptive" counter-violence.

The "rational" goal of the threat of violence is an accommodation of interests, not the provocation of actual violence. Similarly, the "rational" goal of actual violence is demonstration of the will and capability of action, establishing a measure of the credibility of future threats, not the exhaustion of that capability in unlimited conflict.[2]

Journal of Conflict Resolution, 7 (1963), 43–54. Reprinted by permission.

[1] The role of violence in political organizations is vividly demonstrated by a recent event among a group of elks at the Bronx Zoo. A 4-year-old bull elk, Teddy, had his magnificent antlers sawed off to one-inch stumps. He had reigned as undisputed boss of a herd of six cow elks and one younger bull. But the breeding season was on, and he was becoming "a bit of a martinet." With his antlers off, he gets a new perspective on his authority and becomes a tolerable leader. A younger bull may try to take over as paramount leader of the herd, but if he does, the veterinarian will saw off his antlers, too (*New York Times,* September 26, 1962, p. 35).

[2] By "rational" here is meant: having a conceptual link to a given end, a logical or symbolic means-ends relationship which can be demonstrated to others or, if not demonstrable, is accepted by others (but not necessarily all) as proven.

...Within each system there are conflicting values among members which are constantly adjusted as roles change, maintaining a state of tension. Political systems have an objective, dynamic interrelationship, structured into the hierarchy of macrosystems. Within the latter, each subsystem has a role much like that of the individual in smaller constellations. Each subsystem may be part of several macrosystems, imposing conflicting demands upon it. Consequently, within macrosystems there is maintained a state of constant tension between subsystems. This objective tension, existing on all levels, is seen subjectively in terms both of competition and consensus, depending on the comparative degrees of collaboration and conflict which exist in the situation at any given moment.

Any two or more systems may appear as hostile at any given time. From the viewpoint of the participants, the conceptual framework of competition overrides underlying consensus. Decisions and policies of the rival elites are rationalized in terms of hostility to the values and leaders of the other system. However, if events conspire to place a higher value on a hostile tactical situation involving the macrosystem of which both smaller systems are a part, their relationship will be transformed quickly to a conceptual framework of consensus which will override and mute the unresolved competitive elements. Such an event may also bring about internal leadership changes in both subsystems, if the elites were too firmly wedded to the requirements of the now-irrelevant competitive situation.

Objectively, tension is always present among all roles and systems; that is, there are always present both elements of competition and consensus. The subjective emphasis which each pole of the continuum receives depends on the value which the tactical situation places on acts and attitudes of hostility or collaboration among the various systems at various times. Degrees of hostility and collaboration are structured by a hierarchy of values within and among all roles and systems all the time. All are involved in a dynamic process.

Conflict, in functional terms, is the means of discovering consensus, of creating agreed terms of collaboration. Because of the individual's personal role in the macrosystem of nation-states, he tends to view the Cold War in terms of competition. Similarly, because of his role in the subsystem of the family, he tends to view family problems in terms of consensus (until the system breaks down completely).

. . .

The commitment required by a credible threat of violence, able to induce peaceable accommodation, is one of a very high order. Not all individuals nor all political systems are capable of credibily using the threat of violence in order to induce greater deference by others to their values. There is general recognition by all of the kinds of values which can and cannot elicit the high degree of commitment required to make the threat credible.

By and large, all violence has a rational aspect, for somebody, if not for the perpetrator. All acts of violence can be put to rational use, whether they are directed against others or against oneself. This is true because those who wish to apply the threat of violence in order to achieve a social or political bargaining posture are reluctant to pay the costs or take the uncertain risks of an actual demonstration of that threat. Many incoherent acts of violence are exploited by insurgent elites as a means of improving their roles or imposing a larger part of their values upon a greater political system. The greater the logical connection between the act and the ends sought, the easier it is to assimilate the act and claim it as a demonstration of the threat available to the insurgents if their demands are ignored. The rapidity with which insurgent movements create martyrs, often from the demise of hapless bystanders, and the reluctance of governments to give martyrs to the opposition, are evidence of this.

. . .

THE INTERNATIONAL PROCESS

Many people blithely argue for law as a substitute for violence, as though there were a choice between the two. They call for international law and world government to eliminate war. This point of view reveals a blissful ignorance of the functions of violence in domestic legal systems. A viable system based on law protects the conditions of group action. Law always rests on violence. The threat of violence and the fear of the breakdown of law and order act to moderate demands and positions, thereby setting into peaceful motion the informal political processes of negotiation, concession, compromise, and agreement. Although there is no centralized police power in the international forum, the processes of mediation and negotiation operate in much the same way. The credible threat of violence in the hands of the nations has a similarly stabilizing effect, providing statesmen are attentive to maintaining their national capability for demonstrating violence, and providing their ambitions are commensurate to the bargaining position which their armaments achieve. More comprehensive legal codes and a world government may

not improve the stability of the world community in any case, since the possibility of civil conflict exists in all political systems. Civil wars are frequently bloodier and more unforgiving than wars between sovereign nations.

In international politics, the threat of violence tends to create stability and maintain peace. Here the threat is more directly responsive to policy controls. The nation-state has greater continuity than the informal political systems that coalesce and dissolve in the course of domestic social change. The threat of violence can be asserted much more deliberately and can be demonstrated under full control, as in "good will" navy visits, army maneuvers near a sensitive border, partial mobilization, etc. Because of the greater continuity of these macrosystems, the national leaders must strive to maintain the prestige of a nation's might and will. If the reputation of a nation's military power is allowed to tarnish, future bargaining power will be weakened. It may be forced to reestablish that prestige by invoking a test of arms, as a means of inducing greater respect for its position from other nations. All strong nations are anxious to demonstrate their military power peaceably in order that their prestige will afford them the bargaining power they deserve without a test of arms.

Because the threat of violence is a conscious instrument of national policy, it generally lacks the random character which violence has domestically. This means that if the armaments of nations fall out of balance, if the prestige of nations is no longer commensurate with their ambitions, if the will to take the risks of limited military conflicts is lacking, if domestic political considerations distort the national response to external threat, then the time becomes ripe for the outbreak of violence, escalating out of control.

In general, the dangers of escalating international conflict induce greater, not lesser, restraint on the part of national leaders in their relations with each other. Attempts to achieve infinite security for the nation are as self-defeating as such attempts are for domestic regimes.

The functioning of consensus and competition between nations is not fundamentally different from that of domestic politics. The most striking difference is that in domestic politics the level of centralized violence available to the state creates a high threshold of stability against the threats brought to bear within the system by private groups. In the international forum, the closest approximation to such a threshold is the decentralized forces available to the Great Powers. A power interested in modifying the status quo must raise the level of its threat of violence, in order to induce other powers to choose between concessions to its demands or the costs and risks of an arms race. To the extent that the status quo powers are capable and willing to pay the costs and take the risks, their own levels can be raised, depriving the challenger of any political advantages from his investment. When all of the great powers are attentive to the equations of potential violence, no nation can hope to gain conclusive political advantages from an arms race. This situation makes possible international agreements for stabilizing arms and bringing about political settlements.

Diplomatic ceremonials, like the ceremonials of personal relations which we call "manners," serve to minimize the dangers of provocation and threat in the day-to-day relations between nations. Conversely, manners tend to minimize the dangers of provocation and threat in relations between people.

. . .

2. The Uselessness of Certain Kinds of Force

RUSSELL BAKER

Russell Baker is perhaps the country's outstanding satirist. His column is syndicated in many papers throughout the United States.

A tiger who lived in a China shop read in a detective story magazine one

"The Tiger Who Lifted Weights," The New York Times News Service, April 1969. Colorado Springs Free Press, April 23, 1969. Reprinted by permission.

day that he could add six inches to his biceps and double his paw strength in eight weeks by working out regularly with barbells.

"That's what I need to keep mice from kicking sand in my face when I go to the beach with my tigress," the tiger said, and put his check in the mail.

When the barbells arrived, the tiger began a daily routine of weight-lifting and, within four weeks, was able to press 600 pounds while standing over a showcase of Dresden figurines.

"I don't get it," said the bear, who was one of the tiger's business partners, as he watched the tiger straining one day to raise 500 pounds with one paw.

"Use your head," grunted the tiger. "We've got some pretty acquisitive partners mixed up with us in this business. Just the other day I heard the gander telling the tortoise that they were entitled to a bigger share of the profits."

"Oh yeah?" growled the bear. "Just let them try to get it." And he went away for his punching bag, and he gave up smoking and his daily vodka martinis.

The mole, who lived in the cellar, came upstairs one day after the bear had gone six good rounds against the punching bag. "How do you guys expect me to sleep with all that China rattling up here?" he demanded.

"You want sleep?" sneered the bear. "I'll give you sleep." And striking the mole just below the rib cage with a beautiful left hook, he knocked him out for a count of 30, breaking a Wedgwood teapot with his follow-through.

The tiger had always pitied the mole and did not like seeing him bullied. He particularly disliked seeing a teapot broken. "The bear is getting too big for his bearskin," he told himself that night while writing away for a course of karate lessons.

He was correct about the bear who had gained 350 pounds, all of it muscle, under his new regimen. When a customer came in for some China, the bear's great weight made the entire

shop tremble as he moved about displaying soup bowls.

The tiger's muscle-building program had nearly doubled his weight. When he and the bear worked together in the shop floor boards creaked alarmingly and gravy boats rocked perilously at their moorings.

One day they accidentally collided at the storeroom door and smashed a 16-place Spode dinner setting. "This place isn't big enough for both of us," said the bear.

"That's right," said the tiger, "and I'm not leaving."

"Excuse me," said the gander, "but I hope you'll think of the consequences to the rest of us before you two start punching. We have a small interest in the shop, too."

The tiger and the bear saw the justice of the gander's argument, but they didn't like it much. "All right," said tiger, "but tell that muscle-bound bear to stay out of my way."

That night, as the tiger was breaking bricks with his bare paws overhead, the small animals held an emergency meeting in the cellar.

"There's only one way to deal with those louts," said the hare, and he outlined his plan. The next day the hare went to the tiger and then to the bear. He told them that all the other animals had decided to surrender their rights in the business in return for the right to continue living in the shop.

This delighted the tiger. "The world belongs to the strong," he observed. "It shows that preparedness pays off," the bear confided that night to the tiger over the first vodka martini he had had in months. The tiger joined him.

As the two stumbled off to bed, a duck waddled out of a dark doorway and bit the bear on the calf. "I'll murder the bum!" roared the bear. "Easy," cautioned the tiger. "It's our shop now.

We don't want to do anything to wreck it." And the bear saw the wisdom of this.

Next day while the tiger was counting the receipts, the tortoise waddled up and bit a small piece of fur from his paw. "Don't strike at him," screamed the bear. "You'll destroy the whole shop!"

"You're right," groaned the tiger. "Forbearance is the first obligation of great power." Whereupon a rooster lit on the cash register, filched the day's recepts and squawked away to buy wine for the rest of the animals in the back room.

"I could have creamed him," muttered the bear.

"So could I," said the tiger. "But it would have wiped us out." As sounds of revelry came from the back room that night, the bear, who was hungry and frustrated, went to punch his bag and found that the moths had chewed large holes in it.

While the tiger debated whether it would be too dangerous to the shop to smash a few bricks with his paw, some mice came by and kicked sand in his face.

Moral: He who spends his money on barbells gives sport to the mouse.

3. International Structure, National Force, and the Balance of Power

KENNETH N. WALTZ

Kenneth N. Waltz is Professor of Politics at Brandeis University. He is the author of MAN, THE STATE, AND WAR *and* FOREIGN POLICY AND DEMOCRATIC POLITICS.

. . .

The reduction in the number of major states calls for a shift in con-

From IMAGE AND REALITY IN INTERNATIONAL RELATIONS, *ed. by John C. Farrell and Asa P. Smith (New York: Columbia University Press, 1968). Reprinted by permission of the* JOURNAL OF INTERNATIONAL AFFAIRS, *where this essay first appeared.*

ceptual perspective. Internal effort has replaced external realignment as a means of maintaining an approximate balance of power. But the operation of a balance of power, as previously noted, has entailed the occasional use of national force as a means of international control and adjustment. Great-power status was traditionally conferred on states that could use force most handily. Is the use of force in a nuclear world so severely inhibited that balance-of-power analysis has lost most if not all of its meaning?

Four reasons are usually given in support of an affirmative answer. First, because the nuclear might of one superpower balances that of the other, their effective power is reduced to zero. Their best and most distinctive forces, the nuclear ones, are least usable. In the widely echoed words of John Herz, absolute power equals absolute impotence.[1] Second, the fear of escalation strongly inhibits even the use of conventional forces, especially by the United States or the Soviet Union. Nuclear powers must fear escalation more than other states do, for in any war that rose to the nuclear level they would be primary targets. They may, of course, still choose to commit their armies to battle, but the risks of doing so, as they themselves must realize, are higher than in the past. Third, in the nuclear age enormous military power no longer ensures effective control. The Soviet Union has not been able to control her Asian and European satellites. The United States has found it difficult to use military force for constructive purposes even against weak opponents in Southeast Asia. Political rewards have not been proportionate to the strength of the states that are militarily most powerful. Finally, the weak states of the world, having become politically aware and active, have turned world opinion into a serious restraint upon the use of force, whether in nuclear or conventional form. These four factors, it is argued, work singly and in combination to make the use of force more costly and in general to depreciate its value.

Never have great powers disposed of larger national products, and seldom in peacetime have they spent higher percentages of them on their military forces. The money so lavishly expended purchases more explosive power and more varied ways of delivering it than ever before in history. In terms of world distribution, seldom has military force been more narrowly concentrated. If military force is less useful today, the irony of history will have yet another vivid illustration. Has force indeed so depreciated as to warp and seriously weaken the effects of power in international relations? The above arguments make it seem so; they need to be re-examined. The following analysis of the use of force deals with all four arguments, though not by examining them one by one and in the order in which they are stated.

E. H. Carr long ago indentified the error of beliving "in the efficacy of an international public opinion," and he illustrated and explained the fallacy at length.[2] To think of world opinion as a restraint upon the military actions of states, one must believe that the strong states of the world—or for that matter the weak ones—would have used more military force and used it more often had they not anticipated their condemnation. Unless in a given instance world opinion can be defined, its source identified, and the mode of its operation discerned, such a view is not plausible. To believe in the efficacy of world opinion is to endow a nonexistent agent and an indefinable force with effective restraining power. Not world opinion but national views,

---

[1] John Herz, *International Politics in the Atomic Age* (New York: Columbia University Press, 1959), pp. 22, 169.

[2] Edward Hallett Carr, *The Twenty Years' Crisis, 1919–1939*, 2nd ed. (New York: Harper & Row, 1964), p. 140.

shaped into policies and implemented by governments, have accounted for past events in international relations. Changes that would now permit world opinion, whatever that might be, to restrict national policies would have to lie not in the operation of opinion itself but in other changes that have occurred in the world. With "world opinion," as with Adam Smith's "invisible hand," one must ask: What is the reality that the metaphor stands for? It may be that statesmen pay their respects to world opinion because they are already restrained by other considerations.

Are such considerations found, perhaps, in changes that have taken place in the nature and distribution of force itself? If the costs of using military force have lessened its value, then obeisance paid to world opinion is merely a cloak for frustration and a hypocritical show of politeness. That the use of force is unusually costly, however, is a conclusion that rests on a number of errors. One that is commonly committed is to extend to all military force the conclusion that nuclear force is unusable. After listing the changes effected by nuclear weapons, one author, for example, concludes that these changes tend to restrict "the usability and hence the political utility of national military power in various ways."[3] This may represent merely a slip of the pen; if so, it is a telling one. A clearer and more interesting form of the error is found in the argument that the two superpowers, each stalemated by the other's nuclear force, are for important political purposes effectively reduced to the power of middle-range states. The effective equality of states apparently emerges from the very condition of their gross inequality. We read, for example, that "the very change in the nature of the mobilizable potential has made its actual use in emergencies by its unhappy owners quite difficult and self-defeating. As a result, nations endowed with infinitely less can behave in a whole range of issues as if the difference in power did not matter." The conclusion is driven home —or, rather, error is compounded—by the argument that the United States thinks in "cataclysmic terms," lives in dread of all-out war, and bases its military calculations on the forces needed for the ultimate but unlikely crisis rather than on what might be needed in the less spectacular cases that are in fact more likely to occur.[4]

Absolute power equals absolute impotence, at least at the highest levels of force represented by the American and Soviet nuclear armories. At lesser levels of violence many states can compete as though they were substantially equal. The best weapons of the United States and the Soviet Union are useless, and the distinctive advantage of those two states is thus negated. But what about American or Soviet nuclear weapons used against minor nuclear states or against those who are entirely without nuclear weapons? Here again, it is claimed, the "best" weapons of the most powerful states turns out to be the least usable. The nation that is equipped to "retaliate massively" is not likely to find the occasion to use its capability. If amputation of an arm were the only remedy available for an infected finger, one would be tempted to hope for the best and leave the ailment untreated. The state that can move effectively only by committing the full power of its military arsenal is likely to forget the threats it has made

[3] Knorr, *On the Uses of Military Power,* p. 87.

[4] Hoffmann, "Europe's Identity Crisis," pp. 1279, 1287–88.

and acquiesce in a situation formerly described as intolerable. Instruments that cannot be used to deal with small cases—those that are moderately dangerous and damaging—remain idle until the big case arises. But then the use of major force to defend a vital interest would run the grave risk of retaliation. Under such circumstances, the powerful are frustrated by their very strength; and although the weak do not thereby become strong, they are, it is said, nevertheless able to behave as though they were.

Such arguments are often made and have to be taken seriously. In an obvious sense, part of the contention is valid. When great powers are in a stalemate, lesser states acquire an increased freedom of movement. That this phenomenon is now noticeable tells us nothing new about the strength of the weak or the weakness of the strong. Weak states have often found opportunities for maneuver in the interstices of a balance of power. This is, however, only part of the story. To maintain both the balance and its by-product requires the continuing efforts of America and Russia. Their instincts for self-preservation call forth such efforts: the objective of both states must be to perpetuate an international stalemate as a minimum basis for the security of each of them—even if this should mean that the two big states do the work while the small ones have the fun. The margins within which the relative strengths of America and Russia may vary without destroying the stalemate are made wide by the existence of second-strike retaliatory forces, but permissible variation is not without limit. In the years of the supposed missile gap in America's disfavor, Khrushchev became unpleasantly frisky, especially over Berlin and Cuba. The usefulness of maintaining American nuclear strength was demonstrated by the unfortunate consequences of its apparent diminution.

Strategic nuclear weapons deter strategic nuclear weapons (though they may also do more than that). Where each state must tend to its own security as best it can, the means adopted by one state must be geared to the efforts of others. The cost of the American nuclear establishment, maintained in peaceful readiness, is functionally comparable to the costs incurred by a government in order to maintain domestic order and provide internal security. Such expenditure is not productive in the sense that spending to build roads is, but it is not unproductive either. Its utility is obvious, and should anyone successfully argue otherwise, the consequences of accepting his argument would quickly demonstrate its falsity. Force is least visible where power is most fully and most adequately present.[5] The better ordered a society and the more competent and respected its government, the less force its policemen are required to employ. Less shooting occurs in present-day Sandusky than did on the western frontier. Similarly in international relations, states supreme in their power have to use force less often. "Non-recourse to force"—as both Eisenhower and Khrushchev seem to have realized—is the doctrine of powerful states. Powerful states need to use force less often than their weaker neighbors because the strong can more often protect their interests or work their wills in other ways—by persuasion and cajolery, by economic bargaining and bribery, by the extension of aid, or finally by posing deterrent threats. Since states with large nuclear armaries do not actually "use" them, force

5 Cf. Carr, *The Twenty Years' Crisis,* pp. 103, 129–32.

is said to be discounted. Such reasoning is fallacious. Possession of power should not be identified with the use of force, and the usefulness of force should not be confused with its usability. To introduce such confusions into the analysis of power is comparable to saying that the police force that seldom if ever employs violence is weak or that a police force is strong only when policemen are swinging their clubs. To vary the image, it is comparable to saying that a man with large assets is not rich if he spends little money or that a man is rich only if he spends a lot of it.

But the argument, which we should not lose sight of, is that just as the miser's money may grossly depreciate in value over the years, so the great powers' military strength has lost much of its usability. If military force is like currency that cannot be spent or money that has lost much of its worth, then is not forbearance in its use merely a way of disguising its depreciated value? Conrad von Hötzendorf, Austrian Chief of Staff prior to the First World War, looked upon military power as though it were a capital sum, useless unless invested. In his view, the investment of military force was ultimately its commitment to battle.[6] It may be permissible to reason in this way, but it makes the

result of the reasoning a foregone conclusion. As Robert W. Tucker has noted, those who argue that force has lost its utility do so "in terms of its virtually uncontrolled use." But, he adds, "alter the assumption on which the argument proceeds—consider the functions served by military power so long as it is not overtly employed or employed only with restraint—and precisely the opposite conclusion may be drawn.[7]

In the reasoning of Conrad, military force is most useful at the moment of its employment in war. Depending on a country's situation, it may make much better sense to say that military force is most useful when it deters an attack, that is, when it need not be used in battle at all. When the strongest state militarily is also a status-quo power, non-use of force is a sign of its strength. Force is most useful, or best serves the interests of such a state, when it need not be used in the actual conduct of warfare. Again, the reasoning is old-fashioned. Throughout a century that ended in 1914, the British navy was powerful enough to scare off all comers, while Britain carried out occasional imperial ventures in odd parts of the world. Only as Britain's power weakened did her military forces have to be used to fight a full-scale war. By being used, her military power had surely become less useful.

Force is cheap, especially for a status-quo power, if its very existence works against its use. What does it mean then to say that the cost of using force has increased while its utility has lessened? It is highly important, indeed

---

[6] "The sums spent for the war power is money wasted," he maintained, "if the war power remains unused for obtaining political advantages. In some cases the mere threat will suffice and the war power thus becomes useful, but others can be obtained only through the warlike use of the war power itself, that is, by war undertaken in time; if this moment is missed, the capital is lost. In this sense, war becomes a great financial enterprise of the State." Quoted in Alfred Vagts, *Defense and Diplomacy: The Soldier and the Conduct of Foreign Relations* (New York: King's Crown Press, 1956), p. 361.

[7] Robert W. Tucker, "Peace and War," *World Politics,* Vol. XVII (Jan. 1965), 324 fn. For a comprehensive and profound examination of the use of force internationally, see Robert Osgood and Robert Tucker, *Force, Order, and Justice* (Baltimore: The Johns Hopkins Press, 1967).

useful, to think in "cataclysmic terms," to live in dread of all-out war, and to base military calculations on the forces needed for the ultimate but unlikely crisis. That the United States does so, and that the Soviet Union apparently does too, makes the cataclysm less likely to occur. But not only that. Nuclear weapons .deter nuclear weapons; they also serve as a means of limiting escalation. The temptation of one country to employ larger and larger amounts of force is lessened if its opponent has the ability to raise the ante. Conventional force may be used more hesitantly than it would be in the absence of nuclear weapons because it cannot be assumed that escalation will be perfectly regulated. But force can be used with less hesitation by those states able to parry, to thrust, and to threaten at varied levels of military endeavor.

Where power is seen to be balanced, whether or not the balance is nuclear, it may seem that the resultant of opposing forces is zero. But this is misleading. The vectors of national force do not meet at a point, if only because the power of a state does not resolve into a single vector. Military force is divisible, especially for the state that can afford a lot of it. In a nuclear world, contrary to some assertions, the dialectic of inequality does not produce the effective equality of strong and weak states. Lesser states that decide to establish a nuclear arsenal by slighting their conventional forces render themselves unable to meet any threat to themselves other than the ultimate one (and that doubtfully). By way of contrast, the military doctrine of the United States, to which the organization of her forces corresponds, is one of flexible response. Great powers are strong not simply because they have nuclear weapons but also because their immense resources enable them to gen-erate and maintain power of all types, military and other, at different technological levels.

Just as the state that refrains from applying force is said to betray its weakness, so the state that has trouble in exercising control is said to display the defectiveness of its power. In such a conclusion, the elementary error of identifying power with control is evident. Absence of control or failure to press hard to achieve it may indicate either that the would-be controller noticed that, try as he might, he would have insufficient force or inappropriate types of force at his command; or it may indicate that he chose to make less than a maximum effort because imposition of control was not regarded as very important. One student of international relations has remarked that "though the weapons of mass destruction grow more and more ferociously efficient, the revolutionary guerrilla armed with nothing more advanced than an old rifle and a nineteenth-century political doctrine has proved the most effective means yet devised for altering the world power-balance."[8] But the revolutionary guerrilla wins civil wars, not international ones, and no civil war can change the balance of power in the world unless it takes place in the United States or the Soviet Union. Enough of them have occurred since the Second World War to make the truth of this statement clear without need for further analysis. Even in China, the most populous of states, a civil war that led to a change of allegiance in the cold war did not seriously tilt the world balance.

Two states that enjoy wide margins of power over other states need worry little about changes that occur among the latter. Failure to act may

[8] Coral Bell, "Non-Alignment and the Power Balance," Survival, Vol. V (Nov.–Dec. 1963), p. 255.

then not betray the frustrations of impotence; instead it may demonstrate the serenity of power. The United States, having chosen to intervene in Vietnam, has limited the use of its military force. Because no realignment of national power in Vietnam could in itself affect the balance of power between the United States and the Soviet Union—or even noticeably alter the imbalance of power between the United States and China—the United States need not have intervened at all. Whether or not it could have safely "passed" in Southeast Asia, the American government chose not to do so; nor have its costly, long-sustained efforts brought success. If military power can be equated with control, then the United States has indeed demonstrated its weakness. The case is instructive. The People's Republic of China has not moved militarily against any country of Southeast Asia. The United States could successfully counter such a move, one would expect, by opposing military force with military force. What has worried some people and led others to sharpen their statements about the weakness of the powerful is that the United States, hard though it has tried, has been unable to put down insurrection and halt the possible spread of Communist ideology.

Here again old truths need to be brought into focus. As David Hume long ago noted, "force is always on the side of the governed."[9] The governors, being few in number, depend for the exercise of their rule upon the more or less willing assent of their subjects. If

sullen disregard is the response to every command, no government can rule. And if a country, because of internal disorder and lack of coherence, is unable to rule itself, no body of foreigners, whatever the military force at its command, can reasonably hope to do so. If Communism is the threat to Southeast Asia, then military forces are not the right means for countering it. If insurrection is the problem, then it can hardly be hoped that an alien army will be able to pacify a country that is unable to govern itself. Foreign troops, though not irrelevant to such problems, can only be of indirect help. Military force, used internationally, is a means of establishing control over a territory, not of exercising control within it. The threat of a nation to use military force, whether nuclear or conventional, is pre-eminently a means of affecting another state's behavior, of dissuading a state from launching a career of aggression and of meeting the aggression if dissuasion should fail.

Dissuasion or deterrence is easier to accomplish than "compellence," to use an apt term invented by Thomas C. Schelling.[10] Compellence is more difficult to achieve than deterrence, and its contrivance is a more intricate affair. In Vietnam, the United States faces not merely the task of compelling a particular action but of promoting an effective political order. Those who argue from such a case that force has depreciated in value fail in their analyses to apply their own historical and political knowledge. The master builders of imperial rule, such men as Bugeaud, Galliéni, and Lyautey, played both political and military roles. In like fashion, successful counter-revolutionary efforts have been directed by such men

[9] "The soldan of Egypt or the emperor of Rome," he went on to say, "might drive his harmless subjects like brute beasts against their sentiments and inclination. But he must, at least, have led his *mamalukes* or *praetorian bands,* like men, by their opinion." "Of the First Principles of Government," in *Hume's Moral and Political Philosophy,* ed. by Henry D. Aiken (New York: Hafner, 1948), p. 307.

[10] Thomas C. Shelling, *Arms and Influence* (New Haven: Yale University Press, 1966), pp. 70–71.

as Templer and Magsaysay, who combined military resources with political instruments.[11] Military forces, whether domestic or foreign, are insufficient for the task of pacification, the more so if a country is rent by faction and if its people are politically engaged and active. To say that militarily strong states are feeble because they cannot easily bring order to minor states is like saying that a pneumatic hammer is weak because it is not suitable for drilling decayed teeth. It is to confuse the purpose of instruments and to confound the means of external power with the agencies of internal governance. Inability to exercise political control over others does not indicate *military weakness*. Strong states cannot do everything with their military forces, as Napoleon acutely realized; but they are able to do things that militarily weak states cannot do. The People's Republic of China can no more solve the problems of governance in some Latin American country than the United States can in Southeast Asia. But the United States can intervene with great military force in far quarters of the world while wielding an effective deterrent against escalation. Such action exceeds the capabilities of all but the strongest of states.

Differences in strength do matter, though not for every conceivable purpose. To deduce the weakness of the powerful from this qualifying clause is a misleading use of words. One sees in such a case as Vietnam not the *weakness* of great military power in a nuclear world but instead a clear illustration of the *limits* of military force in the world of the present as always.

[11] The point is well made by Samuel P. Huntington, "Patterns of Violence in World Politics," in *Changing Patterns of Military Politics,* ed. by Samuel P. Huntington (New York: The Free Press of Glencoe, 1962), p. 28.

III

Only a sketch, intended to be suggestive, can here be offered of the connections between the present structure of the global balance of power, the relations of states, and the use of force internationally.

Unbalanced power is a danger to weak states. It may also be a danger to strong ones. An imbalance of power, by feeding the ambition of some states to extend their control, may tempt them to dangerously adventurous activity. Safety for all states, one may then conclude, depends upon the maintenance of a balance among them. Ideally, in this view, the rough equality of states gives each of them the ability to fend for itself. Equality may then also be viewed as a morally desirable condition. Each of the states within the arena of balance will have at least a modest ability to maintain its integrity. At the same time, inequality violates one's sense of justice and leads to national resentments that are in many ways troublesome. Because inequality is inherent in the state system, however, it cannot be removed. At the pinnacle of power, only a few states coexist as approximate equals; in relation to them, other states are of lesser moment. The bothersome qualities of this inevitable inequality of states should not cause one to overlook its virtues. In an economy, in a polity, or in the world at large, extreme equality is associated with instability. To draw another domestic analogy: where individualism is extreme, where society is atomistic, and where secondary organizations are lacking, government tends either to break down into anarchy or to become highly centralized and despotic. Under conditions of extreme equality, the prospect of oscillation between those two poles was well described by de Tocqueville;

it was illustrated by Hobbes; and its avoidance was earnestly sought by the authors of the *Federalist Papers*. In a collection of equals, any impulse ripples through the whole society. Lack of secondary groups with some cohesion and continuity of commitment, for example, turns elections into auctions with each party in its promises tempted to bid up the others. The presence of social and economic groups, which inevitably will not all be equal, makes for less volatility in society.

Such durable propositions of political theory are lost sight of in the argument, frequently made, that the larger the number of consequential states the more stable the structure of world politics will be.[12] Carried to its logical conclusion, the argument must mean that perfect stability would prevail in a world in which many states exist, all of them approximate equals in power.

The analysis of the present essay leads to a different conclusion. The inequality of states, though not a guarantee of international stability, at least makes stability possible. Within the structure of world politics, the relations of states will be as variable and complex as the movements and patterns of bits of glass within a kaleidoscope. It is not very interesting to ask whether destabilizing events will occur and disruptive relations will form, because the answer must always be yes. More interesting are such questions as these: What is the likely durability of a given political structure, whether international or domestic? How does it affect the relations of states, or of groups and individuals? How do the relations of constituent units and changes within

them in turn affect the political structure? Within a state, people use more violence than do governments. In the United States in 1965, 9,814 people were murdered, but only seven were executed.[13] Thus one says (with some exaggeration, since fathers still spank their children) that the state enjoys a monopoly of *legitimate* violence. Too much violence among individuals will jeopardize the political structure. In international relations it is difficult to say that any particular use of violence is illegitimate, but some states have the ability to wield more of it. Because they do, they are able both to moderate others' use of violence and to absorb possibly destabilizing changes that emanate from uses of violence that they do not or cannot control. In the spring of 1966, Secretary McNamara remarked that in the preceding eight years there had been "no less than 164 internationally significant outbreaks of violence...."[14] Of course, not only violence is at issue. To put the point in more general terms, strong structures are able to moderate and absorb destabilizing changes; weak structures succumb to them.

No political structure, whether domestic or international, can guarantee stability. The question that one must ask is not whether a given distribution of power is stable but how stable different distributions of power are likely to be. For a number of reasons, the bipolar world of the past two decades has been highly stable.[15] The two leading states

[12] By "structure" I mean the pattern according to which power is distributed; by "stability," the perpetuation of that structure without the occurrence of grossly destructive violence.

[13] U.S. Bureau of the Census, *Statistical Abstract of the Untied States: 1966* (Washington, D.C.: Government Printing Office, 1966), p. 165.

[14] *The New York Times*, May 19, 1966, p. 11.

[15] For further examination of the proposition, see Kenneth N. Waltz, 'The Stability of a Bipolar World," *Daedalus*, Vol. XCIII (Summer 1964), pp. 881–909. On the

have a common interest in stability: they would at least like to maintain their positions. In one respect, bipolarity is expressed as the reciprocal control of the two strongest states by each other out of their mutual antagonism. What is unpredictable in such a two-party competition is whether one party will try to eliminate the other. Nuclear forces of second-strike capacity induce an added caution. Here again force is useful, and its usefulness is reinforced in proportion as its use is forestalled. Fear of major war induce caution all around; the Soviet Union and the United States wield the means of inducing that caution.

The constraints of duopolistic competition press in one direction: duopolists eye each other warily, and each is very sensitive to the gains of the other. Working in the opposite direction, however, is the existence of the immense difference in power between the two superpowers and the states of middle or lesser rank. This condition of inequality makes it unlikely that any shifts in the alignment of states would very much help or hurt either of the two leading powers. If few changes can damage the vital interests of either of them, then both can be moderate in their responses. Not being dependent upon allies, the United States and the Soviet Union are free to design strategies in accord with their interests. Since the power actually and potentially at the disposal of each of them far exceeds that of their closest competitors, they are able to control in some measure the possibly destabilizing acts of third parties or to absorb their effects. The Americans and Russians, for example,

can acquire the means of defending themselves against the nuclear assaults that the Chinese and French may be able to launch by the mid-1970's. Anti-ballistic-missile systems, useful against missiles launched in small number, are themselves anti-proliferation devices. With considerable expectation of success, states with vast economic, scientific, and technological resources can hope to counter the armaments and actions of others and to reduce their destabilizing effects.[16] The extent of the difference in national capabilities makes the bipolar structure resilient. Defection of allies and national shifts of allegiance do not decisively alter the structure. Because they do not, recalcitrant allies may be treated with indifference; they may even be effectively disciplined. Pressure can be applied to moderate the behavior of third states or to check and contain their activities. The Suez venture of Britain and France was stopped by American financial pressure. Chiang Kai-shek has been kept on a leash by denying him the means of invasion. The prospective loss of foreign aid helped to halt warfare between Pakistan and India, as did the Soviet Union's persuasion. In such ways, the wielding of great power can be useful.

The above examples illustrate hierarchical control operating in a way that often goes unnoticed because the means by which control is exercised are not institutionalized. What management there now is in international relations must be provided, singly and occasionally together, by the duopolists at the top. In certain ways, some of them suggested above, the inequality of states in a bipolar world enables the two most powerful states to develop a rich variety

---

possibility of exercising control, see Waltz, "Contention and Management in International Relations," *World Politics,* Vol. XVII (July 1965), pp. 720–44.

[16] On the limitations of a small nuclear force, see Waltz, *Foreign Policy and Democratic Politics* (Boston: Little, Brown, 1967), pp. 145–48.

of controls and to follow flexible strategies in using them.

A good many statements about the obsolescence of force, the instability of international politics, and the disappearance of the bipolar order are made because no distinction has been clearly and consistently drawn between international structure, on the one hand, and the relations of states on the other. For more than two decades, power has been narrowly concentrated; and force has been used, not orgiastically as in the world wars of this century, but in a controlled way and for conscious political purposes. Power may be present when force is not used, but force is also used openly. A catalogue of examples would be both complex and lengthy. It would contain such items, on the American side of the ledger, as the garrisoning of Berlin, its supply by airlift during the blockade, the stationing of troops in Europe, the establishment of bases in Japan and elsewhere, the waging of war in Korea and Vietnam, and the "quarantine" of Cuba. Seldom if ever has force been more variously, more persistently, and more widely applied; and seldom has it been more consciously used as an instrument of national policy. Since the war we have seen, not the cancellation of force by nuclear stalemate, but instead the political organization and pervasion of power; not the end of balance of power owing to a reduction in the number of major states, but instead the formation and perpetuation of a balance *à deux*.

4. Different Responses to Different Types of Violence

KENNETH W. THOMPSON

Prior to assuming his present post as Vice President of the Rockefeller Foundation, Kenneth W. Thompson taught at Northwestern University. He is the author and co-author of numerous works in the field of international politics, including FOREIGN POLICY IN WORLD POLITICS, CONFLICT AND COOPERATION AMONG NATIONS, PRINCIPLES AND PROBLEMS OF INTERNATIONAL POLITICS, CHRISTIAN ETHICS AND DILEMMAS OF FOREIGN POLICY, AMERICAN DIPLOMACY AND EMERGENT PATTERNS, *and* THE MORAL ISSUE IN STATECRAFT.

The major challenge we face in the coming decades is, I would think, the development of an approach or a

"The Challenge of the Future," WORLD-VIEW, *11 (January 1968), pp. 21–24. Reprinted by permission.*

philosophy that would help us to differentiate among types of international and national conflicts and rational American responses. That conflicts will exist, particularly given the sweeping surge of development across the whole southern half of the globe, seems indisputable. That we need intervene or that the U.N. need intervene whenever or wherever the peace is threatened seems a more doubtful question. Secretary of Defense Robert S. McNamara, in his much-quoted Montreal speech in May of 1966, pointed out that over the past eight years there had been 164 outbreaks of violence within nations around the world. Most of these conflicts were civil conflicts; 82 different governments were directly involved. In only 15 of the 164 instances of violence were there military conflicts involving two or more states. In not a single one of the 164 conflicts was there a formal declaration of war. Indeed, since World War II, there has not been a single instance of a formal declaration of war anywhere in the world.

It seems clear that far from having become a safer world in which to live, this planet, over which the threat of potential nuclear warfare hovers, is a world of growing rather than diminishing conflict. In 1958, there were 23 prolonged insurgencies taking place throughout the world, while in 1966 there were 40. Outbreaks of violence, as distinct from insurgencies, also increased from 34 in 1958 to 58 in 1965.

The form and character of violence and insurgency in the world poses a double challenge for the United States. We must think through and develop some consistent and rational view of what role the U.S. and the U.N. can and should play in the face of these conflicts. It must be evident that not every conflict has the same configurations. Conflict anywhere is not necessarily a threat to the peace. Peaceful processes, if they are to be effective, must often be local and long-term. The Charter of the United Nations itself pays tribute to this principle by stating that members should seek to resolve

disputes and differences before bringing an issue to the U.N. The history of the years since World War II highlights the tendency of nations everywhere to throw their burdens on an already over-burdened United Nations or to call upon the United States to assist them even while a fraction of those sending up the call express ambivalence about American involvement.

We have been the recipients of an outpouring of serious thought and worthwhile discussion about the role of the United Nations in maintaining international peace and security. Most, if not all, of this writing has assumed that the task of any international organization would be to preserve the peace in the face of conflicts between two or more nations. However, the serious conflicts which have either engaged the United Nations or have generated discussion of its future role have by and large been civil conflicts. Korea, Berlin, East and West Germany, The Congo, and strife in Lebanon and Vietnam illustrate the emerging pattern.

The U.N., whose architects imagined that most international disputes, as had been the case in the 18th and 19th centuries, would involve sovereign states, has confronted internal conflicts. The involvement of other states has taken the form of participation by sponsors of the status quo or of revolutionary change who, like their forerunners engaged in supporting the Spanish Civil War, have tried to shift the balance of power to one side or the other. The U.N. has faced the problem of being restricted by Article II, Paragraph 6, to non-intervention in domestic affairs. While it has found ways to transcend this limitation, no one has drawn clear and definite lines distinguishing permissible from impermissible intervention.

However, if the problem confronting the United Nations in the elaboration of a doctrine is severe, that of the United States is even more tragic and far reaching. We are spending 30 billion dollars per year intervening to maintain stability within a small Southeast Asian state. Other changes in far more vital and important areas of the world such as China itself did not engage American resources. We have accepted either the maintenance of a tyrannical system or order within particular Eastern European states or have stood by while far-reaching social and political changes took place in Cuba, a few miles from our shores. The best we have been able to do has been to utter a few truisms concerning the Monroe Doctrine, the Inter-American System, and the self-determination of peoples. We seem to follow, like persons caught up in a subway station surge, the onrush of events which force a course of action that at best can be rationalized and at worst seems at odds with any effort at formulating a doctrine of foreign policy. What we do in some areas of the world is often sensible and successful but the grounds on which our choices are made are seldom spelled out or clarified.

The great need, then, or so it seems to me, is for a working theory of foreign policy that would at least formulate the questions in advance: When should our national blood and treasure be committed in the national interest and when should it be withheld? When should we turn to other national or regional or worldwide bodies and when must we, in the national interest, be compelled to carry the burdens ourselves? Is the ancient and historic tradition surrounding the ideas of national security and the national interest still relevant as a guideline to action or does its only purpose arise in rationalizing or justifying action taken in accord

with other purposes? How are we to define our national objectives if having put them in such narrow terms throughout the first three decades of the 20th century we now define them as involving total and indiscriminate preservation of peace and order everywhere in the world? What are the strategic and political differences between the insurgencies which affect our national security and those that do not? What distinguishes the 15 military conflicts out of 164 instances of national violence, and how are both of these types to be differentiated from the seven instances in which American power and military capacity were engaged? Where are the elements of a strategic doctrine which would help us to think through before the fact what policies we should follow in the face of violence and conflict close to our shores or at farflung outposts?

The other aspect of the problem concerns the relationship between the poor nations and conflict. It would be a grievous error to equate lack of economic development or burgeoning population growth with the inevitability of war. We could overnight become the new non-Marxian economic determinists of the 1960's if we embraced this view. Nevertheless, most of the conflicts which have arisen appear to have involved the poorer nations. Secretary of Defense McNamara has pointed out that there are 27 rich nations with a per capita income of $750 a year or more since 1958, and that only one of these 27 nations has suffered a major internal upheaval within its boundaries. However, among the 38 very poor nations with per capita incomes of less than $100 a year, 32 have been victims of significant conflicts. Indeed, nations in this group have had on the average of two major outbreaks of violence per country in the eight-year period. Since

1958, 87% of the very poor nations, 69% of the poor nations and 48% of the middle-income nations have been plagued by internal strife and violence. Secretary McNamara concludes that "there can...be no question but that there is an irrefutable relationship between violence and economic backwardness. And the trend of such violence is up, not down."

IV

The Struggle for
World Order

ARMS CONTROL

AND

DISARMAMENT

Chapter 17

Few states have enough confidence in a powerful neighbor to
rely on that neighbor's self-restraint when it comes to preparation for war. As we have seen in our discussions of force and the military
dimension, even the non-aggressive country has to rely on arms, and establish
the credibility of its willingness to use them if necessary, in order to achieve
either security or a sense of security today. Yet at the same time all but
the most militaristic powers are reluctant to divert over a long period of
time the raw material and industrial and financial resources necessary to
keep abreast of the arms race. Not only does this represent an unproductive
use of capital, but it impedes the advancement of social welfare and the
productive use of national goods and services their people demand. Add
to this the anxiety on the part of statesmen that an escalation of armaments
might well lead to war and it is not difficult to see why so much rhetoric
and energy are spent on attempts to bring arms under control. Indeed many
thoughtful analysts (though not many responsible statesmen) have gone
so far as to argue that the only way to bring an end to international conflict
is to deprive the powers of the means of fighting one another altogether,
that is, to disarm them.

What is readily apparent in any discussion of disarmament and arms
control is that what is needed is some international body to do the controlling.
Thus a military power must not only place its reliance on the capability of
that body to keep other powers' arms under control but must stand ready

to accept that control over its own weaponry. Failing that, the states whose leaders want to limit arms increases must fall back upon bilateral or multilateral agreements among the powers that really matter, that is, those who might in fact threaten one another without such limitations. Even this requires some degree of trust, because no control system is fully foolproof against the state whose decision makers decide to circumvent the system or the agreements they have entered into and to improve their relative weapons capability without outside restraint.

In the history of arms limitation attempts, the story of disarmament has been a dismal one. Prior to the First World War efforts were made as early as 1899 to work out rules and regulations governing the use of weapons in wartime in an endeavor to make warfare more humane, but it was not until after the devastation and costliness of that war made the consequences of an uncontrolled arms race brutally evident that serious international attention was given to the more fundamental problems of control before wars broke out. Actually, however, the discouraging disarmament con-ferences of the interwar years were never designed to bring about *dis*armament at all, in the sense of doing away with any and all means of conducting warfare. The limitation of both military and naval arms, brought about by those conferences seems in retrospect to have been principally an effort to maintain a certain balance between the victorious powers (without too great a strain on national budgets) in a situation where those powers did not really regard one another as very threatening anyway. It was only when the challengers of the entire post-war system which was created at Versailles and Washington embarked upon gigantic arms build-ups and later armed aggression that talk about arms limitation ceased and the arms race was renewed in earnest, only to end after six years of a war which saw the fascist aggressors defeated. Then, as Kurt London has observed, "...it would have been natural, after the exertion of a terrible war, to follow the road to disarmament. The United States, having almost eagerly wrecked its enormous fighting machine, relied on the atomic bomb and the United Nations. Stalin willed it differently, and his initiative stimulated rearmament and the nuclear race."[1]

Fifteen years later President Kennedy, although having no illusions about the chanecs of achieving total peace and understanding with the Communists, nevertheless "did hope that the Soviet leaders, as rational men, might at least agree on the value of moderating the cold war."[2] He was quickly disillusioned, although since that time limited gains have been made, due in all likelihood to a combination of factors in the thinking of Russian leaders. For one thing Communist China has come to be a more threatening challenge to the U.S.S.R. than the United States; partly as a result of this,

[1] Kurt London, *The Permanent Crisis* (London: Blaisdell Publishing Co., 1968), p. 93.

[2] Arthur Schlesinger, Jr., *A Thousand Days* (Boston: Houghton Mifflin Company, 1965), p. 448.

ideology as a basis for foreign policy decisions seems to have been superceded by greater evidence of the kind of rationality which President Kennedy expected but did not find in the early days of his relationships with Soviet leaders. But perhaps the most important determinant of a gradual increase in Russian willingness to enter into agreements limiting nuclear proliferation has been the fear of the possible consequences of these weapons falling into the hands of a growing number of possibly irresponsible leaders among the middle-range powers. In pointing to the "potential havoc of nuclear mini-bombs in the hands of desperate men," Barbara Ward has indicated that:

> It is not alarmist to point to such risks. It is not Cassandra-type gloom to ask whether the sixties may not be just a peaceful lull between the liquidation of Empire and the full onslaught of disillusion in the post-colonial continents. On the contrary, such warnings spring from a sense of how history has dealt with similar crises in the past. For, as Santayana once reminded us: Those who will not learn from history are destined to repeat it.[3]

As is so often true in this age of rapid and widespread communication, propaganda plays an important role in international discussions in this field. In September 1959 the Soviet delegation at the United Nations produced a plan for "general and complete disarmament," which was to take place in three stages. Formal discussion of these proposals took place after the United States countered with its own sweeping plans. In both countries arms expenditures continued at record high levels, while observers of the diplomatic scene were divided on how seriously such fundamental suggestions should be treated. Some argued that the exclusion of Communist China and the refusal of France to cooperate "renders the discussion of general and comprehensive disarmament unpromising,"[4] while others felt that "it will be an eye-opener to them and to us if we take their disarmament proposals seriously and make serious proposals of our own...for we face a common danger."[5] The Russians walked out on the talks in mid-1960.

But whether it makes sense to contemplate anything so breathtaking as general and comprehensive disarmament, there can be no doubt that in the more limited and feasible sphere of arms control, the attention of both civilian analysts and military planners is urgently occupied. As Wesley Posvar has observed, studies about arms policy "reach into the places where decisions are made and into the minds that make them. Nowhere is this influence more apparent and pervasive than in the area of arms control."[6] Whereas disarmament means the elimination or at least the reduction of

[3] Barbara Ward, "Hindsight and Foresight in The World Economy," *Columbia Forum* (Spring 1969), 12, No. 1, 27.

[4] David V. Edwards, *Arms Control in International Politics* (New York: Holt, Rinehart and Winston, Inc., 1969), p. 21.

[5] David Frisch, "Disarmament: Theory or Experiment," *The New York Times Magazine,* July 30, 1961. Cited in the second edition of this book, p. 407.

[6] Wesley W. Posvar, "The New Meaning of Arms Control," *Air Force Magazine,* June, 1963, p. 38. Reprinted in the second edition of this book.

military weapons and forces, arms control encompasses anything which is designed to reduce the probability and destructive results of war (which in the contemporary world may mean nuclear war) and may or may not call for the reduction of armed forces and weapons. Because of the difficulties which exist, both on the intellectual and political planes, in making acceptable qualitative distinctions, the tendency has always been to try to reach agreement on the quantitative level. In the twenties negotiations bogged down over the qualitative differences between offensive and defensive weapons, so accomodation could be reached only on such considerations as the number and tonnage of naval vessels, for example. More recently concepts such as counter-military, counter-population, and counter-civilization measures have complicated discussions, so there has been a tendency to confine the discussions to such quantifiable objectives as "specified ratios for increase."[7] In the selection below J. P. Ruina of M.I.T. shows how both the qualitative and quantitative dimensions of the problem have to be faced in what he terms the "diagnosis and treatment" of the nuclear arms race between the United States and the Soviet Union.

As we have endeavored to demonstrate in many other ways throughout this book, the fundamental questions are not at the level of whether a given weapons system is offensive or defensive, since most systems are both of these (with the possible exception of old-fashioned concrete-imbedded coastal gun emplacements), or even whether arms control should be approached on a qualitative or quantitative level. The real questions are, first, what conditions have to exist before nations are prepared to make serious efforts to control arms, and second, how can those conditions be achieved in a world of limited legal restraints at the international level and of ineffective world organization? Some of these conditions are material, involving the stages of scientific and technological development which the relevant powers have reached or regard themselves capable of reaching. Those powers whose economic and raw material base is insufficient to make successful competition feasible are not only ready but eager to enter into arms limitation agreements with their more powerful neighbors, especially if the neighbors are potential adversaries. Theoretically at least the most super of the superpowers would like to level off its development of more sophisticated and more expensive weapons systems, since beyond a certain point all that is being bought is a greater overkill capability.[8] But in the long run the material conditions which must underlie arms control give way to the political conditions as the real determinants of whether an effective system of arms

[7] Edwards, *op. cit.*, pp. 16–17.

[8] In practice, of course, domestic influences may have just as much to do with arms appropriations as the international environment; on this, see Arthur Herzog, *The War-Peace Establishment* (New York: Harper and Row, 1965), a thoughtful and unconventional treatment of various American schools of thought "from power-thinkers behind massive deterence to the architects of a disarmed utopia, and all the shades of strategy in between."

control is likely to be achieved. These are both domestic and international in nature.

The preamble of the draft treaty on the non-proliferation of nuclear weapons, offered to the world by the United States and the Soviet Union in 1968, contains language (part of which follows) which both defines the problem and expresses the hope that it may be susceptible to solution:

> Declaring their intention to achieve at the earliest possible date the cessation of the nuclear arms race,
>
> Urging the co-operation of all States in the attainment of this objective,
>
> Desiring to further the easing of international tension and the strengthening of trust between States in order to facilitate the cessation of the manufacture of nuclear weapons, the liquidation of all their existing stockpiles, and the elimination from national arsenals of nuclear weapons and the means of their delivery pursuant to a treaty on general and complete disarmament under strict and effective international control have agreed... [to the articles of this treaty].

The key phrase here is "the strengthening of trust between States." This is the most difficult and essential aspect of the struggle to achieve world order, making many observers conclude that without trust no machinery for arms control will succeed but that with trust such elaborate devices are hardly needed.

J. DAVID SINGER

*J. David Singer is Associate Research Political Scientist of the Mental Health
Research Institute at the University of Michigan. His books include* FINANCING
INTERNATIONAL ORGANIZATION: THE UN BUDGET PROCESS *(1961), and* DETERRENCE,
ARMS CONTROL AND DISARMAMENT: TOWARD A SYNTHESIS IN NATIONAL SECURITY
POLICY *(1962).*

In his famous treatise on military affairs, Vegetius advised his emperor: "If you want peace, prepare for war." Theodosius followed this advice, yet within a few years was embroiled in a series of bloody conflicts. This crude doctrine of deterrence failed to preserve the peace in the fourth century, did little better during the fifteen suceeding ones, and has thrice in this century failed to prevent mass bloodshed. Neither the evidence of history nor the application of logic would suggest that the *para bellum* doctrine holds out any peaceful prospects for the present; yet, as Madariaga sadly concluded, "its vitality is incredible." Clinging to the dogma as if in a trance, the Soviet and Western blocs are today engaged in a hypertrophic race for superiority in weapons technique and production: Like the Hobbesian "Kings and Persons of Soveraigne Authority," they find themselves "in the state and posture of gladiators; having their weapons pointing and their eyes fixed on one another; that is, their Forts, Garrisons, and Guns upon the Frontiers of their Kingdomes, and continually Spyes upon their neighbors; which is a posture of War."

I. THE PERILS OF "PARA BELLUM"

The historical and logical inconsistencies implicit in this paradoxical doctrine of national security might be made more explicit by a brief examination of its application to the present bi-polar "balance of terror." No political canon can survive the centuries without some kernel of truth, and that of *para bellum* is no exception. Thus, given the persistence of certain ideal and specified conditions, there might well be some modicum of security in the pursuit of weapons parity or superiority. At the very least, today's military stalemate does make highly unlikely any calculated initiation of large-scale hostilities by either the Soviet Union or the United States. The capacity of each to mount a massive and punishing counterblow, does, in fact, provide a not insignificant deterrent. But any number of technological, diplomatic, or psycholog-

*Journal of Conflict Resolution, II
(1958), 90–105. Reprinted by permission.*

ical developments could, with violent rapidity, reduce this precarious balance to a shambles. Several such possibilities will be alluded to here.

Perhaps the most dramatic illustration of the tenuousness of that balance is revealed in the recent Soviet protest over SAC flights in the Arctic. Despite the patently propagandistic intent, it is difficult completely to ignore the fears expressed by Ambassador Sobolev during the Security Council debate: "But what would happen if American military personnel observing their radar screens are not able in time to determine that a flying meteor is not a guided missile, and that a flight of geese is not a flight of bombers?" Both the Secretary of Defense and the Chairman of the Joint Chiefs of Staff have tried to assure the world that the "failsafe" turnback system is foolproof, but "foolproof" military techniques have been known to fail before; a repetition of the combination of human and mechanical error which laid waste Pearl Harbor could be far more disastrous today. Furthermore, the two hours or more now available for the making of a responsible political decision will, when the Soviet ICBM becomes operational, be reduced to approximately fifteen minutes. And when the Western missile systems are in readiness, there will be no "fail-safe"; once launched, the ballistic missile cannot be recalled. In addition to the dangers inherent in an erroneous reading of the radar scopes or a failure in communication later on, the identical train of events could also be set in motion by the crash of a nuclear bomber or the accidental discharge of its cargo. Before the source of the detonation, if such occurred, could be identified, the retaliatory signal might have been given. Despite considerable precautions and frequent reassurances, these perils cannot be ignored.

A second development which might upset the delicate strategic balance is that of a major technological breakthrough, particularly if it were in the field of defensive weaponry. Were either power or bloc to come up with the means of preventing, or markedly reducing, an effective and devastating counter-blow, it might certainly consider certain types of military adventurism and boldness which are now ruled out by the threat of massive retaliation.

Another possibility which might vitiate the stability of this precarious balance is the rise of "moral disarmament" in either of the camps. Certainty is the very essence of deterrence, and if at any time the willingness of either to make good on its promise of retaliation is called into question, the other might well be tempted to take certain military risks. That such ambiguity already exists in the West is undeniable, and further evidence of loss of "nerve" can only serve to increase the danger. Finally, with the United States administration pressing the Congress for permission to make available the techniques and materials of nuclear weapon construction to its allies, the "fourth-power" problem takes on grisly significance. Nuclear bombs and advanced delivery systems in the hands of certain trigger-happy military leaders is far from a comforting thought.

This represents only a sample of those developments, any one of which could set in train a sequence of events culminating in total war. Faced with such risks, particularly when added to them are a multitude of domestic political pressures, economic limitations, and other policy considerations, those who shape policy in Washington, Moscow, or elsewhere are provided with a powerful incentive to search for other paths to national security. The purpose of this article is to explore several of those alternative paths, especially as they are affected by and might act upon the vicious circle of national armaments and international tensions.

II. THE QUESTION OF CAUSE OR EFFECT

In examining the present pattern of bi-polar hostility in search of a possible avenue of escape from its ominous paradox, one is insistently confronted with the armaments-tension phenomenon. That there is some sort of reciprocity between national military capabilities and international tensions would be difficult to refute, but the problem of illuminating this reciprocal relationship has proved consistently elusive. Positing the desirability of breaking out of this circle, the first question to arise is the old chestnut of "which comes first?"

One view is expressed by a former United States delegate to the United Nations, Benjamin V. Cohen; in addressing a meeting of the International Law Association, he stated that "if we knew of certainty that no nation was in a state of preparedness to undertake a war with any prospect of success... there would be a profound change in the climate of international relationships." In a more extreme form, this view is also expressed by some Quaker spokesmen, who are "convinced" that disarmament "in itself would so change the climate of world opinion that no power on earth could oppose it effectively."

At the opposite extreme is Sir Alfred Zimmern, who concludes that "armaments are not a cause of international tension; they are a symptom. ..." Another Briton, Sir Alexander Cadogan, endorsed this stand when he told a

meeting of the United Nations Commission for Conventional Armaments that "the reduction and regulation of armaments and armed forces depends primarily on the establishment of international confidence; the converse argument is misleading and dangerous."

Rejecting both these polar and mutually exclusive positions would be found most of those who follow closely the pattern of world politics and who are not required to defend any specific governmental policy. For example, in his recent thoughtful study of international organization, I. L. Claude takes the position that "this is a circular problem, in which causes and effects, policies and the instruments of policy, revolve in a cycle of interaction and are blurred into indistinguishability." The circularity view is also put succinctly by Governor Stassen's White House Disarmament Staff in an official publication: "World tensions and world armaments tend to reinforce one another. Each serves as a breeding ground for the other."[1] To summarize, it might safely be held that when students of international politics are in a position to observe dispassionately and are inclined to theorize, they will tend to describe the arms-tension relationship in predominantly reciprocal terms. Despite this, however, when pressed for an opinion, many will indorse either a tensions-first or arms-first approach, frequently to the exclusion of the other; concentrate on one, it is argued, and the other will take care of itself. Each of these broad approaches will be discussed presently, in light of the perceptual setting which is examined in the following section. ...

[1] There is considerable evidence that this has not necessarily been the view held by other, and more influential, presidential advisers.

A. The tensions-first approach

The recent Soviet-American cultural exchange agreement was hailed in its communiqué as "a significant first step in the improvement of mutual understanding between the peoples of the United States and the USSR"; the text then expressed the hope that the agreement would be carried out "in such a way as to contribute substantially to the betterment of relations between the two countries, thereby also contributing to a lessening of international tensions." To many, this sort of program illustrates the most fruitful approach to the arms-tension dilemma; cultural exchanges, educational and literacy programs, increased travel, and expanded trade are all viewed as the way to reduce or eliminate people's "ignorance of each other's ways and lives...through which their differences have all too often broken into war." The reasoning upon which this so-called "UNESCO approach" is based, though not always made explicit, is quite clear: provide the people of the quarreling powers with an opportunity to meet with and learn about one another; this will lead to increased mutual tolerance, understanding, and respect and a consequent reduction in tensions between them. This new set of attitudes will, in turn, influence governmental relations, and, once such inter-governmental tensions have commenced their downward swing, it is contended, the national elites will no longer see any need for the maintenance of expensive and dangerous arsenals. With this realization will come a willingness to disarm or at least a more tractable approach to multilateral disarmament negotiations. Until such a diminution of international tensions has occurred, national armaments will remain as their fearsome manifestation.

Without attempting any thorough diagnosis of the "UNESCO approach," two closely related questions raised by that point of departure will be examined here. First, if the approach is aimed primarily at the *people* of the separate states, what is the connection between popular attitudes and the readiness of policy-makers to engage in bellicose behavior? Second, what are the really effective forces at work in the shaping of those popular attitudes? Regarding the first question, the connection would seem to be unmistakably clear in this "century of total war." Whether it be limited or global, war today requires the fullest mobilization of a nation's resources—military, industrial, governmental, and psychological. Moreover, such mobilization must be undertaken long before the appearance of armed conflict; without preparedness, there can be little deterrence and, without deterrence, no security. The citizenry must therefore, in the name of national security, send its men into uniform, finance the ravenous military machine, adapt to new and dangerous levels of radioactivity, and acquiesce in the inevitable transfer of individual liberties to the agents of the evolving garrison state. That popular attitudes are an essential element of national preparedness would be most difficult to deny.

Less obvious is the answer to the second question; yet it is in the reasoning of the first that we find the answer to the second. If, as has been stated, the public's attitudes are so crucial to national preparedness, can it be reasonably expected that governmental elites will encourage, or even permit, more than token opportunities for the public to develop an image of the potential enemy in other than hostile and menacing terms?

Classically, public opinion is seen

as a resultant of two general sets of factors. One of these is the sociocultural framework or national ideology; vague and amorphous, yet internalized and powerful, the national ideology provides the cognitive and affective setting within which specific attitudes on particular problems are formed. The myths and symbols associated with the ideology need only be tapped and manipulated by those who control the second set of factors: the presentation and interpretation of recent and immediate experiences. By the adept use of the appropriate cues, the elite can readily generate a menacing and hostile image of the potential enemy; given the high concentration of ethnocentrism in most national ideologies, the opinion-maker need merely single out and label the appropriate foreign target. Just as there are techniques for inducing pacifistic attitudes, there are those which are equally effective in creating an atmosphere of tension and bellicosity.

Thus there are three main conditions which come into play. First, there is the dominant preoccupation of the elite with national security. Next there is the urgent necessity for public support of any preparedness program. And, third, there is the relative ease with which this support may be induced. The implications of this threeway interaction are evident. The public's support is contingent upon its perception of a genuine threat to the nation's way of life and political independence; and, since the potential threat may rapidly become an immediate one, some marginal surplus of popular threat-perception must be maintained. Therefore, while tension-reducing programs are exercising some impact upon a selected few intellectuals, artists, farmers, or workers, little permanent headway is made. A visiting group returns from the other country, perhaps with considerably modified views (though this is by no means guaranteed), and disperses among its own citizenry. As the returnee attempts to recount his experiences and demonstrate the peacefulness (or other virtues) of his Russian or American counterpart, he runs headlong into the inevitable reaction from those who have not shared his experience. "Surely," it will be said, "many of those people are indeed peace-loving, but after all, they are not the ones who make policy. Our enemies are the fanatic Communists [or the war-mongering imperialists]. It is their aggressive leaders who drive them to war against us." Within this simplification there is the usual germ of truth. The attitudes of the masses may influence the policy-makers, but the setting within which the people form these attitudes is something less than objective reality. Their simplified and exaggerated definition of the situation is formulated for them to a considerable degree by those responsible for national security.

The logic of the process is inexorable. Each elite perceives the other's military capabilities in terms of aggressive intent. They transmit this perception to their people, and the tension between the governments makes impossible any reduction of tension between the people. As long as each nation retains the capacity to wage aggressive war, mutually perceived threat will continue to flourish, and tensions will be perpetuated and exacerbated, not eliminated. Disarmament based upon a prior elimination of tensions will be a long time in coming.

B. The political-settlement approach

As might be anticipated, not all adherents of the tensions-first school are convinced of the fruitfulness of any direct assault upon the "minds of men." Rather, while accepting the chronological precedence of tensions vis-à-vis armaments, some of them seek to back up a step and look for the indirect source of such tensions. In his *Politics among Nations,* Morgenthau traces them to the "unformulated conflicts of power," while Kennan discovers them as arising out of "substantive political differences and rivalries." Arguing that any direct search for disarmament would be placing the "cart before the horse," such observers stress that the "reduction of armaments must await the political settlement" and that disarmament is "impossible as long as there exist unsolved political issues which the participating nations regard as vital to themselves."

Proceeding from these premises, the political-settlement approach suggests that the first step is therefore to identify the areas of political conflict, define the interests of the protagonists, and then attempt the negotiation of a realistic settlement. As Kennan describes it, this process requires "taking the awkward conflicts of national interest and dealing with them on their merits with a view to finding the solutions least unsettling to the stability of international life." In order to achieve success in this diplomatic pursuit, national decision-makers are advised to *a.* arm themselves with "an attitude of detachment and soberness and a readiness to reserve judgment," *b.* rid themselves of "arrogance or hostility toward other people," and *c.* exercise "the modesty to admit that our [their] own national interest is all that we [they] are really capable of knowing and understanding." So prepared psychologically, the professional diplomatists may then actively engage in "the pursuit of the national interest," an activity which "can never fail to be conducive to a better world."

Of course, in this reasonable pursuit of the national interest, each nation shall rely upon "physical strength, armaments, determination, and solidarity" and meet the other with "unalterable counter-force at every point where they show signs of encroaching upon" the former's conception of a peaceful and stable world. Within the context of this particular approach to world peace, both sides will pursue their respective national interests by the intelligent application of national power; this will eventuate in a series of negotiated political settlements, leading to a relaxation of international tensions; and, from such a tension-reduction, disarmament may legitimately proceed. It is little wonder that Professor Kennan refers to disarmament as a "utopian enthusiasm."

In addition to the inability of the political-settlement approach to get to the heart of the threat-perception problem by ignoring the role of weapons in that perception, it suffers from a further logical contradiction. In their writing and lecturing, Morgenthau and Kennan (with their colleagues of the "realistic" school) assume a sharp and identifiable distinction between political settlements and armament reduction; this distinction is made explicit in their demand that the one must precede the other. Yet this distinction is far from self-evident. In pursuing the national interest, an elite's primary instrument is national power, much of it in the form of military hardware; its other elements might be bases for the stationing of forces and the deployment of the weapons, accessibility to raw materials and industrial products, the strength and viability of the economies and political systems of one's allies, and perhaps the attitudes of the elites and masses in the uncommitted areas. The realist might argue that national power is a vast, complex, and all-inclusive phenomenon and that one cannot separate a single element, such as armaments, and deal with it individually. Yet Kennan has only recently stirred intellectual Europe by proposing a modified disengagement. Apparently the granting of significant politico-strategic concessions differs in some way from scrapping of military hardware. The reduction of bomb and missile stockpiles is "disarmament," but the surrender of the bases from which they might be deployed is merely "political settlement."

C. The armaments-first approach

Believing that no direct attack upon tensions themselves will be successful and that any political settlement which disregards the primary instruments of national power is doomed to failure, some students of international politics have begun to give serious consideration to the problems inherent in the disarm-by-disarming approach. Within this school there is a wide and complex range of alternatives, which, for the sake of clarity in analysis, will be divided into four general categories: (I) unilateral and complete; (II) unilateral but partial; (III) multilateral but partial; and (IV) multilateral and complete.

Alternative I is that espoused by the pacifist movement and is embodied in the proposals of such groups as the Fellowship of Reconciliation and the American Friends Service Committee; their position is based upon two primary and well-articulated assumptions. First, there is no genuine national security in adherence to the doctrine of *para bellum*, and, second, if one major power or bloc were to take the decision for unilateral and total disarmament, "it is entirely probable that other heavily armed powers would follow the lead."[2]

The first assumption has already been discussed here, but it should be emphasized that it is accepted not only by the critics of preparedness but by many of those responsible for the formulation and execution of that very policy. In testimony before the Disarmament Subcommittee, Secretary Dulles himself referred to the "constant menace of destruction," and Commissioner Murray observed that "it is by no means clear that a balance of terror furnishes an assurance that aggression...will not be undertaken.... A balance of terror is too easily upset." Similar reservations have been expressed, not only by those out of power such as Gaitskill and Ollenhauer, but by those currently responsible for their nation's security, such as Eisenhower, Khrushchev, Macmillan, and Nehru; there is today an almost universal recognition of the tenuousness of a peace or a security based upon either parity or superiority in military capability.

As to the second assumption, there is greater room for doubt. While it is true that spokesmen for both blocs continually protest that they arm only for self-defense and imply that their opposites need only demonstrate their peaceful intent by scrapping their weapons and they will immediately follow suit, several obstacles arise. Since it is, by definition, the *other* power which arms for aggression, *they* obviously must disarm first; who will take the first step? Even if one power agrees to begin disarmament unilaterally, how do the

---

[2] The quote is from the testimony of M. Q. Sibley, of the University of Minnesota, an active pacifist. It should be added that the pacifist begins from an even more fundamental premise: violence and the tools of violence are themselves immoral and under no circumstances justifiable. This aspect of pacifism will not be discussed here.

others know that the process has in fact been started? And, in addition, some powers will raise the question of "fulfilment of international obligations" (usually the United Nations Charter is invoked here) without military forces available. In the absence of an effective ethical or legal code assuring high correlation between promise and performance, it is difficult to expect a government elite to commence disarmament on the *hope* that its opposite numbers will do likewise. The responsibility for and preoccupation with the national security assures that such an act of faith will appear far too risky to even the most sanguine policy-maker.

Alternative II, however, is a somewhat different proposition, despite apparent similarities; whereas alternative I calls for disarmament which is both unilateral and complete, down to the last weapon of mass destruction, this requires only a partial reduction and, as a result, has many more adherents. It proceeds from the same first premise as I—the inability of weapons to assure any lasting national security—but it relies to a considerably lesser extent upon the likelihood of one power or bloc following the other in stripping itself of aggressive military capability. Rather, it views such an eventuality as possible, rather than probable, and therefore seeks a modification which might minimize the risks inherent in the unilateral and total scheme.

In fuller terms, the partial unilateral approach takes a less simplistic perspective of the arms-tension dilemma than does alternative I. Recognizing the grip which threat-perception has upon the minds of the decision-makers, the opinion-makers, and the general public, it proceeds to address itself to a relaxation of that grip. It appreciates that protestation and promise will not materially diminish reciprocally perceived

threat and that concrete deed is essential to break the spell. For example, the Committee for a Sane Nuclear Policy, in a series of newspaper advertisements, has proposed that missiles and nuclear weapons be considered separately from other weapons and that all nations immediately suspend their testing and development. While the committee does specifically refer to the need for United Nations monitoring and control, it is nevertheless willing to see the United States take the first step unilaterally and unconditionally, prior to the establishment of any international control system. In this same category are the British Campaign for Nuclear Disarmament and the West German Fight against Atomic Death. Each of these seeks a bilateral or multilateral inspectable agreement prohibiting both the further testing of nuclear weapons and the stationing of delivery systems within their territories; but each is willing to engage in immediate and unconditional unilateral nuclear disarmament in the Western bloc. The assumption of all three movements is that, despite the genuine military risks inherent in such unilateral action, nothing less will suffice to demonstrate Western sincerity and diminish the degree of threat which the Kremlin infers from the NATO military posture.[3]

While it may be reasonable to expect that such deeds *might* reduce the sense of insecurity in the Soviet camp, it does not necessarily follow that diminution of threat-perception will lead the Soviets quickly to reduce their own arsenals. Their policy-makers may hail

---

[3] Obviously, there are other considerations behind these movements, such as fear of nuclear retaliation in a war "not of their making," costs, increasing fallout, and the search for domestic political issues, but these merely supplement, rather than negate, their basic reasoning.

the action as "a welcome step toward the strengthening of peace," yet interpret it as *a*. a reflection of domestic economic, popular, or partisan pressures; *b*. a propaganda device; *c*. a shift in military or technological strategy; or *d*. a ruse to generate complacency. Concern for national security requires that each place the most cynical interpretation upon such a gesture. An excellent example of this array of reactions to a unilateral cutback is found in the American response to Soviet announcements of a troop reduction of 1,200,000 men in May, 1956. A *New York Times* article by Harry Schwartz carried the caption "Domestic Economic Pressure and Desire to Embarrass West Believed Involved," while another by Elie Abel was headed "Russian Arms Cut Laid to Emphasis on Nuclear Power." Any suggestion of a new Soviet peacefulness was quickly scotched.[4] The almost inevitable reaction to such a "tension-reducing" step is found in Prime Minister Eden's letter to Premier Bulganin: "My own feeling is that unilateral reductions of this kind are helpful. I do not think, however, that they are of themselves sufficient if international confidence and security are to develop as we wish." Unless unilateral cuts are followed up quickly on both sides by further reductions, any diminution of threat-perception will be of only the briefest duration. They might make preparedness somewhat less expensive, but they would not make it any less necessary. It might even be argued that if a unilateral reduction on one side were not promptly succeeded by a similar move on the part of the other, the originators might

experience a sharp increase in threat-perception and return to the arms race with renewed vigor; thus the long-range effect of unilateral action might be to heighten, rather than reduce, international tensions.

Turning now to alternatives III and IV, we come across an element which was lacking in I and II—that of reciprocity. In the bilateral and multilateral approach, each side makes its arms reductions contingent upon a similar reduction by the other. Such a reduction might flow from a negotiated treaty, agreement, or convention or possibly (and not to be excluded) a process of "tacit bargaining" proceeding out of a public exchange of conditional statements and communications. Whether such disarmament is partial or total, it is clearly contingent and reciprocal.

Alternative III (multilateral but partial) is that which has been most frequently pursued in the twentieth century. For a variety of reasons, the governments of the major powers might seek to enter into (but not necessarily conclude) negotiations on some measure of weaponry limitation or reduction.[5] Generally, such negotiations would deal with a specific category or type of weapon; during the interwar period of the 1920's and 1930's great importance was attached to the distinction between offensive and defensive armaments; Lord Davies' "principle of differentiation" was based on pre- and post-1914 hardware, and today's dichotomy tends to separate conventional from thermonuclear and chemical devices. In addition,

---

[4] However, after the alleged cut had been negatively interpreted by Dulles, Wilson, and most of the press, Governor Stassen called a special news conference to praise the step as an "initiative we wanted them to take."

[5] Van Dyke asks "why states propose disarmament" and enumerates the following: to save money, to reduce tensions and the danger of war, and to achieve a propaganda advantage. "Of these, only the first is well reasoned and fully compatible with the... objective."

implied is some measure of verifiability, either through reciprocal or third party inspection of territory, bases, or such official records as budgets, which would reflect levels of military preparedness.[6] Such has been the nature of almost all disarmament proposals and negotiations since World War II.

The benchmark against which this type of arms reduction must be measured is the same as that applied to the unilateral alternatives: How effectively does it break into the arms-tension circle? Today there is under consideration a range of possibilities which includes the cessation of nuclear or missile tests, cutbacks in mobilized manpower, or withdrawal of all foreign forces from certain specified areas of central Europe. Let us suppose that one or more of these has been successfully negotiated, that an adequate inspection system has been installed, and that both sides have commenced the required action in accordance with a mutually acceptable schedule.

Such reciprocal and verifiable adherence to the arms-reduction agreement would certainly tend, despite the inevitably cynical interpretations, to produce a more relaxed atmosphere for some measurable period of time. The policy-makers on each side would have rather clear evidence that the other had actually diminished its capacity for armed attack, albeit to a limited extent; each could logically infer that such a diminution of the other's aggressive military capabilities reflected a corresponding diminution of aggressive intent. Furthermore, each would have concrete evidence that, under certain clearly defined conditions, the other would adhere to its

---

[6] Recent French proposals have emphasized the merit of this sort of inspection and verification.

commitments. Though such affirmative interpretations and results are by no means assured, the experience of the early interwar period suggests that they may reasonably be anticipated. Similar limitations and reductions were negotiated in 1922, 1930, 1936, and 1937 (this latter between Germany and Britain), and to some extent they resulted in a temporary reduction of mutually perceived threat and consequently of international tensions.

However, if such a first step were limited to inspected partial reduction (or merely aerial inspection to prevent surprise attack), the impact of the agreement would tend to decrease as time went on and no further reductions in striking capacity were negotiated—or undertaken unilaterally. The agreed and verified decrease in capability would be less and less interpreted as an indicator of peaceful intent and more and more in those cynical terms outlined earlier. Such was the final interpretation placed upon those agreements negotiated in the pre-World War II era, and such is the interpretation already being put upon the several disarmament proposals now being bruited back and forth across the Iron Curtain. Inability or unwillingness to go beyond some limited, partial agreement implies unwillingness to accept total disarmament, and when one side sees the other insisting on the retention of some military capability, it may reasonably assume that such weapons as are retained may be for other than purely defensive purposes. Referring to the reductions and limitations negotiated during the 1920's, Madariaga observed that "so-called disarmament discussions are in fact *armament* discussions, and that whatever the label, the commodity bought and sold in the market is power." Bilateral or multilateral partial disarmament may temporarily mitigate the mutual perception of threat, but to expect any lasting diminution of this ingredient of war is to overlook the transcending preoccupation of the decision-maker with the security of his nation-state.

Finally, we turn to alternative IV (multilateral and total) of the various arms-first approaches. Is there anything in this alternative which permits it to overcome the liabilities inherent in the tension-first, political-settlement, and previous armaments-first approaches? It will be recalled that the crucial element in the latter's inability to break out of the circle was the failure to maintain, over any durable period of time, the temporarily decreased levels of threat-perception. Each time that a halt in the reduction of military capability was reached, the natural tendency was for a sense of national insecurity to reappear, with a commensurate reestablishment of the original levels of mutual threat-perception. The problem, therefore, would seem to be one of *continuing and perpetuating,* once commenced, the gradual diminution of military capability.

This, however, is precisely the core of the problem; two factors arise which might well paralyze this total reduction process even before it had begun. First, even with the establishment of a thorough inspection system, there would always be some possibility of evasion or the development of a new and unexpected weapon or delivery system which would make invalid the assumptions upon which any schedule had been negotiated. Given the pre-existing condition of mutual hostility and fear, each side must and would operate on the premise that such an evasion or development was quite possible, if not probable. Second, some power not covered by the agreement might secure enough military might to become an aggressor-by-proxy for one of the signatories.

While this latter danger might be avoided, in theory at least, by insistence upon universality, the first menace would be much less readily mitigated. Whereas in any partial disarmament scheme the risks of an evasion are significant but not tragic, in a complete and total disarmament program the hazard is almost intolerable. In the former, the nation has not denuded itself completely; its defensive or retaliatory power may be diminished, but it is not eliminated. In any complete disarmament schedule, there comes a time when each government is virtually incapable of self-defense and when, if another has successfully concealed any significant offensive weapons, it may be faced with the choice between surrender and annihilation.

It may safely be said that it is the awareness of this haunting possibility which will, in the final analysis, deter any national elite from agreeing to any total disarmament schedule of the nature described above, no matter how effective the inspection provisions may seem. They may perceive the continuation of the spiraling weapons race as a major gamble, pregnant with dangers, but the other alternative may well be discerned as an invitation to national suicide. Given the choice between the two sets of risks, national policy-makers will probably continue in the path, at least familiar, of their predecessors. It would appear, then, that, whereas unilateral or partial multilateral disarmament could not, if attempted, produce the necessary effect upon threat-perception, complete disarmament implies hazards so great as to preclude even its attempt. Thus, by themselves, none of these approaches would appear to offer a road out of the arms-tension dilemma. Each fails the acid test of national security; each seems incapable of meeting the rigid requirements of those responsible for national self-preservation.

CONCLUSION

Having analyzed the tensions-first, political-settlement, and armaments-first approaches, and finding them separately incapable of escaping the inexorable logic of the arms-tension dilemma, one might conclude that there is, in fact, no escape. Such a conclusion has already been reached by a staggering number of statesmen and students of international affairs, and much of the evidence, historical and logical, would seem to substantiate this gloomy judgment. Yet this writer cannot acquiesce in such a conclusion. Be it tender-minded optimism or ordinary human obstinacy, he is convinced that there exist, within the mind of man, the ingenuity and the persistence to discover a workable solution. Such a conviction leads him, despite the limitations of space and intellect, to hazard a few brief paragraphs suggesting those modifications and combinations of the separate alternatives which might possibly hold the promise of reprieve.

It will be recalled that each approach, considered separately, was ruled out by its inability to cope in any lasting way with the problem of perceived threat to national security. For example, the tensions-first and three of the arms-first approaches failed to provide anything more than a temporary mitigation of threat-perception, while the political-settlement approach, by attempting to ignore weapons entirely at the outset, failed to even initiate a trend in that direction; none seemed to produce a situation out of which might develop an increasingly permanent sense of national security. And the total multi-lateral approach, probably the most promising of the traditional alternatives, appeared to be doomed at the start because of the risks involved later.

Let us suppose, however, that a radical change in the concept of disarmament were introduced. In place of the traditional reliance upon the scrapping of weapons or their conversion to peaceful purposes, let us assume that certain specified national weapons were instead transferred—slowly, cautiously, but regularly and in accordance with a prearranged schedule—to previously designated United Nations depots, where trained members of an international gendarmerie were prepared to receive, account for, maintain, and man such weapons. Further, let us assume that this gendarmerie had been assigned certain clearly defined and limited, yet very real, legal and political responsibilities for their operation and deployment, such responsibilities extending to the protection of the signatory nations as their military capabilities approached inadequacy while those of the United Nations agency were gradually increasing. Might such a procedure not ultimately remove the greatest psycho-strategic barrier to the policy-makers' willingness to engage in any long-range and total arms reduction program? If it is true that the gamble of finding one's nation militarily denuded, while the potential enemy has managed secretly to preserve a part of his striking power, is in fact the single most paralyzing factor in the path of global disarmament, perhaps the substitution of an international agency, armed with the requisite legal, political, and military powers, might serve to eliminate the dread with which that gamble is contemplated.

This brief suggestion probably raises more questions than it answers, but the implication should be clear. No national statesman, Western, Soviet, or neutral, has yet proposed a disarmament plan that has any chance of lasting success, and it is unlikely that any will until the basic, crucial issue is faced squarely. In order to protect the people of a nation which has willingly surrendered its weapons, the United Nations will require a range of powers and a delegation of authority considerably greater than that now intrusted to it.

To deal effectively with the arms-tension dilemma, the Organization will need certain of the powers which have come to be associated with those of a federal government. But that would imply an abrogation of traditional state sovereignty, and, as long as such transfer of sovereignty is perceived as a greater threat than thermonuclear obliteration, disarmament negotiations will remain as before—on top of dead center.

2. The Nuclear Arms Race: Diagnosis and Treatment

J. P. RUINA

J. P. Ruina is Vice-President for Special Laboratories at the Massachusetts Institute of Technology.

If the war in Vietnam ends soon and the vast resources currently allocated to that war are redirected to meet the demanding needs at home, America's strategic policies and goals will undoubtedly be carefully reexamined by the new administration, the new congress, and the press. Today, the United States spends more than $10 billion annually in the strategic area alone, and there is unlikely to be any substantial

BULLETIN OF THE ATOMIC SCIENTISTS, *October 1968, pp. 19–22. Reprinted by permission. The views included in this article were first presented at the April 1968 meeting of the American Academy of Arts and Sciences.*

reduction in this expenditure, regardless of the outcome of the election in November. More than current expenditures are at stake, however. We seek to minimize the risk of nuclear war and, at the same time, maintain our security with minimum expenditures. Both of these goals are dependent on our present nuclear policies.

Since the end of world War II, the United States and the Soviet Union have engaged in discussions on the control of nuclear weapons and strategic forces. From the beginning, we realized that traditional national and military thinking, would, if unaltered, drive us to the brink of total destruction. Despite this fear, the United States remained distrustful of any accommodation with the Soviet Union in this area; we found comfort in "nuclear superiority" while the Soviet Union did not appear to be either serious or reasonable in most of its proposals.

This is not to say that there has been no progress toward arms control. The nuclear test-ban treaty and a treaty which bars weapons of mass destruction in outer space have been worked out, and there is hope that a nonproliferation treaty will soon be signed. However, these agreements are merely "brakes" to the maddening increase in nuclear arms all over the world. None of these steps would, by themselves, affect the increasing size of the nuclear arsenals.

Before discussing the issues facing us today, I would like to outline the current status of American and Soviet nuclear capabilities. Today, the United States' strategic arsenal, exclusive of short-range bombers and tactical and defensive nuclear weapons, includes over 1,000 intercontinental ballistic missiles, over 600 submarine-launched missiles, and about 500 long-range B-52s. Assuming that each missile carries one bomb and each airplane four bombs, there are approximately 3,000 bombs in this American strategic force. If each of these bombs had the destructive capability of the Hiroshima bomb (in actuality, each is at least fifty times as powerful as the Hiroshima bomb) and if only one-third of them reached their target, we would still be able to kill one hundred million people in the Soviet Union.

In the strategic long-range arsenal of the Soviet Union, there are probably some 1,500 bombs, about half the number in our arsenal. The destructive capability of both countries is approximately the same, however, because the Soviet bombs are of greater yield, and

the population of the United States is more concentrated in urban areas.

The current nuclear policy of the United States consists of maintaining the existing number of missiles and airplanes while increasing the technical sophistication of our payloads. To penetrate any Soviet defense system that might be built, the United States has decided to place multiple warheads rather than a single bomb in many of its missile payloads. The total yield of all these bombs taken together is smaller than that of the single bomb they replace, yet several smaller bombs have a greater damage capability than one large one. Within the last few months, we have also decided to deploy a "thin," anti-Chinese ballistic missile defense.

While the United States has not chosen to increase its total number of missiles, the Soviet Union, according to Robert McNamara, is building new missiles at an unprecedented rate; whether the warheads are more sophisticated is not a matter of public knowledge. The Russians are also constructing some kind of ballistic missile defense, the exact nature of which is unclear, and they are developing a number of new space weapons. The one mentioned most frequently is the so-called fractional orbital bombing system (FOBS). FOBS is essentially a depressed trajectory missile that can launch an atomic warhead into a relatively low orbit; a bomb in a low orbit above the earth, reaching the United States via the Southern Hemisphere, would not be detected by the radars of the ballistic missile early warning system until a few minutes before impact. The military usefulness of FOBS can only be for a first strike.

Today, the United States and the Soviet Union are masters of tremendous nuclear forces. How did this powerful capability come into being? One of the forces that has driven the United States up the nuclear ladder is fear of that the other side might be doing. During World War II, the fear that Germany was engaged in the development of an atomic bomb led our government to allocate what was, at that time, a tremendous expenditure—$2 billion—for our own A-bomb program. After the war, when the feasibility of a hydrogen bomb was being debated, it was the overwhelming, and in this case, justified fear that the Russians were already at work in this area that compelled us to embark on a development program even before we knew precisely how to go about it.

The construction of a nuclear bomb is, in itself, a major accomplishment, but a strategic force is not composed of weapons alone. More important, more expensive, and more sophisticated is the design of an effective delivery system—the bombers, missiles, and submarines—that will transport nuclear weapons from one place to another.

In the decade from 1950 to 1960, both the United States and the Soviet Union were involved in the intensive development of bombers and air defense. The United States undertook a long-range bomber program, beginning with the propeller-driven B-36 and extending to the B-47, the first short-range jet bomber; the B-52, a long-range jet; and, finally, the B-70. In the Soviet Union, the intensity of activity was equal to that of the United States. The Soviets, however, placed greater emphasis on defense rather than offense, on short-range rather than long-range bombers. At the end of the decade, each nation had over 1,000 long-range and short-range bombers.

By 1950, there was the realization that, for the first time in its history, the United States was vulnerable to attack by a massive destructive force. The presence of such an awesome threat means that the nature of air defense in the nuclear age must be on an entirely different level from that of World War II. In the days of conventional weapons, a nation that could eliminate 10 per cent of a bombing force each time it came in for a raid was said to have an effective defense system. In the nuclear age, an air-tight defense is essential; even if 90 per cent of the enemy's nuclear bombs are destroyed, the remaining 10 per cent can do untold damage.

The concept of mutual deterrence —the idea that nuclear war is unthinkable—began to take hold within the American government in the course of the 1950s. Yet, while we talked about deterrence, we still insisted on maintaining a superior nuclear force. At that time it was universally accepted that the United States did indeed have some kind of superiority over the Soviets and that our commitment to nuclear supremacy, coupled with our tremendous technical resources and industrial capacity, virtually guaranteed the maintenance of our position of leadership.

In the early 1950s, American intelligence credited the Soviet Union with having a program for the successful development of an intercontinental ballistic missile (ICBM). The use of nuclear weapons with long-range rockets had been considered earlier by this country, but the idea was rejected, principally because we believed that rockets did not possess either the required accuracy or the ability to carry a bomb with enough destructive capacity to make them significant in the military sense. Later developments showed that the guidance system for ICBMs could be made extremely accurate. Then, with the development of the H-bomb, the destructive capability of the ICBM payload was increased enormously. Driven once again by the fear that the Soviets were far ahead in this area, the Department of Defense organized a committee under Von Neumann to assess the feasibility of designing an ICBM capable of carrying a hydrogen bomb. On the basis of the Committee's recommendations, the United States embarked on a crash program to develop long-range ballistic missiles for operational use.

America's confidence in its nuclear superiority was severely shaken when the development of ballistic missiles ushered in a new phase of the nuclear arms race. At its conception the ballistic missile was looked upon as the ultimate weapon. Although missiles had neither the damage capability nor the accuracy possessed by the aircraft of the day, they inspired the overriding fears of surprise attack and no possible defense. With the advent of the ICBM, the time scale for devastation was cut from the ten to twelve hours it takes to fly from the Soviet Union to the United States to only thirty minutes, and nuclear destruction became essentially a push button affair. From the military point of view, the most significant aspect of the ballistic missile was its ability to attack with no warning whatsoever. While the large bomber defense provided us with all kinds of radar warning lines, ballistic missiles made a surprise attack militarily feasible. Finally, the coming of the ballistic missile meant that the recognized nuclear superiority of the United States could no longer be assured; at best the United States and the Soviet Union were starting from the same point, and both would be in approximately the same position in terms of their destructive capability.

Today military technology has brought us to the point where the United States is ready to deploy a complex ballistic missile defense system. We expended over $1 billion on the Nike-Zeus system, yet it was never deployed, principally because it could not cope with a full-scale enemy attack employing decoys and other penetration aids. The Nike-Zeus system simply could not distinguish between "garbage cans" and actual warheads in sufficient time to do anything about it. The scientific community was in agreement on the inadequacies of Nike-Zeus; however, the government felt that, in view of the tremendous importance of an effective ballistic missile defense, it could not afford to give up the development program which in effect let us keep the option of deploying a system. Consequently, the development of Nike-Zeus went on for seven years. It was then declared obsolete and replaced by a technologically superior system—the Nike-X.

As originally developed, the Nike-X provided a two-layer defense. One type of interceptor missile, the Spartan, was designed to intercept a warhead hundreds of miles away. If some missiles eluded the initial intercept or if elaborate decoys forced the radar to delay its discrimination decision, the Nike-X could rely on a second, low-level interceptor called Sprint, the fastest guided missile ever built. The upper tier of the Nike-X could defend all of the United States, while the second tier was essentially a terminal defense system. At present, the United States has decided to deploy only the upper tier of the system as a "thin" defense against China.

A ballistic missile defense (BMD) has never been deployed against the Soviet Union, largely because the cost is too high, the capability too low, and the side effects too significant. The absolute cost of a BMD system is prohibitive in itself, but even more important is the cost of a defense system when compared with the cost of the offense required to nullify its effects. If the United States were to deploy a BMD system, the Soviet Union would undoubtedly increase its missile-building program as a countermove.

The Soviets have always argued, both privately and publicly, that defensive weapons are not dangerous. At the same time, they have continued to detail their accomplishments in the development of antimissile missiles; in July 1962, for instance, Khrushchev boasted of a missile that could hit "a fly in the sky." Much of this was idle bluffing, but, unfortunately, it was effective. If, at that time, an informed observer were asked where the Soviet Union and the United States stood in the development of a BMD, he undoubtedly would have said that the Russians were way ahead.

In the early 1960s, the press reported the existence of an antimissile system around the city of Leningrad. The reports were short-lived, and there is no longer any mention of a Leningrad system. Subsequently, there were reports of a massive deployment of ballistic missiles around other cities including Tallin and Moscow. In addition there were reports that the Russians had conducted nuclear tests in the atmosphere, tests directed toward the deployment of a BMD system. In his last defense-posture statement presented to Congress in January, Secretary McNamara stated that, according to American intelligence, the Tallin system, which apparently has widespread deployment, is not a BMD system. Current assessments still indicate that the Moscow system, whatever combination of radars and interceptors it may employ, apparently is a BMD system. Thus, despite all the Russian boasting and all the American concern, it appears that the Soviets have deployed a defense system only around Moscow.

In the midst of the ever-intensifying race for nuclear supremacy, it is important to examine the conditions that tend toward stability in the nuclear age. We will attain a measure of stability (1) when the United States and the Soviet Union are no longer sensitive about the exact number of nuclear weapons possessed by the other; (2) when neither can miscalculate the outcome of a nuclear war; and (3) when both have absolute confidence in the command and control system of the other side. Recent events have given rise to a concern that, in this nuclear age, the United States (and perhaps the Soviet Union as well) may not always be on top of events. The public record of the crises in the Dominican Republic and the Gulf of Tonkin indicates that the American government may not have been completely aware of what was taking place, and that major decisions were made on the basis of incomplete information. Before any kind of stability can be achieved, both sides must be assured that their command and control systems are working superbly.

There was a short period from 1962–64 when this kind of stability seemed possible. Both the United States and the Soviet Union had a large, invulnerable, and reliable nuclear force. These indestructible forces are, in themselves, a deterrent to nuclear war, and they also have a bearing on the importance of first-strike and second-strike capability. From the military point of view, every first strike is aimed not against populations or industries but against the enemy's weapons. In this case, the weapons were hardened, that is, they had been encased in silos. Unless an aggressor deployed missiles with an accuracy far beyond that of the 1962–64 period, the side attacked first could have launched a counter-attack with a virtually unscathed atomic force. The Defense Department estimated that if we had struck the Soviets first we could have caused 80 million deaths, whereas their counterattack might have claimed 120 million American lives. Thus, the presence of an invulnerable striking force militates against the idea of a first strike.

Unfortunately, the 1962–64 situation no longer exists. Technical developments and political decisions on both sides have made the world of today much more complex. Once one side deploys a BMD system, uncertainty enters into the other side's "assured destruction" capability.

To penetrate what was originally thought to be a heavy Soviet BMD, the United States undertook the development of MIRVs—multiple independent reentry vehicles. Existing launchers are to be retrofitted with missiles carrying several bombs. Each of these bombs is independently guided; that is, each warhead goes to its own target with an accuracy equal to, if not greater than, that of the original warhead. If such a missile were used as a first-strike weapon, it would be as effective as several missiles, thus bringing the advantage back to the power which strikes first.

The development of MIRVs has seriously complicated the whole question of inspection. In the course of all the arms control discussions we have had with the Soviet Union, inspection has always proved to be the most troublesome issue. To determine whether the Soviets have deployed their own multiple warheads requires inspection of the payload of their missile force. Such a thorough inspection is out of the question as far as the Soviets are concerned.

The construction of a BMD system and the development of multiple warheads increase the need for serious efforts to control nuclear weapons. Since the beginning of the arms race, the United States and the Soviet Union have engaged in a continuing dialogue —secret government talks, Pugwash meetings, etc. The United States has always wanted to take small steps with adequate inspection controls at each level. On the other hand, the Soviet Union has consistently advocated general and complete disarmament to be followed by inspection. As suspicion grew, the dialogue faltered, and discussions between the United States and the Soviet Union became interspersed monologues.

Within the last year, however, there has been some evidence of a merging of views on possible first steps. For instance, in the negotiations on the nonproliferation treaty, it is surprisingly the Russians who are worried about the inspection clause.

Given this situation, it is difficult to know whether to be optimistic or not. The dialogue has improved, but recent technological developments may be leading to a new intensification of the arms race. Moreover, the pressure to maintain "nuclear superiority" remains strong in this country. In a recent statement, Senator John Stennis declared that "the United States has no alternative except to zealously guard its military supremacy in the nuclear and strategic field."

Does superiority have any meaning in the nuclear age? How can we compare the relative effectiveness of Soviet and American nuclear forces given the different geography and population density of the two countries? Do alliances have an effect on the arms race—is a Soviet missile aimed at London the same as an American missile aimed at Vladivostok? How do we assess large and small yields against entirely different complexes or the uncertain performance of a limited antiballistic missile? The most that can be said is that there exists today a kind of parity between the two great nuclear powers with each able to kill more than half the population of the other side.

Why must the United States maintain this so-called nuclear superiority? One view is that so long as the United States has the superior force, it will be able to exert its power over the Russians after World War III. If we obliterate 100 million Russians and they obliterate only 50 million Americans we will be that much further ahead. On the other hand, diplomats argue that there will never be a Third World War, but that clear nuclear superiority will place us in a better position to negotiate with the Soviet Union in case a confrontation such as that which occurred in Berlin or in Cuba should arise again. The main ingredient in the public view seems to be prestige: Americans find it difficult to abandon the idea that the country with the greatest gross national product should also be first in nuclear arms. (The fact that we are eighteenth in infant mortality and twenty-second in male life expectancy appears to be of little importance when our international prestige is at stake.) Another view is that the military-industrial complex is engaged in a conspiracy to maintain the government's expenditure of billions of dollars in the arms sector of the economy.

Each of these arguments has some validity, although the conspiratorial view has been greatly exaggerated. Nonetheless, the need to deescalate the arms race should be clear to all: the cost is excessive, the potential damage tremendous, and the commitment to superiority dangerous and unhealthy given the other serious problems we face. Before any progress is made, however, there are two basic difficulties that must be overcome. On the American side, the Congress, the public, and the press must accept the fact that superiority in nuclear weapons no longer has meaning. On the Soviet side, the system of secrecy, whether it be inherent in Soviet society or just an aspect of Soviet military strategy, must be abandoned. Our need for superiority is aggravated by our uncertainty about Russian capabilities which, in turn, is increased by the bluffing techniques employed to exaggerate Soviet nuclear strength—techniques made effective by the rigid internal secrecy of the Soviet Union.

The acceptance of a minimum deterrent has been suggested as the key to halting the arms race and reducing the threat of nuclear war. An agreement providing for a reduction in the American and Russian strike force to a minimal level may not be very difficult and is not nearly as important as stabilizing the level.

Both we and the Soviets must avoid introducing new weapons systems which are of a character which would stimulate the. arms race and we must assure ourselves and each other that our national command and control systems are truly effective.

A RULE OF

LAW AND AN

ORGANIZED WORLD?

Chapter 18

Perhaps the first thing to recognize about international law and organization is that they operate *among* states, not *over* states. The formalization of international collaboration should be thought of as serving and advancing the respective national interests of the participants, as a supplement rather than as an alternative to conventional diplomacy on their part. It recognizes the fact that certain of their interests can best, and indeed *only,* be served within an international legal and structural framework.

In a world of sovereign states international law should not be conceived of as something separate from an existing state system which it might in some way replace. Indeed since international law does not appear to restrain or even affect states in their actual pursuit of "vital national interests," which are often narrow and selfish, doubts are often expressed that *international* law is really *law* at all.

Prevailing assumptions about the relevance, efficacy, or potential utility of world law tend to vary with the degree of stability in the inter-state system. Before the turn of the century there was much more stress upon the universal efficacy of international law than there is today. The reason is clear: Before the outbreak of war among the "civilized states" shattered the illusion, it was widely believed that there existed among the leadership of these Great Powers a consensus of values which could underlie the development of a rule of law throughout the world.

After World War I, interest on the part of those who believed that law had to rest upon the existence of community tended to concentrate upon the League of Nations until that body proved incapable less than twenty years later of meeting the challenge of totalitarianism. The years immediately following World War II even more quickly saw the frustration of any immediate possibility of erecting a world community on the basis of wartime coalition. There emerged not just two but several competing value systems in the world. In the wake of what Hajo Holborn of Yale has called "the political collapse of Europe," the European system of values on the basis of which a structure of law seemed possible of achievement early in this century could no longer prevail. To speak of a world rule of law today assumes that among the several systems of value, particularly but not only between the main protagonists, there is a high enough degree of consensus that a universal legal structure can be created. Such a consensus is difficult to locate in a situation in which each side tends to define error and illegality in terms of whatever the other side does, as is true in Chinese-American and Arab-Israeli relations.

Unless some state or combination of states succeeds in creating a world empire whose legal norms will then be imposed upon all mankind, the development of a world rule will be a gradual process rather than a sudden event. One step in preparing for its eventual acceptance is the creation of a *climate* of legal observance, insofar as this is possible under existing political conditions. Enforcement ability may be lacking, but as long as states or even some states obey the law—for whatever reason—then it is perfectly proper and essential to speak of the existence of an international legal system, limited though it may be in practice.

From the point of view of theory it is still useful to examine the basis for the idea that international law is binding. One view is that states can, as an exercise of their sovereignty, agree to observe certain rules in the conduct of their relations with other states; international law is simply the body of these rules of conduct. According to this consent-theory could not a state, still being sovereign, withdraw its consent to abide by these rules as well? If so, what happens to the *binding* character of law? A contrasting theory has it that, once consent is given, a rule of law is created which henceforth ceases to be a subject of repeal by states. But this view raises the further question of what the *source* of international law really is, if it is somehow beyond the state to decide whether or not to be bound by it. Fenwick and others argue that the theory of consent is inadequate, that law exists because without it there would be anarchy, and that the interdependence of states is a fact, "so that international law may be said to be based upon the very necessity of its existence, upon the very human beings in constant contact with one another under the condition of the present day."[1]

Be that as it may, it is difficult to contest the view expressed by Hans

[1] Charles Fenwick, *International Law*, 3rd ed. (New York and London: Appleton-Century-Crofts, Inc., 1948), p. 27n.

Morgenthau when he writes that to recognize that international law exists is not tantamount to saying that, as a legal system, it is as effective as the legal systems of states. Nor does it follow from the *existence* of international law that it is *"effective* in regulating and restraining the struggle for power on the international scene."[2]

In another, but closely related manner, the United Nations reflects the realities of world politics (or at least some of them). Because of the Soviets' extensive use of the veto, the functions of the Security Council were for several years assumed to some degree by the General Assembly, particularly after passage of the "Uniting for Peace" resolution as a result of the Korean crisis of 1950. Certain observers in the West have viewed recent and probable future additions to the UN of members that give more weight to the Asian-Arab-African bloc in the Assembly as endangering the position of the Western powers in the United Nations. Actually predictions of patterns of voting which are hostile or revengeful toward the Western powers (growing out of anti-colonialism) have not come true.[3] Nor have the alarms often heard, particularly in the United States, that the UN would come to be dominated by Communist countries; Soviet-controlled votes have generally stood alone or merely followed the lead of other nations and blocs. For several years the basic intention of the leaders of the Big Five at San Francisco to control UN action in the crucial area of international security tended to give way to assumption of this role by the General Assembly. But even though these gradual transformations decreased reliance upon the United Nations by the Great Powers in favor of the more traditional methods of diplomacy and of stronger regional arrangements, one authority has recently indicated that "if the nations of the world had been without a place to air their grievances and adjust their differences under a code of international behavior, our civilization might well have been destroyed in a nuclear war."[4] The United Nations *has* been useful in the political field, even if it has fallen short of the expectations of 1945.

Yet in the long run the organization may prove most effective through the extensive but usually unspectacular programs of the non-political agencies in solving economic and social problems which might otherwise lead to war. Here as at the regional level functionalism seems to be demonstrating its practical utility. Coordinated through the Economic and Social Council, which has increased its membership to twenty-seven, these func-

[2] Hans J. Morgenthau, *Politics Among Nations* (New York: Alfred A. Knopf, Inc., 1948), p. 211. See also on this point Percy E. Corbett, *The Study of International Law* (New York: Random House, Inc., 1955), esp. pp. 45–47.

[3] Inis J. Claude, *Swords into Plowshares,* 2nd ed. (New York: Random House, Inc., 1958), pp. 454–57.

[4] Francis O. Wilcox, "The United Nations: the Road Ahead," *Department of State Publication 6712* (Washington, D.C.: Government Printing Office, 1958), p. 20. Dr. Wilcox, who is presently Dean of the School of Advanced International Studies of the Johns Hopkins University, was then Assistant Secretary of State for International Organization Affairs.

tions are performed mainly by Economic Commissions on four continents (Europe, Asia and the Far East, Latin America, and Africa), and by the specialized agencies, each with its own membership, budget, and set of operating principles. Programs of these bodies are supplemented by an increasing number of agencies created by and working directly under the General Assembly, such as the Korean Reconstruction Agency, the Relief and Works Agency for Palestine, and the Committee on Information from Non-Self-Governing Territories. The activities of these bodies seldom make headlines but they may promote international collaboration in a manner never imagined by practitioners of the older diplomacy, nor indeed even by many earlier theoreticians of international organization itself.

Meanwhile the United Nations as an effective force fluctuates between the kind of paralysis that for a time characterized the sessions of the General Assembly, in which formal voting had to be suspended because of the financial crisis over Article 19, and the demonstration of real influence for peace in halting the bloodshed over Kashmir. Two facts need always to be kept in mind when assessing the place of the UN in world politics: One is that the UN can be effective only in matters affecting international peace and security to the extent to which the Great Powers agree, that is, when their interests happen to coincide. And the other is, as Leland M. Goodrich points out below, that the UN is a very different kind of body today than it was when it was founded.[5] With twice as many members, many of which are scarcely viable states by any criterion except that of sheer existence within identifiable boundaries, the Assembly increasingly seems to fail to reflect the hard realities of development and power. Yet what has recently happened in the UN has made this obvious weakness less telling. Whereas the Uniting for Peace Resolution of 1950 had the effect of transferring the peace-keeping authority of the UN from the Security Council to the General Assembly (where the role of the smaller states was thereby greatly enhanced), the financial crisis of the mid-sixties put it back again, not perhaps where it belongs, but certainly back where the framers at the San Francisco Opera House intended it to be. This new phase represents a backward step if movement toward world order means developing the Assembly into a kind of world parliament with authority to make its members, whether they vote with the majority or not, pay for the implementation of its decisions. On the other hand, the decision to add to the membership of the Security Council and the Economic and Social Council was a step forward, if it will make those bodies more reflective of actual political and economic reality than ever before.

---

[5] See also Roberto Ducci, "The World Order in Sixties," *Foreign Affairs* (1964), 42, 379–80.

1. The Maintenance of International Peace and Security

LELAND M. GOODRICH

Leland M. Goodrich, one of the outstanding authorities in the field, participated in the meetings at San Francisco as an adviser to the United States delegation which helped draw up the Charter. He is the co-author of the definitive work, THE CHARTER OF THE UNITED NATIONS: COMMENTARY AND DOCUMENTS *(1949) and is a member of the editorial board of* INTERNATIONAL ORGANIZATION. *At Columbia University he is Professor Emeritus of International Organization and Administration.*

It is a truism that the text of the Charter gives a quite misleading picture of the United Nations as it is today. In no respect is this more true than in the working of the Organization in the maintenance of international peace and security. Those provisions of the Charter which were claimed by its authors to provide the new Organization with teeth that the League of Nations did not have either have never been used or have in practice been of little importance. New emphases and new methods have been developed through the liberal interpretation of Charter provisions. These have not always been equally acceptable to all Members, however. The process of adaptation and development continues, with great present uncertainty as to what the future has in store. . . .

NEW TRENDS IN PEACEKEEPING

The decade of the 1950's saw a new trend in thought and practice regarding the role of the United Nations in keeping the peace. This change was due to many factors no one of which was by itself decisive. The total impact of the Korean experience and the ineffectual efforts to implement certain provisions of the Uniting for Peace Resolution were disillusioning. The balance of atomic terror came to be recognized as the effective deterrent of major power aggression while, with the death of Joseph Stalin, Nikita Khrushchev's emphasis on "peaceful coexistence" seemed to offer some reasonable prospect that the Soviet Union would find it in its interest to avoid war. The breaking of the membership deadlock in 1955, the consequent large increase in the total membership of the Organization, and, more particularly, the increase in the number of Asian and African states committed to "neutralism" in the Cold War struggle made it necessary to find a role for the United Nations which was consistent with the policies and aspirations of the new Members.[1] Finally, and this perhaps

[1] See Laurence W. Martin (ed.), *Neutralism and Nonalignment: The New States in World Affairs* (New York: Frederick A. Praeger, Inc., 1962).

INTERNATIONAL ORGANIZATION, XIX (1965), 429–43. *Reprinted by permission.*

proved to be the most important factor, Dag Hammarskjöld's appointment as Secretary-General in 1953 brought to that office a person who soon demonstrated a capacity for performance that won for him the confidence of governments and led to their vesting unprecedented responsibilities in him.

The new approach to peacekeeping—new in the sense of contrast to the emphasis of the preceding decade, though embodying elements of earlier practice—can best be described in the words of Mr. Hammarskjöld. In a press conference on February 27, 1956, the Secretary-General was asked to tell what kind of "preventive action" the UN might be able to take in an area where war threatened or was "right on the verge of breaking out." After explaining his view in some detail in relation to the current situation along the Israeli-Arab border, he generalized as follows:

In other words, the two lines of preventive action which I think are obviously indicated are, first, to stabilize the situation in the field on a day-to-day basis and to avoid the incidents which may lead to major friction, and, secondly, to be—you will excuse me for using the word—*quietly* helpful by being a third party with which the two conflicting parties can discuss matters and which may help them to bridge the gulf not by formal mediation but by working out a maximum of understanding which, I think, will increase as time goes on if the operation is wisely run.[2]

That these techniques were not new is obvious. In previous cases, the

[2] Wilder Foote, ed., *Dag Hammarskjöld: Servant of Peace* (New York: Harper & Row, Publishers, 1963).

UN had sought to "stabilize the situation" by getting the parties in conflict to agree to a cease-fire, to withdraw forces from dispute areas, and to accept UN observation and report as a means of assuring respect for armistice or cease-fire agreements. Furthermore, the use of "quiet diplomacy" to achieve wider agreement had been practiced, though customarily through formal arrangements involving the appointment of a committee of good offices, a mediator, or a UN representative. The novelty of preventive diplomacy, as conceived and practiced by Dag Hammarskjöld, lay rather in the contrast to previous emphasis on methods of coercion and in the fact that he proposed to exercise or to accept personal responsibility as Secretary-General for initiating and for carrying out such preventive measures.

In the Middle East crisis of 1956, after Mr. Hammarskjöld's efforts to mediate the Suez and Israeli-Egyptian conflicts had been cut short by appeals to violence and after the Security Council had been prevented from taking decisions by the British and French vetoes, the General Assembly authorized the Secretary-General to organize a UN force "to secure and supervise the cessation of hostilities." The UN Emergency Force, in accordance with the Secretary-General's proposals, approved by the Assembly, was to be composed of contingents voluntarily contributed by Members, was to enter Egyptian territory only with the consent of the host state, was not to use force of the host state, was not to use force except in self-defense, and was to be under the executive direction of the Secretary-General. Furthermore, the permanent members of the Security Council were not asked to contribute military contingents. It was made clear by the

Secretary-General that the Force was not to be used in any way to influence the political settlement which was to be the responsibility of the parties with such assistance as they might accept from the UN.[3]

Two years later, when the government of Lebanon complained of intervention in its political affairs by the United Arab Republic, the Secretary-General was authorized to dispatch an "observation group" to insure that there was no "illegal infiltration" of personnel or supplies of arms across the Lebanese frontier. While the UN Observation Group in Lebanon (UNOGIL) was not able to satisfy the United States in regard to the extent of infiltration and thus to forestall United States military intervention at the request of President Camille Chamoun, it did contribute to the eventual stabilization of political power in Lebanon. Furthermore, in this instance the Secretary-General established the important precedent that such a UN group should not interfere in the domestic politics of the host state.[4]

This technique of introducing the UN presence and seeking through it to stabilize the situation and assist the parties in reaching wider agreement received its most vigorous test in the Congo (Leopoldville). In this instance the Secretary-General used his powers under Article 99 of the Charter to bring the situation resulting from the collapse of law and order and the Belgian military intervention to the attention of the Security Council. His motive in part was, by interjecting the UN into the situation, to prevent what might be regarded as a power vacuum from being filled by the major contestants in the Cold War. By its resolution of July 14, 1960, the Security Council authorized the Secretary-General to provide the Congolese government with military assistance necessary to enable the national security forces to perform their tasks. The Secretary-General made it clear that he intended to follow the UNEF guidelines in the organization and conduct of the force. The Congo situation turned out, however, to be much more difficult to handle by techniques of preventive diplomacy than the Middle East or Lebanese situations since the UN Operation in the Congo (ONUC) had to contend not only with the unwanted Belgian and foreign presences but also with the disintegration of the recognized government and the attempted Katangese secession, aided and abetted by foreign influences. In the course of discharging his responsibilities under Security Council and General Assembly resolutions and the Charter of the UN, Mr. Hammarskjöld came under criticism from Congolese authorities for failure to give sufficient support to their political objectives, from the Soviet Union for failure to act with sufficient force to expel the Belgians and other foreigners, and from certain Western powers for excessive interference in the internal affairs of the Congo. Though Mr. Hammarskjöld's successor, U Thant, equipped with more adequate authority to use force, was able to bring the Katanga secessionist movement to an end, the financial crisis caused by the refusal of certain Members, especially the Soviet Union and France, to contribute to the expenses of the military operation made necessary

[3] See Gabriella Rosner, *The United Nations Emergency Force* (New York: Columbia University Press, 1963); and D. W. Bowett, *United Nations Forces: A Legal Study* (New York: Frederick A. Praeger, Inc., 1964).

[4] See Gerald L. Curtis, "The United Nations Observation Group in Lebanon," *International Organization* (Autumn 1964), XVIII, No. 4, 738–65.

its premature ending with the initial mission of the force still unfinished.[5]

Other peacekeeping operations since 1960 have been undertkaen and arranged under the shadow of the financial crisis that the Congo engendered, with the Secretary-General adopting a more cautious attitude regarding the assumption of responsibilities, more particularly insisting that there be reasonable assurance in advance that funds will be forthcoming to cover the costs. In West Irian in 1962, through the United Nations Temporary Executive Authority (UNTEA), the United Nations provided a face-saving device under which the control of the disputed territory could be transferred from the Netherlands to Indonesia.[6] The mission of the UN Authority was determined by agreement of the parties, subsequently approved by the General Assembly. The Authority was supported by a military contingent of 1,500 men provided by the government of Pakistan, and costs were shared equally by Indonesia and the Netherlands. In 1963 the United Nations Yemen Observation Mission (UNYOM) was established by agreement of the United Arab Republic and Saudi Arabia to observe compliance with a disengagement agreement these two countries had entered into with respect to their military interventions in Yemen. The Mission was handicapped from the beginning by failure to get the full cooperation of the parties and the diffi-

cult physical conditions of its work. In this instance also, the parties directly concerned agreed to pay the costs.[7]

The most recent United Nations peacekeeping operation has been the UN Peacekeeping Force in Cyprus (UNFICYP), which is still in process. By its resolution of March 4, 1964, the Security Council called upon Member States to refrain from action that would "worsen the situation" in Cyprus and recommended the creation of a peacekeeping force

> to use its best efforts to prevent a recurrence of fighting and, as necessary, to contribute to the maintenance and restoration of law and order and a return to normal conditions.

It also recommended that the Secretary-General designate a mediator to promote "a peaceful solution and an agreed settlement" of the Cyprus problem. Certain features of the Cyprus operation differentiate it from the UNEF and ONUC operations. A permanent member of the Security Council is a major contributor to the Force, the mandate runs for limited periods of time (three months), extension requires explicit action by the Security Council, and costs have been covered by voluntary pledges. It is too early to say what the success of the Cyprus operation will be; thus far it has succeeded in maintaining an uneasy peace with some difficulty.[8]

---

[5] For good discussions of the Congo military operation, see Arthur Lee Burns and Nina Heathcote, *Peace-Keeping by U.N. Forces: From Suez to the Congo* (New York: Frederick A. Praeger, Inc. [for the Center of International Studies, Princeton University], 1963); and Bowett, Chap. 6.

[6] For a critical account see Paul W. van der Veur, "The United Nations in West Irian: A Critique," *International Organization*, XVIII, No. 1 (Winter, 1964), 53–73.

[7] See *Annual Report of the Secretary-General on the Work of the Organization (16 June 1962–15 June 1963)* (General Assembly *Official Records* [18th session], Supplement No. 1).

[8] For the text of the resolution establishing UNFICYP, see UN Document S/5575. See also the periodic reports by the Secretary-General on the United Nations operation in Cyprus.

LESSONS FOR THE FUTURE

UN experience with peacekeeping to date suggests that the detailed prescriptions of the Charter have in many respects proved to be completely unsuited to postwar conditions, that adaptations that have been developed by Member governments and the Organization in dealing with postwar situations have had some success but have encountered serious difficulties, and that the future is uncertain with various possibilities of future development now open.

Experience on the whole has shown that the emphasis of the Charter on peace enforcement was unrealistic; at least in the conditions that have prevailed since 1945, peace enforcement of the kind that was thought to give "teeth" to the Organization has only been possible, and then in highly modified form, in one case—Korea—and there with only limited succeess. But while peace enforcement has not been practiced, there has been ample demonstration that the assumption of the Charter-makers that peace enforcement requires concurrence of the Council's permanent members, especially the United States and the Soviet Union, and that such measures are· not likely to be effective against a major military power is sound.

It has been possible, however, for the United Nations to play a somewhat more restricted role with considerable success. In a number of instances, with the agreement of the permanent members of the Security Council, or at least in the absence of positive disagreement, the United Nations has been able to achieve agreement of the parties in conflict to the cessation of hostilities, either through a cease-fire or a formal armistice agreement. Furthermore, the UN has assisted in securing the observance of such arrangements through various forms of UN presence, thus providing opportunities for observing, reporting, mediating, and exercising a restraining influence. The possibility of the Organization's playing a limited role of this nature was anticipated in Article 40 of the Charter but has been developed beyond the limits of purely provisional measures. It is important to note that many of the basic techniques that have been utilized in recent peacekeeping operations were developed and utilized early in the Organization's life, for example, in Indonesia and Palestine. Furthermore, Trygve Lie's proposal, which was not accepted, of a United Nations Guard envisaged the establishment of a UN military body with limited police functions.[9]

Limiting the role of the UN in the control of violence to the arrangement and supervision of cease-fires and armistices and to the performance of mediatory functions does not of course eliminate the possibility of UN activities having important political implications and effects. Sponsoring a cease-fire or being willing to assist in implementing one and assuming responsibility for the establishment of internal order and stability, as in the Congo, involve taking decisions that are bound to affect the development of situations in which many states, including Great Powers, have serious interests. The discharge of such responsibilities must consequently be based on an adequate consensus of Members. The need of such consensus cannot be avoided by delegating authority to an international official pledged to impartiality and to placing the pur-

[9] UN Document A/656 (September 28, 1948).

poses and principles of the Organization ahead of national interest. To be more specific, the conclusion can fairly be drawn, from the Congo experience in particular, that vesting discretionary power in a Secretary-General who has demonstrated outstanding qualities as a public servant is not an adequate substitute for agreement of the major powers on critical issues.

In the light of experience, many questions arise with regard to the organization and direction of peacekeeping operations. We have had instances of such operations being initiated by decision of the Security Council, on the recommendation of the General Assembly, with the parties themselves sometimes making the initial request, and with the Secretary-General in some cases taking important initiatives. If the consensus of the major powers is considered important to the success of the operation, obviously the Security Council is in the best position to assure this agreement. Up to the present, there has been no permanent international force available for peacekeeping operations and there is little likelihood that such an international force will be established in the near future. Dag Hammarskjöld was of the opinion in 1958 that peacekeeping forces should be organized on an *ad hoc* basis because of the uniqueness of each situation.[10] Other studies that have been undertaken suggest that the establishment of an international police force with enforcement powers, such as has been envisaged in plans for a disarmed world, are far in the future.[11] In an address at Harvard University on

June 13, 1963, Secretary-General U Thant gave a number of reasons why it seemed to him that "a permanent United Nations force would be premature at the present time."[12] These judgments appear sound. Nevertheless, there are obvious possibilities of advanced planning that would assure smoother and more efficient operations once the need for peacekeeping arises. These include the establishment of a planning staff and the assumption of advanced commitments to make properly trained and equipped units available when needed. It should not be assumed on the basis of limited experience to date that the major military powers should necessarily be excluded from contributing military contingents to peacekeeping forces. The special considerations that dictated exclusion of major power contingents in the Middle East and the Congo will not necessarily be decisive in other situations where the UN is called upon to perform a "peacekeeping" function as Cyprus has already demonstrated. However, since the essence of the UN's task is likely to be that of persuading the major powers to stand aside rather than become more involved in a given situation, it can reasonably be anticipated that the prac-

---

10 See *United Nations Emergency Force Summary Study of the Experience Derived from the Establishment and Operation of the Force* (UN Document A/3943, October 9, 1958).

11 See William R. Frye, *A United Nations Peace Force* (Dobbs Ferry, N.Y.: Oceana Publications, 1957); Lincoln P.

Bloomfield and others, *International Military Forces: The Question of Peacekeeping in an Armed and Disarming World* (Boston: Little, Brown and Company, 1964); and Bowett, *United Nations Forces.*

12 *United Nations Review* (July 1963), p. 56.

13 Canada and the Scandinavian countries have shown interest in these possibilities and the readiness to act. See Per Frydenberg, *Peace-Keeping: Experience and Evaluation* (Oslo: Norwegian Institute of International Affairs, 1965); and Lester B. Pearson, "Keeping the Peace," in Andrew W. Cordier and Wilder Foote, eds., *The Quest for Peace: The Dag Hammarskjöld Memorial Lectures* (New York: Columbia University Press, 1965), pp. 99–118.

tical requirements of preventive diplomacy in the future will be more commonly met by excluding the military contingents of major powers and using the forces of relatively uncommitted states to represent and implement the general interest in stabilizing many situations.

The measure of success that the UN has achieved to date in discouraging and controlling the use of armed force has not been accompanied by equal success in bringing about accommodation of the conflicting interests and demands that are the source of tension. Since the war we have had a progressive accumulation of situations in which serious tension and the danger of open violence continue to exist after initial outbreaks of violence have been brought under control. What is particularly significant is that old areas of tension tend to remain as new ones are created. The failure of the UN in its efforts to promote settlement or adjustment is in all likelihood due to a number of considerations. The major cause may well be the failure thus far to harness the influence and authority of the major powers in support of reasonable accommodations of conflicting interests. Efforts to achieve equitable settlements through the organs and procedures of the UN have thus far had limited success because the proposals of UN organs for peaceful settlement and accommodation have not as a rule been supported by necessary agreement among the Great Powers. Too often these powers have seen it to their advantage to give encouragement to one side or the other as a means of gaining advantages in their own power struggles or at least have so distrusted each other's motives as to be unwilling to join in promoting a result which each might otherwise consider desirable. Thus, in 1948, while both the United

States and the Soviet Union supported the General Assembly's recommendation for the settlement of the Palestine question, they could not agree on using the Security Council as an instrument to implement that recommendation. Furthermore, the Cold War confrontation has permitted the parties in conflict to exploit the situation by playing one side against the other.

It is often maintained that the agreement of the permanent members of the Security Council is not as important to the exercise of its mediatory and conciliatory functions as to the discharge of its responsibilities under Chapter VII. The General Assembly has in fact recommended that permanent members refrain from claiming the right of veto in such cases. While there is much to be said for this point of view, it must be recognized that any UN recommendation that has the support of all the major powers is more likely to be accepted than one that might have the support of only a majority of them. Furthermore, it is clear that if the permanent members use disputes or situations before the UN for airing their own propaganda claims and introducing a major-power confrontation, the result cannot fail to be negative so far as the promotion of settlement is concerned.

The experience of the UN during the past twenty years suggests that those who wrote the Charter were not too far off the mark when they emphasized the need of agreement among the major powers if the Organization was to succeed in performing its peacekeeping function. New techniques have been developed, but these too depend for their effectiveness, as the current financial crisis demonstrates, on agreement among the Great Powers. The authors of the Charter recognized that in an international organization of sovereign states for keeping the peace, while there must be recognition of the interests and possible contribution of each Member, large or small, there must also be recognition of the special position that the major powers must occupy in any system based upon voluntary cooperation. Recognition of this truth may result in limiting the activities of the United Nations in the maintenance of peace but it will assure a more substantial success in what it undertakes.

2. A Pragmatic View of the New International Law

JOHN N. HAZARD

John N. Hazard, Professor of Public Law at Columbia University since 1946, is a recognized authority on Soviet law. Among his many books are LAW AND SOCIAL CHANGE IN THE USSR *(1953);* THE SOVIET SYSTEM OF GOVERNMENT *(1957); and* SETTLING DISPUTES IN THE SOVIET SOCIETY *(1960).*

Let us be candid and pragmatic. What is this new international law of which so many are speaking? It is a philosophical construction which we have misunderstood, because we are not a philosophically-minded people. To the Communists it is new because in their book a legal system must be judged not by the norms it incorporates but by the ends it serves. They purport to see contemporary international law in the service of the exploiters and to anticipate the evolution of a new function for international law which will make it new. For them the new content must change the form as well, because form and content are in dialectical unity.

PROCEEDINGS OF THE AMERICAN SOCIETY OF INTERNATIONAL LAW *(1963), pp. 79–83. Reprinted by permission.*

Thus, a legal system composed of the norms we all know, with but a few changes, can be a wholly new legal system. That is what the Communists are talking about.

For the jurists of the newly developing states of Asia and Africa new international law is also largely the familiar norms, but applied with a new style. They argue that the dignity of men and of states has been degraded by colonialism. Men are not treated as equals, nor are the developing states yet treated as equals, and some are even still colonies. A new international law becomes under this approach a system of norms denuded of those that foster colonial domination. Yet these rules of the past are not many when related to the whole body of law. A new law becomes under this interpretation primarily a new attitude of statesmen in the chancelleries of Europe, an attitude that accepts former colonials as equals, not only in renunciation of the use of force to collect debts and protect materials, but, more importantly, in daily association around the green tables of diplomacy. An African can tell a handshake that is offered by a man who thinks he is being magnanimous in offering his hand from one who thinks nothing of it at all, but assumes that it is routine.

How can we know that our task is less complicated than we thought and that the changes we are being asked to accept are less sweeping than was supposed? The record in print proves it, as does association in the corridors of the United Nations and at scholarly congresses. No one is asking for the complete rejection of what we know as international law. No one is asking that the books be burned and that we start afresh in rejection of the lessons history has given as to the rules which minimize friction. If we approach the problem pragmatically in examination of specific suggestions for alteration of the rules, and avoid the philosophical conceptions of "new" law, we shall be able to proceed. This is our English heritage, and when combined with our American heritage of anti-colonialism, the two forces should facilitate our task as North Americans in reaching our goal of a system of law that can minimize frictions.

This is not to say that we can construct a legal system that will assure the peace if power-hungry statesmen with ample resources to overcome their neighbors turn to the sword. Reluctantly I have reached the conclusion that legal norms cannot perform this task at this moment in history, and we cannot expect either old or new law to save the world from the madman or the zealot or the reckless empire-builder. Yet, inability to assure world peace through world law is no reason to avoid doing what we can to minimize frictions that could lead to conflict of a lesser type, and the place to begin is at the conference table in review of the individual norms of international law against which complaint has been lodged.

Suppose that we begin with the Russians. Many have been suspicious of their aims, and we tend to see a Trojan horse in the innocent-sounding proposals that come from their jurists. But lawyers are used to this problem. Who has not learned in law school to look for advantages which the other side is trying to gain by innocent-looking proposals made in the negotiation of a contract? And when the hidden possibilities are discovered, experienced counsel determines whether to reject them, to counter them with alternatives, or to accept them in expectation that they can cut both ways. Knowing this tradition of the Bar, we need not refuse to look at the proposal.

The legal adviser to the Soviet foreign office has set forth his concept, and, therefore, the concept of his government, of what is needed to improve the law. He divides the norms of international law into three groups: norms to be discarded, norms to be strengthened, and norms to be changed. Into the discard would go: spheres of influence, capitulations, consular courts, unequal treaties and intervention. No American statesman or jurist will object to these proposals. They are principles from the past, superseded by the practice of states and by the United Nations Charter.

To be strengthened as norms of the second category would be: respect for state sovereignty, non-interference in domestic affairs, equality of states and *pacta sunt servanda*. Here we move to a group of issues that have been much debated in the United Nations and elsewhere. No American objects to these principles, and many see in them only problems of interpretation. For example, we see sovereignty strengthened when utilized to join groupings of states organized to resist aggression, or to reduce tariff barriers in expansion of economies, or even to provide judicial assistance to foreign plaintiffs in the courts of the United States. We brook no interference in the domestic affairs of the United States and we propose none on our part in other countries as long as they do not threaten our existence. To us it seems that threat to existence goes beyond domestic affairs and becomes of moment internationally. The United Nations is creating from year to year a new jurisprudence establishing a definition of the seemingly domestic activities that threaten world peace. We can be content to let this process continue.

As to equality of states and *pacta sunt servanda,* we have no quarrels. We have relinquished our few colonies, offered to Puerto Rico complete freedom to choose her future status and begun a program of political education in the few islands we maintain as fortresses. We reluctantly supported colonial empires of allies when their loyalty in the alliance seemed jeopardized by our anti-colonial sentiments, but we sighed with relief when France and Algeria reached accord as to the latter's status. And who would reject the very principle on which law rests, the concept of *pacta sunt servanda?* We might be tempted to recall the 1920's when Soviet jurists argued that in principle Tsarist treaties were not binding, at least insofar as they created financial obligations. But we read that this period is over and that the U.S.S.R. is even more conservative in application

than many others of the *clausula rebus sic stantibus.* Yes, we can accept *pacta sunt servanda* and demand that all nations adhere to it.

It is with the third group of norms to be established anew that we shall want to be most careful, as is any lawyer with concepts for which there are as yet no annotations telling us what the language means. This is the more so since some of these principles have been in discussion for years in the United Nations, and there has been no agreement on definition.

Here are the Soviet proposals for this category: prohibition of aggressive war within the meaning of the United Nations Charter, peaceful settlement of disputes, self-determination of nations, peaceful co-existence, disarmament and prohibition of war propaganda. No one knows what aggression means, since the United Nations committee seeking to define it has had to postpone its work until it thinks agreement possible, and it has not suggested recall of its members. No one knows what peaceful co-existence means, although efforts are being made both inside and outside the United Nations to define it. Everyone is for self-determination of nations and disarmament, but agreement cannot be reached on how these two concepts can be put into effect without increasing the threat of war. Only prohibition of war propaganda presents a case of rejection at the present time in keeping with the Western world's reluctance to silence freedom of speech unless there is a clear and present danger resulting from its use. And up to now, the majority in the West does not believe that the utterings of some military men and sensational journalists would really create such panic in the minds of responsible statesmen as to drive them to war against their considered judgment.

My point in reviewing the Soviet

proposals is to show that they do not require rejection of international law in its totality, or in its major aspects. They are but moves on the chessboard of international politics which can be met calmly in preservation of an international law which has always seemed to Americans to be a dynamic discipline capable of change without loss of its identity.

Let us turn to the second group of states that are demanding new international law, namely, the states of Asia and Africa. The record in the Sixth Committee of the United Nations discloses what is desired. It is first and foremost a recognition of the dignity of individuals and states, regardless of previous condition of servitude, race and religion. This is the matter of "style" of which I have spoken, which requires little new in the way of law. The evil features of colonialism are on the wane, and only a few sore spots remain beyond the nearly one hundred small islands and enclaves for which solution must lie not in independence but in federation or union with neighbors with whom wealth and defense can be shared. The problem is not the breakup of the old empires, but avoidance of the creation of new ones. A candid man cannot look without alarm on some events in parts of Africa and Asia today which suggest that new Alexanders have aspirations out of keeping with the trend of the postwar years.

The details that the developing states wish revised are various. Some fear the use of consular immunities for purposes of espionage and ask that the privileges of the pouch be denied to all but diplomatic representatives. Some fear foreign warships severing communications between islands of an archipelago state. Some want established their right to subsoil resources now owned by foreign interests. Some demand that the former colonial powers return in expiation of their exploitation of colonial resources large sums of money in the form of grants and technical assistance so that economies may be improved. Some demand access to foreign markets currently protected by customs barriers.

The statesmen of the world are already meeting to consider these desires, and the International Law Commission is not only codifying but developing the law. This is an orderly procedure, and the forums are varied in which the claims can be discussed and met to the extent possible. The recently concluded Vienna Congress on diplomatic privileges and the...one on consular rights will resolve some of the issues. More will be heard on the law of the sea. The United Nations has just concluded adoption of a resolution on nationalization of resources, and the financial agencies of the organized world are filling economic needs. These measures probably fail to meet all the desires of the developing states, but no state can expect to obtain all of its aims immediately, and the new states are sophisticated enough to know that fact.

There is one avenue of change that has become popular with the developing states and for which the long-established powers have been slow to rally. It is the resolutions of the General Assembly. Admittedly, such resolutions are not sources of international law, although many speakers in the Sixth Committee from the small states have wished that they were, and some have even tried to pretend that they are such sources. Nevertheless, these resolutions are having increasingly persuasive importance in guiding the conduct of foreign ministers. If we Americans take into consideration that the great majority of states in the

United Nations share the values, if not always the institutions, for which we have declared ourselves, we can hope usually for the statement of desirable guides to action in these resolutions. There are few states, after all, which evidence an expectation that they can lord it over the whole world, although some may talk of hegemony in philosophical terms as an ultimate desideratum of a social system for which they hope to be the teacher. We can expect a majority vote for independence as conceived by nationalistically oriented statesmen for the foreseeable future, and if we work with this majority we can share in strengthening concepts which meet our needs. If they are ill-conceived, as some surely will be, our function will be to point out the shortcomings for consideration by a world public opinion which is increasingly literate and experienced in distinguishing the wolfish aggressor, who seeks to cloak himself in the sheep's garb of peaceful propaganda, from the real peace-lover.

My point is simple. Face the future of international law fearlessly. No one can hope to rend the fabric, and very few seem to want to do so. We have only to attend to patching the garment or to weaving new parts. We are skilled in that process as pragmatic jurists. We know how to be wary and yet receptive of legitimate proposals. I cannot resist a melodramatic conclusion. Why be afraid?